Donald Dewey is a prolific magazine writer, playwright and novelist, and the author of a well-received first biography of Marcello Mastroianni. Dewey's writing has earned him many awards, including the Nelson Algren Prize for Fiction. He lives in New York.

JAMES STEWART
A Biography

DONALD DEWEY

WARNER BOOKS

A *Warner* Book

First published in Great Britain in 1997
by Little, Brown and Company
This edition published in 1998 by Warner Books

Copyright © 1996 by Donald Dewey

The moral right of the author has been asserted.

A CIP catalogue record for this book
is available from the British Library.

ISBN: 0 7515 2160 4

Printed and bound in Great Britain
by Clays Ltd, St Ives plc

Warner Books
A Division of
Little, Brown and Company (UK)
Brettenham House
Lancaster Place
London WC2E 7EN

FOR JEANNE DEWEY
AND VIRGINIA DELANEY

TABLE OF CONTENTS

ACKNOWLEDGMENTS

James Stewart: A Biography is based on material from three principal sources: interviews and correspondence undertaken for this particular project; interviews conducted by the author for other projects but relevant to the present book; and the thousands of articles and profiles on the subject collected in various libraries and special research centers around the country.

Thanks are due, first of all, to the people who graciously set aside time to talk or write about Stewart with the author. These were:

Sheldon Abend
Julie Adams
Eddie Albert
Jane Alexander
Joan Benny
Edward Bernds
Eleanor Blair
Susan Blanchard
Harry Carey, Jr.
Ronald Clint
Rosemary Clooney
Thomas Cook
Jackie Cooper
Linda Cristal
Bryan Crozier
James D'Arc
Doris Day
Rosemary DeCamp
Fred DeCordova
Chip Deffaa
Myrna Dell

Vivian DeVine
Matthew Dingman
Bill Dixon
Melinda Draddy
William Draddy
Buddy Ebsen
Jack Elam
Dana Elcar
Elin Elisofon
Douglas Fairbanks, Jr.
Jane Fonda
Joan Fontaine
Ben Gazzara
Ellen Geer
Leonard Gershe
Lucille Gipson
Farley Granger
Jane Greer
T. Edward Hambleton
Katharine Hepburn
Charlton Heston

Frank Hood
Norris Houghton
Linda Janklow
Ben Johnson
Shirley Jones
Hal Kanter
David Karp
Wendy Keyes
Howard Koch
Howard Kriedler
Hardy Kruger
Jack Lambert
Arthur Laurents
Frank Lawrence
Richard Lees
Janet Leigh
Jack Lemmon
Karin Lopp
Andrew Low
James MacArthur
Tony Martin

Dorothy McGuire
Andrew McLaglen
Burgess Meredith
Marilyn Miller
Robert Mitchum
Lou Mofsie
Bill Moorhead
Jay Morehouse
Harry Morgan
James Morrison
Billy Mumy
Alex Nicol
Mayf Nutter
Barney Oldfield
Diana Onuscheck
Greg Paul
Bud Pease
Gregory Peck
Nehemiah Persoff
Ramsey Potts

Will Prappas
Irving Ratner
James Reid
Gene Reynolds
John Harold Robinson
Laurance Rockefeller
Elizabeth Rogers
Jay Rubin
Janice Rule
Donald Saddler
Victor Samrock
John Saxon
Peter Scaroni
George Schaefer
Robert Schnitzer
Peter Schwed
Lloyd Sharrard
Elizabeth Simpson
Anna Sosenko
John Springer

Robert Stack
Eddie Stanky
John D. Stewart
Ethel Stratton
John Strauss
Walter Strawinski
Paul Tanner
Lewis Van Dusen
Robert Vaughn
Connie Wald
Robert Waskowicz
John Waxman
Raquel Welch
Jesse White
Mignon Winants
William Winants
William Windom
Shelley Winters
Fay Wray
Jane Wyatt

My sincere and very special thanks are owed to the children of James and Gloria Stewart—Michael McLean, Kelly Harcourt, and Judy Merrill—for being willing to scratch their memories to come up with answers for what must have often seemed like uninformed or trivial questions.

James Stewart: A Biography also includes material from interviews conducted by the author in the past with John Huston, Marcello Mastroianni, Gene Kelly, and Billy Wilder for articles and radio programs not directly related to the present project.

Special thanks are owed to: Anthony Lenzi and Ellen von Karajan of the Jimmy Stewart Museum, the staff of the Indiana Historical Society, Frank Hood, and Ray Goss for material on Indiana; Jay Quinn for material on Mercersburg Academy; Mary Ann Jensen of the Firestone Library, Nanci Young of the Mudd Library, and Dave Morgan of the Alumni Records Office for material on Princeton; Kay Ackerman for material on Wilson College; Thomas Bolton of the Iowa Gold Star Museum for material on Camp Dodge; Cynthia Pease of the Falmouth

Enterprise for material on the University Players; Dorothy McGee for material on the subject's summer-stock work on Long Island; Butch Jackson for material related to Thunderbird Field in Arizona; Robert Payne, Carlton McConnell, and Ray Pytel for material related to the World War II years; Gregory Gallant for material related to Senator Margaret Chase Smith; Frances B. Clymer of the Buffalo Bill Historical Center for material related to *Winchester '73* and *Carbine Williams*; and Mark Swope for going through his father's voluminous files to find relevant photographs.

The poring through thousands of old newspaper clippings and magazine articles was made significantly easier by the assistance of the staff at the Lincoln Center Library for the Performing Arts; by Charles Silver and his assistants at the research facilities of the Museum of Modern Art in New York; by Leith Johnson at the Olen Memorial Library at Wesleyan University; by Ruth Spencer at the American Film Institute in Los Angeles; and by Sam Gill and Faye Thompson at the Academy of Motion Picture Arts and Sciences in Los Angeles.

Along the line, the author also had the critical help of dozens of individuals who came up with the right address or phone number, who found the right film, who dug out the right clipping from a local library, and/or who corrected a course erroneously taken. Vital in this area have been Nick Acocella, Rosalind Arnstein, Val Avery, Ken Baldwin, Tim Bergstrom, Luis James Chalif, Shaun Considine, Jim Cyrus, Stanley Dance, Evelyn Dehner, Sheila Dehner, James Draddy, Tom Fenaughty, Denise Figueroa, Peter and Linda Flaherty, Sid Gribetz, Mary Halchester, Shirley Herbert, Dorothy Herrmann, Ed Jaffe, William Jakela, Jill Krall, Joseph Mancini, Joseph McBride, Victor Navasky, John Randolph, Don Rehill, and Mort Viner.

No less important have been the insights and clarifying suggestions of my editor Walton Rawls and his associate Michon Wise.

Lastly, thanks are due to my wife, Marta, for running back and forth to libraries and copy shops and to Martha Kaplan and Mary Maguire for seeing to it that there was a reason for all the running back and forth.

It goes without saying that none of those cited is responsible for any misuse of their help in the pages that follow.

—*February 1996*

INTRODUCTION

INTRODUCED TO A MASS AUDIENCE AS AN ACTOR more than sixty years ago, James Stewart quickly found other, sometimes competing identities: as the Hollywood star, as the World War I hero, as the stalwart family man, and as a paradigm of the small town idealist who brings American simplicity and integrity to encrusted big-city cynics. Harry Truman said he would have made a perfect son, Natalie Wood said he would have made a perfect father, and Gloria Stewart said he *did* make a perfect husband. Depending on the thrust, over the years, of a particular magazine article or press release, we have had Stewart the actor presented as an extension of the private Stewart of Indiana, Pennsylvania; Beverly Hills, California; and several points in between, or the private Stewart of Indiana, Beverly Hills, and elsewhere portrayed as so suffusing his professional material as to suggest that maybe he never really acted at all. For many, Stewart the actor has often seemed like an afterthought; or, as one knee-jerk evaluation of his work would put it, "Oh, that's Jimmy Stewart just being Jimmy Stewart."

There have been many accomplices to "Jimmy Stewart just being Jimmy Stewart." To begin with, there is Stewart himself, who only sporadically has reared up against a confusion of his talent with his image and who even on those occasions has made it clear that he considers parent-of-the-year awards from *Reader's Digest* as important as Oscars— and both of them less important than military honors or election to eldership in the Presbyterian church. His recitation of the benefits of growing up as the son of Alexander and Elizabeth Stewart, of working under the old Hollywood studio system, and of acting for Frank Capra, John Ford, and Alfred Hitchcock—recorded in thousands of newspaper interviews and public appearances—has taken on the predictability of a ritual. Asked directly about his acting technique, he usually has retreated behind a barricade of self-deprecation (though not without firing a shot or two back at acting schools and, more particularly, at disciples of the Method). Asked for his favorite motion-picture role, he invariably has cited the one—George Bailey in *It's A Wonderful Life*—that, thanks to relentless television promotion every Christmas, has been reduced to a Hallmark greeting card character, making Stewart's frequently dangerous performance something more observed than seen. His very survival as practically the last of the studio stars (once counted by MGM as outnumbering those in the heavens) has conferred on him an emblematic significance more conducive to appreciating movie history than the nuances and subtleties of living screen art.

Caricature—well past a point of comic flattery and into another zone of bland reassurance—has long been a Stewart companion. Here again the actor has been no passive recipient of the obviousnesses of others; in fact, there is some evidence to indicate that after World War II, he himself gilded his natural stammerings and elliptical phrase-making as a commercial calculation, as a conscious attempt to help shape a persona that would prove attractive at the box office. However that might be, by the time he was fitfully wrapping his tongue around his jingles for Johnny Carson and the *Tonight Show* audience in the 1980s, Stewart had certainly become the most durable and accurate of the Jimmy Stewart impersonators. Those scores of flinty film performances without an *er* or a *waal* in them? They remained locked away in the basement of the Jimmy Stewart Institution; which is to say, locked behind our own selective memories. In some instances, the passing of years, when not decades, has provided us with a reasonable excuse for seeing only what we want to see; we can be forgiven, for example, for overlooking his reputation as a womanizer in the 1930s and 1940s (before he was hailed as a paragon of the family man), when his incessant prowlings began to worry even his closest male friends. Where other attitudes are concerned—say in the thought that this 1932 graduate of Princeton probably learned to read by memorizing the letters off the label of his bib overalls—we have unwittingly reflected an old MGM publicity slant where Ivy was never supposed to flourish near Innocence. But beyond such oversights are blindered perspectives explained less easily, where what might be folksy, shy, respectful, or trustworthy about Stewart personally has been projected into a broader cultural context that some of us might yearn to believe, but that many more of us mainly perceive as some comfortably removed relic of a quaint past. Either way, Stewart himself remains out of focus.

Take a wider view of Stewart's most parodied characteristic—his speech: specifically the notion that he has found speaking an arduous process, that his every syllable in front of a camera was produced by tapping his brain with a mallet. Once again, he has been the first to abet this impression through, among other things, his praise over the years for Hitchcock, Ford, George Stevens, and others as being "visual directors," for never hesitating to discard reams of dialogue if that was what was required to make a picture work. The fact of the matter, of course, is that however visual they might have been, these directors helped to make Stewart the most voluble actor in American screen history. Nobody has ever been more deaf to John Wayne's fabled advice to a rising actor to "talk low, talk slow, and don't say too fucking much." Where a Wayne grimaced, a Gary Cooper squinted, and a Clark Gable scowled, Stewart launched into a page-long monologue. Cary Grant considered it professional self-protection to have his characters' exposition speeches broken up and reassigned to other actors so that his character would be free to dominate scenes through silent reaction shots; no such insecurity for Stewart. From *Mr. Smith Goes to Washington* to *Anatomy of a Murder*, from *The Shop Around the Corner* to *Shenandoah*, from *Harvey* to his *Hawkins* television series, Stewart has talked and talked and talked.

He has talked off screen, too; and while it has been convenient for some admirers to slough off his glacially conservative opinions on the state of the nation and the human race as inevitable given his age, economic status, and military background, and expedient for others to embrace those views as imperative ingredients of patriotism, there has been nothing in the least abstract or bromidically idealistic about many of his pronouncements. More than fifteen years after the House Un-American Activities Committee had finished its worst work in Hollywood, Stewart could still tell an interviewer that Communists were holding sway in the motion-picture industry. Even before his stepson was killed in Vietnam, he could denounce antiwar protesters as traitors. The civil rights struggles might have happened on another planet, and, to judge from some of his comments, he might have preferred it if they had. At one time or another, he has descried television, long hair, and Jimmy

Carter as undermining the American social fabric. At the very least, in other words, Stewart has felt less than responsible to the twenty-four-hour-a-day benevolent geniality the image-mongers have laden him with.

The development of "Jimmy Stewart just being Jimmy Stewart" has also taken place on a whirligig of ironies and contradictions. The midcentury studios that he always has admired for their organization and what he termed their "passion for movie making," for instance, didn't have the faintest idea for years about how to market Stewart, and it ultimately fell to contracted directors and two actresses rather than moguls who liked to think of themselves as star makers to give him his footing as a screen personality. It was his closest friend, Henry Fonda, who continually called into question the sophisticated labor behind his craft with the backhanded compliment that he was simply a "natural" actor (an assertion that Stewart resented more deeply every time he read it). His genuine aversion to speaking about, let alone exploiting, his war record for career ends reinforced traits of aloofness and secretiveness that would figure prominently in his subsequent (and best) work but never really become part of the accepted persona of the endearing yet quietly righteous, purposeful Stewart. And while that persona might have been built up over a couple of generations of motion pictures and attendant print and radio publicity, it owed its final solidification to the television medium that he always distrusted—to appearances with Jack Benny and on variety shows, to a flop of a comedy series, and to the *Hawkins* mysteries that were only marginally more successful. Even those too young to understand or care about images gratifying to their parents registered the image of a self-lampooning Stewart that channel-surfing washed into their bedrooms.

In the end, however, no matter how they have been nurtured and consolidated over the years, no matter how many presidents of the United States thought of him as a son and how many actresses fantasized about him as a father, the various presumptions animating "Jimmy Stewart just being Jimmy Stewart" don't stand a chance. Stewart is not Will Rogers—dependent on a few preserved quips, old films, and tinnily recorded radio broadcasts for living forever as a lariat-twirler who never met a man he didn't like. Nor is he Abraham Lincoln, to be referred to opportunistically whenever extra inspiration is needed for dressing up some partisan political program as fundamental cultural instinct. Least of all is he George Bailey, Jefferson Smith, Elwood P. Dowd, or any of the other individual characters that he has played. In the long run the entire body of James Stewart's work—beginning with a Princeton theatrical in the 1930s and extending through to an animated cartoon in the 1990s—will have none of that. What he has done, especially in film, is just too available in all its variety to remain a perpetual shadow to what Stewart is supposed to be or what we want him to represent to us.

In black and white, in Technicolor, or in the colorization process that he is on record as despising, Stewart's motion-picture work encompasses a vast emotional and intellectual territory that few other actors have dared enter, let alone negotiate successfully. If comparisons of the kind always smack of the artificial, it is nevertheless still arguable that no other U.S. screen performer—and certainly none of the stars from the big studio era, male or female—has shown as much range or delved into as many emotional nooks and crannies. As inflated as this claim might sound to those who identify him strictly with Capra or a succession of biographical roles in the 1940s and 1950s that seem to add up to merely "a nice guy pitching for the Chicago White Sox," "a nice guy playing the trombone," and "a nice guy flying solo across the Atlantic," Stewart's filmography would argue the case. In five westerns directed by Anthony Mann (*Winchester '73*, *Bend of the River*, *The Naked Spur*, *The Far Country*, and *The Man from Laramie*), the actor not only took on embittered, disillusioned characters bent on wreaking vengeance against brothers and best friends, but along the way became synonymous with a new standard of graphic film violence. In four films for Hitchcock, he abandoned even the ugly visceral justifications of Mann's action heroes to portray people either ambiguously cold and clinical (*Rope* and *Rear Window*), manipulative (*The Man Who Knew Too Much*), or obsessive (*Vertigo*). For Ford, he was the cynic in *Two Rode Together* and the phony in *The Man Who Shot Liberty Valance*; for Otto Preminger, he was canniness incarnate in *Anatomy of a Murder*; for Robert Aldrich, he was jealous obstinacy in *The Flight of the Phoenix*. All those memories of Stewart characters getting tipsy by the pool or holding leaking babies notwithstanding, in the 1950s—the decade of his greatest commercial success—he didn't make a single comedy. He wasn't heard to say *shucks* in local theaters too often, either.

As wide ranging as Stewart's roles have been, they would be little more than memorials to misguided ambition if he had not delivered on them. But for the most part he did, and then some, generally coming off worst in work that required minimal enterprise from him, which effectively demanded only that "Jimmy Stewart be Jimmy Stewart." For Ford, the key to his range was in the fact that, as the actor himself always insisted, he "worked at his trade." In the words of the director: "Wayne, Cooper, and Gable are what you call natural actors. They're the same off the screen as they are playing a part. Stewart isn't like that. . . . He studied acting and transformed himself, very deliberately, into whatever he was doing. He was good in anything." Without subscribing to that last blanket statement, film critic Andrew Sarris has concluded that Stewart's work in such a broad range of parts entitles him to recognition as "the most complete actor-personality in the American cinema." In an essay written in the early 1970s, Sarris observed among other things that Stewart "never really let down even in bad movies, and this unrelenting professionalism and tenacity are qualities often lacking in even the greatest stage actors when they venture into the relatively fragmented screen."

The most common description of Stewart's talent by fellow performers, directors, and critics has invoked his *honesty* or *sincerity*; everyone from Katharine Hepburn and Joan Fontaine to Ben Johnson and Ben Gazzara has used one or the other term. George Stevens reached for another synonym when, asked once to evaluate the actor during the shooting of *Vivacious Lady*, he replied: "To overcome disbelief is the most difficult thing to do in pictures. And Jimmy, with this extraordinary earnestness that he has, just walks in and extinguishes disbelief." For Shelley Winters this translates as "he never did a phony take." Jack Lemmon differs only in emphasis: "The thing you get with Stewart, like maybe before you got from Spencer Tracy and Robert Donat, is that they never give a sense of the film take. What you see coming off the screen is fresh, real, immediate. Maybe they were working at it for the entire day, a hundred times over, or maybe it really was the first go-round. Doesn't make a difference. Either way, they're as honest and direct about it as if they'd done it on some saintly inspiration the first time." Capra, who never needed much prodding to claim his favorite leading man as "probably the best actor who's ever hit the screen," summed it up as: "There is bad acting and good acting, fine performances and occasionally great performances, but there is a higher level than great performances in acting. A level where there is only a real, live person on the screen. A person audiences care about immediately. There are only a few actors—very few—capable of achieving this level of an actor's art, and Jimmy Stewart is one of them."

The esteem for the impact of Stewart's work, however, still sheds little light on its sources, triggers, or techniques. In one of his forays against the assertion that he has always been an instinctual actor who needs only to memorize lines and await a director's call for action to acquit a role, Stewart noted that "there is nothing less natural in the world than to stand out there in front of dozens of people on a sound stage with all those lights and big cameras and equipment surrounding you and to carry on a scene with somebody as though you're completely alone." Or again: "An actor is always sort of traveling a road—from being who he is to being the character he's doing." And the conveyance used for getting from one point to the other? "Imagination."

As a shorthand answer, it is hard to better *imagination*. But that also begs almost as many questions as it resolves, especially within the polarized views with which acting approaches have been debated in this century since Konstantin Stanislavsky exported his first Moscow Art Theater students to the United States and the big Hollywood studios went into the business of creating stars. Stewart himself has usually declined to see any problem. "I am James Stewart playing James Stewart," he has said with the kind of self-obvious tone that has encouraged the perception of the so-called natural actor. "I couldn't mess around with characterizations. I play variations on myself." In the same vein, he has tapped for years the story of a reporter who once reputedly accosted Spencer Tracy to ask him why he was "always doing Spencer Tracy." In the Stewart telling (sometimes with other names in the punchline), Tracy shot back: "Who the hell am I supposed to do—Cagney?"

The more aggressive implication here is that the Hollywood stars of yore, whatever the given roles they have played, remained the box-office personalities the studios were banking on. But in Stewart's allusion to "characterizations" (and in his Tracy anecdote) there is also the suggestion that other performers have had the desire, necessity, and/or training to *become* their characters in some way that he (and Tracy) did not. It is a distinction that has been accepted as fundamental for some time—the line of demarcation established not only by acting methods stressing the need for some total psychic submersion into the character on the page, but also by Hollywood in its traditional separation of stars and "character actors." As a conspicuous beneficiary of this latter division, especially, it should not come as a surprise that Stewart has endorsed its premise. But exactly how real such a division has been beyond the academic rationalizations of the acting schools and the economic priorities of motion-picture companies, and how helpful it is for glimpsing the springs and calculations behind his specific talent, is another question.

Stewart has layered the problem further with a decidedly ambivalent attitude toward the capability that he calls his imagination. Whatever it actually consists of, he has told a number of interviewers, it should be held in check, when not stifled altogether, in nonacting situations. This is particularly so, he has said, in life-and-death contexts, such as those presented in the military; or, in his warning: "Imagination can be a soldier's worst enemy." When he has expounded on this idea, Stewart has made it clear that he is not using imagination solely in the sense of fantasy, daydream, or reverie, but in all its connotations and originality as well. It is also within this framework, he has intimated on more than one occasion, that the multidecorated World War II bomber pilot almost always turned down parts casting him as a fighting man in uniform, including those in star-studded spectaculars of *Midway* and *Longest Day* stripe that offered big money for an in-and-out cameo appearance. "They're just hardly ever the way it really is," he has said of Hollywood war pictures.

Stewart's aversion to being part of a screen fictionalization of war has not extended to other areas where a role of his might be construed as having reflected on some personal experience or deeply held belief. In the 1950s, for example, he lent his presence to two blatantly propagandistic projects conceived in Washington and carried to term in Hollywood—*Strategic Air Command* and *The FBI Story*. Aside from promoting the personality cults of General Curtis LeMay and J. Edgar Hoover, respectively, the films were in tune with Stewart's views on the Cold War threat posed by Communism and with his championing of two institutions he regarded as vital defenses against the Soviet Union. Similarly, he got involved in a trio of comedies for 20th Century-Fox in the 1960s with the avowed purpose of refocusing attention on what he called "traditional family values." None of the five films excited a particularly flexible performance from him; in fact, his work in all of them seems to have been undertaken when he was more concerned with keeping a rein on his imagination than with using it to travel the road from James Stewart to a character, when he was willing to settle for "Jimmy Stewart just being Jimmy Stewart."

One of the trademarks of a working Stewart at ease with his imagination has been the high emotionality of his characters. As a film historian, James Naremore, has observed: "He was the most emotional leading man to emerge from the studio system—perhaps the only one who could regularly cry on the screen without losing the sympathy of the audience." For film analyst Kathleen Murphy, Stewart's persuasiveness in crying has been merely the most obvious of the emotional weapons in his arsenal; "few actors have ever matched Stewart's ability to project flat-out enthusiasm for the fall into love," Murphy has noted, citing another example. And another film critic, Dennis Bingham, has made the point that "just as few actors fall in love as wholly as Stewart, few actors faint as gloriously as he does. . . . [His] lips quiver, his head and shoulders waver, the hand limply reaches for the mouth, and his eyes roll to the top of their sockets just before falling shut." For his part, actor-director Clint Eastwood has admitted to having been affected in particular by the emotional Stewart in the westerns of Anthony Mann in the 1950s. "He had a great way with violence," Eastwood has said. "Most people don't realize that about him, but when he was mad about something, when he had been wronged in a film, when he showed anger, it was much more intense than in most actors. He could be extremely volatile. When he snapped, the danger came on very strong."

Stewart himself has often sounded proud of the emotional immediacy of his best roles, and to a frequent question about the one trait that makes a scripted character appealing to him, has always replied "vulnerability." What Stewart has taken for vulnerability, however, has rarely been taken as just that by the attitudes—hostile, sympathetic, or ignorant as they might be—informing the stories in which he has given vent to his emotions. In fact, no other actor in so many roles has inspired so many characters sharing the screen with him to accuse him of being "crazy" or "nuts." Several times, Stewart's characters themselves have broached the possibility that they were more pathological than emotional—most despairingly in Jefferson Smith's challenge to be adjudged "dead right or crazy," most self-absorbedly in the eccentric aviation scientist's warnings of disaster in *No Highway in the Sky*, most guiltily in the bounty hunter's corpse-dragging in *The Naked Spur*.

Maintaining the courage of one's convictions—an idealistic goal—hasn't always been an attenuating circumstance, either, as the manic characters in Hitchcock and Mann pictures in particular have served to attest. If critic Tom Shales could detect in some Stewart characters "a spirit of abiding sanity even when the sanity was camouflaged under the trappings of a nut," the proposition is no less true stated in reverse.

Even without insinuating mania, the naked emotional charge in Stewart's most accomplished performances has frequently triggered odd responses. Whether meant as positive appreciations, as criticisms of his limitations, or merely as self-serving justifications for the academic disciplines of given researchers, many overviews of the actor's work have zeroed in on the emotionalism as evidence of a feminine quality that is assumed to be extraordinary in itself. In the eyes of fellow actor Richard Dreyfuss, for example, Stewart has been nothing short of "a feminine hero." One popular film reference work claims that Stewart stands in contrast to other leading men of his era because "while his rivals played with masculine understatement, [he] mirrored the vital excesses of those most American of rising actresses—Crawford, Davis, Hepburn." An even denser evaluation of his collaboration with Capra, and particularly on *It's a Wonderful Life*, concludes that "the Italian-Catholic Capra puts his protagonist through a secularized Christian ritual of castration and suffering that does not break violently with Stewart's prewar image, but does derive from the persona's 'femininity.'"

Psychiatricentric banalities of the kind have colored evaluations of Stewart's work for some time. If they managed to illuminate anything at all, it has been the dubious truths that masculinity equals the spare, the laconic, and the inscrutable, that an average Stewart character's loquaciousness is encountered away from the screen most frequently at a party of prattling women, and that any male actor who put himself into the hands of Frank Capra had to be crazy *and* nuts. In the meantime, these disquisitions have had no time for the chief complement to the strong emotionality of a Stewart performance: the actor's pronounced physicality. Unlike the Waynes and Coopers who, for example, could seem at ease with their height even when their heads grazed the ceiling beams of sets, the equally tall Stewart rarely let an audience forget that he had a body problem. He was too skinny. He was too awkward. He was bent over. His ears flopped. His lips were too large. His hair was cut wrong. He had a pondful of frogs in his throat. His knees rose to his chin whenever he sat down. And his hands, especially his hands. They were forever fumbling with something or drawing arcs in the air or erecting steeples of fingers or trying to find some pocket to disappear into. They plied trombones, accordions, pianos, guns, and reins, and still couldn't be quieted.

But the physicality of Stewart's performances has gone well beyond that pertaining to his own person. With a thoroughness normally associated with a Robert De Niro or a Dustin Hoffman, he has been exhaustive about ensuring that the physical objects or motions of a given character's world were as accurate as possible, even when directors, producers, and technical consultants did not think his efforts necessary. Forty years before De Niro hazarded precipitous weight gains and losses to portray Jake LaMotta, Stewart had a painful chemical solution applied to his throat so that Jefferson Smith knew what suffering was all about while filibustering on the Senate floor. He refused to go before the camera as Monty Stratton before he had pitched off a mound for weeks under the tutelage of the Chicago hurler, or as the vengeful marksman in *Winchester '73* before he had mastered the weapon with an expert from the rifle company, or as Glenn Miller before he had learned all slide positions for trombone notes that were going to be dubbed by professional musicians anyway. In what he had counted on as his equivalent of Fonda's valedictory performance in *On Golden Pond*, in the star-crossed cable-TV movie *Right of Way*, he waved off the idea of faking a scene in which he was asked to eat cat food, even though he regurgitated after every one of numerous takes. On one level, of course, such immersions into a part invite the noted Laurence Olivier line to Hoffman after the latter had twisted himself into a knot over the motivations of his character in *Marathon Man*: "Dear boy, why don't you just *act?*" On another level, however, the attention to such detail reflects the need for some actors—and Stewart has certainly been one of them— to inhabit their roles as just one element of an entire, plausible world that has been created by a screenplay and that, to be immediate and authoritative to them, cannot exist only in their imaginations.

Not all of Stewart's film characters have consisted in equal parts of volubility, emotional vulnerability, and conspicuous physicality. But enough of them have for one to be struck by the difference between this combination and the blend of hesitant articulateness, venerable drollery, and tightly wound courtesy that has characterized his nonperforming public appearances, particularly in his later years. Even more noteworthy, there would appear to be little in his biographical dossier to prepare us for the intensity of his work. He grew up in a western Pennsylvania town where his parents not only provided a model for solid domesticity, but also consciously encouraged his personal sense of adventure and creativity. He went to the best high school and prep school then available, where he was an also-ran academically but where he engaged in a routine variety of extracurricular activities. He went to Princeton for four years, impressing some classmates as personable, others as humorous, but none as the student destined to be the most famous alumnus at future reunions. Between semesters he went home to work either in his father's hardware store or at temporary manual jobs. He was handed some things, told to earn others, and didn't find one circumstance stranger than the other. Within his family there were no Eugene O'Neill terrors; within his early circles no Tennessee Williams violences.

There was a similar unexceptional pattern to his professional progress. While awaiting graduation at Princeton, he was asked to join a theater company on Cape Cod, so he joined. He was asked to accompany one of the Cape Cod productions to Broadway, so he accompanied it. He was asked to take a screen test for MGM, so he took it. He was asked to go to Hollywood, so he went. He did small roles because his contract said he was obliged to, then did bigger and bigger ones. He has never been insincere in referring to his climb as a "lucky accident," but on the other hand has also pointed out that he was scrupulous about maintaining a balance between what had been handed to him and what he had earned by exploiting whatever opportunity arose—by working, studying, promoting, and then starting all over again. He has expressed bafflement that anybody would see anything special in that.

Stewart has also done considerable walking between the raindrops. He arrived in Hollywood after the cresting of the fierce labor war that established the Screen Actors Guild and similar talent unions, so did not have to adopt an antagonistic attitude toward his employers. When he did challenge MGM over the film industry's equivalent of the baseball reserve clause, he was already a well-publicized war hero and the studios were terrified of making a move that would play into the hands of congressmen bent on cutting Hollywood down to size. He counted as his closest friends fellow professionals (Fonda, actress Margaret Sullavan, agent-producer Leland Hayward, most prominently) who had hellish private lives, keeping them on a rondo of internecine affairs and ultimately yielding up more than one suicide, but he mainly could think of them in gratitude for how they helped him in Falmouth, Manhattan, or Los Angeles. The women with whom he was involved for extended periods in the 1930s and 1940s—among them, actresses Ginger Rogers and Olivia de Havilland and singer Dinah Shore—did anything but linger once the relationship called for more from him than a capacity for a good time. At first glance, in fact, Stewart's two greatest emotional challenges offscreen would seem to have come through the military—in his own perilous bombing missions over Germany during World War II, when he was already well into his thirties and had such signal films as *Mr. Smith Goes to Washington* and *The Philadelphia Story* behind him, and in the death of his stepson Ronald McLean in Vietnam in June of 1969, when he was already more than sixty and had practically his whole motion-picture career behind him.

None of this offers aid and comfort to those seeking a mechanical correspondence between a traumatic cause and a subliminal effect. Even Stewart's undeniably more profound sense of anguish in the parts he played after the war does not eradicate the persuasiveness of the similar notes he sounded before being exposed to daily life-or-death situations in the skies over Bremen and Brunswick. So where exactly did this passion—and the adroitness to shape it and direct it—come from? Where did Stewart find the resources for becoming, in the opinion of veteran actor Nehemiah Persoff, "a classic example of the actor who's never satisfied with less than the whole truth of the character?"

There are clues.

James Stewart's acting prowess is not the only quality that has made an impression on his professional colleagues over his career; almost every one of them will also mention a behavioral correctness that extends from basic politeness to an old-world courtliness to unsolicited generosity. More than Mary Chase ever knew when she was writing the dialogue for *Harvey*, Stewart understood Elwood P. Dowd's philosophical outlook that "in this world you must be oh so smart or oh so pleasant. For years I was smart, now I recommend pleasant." The actor's daughter Kelly recalls the evening before she and her twin sister Judy were to go off to college when Stewart summoned them down to the living room. While the girls squirmed in dread of having to hear some last-minute paternal advice about sex, Stewart hemmed and hawed unintelligibly for a few moments, then blurted out that the two of them should "just remember always to be nice to people"; with that, he bade them goodnight.

Stewart's refusal to second-guess career mistakes has become legendary; for the most part, he has written off film debacles or trying costars with some variation on "Waal, I suppose that didn't work out the way we all hoped it would." Performers or directors who have driven him to distraction are generally described as "lively" or "fascinating," while cutthroat studio bosses usually come in for no worse a judgment than "hard-nosed." In the particular case of Bette Davis, more responsible than anyone for undercutting the impact of his performance in the cable-TV film *Right of Way*, he has for years excused her manipulative behavior on the set with the story that she was "feeling under the weather" at the time, while in reality the actress was in good health, subject to a series of ailments only months later.

But courteous as he has been to others, Stewart also expected to receive the same courtesy in return, not showing too much tolerance for those who, in his eyes at least, abused the exchange. This has been markedly so of his working relations, where he always has brought along his articulated manual of the Dos and Don'ts of being "professional." One victim of these standards was an assistant director up for that slot on *The Jimmy Stewart Show* in the early 1970s. Stewart, who had a big say in hirings for the show, turned him down because a couple of years before, while working together on a motion picture, the assistant director had given him a 7:30 AM location call and the actor had had to stand around a couple of hours before he really was needed. As Hal Kanter, the producer-director of *The Jimmy Stewart Show*, puts it: "With Jimmy a 7:30 call means only one thing—he starts work at 7:30. Not at 7:35 or 7:45, at 7:30. Anything else is 'unprofessional' to him. Maybe it wasn't the guy's fault that Jimmy had to stand around there waiting to start work. He was just doing what he had been told. But as far as Stewart is concerned, everybody has to be responsible for his own job."

Sometimes Stewart's instinct for tact and his contempt for a lack of professionalism have ended up on a collision course, prompting a bizarre compromise. Mayf Nutter, the singer-actor who was a semiregular on the *Hawkins* television series in the mid-1970s, recalls a situation when Stewart's roundabout way of dealing with ticklish problems had all but convinced him that he was going to be fired from the program.

> We had this sequence in an airplane cabin—me, Jimmy, and the weekly guest star. I had a pretty long monologue—Jimmy and I *always* had pretty long monologues on that show—and the guest star was throwing in a line every so often. We were shooting me and the guest star from over Jimmy's shoulder so that he was standing next to the camera. Well, I'm going through my monologue and I keep getting odd facial expressions from Jimmy. He's trying to tell me that I'm doing something wrong, but whatever it is, I don't get it. I just go on with my speech, and the guest star does his thing. I started getting very nervous seeing these faces Jimmy was making at me. Finally, Jimmy does something very rare for him—he asks the director to break for a few minutes while he talks to me. The director agrees, and Jimmy waves for me to follow him down to his trailer at the other end of the studio.
>
> We get to his trailer, and suddenly he starts to talk about Africa, about his daughter Kelly being an anthropologist and how great she is working around gorillas. By this time I figure it's over: whatever I've done, it's fatal enough to get me thrown off the show.
>
> Then, finally, he looks at his watch. Forty-five minutes have passed since we've walked away from the set. "Well, do you think that son of a bitch has learned his lines yet?" he asks. It wasn't me he wanted to strangle, it was the guest star! "You and I have to memorize the damn telephone directory for every show," he says to me, looking madder than I'd ever imagine he could be. "Meantime, they're paying a ton of money to that guy out there to parachute in here for a couple of days, do a couple of scenes, and he doesn't even have the courtesy to be prepared for that little effort when he comes on the set!"
>
> And of course, by the time we get back to the set, the guest star has used the break to master the lines he'd been messing up. The scene went off without a hitch. Jimmy never said a word to the actor. I don't think the guy knows to this day why we walked off the set.

People who have jobs should do them properly; and that includes James Stewart. Harry Morgan, who appeared with him in half a dozen pictures in the 1950s and 1960s, recalls a similar incident during the shooting of *Bend of the River*:

> Jimmy was together with Tony Mann as director and Aaron Rosenberg as producer for a string of movies at Universal. He wasn't the producer, but

he wasn't just contracted talent, either. He had a hefty percentage deal, so that gave him even more of an incentive to make sure that everything went right on the shooting. Well, one day they hand out the normal box lunch—a sandwich, piece of fruit, something to drink. And in the middle of it all there's also a Baby Ruth bar. Well, before I even get to my candy, somebody lets out a yell. The Baby Ruths are crawling with worms! Jimmy went absolutely ballistic! It was bad enough that he was handed this rotten stuff as one of the cast, but he also felt responsible for having it handed out to us. "Who the hell's catering this goddamn lunch?" he starts yelling. We got a cast and crew working like hell here morning and night, and *this* is what they get???" That was the end of those caterers.

Stewart's expectations of correct behavior—and his indignation at being disillusioned by the contrary—have emerged not only in his working relationships. On one occasion, he slugged a radio journalist for making a crack he thought offensive to his wife. On another, he hoisted a Pentagon representative out of a chair and out the door of his Beverly Hills home for suggesting that the death of his stepson in Vietnam might be made use of to support Nixon Administration policies in the war. The death of Ronald McLean also precipitated extended coolness toward his community church in Beverly Hills because of a mix-up over starting time for a memorial service. Despite being a church elder for whom religion had been formative force since his childhood, Stewart felt slighted enough by what he regarded as sloppy organization that he switched his allegiance away from the church for many months.

Stewart's developed sense of what constitutes proper and professional behavior has also encompassed his belief in the need for discipline in every aspect of life. Repeatedly in interviews over the years, whether the topic has been acting or antiwar demonstrations, he has bemoaned a lack of discipline as the root cause of one problem or another. Of itself this is hardly startling, cohering as it does with the one's-own-bootstraps political and pro-military positions he has taken on public issues across the board. Over and above these contexts, however, discipline—with its significance to him growing up in Pennsylvania, working for MGM, serving in the military, etc.—would also appear to have provided contours clear enough on more intimate levels for him to know just about all the time where he is in relation to them. Put another way, where the stress on discipline as the virtue of virtues might indicate a cage to some, to others it might help create the parameters for a different kind of barred space—one more evocative of a playpen, where the salient feature is not what the occupant is prevented from doing but what he is able to do in safety inside.

For sure, Stewart has never equated the rigor of his acting approach to the quality of its product. In his own words, it is an "indispensable foundation, but still only a foundation, from which you can only hope that luck, rapport, understanding, whatever you want to call it, will kick in and take you the rest of the way in the right direction." In another description of what he has painted as a multistep process, he has said: "You've done everything you can do from the point of view of learning the skills of your craft, and sometimes even that won't be enough. But sometimes a little moment will come when everything is right. You get involved. The sweat glands start to work. You tremble a little. And if you're lucky, people will remember those scenes for years. Maybe they'll forget the whole movie, but remember that scene." Kim Novak has been among those who have accompanied Stewart to the far side of his discipline. Concerning her experiences with him during the filming of *Vertigo*, she has said: "He'd go deep inside himself to prepare for an emotional scene. He was not the kind of actor who, when the director said Cut, would be able to say OK, then walk away. He'd squeeze my hand real hard and I would squeeze his hand, and we would allow each other to come down slowly, like a parachute."

But once back on the ground, Stewart usually wasted little time before returning to another phase of his persona on a movie set. In fact, his reputation for encouraging fellow performers, for making himself available before cameras begin to roll, for shared explorations of scenes and characters, even at the potential cost of his own character's scripted prominence, is matched by another—his withdrawal to what a number of colleagues have labeled "a friendly aloofness" whenever he is not on call or the working day is over. Harry Carey, Jr., recalls having gone to John Ford once with the worry that, despite having worked with Stewart on several films, he still was unable to say that he knew the man. Ford's reply to Carey was that "you don't get to know Jimmy Stewart, Jimmy Stewart gets to know you." Walter Brennan phrased it in his own bald way during the making of *The Far Country*: "It's not that he's unfriendly, it's just that he's always getting bogged down in thought."

From the testimony of fellow workers, only rarely has Stewart allowed himself to be distracted from his work once on a location or on a soundstage, and that includes the down hours. When he wasn't poring over lines with other actors, he was usually in his trailer or hotel room, avoiding as much as possible the social byplay of motion-picture casts and crews. As Robert Mitchum saw it during the shooting of *The Big Sleep*, "he came to work—over and out." Nobody understood better than Gloria Stewart, whose sightings on a set during forty-five years of marriage were few and far between. Conversely, intrusions from the outside world corresponded with some of Stewart's less inspired performances. As Janice Rule recalls from the making of *Bell, Book and Candle*: "He seemed hardly there a lot of the time. We did the dialogue, we did the scenes, period. He looked tired and acted harassed for most of the picture because he was having problems with his teenager sons at home and seemed to be on the phone an awful lot about what was going on. It was just a father having to confront those wonderfully charming teenage years."

Normally, however, as Burgess Meredith, a Stewart roommate in their early days in Hollywood, attests: "His involvement in a thing could get damn eerie. For good and bad, he never permitted himself to go drifting through. Once he took on a project—and God knows some of them were debatable propositions—he was always there at full throttle. The more meticulous he became about his role in a picture, the more he enjoyed the whole of it. I guess it made the world of the picture he was doing more real, more comprehensive, to him."

Nevertheless, between the intensity of his preparations and that of his performance there still yawns the question of the specific contents of Stewart's resources—the alchemical stuff in reserve to be transformed by somebody who, by his own bemused testimony, never felt any special inadequacy *or* superiority in growing up and who, to judge from his offscreen conversation, has preferred the approximate and the deflective for articulating his emotions. (The locutions "kind of" and "sort of" dot every lengthy interview he has given; he has called the phrases into play to cover feelings on everything from the impact of his small-town background on his career to the death of close professional colleagues.) Where did all that emotional precision and the variety of it on the screen come from? Where did he pick up, as director Samuel Fuller once described the art of Barbara Stanwyck, "all those closeted thoughts to be selected at will?"

The obvious starting place for an answer is the life of James Maitland Stewart of Indiana, Pennsylvania—somebody significantly older than both James Stewart the actor and James Stewart the Hollywood star and national icon.

I
HOME
IN INDIANA

THE MUSEUM CASE

I N LATE MAY OF 1995, THE CITIZENS OF INDIANA, Pennsylvania, enthusiastically opened a long-awaited Jimmy Stewart Museum on Philadelphia Street—a tribute to the town's most famous native son that also offered hope for relieving the chronic local economic problems.

Well, maybe not *all* of the town's 17,500 citizens were enthusiastic. And maybe there was not all *that* much confidence that a single museum would attract enough tourists to markedly reverse decades of economic woes and double-digit unemployment in the region.

Still, the museum had finally become a reality after surviving several years of local ambitions that ran the gamut from the well-intentioned to the opportunistic. If not every native believed that the 4,500-square-foot space on the top floor of the municipal library was going to transform Indiana into the Cooperstown of the movies, there were enough of them who were sure that their numbers constituted only a fraction of the international admirers of James Stewart and that those from the outer precincts would sooner or later adjust vacations to include a drive through western Pennsylvania to visit the rather unassuming building. And in the meantime there was for one and all the immediate payoff of a weekend of parades and celebrations to mark the opening.

Indiana has always liked parades for marking national holidays and regional and local milestones. The town's customary way of dealing with events has been to clear Philadelphia Street of its cars and buses, set up chairs on the sidewalks, and prepare to review the latest offerings of local high school bands along a six- or seven-block route. Given the town's size, there is seldom any surprise in the eyes of spectators as the marchers troop by; those proceeding down the street have almost certainly squeezed into old army uniforms, lodge shirts, and majorette tights in homes they share with the people now appraising them. This usually generates loud repartee back and forth between the sides, a great deal of it about waistlines betraying their owners since the passing of the last parade. The unexpected—and the appreciative laughter saluting it— invariably centers around marchers representing nearby towns or outlying districts; without these ringers, in fact, the parades down Indiana's main thoroughfare would last no longer than it takes for a big-city subway train to disgorge its passengers through a turnstile.

The most optimistic advance word on the parade inaugurating the museum had foreseen more than 50,000 western Pennsylvanians paying tribute to Stewart. As the days had grown closer to the opening, however, that number had been consigned to delirium, to a point where the initial prognosticators themselves denied ever having entertained it. When Stewart had been the featured attraction of another motorcade down Philadelphia Street in May of 1983, on the occasion of his seventy-fifth birthday and the unveiling of a statue in his likeness, the actor had drawn crowds generally calculated in the 10,000 range. But the museum opening was operating under a handicap that the birthday fete had not: the absence of the guest of honor. Because of a deep depression that had kept him confined to his North Roxbury Drive home in Beverly Hills since the death of his wife in February 1994, and an accompanying refusal ever to appear in public again, Stewart had left the ceremonies up to his twin daughters. Museum promoters had not exactly suppressed that particular; it had been mentioned (albeit hidden away as part of a subordinate clause) in most local newspaper stories about the museum for some time. But the resulting emphasis on the museum rather than the man who inspired it, had created its own air of uncertainty—a fleeting thought that if the opening wasn't going to be quite as definitive as it might have been, maybe the museum wasn't all that authoritative either.

Of course, a parade was still always a parade. And May 20, 1995— Stewart's eighty-seventh birthday—provided a perfectly comfortable 73 degrees Fahrenheit for the march; even the sun, normally spotted in Indiana as often as a good job opening, showed up shortly before the noon step-off to light up Philadelphia Street. Most of the late morning action revolved around the Indiana Court House lawn, a block down from the museum, where workers were testing the microphones and setting up the last chairs for the official dedication ceremonies that would take place as soon as the parade ended.

The row-seating arrangement for the ceremony surrounded to near-disappearance the nine-foot bronze statue of Stewart that had been guarding the courthouse since 1983. The Malcolm Alexander sculpture depicts the actor in the kind of suit and fedora he wore in some of his less compelling screen efforts (*The FBI Story* and the comedies made with 20th Century-Fox in the 1960s, for example), but more than one gazer has also discerned the metallic likeness of Elwood P. Dowd. Adepts of Indiana geomancy have noted that the statue has been angled in such a way that the figure is facing the former location of the hardware store owned by the Stewart family for generations, which has become a fulcrum for Jimmy Stewart anecdotes. What the statue actually has been peering at is the headquarters of the Savings & Trust Bank, which took over the property after the store was demolished in 1969. A billboard in front of the bank announced YOU ARE NOW IN BEDFORD FALLS. This allusion to *It's a Wonderful Life* might have been more poignant if that institution had looked more like the savings and loan run by George Bailey and less like some late twentieth-century financial fantasy realized by Lionel Barrymore's avaricious Mr. Potter.

The uncertainty about the turnout and the relative brevity of the parade program had doused the ardor of outside concessionaires. For the most part, street vending was restricted to improvised annexes of Philadelphia Street stores—luncheonettes moving freezers with Italian ices out onto the sidewalk, souvenir boutiques clogging their front doors with racks of T-shirts and sweatshirts. Although most of the shops along the four- or five-block commercial nucleus of the street had acknowledged the day by putting posters of Stewart's films (mostly *It's a Wonderful Life* and *Harvey*) in their windows, few of the items being sold bore directly on the actor; even the T-shirts were more concerned with the beer-drinking reputation of students from the local Indiana University of Pennsylvania and with the championship years of the Pittsburgh Steelers. Coming as close as anyone to the man of the hour was a haberdasher who had set out sidewalk racks and tables to peddle suits and hats similar to those worn by the bronze statue standing in front of the courthouse.

With only minutes to go before the start of the parade, the consensus estimate of two organizers, their wives, and a visiting friend from Philadelphia was that there were between two and three thousand people staking out good curb positions, with maybe another thousand lingering on the side streets, grabbing a last cup of coffee, or otherwise being reluctant about showing their faces before the first baton twirler did. Even at that point not everyone had heard that Stewart would be among the missing: An announcement that the proceedings were to be held up briefly because his daughters were still on their way back from another dedication ceremony, at the Indiana County Jimmy Stewart Airport some miles distant, prompted one woman to ask, "Why can't we just begin with Jimmy. What do the daughters have to do with it?" Informed by a companion that Stewart was back in California, the woman looked at the man as though *he* had been Harvey all these years, going invisible every once in a while just to annoy her.

The delay in the start of the parade seemed to irk a WDAD radio announcer who had been set up for the occasion at a sidewalk booth a few steps from the museum entrance. After an hour or more of bubbling patter about Stewart's films and interviews with alternately solemn and giggling passersby, the announcer was more than ready to get on to play-by-play coverage of the parade. Between regular assurances to his audience of Stewart's "critical importance for Indiana, Hollywood, America, and the rest of the world," he had been worn down by the frequent failure of his interviewees to answer trivia questions about Stewart's career that would have netted them prizes donated by station sponsors. The questions were generally of the order of "Which sport did Monty Stratton play—baseball, basketball, or badminton?" and "Who was Jimmy's costar in *The Philadelphia Story*—Katharine Hepburn, Grace Kelly, or Demi Moore?"; but even those who claimed to have seen every Stewart film showed a tendency to give the excuse that "that was before my time." What that prompted was both another reminder from the announcer that "everything Jimmy has done will always be *in* our time" and an even easier question ("To what city did Jimmy's character of Mr. Smith go in the very famous Frank Capra picture?") to aid in moving the goods and services put up as prizes by town merchants.

A free restaurant dinner or not, the overwhelming majority of those on Philadelphia Street that late spring morning could justly have claimed that Stewart's screen work *had* been before their time. It had been a quarter of a century since he had starred in a major feature and only five years less than that since his *Hawkins* television series had been canceled. The community that sported a Hollywood star as its most brilliant bauble had not even had a movie house since the Indiana Theater went out of business under competition from a mall multiplex a couple of miles away. Except for those who had glimpsed the sodden *Magic of Lassie* in the early 1980s or Stewart's cameos in *The Big Sleep* and *The Shootist* shortly before that, there probably wasn't a single person under thirty-five waiting for the parade to start who had ever paid to see James Stewart perform within an establishment that sold popcorn. At best, they had seen the working James Stewart by the grace of their television sets or VCRs; at worst, they had been reduced on those occasions to seeing a colorized James Stewart that the actor always refused to recognize as the genuine thing.

Far more familiar has been the local institution of "Jimmy"—visible immediately in the streets, hospital wing, airport, and other spots named after him. To some degree, in fact, the museum was less an overdue acknowledgment of his artistry than it was an overdue focalization of all the earlier tributes that, with the passing of a few years, had come to seem rushed to the point of tackiness and ubiquitous to the point of prepotency. Local cynics liked talking about the Indiana forces bent on turning the town into Jimmyland. But it wasn't necessary to envision *Mortal Storm* Alpine villages or *Vertigo* bungee jumps to see that there might not be all that much difference between the leeriness of the Indiana teenager who had to walk down Jimmy Stewart Boulevard to satisfy his craving for a Jimmy Stewart Devonshire Sandwich and that of the dusty cowpoke who—as once played by James Stewart—arrived in a new western town and, as he cantered down the main street on his wilting horse, noticed that somebody named Carruthers or Hawley owned everything from the saloon to the blacksmith shop.

Would the museum provide more informed, more energizing access to its towering spirit? There were as many opinions on that as there were neatly manicured church lawns and boarded-up storefronts in town.

On the far end of the skepticism there were those who appeared irritated even to hear the Stewart name. Generally, they were residents who had latched on to the biographical fact that the actor had not lived in Indiana full-time since the 1920s and who didn't believe that his visits over the years entitled him to any special fealty. Among those representing this view was a waitress in a Philadelphia Street luncheonette where sugar was kept off the countertop and booth tables to discourage thieves and where signs warned: WATER WITHOUT PURCHASE 25¢ SMALL, 35¢ MEDIUM, 45¢ LARGE. "Name a single place or person he's ever given a little money to without getting his name up in lights," the woman, in her mid-thirties and with an air of perpetual annoyance, challenged. "He's never done anything for this town except given them some new excuse for a parade. This museum is just a few people trying to make a quick buck. What else is new?"

Actually, Stewart *has* donated money, and more than once, to local projects without receiving publicity for it, but that wasn't the kind of detail that easily fit under the clouds of resentment that seemed to hang over much of Indiana as naturally as the next hour's rainfall. For Elizabeth Rogers, pastor of the Calvary Presbyterian Church that the Stewart family had attended scrupulously for generations, there was nothing at all novel in the bitterness directed toward the museum or toward Stewart. "There is an exhausting whining mentality around here," Rogers, a heavyset blonde in her forties, said. "This is Appalachia. Pick up your self-pity as you enter." At the same time, however, Rogers had some reservations of her own about the museum and what it insinuated about some of Calvary Presbyterian's parishioners. Choosing her words carefully, after noting that she was to deliver the invocation at the dedication ceremonies, she said:

> Let's say I watch all this with interest, but not too much enthusiasm. There's all this hero worship of Jimmy Stewart by people who otherwise strike me as very intelligent. I really don't understand it and I can't see it as a particularly good thing. At bottom, it's that idol worship that I find most disturbing about the museum, not all this other talk about a mercenary attempt by a few people to make money. There's a fine line between respecting somebody for what he's accomplished with his life and becoming a keeper of the flame. I think some people around here have crossed that line.

Robert Waskowicz, operator of a used bookstore on Philadelphia Street, mixed his criticism of what he called "all these nostalgia buffs" with the warning of a small entrepreneur. A thin forty-year-old with a blond ponytail, Waskowicz confessed to being "dumbfounded that some people think they only have to mention the name Jimmy Stewart and everybody will understand. Understand what, exactly? It's absolutely ludicrous that you have them going around saying that Stewart is a great American in a tone that implies anyone who disagrees with his way of life or political beliefs isn't a good American. They want to talk about what a great American Jimmy Stewart is, they should look at themselves and their plans for this museum because what America is all about is *marketing*. If they don't know how to market Stewart, if they just turn him into Indiana's version of Punxsutawney Phil, you're going to see a pretty fundamental contradiction in all their posturing."

But in the eyes of the locals, and not only those connected to the museum, Rogers and Waskowicz shared flawed credentials for their opinions in not being natives of Indiana. (Rogers: "Anybody born here after World War II is still a newcomer in the opinion of the old guard.") It wasn't so easy to dismiss Elizabeth Simpson, a friend of the Stewart family for some eighty years. According to Simpson, "it's a little ridiculous to have a museum for a movie star. Jimmy's a great guy and a wonderful actor, but you erect monuments and dedicate museums to people who remain vivid for centuries, not just for a few decades. Do they really expect somebody in the middle of the twenty-first century to be impressed by a movie actor as a symbol of a town? Far too much has been made of this thing."

Then there was Frank Hood, the Sunday editor of the Indiana *Gazette*, the community daily that assiduously had been reporting every major and minor development in the organization of the museum for some four years. Unlike Rogers and Waskowicz, Hood evinced unadulterated admiration for Stewart; unlike Simpson, the soft-spoken, sixtyish newsman had thought the actor deserved a museum:

The original idea of the museum—at least I think it was the original idea—was that we do something for Jimmy. It hasn't really turned out that way. The whole thing has turned into a platform for Republican Party propaganda, of benefit to a lot of other people before benefiting Jimmy Stewart. It's the same mentality we had in 1983, when they were unveiling that statue for his seventy-fifth birthday. Where else in the whole world can you see a public statue with the names of all the committee members who were behind it spelled out on it? Have even Latin American dictators put their names on the latest statue of Simon Bolivar? Did Mussolini's flunkies do it when they were putting up all those bronzes showing Roman gladiators? The only place you'll find that kind of self-aggrandizement is on the Jimmy Stewart statue out in front of the courthouse in Indiana, Pennsylvania. Except for a couple of individuals on the board of the museum, that's the same kind of provincial politicking and small-minded grabbiness that you'll find going on now, too. I have no time for these people. We haven't done the museum for Jimmy. We've used him.

Even for the critics, though, there was no immediate escape from the museum's reach. With the parade in the offing, the luncheonette counterwoman had taken up a stand next to the store's ice cream freezer on the sidewalk, waiting for some passerby to show an interest in her wares. A few doors down the block, Waskowicz kept a casual eye on another would-be spectator who had grown tired of staring at the still-empty parade route and had wandered over to the sidewalk tables of old Erskine Caldwell novels and grayed accounting textbooks. Rogers had her date with the benediction that she was going to call down on the museum. And Hood, who had been emphatic about how nobody was ever going to see him near the museum, was nevertheless still going to have to oversee every detail reported from Philadelphia Street for the next edition of the *Gazette*.

DARKROOMS

BEFORE JAMES STEWART CAME ALONG, INDIANA DIDN'T have too much practice in celebrating local heroes who were known beyond county borders. About the only previous residents who had gained some national attention were a nineteenth-century labor union pioneer (William Sylvis), a journeyman big league outfielder (Doc Gessler), a journeyman Supreme Court justice (John Elkin), and John Braillier, a long-time claimant to having been the first professional football player and the recipient of the first lifetime pass issued by the National Football League. Even Nellie Bly, a student in town before undertaking such nineteenth-century journalistic escapades as circling the world in seventy-two days, remained relatively anonymous in local records under her real name of Elizabeth Cochrane. Aside from Stewart, celebrity hitchers were reduced for many years to noting that Arthur Godfrey, once the king of network morning radio and television, had toiled as a young man in the mines of nearby Clymer. But if Indiana has a lot to be modest about, it also has evinced an attitude that this is the natural course of things. Since its formal incorporation as a borough of Indiana County in 1816, the community has cast a baleful Scots-English Protestant·eye on attempts to blow out of proportion the individual achievements of residents.

For a place that maintained an active Prohibitionist Party for more than 100 years, all the way into the 1970s, there is a touch of irony in the fact that Indiana's very first building was a log tavern. It was within those walls, on what would become Philadelphia Street, midway between the present intersections of Fourth and Fifth streets, that the community began to take shape in 1805. While tavernkeeper Henry Shyrock kept the ale flowing freely for three days that December, settlers from nearby areas of Pennsylvania and Ohio staked out claims to more than 300 lots up for public sale in the surrounding timber-rich zone. General storekeeper John Denniston was recorded as Indiana's first dealer in nonalcoholic products, and one Peter Sutton decided that there was enough overflow from Shyrock's clientele to justify a second tavern. A year to the day of the lot sales, Indiana held its first court hearing—on the second floor of Sutton's tavern.

Whether or not the founding fathers had planned it that way, the court session in Sutton's upstairs room proved to be a milestone in the town's development since one of Indiana's most important functions thereafter was as a legal center. Through all its economic ups and downs over the next two centuries with agriculture, timber, tanneries, flour and paper mills, and bituminous coal, right up to its current designation as the Christmas Tree Capital of the World, the town preserved a county seat allure for attorneys, judges, and all those dependent on them. Thanks to the visiting litigants, the law business also gave impetus to hotel keeping early in the nineteenth century. Like the original court, a majority of the hotel rooms were on the upper floors of two-story taverns; well into this century, there were separate inns for men and women. As a rule, judges were so expeditious in ruling on the ever-mounting number of legal wrangles brought before them that many of the visitors didn't bother undressing when they checked into the hostelries, being satisfied to grab a nap, show up for their court date, then leave town again right away; this did wonders for the turnover at the hotels.

Because of manipulations and political gerrymanders, it wasn't until a decade after the public land sales at Henry Shyrock's tavern that the community gained its status as a borough. Its growth was hardly precipitous. An 1810 census still registered a mere fifteen families in the town proper and an overall population of only fifty. Although some of that slight number was attributable to jurisdictional maneuvering among speculators and to a reluctance by farmers and woodsmen to have their heads counted for anything outside a village social, it also presaged a perduring uneasiness in Indiana over the town's failure to attract more settlers—a blinking suspicion that maybe not even the court bureaucracy, with its traffic in transient visitors, amounted to a stable center. Even when Stewart was born in 1908, with the town functioning as a significant trading and supply node for the Allegheny coal district, the population was only 6,500. As recently as the 1960s, state tourist officials were reduced to happy-talk consolations in their brochures that "within 500 miles of Indiana, Pennsylvania, lives nearly one-half of the population of the nation." Keeping the *nearly* handy, a similar claim, of course, could have been made for innumerable locations between the Ohio River and the Atlantic. But what very few of these other spots have had to put up with, aside from a succession of economic disasters, has been a meteorological sneer: habitually gloomy skies that have saddled the entire region with a reputation as "the biggest natural darkroom in the world." According to medical experts, this gray corduroy climate has played a cardinal role in helping western Pennsylvania to its dubious distinction over many years of having the highest incidence of mental depression in the country. To put it mildly, Indiana has never struck too many people off the bat as an ideal nesting place.

But for some it has. And practically from the beginning to the present day, many of the same family names have been prominent—Shyrocks, Suttons, Moorheads, Stewarts, Marshalls, Campbells, Wilsons, Whites, Thompsons, Mitchells, Taylors, Nixons, Blairs, Kellys, and others whose forebears trace back to the islands north of the English Channel. It was a Leonard Shyrock, for instance, a descendent of the first tavernkeeper, who in 1854 ceded the Pennsylvania Railroad title to a packet of centrally located holdings, enabling the town a couple of years later to institute a daily train service to Blairsville and lessen its isolation. It was a James Sutton, a descendent of the second tavernkeeper, who operated the largest mill for a good part of the nineteenth century and who, after the

Civil War, channeled some of its riches into building the town's biggest mansion. The annals of Indiana have not had to stray too far from the same nucleus of names to list the valiant natives who marched off to battle in the Civil War, the Spanish-American War, World War I, World War II, the Korean War, the Vietnam War, and in the nation's various other military adventures between them and since. Atypical has been the elected official or local dignitary who has not propagated a line of similars or not boasted a pedigree dating back a number of generations, with or without the assistance of interfamily marriages from within the same core group. The inroads made by some non-WASP groups lately, notably by eastern European immigrants, have not eclipsed that tradition to any conclusive degree.

If England, Scotland, and Ireland have provided the W, A, and S, Presbyterians and Methodists have accounted for most of Indiana's P. Though some sources give a statistical edge to the Methodists, there has been little argument that western Pennsylvania is the heart of Presbyterianism in the United States and that Indiana County is one of that heart's major chambers. The dominant position of the Presbyterians has been a social reality long enough for it to have spawned the—by now—wheeziest of church humor. Elizabeth Rogers, the pastor of Calvary Presbyterian, likes pointing to the church's following as evidence that "Presbyterians have to be the densest people in western Pennsylvania."

In less than two centuries, American Presbyterianism has negotiated as many schisms, secessions, mergers, and reunifications as the Vatican has had to cope with in a bad millennium; Indiana has reflected many of these changes, and on more than a religious level. The church disputes have ranged from the doctrinal and the ritualistic to the political and the regional, generating an often baffling array of organizational names. The 1958 creation of the three-million-strong United Presbyterian Church in the United States of America, for instance, came through the consolidation of the Presbyterian Church of the United States of America with the United Presbyterian Church of North America. Declining to be part of the merger was the Presbyterian Church in the United States, sometimes known as the Southern Presbyterian Church. In addition, there are denominations such as the Orthodox Presbyterian Church, the Reformed Presbyterian Church of North America (Old School), and the Reformed Presbyterian Church of North America

(General Synod). Aside from offering followers the finest nuances of credal harmony, the panoply of churches has left a material mark on many western Pennsylvania communities with a proliferation of steeples and towers that not even the coalescence of doctrine and rituals at the pulpits inside has braked. In some towns, such as Indiana, on the appropriately named Church Street, directly across the street from a Methodist house of worship, rival Presbyterian congregations stream every Sunday into cheek-by-jowl properties of neatly trimmed lawns and formidable scrubbed stone.

For Calvary pastor Rogers, what distinguished her congregation from the adjoining Graystone Church was that "they're much more old-fashioned. Call it the difference between order and ardor—they're the order, we're the ardor. We consider ourselves a liberal church. We pride ourselves on new things. We view religious belief as a vital contribution to the surrounding society, not as a private discipline to be practiced away from it."

Although it has meant widely different things at different times, liberal Presbyterianism has had a foothold in Indiana practically since the founding of the town. In the midnineteenth-century days of the Abolitionists, several leading church members had a big role in making the town a stop-off on the Underground Railroad that enabled runaway slaves to reach Canada. The activity became so identified with moral Christian responsibility that it eased the way toward an organizational unification between two branches of the denomination that previously had been leery of one another; this produced the United Presbyterian Church of North America, which lasted for 100 years until the 1958 supermerger. In the 1920s, the Reverend Frederick Hinitt gained even national attention for sermons inspired as much by the daily newspapers as by the Bible; his homilies had titles like "Problems of the City," "Immigrants and Americanization," "Unchristian Individualism," and "The Problem of Japan at the Disarmament Conference." Among those listening to Hinitt's weekly calls for the church to interest itself in social problems and for members to be aware of their prejudices and smug chauvinism were Alexander and Elizabeth Stewart and their son James. At his seventy-fifth birthday celebration in 1983, Stewart named Hinitt as one of the major inspirations of his life.

But apart from social ills, the liberals also had opponents within the church—as well as failing nerve among their own—to deal with. A criminal trial involving a slave assisted by the Underground Railroad embarrassed some church elders, cooled the abolitionist ardor, and, for a brief period, left the political initiative in town to the Whigs, who sometimes acted as little more than a respectable front for the xenophobic Know-Nothing Party. It was against this background that influential church members, liberals included, embraced the 1856 presidential candidacy of John Frémont, the first Republican to run for the White House. Thereafter, the church often came off as an institutional twin to the Republicans, its most visible spokesmen along the way backing with particular vigor populist standard-bearers such as Robert La Follette and Wendell Wilkie, but also the far more obscurantist party candidates thrown up at local, state, and national levels before, between, and after them. Similarly, an organizational inertia set in after the death of the modernist Hinitt in 1928; in his place came the Reverend Robert Clark, who carried on from the pulpit on such old-time religion themes as personal devils and the need to interpret Scripture literally, while chiding members for thinking that the Great Depression required any special measures beyond the attention of Jesus Christ. Liberal dissent was either muted or ineffective.

Nor, flirtation with the Abolitionists notwithstanding, has even the most activist sector of the Presbyterian Church been particularly consequential in dealing with a deep current of racism and anti-Semitism that one resident has called "Indiana's silent problem." Only by adding in an estimated 600 African Americans and overseas exchange students at the university did the black community number more than 1,000 in the early 1990s; yet, even the few hundred black townies that have represented the norm for decades have been more than sufficient for nourishing enough bigotry to sustain the Ku Klux Klan. At the nadir of the Depression in the 1930s, as many as 50,000 sympathizers and curiosity seekers were reported to have attended a Klan rally in the region, with the now-defunct Indiana *Weekly Messenger* functioning as little more than a mouthpiece for the thugs. If there is nothing like that kind of membership (or even curiosity) today, it isn't that the Klan adherents have felt social pressures to remain incognito. Early in 1995, for instance, one Klansman felt safe enough to parade into a state welfare office in hood-and-sheet regalia to protest a decision to cut off his checks.

While Indiana officialdom has been quick to dismiss the significance of "a handful of crazies," there has been a thick cloud of ethnic intolerance extending beyond the KKK that has hung over western Pennsylvania most of this century. Jews running for public office receive the usual anonymous telephone calls telling them to desist. With regard to blacks, the least of it has been the Come In Person tag lines in want ads aimed at screening out job applicants of the wrong color. As recently as the 1980s, a couple of state agencies had to be called in to deal with protests against a black boy using a school bus in nearby Clymer. In Indiana itself, Frank Lawrence, pastor of Graystone between 1952 and 1960 and now retired to another part of Pennsylvania, recalls a late 1950s attempt to desegregate a public swimming pool: "I got into a lot of trouble over that one. Indiana had some good people, but even they were not exactly militants when it came to respecting the civil rights of everybody. Me, I just didn't think it was a Christian thing to have that pool—a public facility supported by the taxes of everybody, black and white—for whites only. But the more I brought up the issue with the town, talked about it with church people, the harder they came down on me. One of my staunchest critics was somebody who up to then I had considered a good friend. I lost the battle and I lost a friend."

Calvary's Rogers didn't have to go back to the 1950s to cite another example of what she termed her church's "exasperation" with Indiana attitudes toward race.

> I suppose it shouldn't come as a big surprise that the economic conditions around here have been a great breeding ground for the Klan. A couple of years ago, there was a KKK rally scheduled to be held at a farmhouse a few miles outside of town. The Indiana *Gazette* not only reported that it was going to be held, but printed directions on how to get there. I couldn't believe it! It was as if they were encouraging readers to go. So I wrote a letter to the paper in protest. I didn't get an answer. Then we decided to write to the individual editors asking them how they felt about working for a paper that offers directions to a Klan rally. We didn't get a response from them, either.

As well-intentioned as the letter-writing protest might have been, it also suggested to some the bridled way in which the Presbyterians, even those proclaiming themselves as liberals, have engaged social issues in Indiana. To be sure, the church has been hard put to shake its image of a somewhat bloodless, white-gloved sentry to moral responsibility; this in turn has perpetuated doubts about where a profound abhorrence of something like a Klan rally leaves off and where a political concern for the appearance of things begins. For instance, attorney Jay Rubin, the chief promoter of the Jimmy Stewart Museum and a long-time adherent of the American Civil Liberties Union, declared that he didn't see anything wrong with the *Gazette* telling everybody how to get to the KKK rally. "The more the merrier," Rubin said. "Let everybody stand around and see what these imbeciles are all about." A similar line was taken by Frank Hood, one of the *Gazette* editors who received the protest letter and a member of the Calvary congregation. According to Hood, Rogers was "exactly wrong" on the directions issue. "Would Elizabeth prefer that we not tell people that the Klan is alive and well and holding its rallies here? There's a thinner line between indignation and covering up than people sometimes realize. There's too much silence about the Klan, not not enough of it."

If there has been a critical force for change in Indiana in recent decades, it hasn't been the Presbyterian Church (Calvary *or* Graystone versions), the Republican Party, or any of the other institutions that Jimmy Stewart has pointed to at one time or another as a formative hometown influence; that distinction goes to Indiana University of Pennsylvania. Aside from effectively doubling Indiana's standing population during the academic year to almost 35,000, the school has gradually been turning the borough into a university town, with all the business and financial ramifications of such an identity. Without IUP there would have been no need for twenty-one bank headquarters or branches in a community starved for jobs, even considering the estimated hundreds of millions of dollars of "old money" deposited in vaults by the deceptively wealthy. Subtract the teachers, students, administrators, researchers, and support personnel from the university who have had their voting addresses switched to Indiana or some other part of the county and a resurgent Democratic Party would not have edged out the Republicans in every district election held in the late 1980s and 1990s except for the 1994 gubernatorial race. It hasn't been only IUP staffers who have claimed that without the campus's seventy-five buildings spread out over ninety-five acres, Indiana would have joined the Ghost Town Trail for tourists that starts about twenty-five miles away. And it hasn't been IUP staffers who have resented the entire situation.

"You could already see it in the 1950s," according to former Graystone pastor Frank Lawrence. "They were closing down the mines and the college was emerging as a potent force. The old guard really hated that. They couldn't think of anything more deplorable than depending on these outsiders for survival. Being a long-hair intellectual was the least of it. It was just the whole idea of the university itself taking over." The antagonism hasn't abated all that much since, at least among those who remember when there had been other sources of economic health or who are more preoccupied with growing the Christmas trees that have produced at least seasonal business. "The university has become the real economic backbone of the town," said Elizabeth Rogers, "but the town has this attitude that everyone would be better off without it."

In fact, the university, even more than the legal administrative machinery originally installed on the upper floor of Peter Sutton's tavern, has become the town's most conspicuous example of an institution *in* Indiana more than *of* Indiana, of a structuring element and vital economic force that still has not provided a confident center for the community. And, as Rogers observed, "it isn't as though they just came and dumped the campus on Indiana. It goes all the way back to 1875, when they called it the Normal School and it was for teaching teachers. Maybe people are always going to be outsiders if they came here after World War II, but institutions are going to remain outsiders if they grew up any time after the *Civil* War."

As individuals or institutions, on the other hand, the Stewarts have never been outsiders.

THE STEWARTS

ALTHOUGH THE JIMMY STEWART MUSEUM IS NAMED AFTER Indiana's most famous native, he was never the town's most popular Stewart among the locals. Even three and a half decades after his death and a quarter of a century after the razing of the hardware store he used most of his life as a combination cracker-barrel–Hollywood display case, Alexander Stewart, the actor's father, remained a special guest at the inauguration proceedings. Most immediately, there were the reminders in the dedication speeches and museum literature of how often over the years Jimmy had expressed devotion to his father for having been a model parent, storekeeper, eccentric, Presbyterian, dreamer, adventurer, child psychologist, film critic, and patriot. Attendees of a certain age had their own stories about "Alex," "Alec," or "Eck," most of them with the theme that there never would have been an actor in Hollywood if there hadn't first been a ham in the hardware store. There was also a second moral implicit in all the stories: that Alexander Stewart, who died in 1961 at the age of eighty-nine, had been the last of the Stewarts to call Indiana his lifelong home. In that sense, the museum was not only something new, but it provided a measure for the end of a tradition dating back to the immediate wake of the Revolutionary War.

The United States was barely a fact in the autumn of 1785 when the first Stewarts in America had left County Atrim in the northeastern part of Northern Ireland to set sail across the Atlantic. Come to that, the Stewart family itself was barely a fact at the time: When a thirty-year-old William Stewart climbed aboard the passenger ship *Congress* in Belfast, he was accompanied by his very pregnant wife, Margaret Gettys, and a son, Archibald, who had not yet celebrated his first birthday. In the middle of the crossing, on November 15, 1785, Margaret gave birth to her second son, baptized as John Kerr Stewart. Over the next five years there would be three more additions to the family—Martha, Alexander, and William. Subsequent generations would frequently have recourse to the same names.

Martha Stewart, who entered the world on July 6, 1787, was the first Stewart to be born in the United States. But she wasn't born in Indiana County. With in-laws already settled in southern Pennsylvania, a few miles away from present-day Gettysburg, William Stewart initially set up a modest storekeeping business in that area. It was only in 1794, nine years after arriving in America, that he made for the western counties, moving around for a few years before finally establishing a homestead in Armstrong Township, about six miles west of Indiana. In 1810 he died there at the age of fifty-six.

John Kerr Stewart, the son born to William and Margaret in the middle of the Atlantic, was the first to join the Stewart family's genes to those of prominent clans of Scots and English origin in western Pennsylvania. On March 16, 1815, he married Elizabeth Hindman Armstrong, whose roots in the region went back to before the French and Indian War. While homesteading a substantial tract of land nine miles north of the borough of Indiana, the couple produced five sons and five daughters. The first-born was already twenty-three when the last-born, James Maitland, appeared on the scene in 1839. James Maitland was the father of Alexander Stewart and the grandfather of the Hollywood actor.

The first important Stewart presence in the borough proper was that of Archibald, the child born in Northern Ireland. A bachelor with a religious bent, he went into partnership with one of the local Suttons in 1851 to establish the hardware store that eventually was to be known throughout the region as The Big Warehouse for its variety of merchandise. When he wasn't selling hammers or rifles, Archibald Stewart kept busy as a founder of the American Bible Society and as a fundraiser for the building of hospitals all the way down to Pittsburgh. When he died in his mid-nineties in 1877, the small fortune he had amassed through the store and some side investments went to the Bible Society.

Because he didn't have any progeny of his own, Archibald brought in one of his brother John's children, Alexander, to assist him in operating the store. Another one of John's sons, also named Archibald, worked for a short time on the premises, as well. The two nephews shared Archibald's religious fervor. When Alexander died at the age of seventy-seven at the beginning of this century, he left all his money to the Foreign Mission Society of the Presbyterian Church. For his part, the younger Archibald, who ended up as a justice of the peace, left behind a journal that, among other things, recorded in pedantic detail all the Sunday sermon topics he had been exposed to and the names of the ministers who had expounded them.

The Civil War cut a bloody swath through the Stewart family. Two of John's sons, the justice of the peace, Archibald, and the youngest, James Maitland, joined the Union Army; seven grandsons also saw action. Archibald enlisted in April 1861 as a private in the 40th Regiment (11th Reserve) of the Pennsylvania Volunteers and displayed sufficient leadership qualities to be promoted to the rank of second lieutenant within a few months. Two years later, he made first lieutenant—the rank that he held when he was fatally wounded in May 1864 during the fighting at Spotsylvania. One of Archibald's nephews was felled in the same battle, a second was killed during General William T. Sherman's devastating march through the South, and a third lost an arm in an ambush. More fortunate was James Maitland, who, as a sergeant in the Signal Corps, got through the fighting at Winchester, Cedar Creek, Fisher's Hill, and Richmond without sustaining serious injury.

When he returned home from the war, James went to work for his older brother Alexander as a clerk in the hardware store. He also married Virginia Kelly, a member of one of the region's most storied families. Kelly's antecedents included a father killed in the Mexican War in 1847 (about the only hostilities over two centuries that didn't involve the Stewarts), a grandfather who had been a state senator, and a grandmother descended from a couple of combatants in the Revolutionary War. The union between James and Virginia Kelly produced two sons— Alexander, Indiana's future character-in-chief, and Ernest.

When he went to work at the hardware store, James had more to recommend him than nepotism. For one thing, he had received a thorough formal education from elementary school through Dayton Academy to Westminster College. For another, he was regarded by Uncle Archibald, still the principal owner behind the store, as a potentially sharper businessman than his older brother Alexander. Archibald was right; aided no little by a building boom after the war and by the increasing importance of the Penn Railroad to the town (the store was situated at the corner of the railway's Philadelphia Street crossing), James received much of the credit for the unprecedented volume of orders that fell on the business in the late 1860s and 1870s. Although no less respected than Alexander in the community, James demonstrated an easier geniality with customers than his brother did. Particularly good customers usually found an "extra"—a free tool, additional brads, some new pamphlet on a religious or political issue that James found interesting—thrown in with their orders. In his later years, he bought a booklet entitled *101 Famous Poems* by the gross and distributed copies to people who struck him as needing an uplift. His most noted freebie of all, however, was a penknife—a tradition at The Big Warehouse that was carried on by his son Alex. On one occasion he even sent one of his knives to President Calvin Coolidge, receiving a thank-you note from the White House in return. (When Alex sought to emulate this gesture after World War II by sending a knife to Harry Truman, he received nothing in return. According to Alex, the White House silence had probably stemmed from the fact that he had let the Democrat Truman know he was a Republican.)

James's business smarts allowed him to take over as owner of the store in 1883 and to rename the enterprise J. M. Stewart & Co. Although the store continued to thrive for most of the rest of his life, James himself showed a crankier control as the years advanced. He had his reasons. Not only did Virginia Kelly die of illness at an early age, but a second wife also succumbed. He felt compelled to test his deep religious convictions in a protracted debate with his church over what was and wasn't proper ritual, including the use of an organ during services, finally becoming a reluctant defector to what evolved as Indiana's Calvary Presbyterian Church. Even where the store was concerned, he got involved in a series of deals with nephews and banks that, originally intended to finance an expansion, muddied his own ownership role from the late 1880s to the dawn of the new century. What had been regarded as a tart sense of humor began to strike friends and associates as turning progressively sour. Nowhere was this more manifest than in a frequently reiterated crack about his two sons. Noting that Ernest had been born with a leg deformity, James was given to telling customers that "I have one son with a crippled leg and another [Alex] with a crippled head." Eleanor Blair, an eighty-two-year-old resident of Indiana who was always close to the Stewart family, recalls an equally churlish James from her childhood:

When he was old, his main job at the store was bringing all the coins from the till over to the bank. He went through the same ritual every time. He would walk up to the teller and start stacking up all the pennies, nickels, dimes, quarters, and halves in separate, neat piles. Then, after he had counted them all to make sure he had the same total as he had had at the store, he would swipe his hand at the stacks so that they were completely messed up again. He always said that he had earned his money at the store working hard for it, so the bank teller should earn his by doing what he had been hired for—counting. And then he would just stand there with his cackling laugh, watching the teller recount every single coin.

James Stewart died in 1932 at the age of ninety-one. Pallbearers at his funeral included the mayor of Indiana and dignitaries from around the county. A local newspaper editorial noted that his life had spanned most of the history of the United States up to then:

He had seen days when clothing was spun and woven at home, then sewn into garments. He experienced the evolution of transportation from wagon roads to canals, railroads, electric streetcars, and the automobile. Numerous new states had come into being as he saw the United States expand to the Pacific. Four wars had come and gone: Mexican, Civil, Spanish-American, and the first World War. The telegraph, telephone, and electricity were all developed during his lifetime.

Long before James's death, Alex, the son with the "crippled head," had become the focus of Stewart lore in Indiana. Like his father, he had attended the best schools that his family's ample income could provide—studying at Chester and Kiskiminetas Springs School (or Kiski, thirty-five miles east of Pittsburgh) before pursuing a Bachelor of Science degree at Princeton, then still an institution inextricably wound up with the Presbyterian Church. In April 1898, only a few weeks before receiving his degree, however, the burly twenty-five-year-old bolted from the New Jersey campus to sign on with the Battery A, Pennsylvania Volunteers and fight in the Spanish-American War. One of the first of innumerable maybe-fact-maybe-fiction stories about Alex told that he had quit Princeton in the middle of a chemistry class, leaving on a Bunsen burner that almost torched the laboratory. He spent most of his time in uniform in the Puerto Rican capital of San Juan; in later years he did little to amend the rash conclusions of some journalists that he had been involved in the fighting for San Juan Hill in Cuba. He was mustered out of the military only seven months after enlisting, and wore his private's uniform to belated graduation ceremonies at Princeton.

Alex appeared seldom to have doubted that his future rested with the hardware store—an attitude that often was to carry over in an undisguised resentment that his own son preferred acting on the stage and screen to retailing on Philadelphia Street. After working as his father's employee for a number of years, Alex saved enough money to buy a one-third investment in the store in 1905, to James's deepest satisfaction. Among other things, his investment was an attempt to offset a growing reputation as a Good Time Charlie who squeezed his work and weekly church attendance in between regular carousing. Aside from his father, the person he was most concerned with persuading that he had a new sense of responsibility was his fiancée, Elizabeth Ruth (Bessie) Jackson. It wasn't that easy. As Eleanor Blair recalls:

The house I was born in should have been where Alex and Bessie were living. He had bought it for her during their engagement. But then she gave him an ultimatum to put an end to his alcoholic sprees or there would be no marriage. When Alex continued drinking, she went through with her threat, and didn't care who in town knew about the reasons for the break. Alex was as humiliated as he was surprised. Only when he was going through the whole painful thing of getting rid of the house again, I think, did it sink in that he had a problem and that Bessie wasn't going to put up with it. That's when he cut down on the liquor. They were finally married about a year later, but my parents had the original house by then.

Alex and Bessie were married on December 19, 1906. Again, it was Pennsylvania gentry marrying Pennsylvania gentry, although this time with a little more fodder for the scandal chewers. Bessie Jackson's father, Samuel, a former Pennsylvania state treasurer and the founder of a steel company and bank in the town of Apollo, had been sued by Nellie Bly in the 1880s for having abused his position as her legal guardian and misappropriated her trust fund.[1] Although no specific criminal charges were leveled against him, Jackson's ascertained "mismanagement" of the money had forced Bly to withdraw from Indiana's Normal School and had cast a shadow over his own reputation.

But Jackson's court problems had not stopped him from giving his own daughter the best education money could buy for a woman in the late nineteenth century, and Elizabeth, unlike Bly, had continued on through Wilson College in the Cumberland Valley of Chambersburg.[2] Although interviews with her husband and son over the years have suggested that she graduated from Wilson, the college's surviving records are not so definite, establishing her presence only in music and art programs in the 1893–94 academic year. Within that period, however, she was extremely active musically, winning praise for the piano recitals she gave of pieces by Beethoven, Mendelssohn, and Schubert.

Elizabeth Jackson struck most people as a refined woman who preferred to leave the spotlight to her husband, but who wasn't beyond

---

[1] Jackson gained the guardianship by virtue of being a banker and because his sister had married into his ward's family.

[2] Another school with strong Presbyterian ties, where the president had to be an ordained minister, Wilson featured such courses at the end of the nineteenth century as Assyriology, Egyptology, literary and colloquial Chinese, Sanskrit, Zend, Pali, Siamese, and Burmese.

pulling the plug on him when she decided he had gone too far. "In general, I would say she was very unassuming," says Eleanor Blair. "She belonged to a lot of community organizations, for instance, but she always said no to any kind of leadership or elective role. I believe her real center was her music. She sang in the choir, played the piano beautifully. If she lost her patience, though, she could become very firm. The ultimatum to Alex about not drinking was only the first of many times that she laid down the law to him. She didn't make very many demands, but when she did make them, she expected them to be listened to."

Whatever Bessie's boiling point was, Alex seemed dedicated to discovering it. One of his favorite ploys over some forty-three years of marriage was inviting people over to his house for breakfast or dinner, but neglecting to tell his wife about it. Although not an original insensitivity between married couples, it took on an extra resonance in Alex's case for the fact that he sometimes tendered the invitations during meetings of the numerous organizations to which he belonged, prompting as many as forty people to show up on the Stewarts' doorstep looking to be fed. On the other hand, he was known to have suggested to Bessie on more than one occasion that they sample some new restaurant in the area, driven her over to it, told her to wait in the car while he canvassed the interior, and come out again a half-hour later with the verdict that the food hadn't been all that good.

Bessie was hardly the only victim of such whims. As Eleanor Blair tells it: "One time Alex got my father-in-law all excited about a trip to Atlantic City. My in-laws got up bright and early, packed the food for the trip, then sat around waiting for Alex to arrive in his car. One hour, two hours, went by. They waited that long only because Alex never showed up on time for anything. Finally, they rolled over to the Stewarts and heard from Bessie that Alex had gone to Pittsburgh for the day. Obviously, that was also the first she had ever heard of any trip to Atlantic City."

For the *Gazette*'s Frank Hood, who admits to having been always less captivated than others in Indiana by what a half-century of newspaper profiles referred to as Alex Stewart's "colorful" personality, such incidents were typical. "Bessie was an elegant, culturally refined, truly grand woman," he says. "In so many ways he was her direct opposite. Maybe that's what they mean by opposites attract, but, frankly, I never really understood how she managed to live with him."

But live together they did, for almost a half-century. In 1908, they began building their family, and on May 20 of that year, a day after Alex's thirty-sixth birthday, their son James Maitland, named after his paternal grandfather, was born. On January 12, 1912, it was the turn of Mary Wilson—the name taken from her mother's side of the family. Finally, on October 29, 1914, Bessie delivered Virginia Kelly, whose name was taken whole from her long-dead paternal grandmother. It was shortly after Virginia's birth that Alex moved the family from a Philadelphia Street house close to the hardware store to 104 N. Seventh Street in the Vinegar Hill section, a home he would remain in until his death and that his son would always regard as the taproot of his growth. Standing at the end of a cul de sac on a promontory overlooking the commercial center of town, the rather shapeless two-story residence peeked out from behind bushes planted around a steep, fifty-four-step staircase, taking in most immediately a half-dozen Methodist and Presbyterian church steeples. It was something of a sneaky view of a somewhat arid, neat tableau.

With the store and his family defining his responsibilities, Alex gave signs of seeking the life of respectable burgher. He became a joiner. He was a member of the volunteer fire department, of the Salvation Army's advisory board, of a Masonic lodge, of an American Legion Post, and of the Indiana Rotary Club. On top of those organizations there was his activism in the church, as well as his attendance at a Bible class and his fervor about maintaining alumni ties to Kiski and Princeton. The business—and Alex's interest in it—expanded enough to require the purchase of an adjoining building. Even when an oil fire in 1912 ravaged a good part of the store and its stock, there were sufficient funds for repairs and supplies to keep going with minimal disturbance. The strongest reminder of his rambunctious bachelor years was half of an iron bell clapper from the Princeton campus that not only survived the fire, but would survive the store itself and end up in Beverly Hills. Alex and a fellow student had pilfered the clapper in hopes that the lack of morning tolls would excuse the boys from early classes. It hadn't, but the thieves had split their prize in two for a memento that Princeton alumni, including his own son, would always consider part of the Alex Stewart romance.

Alex's apparent contentment with his small-town rhythms ended with a bang when the United States entered World War I. Once again, on October 18, 1917, he enlisted in the Army, this time using his grasp of mechanical skills for an assignment with the Ordnance Department. His wife and father put up only mild protests that his family and age (he was then forty-five) should have exonerated him from military service; neither had any doubts that Alex was going to do what he wanted to do anyway. Overall, he spent nineteen months in uniform, divided almost equally between time in the United States and France. In the U.S., his biggest assignment was in New York City, where he helped to recruit machinists and skilled mechanics for the war effort. Before going overseas, he also spent time at Camp Dodge, near Des Moines at Johnson, Iowa; he was shipped out just before Camp Dodge became infamous as both an epicenter of the lethal Spanish Lady influenza that ripped through the military during World War I and as the site of the summary hanging of three black soldiers on charges of having raped a white woman. Over in France, Alex was attached to the First Company Ordnance Repair Shops in the central town of Mehun-sur-Yevre. He received his honorable discharge with the rank of captain on May 1, 1919.

In case anyone in Indiana had forgotten the steamroller side to Alex's personality, he offered an immediate reminder of it when, barely back home, he decided that the town ought to have a memorial to those killed during the war. More than that, he decided that a neglected German Lutheran cemetery provided the perfect location for such a tribute. Without waiting for authorization from town or county authorities, he had employees from the hardware store dig a hole for the foundation in the middle of the cemetery while he went about securing a marble pillar that had been junked during the renovation of a nearby bank. But then, as his son recalled some time later, a delegation of Lutherans with other designs on the land arrived on the scene: "They read him a court order they had obtained, which prohibited the erection of the tall pillar as a 'threat to life and limb.' Then they marched away again. There was a sadness on Dad's face as he watched them go, sadness over the fallibility of the Lutherans and of the court. However, he resolutely downed this emotion, turned back to his waiting employees, and said crisply, 'Okay, boys, put her up.' "

The Lutherans didn't accept defeat so easily. For a couple of weeks afterward, they sent saboteurs into the cemetery after nightfall to wreck the work done by Alex's employees during the day, while at the same time appealing to the courts for orders with more teeth in them. In the end, however, the combination of the settled cement around the foundation, the greater sway of a Presbyterian lobby over that of the Lutherans, and continuous appeals to patriotism prompted a ruling that the cemetery land belonged to the county, which in its turn endorsed the memorial. Alex's only concession was to go along with the line that his initiative had originated with the American Legion and the Mothers of Democracy.

In the early 1920s, the elder James Stewart relinquished his last formal hold on The Big Warehouse to Alex. His other son, Ernest, who also had been given a financial stake in the store some years earlier, had little problem with that since he had become a successful lawyer with little time for the hardware business. For most of the decade, Alex conducted the store's affairs with little incident. If he had any problems at all, they stemmed from his unrelenting bluster with customers. As his son once described it: "The store was not only his method of making a living, but his forum where he pronounced opinions seldom tailored to the popular style. If he had ever heard of the slogan about the customer's always being right, he would have scorned it as toadyism as well as a falsehood. He constantly assured his customers, friends, and family that there was one correct way to do things—his way." Sometimes, according to Eleanor Blair, that attitude cost him business:

> My mother-in-law never tired of talking about the time she went to the hardware store to buy some green paint. Alex, who had never seen the inside of her house, began telling her to pick another color, that green wasn't right for the walls she had in mind. My mother-in-law insisted that she wanted green. Alex insisted that she was being silly, and obviously didn't know very much about room decor. Finally, she just got tired of arguing and walked out. I don't think she ever went back, either. Alex had a habit of self-starting himself into arguments like that, and the more you argued back with him, the more he seemed to lose himself more deeply into what he was saying. If he hadn't believed what he had been saying at the beginning, he did by the time he was finished.

For the most part, however, the three-story emporium on Philadelphia Street was the last word in the county for hardware supplies, so not too many customers allowed Alex's eruptions of bluster to abort their shopping objective. Far more ruinous was a double whammy delivered at the end of the decade—another fire, which dwarfed the devastation caused by the 1912 blaze, and the Depression. According to one member of the family, that fire was the last blow for Grandfather James, who never quite got over the sight of the business that he had steered for half a century reduced to ashes; for him the costly financing of rebuilding still again represented one attack too many on the family reserves. When the Depression ate up whatever was left, he knew, going to his grave, that Alex's generation of the Stewarts would not be numbered among the old Indiana families who encouraged constant speculation about how many millions they had socked away. That mattered to him.

Alex had his consolations. Through connections, promissory notes, and the gradual rehabilitation of his business, he indulged a passion for horses, raising a string of trotters. He continued to be active in his clubs and associations, continued to sing in the church choir every Sunday, and continued to be the first respondent to any fire-alarm bell. But most of all, Alex had the inventiveness that he had found within his family—not so much Father Knows Best as Father Knows Just About Everything and Wants to Show You How You Can Know It All, Too. For those who saw only his bombast, it came as something of a marvel that, especially with his son and daughters, he often displayed an emotional sensitivity beyond the norm and an open-mindedness that would-be purchasers of green paint at The Big Warehouse had not glimpsed.

BOY'S LIFE

TO HIS MOTHER HE WAS JIMSEY. TO HIS FATHER HE WAS Jimbo—a diminutive of James that struck Alex as suggestive of Jumbo the famous circus elephant. For the Stewart who would spend much of his early movie career fretting about being underweight weighed in at eight pounds upon delivery and more than filled out his clothes for most of his boyhood. "He's a fat little rascal," Alex got into the habit of telling his customers at the store. "But you never saw a boy like him. Stop around and see him." It was an invitation his father would still be extending fifty years later—if not then to his home, to the local movie theater where the boy's latest film was playing. Alex Stewart always made it clear that nothing had ever been more important to him than the birth of his son.

The feeling was hardly unrequited. As James Stewart told *McCall's* magazine once:

> ... the Stewart Hardware Store seemed the center of the universe. It was a three-story structure full to the rafters with everything needed to build a house, hunt a deer, plant a garden and harvest it, repair a car, or make a scrapbook. I could conceive of no human need that could not be satisfied in this store. Even after I grew up and moved away and saw larger sights, the store remained with me. But then I realized that what was central to my life was not just the store but the man who presided over it—my father.

Although Stewart never stinted on praising his mother, in particular as the family's anchor of stability and for tuning whatever ear he developed for music through her singing and playing piano and organ, the very welter of stories shared with journalists over the years about his father has underscored the papa's boy he always regarded himself as being. More often than not, his mother appears in his reminiscences only as a sensible censor to escapades dreamed up by himself and his father—adventures that were carried out frequently behind her back by the two of them anyway. (Largely because of age differences, his two younger sisters usually earn mention, if at all, only as secondary characters during his boyhood.) But on at least two cardinal points, the parents were of a similar mind. The first was in the need for discipline at home; or, as Stewart sought to explain it once: "My folks were strict but somehow they got away with it without being strict, if you know what I mean. Few people I've come across in life had that ability. The rules were there and everyone knew they were there, so even having to refer to them should have been unnecessary. It was just expected that you would be well behaved, be in line."

The other point on which Alex and Bessie saw eye to eye was in the attitude that living in a small town should never be an excuse for having a small mind, that the observed proprieties had to be integrated with intellectual and aesthetic stimulations. Hall Blair, Stewart's oldest boyhood friend in Indiana until his death a few years ago, once described the Stewarts' Sunday routine to the *Tribune-Democrat*, a western Pennsylvania daily:

> The Stewarts had an interesting family life. They were very close, and highly principled. At every meal they all took hands and said Grace. On

Sunday they all went to church. [Alex] was in the choir and [Bessie] was the organist, so they went first and the children came later. They were *always* late. I can still see Jim dashing down the aisle and going sliding into the pew—the third from the front where they always sat. . . . At home they all sang hymns and had musical Sunday evenings. They stayed home the whole day and read. They always had the *New York Times* and magazines like *Atlantic Monthly* and *Scribner's*. They followed theater and opera.

Indiana wasn't allowed to become a physical confine, either. First by train and then by car, Alex organized regular outings to Pittsburgh sixty-five miles to the southwest. Every summer there were more ambitious excursions—to Washington, D.C., to Canada, to Yellowstone Park. What Alex didn't know about their destinations before they got there, he improvised on the spot with enough authority to impress his children with the cosmopolitanism he had picked up during his travels with the military. He was *interested* in things, as was Bessie. The initial fulfillment for the children was the sightseeing, but the more durable one, for a trio that grew into actor, artist, and writer, was the kindling of curiosity.

If there was an Indiana institution that tantalized the young Stewart as much as the hardware store, it was the volunteer fire department. He had little choice in the matter. For one thing, a combination of ramshackle nineteenth-century buildings, open stairwells, oiled sawdust on wooden floors, and a periodic rash of criminal speculation and arson-for-insurance made the town unusually subject to fire. Even a cursory review of its history this century turns up the loss to flame of every conceivable kind of structure—homes, theaters, university buildings, churches, glass factories, furniture stores, paper mills, warehouses—at regular intervals. John D. Stewart, a son of the attorney, Ernest, through a second marriage, remembers one typical incident in the 1920s, when his maternal grandfather was the town fire chief:

His name was Doherty, and twice within a very short time he was called to organize the brigade against a fire in a hotel in the center of town. Both times they got the fire out pretty quickly and both times it had obviously been arson. Well, during the post-mortem after the second try, my grandfather was sitting around telling everybody how stupid the arsonist had been because if he had really wanted to make sure the hotel would burn down, he would have put oil rags here and put them there and done this, that, and the other thing. Two nights later, there was a third fire in the hotel, and this time it succeeded. One of the people who had been listening to my grandfather's expert advice was the owner of the hotel, and he had been setting all the fires to get the insurance.[3]

The Stewarts were in a particularly (dis)advantageous position to know when trouble ignited, since they lived only a block away from the siren that summoned volunteers to bucket and hose. Alex once acknowledged that there were nights when the wailing went on from dusk to dawn, that this became as much a nocturnal sound as the chirping of crickets. For his part, James characterized the nightly blaring as "kind of loud . . . making it hard to sleep sometimes." What he always preferred to accent were the rides his father gave him atop the engines returning from a blaze and the older man's precarious driving of a Packard ladder truck. He has doted in particular on the impact of fire alarms sounded during Sunday church services:

> At the first sound of the siren, Dad would immediately stand erect in the choir loft and then move toward the exit with deliberate speed. He took all eyes and thoughts with him, leaving the minister to flounder, his words unheeded. And desperately as the minister might try, he never could recapture the attention until Dad returned, for each worshipper was full of apprehension for his own house.
>
> When Dad returned, he would enter the choir loft with dramatic unobtrusiveness, pretending to be unaware that all eyes and hearts were awaiting his sign. Only after he had settled himself would he turn to the congregation and solemnly nod his head, indicating that everything was under control. A sigh would go through the church, and now, finally, attention would return to the minister; but by this time he had been routed, and he concluded the service with a muttered prayer.

Another early goad to the Stewart imagination, in more ways than one, were the traveling carnivals that set up their tents and sideshows in Indiana once or twice a year. Alex was as excited as anyone by their arrival, and sometimes shook his son awake barely after dawn to accompany him down to Philadelphia Street to watch the wagons roll in.

---

[3] As recently as the 1980s, Indiana's most-wanted criminal was an arsonist who had set almost sixty blazes over several years; he was finally caught and sentenced to life imprisonment after setting a hotel fire that killed two people.

James was only seven or eight when he started helping the roustabouts unload their equipment, in return for being allowed to feed the animals. ("They couldn't keep me away from the elephants.") On a couple of occasions, the carnival people themselves got fed at the Stewart supper table. The first visit ultimately led to trouble between Alex and the police. James told *McCall's*:

> One evening, there were four guests who had about them a strange pungency. They were circus people who had asked for credit to purchase some supplies. Dad figured if they needed credit, they also needed a square meal. The conversation that evening was a bit racy for Mother, but great for Dad and us kids.
>
> Later, the circus went broke and offered to pay Dad in merchandise. He chose a fourteen-foot python, which was duly delivered to the store in a stout crate. "I figured he'll be good advertising if we put him in the window," Dad explained to his apprehensive clerks. And he was right. It became a town occupation to walk to the hardware store and see what the snake was doing.
>
> One evening, two spinster ladies named Fullerlove strolled down to take a look at the snake, which, unaccountably, took a dislike to them and coiled himself up and struck at them. All he got was a bruised nose on the plate-glass window, but one of the Misses Fullerlove fainted. When she revived, the two of them marched directly to the police station, and once again Dad was charged with being responsible for threat to life and limb.
>
> The Stewart Hardware Company agreed to remove the snake, but then the question arose—how exactly? For once, there was rebellion among the employees, as they defied all orders to enter the window. Finally, late on a Sunday night, Dad and his buddy Doc Torrance went to the store and chloroformed the snake. For years, it was a well-kept secret that they almost chloroformed themselves in the process.

Another carnival performer unable to pay a store bill bartered a far more significant gift—an accordion. Alex took the instrument home and told his son to learn to play it. With critical assistance from what he had picked up at the piano under the tutelage of his mother, Stewart worked for some time at teaching himself the accordion, at least within the key of C. The instrument would figure prominently years later in the circumstances surrounding his decision to become an actor; he would also play it in several films, probably most conspicuously in the western *Night Passage*.

Elephants weren't the only animals that attracted young James. A lifelong affection for horses began the day he realized that his father was spending a lot of time at the edge of town with trotters he had begun to enter into harness races at county fairs. "I didn't get to ride them much," he has said, "but I did get to clean the stables a lot. It wasn't the nicest thing in the world, but it gave me something essential for when you're around horses, and that is an absolute lack of fear."

It was another animal—a dog—that, according to Stewart, helped teach him never to pretend to be someone or something he wasn't. Again, it was a lesson mediated by Alex:

> When a neighbor's dog killed my dog, whose name was Bounce, I vowed to kill that dog in revenge. I vowed it day after day in the most bloodthirsty terms. I never quite did it, but I was making myself ill with my own hate and frustration. "You're determined to kill this dog?" my father demanded abruptly one evening after dinner. "All right, let's stop talking about it and get it done. Come on."
>
> I followed him to the store, to discover that he had tied the dog in the alley. He got a big deer rifle out of stock, handed it to me, then stepped back for me to do my bloody work. The dog and I looked at each other. He wagged his tail, and his large brown eyes were innocent and trusting. Suddenly the gun was too heavy for me to hold, and it dropped to the ground. The dog came up and licked my hand.
>
> The three of us walked home together, the dog gamboling in front. No word was ever said about what had happened. None was needed. Dad had taught me I wasn't really a killer, and I didn't have ever again to try to work it up or pretend. It was a great relief.

At one point, when he was ten, Stewart was so obsessed with animals that he announced over dinner that he intended going on safari to Africa. While his mother laughed at the notion, Alex immediately set about gathering train and ship schedules, books about Africa, and iron bars for the cages that the Great White Hunter in their midst would need. Even his son admitted to being taken aback when Alex set a specific date for a departure, the plan being to catch a train to Baltimore for a connection to New York and, ultimately, the Atlantic. Everything was played out right to the final day, when Alex announced that the line to Baltimore had been blocked by a derailment and suggested a trip to Atlantic City while waiting for the track to be cleared. It was only during the day in Atlantic City that James accepted his father's suggestion that maybe it would be better to wait a few years before undertaking the safari. That decision, too, came as "a great relief."

Given the cornucopia of tools and gadgets to be found in the hardware store, it was probably inevitable that young Stewart would demonstrate a technical side to his imagination. His first triumph, when he was only twelve, was to put together a crystal radio receiver by winding and unwinding loose couplers on oatmeal boxes. It was through an only slightly more sophisticated contraption, worked out with friends Hall Blair and Bill Neff, that he heard the first radio broadcast to reach Indiana—the coverage by Pittsburgh's KDK of President Warren Harding's inauguration. But then he made the mistake of bragging about his achievement to classmates, and word quickly got back to teachers. "I was asked to describe the broadcast at a full school assembly. So I stood up and said, 'It really wasn't much. The President spoke. They all cheered. Then there was another speech.' If I'd stopped then, the other kids probably would have hated me a little, but forgotten all about it by the next day. Instead, I kept talking, and said, 'Then the band played "Columbus, the Germ of the Ocean."' I've never lived that one down."

Alex, who decided early on that his son had the makings of an engineer, certainly did his part to abet such an ambition. On one occasion he drove to Pittsburgh for a sixteen-dollar tube that his store didn't stock, then, later on, ordered a loudspeaker for Jimmy. As much as he did to encourage the developement of a future engineer, he also ended up witnessing a spark of capitalism. As Hall Blair later described it: "After awhile, Bill Neff and I would build the crystal sets and Jim would be our sales manager. We sold a little one-tube set to a farmer near Creekside and he burst into the hardware store one day saying he had picked up station KHJ in San Francisco. It made a big splash. We got our pictures in the paper, and we started getting swamped with orders. We must have put together 30 or more sets and we sold them at $20 apiece."

Eleanor Blair remembers that her husband Hall and Stewart also entertained visions for a while of selling new sideshow attractions to the traveling carnivals. "There was one ride they called the Whizzbang. It was really nothing more than a clothesline with a seat attached that ran from the top of a tree down to the garage. They always used my husband's sister as a guinea pig, shooting her down what was a pretty steep distance. After they got tired of the Whizzbang, they decided an electric chair might be perfect for a sideshow. They built one and it worked only too well. They tried it out on a cat, and the cat's howls as it scrambled away convinced them that they had gone about as far as they could with that particular invention."

Still another early Stewart fascination, shared with Bill Neff, was magic; before leaving Indiana for good, he would even team up briefly with the future professional magician to put on shows. Like the radio sets and the Whizzbang, however, the magic tricks proved to be a passing fancy. The same could not be said for flying, which remained an enthusiasm for the remainder of Stewart's life. As he once told an interviewer: "I think it all started when I was about nine or ten. We took the *Literary Digest*, and it always seemed to have a war scene on the cover because of the war going on in Europe. Action stuff, a lot of bright colors. I'd tear off every cover that had an airplane on it and tack them on the wall of my room. Airplanes were the last thing I thought about every night and the first thing I thought about in the morning. My one ambition was to find out what it was like to be up in one."

He ended up having to wait a few years, until he was already in high school, before realizing his ambition. Jack Law, one of many barnstorming pilots who scraped by after World War I by taking passengers on brief flights, arrived in Indiana behind a lot of tub-thumping about the thrills he could provide. His fee was a then-startling fifteen dollars for fifteen minutes in the air, but Stewart was ready for him.

> I had been saving every cent I could for a long time—mostly money I had picked up working around the hardware store. Both my parents, Dad as much as my mother, were against it. They kept saying it wasn't safe. But I had made up my mind, and I think I knew I would always be able to persuade Dad at the last minute. When the big day finally came, and Law had landed in this pasture outside of town owned by the Bennett family, sure enough, Dad came around. What I didn't know was that he had been asking a lot of store customers if they had ever flown and to tell him what it had been like. They had really helped break down his resistance, assuring him it was perfectly safe for me to go up. He wasn't all that convinced, though. On the way out to the pasture, he insisted on stopping to pick up the family doctor! And even that wasn't enough for him. The whole time I was up in the air, he stayed in the car with the engine running, just in case a wing or something fell off and he had to rush to the crash site!

Regarding the flight itself, Stewart has said that he knew at once "there was nothing to be afraid of—that, just the opposite, it was a wonderfully exhilarating and relaxing experience—and that I would be up again as soon as I could." In the meantime, he went back to a meticulously kept scrapbook in which he preserved any and all printed matter related to aviation. Hall Blair, who had an identical album, liked to note that their collection included a skimpy fourteen-page manual that told the reader everything that he needed to know about mastering and maintaining an airplane.

If there was one casualty to so many interests and activities, it was schoolwork. In fact, from his elementary education at Indiana's Model School all the way to Princeton, Stewart seldom made a mark academically—in one instance having to attend a special summer semester to make up for failing grades. It took pull from both his father and his mother's side of the family to gain entry to Mercersburg Academy and the persistence of Alex and some alumni connections to remain in good standing at Princeton. His biggest moment in the academic spotlight at the Model School came in the ninth grade, just before he graduated, when he was cited for an essay written in conjunction with an annual Red Cross appeal. An altogether average teenage effort, the composition was at pains to distinguish between charity and borrowing even for such an ostensibly charitable organization as the Red Cross, declaring in part:

The American Red Cross and its work in our midst is something that should appeal to every earnest citizen. During the past year, the Indiana County chapter has been doing a great deal toward setting aright the tangled affairs of both civilians and ex-soldiers, be their troubles mental, physical, or economic.

It is very true that a man will not hold long a position in a vocation to which he is not accustomed or which he does not like. A man has had experience as a clerk, as a truck driver, and in various positions of a similar nature, but they do not interest him. His work is masculine-like, but neither he nor his employer profit from it. His ambition is to be an assembler in a large plant such as a Westinghouse plant. In order to secure such a position, he must have vocational training along that line. He does not turn to charity for aid; word of his difficulty reaches the Red Cross, which immediately investigates the circumstances.

To enter school, the man must have money. The money is furnished in the form of a loan by the Red Cross. The Indiana chapter met the need of such a case during the month of October. The man was allowed $35 and sent to the Allegheny Vocational School. At the rate of $5 every payday (which is twice a month), the man is paying back the loan. . . . It must be held in mind that the $35 and the spirit that has taken care of these men must be kept up, in order to extend the great work done by the American Red Cross at the present time, here in our very midst. . . .

Stewart's generally good health as a child included the usual bouts with measles and chicken pox. His most serious illness struck him in his early teens, when a scarlet fever attack degenerated into a kidney infection that forced him to miss quite a few months of school. What he has remembered as his most difficult physical problem from the period just before his thirteenth birthday, however, was his abrupt sprouting up and an accompanying drastic loss of weight. For openers, he grew out of three suits within a year, exhausting the family's clothing budget. ("I didn't get a fourth suit. Indiana was simply treated to a view of a few more inches of my wrists and ankles.") If his height did not come as a complete surprise (both his father and grandfather were tall), his weight did. His mother's solution was extra-large portions of oatmeal every morning. ("I had to eat a mound of it at breakfast. She was always saying that I would look like a rail if I didn't. It didn't put any weight on me, but I came away from that diet with a loathing for oatmeal I kept for the rest of my life.")

Stewart has denied ever coming in for special abuse from his classmates for his gangly appearance, although, in other contexts, he has acknowledged that it was around this period that he acquired a reputation for having "a good right hand." For certain, the mere sight of him walking down the street with Hall Blair (slapped with the nickname of Tubby for an appropriate reason) must have offered an aching temptation to teenage wit. But even without razzing from schoolmates, he had his own preoccupations with his skinny frame to contend with— a complex that made him unenthusiastic about donning a bathing suit and that stayed with him to his World War II service with the Air Corps. Along the way, he crossed paths with high school football coaches, college track coaches, Hollywood physical trainers, and military nutritionists with rival theories about how to bulk him up; but as zealously as Stewart obeyed their diets, the additional pounds did not materialize. Only when he was almost forty did the actor announce what he called "a peace with my physique. I'll always be conscious of it, I suppose, but I'm not going to let it worry me anymore."

Of all Stewart's boyhood activities, none would seem as seminal, at least in retrospect, as those of a performing kind. His public debut was not particularly auspicious: at the age of five, he sneaked a couple of hand puppets into church on Sunday and spent the service in a lot of animated muttering. (Alex: "I didn't know what was going on for a while because I was up there in the choir loft. But as soon as I heard about it, I put a stop to it.") More structured were the evenings at home when his mother, especially, encouraged him to sing or show what he had learned from her on the keyboard. Later on, when his sisters were older, the musical gatherings had him playing the accordion, Virginia the piano, and Mary the violin—all in accompaniment to his mother's singing. One of Stewart's strongest memories of those evenings was of how his father "sang softly, so as not to cover up Mother's clear, sweet voice." He found this noteworthy because, as a member of the church choir, Alex had "a true but penetrating tenor that somebody once described as 'solos by Mr. Stewart with accompanying voices.'"

By Stewart's own account, his first foray into theater came at the age of eight, with his production of *Beat the Kaiser* in the basement of his Vinegar Hill home. "I wrote and played all the male parts, and I made my sisters, who were still practically toddling, play all the female parts. I remember that when we did it, I was afraid Dad was getting sick as he sat there watching us. It wasn't until years later that I realized he just looked the way he did—sort of swelled up and red—from trying so hard not to laugh."

Discouraged by the initial reaction to his straight dramas, he next turned his attention to the role of carnival huckster, working out spiels with Neff that usually served as the prelude to a gag. One production was called *Trip to Mars*, wherein the unwary were inveigled into paying in advance for the pleasure of being put on a waxed board in the Blair household and shot down into the basement. The more benign production *For Men Only* required payment from those eager to open a closet door only to find a pair of men's pants hanging off a hook.

Stewart's biggest early incentive for junior theater, however, came with his father's departure for France in World War I. At the end of the trip to New York to see Alex off for Europe (and during which he had to be stopped from trying to crawl down the nose of the Statue of Liberty), young James asked if he could have a couple of boards from the store for building a theater in the basement of the house. Alex agreed, then went one better by instructing Bessie to give the boy anything he needed for his plays from the store while he was away. The dramatic results were a more elaborate production of *Beat the Kaiser* that was retitled *To Hell with the Kaiser* and another original, *The Slacker*. The latter centered around a man (Stewart) who first refuses to fight against Germany, but who then sees the light and wins the war all by himself. To create an impression of shells being fired, Stewart and his cronies flickered footlights on and off; red lights stood in for fires. There was a one-cent charge, and nobody was exempt, not even Bessie. It was partly in this context that Virginia Stewart would observe years later that her brother was "terribly intense about his plays, just as he is about everything he gets interested in. There are no halfway measures with Jim."

Stewart has acknowledged that his basement theatricals provided solace for his father's absence. He has insisted that it was the older man's absence, rather than a fear that Alex would be killed in France, that preoccupied him. Whenever there was a report of some new Indiana fatality on the battlefield, he has intimated, he trusted in the fact that his father's duty in the Ordnance Department kept him out of immediate harm's way. However true that might have been, he suspended his interest in acting and writing almost as soon as his father came home. With the exception of a walk-on in a Model School production of *The Frog Prince*, in fact, he stayed away from a stage, his own or anyone else's, until his senior year at Mercersburg, almost nine years later.

Stewart began his relationship with the movies at Indiana's nickelodeons. (Unlike radio, films caught on quickly in town. As early as 1896, there were public showings in a library building; between 1906 and 1909, four nickelodeons were opened for a community numbering barely 6,000.) What he was particularly enthusiastic about were such weekly serials as *The Perils of Pauline*. His favorite actress of all, however, was Ruth Roland, who rivaled Pearl White in popularity and athleticism in the cliff-hanger silents made in the late teens. On at least one occasion, he has confessed, he jumped up from his seat intent on running to the screen to help an endangered Roland.

In the summer of 1921, when he was thirteen, Stewart evinced little enthusiasm for spending another school vacation in the hardware store, so Alex talked to Sam Gallo, the operator of a Philadelphia Street movie theater, about hiring a projectionist. As the actor subsequently recalled:

Dad wanted me to do my part over the summer to make spending money, but he wasn't going to be adamant that it had to be at the store. So Sam Gallo took me on at the Strand Theater. Back in those days you actually had to crank the projector, and while you were doing that, you were supposed to be watching out for tint marks. When the tint marks came up, it meant that you had to hold a tinted shade out over the eye of the projector. I concentrated on the stories so much that, once in a while, I'd forget and miss a tint mark. Once, in *20,000 Leagues Under the Sea,* I missed it for an awful long time. People saw the underwater part in black inkiness; then, suddenly, when I remembered, everything became a deep-sea green.

If his son's coolness to the idea of working in the hardware store sounded alarms in Alex's head, he didn't betray them; he preferred thinking of such moments as the normal distractions of growing up that, as in the case of the African safari, were best played out. At the store he continued to recount tales of his progeny's ingenuity to whomever would listen—and even to those who wouldn't. He also made sure that every small crossroads in James's development received an appropriate marker; for example, when it was time for the boy to be fitted out for his first pair of long pants, Alex celebrated the occasion by taking a "men's only" trip to Princeton so that his son could watch his alma mater beat Yale in a football game. Their most-noted trip together in the period, however, took place in August 1923, following the sudden death of Warren Harding in San Francisco. As Stewart has told the story:

The funeral train was scheduled to pass through a town about 20 miles from ours, at the Blairsville Intersection. I wanted desperately to go and see the train, but Mother pointed out that it was due to pass Blairsville at 3:30 in the morning, so that was that. Around 2:30, though, I was awakened by Dad's hand on my shoulder. In a voice as near a whisper as nature would allow, he said, "Jim, get up. It's time to go see the funeral train."

We drove through the night without talking much. I suppose you could say we were bound together by a comradeship of disobedience. When we came to the railroad station, we found half a dozen people already there. They were talking in hushed tones and from time to time stepping to the edge of the platform to look down the tracks. I always remember how silver those tracks looked in the moonlight. Suddenly, the tracks gave off a low hum—the funeral train was coming! Dad shoved two pennies into my hand and said, "Run, put them on the rails. Quick now!"

I did what he told me and jumped back to hold his hand as this monstrous engine thundered past us, pulling a glass-windowed observation car in which we saw the flag-draped casket of President Harding. It was guarded by two Marines, their glistening bayonets at attention. I could hardly breath I was so overwhelmed by the sight and sound.

After the train passed, I retrieved the two flattened coins from the track. Dad put one into his pocket and I kept the other. As we drove home, I examined mine and found the Indian's features had been spread and the few feathers of his headdress had become a great plume. On the other side of the coin, the two slender stalks of wheat had grown and burst, as if the seed had ripened and scattered.

The penny that had been flattened by Warren Harding's funeral train was still in Stewart's pocket when he moved out of Indiana.

OPENING BELLS

CONTAINED WITHIN THE TOP FLOOR OF THE INDIANA Public Library, the Jimmy Stewart Museum is nothing if not modest. That is hardly accidental: It was a condition set by the actor for allowing his name to be attached to it. Even his conditional approval had not come all that easily. Stewart had in fact bridled at the prospect of a museum of any kind after first being approached a few years earlier by a delegation from Indiana University of Pennsylvania. The only thing that wasn't clear following the meeting at his Beverly Hills home was whether his opposition was primarily to the university's grandiose plans for a new convention center, with the museum occupying a prominent niche, or to an unsubtle suggestion that he help finance the entire undertaking.

The university approach hasn't been the only one in recent years aimed at separating Stewart from some of his wealth in the name of Indiana loyalty. Generally speaking, Stewart has deflected these overtures behind polite notes or statements of regret. Occasionally, he has matched posed ingenuousness with posed ingenuousness. Thus, a couple of years ago, a member of the Calvary Presbyterian Church took it upon herself to write to California to point out that the congregation had just bought a new organ for such-and-such an amount. Stewart's reply a couple of weeks later was to congratulate Calvary Presbyterian for getting the organ and to announce that his own Beverly Hills church had also just purchased an instrument for such-and-such an amount.

Following the 1983 bash to mark his seventy-fifth year, a few of the people involved in organizing the festivities sent the actor a message proposing that he return to Indiana for another whirl of celebrations for his seventy-sixth birthday. They had to settle for the consolation prize of being photographed for the front page of the *Gazette* while in the act of reading Stewart's wire claiming conflicting appointments. It was against this background that Jay Rubin succeeded in persuading Stewart that there was more to be said for an Indiana museum than against it. A bantam-sized attorney in his late forties, Rubin was only too aware that the earlier approach by the Indiana University representatives had stiffened the actor's resistance to what some people might regard as "a personal shrine." Rubin:

> The last thing he wanted was to have his name emblazoned all over western Pennsylvania as a kind of Hall of Fame unto himself. When I visited him in California, my pitch was that Indiana—not the university—was in trouble economically and needed the kind of boost something like the museum would give it. I stressed that we'd set up a nonprofit corporation and that all the money would be raised locally. The only thing we wanted from him, I told him, was his authorization. If he wanted to give us some memorabilia, that would be great, too, but we didn't ask. What we really wanted more than anything was his approval.

What Stewart was talked into approving was a series of narrow corridors (called Hollywood Galleries) surrounding a fifty-two-seat screening room for the regular projection of his movies. The corridor walls contain stills, cast lists, and plot summaries of every one of his screen works. (Complete as this filmography is, it goes against Stewart's stated condition for a modest display, since by offering no perspective on what were his major and minor efforts, it makes the implicit claim that *anything* in which he appeared has crucial importance.) In addition to the galleries, there are rooms tracing the actor's roots in Indiana and his World War II service. Another area features European advertising posters of some of his films, with familiar images emboldening such unfamiliar legends as COCKTAIL POUR UN CADAVRE (*Rope*), PASSAGIO DI NOTTE (*Night Passage*), LA FLECHE BRISÉE (*Broken Arrow*), and L'UOMO CHE UCCISE LIBERTY VALANCE (*The Man Who Shot Liberty Valance*). Memorabilia from the Stewart collection includes his Oscar for *The Philadelphia Story* (which had been in his father's hardware store for years), original scripts, a Winchester rifle, and a metal airplane propeller from the cast and crew of *The Flight of the Phoenix*.

Much of the story behind the realization of the museum had to do with the political and personal resentments that regularly attend such ventures; in the words of *Gazette* editor Frank Hood, "some of those people who wanted their names on Jimmy's statue were back in the act." At the same time, there were scores of volunteers from every age group who spent weekends and evenings for months helping to gather everything from the old film posters to the blue velvet curtains that grace the screening room. As for Rubin, Indiana's resident cineaste as well as attorney, he made no apology for bruising some feelings along the way to what he said had been a goal for years: "I admit that I've ridden roughshod over a few people. Yes, I *have* stepped on some toes. But from the beginning I've had a dream about the museum, and I had no intention of allowing it to be undermined by people, however well-meaning, who would have been satisfied to fill up the rooms with papier-mâché Harveys. I guess that's very cute in its place, but Jimmy has been a lot more than that."

What Stewart mainly provided on May 20, 1995, was an excuse for a parade. And, whatever chagrin this caused some people, the most explicit connection between the Philadelphia Street marchers and the man being honored were several participants dressed up as Harvey the no-longer-invisible rabbit. Aside from them and the bannered announcement that the Henry Hall stationery store had opened for business on the same day that Stewart had been born, the parade was totally dependent on the presence of the actor's two daughters to not be mistaken for marking a Day Before a Month Before the Official Start of Summer. There were high school bands, an old trolley car, a state senator and his family waving from another convertible, a couple of military officers uneasy about waving from the back of a convertible, and the top-hatted mayor of Punxsutawney looking absolutely petrified about waving from his convertible in case Phil, the groundhog he held in his arms, took that as cue to bite him.

Bill Moorhead wouldn't have minded at all if the groundhog took a bite out of some people on the museum board. A ninety-two-year-old widower, Moorhead was trudging around with some of the toes that Rubin admitted having stepped on. What made that especially irritating to the former clothing store owner and IUP business manager was that he regarded himself as Stewart's only true remaining friend in Indiana and the real broker for the museum project. "It was me that Jimmy called originally to say he didn't want anything to do with that university convention center. He said to me clear as day, 'Bill, you go right over to that borough council and do whatever it takes to kill that idea.' So that's what I did. And at the same time I told them that if they wanted to do a museum for Jimmy, they had to make it a modest thing, like the man himself. As soon as I said that, some of them started to see the light—and started taking credit for everything."

By Moorhead's account, his friendship with Stewart went back to 1918, when the actor was ten years old. The trouble with that claim, according to some local skeptics, is that it would have made Moorhead an extremely rare fifteen-year-old who considered a boy five years younger a friend. And besides, why hadn't he been able to produce a single photograph dating back before the 1970s that showed him and Stewart together? At best, the skeptics have said, Stewart and Moorhead had been nodding acquaintances as kids, and what was so exclusive about a nodding acquaintance in a community the size of Indiana? Moorhead's answer was usually a twinkle-eyed stare that dared the questioner to get on to more significant business. For sure, even those who doubted the venerability of his ties to Stewart conceded that the two men had been as close as almost-weekly telephone calls between Indiana and Beverly Hills permitted, once Moorhead began looking after the graves of the actor's parents in the 1970s. There was also evidence that Moorhead had been the first outside party contacted by Stewart after the death of Gloria Stewart in February 1994. Some had come to the conclusion that, especially since the death of Hall Blair, Moorhead represented Stewart's last link to the Indiana that he had known as a young man and while his father had been alive, so for that reason the actor had always declined to comment on the age of their bond. "Sometimes I think Bill is the Indiana that Jimmy has to believe in now because there isn't too much else of it left that he's known personally," as Rubin put it.

But with the official opening of the Jimmy Stewart Museum imminent, what Moorhead wanted to know was why his friendship with Stewart, whatever its length, had not gotten the resounding tribute it was supposed to have. Specifically at issue was a twenty-five-year-old collection of bells that overwhelmed the front rooms of his meticulously kept, pine-scented two-story home, situated on an incline below the long-time Stewart family residence on Vinegar Hill. Scattered around the floor, on shelves, and on tables were bells topped with gleaming brass eagles, bakery wagon bells, train bells, church altar bells, African tortoise-shell bells, a British air raid alert bell, even a bell from Albert Schweitzer's hospital in Gabon. One credenza alone had been smothered by almost one hundred glass bells. The problem, according to Moorhead, was that, with the exception of one small set of bronzed figurine bells depicting the likes of Edgar Allan Poe, Blackbeard, and Dorothy of Oz, his collection was still in his home rather than over at the museum. "It shouldn't be," he said, dropping his eyes to his white shirtcuffs so his indignation wouldn't be too bare. "Jimmy made it very clear that the only thing that was supposed to be in the museum besides his stuff was my Moorbells. I even bought showcases and pedestals for displaying them. What do you think Rubin and the others did? They took the showcases, but not the bells! Jimmy is going to be real mad when he hears about this."

Mention of Moorhead's bells brought a volley of sighs from Rubin. "The Moorbells—there's Indiana, Pennsylvania, today in a nutshell," he said exasperatedly. "I showed up a little late for a board meeting one day and I find out they're turning the Jimmy Stewart Museum into a bunch of bells! I exploded. I asked them if they wanted to do a museum honoring a great actor or open a place where anybody could drop off some pet project, maybe even their laundry!" He paused, then came back more dispiritedly. "I finally said okay, you can have some of your bells if Bill is going to make a big thing of it. Just as long as you don't forget what the Jimmy Stewart Museum is really supposed to be about."

One of the things it should have been about, in Moorhead's view, was generosity. "You get all these know-nothings going around town saying Jimmy's never done anything for Indiana," he said. "They don't know about the $23,000 he gave to the Greater Indiana Endowment for community projects, or the $10,000 he donated for a bandstand roof in the park, or all the other money he's given to the hospital and the university. That's just his way—quiet generosity. And that's what this museum ought to be honoring, not just a lot of old movies. I told them from the start, too, that I was ready to give them my bells, not just offer them as a loan, like some other people have done. Sometimes I think the more generous you are around here, the more you end up paying for it."

But for the duration of the official ceremonies, Moorhead kept his reservations to himself. Critics of the entire enterprise, such as Frank Hood, also stayed away, and it might have been just as well. At a dinner the evening before the opening, for instance, apprehensions about identifying Stewart too much with his invisible rabbit costar seemed to have evaporated as Rubin presented a "Harvey," a bronze statue of a lamppost, to the actor's two daughters, Kelly Harcourt and Judy Merrill. No sooner had the women sat down with their trophies than the museum board awarded itself another "Harvey" and Rubin was given a plaque for his organizational work and his contribution of many of the artifacts on display in the museum.

Another example of the names on the statue?

Rubin was unfazed by the suspicion:

For one thing, the board worked hard and earned the Harvey. As for the plaque, I didn't even realize it was coming. But there's no getting away from the fact that we're in a small town here or that you sometimes have to adapt to what that involves. Indiana people like their little perks, their little badges of social prestige. They'll bank with a local outfit because that's the way to get a place on the board, to get invited to this or that function. That kind of person won't be in a hurry to pull his money out and go over to the Mellon Bank, because in Pittsburgh he'd be just another name on a balance sheet. There's no question that being a big fish in a small pond has always been a part of Indiana life.

The formal dedication ceremonies took place about an hour after the end of the parade—time enough for most of the few thousand spectators who had applauded and exchanged wisecracks with the marchers to have scattered back to their homes or to other weekend appointments. There were only a few hundred souls milling around in the middle of Philadelphia Street in front of the courthouse while Calvary pastor Elizabeth Rogers delivered an invocation. If some of them didn't register the somewhat perfunctory tone of her benediction, it was because they were being distracted by a pamphleteer from the Dry Run Gospel

Tabernacle in Duncansville whose literature explored the theme "To Go to Hell Do Nothing Because You've Already Done Enough" and offered graphic descriptions of the morgue sheets and cemetery dirt awaiting every human being, famous movie star or not.

The spectators listened with some interest as Rubin mocked those who wondered what Jimmy Stewart had done for Indiana, but mostly they kept their hands apart when he produced the answer—"Look at that museum. He'll never have to do another thing after that." They were far more fervid about reciting the Pledge of Allegiance, singing the national anthem, and cheering a couple of poems written by school children. President Bill Clinton, the governor of Pennsylvania, and a bevy of local government officials had plaques delivered to the Stewart daughters, and state and county politicians got in plugs for themselves. The grand almost-finale was the singing of "God Bless America" as two jets and two World War II cargo planes streaked across the sky over town.

Through it all, the daughters sat with their chins cocked for any circumstance at all. Forty-four-year-old twins, they represented the two sides of the Stewart family physically—the raw-boned, silver-white-haired Judy suggesting her mother, the solid-jawed Kelly clearly a descendent of Alexander Stewart. Both Judy, a mother of two who had spent years working in Nepal and Tanzania, and Kelly, an anthropologist only recently returned to the University of California after years of field work in Kenya, were practiced enough in public ceremony to know when there was room to roll their eyes or affect goofy reactions and when it was time to be solemn about what was being said or given to them. Finally, though, it was time for them to do more than say thank-you and shake hands, and both of them blanched at the sight of a hook-and-ladder parked in front of the library and the third-floor banner that would have to be cut down to symbolize the museum's opening. As Rubin explained that the two would be lifted up to the banner by the vehicle's cherry picker, Kelly flashed the grin of a good sport. Judy, however, couldn't resist clowning a barf threat.

"Jimmy would've never done that," an elderly woman stated.

"Yes, he would," her husband said implacably. "He always hated fire engines."

"He did not," the woman replied testily. "He loved them. He was always riding on them with Alec."

The husband shrugged. "Who remembers that long ago?"

The cherry picker slowly raised the women to the third story of the library. They cut the strings holding the banner, then raised their huge scissors in triumph. The crowd applauded.

The elderly couple didn't wait for the hook-and-ladder bucket to return the women to the ground. They started off down Philadelphia Street, away from the museum, wondering aloud why it had taken the daughters of the town's favorite son forty-four years to make a first visit to Indiana. "They had bigger places to see," the woman guessed. The husband merely nodded. "That's not hard," he said.

II
FIRST FLIGHTS

ACADEMIC EXERCISES

I N ONE OF HIS RARE SCREEN ROLES AS A YOUNG
rebel—the son of a poor preacher in Clarence Brown's *Of Human
Hearts* (1938)—Stewart has a scene in which he bitterly tells
Beulah Bondi, in the part of his mother, that he has had enough of
the hand-me-down clothes and miserable food donated to the family by
fellow townspeople and that he intends striking out on his own to study
medicine. It is the kind of tirade that James Maitland Stewart of Indiana,
Pennsylvania, never had to unleash against his own parents to get an
education; on the contrary, Alex and Bessie were the ones who took the
initiative to enroll him at Mercersburg Academy at the age of fifteen in
1923.

It wasn't easy. Stewart's less than brilliant grades at the Model School
had not exactly caused Pennsylvania's most prestigious preparatory
institutes to go into a bidding war for his enrollment. His teenage
physique of an upright shoelace didn't make him a natural candidate,
either, for a football-obsessed school such as Kiski, where not only had
his father gone, but where his friend Hall Blair was already studying. Even
when the family had decided on Mercersburg, there was the barrier of an
academy response that it was too late, that the school had "full capacity
enrollment" for the coming semester. In the end, it took both Bessie's
family connections and Alex's pull through the Presbyterians to have
room made for another student.

Situated among the elms and beeches of the Cumberland Valley in
southern Pennsylvania near the Maryland border, Mercersburg Academy
had had earlier identities as a German Reformed seminary and as a
college with a strong religious bent. That influence remained palpable

during Stewart's days on the campus. Not only were prayers intoned before every meal in the dining hall and chapel attendance compulsory (and remained so until a mass student protest in 1969), but there was little to be heard in the classroom that contradicted academy developer William Irvine's perspective that "we emphasize the religious note more than does almost any other school in America because I look on religion as the Queen of all Sciences." This expressed attitude notwithstanding, Stewart could still insist in later years that he was "never conscious of religion being forced on anybody," that it was "just there as a natural part of the educational foundation."

Another prominent feature of Mercersburg, related to its religious concerns, was its nestling relationship to Presbyterian-maturated Princeton: Of the 104 students who graduated in Stewart's 1928 class and then went on to a university, for instance, an astonishing fifty-four headed for the New Jersey campus. The line was so direct that it undercuts one of Stewart's yarns to interviewers over the years—how, after graduation from Mercersburg, he was a naive bubble while his father drove him around on a scouting trip of several eastern colleges, not realizing until they had arrived in Princeton that this had been Alex's destination from the start. He probably came much closer to the actual unfolding of events in the course of narrating *Boys Will Be Men*, a short film put together to raise funds for Mercersburg in the late 1950s. Talking about entering the academy as a freshman in 1923, the actor abruptly veers off to remark: "I had always rather fancied myself going to Annapolis. But my Dad, who prided himself on letting me make my own decisions, he said that I was going to Princeton or he'd shoot me." Since there was no educational impediment to going to Mercersburg and *then* to Annapolis, the apparent non sequitur would argue, in a sardonic tone or not, an awareness of having been steered onto the fast track to Princeton from his very first day at Mercersburg.

Stewart entered the academy just as it was gearing up for an enrollment explosion. After a couple of decades of accepting only a hundred or so applicants a year, expanded facilities and endowments permitted receiving five times that many in the mid-1920s. Tuition for boarders hovered around the $1,000 mark. During his administrative run of 1893 to 1928, Irvine, a puritanical man with more than his share of pompous quirks, touched everything. To encourage Mercersburg's distinction from other preparatory schools, for example, he even coined his own terms for referring to undergraduate classes: freshman were known as juniors, sophomores as lower middlers, and juniors as upper middlers. He also felt better not hearing the words *bathroom, toilet,* and *lavatory,* so anyone in need of that facility had to be directed to "The Ten" (for the number posted on the door of all campus toilets).

Although school literature boasted of student representatives from "37 states and 14 foreign states" in the 1920s, there were also clear restrictions about who those students could be. For one thing, they had to be boys, since Irvine had ended an experiment with women students as soon as he had taken over as head administrator in 1893. (The school returned to a coeducational basis only in 1969.) Native Americans, considered to be too indecorous, unscholarly, and immoral, got accepted only as exceptions to the rule, and African Americans didn't need to apply at all (there were no blacks until 1964). As for Jews, a school history published in 1993 observed:

> Records indicate that as late as the 1930s there was a quota for Jewish students. . . . A few Jewish students (had been) enrolled at Mercersburg nearly every year from the beginning of Dr. Irvine's administration. In 1917, however, disciplinary problems with several Jewish boys convinced Dr. Irvine that Jewish students generally did not fit in at Mercersburg. He decided to discourage Jewish applicants. But a furor erupted when the application of a Jewish boy was rejected in 1918. The boy's parents enlisted the support of various influential people to put pressure on Dr. Irvine. After consulting the headmasters of other schools, Dr. Irvine eventually decided that Jewish students could attend Mercersburg after all, but only as a small percentage of the student body.[1]

While he admitted to being "plain scared that I wouldn't measure up" the first night he spent in an academy dorm bed, Stewart had few adaptation problems. He didn't have much room for indulging them, in any case. All the more emphatic for its still relatively contained size in 1923, Mercersburg couldn't help but impress for its minutely structured regimen, in terms of both the average class day and the school year.

---

[1] Even published in 1993, the academy history declines to use words like racism or anti-Semitism in connection with such policies. It refers, instead to the "school's general uniformity" in once having been white, male, and Protestant, attributing this in part to the social realities and "traditions of the age" and in part to the "school's location, its early church affiliation, and its cost."

Behind a motto of *Integritas, Virilitas, Felicitas*—rendered by Irvine as Clean Life, Hard Work, Fair Play—the academy made sure that all its students were involved in the activities—from formal dances to Field Day—that served as social or extracurricular markers from fall to summer. Every student, for example, had to belong to one of the school's two literary societies—Marshall or Irving. The annual climax to membership was Midwinter Weekend, in which, after preliminary competitions in such sports as wrestling, basketball, rifle shooting, and swimming, representatives of the two societies engaged in a formal debate on some political or social issue of the day. A panel of faculty judges gravely declared a winner, setting off a night of celebration and two semesters of bragging rights.

By his own estimate, Irvine averaged twenty-five expulsions a year, most of them precipitated by gambling, drinking, or never-better-defined "immorality." The school's principal disciplinary tool for dealing with minor offenders was called "walking guard"—a Saturday afternoon detention in which the week's culprits had to quickstep their way around the campus while classmates were off in town. Those sentenced to walking guard usually learned their fate by consulting the Dean's Disaster List. Most infractions were reported by housemasters, charged with enforcing the school penal code; for instance, ten hours of walking guard for anybody caught smoking inside a school building, and a similar punishment for anybody even sitting in a dorm room where smoking was going on. Stewart has suggested that this particular rule was one of the reasons why he never became a serious smoker.

Campus contact with women was generally confined to periodic afternoon tea dances or to a formal ball in which the students were expected to wear tuxedos. (Band leaders like Jimmy Dorsey often provided live music for the dances.) The women were generally bused in from Penn Hall in nearby Chambersburg. Those who wanted to get away with their dates from the hall where the dances were held had to remain within a proscribed and patrolled patch of grass. What passed for sex education was an occasional visit from an outsider, more likely than not a minister. One such lecturer in Stewart's era told his audience that the best way of dealing with hormonal rushes was to "get a portrait of Roosevelt up on the wall, and when temptation comes, look up and inquire, 'How about it, Teddy?' I can't think of Theodore Roosevelt in connection with sex wrongdoing."

By the time he arrived at Mercersburg, Stewart had developed a strong attachment to the accordion that his father had taken as payment from the hard-up carnival performer. Even his class yearbook singled that out as a defining characteristic, declaring in part: "Venturing into a certain well-known room in Main you are likely to think you are interrupting the prologue of a miniature Roxy, for such is the disconcerting impression created by the moving strains of Jim's accordion and the bellowing efforts of his companions." On the strength of his accordion playing, Stewart was drafted into the school's Marshall Orchestra in his final year. Musical influences from Indiana also led him to join the choir and glee club in his senior semesters.

But music was hardly Stewart's only extracurricular activity. Despite standing almost six feet four and weighing a mere 130 pounds, he was selected for an underclass football squad three years in a row, managing to survive as a so-so center within the academy's accent on "muscular Christianity." In 1926, he doubled his athletic activity with a stint on the track team. None of his pastimes enthused him quite as much, however, as his drawing for the yearbook *Karux*. His adroitness at caricature and abstract conceptuals earned him the position of the book's art editor from 1926 to 1928. It was an activity that he carried on from home in 1927, which kept him connected to the school when his scarlet fever and kidney ailment forced him to stay off the campus for long months. It was also this artistic facility that he sought to direct down more practical architectural avenues during his subsequent studies at Princeton.

With his accordion, his art, and his willingness to be buried under a pile of bodies on the football field, Stewart had little trouble socially at Mercersburg. If he came in for any teenage derision, it was largely because of his height and the full blooming of his slow, deliberate speech; this prompted some classmates to tag him "Elmer," but not with any cruel consistency. The speech patterns that were to become his professional trademark were inherited from his mother, whose striving, methodical wording was attributed by many in Indiana to lifelong problems with her hearing.

Academically, the Model School's fair-to-middling student grew into Mercersburg's fair-to-middling student. Defending his classroom abilities on one occasion, Stewart acknowledged that he had not been a very good student, but equally insisted that he had "not been the worst one, either." On the other hand, he said he had never had one favorite subject because "they were all tough." He experienced excruciating anguish the evening before he was scheduled to receive his diploma, when he found himself at the dining-room table of his Latin teacher trying to pass a makeup examination so that he could graduate with his class. "The worst part of it," he recalled, "was that my father and mother were already on the campus for the ceremonies the next day. I have thought a lot of times about what I would have said to them if I'd failed the makeup test. It was very embarrassing."

The surrounding town of Mercersburg was Indiana writ still smaller. It too had been settled by Scots-Irish and English, waxing and waning economically until the academy had come along and provided a modest regularity in business traffic. The most popular hangout in Stewart's day was a combination Greyhound station–lunch counter–drug store named McLaughlin's; most Saturday afternoons found the place jammed, particularly around the several pinball machines on the premises. Only doors away on West Seminary Street was the Star Theater, which drew almost exclusively from the academy for patrons on the weekend. But as routinely as he attended the movies at the Star, Stewart confessed to not having been the same captive audience for the silent heroines as he had been back in Indiana. "Most of the fun in going to the Star on Saturdays," he has said, "was in coming up with wisecracks you could shout back to the screen. The guy with the best wisecrack was that afternoon's real hero."

Stewart's studies at Mercersburg coincided with two acts of destruction and two celebrations that have reinforced some notable running motifs over much of his life. The disasters were both fires officially caused by faulty wiring—a 1924 blaze that gutted a dormitory building and, three years later, an inferno that not only devastated the central campus edifice of Main Hall, its library of 5,000 books, and most historical records, but also forced teachers to conduct classes in hastily erected cabins for several years and, as in the case of Stewart's grandfather James after the fire at the hardware store, dealt a blow to Irvine that he never fully recovered from over the final eighteen months of his life. Casey Collison, a student at Mercersburg at the time, described how some students initially seized upon a piano salvaged from the blaze to play some jeering tunes to the flames, but then noticed Irvine: ". . . our dearly beloved headmaster plodded back and forth, head bowed, hands locked behind him, tears streaming down that always so strong face. The sight of that great man—suffering—as only one can suffer who has put his heart and soul into building for the future and sees his hopes virtually destroyed, had its sobering effect on me and many fellow students. There was no joyful singing. A great sadness blanketed us all."

Irvine dropped dead of a stroke while leading some musical exercises only days before Stewart's graduation.

The single biggest ceremony in the school's history also took place during Stewart's student days—the October 1926 dedication of the campus chapel. More than 3,500 people, including the wife of President Calvin Coolidge, were on hand for the unveiling of a structure that owed more to the dreams of cathedral architects than to the assignments of chapel builders. Having watched the limestone-and-granite edifice go up piece by piece for years, Stewart had it vividly in his mind a couple of years later at Princeton, when he was working on his first architectural designs.

The second significant celebration was that one marked around the world in May 1927, when Charles Lindbergh completed his 3,600-mile solo flight across the Atlantic from Long Island to Paris. Stewart's exceptional interest in the feat wasn't just because of his boyhood fascination with aviation. The actual builder of Lindbergh's craft, *The Spirit of St. Louis*, was Benjamin Franklin Mahoney, a 1918 graduate of Mercersburg. Moreover, Lindbergh undertook his crossing on May 20, Stewart's nineteenth birthday. With those coincidences fueling his enthusiasm, Alex and Bessie knew that they were wasting their time by trying to keep Stewart, at home and still not completely recovered from his kidney problems, under lock and key. As the actor described it:

I followed Lindbergh from even before he got to New York, from San Diego. . . . On the night of the flight, I made a model of *The Spirit of St. Louis*, and I cut out a round thing out of beaverboard, with the Woolworth Building here and the Eiffel Tower there, and I put it in the window of my Dad's hardware store. . . . Then I hung *The Spirit of St. Louis* up on a wire and asked my Dad to keep the lights on it. The Indiana *Evening Gazette* was right across the street from the store. So I'd go over there and I'd say, "Where is he now?" And then I'd go back to the store and move the airplane farther on. . . . I had people in front of the window watching the thing all night.

The absorption with Lindbergh would have several more chapters, spanning thirty years, and culminating in Stewart's strenuous campaign to portray the aviator in *The Spirit of St. Louis* when he was almost twice the age the Lone Eagle had been in crossing the Atlantic.

Summer vacations from Mercersburg did not mean idling around Indiana, or even returning to the counters or backrooms of The Big Warehouse. For the most part, Stewart picked up extra money working as a brickloader for an Indiana company specializing in highway and road construction work; he also loaded bricks for the building of a Philadelphia Street bank still in business. But whatever his salary for manual labor, it was rarely spent on his friends. Seconding an assessment once made by her husband, Hall, that "Jim still has the first dollar he ever made," Eleanor Blair recalled a "reputation in town for being particularly tight," saying:

> He'd go to a movie with a girl, then afterward go to a soda shop or something. As soon as the two of them sat down, Jim would take out a dime and put it on the counter between them and say, "Okay, this is what we have to spend." He was so infamous for this that Hall and the others would laugh, even be disappointed if he didn't do it. The same thing happened whenever they'd go to the carnival together. The girl would want to go on this ride or that ride, but Jim would say that he didn't have the money for it. Let him see something that he wanted to go on, though, and he would suddenly find the money for it in his pocket.

At least in part because of his penchant for throwing dimes around like manhole covers, Stewart was never considered Indiana's hottest date—and this despite what Eleanor Blair calls "a good eye for stylish women. Let's just say that he had very good taste, but didn't always know how to go from there." Most of his leisure time, according to Blair, was spent "in non-spending situations" with Hall Blair and Bill Neff. Another member of the group was Emma Stewart, daughter of attorney Ernest Stewart, who was said to have been accepted as "one of the boys" for many years. But the friendship among the four narrowly missed a tragic conclusion. Sitting at a table one day in the Blair home cleaning a .22 rifle that he had been hunting with, Stewart accidentally discharged a bullet, barely missing Blair's head. The incident terrified the actor, causing him to stay away from guns for several years. Sixty years later, during the celebrations for his seventy-fifth birthday in Indiana, he admitted to having been so traumatized by the misfire that he "went out the back door" whenever he felt an invitation coming on from Alex to go hunting. "He said he couldn't even stand the idea of holding a rifle, let alone shooting one," reported Eleanor Blair. "Alex never pushed it. I think he understood. For a man who could be so irresponsible in so many other ways, he always let Jim play things out to their conclusion by himself. I suppose it worked because he eventually resumed hunting when he was older."

Although he didn't know it at the time, Alex's strategy of letting his son "play things out to their conclusion by himself" began to break down during Stewart's senior year at Mercersburg. It was then that, in a raptus of taking on extracurricular activities to make up for the time lost to his scarlet fever and kidney illness, the one-time writer-producer-director of *The Slacker* and *To Hell with the Kaiser* also agreed to join the academy's Stony Batter drama club. Among the other members of the cast was an upper middler (junior) who would also end up in Hollywood, as the star of dozens of low-budget musicals, westerns, and dramas—Nick (later Dick) Foran.

Stewart's theatrical debut, in *The Wolves*, playing the role of a French revolutionary named Buquet, drew decidedly mixed reviews. The campus newspaper, the Mercersburg *News*, was impressed by both future film actors: "[Foran's] gruff but honest voice fitted his role in good manner and he acquitted himself well. . . . As Buquet, James Stewart was excellent. He swaggered around the stage in the accepted manner for the revolutionary citizen and spoke his lines in the most confident manner of a polished star."

On the other hand, the director of *The Wolves*, Carl Cass, was hardly taken with what he had loosed on the stage of the campus gymnasium, telling an interviewer some years later: "Jimmy Stewart was about as clumsy a young adolescent as a play coach ever had to work with. . . . He was a long-legged kid who looked funny in any kind of clothes he wore. I had to find a role in which he wouldn't wear near-fitting clothes. And he had to be coached so that he wouldn't fall when he walked on stage."

As for Stewart himself, he recalled the experience as a lark verging on chaos. As he once told Jahn Robbins:

> A big sophomore named Angus Gordon was the narrator. His job was to tell the audience there was going to be a fierce battle at midnight. He got so enthusiastic with the announcement that he took out his sword and brandished it around violently. Most of the props had been borrowed

from local residents. As he swung it over an eighteenth-century table, a lady in the audience screamed, "Stop! That belongs to me!" But it was too late. Gordon had sliced the table in half. After that catastrophe, it was tough getting the audience back in the proper frame of mind.

Stewart's mind wasn't converted too easily, either: Even after his years at Mercersburg, with all the implications for proceeding on to Princeton, he still harbored hopes of going to Annapolis.

TIGER TALES

UNLIKE MERCERSBURG ACADEMY, PRINCETON UNIVERSITY has gained enough stature with the passing years to look back on part of its history with something approaching candor. Thus a 1947 review of Stewart's 1932 class, published by the school under the title of *Fifteen Years Out*, could declare about that typical graduate that "in knowledge and experience of the practical world, he was about as badly equipped as it was possible to be, reflecting the narrowness of his prep school education and the sheltered nature of his early environment. . . . When he entered Princeton in the fall of 1928, he was already one of a small, privileged, tightly knit group."

Alex Stewart wouldn't have had it any other way. Long before enrolling him at Mercersburg, in fact, he had made sure that his son was aware of the singularity of being a Princetonian. There had been the regular bustlings around the house on Vinegar Hill whenever another reunion of Alex's Class of '98 or of his campus eating club had been in the offing. There had been the periodic jaunts by the male members of the Stewart family to see Princeton tackle Ivy League football adversaries. There had been the visits to Indiana by some of Alex's classmates and the ensuing, weekend-long reminiscences. There had even been ill-advised attempts at having James soak up the atmosphere of reunions directly on the New Jersey campus. As attorney Lewis Van Dusen recalls it: "My father and Alex had been pretty close, so they decided a couple of times to bring us along when they had their bashes for their eating club, the Cottage Club. But Jimmy and I behaved badly both times, and they didn't invite us back another time. We were both kids, maybe nine or ten, and we did a lot of cutting up. Obviously, that made it hard for Alex and my father to have the good time they had been looking forward to."

Worse from the young Stewart's perspective, Alex wasn't alone in Princeton ambitions for him: Won over especially by the university's Presbyterian traditions, Bessie also wanted him to matriculate there. Nevertheless, keeping at bay the implications of his having gone to Mercersburg, James continued to hold out for Annapolis. So once again, Alex, whose promotion of Princeton had found auxiliary energy from an Army background that did not suffer the Navy easily, opted for the tactic of having his son "play things out to their conclusion."

Stewart's accounts of what happened next have differed in various tellings with regard to the itinerary, but the gist of the tale has always been as related during a Princeton press conference he held in 1990:

> After I squeaked through at Mercersburg, I told my father I still wanted to go the Naval Academy. So that summer he said, "Okay, let's take a look." We got in the car and went to the Naval Academy, and I must say I was very impressed by what I saw. Then my father said, "Let's keep going." So we drove to Duke and the University of Pennsylvania and Harvard and Yale and Dartmouth. The last stop was Princeton. By then it had become pretty obvious that he had planned everything from the beginning. We got there in the evening, and the next morning he took me out and introduced me to Princeton in the best way anybody can be introduced: through the front gate, Nassau Hall rising up ahead, the sun set perfectly in the morning sky. I'll never forget it. And I suppose that was the whole idea to begin with.

Whatever his immediate feelings were about being manipulated, Stewart has preferred over the years to stress how grateful he grew for his Princeton education; he has also seen his submission to Alex's will as an opportunity to gather stories to add to his father's lore. As he told one magazine:

> During my first week at college, the proctor of my dorm came to me and he said, "My father knew your father, and I'm keeping an eye on you." At the moment, I couldn't imagine what he meant. I learned over the following months, though, for Dad's reputation as an undergraduate

hell-raiser still clung to those venerable ivy walls. For instance, he and his friends had been the first of many generations to take a cow to the top of Nassau Hall. Another time, when he had a dispute with a Chinese laundryman about the quality of [the man's] ironing, he and his friends ironed the laundryman. The Chinese Ambassador demanded and received an apology from the president of the university.

If Princeton did not represent to Stewart the most desirable progression from Mercersburg, it certainly did for scores of fellow graduates who accompanied him from there to New Jersey, for graduates of similar prep schools, and for the university's own administration, faculty, and alumni. Like Mercersburg, the Princeton of 1928 was an all-male institution that had origins in a Protestant seminary and that counted some of the richest people in the East as parents and grandparents of its students. If it conveyed any atmospheric difference from other Ivy League institutions, it was in the hovering sense that it held "connections" in even higher esteem than did its sister schools, as epitomized by the hoary distinction that "the Yalie walks into a good salon as if he owns it, a Harvard man as though he couldn't care less who owns it, and a Princeton man as though he knows the owner."

Also like Mercersburg, Princeton remained vigilant against attempts to taint its WASP character. Despite having served as a forum for higher learning (if under various names) since the middle of the eighteenth century, it was not until after Woodrow Wilson took over as school president in 1902 that the first Catholic and first Jew were accepted as faculty members. (Women would have to wait until 1944, but even then it was only because during World War II there wasn't an alternative to hiring the Russian wife of a tenured professor to teach her language.) Wilson himself had been the first university president not to have been ordained, but his having descended from ministers on both sides of his family was perhaps pedigree enough.

In addition to the Mercersburg-like discriminations dictated by sex, religion, economic standing, racial and ethnic background, Princeton contributed an original one to its campus life: the line drawn between students who had arrived there from preparatory academies and those who had come from normal secondary schools. In the case of Stewart's freshman class, the division showed 515 from the private boarding schools, as against a mere 98 from regular institutions. Among the latter the feeling of being a minority wasn't just numerical. When they weren't simply being snubbed, they were being reminded in myriad ways that they never had studied Latin and Greek, that they had mingled with low (economic and ethnic) types, and that even their table manners left something to be desired for admittance into one of the campus's eating clubs. Without singling out Stewart, no less a symbol of American wealth than philanthropist Laurance Rockefeller, another 1932 graduate, said it took him most of his life to overcome the "low self-esteem" he had been made to feel because he had not gone to an academy such as Mercersburg or Lawrenceville in New Jersey, Princeton's two largest sources of recruits. "I don't think there's any question that the prep-school kids were more arrogant, felt that Princeton was their due. We didn't have their entrees, even with a name like Rockefeller. In fact, and at the risk of sounding like I'm copping a plea, I think it was tougher having a name like mine and being only a normal high school graduate because that gave the preppies even more of an excuse for their airs. 'How significant can he be if he didn't go to prep school like we did?' that kind of thing."

According to Rockefeller, the arrogance of the prep-schoolers even extended to the teachers.

The prep-school mentality was Happy Times, Togetherness with their own, and let the rest of the world take care of itself. There wasn't any team sense about them. They included the faculty in that attitude, too. You'd rarely see one of them get friendly with a teacher the way the majority of college kids will. Their outlook was that a teacher was only as good as the prep school he had come from. And sometimes not even that was enough. How could even an instructor *with* the background of a fancy academy impress them as a role model when, after all, he'd just ended up as a teacher?

For sure, Stewart didn't have the social nightmares at Princeton that Rockefeller said he encountered. Even discounting the retrospective tributes he has paid to the university for decades, he slid into enough extracurricular activities (track team, the *Tiger* newspaper) in his first year to suggest immediately picking up where he had left off at Mercersburg. He might have even found the familiar in the worst fire in the university's history shortly after he arrived—a blaze that reduced to ashes the Victorian structure known as the Science Building. His nightmares were—again—of the academic variety, and he didn't have to close his eyes at night to see them. Informing his parents that he intended working in aviation after graduation, he embarked on his college studies in pursuit of an engineering degree—civil or electrical, depending on the mood that his most recent test results had triggered. But either way, he found his path blocked by mathematics, and the outcome this time was not as face-saving as that of the Latin makeup exam on the eve of graduation from Mercersburg: He had to attend summer school in 1929 to wipe out failing grades in several subjects. As Stewart remembered it, he eventually "survived" algebra and calculus, but not to the extent of being able to maintain plausible hopes of becoming an engineer. "I was called aside by my math teacher just after I'd gotten the word about summer school, and he said, 'I think you better think very seriously about something else, or you'll be in deep trouble.' I took the hint."

Abetting his second thoughts were his talent for drawing and a facility for one branch of mathematics—descriptive geometry—that he discovered in summer school. His new career, he announced to Alex and Bessie, was going to be architecture.

At first, he embraced his new course enthusiastically. It was of some help that his scrupulous study of the Mercersburg chapel during its stage-by-stage erection dovetailed with a Princeton academic accent on church buildings. But the more his instructors dwelled on apses and naves, the more the practical Stewart—the one who had worked at the hardware store since he was a child, who had made a profit from his crystal sets, and who had listened to the Reverend Frederick Hinitt talk about "relevant Christianity" back in Indiana—grew restless. Peter Schwed, a member of the 1932 Class who went on to a career in publishing, had the same reaction: "Aside from both of us wanting to study architecture, Jimmy and I were thrown even closer together for a while by the fact that we were always next to each other in the classroom because of the alphabetical seating system they had. I could tell that he was bored as I was by all the ecclesiastical architecture. What did the cathedral at Chartres have to tell *us*? We waited in vain that first year for a discussion of building houses and other practical things of concern to the budding architect of the 1930s. Far too much aesthetics. That's why I got out of it."

But Stewart stayed. And as his courses became more intricate and he was able to demonstrate his mastery of detail on a broader range of assignments, he settled in to an unprecedented sense of ease with a classroom subject. The rest of his curriculum remained a daily trial ("Spanish was another Waterloo; about the only thing I learned to say was 'Please hand in your exercise notebooks' "), but he became so proficient at his architecture studies that he received a scholarship in his senior year for graduate work. What especially impressed his instructors was his thesis—the plan for an airport, including terminal building and adjoining hangars.

Even in his academic prime, however, Stewart was assailed by doubts about the long-term value of the road he had taken. No doubt was more enervating than that prompted by the crash of the stock market in 1929, only weeks after he had switched away from his engineering goal. With the hardware store already staggered by its fire losses a short time before, there was suddenly some question whether, with the onset of the Depression, he would be able to continue his studies at all. Certainly, it didn't take long for the sons of even more affluent families to begin dropping out of Princeton because of financial difficulties. On top of that, there were the direct implications of the Depression for the building industry: If there was no capital for construction, who needed more architects?

If nothing else, the country's economic crisis crystallized for Stewart the difference between Princeton's Haves and Princeton's Other Haves. For some members of the student body, even the financial collapse was something happening only to people who resided outside the rails of the campus. According to Thomas Cook, a Greek and philosophy student who later earned a law degree, "campus life insulated most of us. All those bankruptcies and suicides, selling apples on the street, that was something you heard about only when you went home to visit." For Jay Morehouse, another member of Stewart's class who made his career in oil sales, not even visits home brought any true understanding of what was happening to families. "My own father was going broke," Morehouse says, "but I didn't pay any attention. The Depression was simply something you ignored. We were nineteen, twenty, twenty-one. We were living in this pretty little town. Plenty of grass and trees. Reality was somewhere else—across the Hudson, over in New York City."

Stewart didn't have the luxury of such a conceit. What he did have, aside from his willingness to work at brickloading and roadway line painting and delivering for The Big Warehouse whenever he was home, was a father who had no intention of seeing so many years of his wiles in placing him in Princeton go for nothing. Extra loans were made. Additional friends were contacted. Longer hours were worked at the store, and with fewer employees who had to be paid. In Lewis Van Dusen's view, some of the emergency aid almost certainly came from people who had graduated with Alex and with his own father. "Princeton graduates have always had an extended family feeling about themselves," says Van Dusen, "and I think that was especially true of the Class of '98. I know that some of my father's classmates pitched in when *he* was scraping the bottom of the barrel, and I can't imagine they wouldn't have helped Alex as well, particularly if it was a question of keeping Jim at the university."

If the Depression posed the most immediate threat to Stewart's projected career as an architect, his evolving pleasure in performing in public represented a deeper danger. In countless interviews over the years, the actor has left the impression that he was practically whisked off to the theatrical life upon graduation after only minimal stage experience at Princeton. Actually, he was exposed to audiences many times during his upper-school years, if not always as an actor performing in a scripted play at Princeton. What was arguably the most seminal of all these experiences was a summer vacation job as an assistant to his friend, the professional magician Bill Neff.

To make ends meet in the 1920s, Neff played Pennsylvania's dwindling Chautauqua circuit. One summer, he took Stewart and his accordion along to cover up any awkward moments in extracting pigeons from his pockets. The routine was for the pair to enter a new town and head right for the tallest building, where Neff would tie a rope around his ankle and hang upside down while Stewart played and barkered out details of that night's performance. On the stage, however, their partnership became more noted for dispelling illusions than creating them. One evening, for example, Stewart had only to walk onstage to hand a guinea pig to Neff. Stretched on the stage at the time was a fine wire invisible to the audience. Unfortunately for Neff, however, it was not at all invisible to Stewart, so he ducked under it, provoking gales of laughter from the audience and making the delivery of the guinea pig superfluous.

Another evening, Neff and Stewart were both onstage doing a number in which they made a woman "levitate" through their joint "hypnotic powers." The key to the trick was a local stagehand stationed in the wings who, at a given signal, carefully worked a lever that slowly raised an apparatus, unseen by the audience, underneath the woman. To the dismay of the mentalists, however, neither their frustrated energies nor their accompanying gibberish succeeded in elevating the woman— because the stagehand had fallen asleep. Leaving Neff to improvise for the audience the reasons why some souls were more earthbound than others, Stewart worked a concert of coughs, hisses, and whispers behind his hand to wake the man up. When he finally did, he immediately wished he hadn't: The startled stagehand gave a hard shove to his lever, hurtling the woman into the air as though she were riding an express elevator. Only Stewart's quick move amid the bewilderment of the audience prevented the man from compounding his error by yanking the lever back up and depositing the woman back down on the stage with a thud.

The "fun and excitement" with which Stewart has characterized his forays with Neff have been shared by numerous actors who were involved in magic acts in their early years. From James Stuart Blackton, America's first combination actor-director-producer and founder of the first motion-picture studio, to Orson Welles, the opportunity for baffling audiences through illusions became a basic part of the actor's professional demeanor. Stewart, on the other hand, has insisted that audiences were his "partner" in the most consciously collaborative sense of the term. But there are partners and there are partners: those whose presence and participation excite the best from a performer and lend him a feeling of security about his profession, and those who are needed for nothing more than to hand over one penny so they can discover that *For Men Only* means an old pair of pants hanging in the closet.

Within Princeton as well, Stewart performed in public at regular intervals. His first two appearances he owed to his accordion, which, as at Mercersburg, was seldom out of his hands when he wasn't doing schoolwork. In his first year, he was helped around a ban against freshmen appearing in productions staged by the university's Triangle Club, by doing a walk-on in something called *The Golden Dog*. What he walked on with—and the reason he was allowed to ignore the freshman restriction—was his accordion. The following year he was back with his accordion for the Triangle, doing a solo of "So Beats My Heart for You." In his junior year, he performed far more prominently in a production called

The Tiger Smiles and also made one of the most important connections of his life—with future director-producer Josh Logan. In his senior year, he did two plays—one with the Triangle Club and another with the university's Theatre Intime.

Through it all, Stewart laughed off the idea that he was attracted to the theater in any serious way. He told both classmates and friends at home that, as far as he was concerned, working on the stage was just another extracurricular activity, such as the drawings he did for the *Tiger* and for special programs (among other things, the cover of the scorecard for a 1930 football game between Cornell and Princeton). Otherwise, he was still bent on becoming an architect . . . and having a good time.

Stewart's social life at Princeton was conditioned not only by the Depression, but also by a university ban against student driving and by Prohibition. If all these factors should have added up to all work and no play, the actual sum turned out differently.

With regard to the driving ban, Laurance Rockefeller, for one, viewed it as a blessing in disguise, as one of the campus's few levelers between the graduates of prep schools and normal secondary institutions: "The rule against driving came in because there had been too many accidents involving students. This really became a democratizing element because it made it difficult for anyone to leave on weekends, even to go home. There was a common sense of everyone having the same problem, if only at a level of complaint. This didn't mean that the campus exhibited any particular signs of the Depression, but it did prevent the car owners from exhibiting one sign of their wealth."

Automobiles were not needed, however, to aid students in their search for illegal liquor; as often as not, suppliers could be located directly in front of the university campus on Nassau Street. Josh Logan, a year ahead of Stewart, once described the Friday ritual during Prohibition: "At five in the afternoon hundreds of undergraduates crossed the quadrangles with little brown paperbags filled with ice and mixes. Outside the ground-floor windows, bootleggers delivered expensive bad whiskey and cheap worse gin." According to Jay Morehouse, it was also "a common practice among everybody but teetotalers" to take the Nassau Street trolley to Trenton to buy beer from speakeasies in the capital. For Thomas Cook, there was the alternative of using public transportation to the nearby community of Kingston for speakeasy beer and applejack. Even the teetotaling Rockefeller concedes that he was "left out of campus life further" by never joining such excursions.

Stewart went on the speakeasy hunts as often as his budget—and thriftiness—allowed. It wasn't unknown for him to heft along his accordion for some improvised entertainment for fellow trolley riders. In those pre-"Lady of Spain" days, there was apparently more appreciation than irritation for his efforts. In fact, next to the piano, the accordion was the most popular musical instrument in Stewart's class. Another who played it was Robert Moorehead Perry, who in 1944 would marry Stewart's sister Mary.

Less amused than his classmates and trolley passengers by the accordion playing were some of the actor's dates for dances and house parties. As he once told gossip columnist Sheilah Graham: "I got to taking the accordion with me whenever there was a party. A lot of times they would just ask me to bring it. Almost every time I'd end up playing all night. When I looked around to find my girl, she was usually gone. I could never understand why. I soon discovered it was better to go to a prom stag, and I generally did. Take a girl, and she'd likely be whisked away. . . . "

One major difference between Princeton and Mercersburg, however, was that, despite Prohibition and the Depression, Stewart had any number of social opportunities to make up for those squandered. This was especially so in the fall and spring, when the campus's principal social institution, the eating clubs, competed with one another to stage the semester's most memorable party.

The eating clubs had come about as an alternative to fraternities, condemned by nineteenth-century administrators as far too secretive for the university's good. During his Ivy reign, Woodrow Wilson came to the conclusion that the clubs did not mark much of an advance on fraternities, that they merely substituted an undesirable rivalry in snobbishness for secretiveness while otherwise leaving intact a decentralizing campus force. His attempts at abolishing the clubs, however, failed before the pride of trustees and other alumni who had their own past memberships to reminisce about. By the time that Stewart got to Princeton, there were some nineteen clubs operating, and a number of them on a residential scale that shamed the physical facilities of the university itself. One 1912 critic took specific issue with Alex Stewart's Cottage Club, asserting that "what is most regrettable in the

Princeton club system is the luxury of the houses, which notably in the Cottage and Ivy clubs reaches a degree of extravagance which might lead an outsider to believe he was in the homes of millionaires." Not that anyone should have conjured up a tool shed at the thought of a *clubhouse*: Among the architects hired to provide new club quarters for one eating society was Charles Follen McKim, who supervised the rebuilding of the White House in 1902 and designed any number of private clubs in the New York area.

Students were recruited for the clubs at the end of freshman year, with membership open only to sophomores, juniors, and seniors. As their name implied, the clubs' ostensible raison d'être was offering a common table for meals, at which ties and jackets were usually necessary. Aside from this practical function and a calm atmosphere for study and conversation (sleeping on the premises was not allowed), what the eating clubs mainly provided was another specific identity for their members— organizationally as well as personally. Distinguishing some of the characteristics of the more prominent clubs on one occasion, novelist F. Scott Fitzgerald thought "Ivy, detached and breathlessly aristocratic; Cottage, an impressive melange of brilliant adventurers and well-dressed philanderers; Tiger Inn, broad-shouldered and athletic; Cap and Gown, anti-alcoholic, faintly religious, and politically powerful; flamboyant, literary Quadrangle." Josh Logan admitted particular impatience with members of the Ivy Club, writing in his autobiography: "Up and down McCosh Walk pranced that special breed of student—nose in the air, torso bent forward, rear end protruding—wearing white saddle shoes, gray flannel trousers, and a tight-fitting tweed jacket. This said clearly that the wearer was bucking ('whoring') for Ivy, the most distinguished club of them all."

Neither Fitzgerald nor Logan had much to say about Charter, the club to which Stewart was admitted in 1929. Like several other clubs, Charter had no emphatic characteristics: It accepted a little bit of this and a little bit of that, sometimes after candidates had been turned down elsewhere. Asked once why he had not tried for Cottage, the "impressive melange of brilliant adventurers and well-dressed philanderers" to which his father had subscribed, Stewart confined himself to saying that "only Charter asked me."

If the Charter Club did not have one defining characteristic, it helped for members to like music. When Stewart wasn't entertaining with his accordion, he was swapping musical notes in the club's quarters with Jose Ferrer, the future actor, then preoccupied with leading a dance band.[2] He also had a hand in planning the club's elaborate jazz weekends for which some of the biggest names in the business were hired. On May 2, 1931, for instance, Charter sponsored a weekend party bill that included Bix Beiderbecke, Bud Freeman, Jimmy Dorsey, and Charlie Teagarden. The weekend gained a footnote in the Beiderbecke story when the trumpeter, already oiled by a flask from which he had been sipping all evening, wandered off to another house, where he sat down at a piano and began to play a series of original, mesmerizing compositions that were never written down, let alone recorded. Later that Sunday morning, he had to be pulled off the street for flashing his flask before scandalized Princetonians on their way to church. It was partly because of this incident that a campus periodical admonished Charter a few weeks later for its spending on the weekend parties. "Just when the time will come when the clubs realize that they do not have to vie with New York debutante parties in elaborateness and splendor, is problematical, but it is bound to come," warned the *Prince*.

At one time or another in the period, the eating clubs also hired Louis Armstrong, Duke Ellington, and Cab Calloway for spring festivities. It was around the same time that Glenn Miller was making a few thousand dollars by hustling pool on Nassau Street (though nothing indicates that Stewart ever met the orchestra leader he later played on the screen).

Stewart had no regular attachments to women during his university years. Most of his dates at dances and parties—at least before he whipped out his accordion—were women he had met at an earlier function, usually as the dates of other Princetonians. In fact, notwithstanding the blame he has placed on his accordion for showing up stag at social events, he appeared to have enjoyed the role of sexual poacher. What struck some people even back then as shyness, impressed others as guile. Even after more than sixty years, one classmate refuses to pin his name to "a resentment that I can still feel about the way he once came in to a party and waltzed away with a girl I was stuck on. All that hick-from-the-woods manner he had was a lot of crap."

When the Charter Club wasn't providing the entertainment, it was

---

[2] Although he entered Princeton with Stewart, Ferrer took a year off to tour with his band, so he didn't graduate until 1933.

the Triangle Club. Although the productions were all-male affairs, with boys playing distaff roles, they offered a number of opportunities for meeting women, especially during an annual tour of several cities around Christmas. On several occasions, Stewart has made it sound as though the holiday tour was the main reason he continued to appear in the club's operettas and plays, such as when he told the New York *Herald Tribune* in 1939: "The main inducement [for joining] was a tour at Christmas, the seventy-five of us in the troupe, all congenial, traveling and being met at trains by Princeton alumni, the perfect hosts. It offered the chance of getting down to New York at no expense, and that was the highlight." Another time, he recalled the specific tour he took as part of the cast for the 1931 production of *The Tiger Smiles*:

> You were thrown into close activity with a large group of boys from different classes and different parts of the country. You traveled for three weeks with them. You met their sisters, their mothers and fathers, and you returned after the holidays with a host of names in your book. . . . Traveling was a romantic adventure. Silly though it may seem, names like Memphis, Nashville, St. Louis, Louisville and all the others had each its special glamour in my mind, and as we pulled into each town, I would be standing on the platform, wide-eyed and thrilled. . . .

With Logan providing the script, *The Tiger Smiles* pushed Stewart stage center with song-and-dance material that, he said years later, should have shamed any sentient adult. The highlight of the show was a duet entitled "Minnie Ha Ha," in which the Indian-togged Logan and Stewart shared such gems as:

> I be Papa, you be Mama.
> Boom, boom.
> We will have much papooses, no excuses.
> Boom, boom.
>
> We will sleep–ee in a big teepee.
> Boom, boom.

In his senior year, Stewart was drafted for the Triangle production of *Spanish Blades*, a spoof about Don Juan and Don Quixote in which he was an accordion-playing troubadour who also sang two songs. Aside from the Triangle musicals, he performed twice for the university's smaller Theatre Intime drama group—in his junior year as a butler in *The Play's the Thing* and, only two months before he graduated, as a contemporary blue-collar type named McNulty in *Nerissa*. Campus periodicals preferred his butler to his proletarian, and his singing and playing in *Spanish Blades* to both.

In Stewart's telling, *Nerissa* ought to have marked his swan song as an actor. But already in place were a couple of conditions that would make him receptive to Logan's invitation to change his mind. One had taken root during his junior year, when Margaret Sullavan had starred at Princeton in a visiting production of *The Artist and the Lady*. Stewart, the show's stage manager, was so smitten by her that, his supposed shyness toward women notwithstanding, he immediately invited her as his date to a reception hosted by the Charter Club. The actress accepted, initiating a twenty-year relationship that was the most important—and most embroiling—that Stewart would have with a woman until his 1949 marriage. (It was also during the Princeton presentation of *The Artist and the Lady* that Sullavan was spotted by an associate of the Shuberts, who produced her Broadway debut only a few weeks later.)

The other significant shaping event was the deepening of the Depression, which made Stewart even more skeptical of his work prospects as an architect. In the late spring of 1932, the nation's jobless had grown to nine million, with daily newspapers carrying regular reports of suicides and murders precipitated by the economic crisis; it was also on the eve of the graduation of the Class of '32 that a 15,000-strong Bonus Army of aggrieved veterans descended on Washington, culminating in bloodshed. Even though he had already secured a scholarship for his Master's studies, Stewart struck several classmates at the time as being particularly dour whenever the talk turned to postgraduation intentions. Certainly, it didn't lighten matters to have his boyhood hero, Charles Lindbergh, back on his mind—but this time for the kidnapping of the aviator's son. "That happened only a short distance from the university," Jay Morehouse recalls, "so that it really became a constant topic of conversation for everybody. You'd hear more people talking about Lindbergh's baby than about the Depression." For his part, Stewart admitted once to having felt "this tremendous sense of cruelty and tragedy" over the abduction and having tried to imagine what Lindbergh must have gone through when the hunt for his son ended with the discovery of the boy's dead body.

The other shoe dropped about two weeks before graduation. As Stewart was passing the university gym, he was approached by Logan, back for a visit after having graduated the year before. The director got right to the point, inviting him to join the University Players, a summer-stock group that had taken up quarters at West Falmouth on Cape Cod. "I know you're going to graduate school," Stewart remembered Logan as having couched the invitation, "but why don't you come up, play your accordion in the tea room next to the theater, and we'll give you some small parts in the theater as the summer goes on?" For what both men estimated must have been close to three hours, they went back and forth about the idea until Stewart, evidently not ready to take on the assignment himself, said that he would go only if Logan succeeded in persuading Alex that it was a good idea. The next day, Logan called Indiana to make his pitch. Only then, and after a subsequent conversation between father and son, did Stewart agree to join the University Players.

Given the fact that Alex already had impressed some Indiana friends and neighbors as ambivalent about losing the next generation of Stewart storekeepers to architecture, his receptivity to Logan's blandishments might have seemed strange. Actually, there wasn't all that much risk involved: Aside from adopting his customary strategy of letting his (now twenty-four-year-old) son pursue things to what he hoped would be their end, there was now the objective reality of a squeezed job market at home for the summer. The younger Stewart also saw something less than binding commitment to acting with his acceptance of Logan's offer: Aside from the same practical job considerations apparent to Alex and the opportunity to make a living for a couple of months by playing his accordion, it certainly had not been lost on him that going to Cape Cod offered the chance of renewing his proximity to one of the leading ladies of the University Players for several years, Margaret Sullavan.

In reviewing the Class of '32 in 1947, the authors of *Fifteen Years Out* regretted that "our own participation in the arts is spectacularly low. We have ourselves produced no great novel, no poem, no essay, no historical work, no symphony, no play, no skyscraper, no painting, etching or fresco. We have among us no singer, no violinist or pianist of note. In fact, we have produced only one man who is known to America for his artistic works, Jimmy Stewart of the movies."

If there is a hint of condescension toward motion-picture actors in this lament, the Stewart who received his sheepskin in June of 1932 would have understood. After all his time at Princeton, he too remained uncertain about what to take seriously.

THE
UNIVERSITY PLAYERS

STEWART JOINED THE UNIVERSITY PLAYERS JUST IN TIME TO be part of the group's last act. Somewhat like his pressured decision to attend Princeton instead of the Naval Academy and to study architecture instead of engineering, his arrival at West Falmouth, accordion over his shoulder, initiated a cycle of best alternative, apparent debacle, and actual opportunity. The difference was, he would manage to complete this cycle in considerably less time than the four years he had spent at Princeton.

The University Players had been born at a 1928 Manhattan cocktail party held in honor of a man who stood for everything the new company would not. The guest of honor had been Vladmir Nemirovich-Danchenko, cofounder of the Moscow Art Theater and an early exponent of the drama and acting theories of Konstantin Stanislavsky. While the visiting Nemirovich-Danchenko was accepting the welcoming toasts of his American hosts, would-be directors Bretaigne Windust and Charles Crane Leatherbee swapped ideas about establishing their own summer-stock company. It was more of an untried idea at the time than it might seem now. With Mickey Rooney and Judy Garland still years away from wanting to "put on a show," there were in fact only four summer theaters then operating in the entire country—Elitch's Gardens in Denver; the Lakewood Playhouse in Skowhegan, Maine; another group calling itself the University Players at East Hampton, Long Island; and the Cape Cod Playhouse at Dennis on Cape Cod.

The core of the new company came from Leatherbee's Harvard theater group, the Juniper Point Players. Other recruits came from

Princeton (Windust's alma mater), Smith, Yale, Radcliffe, and Vassar. With an initial treasury that amounted to merely a couple of hundred dollars, the group set up quarters around the rather exclusive Cape Cod hilltop home of Leatherbee's mother, Frances Crane. Over their first summer in 1928, the male members of the company lived aboard the Leatherbee yacht in Falmouth harbor, while the women lived with a chaperone in a cottage at nearby Quisset. Performances that first season were given two nights a week, on Mondays and Tuesdays, at a local movie house called the Elizabeth; in exchange for leasing his space on his two slowest nights, the owner of the theater, Ike Robbins, collected 55 percent of the receipts. If there were sorrows to be drowned over that arrangement, Leatherbee, Windust, and the other members of the company knew where to find the liquor: at the Crane hilltop home where—because Leatherbee's mother had found a new husband in Jan Masaryk, the son of the president of Czechoslovakia and himself later to become his homeland's foreign minister—unofficial receptions, cocktail parties, and dinners for visiting American and European dignitaries were a regular occurrence.

For much of the company's stay in Falmouth, its chief leading man was Kent Smith, a member of the Harvard Juniper Point Players who in the 1940s became a familiar screen face for starring in such fright tales as *Cat People* and *The Spiral Staircase*. Other important early members of the troupe were Myron McCormick, who would alternate steady work on Broadway with key supporting roles in the movies, such as those of Andy Griffith's tormented sergeant in *No Time for Sergeants* and Paul Newman's friend in *The Hustler*; Barbara O'Neil, who won screen attention as the mother of Scarlett O'Hara in *Gone With the Wind* and a Best Supporting Actress Oscar nomination for the 1940 soap opera *All This and Heaven Too*; Mildred Natwick, who would make a career of portraying comical, eccentric mothers, most notably in *Barefoot in the Park* and in the television series *McMillan and Wife*; and Logan, who would end up shuttling between Broadway and Hollywood most of his life. Also among the original members were Johnny Swope, who would later devote his talents to photography and marry actress Dorothy McGuire, and Harvard premed student (and future doctor) Bart Quigley. Quigley's most lasting contribution to the theater would be his daughter, actress and National Endowment for the Arts chief Jane Alexander.

The troupe's two most magnetic players, however, were recruited after the curtain at Ike Robbins's movie house had been raised and lowered a few times; moreover, neither was an Ivy Leaguer—a stipulation previously adhered to by Windust and Leatherbee. The first of these exceptions was Henry Fonda, who dropped in on a performance at the Elizabeth during an off-night from his work with the Cape Cod Playhouse company in Dennis, a few miles away. As Fonda himself told the story, he grew so hysterical at a Logan comic turn during a production of George Kelly's *The Torchbearers* that his laughter infected a previously apathetic audience, salvaging the evening for one and all. After the performance, he met with Logan, Windust, and Leatherbee and, despite admitting to having flunked out of the University of Minnesota as a journalism student, was offered a place with the University Players for five dollars a week; he accepted because that was five dollars more than he was getting at Dennis.

The second pickup was Margaret Sullavan, the daughter of a well-to-do Virginia family who had been going to secretarial school in Boston and supporting herself by working at a cooperative bookstore on Harvard Square. Leatherbee met her in the store, saw her act with a Harvard drama group, and invited her to join his company for the 1929 season. He also began telling everybody that she was his girlfriend—something Sullavan didn't deny, but a number of other Harvard men found this strange since they had assumed she was their girlfriend. One of her earliest critics was Fonda, who did a walk-on with her in a Harvard musical comedy in April 1929, shortly before both of them were due to go to Falmouth. Their early scene together called for Sullavan to slap him across the face for a suggestive look—a piece of business that she worked at so assiduously during both rehearsals and performances that the physically hurting Fonda decided, as he warned Leatherbee, that she was "a ball-breaker from way back." Leatherbee's own warning was that Fonda, despite his current perception, would end up loving her as much as he and everybody else did—a prophecy borne out when the actor married Sullavan a few years later.

At the Elizabeth in their first year and then at more stable quarters at Old Silver Beach over the next several summers, the University Players[3] offered a melange of thrillers, comedies, and straight dramas whose

---

[3] Between 1928 and 1932, the troupe was variously known as the University Players Guild, the University Players, the University Repertory Theater, and the Theatre Unit, Inc.

common denominator was an attempt to offer something for everybody—as long as there were enough everybodies every week to meet expenses and produce a little profit. In absolute contrast to the Group Theater, the Stanislavsky-inspired company of Harold Clurman and Lee Strasberg that viewed its efforts as a political weapon in the struggles of the 1930s, the Players ridiculed the notion of an ideological agenda. That seemed inevitable to Jane Alexander, who heard about the troupe's activities not only from her father around her house, but also from Fonda, a costar in a couple of plays in the 1960s and 1970s: "The University Players were in it strictly for the fun. It was really only a step above a college lark. How could it not have been, when they were mostly together for summers, like some kind of extended, organized vacation? That's hardly the atmosphere for considering serious political and social goals, like the Group was doing. It was really the season—the summer— that shaped their priorities."

Norris Houghton, a set designer on Cape Cod who became the company historian through his book *But Not Forgotten*, has also noted the near-obliviousness of the Players to surrounding conditions in preparing annual programs: "To begin with, working in Falmouth was not exactly a constant reminder of how tough the nation as a whole had it. Roughing it aboard a yacht, like we did the first year, might not have been as luxurious as some people believe, but it wasn't sleeping on a Manhattan sidewalk or park bench, either. Above that, though, I'd be tempted to say that the company as a whole was less aware of the social, economic, and political trends of its times than any other intelligent, educated group of young people in America."

To Logan, however, the difference from an enterprise such as the Group Theater wasn't merely in what the University Players were not, but also in what they reflected, if not always consciously, about the very nature of a stage company. As the director put it: "It was in this group that I discovered that good theater is not collaboration. Artists cannot truly collaborate. To be good they must follow their inspiration, their urge, their ego, to the limit. And that limit is only when the venture will collapse if they push themselves one inch further. Only then must they make an adjustment—a creative compromise—but just enough of a compromise to avoid disaster."

By the time Stewart arrived in Falmouth, most of the group's big battles had been fought. There had been almost as many reversals as victories; on occasion, the victories *had been* reversals, at least after the lifting of an initial sense of triumph. For one thing, the latest recruit from Princeton didn't have to worry about sleeping on a yacht or performing in a movie house. After the company's initial season, in fact, theater-owner Robbins decided that his comfortable profit wasn't comfortable enough and declared the Elizabeth off-bounds. When the Falmouth town council vetoed their attempt to rent out an abandoned power plant, the University Players reached the brink of extinction, until Leatherbee's grandfather advanced $20,000 for the construction of a 395-seat auditorium at Old Silver Beach. Making the new facility more attractive was a flanking tea room that, in addition to offering such daily fare as sandwiches and sundaes, hosted university jazz musicians on weekends; patrons were legally forbidden—and tacitly encouraged—to pack flasks in their pockets. With the theater established, it also became easier to find land lodgings for the company, with the men and women still separated.

The plays presented in the new quarters between 1929 and 1931 continued to exasperate for their inconsistency in both production and performance. At one point, Fonda became so discouraged by a bad performance that he announced that he was quitting acting for set designing; however, most of his artwork went into the tea room, where he painted panels swirling with modernistic fish motifs. The company was also beset by power problems at the top, especially by Windust's emergence as the first among equals. So authoritative was he that one actress practically gave up her career on the spot because of his judgment that she was inept, and Houghton, although already underweight, went around for weeks worrying about putting on extra pounds simply because of some incidental remark from Windust. Not even Windust, however, was able to steer the company above the practical pitfalls of trying to turn raw performers into a technically astute company. In one rehearsal of a fight scene, for example, Fonda and Swope were so maladroit about faking punches that the two of them ended up going at each other for real. The constant feeling of always having to start from scratch to find subscribers also began to weigh, prompting Leatherbee and Logan to take off for Europe during the winter of 1930–31 in hopes of picking up pointers about maintaining a company from the Moscow Art Theater and from Max Reinhardt in Vienna.

Ultimately, the greatest threats to the company came from success.

First, there were the individual performers who waited only for their graduations from Ivy League schools to attempt to use good reviews at Falmouth as calling cards on Broadway producers. This became such a pressing problem that Windust and Leatherbee were soon accepting Fonda and Sullavan as forerunners rather than as exceptions to their policy regarding Ivy League applicants; over the objections of Windust in particular, the company decided that even enrollment at the Katherine Gibbs secretarial school met the standards for being a "university" player. In the winter of 1931, in its first significant foray away from Cape Cod and as more than a summer group, the Players became the talk of Baltimore for a spirited production of *Lysistrata*. The success of that production and a couple of others, however, was dwarfed by the marriage of Fonda and Sullavan on Christmas Day and the actor's announcement that, as soon as the group wound up its engagement in Maryland, he intended following Sullavan to Broadway, where she had already gained a niche. Among the other defectors that year were Smith and Swope.

According to Houghton, so many crucial departures had left a "great emptiness" in the company. In addition, the set designer has said, despite Logan's theories about noncollaborative art, the relentless, practical scrambling to put up a new show (during the summers) every eighth day had left him feeling as if he had "acquired the expertise of the journeyman but few creative insights." It was in the throes of this gloom, when the company stopped in Princeton on the way back to Falmouth from Baltimore, that Logan tendered his invitation for Stewart to join the Players. Later on, both men would concede the possibility of there having been a pinch of desperation on Logan's part about keeping the remnants of the group together.

At least with one interviewer, Stewart said that it had taken but a single glance at the Old Silver Beach theater to make up his mind that he was going to build roles rather than skyscrapers or airports. In 1936, he declared: "My first glimpse of the Falmouth Theater decided my future. Built practically on the water, it is one of the most beautiful theaters in America. Cape Cod in the summer is a paradise."

Although he would qualify the significance for him of that initial impression in other recollections, the actor wasted little time in embracing the company's routine. Not only did he perform in the tea room with his accordion before and after shows at the theater, but his tinkerings in the Indiana basement, drawing talents, and architectural eye made him a natural presence around the property rooms, design drafting rooms, and set workshops that had been added to the complex since the theater had gone up. As much as any of his specific tasks, he was also drawn to the general regimen of the activities: "The enthusiasm of Leatherbee, Logan, and Windust was catching. They did their own casting, directing, built scenery, arranged lighting effects, and had unbounded energy in running the theater. It proved to be an ideal training school."

As often as he has referred to his accordion playing at the tea room, Stewart has mocked it, typically asserting that he was eventually "let go because people . . . complained that my playing interfered with their digestion." At other times, he has claimed that his musical stint lasted merely one evening. Houghton denies anything of the sort: "He's always exaggerated about that, possibly because he prefers thinking about himself as an actor up there. We hung out there the entire summer of 1932, and Jim was there with his accordion the entire summer. Maybe there was a customer or two who winced at what came out of his accordion, but he was not at all untalented."

Before going to Falmouth, of course, Stewart had heard about Sullavan's withdrawal from the company and about her marriage to Fonda. But he had also heard how the Battling Fondas had split up a mere few months after exchanging vows and how she had been cavorting with producer Jed Harris and other Broadway types since. Her absence from the unit hadn't completely deflated him, either, since he was now working with several people (especially Logan, Leatherbee, and McCormick) who remained in fairly regular contact with her. It might have been only food for thought, but his coolness toward group members when, on several occasions, they recounted Sullavan Terror Tales, persuaded those around him that he hadn't pushed himself away from the table altogether. Kent Smith, for one, would insist later that Stewart was "always in love with Sullavan," that the feeling had started long before she demanded him as a Hollywood costar. In the meantime, though, there were the distractions of helping to get a new play on its feet every week, serving as a theater usher, and playing his accordion in the tea room. Such a schedule, according to Logan anyway, made it next to impossible for any members to moon too long over would-be or might-have-been lovers: "It was a monastic life. . . . The town looked on us as wild kids having a crazy time and sinful summer together on the Cape. Would that that were true. Sin would have been welcome and relaxing.

But learning lines, rehearsing, helping to build sets, plus lack of sleep or food, left little time or energy or even opportunity—to say nothing of privacy—for such bliss. Physical love had to wait in line."

For Houghton, however, Logan was laying it on a bit thick. His memories of the relationships between male and female members of the company are somewhat less austere.

> Certainly, everybody always had a lot to do. And in 1932, when Jim was there, the living conditions seemed especially bizarre—Windust and Leatherbee living in one place near Charlie's mother, the rest of the men in one dormitory-style cottage, the women in another one, and both groups a good ten- or fifteen-minute drive away from the theater. But Jim and an actress named Merna Pace seemed to hit it off very well, and I wouldn't be surprised if he wasn't also involved with another actress named Cynthia Rogers. But Stewart aside, I never had any impression of monks and nuns. Kent Smith, for example, was very much a ladies man up there. There was more than one entanglement where he was concerned. And you not only had Fonda and Sullavan getting married, but Logan himself married Barbara O'Neil, if briefly, after awhile. I don't know how Josh thought of that as the monastic life. An ongoing orgy, hardly. But not a bed of nails, either.

Stewart made his acting debut at Falmouth in a walk-on role as a Good Ol' Boy from the South in Booth Tarkington's satire *Magnolia*. Shortly afterward, he was given some lines in the comedy *It's a Wise Child*; his role was that of an iceman appropriately named Cool Kelly whose defining character moment came when he announced that he would consider marrying someone only if she were "100 percent pure." Houghton remembers Stewart as receiving laughs in all the right places; moreover, according to the veteran designer, the reactions of Leatherbee and Windust to the performance immediately established a pattern that producers and directors would follow in New York and Hollywood for many years afterward. Houghton: "The fact of the matter was, he was not a typical, good-looking juvenile. In his shambling and somewhat awkward way, he was far more striking and he presented a challenge to directors and producers. Like Leatherbee and Windust, a majority of directors saw he had a quality that they *had* to include in what they were doing, even though they frequently didn't have the slightest idea *how* to include it."

For the rest of that summer, he certainly wasn't cast as a leading man.

Although stories about Stewart's stay with the University Players have sometimes sparked the idea that he was there as a successor to Fonda, he was not yet anywhere near that level of preparation—a fact only too clear to the company directors. It was as a bit player that he contributed to the company's presentations, and as a bit player that, sooner than anyone had a right to expect, he proceeded from Falmouth to Broadway. It was also in having to work up from that status that he consolidated his views of acting as craft rather than art, with all the patient, piecemeal, manual associations of the former as opposed to the more epiphanous abstractions frequently implied by the latter. In this, he was hardly departing from some received attitudes: Even the two largest talent pools for the original company of the University Players, Harvard and Princeton, did not then recognize drama as being worthy of formal department study. But it was an outlook that made almost inevitable his future railing against the value of acting schools. Like the self-made man who has never quite understood those who haven't made their way through life as he has, Stewart ended up turning his humble beginnings at Old Silver Beach into a banner of pride. Typical were remarks made in a letter to Princeton professor Alan Downer in 1962: ". . . the first thing a youngster should do who is interested in making the theater a career is to find out whether he can act, and the only way you can do that is to act; and it really doesn't matter whether it is in the Triangle show or the Intime or the little theater groups during the summer."

In 1977, he told Tobi Nyberg: "The most important thing about acting is to approach it as a craft, not as an art and not as some mysterious type of religion. You don't have to meditate to be an actor. And for heaven's sake, stay away from acting schools. Acting schools take up all your time. Sure, a lot of successful people came out of acting schools, but they knew how to act before they went in. They had the talent, you see. All they needed was a chance to acquire the skill. Acquiring the skill is what acting is all about."

Inching along from line to line, from play to play, Stewart was still sufficiently ambivalent about his acting aspirations not to put together an audition piece for New York producers once the season ended in Falmouth.[4] As it turned out, he didn't have to: Broadway came to him.

---

[4] Fonda, for instance, became noted for his rendition from *Merton of the Movies* in which the hero of the title kneels down and prays desperately that God will make him a good movie actor.

The price was the end of the University Players.

In midseason 1932, Windust, Leatherbee, and Logan met in New York with producer Arthur J. Beckhard, then enjoying a (for him, unusual) hit called *Another Language*. An arrangement was made under which Beckhard would try out a handful of new plays in August, with the University Players footing the production costs on Cape Cod. For Beckhard, whose reputation as a smalltime promoter and concert manager who had graduated to producing flops was second only to that for being a penny-pincher, the agreement was a career preserver; what he had, in fact, not told Windust, Leatherbee, and Logan was that the profits realized through the Broadway production of *Another Language* had been swallowed up and then some by bad road-company presentations of the Rose Franken play. For their part, Windust, Leatherbee, and Logan saw Beckhard as the first Broadway representative who appreciated their efforts at Falmouth and who could help them *as a company* gain exposure to New York audiences. As far as the producer's reputation was concerned, they preferred not to dwell on that too long. "There was no question that he was a shifty individual," Houghton says, "but I don't think he was completely faking it when he said he was enthusiastic about what the Players had been doing. He really believed he was on to something with us. At first, at least."

Certainly, Beckhard's opening move, an announcement of his affiliation with the Players, increased the optimism at Old Silver Beach. "Henceforth," the announcement said in part, "instead of remaining a small company of young people performing a tried and tested play each week, the Theatre Unit enters a fascinating field of trying out new plays and producing, perfecting, and polishing them for that mecca of the theater—Broadway."

The importance of the name change from the University Players to the Theatre Unit only began to sink in a few weeks later; similarly, Windust and Leatherbee played down the significance of the theater programs that began to list Beckhard's name first as the company producer. What was more difficult to ignore was a mid-August invasion by the hapless road company of *Another Language*; while the unit rehearsed and then performed for Falmouth prior to an engagement in Chicago, the Players grumbled away their days at the beach, wondering how Windust and Leatherbee could have agreed to their effective eviction from their own theater. Depending on who told the story,

Windust either persuaded Beckhard that usurpation had not been part of their deal or Beckhard claimed the *Another Language* experience as an emergency exception to his intention of working with the University Players. In any case, the producer immediately began rehearsals on two other original plays that would prove influential in Stewart's decision to become a professional actor.

The first of the originals, *Goodbye Again*, was a comedy by Allan Scott and George Haight. Although Beckhard insisted that Howard Lindsay, an outsider, be given the lead, he entrusted the direction to Windust, who in turn integrated Players Stewart, McCormick, Natwick, and O'Neil into the cast. Playing a uniformed chauffeur, Stewart had only a walk-on line, but it brought one of the biggest laughs of the evening, and for once he was mentioned in the local notices for reasons other than courtesy.

The second production—and the last at Falmouth for the season—was Frank McGrath's *Carry Nation*, an episodic drama covering the life of the militant prohibitionist from 1846 to 1910. If there was one problem with *Carry Nation*, there was a saloon full of them. To begin with, Beckhard sought to resolve territorial tensions with the Players by imposing his own director, actress Blanche Yurka, but making Logan an assistant director. That chagrined Yurka, who had never before taken on such a big production as a director, and infuriated Logan, who made it obvious that he didn't like working under somebody less expert than he considered himself to be. Making matters worse was the casting of Esther Dale, Beckhard's wife, in the title role. The consensus among the Players, already restive with the end of the season and more job hunting in New York on the immediate horizon, was that Dale knew even less about acting than Yurka knew about directing. Some members went so far as to divine a Beckhard plot for getting his wife to Broadway as being the principal reason for his agreement with the Falmouth company. Houghton, for one, didn't go that far. "She was hardly the best-equipped actress in the world," according to the set designer, "but even Beckhard had to have realized no amount of manipulation was going to make her a Broadway star in something like *Carry Nation*. Nobody was to remember her as an actress for anything but that, and who wants to remember even that much?"

Houghton himself had his hands full with the production, having to design sixteen sets for what he later called "one of the most complicated, bizarre, and lugubrious plays anyone ever attempted." One dress rehearsal lasted so long into the night, because of a combination of technical problems and Dale's difficulties with lines, that McCormick proposed that it be timed "not with a watch but with a calendar." Although he had more lines than he had had in *Goodbye Again*, playing a policeman named Gano, Stewart was ready to call it even that he had been noticed at all.

The final fiasco took place on opening night as the cast was clearing the stage hurriedly so Dale could take a solo curtain call. Forgetting what had been rehearsed, Natwick exited downstage between the scenery and the curtain, realizing too late that she had walked into a corner. Worse, a pipe along the hem of the curtain immediately snagged her skirt as the drape began to rise. With no alternative except to have her clothes pulled up over her head, the actress jumped up on the bar and rose toward the flies like a trapeze artist on her way up to the high wire. The audience thought it was funny, company members already offstage thought it was hilarious, and Dale thought it was the culmination of a cast conspiracy against her. The leading lady waited none too patiently while the curtain was lowered and Natwick, looking not at all embarrassed, hurried off into the wings. Dale received only a smattering of applause when she finally took her bow.

Ironically, at least vis-à-vis charges that Beckhard destroyed the University Players, the cut-rate producer turned out to be the only person associated prominently with *Carry Nation* who would be linked again with Falmouth theater. Over the next three years, he leased out the facilities to various fly-by-night parties, some of whom were more interested in the tea room than in the theater and some of whom wanted the theater more for a meeting hall than a stage. On the eve of Labor Day in 1936, the complex burned down, triggering an eleven-year emphasis in the community on movies for summer-evening entertainment. Then, in 1947, Beckhard reappeared on the scene, bought some land cheaply near the railroad station, and tried to relaunch a theatrical center. But his wary ways with a quarter doomed the project almost from its inception.

But that was still in his mottled future. Impressed by what he had wrought with *Carry Nation* at Old Silver Beach and vulnerable to a daily pep talk from Dale, Beckhard decided to bring the play to Broadway. Moreover, he wanted to keep the Falmouth production intact, down to such minor performers as Stewart, if for no other reasons than the savings to be gained from less rehearsal time and a low-paid company.

For Stewart, it was another crossroads. With the academic year beginning and his scholarship for pursuing his architectural studies waiting, he was now being asked for the first time to consider acting as more than an extracurricular activity. For both himself and Alex, he came up with a lot of rationalizations for what he did—starting with the reality that the market had gotten no better for architecture and ending with the realization that his parents also had the schooling of his sisters to worry about. As he once told a magazine interviewer concerning the latter point: "Mary and Virginia were growing up right behind me. Mary was scheduled for an art course at Carnegie Tech. Virginia was going to Vassar. If I went back to Princeton, my tuition would cost nothing, but I would need food and clothes. I'd be an added expense. Dad didn't seem to worry about it, but I did. Money at home wasn't limitless. I knew that and I felt I had had my share. I wrote the trustees expressing my appreciation for the scholarship, and I wrote Dad telling him what I had done."

But even with the added financial problems posed by his sisters' schooling, there was also little doubt, to judge from his comments over the years, that Stewart had no intention of pulling out of the theater company when it was only a few weeks away from reaching a goal he had come to understand obsessed most of his working companions. For himself, he insisted, he just thought it would be "awfully nice" to get to Broadway so quickly. "Lucky," too.

According to Jane Alexander, it was mainly because of her father's stories about the University Players that she got "caught up in the romance of the theater." Directly on the scene, Stewart still wasn't ready to admit to that yet.

BROADWAY

ASIDE FROM SIMPLY TESTING HIS CONFIDENCE THAT HE could do it, Stewart arrived in New York in September 1932 with two big questions about acting. The first was whether it could give him the kind of a living that his parents had expected his education—and their sacrifices in financing it—would assure. The second question was whether it would continue to hold out the sense of adventure that working in Falmouth had ripened in him; after apprenticing with the University Players for only a single summer, in fact, he had been heard to mutter to company members that the prospect of working in an office as an architectural draftsman had begun to lose some of its appeal. The possibility of an intractable conflict between his sense of responsibility and desire for exploration wasn't lost on him, either: He had only to think of Alex. Nowhere has he been more explicit about this than in a conversation with *McCall's* reporter Floyd Miller in the 1960s, with specific reference to his father's reputation as a hell-raiser at Princeton:

> As I heard these stories and looked at his undergraduate pictures, his square young face both pugnacious and gay, full of thirst for adventure, I realized what it had cost him to return to the family hardware store in a prosaic little town. What had made him do it? I thought I knew. A great part of him was the swashbuckling soldier of fortune; but there was a quieter and deeper strain, his desire for fatherhood. When he decided that these two sides of his nature were generally incompatible, he chose the second. I don't think he ever regretted his decision; certainly, he invested his fatherhood with all the excitement that was in him. Just to be near him turned ordinary events into adventure.

Whether viewed as an expression of gratitude or as a self-serving lament, Stewart's perspective did nothing to win Alex over to the decision to go to Broadway with *Carry Nation*. By the actor's account, his father's initial dismay soon degenerated into "annoyance," then into "disappointment," when it dawned on him that he had encouraged his son to play out one impulse too many. What irritated Alex still further, and not for the first time, was the passive note in the response he received every time he asked about future plans: Just as James hadn't sought membership in Princeton's Cottage Club because "only Charter asked me," now the younger Stewart described himself as "only being along for the ride" in the transfer of *Carry Nation* to Broadway. About the only thing that father and son agreed on as they stood on the rejected opportunity of the Princeton scholarship offer was not knowing how long the ride would last.

Not long, at least by the measure of *Carry Nation*. As though the play needed any more handicaps, it opened at the Biltmore Theater on October 29, just days before the election of Franklin Delano Roosevelt as president. Throughout his campaign, Roosevelt had vowed to repeal Prohibition once he entered the White House—making Carry Nation as untrendy a figure as November 1932 New York could devise. On top of the play's script and performance problems, the election results saw to it that the production barely survived four weeks—and half of that time to houses with only a handful of people. The drama's ultimate claim to fame was that it introduced Stewart, Logan, Natwick, McCormick, Houghton, and the other University Players to New York audiences. Then and there, however, Houghton, for one, was convinced that *Carry Nation* would be remembered only as the death knell for the Cape Cod company: "This time we couldn't return to the Cape, for it was the beginning of December. We couldn't immediately sustain ourselves in New York as an organization. Anyhow, we were no longer a group in the complete sense that had characterized our communality of spirit the year before. We were a bunch of uncertain, bewildered, broke youngsters, like all the others who were trudging the pavements of Manhattan."

For Stewart, though, what he has repeatedly called his "luck" held. No sooner had Beckhard conceded defeat with *Carry Nation* than he announced that he also wanted to give the Broadway treatment to *Goodbye Again*, the Scott-Haight comedy that had shown the actor off to relatively better advantage in Falmouth. The producer also made a point of telling Stewart that he wanted him back in the role of the chauffeur. Victor Samrock, who worked with Beckhard on both *Carry Nation* and *Goodbye Again*, didn't think it was only because Stewart had gotten laughs in the right places at Falmouth or because the producer regarded him as a great actor. Samrock, who passed away in 1995 after more than sixty years in the theater, including a stint as general manager of the Playwrights Company, said that Stewart's offstage personality was an equally significant factor:

The last thing Beckhard needed with all his ongoing financial problems was a company of prima donnas. The theater creates extravagant tendencies and sometimes they become awfully neurotic. You're always having to put up with some people because they know their business, not because they're a pleasure to be around. Jimmy wasn't like that at all. He may have been the least neurotic actor I've ever been around. He was almost too nice. No airs, never demanded special attention, seemed to always keep his insecurities to himself even when he was a kid in his twenties. Beckhard needed at least *someone* like that, someone who wouldn't be driving him crazy or, just as bad, driving the director or the other actors crazy, so they would start to harass the producer. About the only thing that Beckhard hadn't predicted with Jimmy was that some of the other actors would see he wasn't using his neuroses, so they figured they were entitled to his portion of them, too. Like the guy who's sitting at a table who's courteous about grabbing for the meat, so the one who's next to him grabs for doubles.

With Osgood Perkins, the father of Anthony Perkins, replacing Howard Lindsay in the lead, *Goodbye Again* opened at the Masque Theater on December 28. With holiday cheer as an ally instead of imminent repeal as a nemesis, the comedy received generally fair to good notices—sufficient to drum up business for 216 performances over six months. As at Falmouth, Stewart was singled out for his droll delivery of limited dialogue in Act One. As he was to recall it:

> It wasn't what you would call a taxing part. I had to bring a book into the living room of a famous author and give it to the author's butler. My first line was, "Mrs. Belle Irving would sure appreciate it if she could have this book autographed." My second line was when the butler returned with the book and said the author couldn't do it, he was too busy. "Mrs. Belle Irving," I said to him, "is going to be sore as hell." Nothing more, that was it. But I got all the mileage out of it I could. The worst part of that role was that I did it in Act One, then had to wait around for the rest of the play to take a curtain call.

Among those who saw Stewart in the role of Mrs. Belle Irving's chauffeur was actor Burgess Meredith, then appearing in another play on Broadway. Like many others, Meredith admits to having been baffled for some time by the immediate connection Stewart made with the Masque audience despite the brevity of his appearance; unlike many others, he thought he had figured it out after awhile:

> Here was this tall, lanky guy bringing down the house with this line or two. He's bemused, he's bewildered looking, he's stuffed into this ugly uniform. The more I thought about it, the more I decided you couldn't have two better lines to make an impression. "Mrs. So-and-So would sure appreciate it. . . . " Jimmy stayed on that sure like a teletype machine that's stuck on typing out *r*. Then he's just standing there and looking awkward while the butler goes off. Then he gets the no, and we're back to another

endless *r* with the word *sore*, followed by the always crowd-pleasing *hell*. He was really quite brilliant in bringing out all those possibilities.

The success of *Goodbye Again* might not have completely persuaded Stewart that his future lay with acting, but it certainly pushed The Big Warehouse in Indiana down on his list of urgent priorities. His thirty dollars a week also went a long way toward making ends meet at the West 64th Street apartment that has become another staple of Stewart lore.

Shortly after arriving in New York in September, even before opening in *Carry Nation*, Stewart got to know Henry Fonda much better than as an alumnus of the University Players, as a regular visitor to company productions, or as the former husband of Margaret Sullavan. He had little choice in the matter since in that period Fonda, as Burgess Meredith recalls, was "letting a great deal hang out." If the actor wasn't still showing his pain from his breakup with Sullavan, he was bemoaning his lack of significant work or, turning the knife in him even more deeply, his ex-wife's ability to jump from one flop to another on Broadway while collecting only steadily more complimentary reviews. Whatever his own feelings for Sullavan, Stewart had little choice but to quash them during the long nights when, invariably to an audience that also included Logan and McCormick, Fonda unburdened himself about the Virginia "ball-breaker from way back." For certain, he showed enough sympathy and solidarity to be invited in as a fourth on the two-room apartment available on West 64th Street, now the Manhattan area dominated by Lincoln Center.

As Stewart, Fonda, Logan, and McCormick have all told the story over the years, the building housing the third-floor apartment was notorious as a pit stop for prostitutes working the neighborhood. Even worse, however, was a hotel two doors away that gangster Legs Diamond was known to use as a base of operations. The only thing more common on the block than drug busts, according to Stewart, was the changing of the name of the hotel where Diamond operated. "At least four times in as many months," he has said, "they changed the name. The West Sixty-Fourth Street Hotel, the West Side Hotel, that kind of thing. I don't know why they bothered. It certainly didn't seem to confuse the police. They were *always* in there," as hoods looking for a good time always seemed to be in the actors' apartment. Fonda once described the situation to Howard Teichmann in his as-told-to autobiography, *Fonda—My Life*:

We'd be sitting there, after the theater, drinking a beer or two and the door would open. We'd turn around and three characters that looked like they'd just walked in from a Warner Brothers gangster movie would appear: Chesterfield coats with black velvet collars up and white Borsalino hats pulled down, dark glasses, hands in their pockets; they'd walk over to the bedroom, glance around, shrug, never open their mouths, and leave. It happened so often, always with different guys, but they were all after the same thing. When they couldn't find the girls, they'd go down the hall or the floor above.[5]

When they weren't worrying about hoodlum johns walking in unannounced, Stewart and his roommates were trying to keep their landlord at bay. "There were periods there when all of us together barely had $35 a week," he has said. "A couple of times we came home to find the place locked because we hadn't paid the rent. I called Indiana more than once. We practically lived on milk toast. It was very cheap and very filling the way we made it. A little of it went an awfully long way."

Despite such practical problems, however, Stewart maintained a distance from his surroundings. Even when a neighborhood shooting deposited a body in front of his apartment building one night, he has said, "none of it was all that real. We were all in our own world up in the apartment. Even with the prostitutes in the building, it was mostly out of sight, out of mind. They didn't bother us, we didn't bother them. We'd still mainly be thinking about people like Arthur Beckhard."

When the milk toast became too much to bear, there was alcohol. Because the West Orange, New Jersey, theater where he was working in late 1932 couldn't produce enough income to pay him as stipulated by contract, Fonda accepted demijohns of applejack instead. When even the hard cider began to pall, there were the still techniques the roommates had picked up in college. As Fonda told Teichmann: "For serious drinking we'd buy raw alcohol and mix it with gelatin. There was always a question if the stuff was raw alcohol or grain. We'd test it by pouring just a little bit on the metal running board of a car. Then we'd light it. If the flame was blue, we'd drink it. If it was red, we'd throw it away."

---

[5] First MGM publicists, then Stewart himself, sought to "sanitize" the hooker-hunt point of Fonda's reminiscence in later years. At times, the actor has even hinted that the four roommates were primarily afraid of having been mistaken for the targets of contract killers.

Thanks to *Goodbye Again* and other jobs snagged by Stewart's roommates, the group had enough spare change in early 1933 to rent a basement speakeasy on West 40th Street across the street from the *Herald Tribune* once a week. In a variation on a Princeton afternoon society that had met weekly over coffee and tea, the actors labeled their forum the Thursday Night Beer Club. For two dollars a head, a guest could have beer and hobo steak, with Fonda usually doing the grilling. Stewart's principal task was organizing weekly musical interludes around his accordion. Dick Foran, who had followed him from Mercersburg to Princeton, and Meredith, a tenor before discovering acting, sang regularly. But what especially excited Stewart and Fonda, both jazz enthusiasts, was that word of their weekly gatherings soon got out among the musicians playing for the radio and hotel orchestras in the Times Square area. Stewart has recalled with particular delight the evening a clarinet player from the NBC house band walked in: "When he came around, I tossed my accordion into a corner and listened with the rest. He was truly an artist and after awhile became our biggest attraction. We kept him tooting the clarinet so late week after week that he couldn't pucker anymore. There wasn't a person in the place who had any doubt about him succeeding." In addition to musicians like Benny Goodman, actresses Katharine Cornell, Helen Hayes, Rose Hobart, and Ruth Gordon were familiar Thursday night faces. Then, too, there were the actresses who had belonged to the University Players, such as Natwick, O'Neil—and Sullavan.

It was during a casual conversation one Thursday night that, according to Meredith, Sullavan made her first public prediction that Stewart would become a major Hollywood star. Some of those present decided that she was taking another shot at Fonda just to keep her hand in; others saw the remark as merely a reflexive courtesy following a disclosure that she herself had just been signed to go to California for a picture; the severest of all preferred to hear nothing but cynicism, to deduce that what she had really meant was that, of all the actors sitting around in the West 40th Street basement, Stewart stood the *least* chance of making it in Hollywood.[6] Meredith was one who assumed she was

---

[6] Sullavan's ability to incite criticism hardly depended on solidarity with Fonda, or on her periodic forays into questioning his professional or sexual gifts. Her unabashed bed-hopping with everyone from producers to extras, her regular blowups during rehearsals, the view that she reduced every play to a vehicle in which only she would shine, even her taste for wearing slacks, alienated many.

sincere. "God knows she may have had a hundred agendas with Hank," the veteran actor says, "but as far as Jimmy was concerned, I never heard her say anything about him that wasn't what she said that night. She really believed in him—maybe sooner and much more than a lot of the rest of us, including Jimmy himself."

McCormick was another who never doubted Sullavan's championing of Stewart. "Oddly, her attitude toward him was never predatory," he once told Lawrence Quirk. "She was protective, loving, maternal. She wasn't usually like this with men. When she wasn't getting sexually predatory with them, she was indifferent, or contemptuous, or good-naturedly casual."

Sullavan also had formed her own romantic stereotype for Stewart; as she would say many times over the years, he was "Booth Tarkington" or a "Booth Tarkington character" to her. The reference to the author of such novels as *Alice Adams, The Magnificent Ambersons, Penrod,* and *Seventeen,* with their emphasis on adolescence, ambition, or both, did not drop completely from the sky. Sullavan had first met Stewart when he had been a member of the Triangle Club, the Princeton drama group founded by Tarkington in the nineteenth century. The first play presented at Falmouth in Stewart's only year there and seen by Sullavan, *Magnolia,* happened to have been written by Tarkington. And it didn't damage the actress's creation, either, that the novelist had been from the state—if not the town—of Indiana.

Stewart's only recorded responses to his framing as Tarkington have been shrugs and wry remarks aimed at changing the subject. At the very least, however, it was a particular identification that seemed to distinguish him in her mind from the droves of other men he was constantly hearing about her being involved with. For his part, he was on somewhat familiar terrain in defending her whenever someone criticized the husky voice that made her almost toneless in some registers: What many initially thought (and others hoped) would be an impediment to her career, he knew, was the result of a hearing problem that had never prevented his mother, with a similar affliction, from singing and playing the piano.

Sullavan was not the only guest of the Thursday Night Beer Club who would figure prominently in Stewart's later career. Also showing up from time to time was a stage manager from the Theater Guild named Emil Bundsmann. Although he would hold on to that name for a while longer while he graduated to directing a few short-lived plays around town, Bundsmann would subsequently change it to Anthony Mann; as Mann, he directed Stewart between 1949 and 1955 in eight pictures, including the actor's most successful westerns.

It was also within the casual atmosphere of the West 40th Street basement that Stewart made the acquaintance of actress Jane Cowl, deemed by many to be the greatest Juliet of the American theater. In her late forties at the time, Cowl had gone from Shakespearean ingénue to a publicity-aided image as the last word in grace, poise, and body-pampering advice. A typical profile of the period found that "cleanliness is her complexion credo and perfumes are her passion." But Cowl still had her passions on the stage, too, one of which was playing the title role in *Camille*. When she heard in the spring of 1933 that *Goodbye Again* was about to close and that Stewart had nothing else lined up, she invited him to go to Boston with her as the stage manager for her latest production of the Dumas classic. With only the hardware store looming as an alternative, plus Cowl's assurances that his previous lack of experience as a stage manager was hardly prohibitive after his time with the University Players, Stewart agreed.

Back in Massachusetts, Stewart took to his new role without incident or enthusiasm for a couple of performances. But then one evening, with Cowl in the middle of her climactic deathbed scene, disaster ensued. Standing near the control board, the novice stage manager suddenly heard a steady series of "plop" sounds against the stage door. Leaving his post to investigate, he discovered an old tramp idly tossing chunks of wood at the metal door. The exertion in chasing away the man proved to be a little too much: Running back inside to his levers, he interpreted a momentary silence from the stage as an indication that Cowl had finished her dying, so, not unlike the stagehand who had once fallen asleep during his magic act with Bill Neff, he pulled down the curtain. The stir from the audience was nothing compared to that of Cowl, who jumped up from her bier with rage and tears in her eyes. The actress had still had plenty of dying to do. "Young man, you don't know what you have done to me!" Stewart has recalled Cowl as having fumed. "You have ruined my performance! I can never face an audience again!"

But Cowl did, the very next night. And Stewart was also back at his post in the wings.[7] Back in New York, though, the incident became a source of laughter in theater circles for some time, doing nothing to hurt the celebrity of an actor whose most memorable foray onto the stage was still that as Mrs. Belle Irving's chauffeur. As Meredith recalls, it was also around the telling of the *Camille* curtain that he began to wonder about how much shrewdness there was behind Stewart's apparently off-the-cuff anecdotes: "Jimmy has a gift for storytelling, though he pretends he doesn't. He launches into one of his yarns in that uneven, faltering tempo of his, until he stumbles. But is it a stumble? Somehow he always stumbles at the right spot. And it brings down the house. The truth is Jimmy is a self-satirist—he pokes fun at himself."

One of those entertained by the tale of the prematurely dropped curtain in Boston was Blanche Yurka, who had directed the ill-fated *Carry Nation* and who had crossed temperaments with Cowl when both had been working for producer David Belasco some years before. Yurka, too, asked Stewart to work as a stage manager, as well as to do a small role, for a fall production of a Spanish comedy, *Spring in Autumn*, that she was scheduled to star in; in this, she had the support of her director, former University Players organizer Bretaigne Windust, and her producer, Beckhard, who still valued the actor's relaxed deportment. If there was any allure for Stewart in returning behind the scenes, it was the one of having little alternative: Nobody was offering him bigger roles than the bit he could squeeze in between his duties in the wings. Waiting back home that summer for the *Spring in Autumn* rehearsals to begin, in fact, he came as close as he ever would to committing himself to the counters of The Big Warehouse once and for all. Alex was content to hold his fire as long as his son put in a few hours at the store while he plotted what to do next.

Shortly before Labor Day, Stewart returned to New York after leaving a clear impression with his parents that this was going to be his last shot. He and Fonda, who had spent the summer in stock at Mt. Kisco, rented rooms at the dog-eared Madison Square Hotel in the East 20s. The Fonda that Stewart took up quarters with was not altogether better for his Mt. Kisco experience. On the one hand, he had worked regularly in R. C. Sheriff's *Journey's End*, so had money for scraping by awhile; on the

---

[7] On occasion, Stewart has told the story with the punchline that he was fired. Most evidence is that he was not.

other hand, he had played a relatively minor role of a stretcher-bearer in the World War I drama, had only gotten even that part through the intercession of the summer theater's leading lady, Hollywood's newest star, Sullavan, and had spent most of the stock season stoking his resentment at the chasm that had opened up between his career and that of his ex-wife. Once again, when not working on the Yurka play, Stewart was called upon to be a sympathetic ear to the travails of knowing and loving Margaret Sullavan.

Stewart got through *Spring in Autumn* without missing any big cues and without any critic noticing his on-again, off-again appearances in what was generally regarded as a "tiresome" comedy. In the role of an opera singer, Yurka's biggest moment came when she sang the aria "Vissi d'arte" while standing on her head. The play ran a mere four performances before the Henry Miller Theatre brought in a new tenant. According to Norris Houghton, it was a typical Beckhard production in which "the savings were as important as the play or the talent." The designer himself was a primary target: "Since I wasn't a member of the union, they had to bring in a front for me from the union. The good news was that the front didn't get paid, and shouldn't have. The bad news was that I didn't get paid, either."

The closing of *Spring in Autumn* didn't leave Stewart on the street too long—again thanks to his oldest ally, his accordion.[8] The rescue came at an October casting call for *All Good Americans*, a romance with airs about American expatriates who hang around a Paris bar making heavy-handed observations about American tourists. If Fonda snared the assignment of understudying the lead, professional magician and would-be dramatic actor Fred Keating, purely on the basis of his demonstrated acting ability, producer Courtney Burn left no doubt with Stewart that his only appreciable cachet was his accordion. As the actor was to recall:

> They needed somebody who could play the thing, and I was it. But then I read further into the script and I came across this scene where I'm supposed to throw the accordion out a window. This was *my* accordion we were talking about because I was expected to provide my own. It wasn't even paid for, but here they have me throwing it out a window every night. So as soon

---

[8] He had even played the instrument as part of his performance in *Spring in Autumn*. In that case, it was a piece of business added by Windust after Stewart had been named stage manager and been given his small role.

as I had the part, I started working on them, talking them into having me play a banjo instead of the accordion. Tossing a banjo out the window is a lot less expensive than tossing an accordion.

Rehearsals on *All Good Americans* kept the two actors busy—and solvent—through November and the first few days of December. If Stewart was looking for a symbol of some progress from his debut in *Carry Nation*, he found it when *All Good Americans* opened at the Henry Miller on December 5, the day that Utah became the thirty-sixth state to ratify the Twenty-first Amendment and formally put an end to Prohibition. The openly alcohol-filled party that followed the premiere helped to blot out tepid reviews. Less than a month later, there was another party—to mark the play's closing. As ever, Stewart entertained during the festivities with his accordion; he still had it when he and Fonda left the party and headed back toward their hotel. "It was three o'clock in the morning . . . and we were on our way across Times Square to get a subway to go home. And Fonda stopped in the middle of Times Square—there was nobody, it was completely deserted, and he said, 'I wonder if you started playing your accordion now if you'd get an audience.' So I took out the accordion and began. And in two or three minutes a couple of people came up. And I played another number and some more people came up. Pretty soon we were surrounded and they started giving requests."

It was at this point that Fonda took off his hat and began to pass it around. Over the years, he would say that he collected merely twelve to fifteen cents; Stewart would contend that the receipts were at least triple that. Either way, the collection was rudely interrupted. As Stewart has told it: "I felt somebody hit me on my backside with a club and it was a policeman and he was furious. He said, 'It's taken me three, four hours to get all these people asleep in those doorways, and you come along and start that noise. Now it'll take me another four hours to get them to sleep again.' "[9]

---

[9] As central to Stewart-Fonda lore as this anecdote has become, it, like many others, has had censored versions. Some tellings, for instance, have described the crowd as having come from passersby on their way to the subway rather than from the homeless and the destitute forced to sleep in doorways. Stewart, especially, has always been sharply attuned to the readership of the reporters asking him questions; according to intimates, few things set him off more vehemently at the crest of his career than the feeling that he had not been sufficiently "prepared" for an interview.

Although unemployed again at the beginning of 1934, both actors still had a little more self-confidence—and another credit for their résumés—as a result of their run with *All Good Americans*. Stewart thought that he had even more than that after auditioning for the key role of the idealistic Sergeant O'Hara in Sidney Howard's *Yellow Jack*, a drama about the soldiers who became human guinea pigs to test Walter Reed's theories about the origins of yellow fever. But though he impressed producers with his grasp of the role, he was turned down because of his inability to affect an Irish brogue. For the first time since he had entered the theater, however, Stewart didn't leave it at that. Still hopeful that the producers would have second thoughts, he got in touch with Frank Cullinan, a onetime member of Dublin's Abbey Theatre, asking for a crash course in brogues. Even with *Yellow Jack* already in rehearsal, the two actors went at it, as often as not in the lobby of a midtown hotel and more than once to the consternation of other guests trying to read their newspapers in peace.

Fonda, meanwhile, had scored what appeared to be a much more definite breakthrough, getting what would turn out to be the leading male role in Leonard Sillman's 1934 version of *New Faces*. Stewart, under the prodding of his hotel mate, and knowing that his sessions with Cullinan were no guarantee of anything, also sought a part in the review, "accidentally" running into Sillman in the lobby of the producer's Algonquin Hotel residence and improvising a comic turn. As Sillman later told an interviewer, he was impressed by the unexpected audition, but had to tell Stewart that "I had already signed another underweight young comedian whose style and delivery were very similar." It wasn't the last time that others in the profession would respond to Stewart and Fonda as competitors.

A few days later, however, Stewart couldn't have cared less about *New Faces*. The producers of *Yellow Jack* had indeed decided that their original casting choice for Sergeant O'Hara was not working out and, astonished by the results of Cullinan's tutoring, gave the role to Stewart.

Yellow Jack, which opened under the direction of Guthrie McClintic at the Martin Beck on March 6, 1934, established Stewart as an actor— not only with Broadway critics and with the theatrical fraternity, but, no less importantly, to himself and his parents. One evening, while standing in the wings early in the drama's ten-week run, he has related, he noticed

Sam Levene and his other cast colleagues[10] in a way that he had never seen the other companies he had shared stages with in Falmouth and New York, let alone at Princeton: "For the first time, I could see these men—good, mature men—out there working and concentrating, and this really meant something to them—creating something on the stage. I think it's when I sort of got serious about it."

Leaving aside the (characteristic for interviews) half-pregnant implications of "sort of got serious," the statement impresses as a bald acknowledgment of how Stewart had tended to view acting prior to that moment; that is, as an activity not to be associated with "good, mature men," as one that he had never particularly understood might have "meant something" to them. If it is reasonable to assume that this awareness was aided by his unprecedentedly prominent role in the proceedings, it doesn't seem much more hazardous to suggest that the very *ambiance* of *Yellow Jack*—American military settings in the tropics at the beginning of the century—helped to promote in him a "responsible" sense of working collegiality. He had even seen his costume before: in the photos of Alex in his Spanish-American War uniform.

Typical of the reviews of his performance was that of the New York *World Telegram*, which declared in part: "James Stewart will not find it necessary to impress casting directors with his autobiographical data after this. Entrusted with a delicate and difficult acting task, he obliges us with as splendid a performance as any youthful player has turned in this year." More than aware of the actor's previous credits, critic Robert Garland essayed: "Especially do I admire the O'Hara of James Stewart who was the man with the banjo in *All Good Americans*, the man with the accordion in *Spring in Autumn*, and the man with the automobile in *Goodbye Again*. Here is a performance that is simple, sensitive, and true. And replete with poetic underbeat." Critiques of the kind weren't lost on Indiana, either. Customers at The Big Warehouse now heard incessantly about New York City's newest star while negotiating their purchases. If Alex continued to think of Broadway's gain as Philadelphia Street's loss, he didn't allow that to obscure his pride in what appeared to be his son's success in an individually undertaken venture. Besides, he could always

---

[10] The cast was a treasure trove of future Hollywood supporting players: Levene, McCormick, Millard Mitchell, Lloyd Gough, Eduardo Ciannelli, Barton MacLane, Robert Keith, and Robert Shayne.

blame himself if he wanted to share in the credit.

Another believer was McClintic, the husband of Katharine Cornell, who, prior to casting Stewart in *Yellow Jack*, had mostly known him as the accordion player and sometime pianist at the Thursday Night Beer Club gatherings. When not even the good reviews appeared able to raise *Yellow Jack* above the word of mouth that it was too depressing and harrowing to be entertaining, the director-producer asked him to be part of his scheduled fall production of a Judith Anderson play, *Divided by Three*. In accepting the offer, Stewart let himself in for three things: his first feeling of security about having a big acting job waiting for him after the summer, a major actress who didn't like him, and a minor actress who would have as much of a hand as anybody in disseminating the image of *Jimmy* Stewart.

Between the closing of *Yellow Jack* and the opening of *Divided by Three*, Stewart put in a few more weeks of summer stock, this time at Long Island's Red Barn Theater. According to the actor, the stint at Locust Valley was mainly memorable for the warfare that erupted between a Long Island Railroad motorman and the theater. Since the railroad tracks were so close to the Red Barn, causing the building to shake every time a train passed, directors were warned to have first acts completed by 9:05 so that there would be nothing happening onstage when a 9:10 express rushed by. This directive seemed to annoy the motorman when he heard about it. Stewart:

For whatever psychological reason, he resented it. He put every conceivable kind of whistle on his engine and blew them all at once as he neared the theater. . . . One Fourth of July night he was late. We held the curtain for the second act until the audience began threatening to leave, so we started again. It was a highly dramatic play, with the second act taking place in an airplane. There were terrific airplane effects. Halfway into the second act, here came the train, all whistling and puffing. There's something awfully comical about an airplane with a train whistle. At least the audience thought so, and howled. There was no recapturing the mood. From then on the play was a complete dud. The motorman had outfoxed us. For a long time, I thought about him whenever a plane would fly over a movie set.

Divided by Three turned out to be an appropriately titled undertaking for more than one reason. Judith Anderson, whose onstage haughtiness was never much of a stretch, went into rehearsals smarting over what she deemed a flawed play that had not received promised rewrites during the summer. She wasn't much more appreciative of McClintic's decision to entrust a key supporting role to Hedda Hopper, then known as Hollywood's Queen of the Quickies for her constant work in negligible B pictures, later known as a particularly vituperative gossip columnist, and always known as an aggressive seeker of attention. When Stewart showed no resistance to being befriended by Hopper, Anderson added him to her list of grievances: When she wasn't questioning McClintic's judgment in not hiring a more experienced actor for the pivotal character of her son, she was pointing out to the director that Stewart was merely ten years younger than she was. Complaints of the kind only made Hopper more protective of Stewart, and made him seem all the more of an ally of hers against the leading lady from Australia. For sure, Anderson believed the appearances. Even years later, in a conversation having nothing to do with Stewart, she abruptly volunteered to an interviewer: "It's too bad they don't have voicelifts. Jimmy Stewart's voice was barely tolerable when he was young. Now it's a trial to listen to. Fortunately, he never has anything interesting to say."

At the opposite extreme, Hopper might be suspected of having dreamed up some interesting things for him to say. In her 1952 book, *From Under My Hat*, she claimed that it was at least partly because of McClintic's failure to heed Stewart's warnings about the moral dubiousness of some of the dialogue in *Divided by Three* that the play failed. Specifically, she cited an instance of Stewart refusing at one point in the drama to denounce his mother as a whore. "I can't do that, Mr. McClintic," the actor was said to have protested. "Under no circumstances could I bring myself to call any woman that—and my mother, never! Especially with the girl I love standing next to me."

Although Stewart has acknowledged "difficulties" during the rehearsals for *Divided by Three*, he has never confirmed that particular remonstrance to McClintic. That is not to say that it didn't happen. But such a protest would also fall neatly within Hopper's purview in the 1940s and 1950s, when she liked to think of herself as Hollywood's major force against immorality and Communism and when she was regularly promoting Stewart as the epitome of American Christian values. Hardly a week went by that her column didn't feature some tidbit about the actor or his family aimed at showing that he was more American than

George Washington, the Legion of Decency, and Senator Joe McCarthy wrapped into one. In one column, she went so far as to relay warnings about immorality in America purportedly given to Stewart and his wife during a private papal audience—though the actor himself was never directly quoted on what he was told. Even his silence, however, was good enough for furthering Hopper's purposes of fine-tuning the persona of Jimmy Stewart.

As for *Divided by Three*, it ran a mere thirty performances at the Ethel Barrymore Theater. Stewart's consolation was another packet of laudatory reviews, including one from his fellow roomer down at the Madison Square Hotel. Fonda:

> He was playing the son of Judith Anderson, a formidable actress. But he was standing up there eye-to-eye with her and he was just marvelous. In his dressing room I looked at him and sat there shaking my head, wondering, "Where did this come from? How the hell did he get to be so good?" I guess by this time it dawned upon Jim himself that he was pretty good at what he was doing, so he decided to stay in the business and go from there. But it ruffled my feathers a little. Here I was busting my shoe leather trying to make it in the theater, and this lackadaisical fellow Stewart just stumbled into it.

It was the kind of appreciation from Fonda—especially the "lackadaisical" and "stumbled into" parts—that would irritate Stewart with repetition over the years, but in the fall of 1934 it was primarily another affirmation that he had chosen the correct path. It also came from an actor who had recently made strides of his own, finding an agent in the swaggering Leland Hayward, then soon afterward signing a contract to go to Hollywood the following spring. And this despite Fonda's often-stated aversion to leaving the theater to make movies.

Stewart had his own reservations about such a move. As early as his days at Princeton, he had confided to friends that the worst part of being on a stage was worrying about audiences zeroing in on his gangling arms and legs and lamented that he could never make movies because then he too would be forced to see his awkwardness. But that was before he had begun killing afternoons with other actors in a midtown Manhattan coffee shop that was also patronized by Hollywood talent scouts. Whatever apprehensions he had about his looks, he had said yes to more than one screen-test offer extended over doughnuts. In some cases, the invitations reflected a genuine hunch by a scout that he might be screen material; in other instances, the offers appeared aimed mostly at allowing the scout to show his superiors that he was busy on the job. During the summer of 1934, while working in summer stock on Long Island, he had even made a two-reel comedy for Warner Brothers, *Art Troubles*, that did little for his résumé except to enable him to say in later years that he had once worked with one of The Three Stooges, Shemp Howard. "I wasn't really interested in doing the picture," the actor has said of the twenty-minute short, "but their offer of $50 a day seemed unbelievable to me at the time. I guess I just had to know if it was a joke. It wasn't."

During the brief run of *Divided by Three*, Al Altman, MGM's chief talent evaluator on the East Coast, dropped backstage with another screen-test invitation for Stewart. What prompted Altman to do so has never been particularly clear. Hopper always asserted that she was the one to push the studio representative into it, and on at least one occasion Stewart credited her with having done so. On the other hand, he has never explicitly contradicted MGM casting director Bill Grady, who insisted that the actor had been under the close watch of the studio since *Yellow Jack* and that, without any need of Hopper, the reviews for *Divided by Three* triggered the visit by Altman. Either way, Stewart agreed to give the camera another try.

The test took place on the soundstages owned by 20th Century-Fox in Hell's Kitchen on the West Side and leased to other studios when the situation permitted; the facility lacked for little, even containing a swimming pool for underwater shots. Whatever direction Stewart was anticipating from Altman from behind the camera he didn't get; instead, as the scout would recall, he instructed: "Imagine that I have a large horse in the palm of my right hand. I'm going to release him so he can gallop up to you. He goes obediently, but the path he chooses is to go up the wall, across the ceiling, and down the other wall. After that, he will come back to me and climb into my hand."

Other tests followed over the next few days (what Stewart later called "all that neck craning stuff"), then nothing for several weeks. Finally, Altman came back with an offer—the standard MGM beginner's contract for six months with unilateral studio options that could extend up to seven years; starting salary $350 a week. The actor, who had yet to turn down anything significant offered to him, didn't start with Altman; he signed.

MGM still had to wait, however, because while he had been awaiting the studio verdict on the tests, Stewart had committed himself to two more plays. The first, *Page Miss Glory*, was a bland comedy about a couple of hustlers rigging a beauty contest. It opened at the Mansfield Theatre on November 26, 1934, with little critical notice of Stewart except for the observation that he had taken more ambitious roles in the past. *Page Miss Glory* closed after sixty-three performances. In retrospect, it was a glorious run compared to his following venture, *A Journey by Night*.

A Journey by Night, which opened at the Shubert on April 15, 1935, brought the actor his first critical trashing, for attempting to play a Viennese in what programs described as "a German drawing room comedy." For many years, Stewart liked to whip out the review of his performance given by Brooks Atkinson of the *Times*, contending that it was his best protection against ever feeling smug about his abilities. (Among other things, Atkinson, who called the play as a whole "hackneyed to the core," slammed Stewart for "wandering through . . . like a bewildered Austrian tourist just off the banks of the Danube.") Actually, he could not have had much confidence in *A Journey by Night*, which lasted only seven performances, to begin with: With rehearsals already under way, he had gone to noted diction and voice teacher Frances Robinson-Duff in the hope that she could do for his Central European accent what Frank Cullinan had done for his brogue. Robinson-Duff, whose pupils over the years included Ruth Chatterton, Ina Claire, and Katharine Hepburn, had despaired of the assignment, sending the actor away with the backhanded invitation to return if he was "interested in learning how to speak English."

By the spring of 1935, however, what Stewart was most preoccupied with learning how to speak was Movies. And the medium would pay back his interest eventually by asking him to portray non-Americans only three times for the rest of his career, with no ethnic verisimilitude required for even two of those films (*The Shop Around the Corner* and *The Mortal Storm*). What Atkinson and Robinson-Duff perceived as limitations, Hollywood would decide was Stewart's greatest appeal.

III
HOLLYWOOD

THE REGIMEN

I N JUNE 1935, WHEN STEWART ARRIVED THERE, Hollywood was a company town divided between those who were licking their wounds following several years of bitter labor and political battles and those who were determined to demonstrate that the strife had changed absolutely nothing. The victories for the pro-union forces had included the formation of guilds for writers and actors and the eclipsing of the Academy of Motion Picture Arts and Sciences in its role as a puppet corporate union. On the other hand, The Big Eight of Metro-Goldwyn-Mayer, Warner Brothers, 20th Century-Fox, Columbia, Paramount, RKO, Universal, and United Artists still controlled every facet of the movie industry—from the signing of extras for lunch money to the worldwide distribution of its films for profits in the millions. If the studios had been dragged kicking and screaming to the negotiating table to recognize the Writers Guild of America and the Screen Actors Guild, they had also quickly seized the opportunities implicit in dealing with a restricted circle of talent spokesmen. Every new capital letter that was stenciled upon the door of a Hollywood office ultimately consolidated rather than sapped the strength of the studios. One and all had to concede that company towns weren't much without the company.

MGM was the Cadillac of the studios, and worked its publicity office overtime to remind everyone of that fact. In logos and mottoes alone, the company was an encompassing superiority complex. For those who like visceral symbols of power, there was the insignia of Leo the Lion. For the aesthetically minded, there was the promise of Ars Gratia Artis. Producers and directors under contract lived with the admonition that their task was to Make It Good, Make It Big, and Give It Class. Movie audiences were told what trademark to look for if they wanted to see More Stars Than There Are in the Heavens.

The head of MGM's West Coast operations was Louis B. Mayer, a Russian-Jewish immigrant and onetime junk dealer in Canada and Boston who had changed his birthday to July 4 to prove his attachment to his third home. As ruthless and tyrannical as most of his counterparts at the other studios, Mayer also indulged an image of paternalism aimed at persuading his employees that they were all part of the same family— whose rewards and punishments would be measured by their loyalty to him. In 1935, the employees at MGM's Culver City headquarters numbered more than 4,000. Included in that total were the medium's most acclaimed art director (Cedric Gibbons), costume designer (Adrian), sound engineer (Douglas Shearer), and cameramen (William Daniels, Karl Freund, and George Folsey), as well as seventeen directors, sixty screenwriters, and more than sixty actors under exclusive contract. Directly in charge of production was Irving Thalberg, the studio's Ars Gratia Artis face who was known as The Boy Wonder during his lifetime for his ability to choose successful commercial (and sometimes artistic) screen material and as The Last Tycoon after his death for having served as the model for the protagonist of F. Scott Fitzgerald's uncompleted novel of that name.

As Stewart quickly discovered, the key to MGM's smooth functioning was a detailed daily schedule that kept employees busy whether or not they were involved in the making of a specific picture. A performer was expected to spend the time not in front of the camera working out in a gym under a physical trainer, attending acting, dance, music, speech, or fencing classes, assisting at screen tests for contract candidates, promoting studio features, and, when necessary, getting into formal wear to act as an escort at a premiere or to fill an unexpectedly empty chair at a studio dinner. A director, even one with a name, knew better than to regard himself as an *auteur*, because his ostensibly completed work was subject to expensive retakes under the guidance of somebody else. A line producer was careful about flexing his muscles during a shoot because he was never further than an intercom call away from Mayer or Thalberg acting on a complaint or conveying some executive-suite inspiration or whim. Everyone—including the star roster of Greta Garbo, Spencer Tracy, Clark Gable, Norma Shearer, Jean Harlow, Joan Crawford, William Powell, Myrna Loy, Jeanette MacDonald, Robert Taylor, Franchot Tone,

Robert Montgomery, Nelson Eddy, and the three Barrymores—was subject to the studio as a whole; or, in the words of film historian Edward Wagenknecht: "The efforts of the producers were concentrated not upon the players, hardly even upon the individual film, but rather upon the firm name."

After attending Mercersburg Academy, especially, Stewart was no stranger to an institution that presumed to account for most of his waking hours. If anything, he would show a readiness over the years to allow everyone from Louis B. Mayer and Uncle Sam to an assortment of advisors and his wife to program his general time, just as long as he was able to work undisturbed on the specifics that he deemed important. As his train pulled into Pasadena, however, MGM's regimen was still just a rumor to him. His most immediate problem was Fonda, who stood on the station platform as a one-man welcoming committee—and not a very happy one. Fonda had been waiting with growing impatience through hours of earlier, missed trains, and not merely to help his old roommate with his bags. As Stewart has recalled:

> All he wanted to know about was this model for a Martin Bomber that we bought back in New York. We had been building model planes for some time. After awhile, the places we had at the Madison Square Hotel had begun to stink of glue, and you couldn't look anywhere around without seeing balsa wood shavings. The Martin Bomber was really something special, though, and it had really annoyed Fonda that he had to go to Hollywood to make *The Farmer Takes a Wife* before we had finished work on it. He was calling me all the time from California to find out how the thing was coming along.

Reassured by a machine-gun-shaped packing crate that the model hadn't been left behind, Fonda brought Stewart over to the Mexican-style farmhouse in Brentwood that his 20th Century-Fox contract had enabled him to rent. The latest accommodations to be shared by the two actors had several features that neither the Madison Square Hotel nor the West 64th Street apartment had been able to claim: spiffy new furniture, a patio nestled under trees, Greta Garbo for an immediate neighbor, and an ever-swelling band of ferocious alley cats. Fonda told Howard Teichmann about the animals: "It didn't take us long to discover that they weren't pets at all. They were wild. . . . We'd put food out for them, but the cats never would come close to a human being. . . . A good ballpark estimate after a year or so was thirty to thirty-five cats."

The cats paid for their keep by supplying both Stewart and Fonda with stories that they would be telling for the rest of their lives. One favorite anecdote concerned Garbo's decision to build a high fence to separate her property from theirs. The Swedish actress didn't want to be alone so much as she wanted to discourage the cats from engaging in their nightly caterwauling under her trees. This gesture in turn provoked Stewart and Fonda, tanked up on beer one night, to begin burrowing under the fence to penetrate the actress's defenses; although both admitted they didn't get very far, Stewart has attributed their aborted project to a water duct that ruptured with their shoveling, as against the Fonda version that they simply got tired and decided to quit digging. Soon afterward, Garbo discovered that her fence was useless against the plague of fleas that the cats had loosed over her house, and she sold her property and moved elsewhere. If nothing else, it was a wakeup call to Stewart and Fonda to take action against the fleas, which had long since penetrated their house. But despite many evenings spent mulling over crackpot schemes for disposing of both the bugs *and* the cats, they still hadn't found a solution in the summer of 1936, when Stewart's cousin John D. Stewart came out to visit with a Princeton classmate before beginning his senior year. John D. Stewart:

When my friend and I arrived at the house, only Jim and Myron McCormick were there. I could stay as long as I wanted, Jim said, but I had to figure out a way of getting rid of the cats without hurting them. At the time, my friend and I were boasting that we were the Do Anything Corporation—walk your dog, clean your windows, build a suspension bridge—so this was right up our alley. But every time we'd grab one of the cats, and they weren't the easiest animals in the world to get your hands on, the housekeeper would come running out and say, "You can't get rid of that one because he's Mr. Fonda's favorite." As far as she was concerned, they were *all* his favorites. Well, one day, we finally caught one and decided to paint it purple, figuring that the other cats would be frightened by such a bizarre creature and leave on their own. Just as we finished, who arrives but Fonda, who'd been out of town for a few days. We handed him the cat, and he gave us one of those long, slow looks of his that seemed to go right into your soul, up, down, and everywhichway. From that day on, whenever I'd see him give one of those looks to somebody in a movie, I'd think that somebody had just handed him a purple cat.

The actors finally decided that Garbo had had the right idea, and they put up their place for sublet. But the only consequence of that ploy was a house-hunting visit by Jeanette MacDonald, who took one look at the clouds of fleas attracted to her ankles and went off to shop elsewhere. With no takers for the house, Stewart and Fonda simply left it vacant— and to the cats—when they moved to another Brentwood location a few blocks away.

As much as he had relied on Fonda for having a roof over his head when he arrived in California, Stewart depended on MGM casting director Bill Grady for his orientation at the studio. An incessantly fidgety, red-cheeked man, Grady had arrived at MGM after several years as a vaudeville booking agent. One of his closest friends was W. C. Fields, and he struck many people as a cynical twin to the comedian, not even beyond macabre lies when it suited his ends. On one occasion, after Stewart had become established, for instance, Grady was having a hard time dissuading an MGM producer from insisting on the actor for the lead in a picture about to begin shooting. Certain that the producer was just looking for a quick fix and that any number of other contract players could have handled the part under discussion, the casting director excused himself from a meeting, saying that he wanted to check whether Stewart was even available. After a few minutes, he returned to the meeting room, his face ashen, with the announcement: "I've just gotten terrible news. Jimmy was in an auto accident this morning, and the poor bastard's dead." The startled producer sat silently until Grady shrugged that not even the death a major movie star should be allowed to shut down MGM, so back to the casting problem at hand. Only after the producer had agreed that several other MGM actors mentioned would have been right for the vacant part did Grady admit that there had been no automobile accident, that he had just wanted the producer to use his imagination a little.

In June 1935, however, Stewart was far from being at the top of every producer's wish list, and it was Grady's task to nudge him along through the regimen that covered six days a week, frequently for twelve or fourteen hours a day. By the actor's own estimate, he appeared in more than 500 screen tests over a four-year period, going from aspiring actress to aspiring actress in regular morning sessions. Publicity caravans ("mostly for pictures that I'd never even seen") were another part of his duty. Did all that lead to doubts about going to Hollywood? "Oh, there were some every so often, but Grady got me through it all in pretty good shape," he once admitted, making the studio executive sound somewhat like a drill sergeant.

The studio had more doubts than Stewart. Ted Allan, MGM's publicity photographer, said that nobody in the hierarchy had a clue about what image the actor was supposed to fulfill. "Was he a comedian, or a romantic leading man? We tried photographing him outside, leaning over fences, working with a shovel, with a tennis racket. But while that worked with Robert Taylor in helping to make him look more athletic, it didn't work with Stewart."

Even two years after his arrival, he would suggest nothing to an MGM producer so much as a starving Chinese, precipitating a ludicrous attempt to have him play the role of the peasant Chang in *The Good Earth*. Stewart: "The make up took all morning. They put a bald cap on my head, yanked up my eyelids with spirit gum, and trimmed my eyelashes. That was bad enough, but I was too tall, so they had to dig a trench which I walked in as I trudged alongside the film's star, Paul Muni. Then Muni started losing his balance, and one time tripped and fell right down into the ditch. After three days of tests, Mayer finally called a halt and gave the part to Keye Luke."

Grady got considerable mileage out of a crack that the reason the studio had even embarked on the absurd test was that Stewart was the only actor under contract who looked like he had come through a famine. Indeed, MGM's image makers were as perplexed as Bessie Stewart and various school athletic coaches had been by the nagging problem of the actor's weight—a mere 138 pounds when he landed in California. Fattening diets were supplemented by daily sessions in the studio gym with Don Loomis, a physical trainer, for hardening Stewart's muscles. Although he would write letters home to his parents and sister Mary for some time bragging about how much better the Loomis sessions were making him look and feel, he admitted later on that the trainer mostly intimidated him:

He was a great, enormous muscleman with a gym shirt on and his neck just came right down. And every time he talked, muscles seemed to come out. He was a weight lifter, and for a while there I got hooked on weight lifting. I went three or four times a week, and he got me on health food— blackstrap molasses, wheat germ, that kind of thing. It took a long time, but I had to buy all new shirts. I grew out of my coats. And I gained 20 pounds and had muscles. But then one day, when I had gotten up to pressing 200 pounds 50 times, I saw that Loomis was still standing there like in the galley with a whip, saying, "More, more. Two more. Three more." And I finally just dropped the thing and said, "I can't do this anymore. I can't lift it again. . . . .There's something a little screwy about all of this. I don't know." And in two weeks I was right back down to 132 pounds soaking wet.

The flip side of his workweek regimen was a desire bordering on compulsion to let loose on Saturday nights and Sundays. According to Douglas Fairbanks, Jr., however, even socializing had a few distinct frontiers in the Hollywood of the 1930s. "The fact of being an industry town reinforced a separation between the actors who had arrived in Hollywood from the stage and the actors who hadn't. A performer who had gotten there from vaudeville or the drug store or a beauty contest was unlikely to have a lot to contribute to a conversation about the Barrymores or the Belascos. Another divider was the studio. The MGM players were always billed as stars and some of them acted in that way even in restaurants. The more hard-nosed Warner Brothers people also seemed to reflect their employers all the time."

Stewart, though, still had a way to go before he was accepted as a fellow diner by either the Barrymores or the Crawfords. Usually accompanied by Fonda and another refugee from the University Players resettled in Brentwood as an assistant director, Johnny Swope, he became a familiar weekend face at the back tables of such clubs as the Cocoanut Grove and Ciro's. His own favorite haunt was the Trocadero, where the dance bands were led by the likes of Harry James, Glenn Miller, and Phil Harris. It was there that, among other things, he saw Judy Garland give her first (unsolicited) conspicuous public performance as a singer.

One of the most obvious perks of being a young male contract player whom a studio intended promoting was the entree it provided for meeting young actresses. Although a great many couples publicized as "dates" for a film premiere or for periodic "on the town" evenings sponsored by the studios were little more than two employees thrown together for a picture opportunity, many other pairings did not end when the flashbulbs stopped popping. Stewart's first serious alternative to model planes after arriving in California was Ginger Rogers, already established as Fred Astaire's dancing partner in a series of RKO musicals. It aided his career—as well as his love life—no little when Rogers started telling the Hollywood press that Stewart ranked with Astaire as a ballroom dancer.

Since the demise of the big studios in the 1950s, nobody has lamented their passing with more regularity—or with more sorrow—than Stewart. His defenses of the operating ways of MGM and its seven sisters has included comments such as: "I've always felt that the studio system is the *ideal* way to make pictures. Everyone calls them the moguls—the Harry Cohns, the L. B. Mayers, and the Warner brothers—and there have been books written about these terrible people that had charge. . . . This is just a *lie*. This is not true. These men were completely in love with the motion picture. And they *believed* in the motion picture. And worked for quality. They didn't need censorship. They did their own censoring and were very good at it."

And, regarding Jack Warner: "I thought he was fine, in the same way that Louis B. Mayer and Darryl Zanuck were fine. They loved the business, and they had a tremendous capacity of knowing what would be right for the audience at a particular time."

And: "You hear so much about the old movie moguls and the impersonal factories where there was no freedom. MGM was a wonderful place where decisions were made in my behalf by my superiors. What's wrong with that?"

Stewart has hardly been alone in such evaluations. It has in fact been a rare month in recent years that television documentaries haven't presented former contract players reminiscing about the old Hollywood days in tones suggesting that their personal glories ended around the same time that the federal courts broke up the production-distribution-exhibition vise maintained for decades by the studios. MGM actresses with personalities as diverse as Joan Crawford, Judy Garland, Lana Turner, and June Allyson have admitted at one time or another to having listened to Mayer with the filial submissiveness that he expected of them and to having felt a loss with his removal from the scene. Singer Tony Martin, who costarred with Stewart in the 1941 production of *Ziegfeld Girl*, still argues that "being an actor at MGM was the movie equivalent of being a pitcher on the New York Yankees—you were first-class, everybody knew you were first-class, and there was no reason not to be grateful for having the privilege." Even director-writer-producer Richard Brooks, a studio system product who made his most conspicuous films (*Elmer Gantry*, *Lord Jim*, *The Professionals*, and *In Cold Blood*, among them) only after becoming an independent, sounded a great deal like Stewart when he declared to *The New York Times* in 1970: "I'll tell you about those men. They were monsters and pirates and bastards right down to the bottom of their feet, but they loved movies. They loved *making* and they loved *seeing* movies, and they protected the people who worked for them."

The preponderant view, however, is still that of such other onetime MGM employees as Ava Gardner, who once cracked that the studio's actors were "the only kind of merchandise allowed to leave the store at night," and Elizabeth Taylor, who characterized Mayer as "an old dwarf with a big nose," and variously attributed writers and directors who declared they would "rather have TB than LB." Actor Ralph Bellamy went even further, telling one interviewer, "Louis B. Mayer was a Jewish Hitler, a fascist. He had no feeling for any minority, including his own. No feeling for people, period. When he found out that MGM contract player Lew Ayres was a conscientious objector [in World War II], he was furious. He informed everybody that 'Lew Ayres has some kind of phobia about killing people.' And he killed his career."[1]

Closer to his own circle, Stewart could have heard similar appraisals from Fonda, who depended on his agent Leland Hayward to keep him out of the kind of long-term contracts that were the norm at MGM, and Margaret Sullavan, who once accused Robert Taylor of being "gutless" not only for not standing up for his rights with Mayer, but for rationalizing to himself that he was being a "good company man" by not doing so.

More than one fellow veteran of the old studios has attempted to understand Stewart's particularly emphatic retrospective defenses of the Mayers and the Zanucks.[2] Former Universal player Jane Wyatt, for

---

[1] Until he made known his pacifist principles, Ayres had been an MGM box-office staple in the *Dr. Kildare* series. After the war, he took an Oscar nomination for *Johnny Belinda*, produced by Warner Brothers, then had a long career as a featured player in films and television. He also produced and directed his own religious films.

[2] Not that Stewart had anything critical to say about MGM while he was working there, either. But his assertions about how "excited" he was usually pertained to publicity around a specific picture.

instance, believes it comes down to a question of age. "People like that were brought up in the studio system, so they tend to adore it," says the actress who always had to acknowledge on television that *Father Knows Best*. "The older they get, the more they extract the old feelings of order and security they had back then from some of the more sordid details. Order and security mean a great deal more to people who are getting on. Plus, maybe we all just like to think that a lot of what we did in the past was the only way to do it."

According to MGM child star Jackie Cooper, Stewart had significantly less reason to harbor bad memories of the Hollywood bosses simply because he was a man:

> If you're using Mogul Patience as your barometer, you had night and day differences in the readings if you were a man or a woman. The men would go to somebody like L. B. Mayer to bitch about something, but there was always a pretty good chance that their complaints would get sidetracked by a conversation about baseball or hunting or fishing or something like that. Mayer used to pull that kind of thing all the time with Robert Taylor and Clark Gable. With women, on the other hand, the executives were usually much more uncomfortable. They couldn't even *fake* it that they thought they were talking to equals. The girls—and they were that, even if they were fifty—unburdened themselves about what was bothering them, then they were told how they had pleased or displeased Papa, then they got their reward or their tongue lashing, then they got a little pat on the head or elsewhere, then they walked out of the office resolved to stay on the straight and narrow. I think there was a hovering atmosphere of sexual conspiracy sometimes, and it even cut through the caste of male employer standing over the male employee. For sure, it did wonders for the egos of the male actors.

Eddie Albert warns against underrating the disposition Stewart brought to MGM in 1935. Albert, who worked with him in the 1948 comedy *You Gotta Stay Happy*, says it's "almost inevitable" for a person of Stewart's personality to think well of Mayer:

> The studios created problems for anybody who railed against the boss mentality. If you detested some idea that a boss had, or detested that he was a boss period, you were in for a lot of aggravation. Jimmy was never like that. Nobody struck up friendships or put people at ease faster than he did. And that goes for executives, other actors, people on the crews. So

if he wasn't going around saying disparaging things about them or rebelling against a decision of theirs, and they acted decently toward him as a result, why the hell *should* he have a bad memory of them?

But Robert Stack, a cast member of *The Mortal Storm* (1940), calls the design traced by Albert the residue of luck.

> I've never admired anybody more than Jimmy, but the whole point is that you *couldn't* expect decent behavior coming back even if you did try to get along. The simplest things that would never occur to a normal human being as representing rebellion, they would interpret them in that way. The plain fact of the matter is that Jimmy can still talk so highly of the studios because he was lucky. If he had ever been suspended, he wouldn't be so quick to go around endorsing how great the Mayers of the world were. L. B. Mayer was the guy who kept Judy Garland on diet pills to the point of addiction. I don't see anything great in a man like that. If Jimmy managed to walk between the raindrops, more power to him. But I think it was pure luck.

The irony in Stewart's undiluted endorsement of the old studios over the last few decades is that, owing first to his successful challenge to the duration of his MGM contract at the end of World War II and then to his profit-sharing deal with Universal at the end of the 1940s, no single Hollywood luminary was more responsible for the collapse of the system. But that said, his often passionate apologies for the old motion-picture industry power structure have also always seemed to reflect more than the nostalgic crabbiness of old age, the insider arrogance of a male, a noblesse oblige rooted in mutual amiability, or simple good fortune

For one thing, Stewart suffered little from the sense of intimidation that most other young actors in his situation experienced in being introduced to the MGM routine. There was no reason that he *should* have felt it keenly. In less than three years, he had advanced from the clouded professional prospects offered by architecture to a position where people supposedly in the know regarded his potential as being as intriguing as that of others (among them, Fonda) who had sweated ambitions of a full-time acting career night and day for much longer. Without any great life plan, he had impressed Broadway critics, producers, directors, and, of essential importance to him, other actors whom he himself respected. He had done all that impressing without any appreciable sacrifice of his

Indiana constitution; on the contrary, it was precisely because of his personality that he had ingratiated himself to people like Beckhard and Yurka. If his father could lament his gradual withdrawal from Philadelphia Street, in geography as much as mind, he could point to any number of things—from the accordion that had become something of a talisman to the fervor of his airplane model building with Fonda—as evidence that he had really brought a great deal of Indiana with him, *and* discovered along the way that his boyhood passions had not been isolated provincialisms of no interest to anyone else.

And there was more. Not even Hollywood was all *that* strange, not with Fonda, and then Swope, Logan, Sullavan, Meredith, and McCormick always circulating near his Evanston Street quarters when they weren't actually sharing his Brentwood house itself. Other actors could worry about pleasing L. B. Mayer, the Surrogate Father of MGM, but as long as Alex Stewart was walking the planet, James M. Stewart didn't need any surrogate fathers. Anyway, he had been raised to be pleasant and polite, so no big problem. And as far as the daily regimen was concerned, he never, not even in the depths of quandaries about career opportunities or going through his worst attacks of restlessness about specific jobs, disdained work itself; it was always his pride on this point, in fact, that would provoke his testiness in the years ahead at the suggestion that he was a "natural actor"—that was to say, somebody who merely had to show up to give a persuasive performance.

In short, whatever feelings of security Stewart has attached to the old studios in his defense of them over the years, they were feelings that he *brought* to Culver City as much as received there. MGM's experts could give him a lot of things, but they couldn't give him an emotional footing; that he already had. At his back was not just The Big Warehouse, but the warehouse that he had begun to stock with his own tested supplies.

The actor's most frequent description of his years at MGM has been a comparison to a professional baseball player in the era before free agency. (For instance: "The studios treated us like ballplayers; I was once traded to Universal for the use of their backlot for three weeks.") The analogy isn't all that wayward, especially in light of the fact that the average studio contract player was developed gradually through bit parts and promotional assignments for up to five or six years before being weighed for a major screen assignment; that was also about the length of time that big league teams of the 1930s kept their prospects in the minors before giving them a serious trial with the parent club. Eddie Stanky, an eleven-year major league infielder in the 1940s and 1950s and a technical consultant for the baseball sequences in *Strategic Air Command* (1955), praised the actor more than he knew in describing him as "down to earth as a minor leaguer."

On the other hand, however, Stewart did not sign with MGM only to run out the ground ball. Nor was he of Alex's mind to be content with playing things through to some end that would reveal the disappointments inherent in the undertaking. The talents and industry of his fellow players in *Yellow Jack* and his subsequent plays were not dissipated so easily. Still, MGM was not Broadway. He needed another goal.

He found it in the appropriate place—not in the organizational structure of his place of work or in his relationship to it, but in the roles he performed on the screen.

THIN MEN

MGM HAD PLANNED TO UNVEIL STEWART IN *AFTER THE Thin Man*, the second in the series of screen adaptations of Dashiell Hammett's sophisticated Nick and Nora Charles mysteries. But that intention was thwarted when Myrna Loy dug in her heels at being paid at a supporting player's level for the costarring role with William Powell. The threat of a long contract tussle with Loy over the *Thin Man* picture induced Grady to propose to producer Harry Rapf that Stewart be dropped instead into *The Murder Man*, a B-budgeted melodrama already in production but with one of the chief featured roles, that of a reporter, still unfilled. Rapf took one look at the beanpole Stewart and decided that Grady had been out too long the night before with his crony W. C. Fields. But then he took a second look and concluded that *The Murder Man* could use all the bizarre touches possible. The script name of the reporter needing an actor was Shorty.

The Murder Man (MGM – 1935)

The Murder Man starred Spencer Tracy as a wisecracking newsman who has earned the sobriquet of the title for his scoops on big homicide cases. His Good-Time-Charlie personality keeps the world at a comfortable distance until his father's second wife kills herself after the old man has been wiped out by a couple of con men. A short time later, one of the frauds himself is murdered, and Tracy's revelations lead the police to arrest the surviving partner for murder. When the accused is about to be executed for the crime, however, Tracy's reporter admits that he is the killer, that he was motivated by revenge for what the two con men had done to his father and stepmother.

Stewart's character of Shorty received relatively little exposure within the gallery of *Front Page*-type reporter stereotypes, among whom were such veteran players as William Demarest, George Chandler, and Fuzzy Knight. Still, some did notice him. One reviewer, for the New York *Herald Tribune*, observed that "that admirable juvenile, James Stewart, who was so fine in *Yellow Jack*, is wasted in a bit that he handles with characteristically engaging skill." Another critic was Stewart himself, who confirmed all the apprehensions he had had back at Princeton, emerging from a screening with the verdict that "I was all hands and feet. Didn't seem to know what to do with either." His most important impression, however, was made on star Tracy, who was called on to answer a volley of questions from the novice whenever they were due to do a scene together. "I told him to forget the camera was there," Tracy would say later. "That was all he needed. In his very first scene he showed he had all the good things."

The accepted wisdom among MGM's unknown contract players was that the only way to get noticed upstairs—and by the public—was to do a big scene with one of the studio's thoroughbreds. Unfortunately for Stewart, Tracy was still about a year away from such status, so that their scenes together swirled down the drain of the modest programmer that *The Murder Man* was. On the other hand, somewhat as in the case of his inept curtain-calling with Jane Cowl in Boston, the actor had the consolation of being the butt of commissary cracks for his ill-suited casting as Shorty. It wasn't a tribute, but it wasn't ignominy, either.

Rose Marie (MGM – 1936)

For more than three months after completing *The Murder Man*, Stewart was kept away from the cameras except to assist in making screen tests. But with *Rose Marie* he began a grind that saw him appear in eight films within a year.

Rose Marie was the second teaming of singers Jeanette MacDonald and

Nelson Eddy after their success in *Naughty Marietta*. A remake several characterizations removed from a Joan Crawford silent film, the operetta told a distracted tale about a famous diva who sets out from Montreal to the wilds of the Canadian Northwest to aid her fugitive brother, wanted for killing a Mountie. Because of several misadventures, she becomes entangled with a Mountie sergeant, who, when he is not falling in love with her and sharing such duets as "Indian Love Call," is counting on her to lead him to the wanted brother. The diva does just that, and when not even another refrain of "Indian Love Call" can dissuade the sergeant from taking her brother off to the hangman, she suffers a nervous breakdown. She is still in pretty delirious shape when the Mountie walks in unannounced into her deluxe apartment and professes his eternal love for her. Neither one of them mentions the by now presumably executed brother as they sing and clinch before the final fade-out.

If Stewart didn't have the starring role in *Rose Marie*, he had the next best thing—the part (that of the fugitive brother) that all the other characters talk about and that gives him a big scene near the end. That, and some professional generosity from MacDonald in giving him the best camera angles in their scenes together, allowed him to make the most of his badly written moments. He was also cut some slack for some undeniably awkward readings because of director Woody Van Dyke's reputation for brisk, one-take recordings of scenes in the interests of saving money. Stewart wasn't likely to have complained anyway; during some location shooting, he ended up as Van Dyke's roommate, and usually had to put the director to sleep with his accordion playing.

Next Time We Love (Universal – 1936)

Next Time We Love was the film that helped Stewart feel like a baseball player—the one that he did for Universal as part of a trade between studios. The deal would never have been made, however, without the insistence of Margaret Sullavan, who backed up her predictions of a big Hollywood career for the actor by demanding him as her costar in what was essentially a soap opera. Universal, which had barely heard of Stewart, gave in to her demand only out of fear that she would stage a threatened strike.

Next Time We Love again has Stewart as a newspaperman, but this time as an international correspondent who goes back and forth between his career and his wife's own success as a Broadway actress.

Caught between the couple is an unplanned child, who, if unwittingly, is blamed at various points in the story for compromising the ambitions of both parents. In the end, Stewart's correspondent dies of a disease picked up in China, making it unnecessary for the Sullavan character to ask for a divorce so she can marry a long-mooning suitor (Ray Milland). Before the newspaperman expires, she tells him that "next time we love, maybe we'll have time for each other."

Stewart's journey to an applauded performance was guided every step of the way by Sullavan. When journeyman director Edward Griffith threw up his arms at Stewart's stage mannerisms in some early scenes, the actress took it upon herself to rehearse with her costar long into the night. The odd man out in all the overtime was Sullavan's second husband, director William Wyler, who didn't mind admitting his suspicions about the relationship between the two former University Players. Invited on one occasion to see some rushes on *Next Time We Love*, Wyler allowed out loud that "she sure got something special out of him" in anything but a complimentary tone. The critics generally agreed, with *Time* magazine calling Stewart's performance "natural, spontaneous, and altogether excellent." The MGM brass was also impressed by the results of the loan-out; Grady, for one, told some interviewers: "That boy came back from Universal so changed I hardly recognized him. In his next few pictures at MGM, he shows a confidence, a command of film technique, that was startling. Sullavan had taught him to march to his own drummer, to be himself, completely."

Wife vs. Secretary (MGM – 1936)

Despite his acquired screen presence in *Next Time We Love*, MGM still wasn't ready to tear apart its own formula for developing performers by giving Stewart another starring role right away. Instead, it worked its traditional gradual exposure ploy by casting him as a fourth to three of the studio's biggest box office names—Clark Gable, Jean Harlow, and Myrna Loy. A somewhat crass comedy, *Wife vs. Secretary* basically portrays all secretaries as tramps who can't wait to hop into bed with the boss; if the picture has any thematic engine, it is that enunciated by the character of Gable's mother (May Robson), who at one point warns daughter-in-law Loy to insist on the firing of secretary Harlow since "you wouldn't blame a little boy for stealing candy, would you?" The rest of the film limns a series of misunderstandings that win Loy over to the mother-in-law's attitude and even prompt a resigned Gable indeed to invite Harlow off for a good-time cruise. Only after Harlow explains all the misunderstandings to Loy is there the requisite happy ending. It falls to Stewart, in the role of Harlow's constantly dangled boyfriend, to seal over everything with the concluding moral of "don't look for trouble when there isn't any, because if you don't find it, you'll make it."

As a product of its time, *Wife vs. Secretary* detonated a lot of the social nastiness that accompanied the increasing need for women to enter the job market because of the Depression; but the typical MGM gloss, as opposed to, say, the rhetorical melodramatics that would have been part of a Warner Brothers treatment of the material, left the sense that the filmmakers were as beguiled by their insinuations as by their resolution. Stewart, on the other hand, emerged from the film with reviews as good as he obtained for *Next Time We Love*. The London *Observer* went so far as to say that he "acts Gable and Harlow off the screen." With *Wife vs. Secretary*, the actor also established one of his performing trademarks— the monologue, going on at length in this specific case about the wonders of a twenty-dollar raise.

But reviews and speeches aside, what Stewart himself remembered most vividly from the picture was a kissing scene with a braless Harlow, and not just because it was a classic instance of MGM's policy of promoting unknowns through scenes with studio stars. As the actor recalled:

> It was high voltage stuff. . . . We sat in an automobile while I told her my plans. The scene ended with a kiss. The lines weren't much, and neither of us paid much attention to them, but in the first rehearsal, she took charge of the kissing. It was then that I knew that I'd never really been kissed before. There were six rehearsals. The kissing gained each time in interest and enthusiasm. By the time we actually shot the scene, my psychology was all wrinkled. She was a stunning girl with a dress so low cut you had to bend down to pick it up. I was just a guy from Pennsylvania. She had platinum hair and a beautiful face. And she slouched. Slinking was fashionable then. Her dresses were tight. She wore nothing under them. Shooting that scene made quite a night!

Small Town Girl (MGM – 1936)

What MGM gave with one hand, it took back with the other. No sooner had Stewart benefited from the studio's policy of giving its top prospects scenes with the likes of Harlow than he was brusquely reminded that he wasn't the only young actor on the lot being developed. In *Small Town Girl*, he was an all but laughable romantic rival to Robert Taylor for the affections of Janet Gaynor; in fact, his character of a bumpkin named Elmer who has a tic of asking everyone he meets "Keeping your chin up?" was the kind of role Grady Sutton was then making a career out of in W. C. Fields's pictures. On the other hand, *Small Town Girl* did reinforce the Stewart persona that MGM was stumbling toward insofar as he was once again (as in *Wife vs. Secretary*) playing a man who wanted his girlfriend to give up whatever she thought was important (in this case, Gaynor's decision to leave her small town) to settle down as his wife. The major difference from other screen males of the period was that a Gable would win the immediate gratitude of a lover for rescuing her and an Edward G. Robinson would order his mistress to get out of the rackets, but the typical Stewart character would hang his head in disappointment when the woman rejected his assumptions—at least until the final reel.

Speed (MGM – 1936)

Speed was Stewart's semireward for playing the goofus in *Small Town Girl*. Although a decidedly low-budget effort with significant amounts of screen time taken up with the characters gaping at backscreen projections of industrial film footage, it was the actor's first starring role for MGM. In *Speed*, Stewart plays a mechanic and test driver who is obsessed with developing a high-speed carburetor. His passion is constantly frustrated—first, by some failures of his invention, then by the ambiguous actions of a public relations officer (Wendy Barrie) newly hired by his company, then by the jealousy of a company engineer (Weldon Heyburn), who is also his rival for the attention of the public relations woman. Everything is sorted out after a crash on the Indianapolis Speedway almost takes his life: the carburetor is found to work, the engineer turns out to be a hero for saving the Stewart character's life after the speedway crash, and the PR woman assures him that he has never had a serious competitor for her love.

The most interesting parts of *Speed* are some periodically good lines ("An idea just came into my head." "How's it getting along with the bats?") and an automobile unveiled at the end of the picture as a new assembly-line product—but which looks like the prototype for the Batmobile. The uninteresting things are everything else. In addition to the relentless stock footage of the inside of a car factory and of an

Indianapolis Speedway race, the central characters played by Stewart and his best friend (Ted Healy) run the gamut from sulky to crabby throughout, making it clear why they would need a public relations woman in their lives, but not much else. The consensus was that the picture did what it was supposed to do—fill out a double feature and keep Stewart working—without lasting harm either to audiences or the actor.

Speed was about the only film that showed some physical results from Stewart's diet and exercising regimen with Don Loomis; in the closing scenes of the picture, he appears almost apple-cheeked. It was also during the making of the melodrama that he claimed to have received the single best piece of advice he ever received in Hollywood, from costar Healy who told him "To think of the audience not simply as watchers but as collaborators, as sort of partners in the project."[3]

The Gorgeous Hussy (MGM – 1936)

On paper, *The Gorgeous Hussy* looked like an even worse idea for Stewart than *Small Town Girl*; in actuality, it was even worse than that.

The Gorgeous Hussy was a star-filled extravaganza purporting to tell the story of a onetime mistress of President Andrew Jackson who ended up compromising his administration with her frequent nocturnal visits to his cabinet and Senate supporters. Although there is some lip service paid to the heroine's "liberal ideas," her embodiment in Joan Crawford makes her come off as an early version of one of the actress's Warner Brothers toughs in the 1950s, where she ineluctably rises with David Brian from a backroom gambling table to a chandeliered mansion—only to have everything come down again in a fire. In this particular instance, Crawford's Peggy O'Neal realizes that she has embarrassed the president of the United States and, despite winning exoneration from an investigating committee, simply leaves Washington in the interests of national security. Among those she leaves behind is a smartly frocked suitor named Rowdy Dow (Stewart).

If Stewart learned anything from *The Gorgeous Hussy*, it was to keep a low profile around a palisade of egos. He himself was an indirect cause of one explosion when Crawford protested to Mayer about her husband

---

[3] Stewart has also credited MGM executive Howard Strickling with tendering that advice to him.

Franchot Tone having only a handful of lines and the studio boss implored her to show some self-discipline around relative beginners such as Stewart. Crawford's reply was to point to another member of the cast and ask, "What about Robert Taylor? Do I change his diapers, too?"

Born to Dance (MGM – 1936)

Born to Dance was Stewart's introduction to the MGM musical department, as well as to star hoofer Eleanor Powell. Equally significant, it allowed him to don the Navy uniform he had aspired to put on since graduating from Mercersburg Academy.

Although Born to Dance has a semblance of a plot centering around the intrusion of a Broadway star (Virginia Bruce) into a developing romance between a sailor (Stewart) and a stage aspirant (Powell), it is mainly a succession of production numbers featuring the two leads, Buddy Ebsen, Una Merkel, Frances Langford, and cowriter Sid Silvers. Stewart got his role, which included singing "Easy to Love" and "Hey, Babe" with Powell, through the help of Cole Porter; although the composer acknowledged that the actor "sings far from well," he also conceded that he had "some nice notes in his voice." Porter also helped to quash a postproduction decision to have Stewart's pipsqueak tenor dubbed by a professional singer.

The picture's chief strengths were the dancing of Powell and Ebsen, and humor—both intentional and unintentional. The vaudeville background of cowriters Silvers and Buddy De Sylva was particularly evident in the dialogue, as when Merkel explains why she decided to marry somebody she had just met during a marathon dance contest ("I thought I was in love; I was just tired") or when Silvers is asked about his birthplace ("I understand you were born in Brooklyn; what part?" "All of me"). On the other hand, the film's indifference to reality generates a scene where Stewart is depicted as living it up all night with Bruce in a ritzy nightclub—then being hit with a bill for $11.80. Shortly afterward, Merkel wants to have a heart-to-heart talk with Powell, so tells her small daughter to "go along and play"—which the girl does, while everybody is standing on the George Washington Bridge!

The perfunctory nature of the plot of Born to Dance was the only thing that prevented it from becoming another prime example of a Stewart character wondering how his love can be thinking of a career instead of settling down with him; still, he manages to press Powell about whether she "really wants to go on the stage" before the dancer goes off tapping on everything from a table to the deck of a submarine.

After the Thin Man (MGM – 1936)

Stewart has always considered himself lucky that, because of the contract squabbles involving Myrna Loy, *After the Thin Man* was his ninth rather than his first Hollywood picture. Among other words he has used to describe his performance in the Nick and Nora Charles whodunnit is "ludicrous." Certainly, it was the first time that he was asked to open all his blasters.

Nick and Nora Charles are asked to find the no-good husband of one of her wealthy cousins (Elissa Landi). They do, in a nightclub where the wastrel has been having an affair with a singer. Stewart, in the part of Landi's spurned suitor, offers the husband $25,000 if he will leave town and open the field for him again. The husband accepts, but is then shot dead. More bodies pile up until Nick realizes that the murderer is Stewart. The climactic scene has the gun-toting Stewart raving that his motive all along has not been love for Landi, but hatred and contempt for her for having jilted him originally. "I want to see you go mad and madder and madder until you hang!" he screams at her before finally being overpowered.

In terms of the *Thin Man* series, the identification of Stewart as the murderer was about as surprising as the mysteries ever got. Much of this stemmed from the innocent youth roles that the actor had been asked to play earlier, and arguably would have had considerably less impact if *After the Thin Man* had indeed marked his screen debut for MGM. What clearly disconcerted Stewart, however, was the abrupt motivational monologue he was called on to deliver at the film's finale— one that the mystery genre could not set much of a foundation for. Unlike the obsessive man's monologue that he rattled off at the conclusion of *Vertigo* twenty years later, he had to pluck his near-dementia for *After the Thin Man* practically out of the air—an already uncomfortable exercise, without tossing in the specifics of hatred and contempt, for a personality who would not feel himself ready as an actor to confront such emotions until after World War II. It was within this context that he has sometimes sounded almost pleading in a surmise that "people must have been laughing" at his confessional scene.

MGM wasn't so sure. To hedge its bets just in case, though, it had a goggle-eyed George Zucco comment on the Stewart outburst by looking directly into the camera and exclaiming, "Good Heaven, I was right! The man *is* crazy!" It was far from the last time that an emotional explosion from a Stewart character would raise the issue of sanity.

Seventh Heaven (20th Century-Fox – 1937)

If *Next Time We Love* represented the benefits of the studio loan-out system for Stewart, *Seventh Heaven* showed the disadvantages. The calculation behind the picture was simple: 20th Century-Fox was counting on some easy revenues from remaking as talkies some of its most successful silent films. Few had been more successful than a 1927 adaptation of Austin Strong's play *Seventh Heaven*; not only had it won Oscars for actress Janet Gaynor, director Frank Borzage, and writer Benjamin Glazer, but it had made Gaynor and leading man Charles Farrell the next best thing to Garbo and John Gilbert as screen lovers for a while. Unfortunately for all concerned, however, Gaynor, Borzage, and Glazer had nothing to do with the 1937 remake. Instead, and in the avowed interests of ethnic "authenticity" for a story concerned with Frenchmen of the World War I era, producer Darryl Zanuck and director Henry King recruited James Stewart of Indiana, Pennsylvania, Austrian Mady Christians, Russian Gregory Ratoff, Dane Jean Hersholt, New Jerseyite Victor Kilian, German Sig Rumann, and Norwegian-Canadian John Qualen. The one concession to France in the cast was Simone Simon, who took on the Gaynor role.

Seventh Heaven follows the turgid adventures of a Paris sewer worker named Chico (Stewart) and a prostitute named Diane (Simon) who, between them, don't believe in God, have been thrown out of a brothel for not engaging more customers, and are growing weary of all the rats running around under the French capital. Nevertheless, after some false starts, they have enough spark left for one another to live together in his garret and even go along with the advice of a neighborhood priest (Hersholt) to make their union official. But just before the wedding takes place, World War I breaks out, Chico runs off to get in uniform, and stays away for four years. In spite of reports that Chico has been killed, Diane stays faithful to him throughout the war. Her reward is his return— though now blind. She assures him that this doesn't make any difference to her love for him, and the two of them settle down again in the garret that they have dubbed Seventh Heaven.

Stewart's in-and-out attempts at affecting continental ennui are about as energetic as his performance gets in *Seventh Heaven*, and few who have seen it have disputed his verdict that "they ought to have left the first picture alone." Because of the accents of a number of his fellow players, his own characteristic delivery made him seem *twice* removed from the proceedings—not only from some representation of France (which only Simon could claim as her own), but even from whatever generic foreign fantasy the other cast members occasionally insinuated.

The Last Gangster (MGM – 1937)

Aside from his teamings with Sullavan, *The Last Gangster* was the most striking film that Stewart appeared in prior to *Mr. Smith Goes to Washington*. Its impact, however, depends not on him, but on star Edward G. Robinson and a couple of supporting performances.

In full *Little Caesar* form, Robinson swaggers into *The Last Gangster* as the vaguely Slovak Joe Krozak who has returned from Europe with a wife (Rose Stradner) he is mainly interested in as a breeding farm. In between winks over his sexual skills to his chief henchman (Lionel Stander), he proceeds to gun down his chief rivals for control of the rackets. Just when his wife delivers him his long-desired son, however, Krozak is arrested for tax evasion, found guilty, and sentenced to a long prison term in Alcatraz. The imprisonment comes as a double shock to his immigrant wife, who had not only been unaware of Krozak's criminal activities, but is forced to face, during a visit to Alcatraz, that he is more interested in seeing his infant son than he is in seeing her. In her confusion, she is duped by a newspaper editor (Sidney Blackmer) and reporter (Stewart) into a photograph showing the baby with a gun on his lap.

While Krozak rages in jail, his wife divorces him, remarries with the reporter who has seen through his cynicism to her sincerity, and moves to a small town in the hope of protecting her son and starting anew. It works, with the son thinking that the reporter is his father, until the still-vengeful Krozak is released from prison. The gangster is detoured, however, by his former henchmen, who want to know the whereabouts of some old loot. When torturing Krozak gets them nowhere, they kidnap the boy, betting that the gangster will surrender the money rather than see his son hurt. The gangster and the boy eventually escape the thugs, surviving in the wilds thanks to some tips the boy has picked up from his stepfather. By the time Krozak gets the boy back safely to his ex-wife and the reporter, he has lost his taste for vengeance. He leaves the house with the boy no wiser about his actual father. Outside, he encounters an old rival who announces his intention of avenging an old murder by first killing Krozak, then his son and ex-wife. Krozak and the rival both go down in a shootout.

Stewart's conversion from a trash journalist to an understanding husband vis-à-vis Stradner is little more than a plot convenience, and he has very little to do except look like a contented father of the family in the second half of the film. The closest he comes to a moment on the screen is when he asks Stradner to marry him, then comments wryly during her silence: "Now my heart is going to stop beating for ten seconds while I find out if I can do this forever." His later scenes weren't helped, either, by a studio decision to give him a fake mustache to make him look older.

Navy Blue and Gold (MGM – 1937)

Navy Blue and Gold went one better than *Born to Dance* in not only putting Stewart into the Navy, but in the Annapolis of his teenage dreams. It was, in fact, only one of numerous films made by Hollywood in the 1930s that were set in either the Naval Academy or in its Army equivalent at West Point.[4] In one sense, the pictures were college dramas or comedies dressed up in military uniform, but on another level they worked as recruiting posters for the next generation's officer class.[5]

Navy Blue and Gold follows the Annapolis trials of roommates Truck Cross (Stewart), Roger Ash (Robert Young), and Richard Gates (Tom Brown). Aside from a common interest in football, the three are markedly different. While Ash is a cynical, calculating cadet indifferent to Navy tradition except for what it can do for him financially and socially, Gates is an already arrived socialite who wants to be taken seriously by

---

[4] Among the other films of the 1930s set at Annapolis were *Midshipman Jack*, *Annapolis Farewell*, *Annapolis Salute*, and *Hold 'Em, Navy*.

[5] They also served as something of an olive branch by Mayer and the other studio bosses to a New Deal administration that had been perceived by Hollywood as hostile to its industry interests, but that by the mid-1930s was too settled in power to be baited. At the very least, the Annapolis pictures, particularly, were counted on as signs of goodwill toward President Franklin Delano Roosevelt, himself a onetime assistant secretary of the Navy.

somebody besides his valet, and Cross is a former enlisted man bent on wiping out the blemish caused by his father's dishonorable discharge from the Navy. Complicating their relations is Gates's sister Patricia (Florence Rice), pursued by both Ash and Cross. Most of the first half of the film is taken up with recitations of Annapolis tradition, usually prompted by some infraction or other committed by Ash. The main drama begins only when Stewart's Cross listens to an instructor glibly use his disgraced father as an example of what the Navy *doesn't* need and blows up at the teacher, insisting that the charges against his parent were always lies.

This leads to his suspension from the big game against Army and even threatened expulsion from the academy. In the end, however, wiser heads prevail, and Cross joins the by now smartened-up Ash and Gates on the gridiron in time to defeat Army. Among those rooting him on are his conquered love Patricia and his exonerated father.

Stewart's tirade against the instructor offered him a film-stealing moment, and he didn't waste it. The New York *Herald Tribune* led a chorus of approval in declaring in part: "Although [Stewart] has been denied Robert Young's beauty and has been endowed with none of the strong, silent intensity of Gary Cooper, he breathes life into his character to hold a formalized theme to a strict pattern. It is due to his expert rendition of a rather preposterous part that a rather preposterous show becomes generally exciting."

Of Human Hearts (MGM – 1938)

By 1938, Stewart had worked his way to the top of the list at MGM for "adult son" roles. In a studio that had actors twenty-deep for most other types, he really didn't have all that much competition for an adult son. His most obvious rival, Robert Taylor, might have been three years younger, but both his more limited acting range and his persona as the slick romantic militated against the studio giving him parts that called for open, conflicting emotions. Thus, it didn't come as too much of a surprise when Clarence Brown insisted that Stewart play Walter Huston's son in a project that had been close to the director for quite some time.

Based on Honore Morrow's *Benefits Forgot*, *Of Human Hearts* records the tribulations of a minister (Huston), his wife (Beulah Bondi), and their son (Gene Reynolds) after they arrive in a poor, narrow-minded frontier community. When the humorless, tyrannical minister is not negotiating the town's spiritual problems, he is accepting charity to keep a roof over his family's head and dealing stern lectures to an increasingly rebellious son. Grown up, the boy (now Stewart) wastes no time in escaping the petty tyrannies of his father and the surrounding town to go off to study medicine in Baltimore. With a perpetual callousness, he takes it for granted that his mother will sell her most precious possessions to help finance his schooling; not even his father's death changes his attitude. When the Civil War breaks out, he is assigned to a field hospital on the front lines with the Union Army. But one day he is summoned to Washington by Abraham Lincoln himself, who wants to know why he has not responded to years of letters from his mother, a fact she has disclosed to Lincoln in a letter. A mortified son, after listening to Lincoln sermonize about his lack of gratitude for all the sacrifices his parents have made for him (the "benefits forgot" of the original title), then sits down to write a letter home that signals the beginning of his redemption.

Of Human Hearts belonged to a Hollywood era that evoked Abraham Lincoln at the drop of a stovepipe hat. But largely because of a makeup job that had John Carradine looking like the Frankenstein monster, the Great Rail Splitter comes across as a grotesque while making such pronouncements as "There's no finer quality than gratitude." For all his championing of the material against years of studio resistance to what was considered a Civil War story, and therefore box-office poison, director Brown seemed much more comfortable with the son's early years as played by Reynolds and with the balking of Stewart's older boy before he goes to Baltimore than with the heavy-handed moralisms served up over the final third of the film. Working within a studio where the prevailing attitude was that fathers always knew best, he certainly shied away from drawing the obvious dramatic parallels between the cold stubbornness of the minister and that of his grown son. Thanks in part to one of Huston's more nuanced performances, in fact, even the impenetrable father is made to appear at the end as paternal wisdom incarnate.

Of Human Hearts was one of the rare times that Stewart was asked to portray a rebel, and his emotional persuasiveness in a monologue to Bondi that veers back and forth from contempt for the family's living conditions to a wonder at the mysteries contained by human bones, rates as one of his best screen moments before World War II. His character at that moment also happens to be *right*—a particular that gets quickly lost amid all the ensuing preachments.

The film also marked two firsts for the actor—riding horses on the screen and playing Bondi's son. The actress would take such a role several more times in both motion pictures and television.

Vivacious Lady (RKO – 1938)

Vivacious Lady marked Stewart's first association with one of the directorial elite of Hollywood. His loan-out to RKO to work with George Stevens was due to Ginger Rogers, a frequent companion during the period, who asked for him as a costar. For Rogers, the film was intended as a demonstration that she could hold her own on a screen without dancing and without Fred Astaire.

Vivacious Lady concerns an assistant botany professor (Stewart) from a small-town college who goes to New York to persuade his brother (James Ellison) to give up his playboy ways. He ends up in a nightclub where he falls immediately in love with a singer (Rogers) and marries her. Arriving back home with his new wife, however, he gets cold feet about announcing their marriage to his stuffy parents (Charles Coburn and Beulah Bondi) and to his former fiancée (Frances Mercer), and while he works up his courage, passes the singer off as somebody he just met on a train. Complications are piled on complications until the professor finally locates the strength to tell the truth to everybody.

Although the picture was treated kindly by critics of the day, enabling Rogers to make her professional point, it wouldn't make any Top-Ten—or even Top-Thirty—list of the best comedies of the 1930s. Stevens's notorious deliberateness as a director blunts one promising situation after another, so that a presumably desired zaniness is rarely achieved. The supposed nemeses of the plot don't come off particularly well, either, with Coburn mainly oppressive, Mercer nondescript, and Bondi nonsensical. There is also an especially embarrassing scene near the end of the picture, where, even within the context of the period's racial stereotypes, a train porter named Sambo (Willie Best) is made to mug to a new low. About the only major comic moment that comes off is an escalating slapping and kicking scene between Rogers and Mercer. Before it was done to Stevens's satisfaction, the actresses swapped a reported 168 blows.

After Rogers, Stewart drew most of the critical praise. *The New York Times*, for one, called his appearance "a priceless bit of casting." Especially in his early scenes, the actor also called to mind Stan Laurel, suggesting what *Vivacious Lady* might have become.

The Shopworn Angel (MGM – 1938)

Because her newest husband, agent Leland Hayward, had secured her a highly favored contract with MGM, Margaret Sullavan didn't have to demand a loan-out arrangement to have Stewart costar with her in *The Shopworn Angel*; this time her demand was strictly intramural.

Based on a 1918 *Saturday Evening Post* story entitled "Private Pettigrew's Girl" and already adapted for two silent pictures,[6] *The Shopworn Angel* focuses on the emotional ambiguousness of a flippant New York entertainer (Sullavan) toward an innocent Texas farmboy (Stewart) who is about to be shipped overseas to World War I combat. The pair meet after the actress's car accidentally knocks down the soldier, then keep meeting because of his hopes that she has become as smitten with him as he is with her. In spite of her attempts to tell him that she has no room in her life for a farmboy (He: "Can I walk home with you?" She: "So long as you don't ask me to skip"), he eventually works her into a corner where she can rationalize that marrying him might keep him safe while on the battlefield and that she can always divorce him when he returns home. Her attitude is seconded, after some initial jealousy, by a Broadway producer (Walter Pidgeon) who has been her lover for some time. The ploy fails: While performing in a New York club, she gets word that the soldier has been killed in Europe. The actress and the producer are left gaping at one another with guilty consciences.

Most critics agreed that everything from the soap-opera incredibility of its premise to the glibness of its ending was wrong with *The Shopworn Angel*. But there was an equal consensus that one thing worked mightily in the film—the chemistry between Sullavan and Stewart. Even Mayer was stunned by what he saw in the screening room, telling aides: "They're red hot when they get in front of a camera. I don't know what the hell it is, but it sure jumps off the screen." The New York *Herald Tribune* agreed: "[Sullavan] has invested scene after scene with eloquence and vigor. There is a quality to her voice and an authority in her every gesture. . . . In much the same manner James Stewart brings the Texas private to glowing life and keeps the characterization solid and appealing even when the script gives him little aid. . . . *The Shopworn Angel* boasts of two of the finest actors appearing on the screen today."

---

[6] It would be adapted still again in the 1950s under the title of *That Kind of Woman*, with Sidney Lumet directing Sophia Loren, Tab Hunter, and George Sanders.

The Sullavan detractors weren't to be left out, however. Many snickered that she owed the effectiveness of her performance to the parallels between her man-manipulating character on the screen and that in private life. It was noted in particular that her film entertainer shifts abruptly from a decided spikiness to an angelic sympathy as soon as she realizes that the producer played by Pidgeon is jealous of her attentions to the young soldier—another trademark of the private Sullavan.

You Can't Take It With You (Columbia – 1938)

No single director dominated a big studio in the 1930s more than Frank Capra did Columbia. While studio boss Harry Cohn liked talking about how he "spits a picture out every Friday to have 52 for the year," he also came to rely on Capra for the higher-toned films that would give Columbia an identity beyond that of a movie mill, thereby not only winning awards (which the executive prized minimally), but attracting more prestigious talents for the box office. In the decade of the 1930s, eleven of Columbia's thirteen Oscars and forty of its sixty-five Academy Award nominations stemmed from Capra pictures. As Barbara Stanwyck put it on one occasion, "Every time Capra made another film, Columbia built another sound stage."

It was the Italian-born filmmaker who requested Stewart from MGM for the film adaptation of the George S. Kaufman–Moss Hart play *You Can't Take It With You.* The studio saw nothing to lose by having the actor associated with a piece that had just won a Pulitzer Prize, especially after learning that his character had been beefed up from the Broadway version of the story.

The never-modest Capra claimed everything for *You Can't Take It With You,* from its being a Hollywood blow against the ideological "isms" prevailing in the 1930s, to its being "the first hippie movie—years ahead of its time." The story is set within the eccentric home of Martin Vanderhoff (Lionel Barrymore), a former businessman who is convinced that the best things in life are free (and who apparently has the savings for supporting his twenty-four-hour-a-day ruminations on the imaginative nature of man to prove it). Among those sharing his home are a daughter (Spring Byington) who fancies herself a playwright and a painter, a son-in-law (Samuel S. Hinds) in quest of the perfect firecracker, a granddaughter (Ann Miller) who wants to be a ballerina, her xylophone-playing, anarchist husband (Dub Taylor), and a second grand-daughter (Jean Arthur) who works as a secretary. About the only cloud hanging over the carefree existence of this menage is an industrialist (Edward Arnold) who needs the house to complete some land clearing for the building of a munitions plant.

The plot is triggered when the working granddaughter falls in love with her boss (Stewart), who also happens to be the son of the industrialist and a snotty socialite (Mary Forbes). To announce their marriage plans to both sets of parents, the couple decides to hold a dinner at the Vanderhoff house. But wary that his fiancée will instruct her family to act stiffly, the well-meaning son deliberately mixes up the dinner date so that his parents can see the Vanderhoffs *au naturel*, the way he admires them. A fiasco of an evening ensues, climaxed by an explosion of the fireworks that lands everybody in jail. Although Vanderhoff's popularity with neighbors packing the courtroom makes it easy to raise the money for the fine assessed for illegal possession of fire-works, the shamed granddaughter breaks off her engagement and flees to Connecticut. This leads Vanderhoff to sell the house, clearing the way for the building of the munitions plant. But when his son announces that he wants nothing to do with the new factory and goes off to find his fiancée, a bewildered industrialist begins to realize that there is more to life than business coups. All of the characters end up back at the disputed house, with the industrialist joining Vanderhoff in a harmonica duet that symbolizes his acceptance of his new daughter-in-law and his spiritual rebirth.

The principal change from the Broadway version of the Kaufman-Hart work was in building up the part of the munitions industrialist from a cardboard heavy to what Capra liked to call that of a "villain-hero." It was an alteration wrought by dramatic sledgehammers. Over the last forty minutes of the film, in fact, the industrialist is: (1) lectured by Vanderhoff for being a spiritual desert; (2) told by his future daughter-in-law that he and his wife are a spiritual desert; (3) berated by a business competitor he is about to squash for being a spiritual desert; (4) vowed to by his son that there will be at least one less spiritual desert in the family; and (5) informed that his business competitor has died from heart failure. Not for the first time or last time in his pictures, Capra's ride through this kind of dramatic repetition creates an atmosphere of inevitability that amounts to more of a political statement than any dozen speeches made by characters on the screen: to wit, munitions industrialists are *bound* to see the light. However dubious this proposition, it is matched by the faith displayed by Capra in the film's other conspicuous authority figure, the judge played by Harry Davenport. Just as Harry Carey's Senate president in *Mr. Smith Goes to Washington* bestows a series of benevolent smiles on Jefferson Smith, the jurist of *You Can't Take It With You* grins reassuringly that everything will turn out fine for good people, and even contributes a coin of his own to the collection for paying off the fine he has just levied against Vanderhoff.

Although Barrymore had the most lines and Arnold had the juiciest role in *You Can't Take It With You*, Stewart was hardly slighted. Especially in his scenes with Arthur, his spontaneity and buoyancy marked an advance on even what Sullavan had taught him, triggering the first avalanche of critical opinion that he was a "natural because he was honest." In the words of one weekly, "No actor on the screen today manages to appear more unconscious of script, camera, and director than Mr. Stewart." Henry Fonda was so taken with his performance that he would always say that, together with George Bailey in *It's a Wonderful Life*, it was the closest that the screen Stewart ever got to the private Stewart.

Capra had other reasons for appreciating the actor, as well. Reminiscent of his extra value to Arthur Beckhard on Broadway, Stewart was one of the few stable points that the director had going for him during the production of *You Can't Take It With You*. Arthur, for instance, had been signed only after protracted attempts to borrow Olivia de Havilland from Warner Brothers had foundered; what Arthur brought with her was one of the most fabled cases of anxiety in Hollywood. When she wasn't looking at mirrors to reassure herself that she hadn't aged significantly since her previous glance, she was vomiting in her dressing room. Arnold, by contrast, exhibited his notorious weakness only when the cameras were on—blowing one line after another in a habit that, despite his acting abilities, had made him anathema to the industry's cost-conscious producers and directors. Barrymore was a third question mark for the undefined illness that had reduced him to crutches and a wheelchair and that had inspired him to suggest to Capra that he wear a cast on one foot to alibi his immobility within the film as having been the result of a faulty slide down a banister. The actor himself always claimed that he had broken his hip in a fall and then been assailed by laming complications. Although general wisdom in Hollywood was that he was suffering from arthritis and was too proud to admit it, there was also a nagging rumor over his final years that he was the victim of a venereal disease that had spread to his joints. Capra's only comment on Barrymore's condition was that "his body was a mess, but not his nerve."

Despite being one of the few sources of calm during the production of *You Can't Take It With You*, Stewart also observed the kind of professional behavior—"friendly aloofness"—that grew into a basic characteristic with the passing of years. What surprised one member of the crew, especially in light of all the admiration the actor has expressed for Capra over the years, was that he included the director in that attitude. According to sound engineer Edward Bernds, "Jimmy was respectful toward Capra, but hardly worshipful in the way that, say, Clark Gable was during *It Happened One Night*. Same thing with regard to the crew. After a single day's work, Gable was on a first-name basis with everybody, but not Jimmy. He was professional and friendly, but always a little removed."

For Bernds, there were two possible explanations for the contrast in the behavior of the actors:

> They both had come over to Columbia from MGM, and I don't think either one of them was used to the free-and-easy style at Columbia. Over at MGM they were always throwing knives at your back. In Gable's case, I think he saw what a golden opportunity he had, and he was giddy with satisfaction at not having to be in a typical MGM atmosphere. With Jimmy, I wonder whether he didn't actually *miss* Metro, whether he didn't find Columbia a little *too* free and easy. But I think there's another possibility too—that Jimmy already had his own center in his work even back then. I think he came to work, and everybody, from a lighting man to Capra, was there only to aid in that.

You Can't Take It With You was the first award winner with which Stewart was associated. It won Oscars for Best Picture and Best Director, also snaring nominations for Byington (Best Supporting Actress), Robert Riskin (Screenplay), and Joseph Walker (Cinematography). The prizes came with controversy. Only a week before the ceremonies, Capra, recently elected president of the Academy, had threatened to instigate a boycott of the proceedings if the Association of Motion Picture Producers didn't accord formal recognition to the Directors Guild. The producers bowed to the demand, and Capra's Oscars triggered roaring ovations on presentation night. Among the films that lost the Best Picture award to *You Can't Take It With You* was Jean Renoir's *Grand Illusion*.

Made for Each Other (United Artists – 1939)

Even after sixteen films, MGM had very little idea of what, in industry parlance, a "Stewart picture" was. Other producers had better ideas, so for the third time in four undertakings, the actor hit the loan-out trail. Requesting his services this time was David Selznick, who had briefly run production at MGM after the December 1936 death of Irving Thalberg and who had subsequently gone out on his own.

As *Vivacious Lady* had been aimed at demonstrating that Ginger Rogers could do more than dance with Fred Astaire, *Made for Each Other* was born of Carole Lombard's desire to show that the comic actress of *My Man Godfrey*, *Nothing Sacred*, and *Twentieth Century* also had her dramatic strengths. Also like Rogers, Lombard made her point in difficult circumstances.

Made for Each Other follows the storm-tossed marriage of lawyer John Mason (Stewart) and his wife, Jane (Lombard). Most of the heavy winds come from his mother (Lucille Watson), who resents the fact that her son hasn't married the boss's daughter, and the boss (Charles Coburn), a hard-of-hearing despot who thinks about nothing except his firm's balance sheets. When the couple have a child, an already-shaky economic situation worsens, primarily because the lawyer doesn't have the gumption to demand a raise and a promotion, but on the contrary meekly accepts a pay cut and the seating of a rival in the vice-presidency he had sought. When his son falls gravely ill of pneumonia, however, Mason finds courage in his desperation, barging into his boss's home late at night and practically demanding the money needed to fly some life-saving serum in from Colorado. The remainder of the film goes back and forth between scenes of the devastated parents and the suddenly sympathetic mother waiting for word of the serum's arrival and of a pilot's dogged attempts to negotiate weather from hell to deliver the cure. Although the pilot's airplane finally conks out on him, he parachutes down to a house less than an hour away from the hospital, assuring the safe delivery of the serum and the saving of the child. The last scene shows the now-aggressive Mason telling his boss about the changes he intends implementing as the firm's newest vice-president.

The first three-quarters of *Made for Each Other* gets by largely on the strength of Lombard's winning injections of humor into what might have been a drip-dry character. Stewart also has his moments in an unusually mousy role, not least when he affects a W. C. Fields drawl in an early scene with the dimly hearing boss. But even these assets are ultimately overwhelmed by the ludicrous finale of the rescue plane sequences—not only unbelievable in themselves, but seeming to have been imported from another picture. In actuality, they emanated from the often overripe imagination of Selznick, who, contrary to his reputation as a meddler, had been initially content to leave the shooting of *Made for Each Other* to director John Cromwell while he concentrated on the preparations for his next project, *Gone With the Wind*. But following a tepid sneak preview of the film, the producer ordered the rescue portion of the story expanded, rebuffing Cromwell's protests with the argument that his own brother, Myron Selznick, had once been saved by a mercy pilot and he wanted to pay tribute to such heroes. The picture's potluck style is also evident in the hospital sequences, where the set seems to have been borrowed from *The Cabinet of Dr. Caligari*. Collectors of Hollywood's racial stereotypes weren't disappointed, either, particularly for a scene in which black housekeeper Louise Beavers counsels Lombard to "never let the seeds stop you from enjoying the watermelon."

If nothing else, Stewart and Lombard came away from *Made for Each Other* as members of a mutual admiration society. According to the actor, his costar was "the only girl I've ever known who could let out a stream of four-letter words and not embarrass you. In fact, I'd have to say it was ladylike the way she did it." Asked to compare Stewart to such other leading men as William Powell, Charles Laughton, Fredric March, and John Barrymore, Lombard told an interviewer shortly before her death in a 1942 plane crash that he was "more sincere than any of them, and just as talented—his talent is perfection itself."

The Ice Follies of 1939 (MGM – 1939)

For Louis B. Mayer, a good picture was one that made money, a better picture was one that made money and featured the character of a benevolent show-business entrepreneur such as himself, and the best of all pictures was one that made money and featured the character of a benevolent show-business entrepreneur such as himself played by actor

Lewis Stone. With *The Ice Follies of 1939*, he had two out of three reasons for liking a picture: It died at the box office.

Follies traces the show-business career paths of skater-choreographer Larry Hall (Stewart), his wife, Mary (Joan Crawford), and his best friend, Eddie (Lew Ayres). While Larry tries, unsuccessfully, to find financing for an ice extravaganza, Mary charms studio boss Tolliver (Stone) into giving her a screen test, and is soon on her way to stardom. Larry's perpetual sulking about being in Mary's shadow leads Eddie to break up their years-long partnership, after which Larry himself also leaves Hollywood to rediscover his footing on the ice. After a year of merely parallel lives at opposite ends of the country, Mary suddenly comes to the conclusion that her career has been harmful to her marriage, and she asks out of her contract. But Tolliver is much too wise for that: Having seen the ice show that Larry has finally managed to produce, he announces a major motion picture built around the extravaganza, starring Mary and featuring, among others, Eddie. Everybody is happy.

The chief distinction of *The Ice Follies of 1939* is its narcissism. Those who miss the allusions to Leo the Lion in the naming of Tolliver's company as Monarch have to be doubly dense to go by a lengthy parking-lot scene in which, against a foreground exchange among Stewart, Crawford, and Ayres, a valet announces the arrival of cars belonging to such MGM players as Clark Gable, Spencer Tracy, Robert Taylor, and Robert Young. What the in-jokes fail to cover over is that the paternalistic studio boss figure is mainly on hand to alibi another large chunk of film turned over to the nondramatic; the only difference between the Indianapolis Speedway footage that concludes *Speed* or the Army-Navy football game newsreel that occupies the last half-hour of *Navy Blue and Gold* is that at least the lengthy ice show winding up *Follies* didn't come from a film library.

Despite the presence of three actors who were known to the public, MGM sensed that ice spectaculars were a harder sell than musicals (or the swimming epics of Esther Williams at a later date), so resorted to some unusual publicity pitches. One angle was the sudden introduction of color for the concluding ice show after more than an hour of black-and-white action—all the better for underlining the supposed excitement of triple axels. More threadbare were attempts to present Stewart, Crawford, and Ayres as skilled skaters and the leading lady as an accomplished singer. In fact, there is only one brief scene of Stewart and

Crawford maneuvering over the ice at the beginning of the picture, and a fairly unimpressive demonstration of Ayres's talents in an additional sequence near the end. Studio publicists came even more a cropper with endeavors to promote Crawford as the latest incarnation of Nellie Melba. After a flood of press releases boasting that the actress sang six songs in the picture and was contemplating making her debut at the Met, the actual film showed four of the songs eliminated altogether and the other two dubbed by a professional singer. Crawford, never one to suffer quietly what she regarded as a slight, retaliated by accusing Jeanette MacDonald of having pressured Mayer into dropping her musical contributions because of fear of competition. MacDonald laughed, and the picture had another reason for failing at the box office.

About the only thing *Follies* gave Stewart was another opportunity for a screen monologue. Critics who wanted to delve that far into the tissue of the forgettable production decided that his lengthy disquisition on astronomy, and particularly on how stars are "cold" and "a million miles apart," was intended as some kind of thematic commentary on the picture's alleged plot.

It's a Wonderful World (MGM – 1939)

The commercial success of the *Thin Man* series starring Powell and Loy made MGM giddy. On a general level, the profitable reception accorded the pictures reinforced the view of Mayer and his top aides (decades before television movies and miniseries) that series were a shortcut to audience interest, that solidly established characters in one story had a foot up in drawing the public back to theaters as much for the reassurances of familiarity as out of curiosity; after all, the *Tarzan*, *Andy Hardy*, and *Dr. Kildare* series hadn't been doing too badly, either. More specifically, the Nick and Nora Charles stories revealed a vast number of fans of urbane, comic mysteries who sat on their dollars between *Thin Man* releases. In order to vacuum up that disposable income, the studio began producing other features that, to hear company publicists, Dashiell Hammett would have also inspired if he hadn't been so busy worrying about the Charles couple. Particularly transparent as Nick and Nora clones were Joel and Garda Sloan, who did their crime solving between exchanging witty repartee with customers at their rare book shop. The Sloan series became known around Culver City as the Fast Flicks because of the titles *Fast Company*, *Fast and Loose*, and *Fast and Furious*.

It fell to company accountants to refer to them eventually as the Slow Flicks because of a waning public interest from picture to picture.[7] Occasionally, as well, the studio plugged in individual sophisticated mysteries to bridge the gap between *Thin Man* features. One of these pictures was *It's a Wonderful World*, with Stewart and Claudette Colbert.

Wonderful World casts Stewart as a hard-bitten private detective named Guy Johnson who is assigned to keeping a much-married and philandering playboy (Ernest Truex) out of trouble. He is shown up as less than effective at his task when he discovers the playboy, reeling drunk and holding a smoking gun, with the dead body of one of the girls he has been seeing on the sly. Johnson suspects that the playboy is the victim of a frame, but before he can prove it, his client is arrested and he himself is taken away as an accomplice after the fact. The playboy is tried, found guilty, and sentenced to be executed, while Johnson draws a one-year term for complicity. On the way to prison, however, the detective escapes and runs into Edwina Corday, a poetess bound for a lecture. Because he needs her car, Johnson drags Edwina along on a chase that is as much toward the real murderers as away from the pursuing police. His situation only worsens when her disappearance adds a charge of kidnapping against him. Gradually, and despite a continual defensiveness by Johnson, Edwina comes to believe in his innocence and falls in love with him; more than that, she contributes some key logic to his thinking about the murder. The pair eventually end up at a Connecticut summer theater where, after some zany complications that have Johnson trying to pass himself off as an actor from Alabama and one wrong person after another getting bopped on the head, the killers are caught.

Written by Ben Hecht and Herman Mankiewicz, *Wonderful World* was directed by Woody Van Dyke who, working for the third time with Stewart after *Rose Marie* and *After the Thin Man*, more than lived up to his label as One-Take Woody by shooting the entire picture in twelve days. The haste was not without its benefits—especially in the hair-trigger exchanges between Stewart and Colbert at the beginning of their

---

[7] Unlike the stability offered by Powell and Loy, the *Fast* films went from Melvyn Douglas and Florence Rice, to Robert Montgomery and Rosalind Russell, to the markedly miscast Franchot Tone and Ann Sothern.

relationship. The often-perfunctory treatment of individual scenes in the interests of keeping everything moving along also obscured to some degree the basically embittered and misogynist character of Stewart's detective—arguably from the same litter as the killer in *After the Thin Man*. Aside from belting the poetess at one point, the private eye makes it clear that he's mainly interested in proving the playboy innocent so he can collect a promised fee of $100,000, delivers himself (frequently) of such lines as "dames are dead from the neck up," and otherwise does a lot of grumbling about his lack of good luck. From a professional standpoint, the detective was a departure for the actor, insofar as he had to maintain the hardness explicitly and for most of the picture. By the time he was called upon to reveal some softer sides, the haste in the production had begun to take its toll, fatally entangling the mystery and screwball comedy genres of the 1930s and reducing the concluding slapstick sequences at the summer theater to punchlines desperately in need of more appropriate setups. Not too many reviewers disagreed with the assessment of *The New York Times* that *It's a Wonderful World* was "almost too strenuous for relaxation."

With the completion of his nineteenth Hollywood film, Stewart didn't have to be told that he had come a very long way from playing the accordion for the Triangle Club. In less than four years, he had played— more often than not successfully—a doctor, lawyer, teacher, news-paperman,[8] mechanic, executive, hayseed, sailor, soldier, skater, farmer, football star, speed driver, detective, and murderer. Within those roles he had been asked to impersonate summer-stock actors, horsemen, students, Manhattan partygoers, fugitives, dreamers, idlers, liars, ingrates, gallant beaus, and prodigal sons. He had been killed, jailed, married, hospitalized, jilted, and lionized. He had sung, danced, loved, fallen out of love, had children, lost parents, gotten drunk, and gone blind. He had done all these things with most of the acclaimed actresses of the 1930s— Crawford, Sullavan, Harlow, Lombard, Rogers, Colbert, Arthur, and Powell. In the final analysis, about the only thing he seemed not to have done over his first score of screen roles was to portray the perfecter of his old backyard Whizzbang.

---

[8] In addition to playing reporters in several of his first features, he had the role of a typesetter—aspiring newsman in a ten-minute Chick Sale short, *Important News*, shot in February 1936. The MGM Miniature, as the shorts were called, was a common showcase for young studio talent.

INDUSTRY CIRCLES

AS OF THE MID-1930s, STEWART WASN'T IN DEMAND IN Hollywood only in the movies. His richly colored voice, for instance, made him a natural for the radio—especially for the abridged versions of popular motion pictures that were presented weekly by the networks under various programming names. For the studios, such shows as *The Lux Radio Theatre*, *The Silver Theatre*, *Good News*, and *The Screen Guild Theatre* were important cogs in the publicity machine; for the radio networks, they were relatively low-cost means of attracting famous names for audiences and sponsors.[9]

The most prestigious of the film industry-linked radio shows was the *Lux* program, hosted by producer-director Cecil B. DeMille. Stewart made his debut on that show on June 14, 1937, portraying Ann Harding's son in an appetite-whetting version of *Madame X*, an MGM production then circulating in theaters with Gladys George and John Beal. He also appeared in various roles on *The Silver Theatre*, a Sunday afternoon presentation on CBS that was hosted by actor Conrad Nagel and that sold itself as a springboard for new talent. But for MGM, neither *Lux*, with a DeMille who was too associated with Paramount, or *Silver*, with its mere half-hour length, represented a secure enough showcase for its productions, so the studio created *Good News* in partnership with NBC and Maxwell House coffee. The first time that a network and a major film studio combined forces in a joint pitch to a commercial sponsor, *Good News* went on the air in November 1937 with the announcement that every one of MGM's stars "except Garbo" would make an appearance eventually. With Stewart acting as host, there was little attempt to disguise the purely promotional aims of the broadcasts. Every show began and ended with the roar of the MGM lion. A segment entitled "Backstage at the Movies" purported to let listeners play flies on the wall at a studio story or casting conference; when this conceit was exhausted, there were more straightforward tours of the makeup, costuming, or special-effects departments. The heart of every show was the background

---

[9] While *Lux* would pay up to $5,000 for a star actor, for example, *The Screen Guild Theatre* was a charity show, with fees going to the Motion Picture Relief Fund to build a home for industry indigents.

to the purchase and filming of some recent property, with studio players then drafted into presenting a mini-version. The only name mentioned as often as MGM during the proceedings was Maxwell House. So much blatancy deprived *Good News* of the benefit of the doubt that a majority of radio critics accorded the other programs. *Newsweek*, in a typical comment, wondered "whether Metro-Goldwyn-Mayer was trying to sell Maxwell House, or if the coffeemakers were putting out Metro-Goldwyn-Mayer in airtight containers." The program limped along for several years under several format changes before NBC and Maxwell House cut ties with their third partner.

There would seem to be little doubt that Stewart's work as a radio actor sped up the familiarity of his voice to the American public; it also helped hasten the caricatured presentation of that voice. Speaking about his own days as a radio performer in the 1940s, Gregory Peck notes that "you had to exaggerate in a way that you wouldn't do vocally on the screen. The really good actors on radio were the ones who knew how to exaggerate, and Jimmy learned how to do that quite well." As Peck and other veterans of the microphones point out, the exaggeration required was not only inherent in a conceptually more emphatic reading of lines, but could also be the practical consequence of the medium's timing constraints. As Robert Stack explains it:

> You would have situations where the play threatened to be finished too soon, maybe four or five minutes before it was supposed to. To avoid that empty air, you would get a signal to draw out your lines ever so slowly. That makes for a lot of drawling. Or, vice versa, you were told that you were going too slowly, so the climax of what you were doing might be performed like the Road Runner ripping toward Hell. Either way, you got to be very conscious of your delivery pace. I think that's one of the reasons those old studio stars—the Stewarts and Grants and Hepburns, for example—are thought of today as much in terms of their voices as anything else. Working in radio could make you feel very naked with your voice in a way that television-trained performers have probably never felt.

Radio wasn't the only medium that MGM used to make sure that Stewart wasn't forgotten as soon as THE END flashed across the conclusion of his most recent picture. Especially after he had displayed his acting mettle with Sullavan in *Next Time We Love*, there was hardly a month that went by without fan magazines such as *Modern Screen*,

Silver Screen, and *Motion Picture* publishing a studio-inspired piece on him, and many months when several of them competed with similar features. Most of the articles gurgled over him as "Hollywood's most fascinating bachelor," assured readers that he was the authentic goods in small-town innocence, and practically copied from Mayer's private address book to list the famous actors and actresses reputed as craving to work with him. Once made available by the studio for such interviews, Stewart played along with appreciably more zest than some other contract players, and by so doing gained even more points with both the magazines and the MGM publicity department. At the same time, however, he also showed a touch of the evasive long-windedness that became so much of his title character in *Destry Rides Again.* Particularly when the fan magazines' questioners broached the subject of women, and specifically about how serious he was about the one he was then reported as seeing, he frequently rattled off some generalization about a bachelor's life, segueing from there into lengthy anecdotes about the trials of—and with—housekeepers who had been managing his bachelor quarters. Insofar as he repeatedly came off in the resultant profiles as an overgrown boy who made movies with the most glamorous actresses in the industry but who didn't pick up after himself, the tactic worked.

With Sunday newspaper feature editors, the studio took a more sinuous (and maybe more confessional) approach at times, posing the question of how somebody so classically *un*handsome could be in a position to claim the stardom that industry experts agreed was so imminent. The result was a burgeoning file in MGM's publicity offices of newspaper clippings from Seattle to Montpelier describing all of Stewart's physical limitations, but inevitably ending with the view that these just made him more of an original. Typical was a syndicated feature by gossip columnist Sheilah Graham that ran in papers from coast to coast, including the Cleveland *Plain Dealer,* on July 11, 1937, and that declared in part:

> Practically every feminine film star has asked this question: What is [James Stewart] like? Well, first of all, he is not like the traditional movie star. He is too thin . . . too tall . . . and not at all handsome. His brown hair is straight, straggly, grows low on his forehead and won't stay brushed. His nose is bumpy and rather wide. His steel gray eyes are attractive, but

nothing to rave about. His lower lip would be almost repulsive on another face. He is awkward and looks like an overgrown, gangling schoolboy. . . .

But:

> . . . There has never been a film star like him before. The nearest to approach him for figure and temperament is Gary Cooper. They are both too tall by screen acting standards. They are both real gentlemen and they are both unbelievably simple and modest . . . to Hollywood producers Stewart is more than a sweet dream. He is a gilt-edged gold mine.

Graham wasn't the only one to compare Stewart to Cooper; for a good part of 1936 and 1937, in fact, MGM publicists at a loss to portray their prospect otherwise, leaned heavily on the star of *A Farewell to Arms, The Lives of a Bengal Lancer,* and *Mr. Deeds Goes to Town.* It became such a commonplace that Cooper, who later regarded Stewart as his closest friend, liked referring to him as "the Gary Cooper of 1936." Stewart himself waved off such comparisons in his meetings with the press, more than once likening himself instead to the diminutive, fastidious Donald Meek in his acting aspirations, if not accomplishments. The publicity department had little alternative but to try to make the best of such image subversion, suggesting to reporters that the comparisons to Meek were indicative of Stewart's modesty. Judging by some of the actor's other remarks in the period, there was certainly nothing ironic, and even less mean-spirited, about his allusion to a supporting player who had been born to play the March Hare in *Alice in Wonderland* and who probably made his strongest screen impression as the nervous passenger in *Stagecoach.* Always uncomfortable with his own looks, or at least with the way he suspected others saw him, Stewart hinted more than once in the mid-1930s that he wouldn't have minded a career of small, supporting roles followed by directing. In one August 1936 interview, for instance, he said: "I hope and pray I will learn something about acting so I can play different characters. Then I want to direct—a screen player's life is short, at best. I love the mechanics of this business; when I'm not working on a picture, I'll hang around the cameramen, the directors, like Woody Van Dyke, Clarence Brown, Henry Hathaway—the men who have the real job that thrills me. Those who are able to create. I want to be a director—a big director who has everything!"[10]

More interested in setting down the foundations for a new MGM star, however, the studio made sure that Stewart was always one of the major attractions of Culver City tours by out-of-town newspapermen. Barney Oldfield, who would later cross paths with the actor as both an industry publicist and a fellow member of the United States Air Force, remembers visiting the studio in 1938 as part of a junket by reporters from the Midwest. Oldfield:

They always brought you into the commissary so you could be impressed by watching all these big names eating sandwiches and drinking coffee at separate tables. Maybe your typical company cafeteria except for the fact that it was Spencer Tracy slurping soup near you instead of someone from accounting taking a lunch break and that the soup was always chicken noodle since Mayer liked it and insisted it be on the menu every day. Stewart's job was to tablehop from group to group, asking us all about our hometowns and answering whatever we asked about how the studio operated. I thought he was awfully articulate, the right man for the job. The studios were very shrewd at that kind of thing. Later on, MGM used George Murphy in that role and Warners had Ronald Reagan—both of them very glib for impressing visitors. Jimmy, though, he'd never have that look in his eye that said he couldn't wait to get up from the table, get over to the next one, and get the whole thing over with. Very sincere, totally conversational. Maybe that's why he never went into politics.

Which was not to say that he hadn't been developing his own strategies for dealing with the way MGM had been using him. And no one was more crucial to him in this than Leland Hayward, his first powerhouse agent and also the first of several motion-picture industry figures who would help to insure the lucrativeness, as well as the longevity, of the actor's film career.

Almost as tall and thin as Stewart, but six years older, the flamboyant Hayward had risen through various jobs in Hollywood and New York (United Artists publicist, press agent, talent scout, inventor of stories for fan magazines) to become the industry's most prestigious talent agent by the second half of the 1930s. He had gotten into the representation business after selling a script by friend Ben Hecht to

---

[10] Although he directed on television in the 1950s, Stewart never called the shots on a motion-picture feature.

Irving Thalberg at MGM, soon afterward picking up Fred Astaire as his first actor client. At the height of his success, he would be collecting 10 percent from Greta Garbo, Edna Ferber, Ernest Hemingway, Ginger Rogers, Dashiell Hammett, Lillian Hellman, Judy Garland, Myrna Loy, Gene Kelly, Fredric March, Gregory Peck, Boris Karloff, Kurt Weill, Charles Laughton, Billy Wilder, Helen Hayes, Charles MacArthur, and innumerable others. He also had a client considerably closer to home—Margaret Sullavan, who had married him almost immediately after divorcing William Wyler in 1936. Not to be left out were Wyler himself, Sullavan's first husband, Fonda, and even Katharine Hepburn, who had been seeing Hayward right up to his marriage with Sullavan and who would always regard the new Mrs. Hayward as a poor substitute for herself on any level anyone cared to mention. When Stewart also signed on with Hayward, more than one circle was closed.

According to Billy Wilder, the secret of Hayward's success was that, together with his intelligence and encyclopedic knowledge of the film business and its most important executives, "the wives of the moguls were crazy about him." "I do not mean to imply that he had an affair with Mrs. Goldwyn," the director once told the agent's daughter Brooke, as reported in her bestselling book *Haywire*, "but Mrs. Goldwyn was just crazy about him. So was Mrs. Warner. All the wives were crazy about him and kept talking about him, because was a very attractive, handsome, dashing man." Another agent of some renown, Irving (Swifty) Lazar, called Hayward his "idol." "He had a gift for closing deals, he never had time to dicker," declared Lazar. "*He* should have been called Swifty instead of me." Fonda, who owed his first Hollywood contract to Hayward, asserted that his representative "could sell the proverbial snowball to an Eskimo."

Describing his own negotiating tactics on one occasion, Hayward told an interviewer:

> It works like this. You call the executives of five or six studios—Warners, Columbia, Paramount, MGM, RKO. You sound excited. Then you tell them they should check the box-office receipts and the reviews of some plays that have opened in New York, having made sure that you have arranged to handle the motion picture sales of these just an hour before. Then, having charged up the atmosphere, you leave the office before they

can call back. You have a relaxed lunch with a client at the Brown Derby, and then maybe do an hour or two's leisurely shopping. By the time you get back to the office there will be twenty hysterical telephone calls waiting from the studios—all of them bidding against one another. You then close the deal calmly at a record price.

Even allowing for his hyperbole (one of his most important professional assets), Hayward brought to Stewart's career management a canniness that the actor had not previously demonstrated in his dealings with show-business employers, whether at MGM or on Broadway. On the level of working relations, Stewart remained as cooperative and efficient as ever—accepting assignments on and off the screen while somehow still eluding even the rudimentary labor-management profile that Mayer had been able to compile on the actors, writers, and directors who had challenged or defended his take-it-or-leave-it rule during the union wars. While he might not have been everybody's friend, he wasn't anybody's sworn enemy, either. But Hayward's cynicism about the movie business was also a shield behind which Stewart could take a closer look at his satisfaction with the "pure luck" that had made him an MGM player. This was especially so when he was depressed (during the filming of *Seventh Heaven*) and exasperated (after the filming of *Of Human Hearts*)—when the studio's bad casting (in the first case) and good casting without an immediate follow-up (in the latter instance) worried him that he was going nowhere fast. Hayward's response was one part counsel and one part action. The counsel was that Stewart keep calm, that he realize that MGM was so uncertain about what to do with him that it could hardly raise objections to lending him out to other studios that had more ambitious (and instructive) plans for his talents; and in fact, it was immediately after *Of Human Hearts* that the actor made three of his next four pictures for RKO, Columbia, and United Artists. Hayward's action was a sweetheart deal that he worked out with MGM for Sullavan, which permitted her to work at the studio on a picture-by-picture basis, allowed her to return to the stage at any time other than in the middle of a shooting, and effectively ceded her approval rights over her leading men. Sullavan's second film under the contract was *The Shopworn Angel* with Stewart, her fourth was *The Shop Around the Corner* with Stewart, and her fifth was *The Mortal Storm* with Stewart. While Stewart had Hayward looking after his career interests, a relationship for which he would be even more grateful in the 1940s, he had others around to make sure that those interests didn't go too much to his head. At the beginning, at least, it appeared to be a dicey proposition where the actor's attitude was concerned. During his late 1935 visit to Stewart and Fonda in Brentwood, for instance, Josh Logan got into an argument with them over the worth of Max Reinhardt's recently released *A Midsummer Night's Dream*. As Logan related the story in his autobiography, he defended the film as a work of art, with Stewart, in particular, replying that "it stinks" and "it won't make a nickel." The future producer-director said that he was so astounded to hear Stewart talking like an industry distributor after only a few months in Hollywood that he got drunk at a party later in the evening, then blasted both his hosts for having "sold out."

Where consciences were concerned, however, Logan, like everybody else, was a distant second to Alex. As Stewart recalled, his father wasn't dissuaded from his ambivalent attitude toward the acting profession even after seeing the solid notices for the first two Sullavan films and *You Can't Take It With You*—on the one hand, making sure that all his Philadelphia Street customers were aware of his son's success, on the other hand, still questioning movie making as "fit work for a grown-up man." Then, when fan magazine and newspaper profiles began mentioning The Big Warehouse and visitors started dropping in for a close-up look at the father of a big Hollywood star, the senior Stewart decided that the time was ripe for more direct balloon puncturing, involving the regular handyman around the store. The younger Stewart told Floyd Miller of *McCall's*:

> Andy was the stove man. . . . He was old and spavined and never quite sober, but in good enough condition to keep the large potbellied stove going through the winter months. Tobacco juice stained his whiskers, and when his eyes were open, they were red-rimmed from long years of looking down the neck of a whisky bottle. . . . From time to time tourists would stop by the store and ask to meet Jimmy Stewart's father. Whenever this happened, Dad would point to old Andy in a chair beside the stove, asleep and drooling, surrounded by a cloud of cheap whisky. "There's Jimmy Stewart's father," Dad would say. "A very sad case." Confused and embarrassed, the tourists would flee.

As insinuating as such a tale is about Alex's own self-esteem vis-à-vis his son's growing celebrity, it spoke primarily to Stewart in the late 1930s as a reminder that his world was never going to be described fully by Beulah Bondi and Lionel Barrymore—or even by L. B. Mayer. The clearer his professional contours (and nobody worked harder in helping him define them than Hayward), the more distinct his working and nonworking activities—calculated separations in everything from party piano playing to learning how to fly, to the point of compartmentalization. As the Richmond *News Leader* observed in a July 12, 1938, feature story: "His whole life is guided by a system. All his earnings are carefully budgeted into savings, annuities, and living expenses. He lives plainly but well. His car is a plain, inexpensive model, and his clothes simple. . . ." It wasn't even so much that it was easier to take the boy out of Indiana than it was to take Indiana out of the boy. More to the point, Hollywood, at least the nonacting part of it, could be *incorporated* into Indiana.

Except for one area. And Alex had plenty to say about that, too.

LOVERS
AND OTHER LOVERS

STEWART'S REPUTATION AS THE MODEL HUSBAND AND family man over his forty-five years of marriage to Gloria Hatrick between 1949 and 1994 has left scant trace of his earlier notoriety as one of Hollywood's most ardent womanizers. In fact, it has become almost a mandatory step in acceding to the image of folksy Jimmy Stewart to wink at his earlier sexual adventures, to be satisfied with the assumption that, whatever they consisted of exactly, they were healthy, moderate, and American. This attitude has held sway over the last few decades despite numerous hints from the actor himself that he has never minded all that much being called a Don Giovanni, being confused with a Casanova, or being accused of being a Lothario. Right up to Fonda's death in August 1982, he could still indulge in nostalgic spitting matches with his onetime roommate about who had had the thicker black book in Brentwood. In the midst of some of his most heated diatribes before interviewers about violence and sensationalism having overtaken the film industry since the fall of the traditional studios, he could crack that he wasn't all that much against nudity on the screen.

Stewart's little black book in the 1930s had names written on the alphabetical pages and others consigned to the back. Among the latter were the numerous starlets that MGM paired with the actor for premieres, formal dinners, promotional tours, and other photo opportunities. These "dates" paid off for the studio twice over: in prompting fan magazines and photojournalists to give coverage to couples who might not have aroused much interest singly and in reinforcing the aura of a young player whose eclectic romantic appetites had been unleashed on Hollywood (and, soon, on a neighborhood theater screen near you). Unless there was a special publicity anchor, such as the joint appearance of a couple in a picture about to be released, the official dates were a constant mix-and-match of contract players, thus opening up even more ancillary story possibilities along the lines of How Come We Saw Him with Her at Ciro's Last Night? What Led the Other Her to Ditch Him After They Attended Last Week's Premiere Together?

Even more fertile source of gossip were the romances that allegedly took place between the leads in a movie in production. Aside from Sullavan, Stewart was linked in this category with everybody from Virginia Bruce from *The Murder Man* and *Born to Dance* and Wendy Barrie from *Speed*, to Eleanor Powell from *Born to Dance* and Rose Stradner from *The Last Gangster*. However exaggerated some of these ties might have been, they maintained some credibility with the enigmatic and evasive comments of the principals themselves; a favorite Stewart rejoinder when Bruce or Powell came up, for example, was to note that they were "great dancers and I love to dance." Even thirty years later, the actor and his wife, Gloria, made it a regular part of an interview routine to joke that he had "always fallen in love" with his costars before she had come along. Burgess Meredith doesn't think that's too far off. "Nobody *always* does anything," says Meredith, "but it was my experience that he had an enormous number of what gentility might call 'light love affairs.'" In addition to his film costars, and such radio drama partners as Rosalind Russell, those most mentioned in this context by one source or another over the years have been Loretta Young, Ilona Massey, Anita Colby, Kay Aldrich, and Phyllis Brooks. Shirley Ross, whose most conspicuous claim to fame was in introducing the song "Thanks for the Memory" in a duet with Bob Hope in *The Big Broadcast of 1938*, also dated Stewart after an earlier involvement with Fonda—an attraction helped by her background as a concert pianist.

But if for different reasons, Stewart's most notable attachments in the 1930s were with five women who had considerably more status in the Hollywood community for their screen accomplishments. One—Norma Shearer—worked so hard at reducing him to a Boy Toy that he was stunned into realizing that his shambling, ingratiating tactics as a would-be lover sometimes exacted a heavy social price. The second—Ginger Rogers—took on a role as his favorite port in a storm—a pal with whom he would make sure to spend his final hours years later before being inducted into the military. The third—Marlene Dietrich—was one of the storms for which he needed a port; she overwhelmed him during the shooting of *Destry Rides Again*, gave him a finishing course in film acting, and broke up with him on one of the ugliest notes of his life. The fourth—Olivia de Havilland—was the only one who received a proposal of marriage from him, at least before World War II. And the fifth—Sullavan—was, according to some on the scene at the time, the major reason for all his other gallivanting.

Although they had crossed paths at MGM before, Stewart had never really talked to Norma Shearer until they met at a costume party some months after the death of her husband, Irving Thalberg, in December 1936. Because of her marriage and a resulting freedom to treat even Mayer somewhat cavalierly, Shearer had been regarded around Culver City for some time as second only to Greta Garbo in majestic aloofness; since the death of Thalberg, she had added a reputation as The Merry Widow for her eagerness to make up for lost time with contract players. After fortifying himself with a few drinks at the costume party, Stewart accosted the actress, announcing for all to hear that she was the most beautiful woman he had ever seen. According to Josh Logan, who was present at the party, "the remark hit her like a thunderbolt, which was more than he reckoned on." What followed was a six-week affair in which, Logan asserted, "she took royal possession of him."

The problem was, however, that Shearer, eight years Stewart's senior, no longer protected by Thalberg, and growingly anxious about her middle-aged place in MGM's constellation of stars, wanted her possession to be as public as it was private. "Jimmy gave Norma what she wanted: proof that she was still young, beautiful, and desirable," said Mickey Rooney, who had his own affair with the actress a couple of years later, "but that wasn't enough for her. She also wanted Jimmy to play a more public role, as her beau." When that entailed arriving for premieres or simply at restaurants in Shearer's yellow limousine, Stewart took to slumping down in the back seat so he wouldn't be recognized. Douglas Fairbanks, Jr., remembers that tactic ending only one night at an Ice Follies opening. "We were a foursome—Norma and Jimmy, Merle Oberon and myself. Norma and Jimmy had clearly had words about the way he had been slinking back whenever a photographer came near. I don't know what she said to him, but, at least that night he acted a lot less bashful when we were being photographed. Norma was not someone you trifled with."

But if Stewart lost the battle of the limousine and the photographers, he won the duel of the cigarettes. As Logan related it in his auto-biography: "As proof of her 'ownership' she gave him a gold cigarette case sprinkled with diamonds. That meant that whenever she asked for a cigarette in front of others, the gift would advertise the giver. Jimmy didn't want any sly looks. He would fumble in every pocket until he came up with a crumpled pack of Lucky Strikes. It was his badge as a free man."

The affair ended without tears on either side, although Shearer, whose career started going downhill after she declined to appear in *Gone With the Wind*, subsequently always named Stewart as the one actor she regretted never having had as a screen costar. As far as the actor himself was concerned, he once confided to Meredith that Shearer "could scare the wits out of you" and stood as a reminder to him that "some old gambits could get you into trouble." Logan profited from the relationship as much as anybody: In the 1950s, he used the Stewart-Shearer affair as the basis for his Broadway musical *Stars in Your Eyes*, which featured Ethel Merman as a movie queen who owned a studio and fell in love with a young director.

If Stewart felt fatally maneuvered by Shearer, he had already had experience with another kind of manipulation that had turned out more benignly. In moving in with Fonda upon arriving in California, he became, unwittingly, fodder for that part of the movie rumor mill that churned up homosexual affairs to keep itself palpitating. The more gossip columnists and fan magazines, in particular, had to confront their lack of nerve in writing explicitly about gays, in fear that an enraged studio would cut off their access to big names, the broader the stain from their off-the-record "scoops" or from the whispered "inside information" of

One of the earliest
photographs of Stewart.
(Below) Stewart as a
young boy with (left
to right) his mother
Bessie, sister Mary,
father Alexander,
and sister Virginia.

Stewart's slight physique didn't prevent him from playing football at Mercersburg Academy.

The actor shown here with his grandfather (third from the left), father (farthest in rear), and several employees from the hardware store during his college days.

(Above) Stewart enjoyed his "high voltage" scenes with sexy Jean Harlow in the 1936 production of Wife vs. Secretary, his fourth feature film. (Below) Aside from scripts, Stewart's greatest reading interest throughout his life was aviation magazines, as shown here on the set of The Last Gangster (1937).

(Above) In the 1938 production of Of Human Hearts, Stewart was cast as Beulah Bondi's son for the first of several times both in big-screen features and on television.

(Right) No one was more responsible for launching Stewart's success in Hollywood than Margaret Sullavan, shown here with the actor in The Shopworn Angel (1938). It was the second of four films the pair made together.

(Below) The actor's droll performance with Marlene Dietrich in Destry Rides Again (1939) disguised a much more tormented relationship with the German star offscreen.

Actress Margaret Sullavan and her third husband, agent Leland Hayward, circa 1940.

(Left) Although Stewart and Fonda liked to clown around with their instruments, as seen here, they also used their musicianship to raise money for the British war effort, and as an excuse for costarring in the popular postwar film On Our Merry Way.

(Below) The actor and Olivia de Havilland, resting after some heavy picnicking.

(Right) Director Frank Capra dubbed Stewart his favorite leading man. The two would make three films together.

(Below) Mr. Smith Goes to Washington (1939) offered Stewart his first major showcase for highly charged emotional performances. Here, under the watch of Claude Rains, he takes in the telegrams that, by Jefferson Smith's definition, appeared to establish that he was more crazy than right.

(Above) Stewart, shown
here with Ruth Hussey,
Cary Grant, and Katharine
Hepburn, shines onscreen
in The Philadelphia Story.

(Left) Ginger Rogers was
probably Stewart's closest
"gal pal" in Hollywood
for many years. Here, the
actors celebrate after winning
Oscars in 1941— she for
Kitty Foyle, he for The
Philadelphia Story.

*(Left) A dashing officer in military uniform.
(Above) Captain Stewart and First Lieutenant
Lloyd Sharrard hunker down before other officers
on the crew of Tenovus, in Marrakech en route
to Tibenham, England. Back row, left to right:
2nd Lt. Jim Kidder, 2nd Lt. Charles Wolfe,
1st Lt. Rowland Swearngin, 2nd Lt. Donald
Daniel. (Below) Stewart going over bombing
mission details with men under his command
at the 453rd Bombardment Group at Old
Buckingham, England.*

individual writers and editors. If it seeped into print at all, it was usually in the form of a passing, snide query about an actor who hadn't been seen in public lately with an actress or about an actress who had listed marriage and motherhood as being 98th and 99th among her priorities. The game wasn't completely unwelcome in the offices of the Mayers, Cohns, and Zanucks, since they could always use the threat of more specific revelations as a negotiating factor in their dealings with rebellious players. Still, especially when it concerned young actors being peddled as the latest paradigm of heterosexual romance, even the vaguest insinuation could bring on a case of business hives. Among those who triggered rashes in the mid-1930s, and with some regularity, were Cary Grant, Randolph Scott, Robert Taylor, and Katharine Hepburn.

Given the press and studio mentalities involved, it was probably inevitable that Fonda and Stewart also would be included in the rumors, not least because of what seemed to be common, braked-down person-alities in public. For many who claimed to be in the know, they were simply younger and still less famous versions of the housemates Grant and Scott. Even Orson Welles once acknowledged that he had bought into the rumors. "I thought these two guys were either having the hottest affair in Hollywood," Welles declared, "or were the two straightest human beings I ever met in my life. I came to the conclusion that they were the two straightest human beings I'd ever met in my life."

Another who had come to that conclusion was Lela Rogers, who was Ginger's mother and known to many as The Stage Mother from Hell. A member of the RKO publicity department at the time, she saw Stewart and Fonda as the perfect vehicles not only for gaining more media exposure for potential studio star Lucille Ball, but also for taking her daughter's mind off estranged husband Lew Ayres, whom the older Rogers had never particularly liked anyway. Oddly enough, the foursome hit it off, if at the price of more stories about the miserliness and quaint romantic notions of the actors from Indiana and Omaha. As Ginger Rogers told it in her autobiography:

> The boys took us dancing at posh places like the Cocoanut Grove and the Trocadero, but they were too cheap to stay there for dinner. Instead, we always ended up for dinner at a little hole-in-the-wall called Barney's Beanery on Santa Monica Boulevard. One night, after a hearty meal at Barney's, the boys took us back to their apartment. Everything appeared

very romantic, as the lights were turned down low and soft music played in the background. Before Lucy and I knew what had happened, we were danced into the kitchen to wash a week's stack of dirty dishes. So much for romance; maid duty was uppermost in their minds.

Stewart and Fonda have offered more exculpating versions of how the women ended up in the kitchen with the dirty dishes. But in his told-to biography with Howard Teichmann, Fonda also added the particular of having reacted with a disgusted "Yuk!" to the reappearance of Ball after she had spent a long time in the bathroom reapplying her makeup. That was enough for the actress to take off and for him to lament that if he had kept his mouth shut at seeing her, "they might have named that studio Henrylu not Desilu." Stewart and Rogers, on the other hand, continued to see one another on and off for years, both evenings on crowded Hollywood dance floors and Sunday mornings and afternoons at her Malibu home. Although Stewart had little to say about the relationship then or in the future, aside from stressing their mutual passion for dancing, Rogers indicated that it didn't maintain as much fervor as she had hoped initially. Asked point-blank by Sheilah Graham on one occasion whether she was in love with the actor, for instance, she communicated more than one sigh with her response of, "If I'm not, I ought to be. He's the nicest man in Hollywood."

By the time he had completed shooting *Vivacious Lady* with Rogers in 1938, the prattle about Stewart's living arrangements with Fonda had long since been replaced by magazine titles about the "Blade of Brentwood." Within that premise the industry press and satellite fanzines, which were as subject to the moralistic winds of the Hays Code as the pictures turned out by the studios, looked upon Stewart's rovings far more benevolently than they did enduring liaisons between other unmarried couples in the Hollywood community. A 1938 article in *Photoplay*, for example, ripped into such obvious partners as Clark Gable and Carole Lombard, Robert Taylor and Barbara Stanwyck, George Raft and Virginia Pine, and Charles Chaplin and Paulette Goddard for living in adjoining houses while always spending their nights out together. "For nobody, not even Hollywood's miracle men, has ever improved on the good old-fashioned, satisfying institution of holy matrimony," the monthly scolded. "And until something better comes along, the best way to hunt happiness when you're in love in Hollywood or anywhere else is with a preacher, a marriage license, and a bagful of rice."[11] By showing little long-term interest in any of the women he dated, Stewart, by contrast, usually came in only for winks for being "the Prince Charming of the local socialites."

Not that he escaped censure altogether. As early as July 1936, *Silver Screen* painted the picture of a footloose young man who maybe just didn't understand how to act with a woman, saw Hollywood as nothing more than a California extension of Indiana, Pennsylvania, and might have been terminally solipsistic in the bargain. "If you happen to be the type who loves the haphazard, then you must meet James Stewart," the magazine advised its largely young female readership. "There's a mad young man for you. You can be quite sure that Jimmy won't 'dress' unless you insist upon it, that he'll arrive in an open roadster which will make short work of your wave, and he'll never remember the flowers." As well, and toward the end of the decade in particular, there was seldom a profile that didn't set off from, or head toward, the question of the actor's vision of an "ideal wife," the implication being that he too had to consider himself as being on the clock for making a domesticating choice. When Stewart generally parried such questions with talk about the "excitement of show business" consuming all his time or with backhanded compliments to the actresses he was seeing for "understanding as fellow professionals that I might be told at the last minute that I have to work until midnight," the would-be marriage brokers fell back on anonymous quotes from women asserting that he didn't have a clue about what an ideal woman might be and that was why he was still searching. In fact, whether this was the conclusion of an actual interviewee or of the writer, it was only half-right: As friends such as Johnny Swope and Burgess Meredith had already gleaned, Stewart might not have known at the end of the 1930s who his ideal wife was, but he had certainly made up his mind who she wasn't—a Hollywood actress.

Marlene Dietrich didn't care about altars. What she initially cared about in agreeing to do *Destry Rides Again* with Stewart at the end of 1939 were a revived screen career after a couple of years of box-office flops and the $75,000 fee that would allow her to pay off some of the bills that had accumulated during her slide. According to producer Joe

---

[11] Within a short time after publication of the *Photoplay* article and others like it, all the couples but Raft and Pine did get married.

Pasternak, however, she developed another interest as soon as she saw her costar on the set the first time. "She took one look at Jimmy Stewart and began to rub her hands," Pasternak declared. "She wanted him at once." The producer, who had insisted on hiring Dietrich for an atypical role as a western saloon singer at least partly because he counted on her showing her gratitude in his own bedroom, said it was Flash Gordon who triggered the offscreen affair between the *Destry* stars: "He was just a nice, simple guy who loved Flash Gordon comics. That was all he seemed to read on the set. . . . When he was in his dressing room, she locked the door and wouldn't let him out. But she promised that she would come back with a surprise. The surprise was a doll—a life-sized doll of Flash Gordon. She had persuaded the art department to come in over the weekend and make it up for him. It was correct in every detail."

To judge from Dietrich's autobiography, nothing more serious ever developed between the actors. About her only acknowledgment of him in *Marlene Dietrich: My Life* is the sardonic: "He belonged to the 'whatever happened to the other shoe' period. Jimmy Stewart was the original inventor of this style. Even when he made a visible effort to play a love scene, he always gave the impression he was wearing only one shoe and looking for the other one while he slowly droned his lines. One day I told him about these ruminations of mine and he answered: 'How's that?' He performed this way throughout his life and became very rich and very famous. Now he no longer has to look for his other shoe."

Stewart has been only slightly more forthcoming, telling one interviewer that he was taken off guard by what he termed Dietrich's "adult concept of life" and admitting to another, decades after the fact, that "I liked taking Marlene out to dinner and to dance back in the days of *Destry* . . . and so we dated quite a few times, which was fairly romantic." For the most part, mention of Dietrich has elicited his praise for how she taught him to address actors on camera in one eye, as the most effective means of conveying an intimate exchange and avoiding a magnified look of splayed attention:

> She knew the business inside out. There is one thing that she said to me that I will never forget. It's really so simple, and you see it all the time, but it's so distracting when you're acting on camera. . . . She said, "Now if you've got an over-the-shoulder shot, and you're talking to the person, never try to look him or her in both eyes, because you really can't do that.

You've got to look at the man or the woman in one eye or the other, without switching your focus back and forth between eyes. Trying to look into both eyes simultaneously is impossible, and it's not only distracting, it also destroys the effect of concentration." She was right, of course. . . . It was excellent advice, and I've used it ever since.

But Dietrich's "other shoe" mockeries and Stewart's gratitude for picking up another camera trick notwithstanding, their relationship involved a lot more torment than lunch-break dalliances during the shooting of *Destry Rides Again* would have allowed and lasted for many months after the completion of the picture. Although this was never a secret to associates of the actors or to anyone connected to *Destry*, and has in fact been Hollywood boilerplate for more than a half-century, the story gained new life in 1995 with the publication of a number of extracts from the diaries of German novelist Erich Maria Remarque.

Remarque was anything but a neutral observer; a Dietrich lover for some time, he had pursued her to the Universal set where *Destry* was being shot so he could keep an eye on her and Stewart. When director George Marshall decided that he was becoming a distraction and asked Dietrich to keep him away, she shrugged that it was no business of hers, leaving the clear impression that she didn't mind in the least having the author of *All Quiet on the Western Front* notice that not everything was quiet on her front. Marshall finally had enough when Remarque started pestering him with suggestions for rewriting scenes in the picture, and had Pasternak bar him. This did little for Remarque's jealousy, especially after he saw that Dietrich had assembled flowers from Stewart and photographs of the actor into "a kind of shrine" in her apartment. The actress's obsession, according to the writer, ultimately caused her to hire private detectives to watch Stewart's house and that of perceived rival Olivia de Havilland.

The published diary extracts also include in details gratuitous to everyone but Remarque corroboration of the long-bruited Hollywood story that Dietrich once became pregnant by Stewart and underwent an abortion at his insistence. The actress is cited as having explained to the novelist:

She'd slept with him from day one. It was a dream: It had been magical. For him, too. Suddenly, she was able to speak about it. It had all been poetic and romantic, hour by hour. That had held her bound to him, making her happy and unhappy. She never knew from one week to the next. He had never talked about love, but told her he was not in love, couldn't afford it. She had broken down because he didn't want to be loved. It had bothered him to be responsible for anybody. She had become pregnant by him the first time they'd slept together. Didn't want to abort the child, in order to continue sleeping with him. But she gave in to his wishes.

If de Havilland entered the picture originally as a buffer against Dietrich, she didn't stay in that role too long. Well into the spring of 1941, she was Stewart's regular companion at night spots in both Hollywood and New York. Under his prodding, she also took up flying.[12] It didn't take long for the sighting of the couple to stir up speculation that they were headed for marriage; through a good part of 1940, many gossip columnists and magazine writers took that outcome for granted. In May of that year, for instance, *Motion Picture* entitled an article "What Kind of a Husband Will Jimmy Stewart Be?" going on to claim sources in de Havilland's "immediate family" for a "scoop that . . . Livvy and Jimmy *are* serious, *are* in love, and *will* be married."

Stewart wasn't nearly so sure. In many respects, de Havilland was the direct opposite of Dietrich—a demure, somewhat fragile front for a deep toughness. Following her success in *Gone With the Wind*, however, the toughness wasn't always so subterranean, being interpreted by an increasing number of professional associates as simple imperiousness. Although not normally a reliable witness when it comes to her long-estranged sister, Joan Fontaine reflected the attitude of many in Hollywood toward de Havilland in a testy account of the birthday dinner that she and her husband Brian Aherne prepared in 1941. As Fontaine tells it: "I invited her and her current escort Jimmy Stewart to dinner, planning a menu with her favorite dishes, even baking the cake myself. Two hours after the time they were asked for, Olivia and Jimmy rang our doorbell. When I remonstrated that the dinner was hardly palatable any longer, Olivia answered, 'It's my birthday. I can arrive whenever I like.' Brian and I did not make a habit of inviting her to our dinner parties after that."

---

[12] Although not as his pupil, as has been frequently written.

Stewart gave little evidence of being bothered by such incidents, even after de Havilland had fired their mutual agent Leland Hayward for not being aggressive enough about getting her meatier roles at Warner Brothers. He also kept his own counsel in the face of her willingness to play along with interviewers who assumed that he was her husband-in-waiting. By the actress's own account, in fact, Stewart finally did get around to proposing marriage, and it fell to her to say no. "He was great fun to be with, a bit like a grownup Huck Finn," she told one reporter years afterward. "I think his offer of marriage was just a frivolous thing on his part. Jimmy wasn't ready for a wife. I guess he still had a few more wild oats to sow."

Burgess Meredith, for one, thinks that assertion gives both principals the best of it. "She wasn't nearly as casual about him as she sometimes wants herself to sound," says Meredith, who shared living quarters with Stewart around the time of the de Havilland breakup. "She always seemed to like him a lot more than he appeared to like her. Or maybe *like* isn't the right word. The main thing about Jimmy's relations with women, including Olivia, was that it was very, very difficult to light him up. They were there or they weren't there. He could always show them a good time, but it was never the center of his universe to do so."

For some who knew him in the late 1930s, the center of Stewart's universe was 12928 Evanston Street in Brentwood, the colonial home where Margaret Sullavan had taken up residence with her third husband Hayward. The house was only a block away from where Stewart and Johnny Swope maintained bachelor quarters and even closer to a place where Fonda had moved with his second wife, Frances Seymour. Especially when Hayward was out of town, Sullavan encouraged her neighbors to drop in to help her create something of a salon setting; the newly married Fondas weren't nearly as enthusiastic about the standing invitation as were Stewart, Swope, and, when they were in California, Logan and McCormick. Stewart's regular presence in the Hayward house inevitably restoked the rumors of his romantic designs on Sullavan, especially after the release of *The Shopworn Angel* had demonstrated that the chemistry between the players in *Next Time We Love* had been no fluke. Walter Pidgeon, the apex of the triangle in *The Shopworn Angel*, could still laugh about the heat on the set of that picture decades later. As he told Sullavan biographer Lawrence Quirk: "I really felt like the odd-man-out in that one. It was really all Jimmy and Maggie. . . . It was so obvious he was in love with her. He came absolutely alive in his scenes with her, playing with a conviction and a sincerity I never knew him to summon away from her."

For Pidgeon, it was all "front" that Stewart and Sullavan had "purely platonic affection" for each other. While subscribing to the majority view that his costars had never actually found themselves in one another's arms away from a movie set, the veteran actor also dismissed the suggestion that Stewart was generating the sparks for both ends of the couple. "I thought she was more emotionally involved [with him] than she consciously was aware she was," Pidgeon said. "It was far more on Jimmy's side than hers, but . . . Maggie was in love with love, and she loved Jimmy's being in love with her. It enhanced her feelings about herself as a woman, and gave her a feeling of—well, power is the best word I can come up with."

Stewart friend Bill Grady came to a similar conclusion. Grady, who never particularly warmed to the actress despite being dragged along by Stewart several times to her weekend gatherings, contended that it "embarrassed Jimmy to have so many people whispering that he was carrying the eternal torch for Maggie. And certainly she encouraged it. . . . It salved her vanity, for when it came to men, she was a very vain woman."

She was also a very blunt one, and didn't bother sugarcoating potentially bruising opinions even for Stewart. When the actor tried to sway Sullavan to join him at MGM by mentioning that Grady would be a good Culver City ally for her in dealings with Mayer, she told him that, friend or not, a casting director was a casting director and she had more clout than that in both her husband and in her own little fist. Whether the topic was the motion-picture business or sex, she also seemed to savor the role of the kettle that called the pot black. Protected by Hayward's shrewd negotiating on her behalf, she regularly tore down actors who didn't have the nerve to take on their bosses personally over contracts and picture assignments. She always defended gays, pointing out sardonically that her own promiscuity didn't leave her much room for criticizing the sexual tastes of others. The out-of-wedlock birth of her first daughter, Brooke, inspired denunciations of those who didn't use contraceptives. Whether or not she was the most intelligent woman Stewart was exposed to in the Hollywood of the 1930s, as some have asserted, she was certainly the most resolute, Norma Shearer included.

The whispers about Stewart and Sullavan weren't blanketed even by the birth of her two daughters—Brooke and then Bridget—with Hayward in the late 1930s.[13] But after awhile, Stewart was drawn to 12928 Evanston Street at least as much by a more viable passion—flying. It was, in fact, Hayward, himself a pilot, who talked the actor into taking aviation lessons and getting a little closer to those fantasies once entertained in Indiana and then elaborated upon with Fonda at the Madison Square Hotel. Making this easier was that Sullavan also had a pilot's license and was as ready to talk about altimeters and trim controls as the men were.

Nevertheless, there were many, including Grady and Louis B. Mayer's right-hand man, Eddie Mannix, who went to their graves certain that the single greatest impetus for Stewart's womanizing in Hollywood was his need to forget about Sullavan. The same talk was heard ten years later when, at the age of forty-one, the actor announced his marriage to Gloria Hatrick; the only reason he hadn't married sooner, it was said, was some lingering hope that he might still find a way to be with Sullavan other than as a costar and frequent visitor to her home. Other indications are, however, that by the time he walked down the aisle, Stewart had long since made another critical compartmentalization between his feelings for Sullavan and the practical means at his disposal for expressing them. On the one hand, his fervor for her as an actress—*and as somebody he thought made him a better actor*—never lost heat. As late as the 1970s, many years after Sullavan's suicide, when he was playing country lawyer Billy Jim Hawkins on television, he went to producer David Karp and fellow series cast member Mayf Nutter on separate occasions and about different roles to observe wistfully that "Maggie Sullavan would've been perfect" for a character in the script being shot. During the shooting of the cable-TV movie *Right of Way* in 1983, he was heard exuding a similar sigh about the daughter character being played by Melinda Dillon. In a talk with Brooke Hayward when she was preparing her book *Haywire*, he also made it clear that working with Sullavan had been a galvanizing experience:

---

[13] Some of this was due to the fact that their two most noteworthy teamings on the screen—*The Shop Around the Corner* and *The Mortal Storm*—were still ahead of them.

Humor. She had great humor. It wasn't mechanical with her. It was a part of her. This was one of the things that made her great. When you'd play a scene with her, you were never quite sure, although she was always letter perfect in her lines, what was going to happen. She had you just a little bit off guard, and also the director. I've always called what she did planned improvisation—she could do just moments that would hit you, maybe a look or a line or two, but they'd hit like flashes or earthquakes; everbody'd sort of feel it at the same time. It's a very rare thing.

But away from the camera was something else—even with Sullavan. He was no longer a Broadway bit player dependent on his accordion for work and grateful for her encouragement that he would find more significant work. Like Sam Levene and the rest of the *Yellow Jack* cast he had once taken in from the wings of the Martin Beck Theatre, he too had found an occupation that "really meant something." As Remarque cited Dietrich as having told him, Stewart could not "afford" love in his private life. As Rogers had come to understand, "nice" was about as nice as things were going to get. As de Havilland had concluded, even a marriage offer was something "frivolous" out of his mouth. As Meredith had sensed, there was nothing vital to him in his progress through the women he encountered. But even with his biggest roles yet to come, he could sculpt a space for himself with the more significant work that he already had done and that Sullavan had predicted. In that, he had the security of knowing that he hadn't disappointed her, and she had the satisfaction of knowing that she had called another one right. Some couples stayed married for decades with less compatibility going for them.

But the exclusion of Sullavan from everything except professional incitements was hardly a one-sided coin. It made it all that much easier, as well, to begin telling interviewers that, contrary to some opinion, he *did* have an idea about the kind of woman that he wanted to marry; specifically, she was someone "who understands that married couples have to adapt their actions and thoughts to each other," "who [doesn't] want to hear all the latest talk about an actor or actress on the set," and, especially, "who'll make a home like my mother made for my father." What was no longer listed as a qualification was one of those fellow professionals who understood that actors could be put on call at the last minute and might have to work until midnight; on the contrary, as

Stewart's remarks with interviewers made increasingly clear, for the position of what he called "the right woman" no actresses needed to apply. This attitude hardly came as a surprise to housemates such as Meredith and Swope, who had been observing the comings and goings of both starlets and accomplished actresses not only as emotional nonevents in themselves, but also as part of a broader pattern of denying to Hollywood as a whole any right to a serious involvement beyond that required by a script. "Jimmy never basically trusted anybody in the film industry," Swope, who married actress Dorothy McGuire, told a reporter in 1970. "He never found anyone before Gloria who could separate him from his film image."

Well, maybe one other person, at least.

It didn't take Stewart long to realize that moving to California didn't mean less vigilance from Philadelphia Street. When a wire-service photographer shot a picture of Stewart and Fonda having a drink to toast their latest reunion as housemates in Brentwood, Alex immediately got off a wire to remind his son that "your mother's side of the family is Irish and the Irish have never been able to hold their liquor." The nagging was even more questionably humorous during Alex's frequent visits to Brentwood before the war. When he discovered on one occasion that Stewart had not been going to one of the local Presbyterian churches, he took it upon himself to round up some ministers, bring them over to Evanston Street, and announce that "they need your help." An even more constant lament to Swope, Logan, Fonda, and anybody else who would listen—was the need to "find a mate" for his son.

Stewart suffered most of these digs in silence, at least in the presence of Alex. But on the marriage question especially, he didn't disagree with some of his father's premises. Talking about himself when he was already more than thirty years old, he told Floyd Miller of *McCall's*:

Dad made trips to Hollywood, not because he liked the place, but because his son lived there and I needed a father's help. His pressing concern was that I get married; he wanted me to know the fun of fatherhood. I was dating a variety of starlets, who seemed to me to be beautiful, talented girls. Dad never spoke against them, but he sure walked beside me to nudge me away from them. His ideal was his own wife, and I guess she was really my ideal, too.

JEFFERSONISM

WHEN IT CAME TO PHILOSOPHER-PRESIDENTS, ABRAHAM Lincoln wasn't the safest oracle to be approached by Hollywood in the latter part of the 1930s; for all his self-evident truths given a screen platform in the period, Lincoln wasn't quite enough above the fray as the unimpeachable symbol of democratic continuity. Most obviously, the sixteenth president remained the foundation stone for the Republican Party in a nation that had already elected Democrat Franklin Delano Roosevelt to the White House twice. As well, it was difficult to disassociate Lincoln from war at a time when any politician who knew what was good for him was vowing that the United States would never get involved in the European hostilities unleashed by Germany and Italy. Commanders-in-chief who had been assassinated also lacked something when it came to reassuring figures. Much safer was Thomas Jefferson. As a contemplative, scientist, architect, and patron of the arts, Jefferson was America's Renaissance Man. Beyond that, less was known about him than about Lincoln by the public, so more could be claimed for him without fear of contradiction from anybody but academic specialists. Most importantly, Jefferson went back to the beginning—back through Lincoln, all the way back to what historian Richard Hofstadter has called "the agrarian myth . . . a kind of homage that Americans have paid to the fancied innocence of their origins." Put another way, Jefferson stood for every patriotic confidence that no longer existed—and might never have existed.

In 1939, in back-to-back pictures, Stewart portrayed characters supposedly inspired by the values of Thomas Jefferson. They were easily the two biggest films of his career up to that point.

Mr. Smith Goes to Washington (Columbia – 1939)

With the possible exception of *Confessions of a Nazi Spy*, no Hollywood film caused more political consternation in the immediate prewar period than *Mr. Smith Goes to Washington*. But whereas the Edward G. Robinson melodrama about fifth columnists stirred up Berlin and Rome, the Frank Capra saga created a stink in Washington and in selected U.S. embassies abroad. The controversy was a godsend. Politically, it ensured for the Columbia feature an ideological significance that is hard to discern on the screen; cinematically, Stewart's dominating performance as the quintessential idealist covered over both erratic direction from Capra and some wildly inconsistent playing by other cast members.[14]

As Jefferson Smith, the head of a chain of boys clubs in a midwestern state, Stewart is maneuvered into filling out the term of a deceased U.S. senator. Doing the maneuvering are a local party boss (Edward Arnold), the governor of the state (Guy Kibbee), and the state's senior senator (Claude Rains), who has always been a hero to the drafted congressman. The three are actually counting on Smith's naiveté for rubber-stamping their plans for an irrigation project that will make them rich. When he realizes that he has been manipulated by the party boss, Smith makes another mistake in still trusting the senior senator, going along with the idea of overcoming his disillusionment and sponsoring a bill for his pet project, a national boys camp. Again, he wakes up too late to a deception—that the camp legislation is merely the latest front for the irrigation bill corruption; before he can carry through on vows to expose the crooks, they nimbly pass the blame on to him, triggering a Senate expulsion inquiry. Acting on the idea of an aide of the senior senator who has fallen in love with him (Jean Arthur), Smith resorts to a filibuster against the united antagonism of the rest of the Senate, hoping that it will give people back home enough time to confirm that he has been framed. But back home, the party boss clamps down on the press and sends thugs into the street to quiet dissenting voices. The apparent coup de grâce for Smith comes when thousands of telegrams are delivered to the Senate floor, demanding that he end his filibuster and resign. Not realizing that the wires have been organized by the party boss, the weary and vanquished junior senator collapses. But just when everything appears lost, the senior senator succumbs to a crisis of conscience—first trying to shoot himself, then raving aloud on the Senate floor that Smith has been telling the truth all along.

In a vast gallery of characters who wore their feelings on their sleeves, Stewart was seldom more emotional than in playing Jefferson Smith. More than anything else, in fact, it was inklings of his greater credibility for first looking in awe upon the Lincoln Memorial and then later breaking down there that persuaded Capra to give the part to him rather

---

[14] Despite the fact that it was *Mr. Smith* that established him on the Hollywood map as a country rather than as just a big island, Stewart has always spoken about the film somewhat gingerly; usually he has required the prompting of an interviewer to include it on his short list of favorite pictures.

than Gary Cooper, who had starred for the director in *Mr. Deeds Goes to Town*.[15] But even the scenes at the Lincoln Memorial were merely warmups for the filibuster sequence, which required close to three weeks of shooting with a Stewart physically degenerating almost as progressively as the character he was playing. According to Edward Bernds, the sound engineer on the film, the actor spent a good part of the production checking off the days until he had to begin his scenes of nonstop talking. Bernds:

> He knew from the beginning that that was going to be the whole ball of wax as far as he was concerned. It wasn't that he wasn't focused all the time. But the closer we came to the filibuster, the more contemplative he became between takes. He told me later that he would even get a little apprehensive about driving to work in the morning. He said he never drove so carefully in his life. He made it sound like he was just afraid that an accident might interrupt the picture. But I think there was something else there, too—like not wanting to tease Fate.

One of the more noted stories about *Mr. Smith* stemmed from the actor's response to Capra's exasperation that he couldn't get down a convincing enough hoarseness during the filibuster. After hearing the criticism once too often, Stewart went to a doctor to ask for something that would give him a sore throat, at least temporarily. The astounded doctor applied a dichloride of mercury compound that produced the requested inflammation and a more persuasive rasp, then hung around the set in case reapplications were needed during the day.

Although the filibuster scene has become something of a signature image for the screen Stewart, showing his very youth being swallowed up by the harrying forces of political corruption, he also had a line of dialogue that became equally fundamental to many of his subsequent characters—the desperately defiant cry of "Either I'm dead right or I'm crazy!" Working under Capra's direction and with Sidney Buchman's script, it was a choice resolved by his being shown to be more dead right than crazy; working under directors such as Anthony Mann and Alfred Hitchcock in the 1950s, the verdict on a similar choice wasn't all that

---

[15] Aside from Stewart's greater emotional effusiveness, Capra always regarded his Princeton background as a casting factor, on more than one occasion describing him as "an educated Cooper."

clear even at the close of the stories. What exactly even Jefferson Smith was dead right about has been at the core of debate over the significance of *Mr. Smith Goes to Washington*.

Capra was the first to admit that he was taken aback by the reception accorded the picture at its Washington premiere in October 1939. "All the elite of Washington was there, four thousand of them," he once told Richard Schickel. "Two-thirds of the way through the picture, they started walking out—booing, disgusted. About the time of the filibuster, they really began to walk out in droves. And the newspapermen were just vicious about it and the Senators were all vicious about it."

He wasn't exaggerating. Senator Alben Barkley, a future vice-president under Harry Truman and then the Democratic majority leader, couldn't get to Capitol Hill fast enough to lash out at the film as "as grotesque as anything I have ever seen." Another vote molder, Democrat James Byrnes of South Carolina, declared that Capra had betrayed just about everything sacred to a 1939 American, asserting:

> Halfway through the picture I said to myself this is a masterpiece—a fine film that will go out to the nation as an inspiration for democracy. But when it was over, I said, here is a picture that is going to the country to tell the people that the federal and state and municipal governments are corrupt, that one corrupt boss can control the press of an entire state, that the newspapers are corrupt, that the wire services are corrupt, that the radio is corrupt, that reporters are corrupt, and that the trucks of city newspapers will intentionally run down boys in the streets. The thing was outrageous, exactly the kind of picture that the dictators of totalitarian governments would like to have their subjects believe exists in a democracy.

Equally scandalized was the U.S. ambassador to Great Britain, Joseph Kennedy, who warned Columbia that *Mr. Smith* would be interpreted by Europeans as Nazi propaganda and put the United States in such a bad light that the morale of the British-led Allies would be seriously undermined. Kennedy, who had never previously been listed as a pioneer opponent to the Hitler and Mussolini dictatorships, even offered to buy the negative of the picture personally so it would be kept out of circulation. A similar proposal came from the other Hollywood studios, which put out feelers to Columbia boss Harry Cohn to accept a pooled sum from them (said to have been $2 million) in exchange for his commitment to shelve the picture. Their worry was that the antagonistic Senate would step up efforts already under way to break up the production-distribution-exhibition monopolies maintained by The Big Eight.

To hear Capra tell it in *The Name Above the Title*, the autobiography that was more of an autohagiography, what turned the tide was his own rallying of Cohn to stand tough and the Columbia boss's adamance that it was his money at stake, not that of ninety-six senators, the U.S. ambassador to the Court of St. James's, or Hollywood's other seven sisters. But what Capra and Cohn also had going for them even in the midst of the gale blowing down from Capitol Hill were enthusiastic audiences in other parts of the country that had seen the picture before its Washington premiere, some of the best critical notices that a Capra film had received since *It Happened One Night* five years earlier, and, hardly negligible, more publicity exposure than the studio could ever have dreamed of. Because of the outcry from the Senate, *Mr. Smith* was also able to avail itself of double doses of favorable reviews—the editors of many newspapers balancing their reports of the congressional indignation on the same page with reprinted or reiterated critiques under titles such as The Other Side. On October 28, 1939, for instance, *The Christian Science Monitor* flanked all the Barkley-Byrnes kind of fuming with reviewer John Beaufort's endorsement that "if those scenes about the capital landmarks, eloquently written, spoken, and photographed, stir something deep in the average American about which he is generally inarticulate, then Mr. Capra has not only put the Emily Posts of officialdom to rout, but he has made a fine and useful contribution to current thought."

Advocates of the special political significance of *Mr. Smith Goes to Washington* have invariably landed on the concept of "populism" to explain its dust-stirring appeal. What that means, however, aside from some generic and institutional cynicism about the deeds of elected officials has never been easy to pin down. Sound engineer Bernds, for one, finds it ridiculous that anyone has ever ascribed to Capra any deliberate radicalism in the presentation of Jefferson Smith:

> I worked with the man quite a bit in the 1930s and 1940s, and I can say that he was about as reactionary, as much of a Roosevelt-hater, as any of the big bosses in the Hollywood Studios. He thought it was funny as hell, for

instance, when Adolphe Menjou, the model of reaction in the business back then, told him that he had already hoarded all his gold in expectation of the day that Roosevelt would lead the Reds to taking over the country. I don't think it was an accident that you had the majority group characters in the Senate, like the one played by H. B. Warner, so clearly Democrats. That's what got all the Barkleys so hot. But over and above the specifics of which party characters like Rains or Arnold might have belonged to, the important thing is that they represented the political establishment, the political establishment around the time of the picture was Democratic, and Capra never worried about offending Democrats. I think it's ludicrous to think that he was being radical in that.

Even on its own fictional screen terms, the supposed populism of Smith remains a dubious alternative to effective political action. As with *You Can't Take It With You*, Capra seems far more interested in mounting what he deems the inevitability of a certain outcome. And whereas that *inevitability* in the earlier film with Stewart had been geared toward ransoming his faith in the redemption of a munitions manufacturer, in *Mr. Smith* it is turned toward demonstrating that the idealistic senator hasn't got a prayer of winning. When Smith discovers that he has been victimized by the Arnold character, he continues to trust the Rains one. When he realizes how Rains has betrayed him and sets out to do something about it, he has to take on the entire Senate. When he tries to get the people back home, including his own enthusiastic Boy Rangers, to help him, they turn out to be powerless. His only real allies at the end are the woman who loves him but who is herself compromised by having been part of the early conniving against him, and the vice-president of the United States (Harry Carey, Sr.) who, in his role as president of the Senate, can support him only with a series of benevolent smiles. Finally, he and all his ideals are unconscious when the Rains character admits the truth of everything. He has to be awoken and *told* that his obstinacy has won the day.

Some critics have detected a "darkness" in such a vision by Capra—a pessimism that his own idealistic attitude can triumph in the real world. But both off and on the screen in relation to *Mr. Smith*, the director himself never appeared so committed. When *The Hollywood Reporter*, for example, asked him whether he was concerned that the negative reaction to the film might accelerate the legislative moves to break up the studio combines, he immediately jumped to the defense of the institution that had so recently accused him of near-subversion. In a letter to the paper only a few days after the Washington premiere, Capra declared:

> If members of the motion picture industry think that the United States Congress will pass a bill detrimental to the industry because of the fact that they did not like a certain picture, I think it is an insult to the United States Congress. No one could make me believe that Congress passes bills of national importance because of personal pique, and if members of the motion picture industry think that such will be the case, it is taking a very low viewpoint of our legislative body. If Congress passes [the bill], it will be because it thinks that it is to the best interests of the country, and not because of the desire for any personal retaliation.

By itself, such a protestation might be read as an attempt at appeasing Capitol Hill, at defending Columbia to the other Hollywood studios, at disavowing personal responsibility for future actions by Congress, or all three together. But there is also plenty within *Mr. Smith* itself, not least the treatment of the three principal villains, that suggests that, as in the case of *You Can't Take It With You* and other pictures not involving Stewart, Capra had, at most, an equivocal attitude toward seated authority, that he did not consider heroes with a penchant for "fighting lost causes" as alter egos.

As the machine-picked governor, Guy Kibbee contributes one of his trademark venal buffoons. The dramatic onus of his character is on being the one who comes up with the idea of drafting Jefferson Smith as the fill-in senator in the first place—a premise that doesn't bear too much scrutiny and that might as well be acquitted in scenes played close to a slapstick style. As the state political boss, on the other hand, there is nothing at all humorous about Edward Arnold; from beginning to end, he is all organizational thuggery, with no redeeming feature. He also happens to be the only one of the three villains who doesn't hold elective office, whose corruption doesn't reflect badly on an electorate. But the character most symptomatic of the Capra vision in *Mr. Smith* is Claude Rains's Senator Joseph Paine.

Although Rains received an Oscar nomination in the Supporting Actor category for his performance, it is one of the most haphazard of his career, virtually without subtext from one moment to another. In some scenes, he is presented as the essence of patrician subtlety and sympathy; in others, he comes across as just one more of Arnold's pigs feeding from the public trough; and, with the finale, he is a raving lunatic. Rather than offering a wide character range, these various sides of Paine are completely independent of one another, as though it had never occurred to either Capra or Rains that a Joseph Paine could be subtle, sympathetic, and corrupt simultaneously. Similarly, there are none of Capra's ineluctable buildings toward the Paine character's climactic act of desperation, even though a suicide attempt and a derangement might seem to require, dramatically, as much progressive attention as the relatively more innocuous swoon by the protagonist. Figure of authority that Paine is, there appeared to be nothing at all inevitable about his downfall, at least to Capra; on the contrary, his confession at the end comes almost as a deus ex machina.

On the other hand, there is the sympathetic character of Harry Carey, Sr.'s vice-president—not only the most authoritative of all the story's figures, but an institutional emblem beyond even biases about Democrats and Republicans. According to Harry Carey, Jr., Capra knew exactly what he was getting when he asked the senior Carey to "do a bit" in *Mr. Smith*. Carey Jr.: "There were some stories that Capra offered the picture to my father because he was grateful about some work that Dad had gotten for him back in the 1920s. But he really wanted Dad because he struck him as a typical Democratic politician from the Midwest in the 1930s who looked like he had been born to carry the Capitol around on his back. What's funny about that, of course, is that my father was an arch New Yorker right down to his New York accent. But for Capra, he was more than a New Yorker and more than a Democrat."

In defense of the film's political virtuousness, Capra liked to point out in his later years that *Mr. Smith* was the last English-language picture shown in France prior to a 1942 German-ordered ban on all American and English features. In fact, some provincial French theaters ran it every day for the month leading up to the preannounced proscription. By that time, however, the event of *Mr. Smith*—including its riling of recognized authority—had become central to its distribution. Widely reported scenes of Frenchmen standing up in theaters applauding the appearance of the word LIBERTY on the screen during the sequence at the Lincoln Memorial might not have been inevitable, but they could hardly be called a surprise, either, in a land under military occupation.

In the last analysis, what held all the lines of the picture together, frayed as many of them were, was Stewart's passionate development from the callow leader of local scout groups,[16] to the self-pitying, disillusioned senator, to the emotionally ravaged critic of congressional process. For *The New York Times*, the actor was "a joy for this season, if not forever." The weekly *Nation* agreed, saying that Stewart's performance had put him in the front rank of Hollywood stars, then continuing: "Now he is mature and gives a difficult part, with many nuances, moments of tragicomic impact. And he is able to do more than play isolated scenes effectively. He shows the strength of his character through experience. In the end he is so forceful that his victory is thoroughly credible. One can only hope that after this success Mr. Stewart in Hollywood will remain as uncorrupted as Smith in Washington."

The actor had a few incentives for not getting a big head. A total absorption in the character of Jefferson Smith during shooting alienated him from costar Arthur, who sought perpetual reassurance when she wasn't vomiting in her dressing room or driving away visitors to the set (because, as she told Edward Bernds after ousting one group of teenage girls, "they are so young and beautiful and make me remember I'm not"). In later years, the actress always compared Stewart unfavorably to Gary Cooper, saying that she preferred the latter's "Rock of Gibraltar" quality to the former's readiness to spew out everything in front of a camera. Arthur wouldn't be the last woman who lived close to open nerves who would find the actor short in his charm.

Stewart might have done a little better in the recognition department, too. Although he captured the New York Film Critics Award as the best male performer of the year and was an odds-on favorite to take the Oscar as well, the Academy Award ended up going to Robert Donat for *Goodbye, Mr. Chips*. In fact, despite eleven nominations, *Mr. Smith* fell before the *Gone With the Wind* juggernaut, taking the prize only in the Original Story category.

Then there was always MGM—for reminding Stewart that, Capra or not, it wasn't easy finding parts for him.

Destry Rides Again (Universal – 1939)

While radically different in story, *Destry Rides Again* had a few points in common with *Mr. Smith Goes to Washington*. As with the Capra film,

---

[16] The boys camp project attributed to the Jefferson Smith character in the film is presented in terms markedly similar to the no-free-ride vision of the Red Cross offered by Indiana high-schooler Stewart.

Stewart got to do the George Marshall western as a result of another MGM loan-out, the home studio still not knowing how to showcase its contract player to best advantage. As well, Stewart obtained the role after some earlier consideration of Gary Cooper.[17] Third, despite playing the protagonist and dominating screen time, he was billed after his female costar (the justification in this case being that he was hired for *Destry* before the release of the Capra picture). And fourth, he was once again, as Thomas Jefferson Destry, associated with the patriotic endowments of the third president of the United States.

The origins of *Destry* were as tangled as some of the personal relations on the set during production. Producer Joe Pasternak's initial idea had been to remake a Tom Mix western with Cooper. When that didn't pan out and Stewart was made available, writer Felix Jackson decided that the actor wouldn't be credible as an avenger out to even the score for his slain father, so he reversed the Mix character and made him somebody who didn't believe in using his gun for taming an unruly town. For his part, Pasternak had undertaken the project with Dietrich as his one and only choice for the barroom girl, having been attracted to this idea since the German actress had lost out to Claire Trevor for the role of the prostitute in John Ford's *Stagecoach*. The producer didn't disguise his personal designs on Dietrich, either, prompting her retort that she would go to bed with him only after Hitler was dead. (Following the fall of Berlin, he tried to collect on this promise, but she kept him at a distance by saying that Hitler was still alive in Argentina.) The saloon singer was named Frenchy for no better reason than that Dietrich happened to be living in Paris during the negotiations for her services.

Destry takes off when Kent (Brian Donlevy), the boss of Bottle Neck, appoints town drunk Dimsdale (Charles Winninger) as the sheriff, assuming that this will leave him a free hand to continue strong-arming local homesteaders for their land. But Dimsdale takes the job seriously and imports Destry, the son of a noted peace officer for whom he had once worked, as his deputy. He is astonished to discover that, unlike his father, Destry believes more in the persuasions of the legal system than in the

---

[17] Indicative of the range that directors and producers perceived in Stewart, he either replaced or was replaced by Gary Cooper or Cary Grant in more than thirty film projects throughout his career. Even allowing for script changes made to accommodate an actor brought in as a second choice, the spread between typical Cooper and Grant characters was enormous.

threats of a gun to impose justice, and doesn't even wear a six-shooter. This makes both Dimsdale and Destry laughingstocks around town, especially after the new deputy appears to take at face value a dubious deed turning over a farm to Kent. What nobody realizes is that Destry has been methodically setting the foundations for exposing Kent and his gang as the murderers of the sheriff who had preceded Dimsdale. When his designs finally become clear, Frenchy, the mistress of Kent and an accomplice in his extortions, tries to warn Destry off. But it is too late to save Dimsdale, who is killed while guarding a prisoner involved in the murder of his predecessor. Seeing that Dimsdale was shot in the back as his father once was, Destry overcomes his aversion to guns, puts on his gunbelt, and goes marching after Kent. The finale shows the homesteaders and lawful citizenry in a pitched battle with Kent's gang. Frenchy, who has fallen in love with Destry, takes a fatal bullet meant for him from Kent, dying in his arms. Destry kills Kent, and peace is restored to Bottle Neck.

Taken as a whole, *Destry Rides Again* can't seem to make up its mind whether it's a western or a satire on the kind of Tom Mix action adventure that inspired it. In the sheer volume of its various elements, the latter would seem to be the case: the knock-'em-down-drag-'em-out saloon fight between Dietrich and Una Merkel, the clowning of Mischa Auer, the casting of mugging-happy Warren Hymer and Allen Jenkins as Kent's two top gunslingers, and Stewart's endless storytelling (which even includes the old joke about the boy who killed his parents and sought leniency on the grounds of being an orphan). On the other hand, the smiles are regularly frozen by the killing of prominent characters and some hard-knuckled exchanges between the Stewart and Dietrich characters. In the end, the film's staying power, for both good and bad, rests with collectible moments in Hollywood history. One of these was Dietrich's singing, especially of the rowdy "The Boys in the Back Room," which she ended up having to perform around the world almost as much as "Lili Marlene." Another was the barroom brawl between Dietrich and Merkel; according to Stewart, it wasn't an altogether fake fight, either: "[It] turned out beautifully, primarily because Una got mad at Marlene when she realized that Marlene was really fighting. They were all over the set, kicking and slapping and scratching and biting, and it was all Marlene's idea. . . . I believe it was the best female fight ever filmed. They both got carried away, especially Una, who had been entirely in favor of having the doubles do the fighting for them . . . until she realized that Marlene wasn't fooling around."

As frequently recalled, *Destry* has also contributed an important building block to the screen image of Jimmy Stewart—the folksy, pleasant young man for whom an aversion to guns is perfectly logical. In fact, however, Stewart's portrayal of Tom Destry is a great deal more nuanced than that, and owes nothing at all to the virtue of meekness. From his very first scene, he plays Destry as sly, edgy, and cocky. He smiles only when other characters look directly at him, otherwise studying them with marked irony. He is so astute and confident in dealing with the other characters through most of the film that his resort to a gun at the end seems almost superfluous. It was a complex reading that was not lost on film critics, some of whom went so far as to say that Thomas Jefferson Destry was a better realized character than even Jefferson Smith. *Time* magazine, for instance, found that "James Stewart, who . . . just turned in the top performance of his cinematurity . . . in *Mr. Smith Goes to Washington*, turns in as good a performance or better . . ." in the Universal western. *New York Times* film reviewer Bosley Crowther called the rendering of Destry "a masterpiece of underplaying in a deliberately sardonic vein—the freshest, most offbeat characterization that this popular actor ever played. It was, in my mind, even better than the rampant young senator . . . " in the Capra feature.

At least as far as Stewart was concerned, Jeffersonism was anything he could make out of it.

IN THE AIR

THERE WAS NOTHING UNUSUAL ABOUT A HOLLYWOOD actor of the 1930s taking up flying. Aviation had been something of a motion-picture industry passion since the days of silent film actress Ruth Chatterton, and so many performers had followed her example that air mishaps had become a boilerplate clause in studio insurance policies. Aside from Stewart, Margaret Sullavan, and Leland Hayward, the pilots of the period included Joan Fontaine, her husband Brian Aherne, Tyrone Power, Robert Taylor, Robert Cummings, Robert Young, Olivia de Havilland, Frances Langford, Jon Hall, and Wayne Morris. Johnny Swope, Stewart's housemate in Brentwood, also had a license.

For sure, there was a whiff of the idle rich at play in the hobby, especially since most of them owned their own aircraft. That image was also abetted by actors (Cummings was one of many) who decided that there were few ways more entertaining to spend a day off than to climb into a cockpit and buzz some exterior location shoot so that a studio would waste a lot of time and money. But many of the actors also made it sound like necessary therapy for people in the public eye. As Joan Fontaine puts it: "It was simply the best way to get away from everything. I think I crossed the continent five times with Brian. Imagine it: You're being harassed by the studio for one thing, by magazines and columnists for something else, and suddenly you have this power to get into a plane and within a few minutes to be in another state altogether! There's nothing more peaceful in the world at a moment like that than the sky."

Stewart has spoken in similar terms: "You're like a bird up there. It's almost as if you're not a part of society anymore. All you can think about is what you're doing and you have a complete escape from your worldly problems. You have a feeling of real power up there—that we human beings aren't really that helpless, that we can be completely in command of an amazing machine, that we do have some control over our destiny. And of course, it's the only place where one can really be alone."

In response to goading from Hayward (and the spirit of Charles Lindbergh), Stewart undertook his pilot training shortly after arriving in California. He would eventually obtain both a private pilot's and commercial pilot's license, log some 400 hours in the air, and buy a yellow-striped Stinson 105 two-seater for himself. ("I think the 105 was supposed to be its speed; but *may-be*, just *may-be*, when you put the nose down, it would go 105.") His initial hours aloft, however, did not come as much like second nature to him as somebody obsessed with aviation since childhood might have expected. While a majority of students were weaned off dual instruction for solo flying after about eight hours, he needed almost double that before being adjudged ready to go it alone. As in the past at the Model School, Mercersburg, and Princeton, one of the major problems appeared to be impatience with having to listen to others instead of being able to do it by himself at once.

But even with his extra time in a cockpit classroom, Stewart left little doubt from the beginning that he had the nerves necessary for becoming a pilot. According to Beirne Lay, the screenwriter of *Strategic Air Command, Twelve O'Clock High*, and other films with an Air Force background, that became particularly evident after a misadventure on a 1936 practice flight.

His instructor jerked back the throttle to give Stewart a simulated forced landing. Jimmy picked an emergency field and executed a power-off approach. As he glided toward a potato patch, he saw that he was going to hit right on the button. He sat there grinning, waiting for the instructor to give her the gun and climb. But the biplane continued to settle toward the ground. Finally, Jimmy grabbed the throttle, but it wouldn't budge. He thought the other man was holding it back. They were skimming the grass now, so Jimmy set her down in a normal landing on the rough furrow. The instructor was furious at Stewart for holding the throttle back, until he discovered that it had jammed so that neither of them could move it. The simulated emergency had become a real emergency without either man realizing it until they were safe on the ground.

Once he had his license, Stewart made a practice of getting up before dawn on weekdays and driving out to Clover Field to get in an hour or so in the air before reporting to the studio for work. Often, he was accompanied by Hayward—though with the understanding that they would get into their separate craft once they reached their destination, leaving one another alone up in the clouds. When he was dating de Havilland, Stewart and the actress scarfed down breakfast at the airport, then he would leave her to her lesson with her flying instructor while he went up elsewhere in his Stinson.

But he didn't find Katharine Hepburn, his costar in *The Philadelphia Story*, quite so accommodating about the rules of the air. As he once described it to the New York *Daily News*:

One Friday night, just before we quit shooting, Katharine came up to me and said ... "I'd like to go flying with you, and I'll be out at Clover Field at eight o'clock tomorrow morning." Well, from the time I started the engine, she asked about everything. When I started it up, she said, "Wait! What about the oil? Why is the gauge below the red?" I said, "But Kate, it always works this way. It's okay." "But it's not supposed to be below the red marker," she insisted. . . . So I ran the engine a bit longer. Then she started on something else. . . .

The lecturing from somebody who had never been in a two-seater before continued through the taxiing and the liftoff. It didn't stop in the air, either.

> I thought I would take her up to Saugus. Well, when I got ready to turn, she said, "Don't turn!" I got up to 500, then 800 feet, and then 1000 feet, when I started to turn again, and she said no again. She kept on, so finally I said, "Kate, if we don't turn, we'll be in China!" "All right, you can turn now," she said. I told her I thought we'd go up over Saugus, and she replied, "I want to go back." So I circled around and lost altitude in order to land. She kept on until the landing, her eyes never moving from the oil gauge. In fact, the landing wasn't really a landing, but more like a controlled crash.

Once back on the ground, Hepburn delivered herself of a curt "thank you," climbed out of the plane, strode over to her awaiting car, drove off, and never again during the shooting of *The Philadelphia Story* mentioned either flying or her morning excursion.

Whatever Hepburn's impressions about taking off with an apparent insufficiency of oil, Stewart struck others in his circle as having found in flying a perfect outlet for his sense of detail and discipline. "Before Jimmy took off on a flight," Burgess Meredith observed in his autobiography, *So Far, So Good*, "he studied every mile on the maps littering the living room floor. By the time he climbed into his eccentric little plane with its yellow-striped tail, he was as well posted on emergency landing fields as J. Edgar Hoover was in those days on Fifth Columnists. 'Anticipation— that's the key to flying,' he told me with total simplicity. 'The only other thing you need is luck.'"

Hayward's influence on Stewart's flying career didn't stop with egging the actor into obtaining a pilot's license. The agent also involved him, financially, in a pre-World War II enterprise that was to prove crucial to the defeat of Germany and Japan in the ensuing hostilities in Europe and the Pacific.

In July 1939, the United States ranked only seventh in air power and could boast of merely one permanent military installation for training pilots. General "Hap" Arnold, an advocate of air superiority, sought to outflank a Congress hostile to more appropriations by enlisting eight civilian associates for setting up airfields, hangars, and mess halls in various parts of the country as additional instruction centers; the civilians, the majority of whom had been Army pilots with Arnold during World War I, even had to pay out of their own pockets for the gas and oil consumed during the schooling. Within a year, the private operations were so successful that there were too many applicants for the eight centers to train; moreover, an increasing War Department nervousness about events in Europe and Japan had prompted some radical revisions upward in the number of pilots who would be required if the United States did enter the war. With the isolationist Congress still not prepared to underwrite significant additional funding, Arnold expanded his call for civilian help. Among those responding the second time were Hayward and Jack Connelly, an engineering inspector for the Civil Aeronautics Authority and a noted test pilot.

In order to qualify even for spending their own money, civilians had to be active operators of a flying-school business, as the original eight had been or had immediately become. To this purpose, Hayward and Connelly set up a corporation called Southwest Airways; Hayward elected himself chairman, Johnny Swope came in as treasurer, and Connelly took over as chief instructor. For a purchase price of $15,000, they set up at the Sky Harbor Air Service in the Salt River Valley near Phoenix, Arizona. Among those contributing seed capital were Stewart, Aherne, Henry Fonda, Cary Grant, composer Hoagy Carmichael, and producer William Goetz. They would never be able to contribute quite enough.

Hayward being Hayward, he wasn't about to be satisfied with clearing a few cacti out of the way and slapping down some Nissen huts for housing and administrative accommodations. As his daughter Brooke described it in her book *Haywire*:

> Father, with his indomitable sense of the aesthetic, lined up Millard Sheets, a well-known Western artist, to design it. It was dazzling. Sheets laid out the entire training field in the stylized shape of a gigantic thunderbird, the Indian god of thunder, lightning, and rain, so that viewed from the air the observation tower formed the head, the administration building the body, the barracks the wings, and the gardens the tail feathers. He eschewed traditional drab Army colors for those of the Southwest desert, the green of sage and cactus, the cream of yucca in bloom, the streaked gray browns of sand, the terra cotta of adobe, and everywhere the tomato-red insignia—a thunderbird with lightning bolts of plumage.

Thunderbird Field, as the facility was inevitably called, was constructed within three months. Before the war would end, it would spawn Thunderbird Field II and Falcon Field in nearby desert areas. Under the tutelage of Connelly and his staff, the facilities trained tens of thousands of pilots—not only from the United States, but from Britain, China, and other Allied countries.[18]

Although Southwest Airways lost what Hayward estimated as a million dollars during the war, it made some of that money back by selling the Arizona airfields after the hostilities and then operating a viable commercial line in California between 1946 and 1958. It attracted travelers between Los Angeles and San Francisco and between San Francisco and Medford mainly through a pitch about not wasting anybody's time, and employed innovations such as having a purser issue tickets in flight. In 1958, the company was sold and renamed Pacific Airlines.

For Stewart, the importance of Southwest Airways went beyond that of his role as an original investor. The emergency training enterprise underlined for him the imminence of a U.S. entry into World War II, at least as anticipated by Arnold and other Washington officials. It also made clear to him the vast difference in skills needed for configuring loops in a Stinson 105 in the skies of California and for maneuvering heavier aircraft on military missions in Europe and Asia. And, especially after he had avidly read in detail about the German dive-bombing attacks on Warsaw, the Japanese air assault on Nanking, and the R.A.F.'s defense of Britain against the Luftwaffe, the skies didn't seem so idyllic to him as a haven for escaping daily worries. To some degree, in fact, the Southwest Airways venture with its various implications released within him the same kind of trickling directive that he had heard the evening that he had stood in the wings watching *Yellow Jack*: Now he, too, had to act.

CONSOLATION PRIZES

MGM CONTINUED TO DITHER ABOUT WHAT TO DO WITH Stewart even after *Mr. Smith Goes to Washington* and *Destry Rides Again*. If it was true that five of the last seven pictures he made before World

---

[18] They were also used for making such films as *A Yank in the R.A.F.*

War II were introduced by the roar of a lion, it was equally true that no one in the industry needed to consult with a think tank to find an appropriate costar for Margaret Sullavan in two of them and that Katharine Hepburn demanded his inclusion in a third. The remaining two pictures were among the most negligible in the actor's career.

At that, Stewart emerged in better shape from MGM's *Come Live with Me* and *Ziegfeld Girl* than he did from the two pictures that he did for other studios at the beginning of the 1940s. In one of them, *No Time for Comedy*, he came up against the only performance by a female costar that routed him; the other, *Pot o' Gold*, he has named a number of times as the single worst film he ever made.

The Shop Around the Corner (MGM – 1940)

Director-producer Ernst Lubitsch was acutely aware of the relationship between Stewart and Sullavan when he agreed on them for the leading roles in *The Shop Around the Corner*; he even confided to aides that he expected their greater detachment from one another, after Sullavan's motherhood and Stewart's involvement with other women, to give his picture the sophisticated weight it needed. Nevertheless, it wasn't until the German-born filmmaker actually began production that he could rest easy, seeing that the "puppy love" aspects of the Stewart-Sullavan teamings in *Next Time We Love* and *The Shopworn Angel* had indeed grown into more subtly deployed yearnings.

Based on Nikolaus Kaszlo's Hungarian play *Illatszertar* (*The Perfumery*), *The Shop Around the Corner* transforms the major setting into a leather goods gift store within a deliberately artificial-looking soundstage Budapest of the 1930s. The store owner, Matuschek (Frank Morgan), is a bastion of middle-class propriety who likes to believe that his employees look upon him as a fair, benevolent man; at the same time, however, he harbors nagging insecurities about his marriage and even about his control over his business, where the head clerk, Kralik (Stewart), seems to have more commercial sense than he does. To help cope with an expected Christmas rush, Matuschek hires Klara (Sullavan), outwardly self-confident but privately reduced to exchanging letters with an anonymous, poetry-spouting pen pal for a little romance in her life. What she doesn't know is that her correspondent is Kralik, as lonely as she is when he is away from the shop and a regular target of her barbs for being "only a clerk."

Kralik's routine at the store is brusquely interrupted when Matuschek suspects him of having an affair with his wife, and fires him. After a suicide bid thwarted by another store employee (William Tracy), however, Matuschek realizes that he was wrong, that his wife had been carrying on with the assistant clerk, Vadas (Joseph Schildkraut), not with Kralik. He not only restores Kralik to his post as head clerk, but leaves the store entirely in his hands until he has recovered from his suicide try. All these ups and downs in Kralik's life make Klara think twice about the way she always has cold-shouldered him, so she begins confiding in him about the wonderful lover she has met through the mail. Kralik, who has already figured out whom he has been writing to for so long, seeks the best way to break the news to her. He finally manages it in the store on Christmas Eve, after she has admitted that she had found him attractive when she first started at the store. He makes a similar admission, and the lovers are no longer anonymous to one another.

Lubitsch made little attempt to disguise the stage origins of *The Shop Around the Corner*, often even underlining what in a theater would have been "curtain" moments. Never accused of having a working-class sensibility, the director of *The Student Prince*, *The Merry Widow*, *Design for Living*, and *Ninotchka* used this device for gaining a stylistic distance from his store clerk subject matter as pointedly as he did the backlot set that could never be confused with a real Budapest street. Still, it wasn't an altogether serene distance: Particularly through the clerical character played by Tracy, the director added some jarringly crass touches at intervals that, coming from a Berlin native who had never wanted for much, echoed some of the upper-class German laments of the time about the social "rudenesses" unleashed by Naziism. In this sense at least, *The Shop Around the Corner* was a fantasy very much aware of its own artificiality.

The relatively more mature relationship between Stewart and Sullavan also enabled the actress to take the gloves off in dealing with her costar over shooting snarls. As Stewart recalled to Brooke Hayward: "We were in a little restaurant, and I had a line: 'I will come out on the street and I will roll my trousers up, to my knees.' For some reason I couldn't say the line. [Sullavan] was furious. She said, 'This is absolutely ridiculous.' There I was, standing with my trousers rolled up to the knee, very conscious of my skinny legs, and I said, 'I don't want to act today. Get a fellow with decent legs and just show them.' [Sullavan] said, 'Then I absolutely refuse to be in the picture.' So we did more takes."

Despite that incident, Lubitsch told anyone who asked over subsequent years that Stewart and Sullavan were the only actors whom he had directed who not only didn't try to upstage one another, but who went out of their way to make the other look good. Nowhere is that more evident, according to critic Andrew Sarris, than in a scene in which a bedridden Sullavan reads a letter she has received from her anonymous pen pal and Stewart, who has actually written the missive, has to sit by the bed and pretend the interest of a sympathetic confidant in what he is hearing. "It is a dangerously delicate moment," as Sarris notes. "It would have been very tempting for a flickering triumphant expression to have passed over Stewart's face, but instead an intensely sweet and compassionate and appreciative look transfigures the entire scene into one of the most memorable occurrences in the history of the cinema. . . . I could not think of any other actor who could have achieved an effect of such unobtrusive subtlety."

The Sarris view was anything but unanimous when the picture was released. Some critics found *The Shop Around the Corner* an irrelevance given the conflagration in Europe; others thought it much too "small" for Lubitsch after *Ninotchka*. Stewart also had problems with some reviewers who, while somehow finding Frank Morgan's Manhattan inflections and Felix Bressart's German *Weltschmerz* perfectly adaptable to a Neverland Hungary, decided that he wasn't Magyar enough for the role of Kralik. As in the case of *Destry Rides Again* and innumerable other films, there was also the curious characterization of Stewart's role by some critics as a basically innocent and pliable man, while on the screen the head clerk is actually portrayed as increasingly self-confident, when not altogether manipulative, even as he moons over Klara.

Lubitsch and Stewart both had their compensations. For the director, it was in such verdicts as that of the weekly *New Yorker* that *The Shop Around the Corner* was "close to perfection—one of the most beautifully acted and paced romantic comedies ever made in this country." For Stewart, it was in taking one of the National Board of Review's Best Actor awards in 1940.

The Mortal Storm (MGM – 1940)

Even though it was made after *Confessions of a Nazi Spy* and Charles Chaplin's *The Great Dictator*, *The Mortal Storm* continued to observe the geopolitical proprieties by not explicitly identifying the setting for its anti-Nazi story as Germany. But though laid only "somewhere in Europe," the story of political repression based on a novel by Phyllis Bottome and directed by Frank Borzage excited the Third Reich enough to dispatch a diplomatic messenger to the MGM set to warn about repercussions if production on the film went ahead. This threat turned out to be academic but other factors related to the Nazi onslaught ended up blunting the impact of the picture.

The Mortal Storm centers around the family of biology professor Viktor Roth (Frank Morgan), whose sixtieth birthday is marked first by his admiring students, then by a dinner at home. Attending the dinner are his wife (Irene Rich), his daughter Freya (Margaret Sullavan), his natural son Rudi (Gene Reynolds), adopted sons Otto (Robert Stack) and Erich (William Orr), and Freya's rival suitors and Roth students— Martin Breitner (Stewart) and Fritz Marberg (Robert Young). The dinner is interrupted by news of the appointment of Adolf Hitler as chancellor—revealing Otto, Erich, and Fritz as enthusiastic Nazis, Martin and Roth as anti-Nazis, and Freya as a skeptic who can't believe that her brothers and suitors would get excited one way or the other. She begins to see the light after Otto, Erich, and Fritz begin stomping around in Brown Shirt uniforms, allow a Jewish professor to be beaten up outside a beer garden, and start menacing Martin for his defense of the professor. When Fritz begins pressuring her to become his wife in an Aryan Eden, she rebuffs him. That makes it only easier for Fritz to do nothing about the firing of Roth from the university for being an undesirable.

Freya's only moments of relief come when she visits Martin and his mother (Maria Ouspenskaya) at their mountain farm. Just as she realizes that she has fallen in love with Martin, however, he has to assist the beaten Jewish professor over the Alps to the safety of Austria, and by doing so also seals his own fate as an outlaw. With Martin gone, Freya can do nothing but watch the disintegration of her family—first with Otto and Erich moving out of the house because of the political embarrass-ment of their disgraced father, then with the arrest, confinement in a concentration camp, and, finally, the death of her father. Freya attempts to leave the country with her mother and brother Rudi to rejoin Martin, but is left behind when border guards discover her in possession of one of her father's biology manuscripts refuting the Aryan blood superiority thesis. Martin then slips back into the country to lead her over the Alps along the same secret trail he used for helping the Jewish professor flee.

But the Nazis, led by Fritz, pursue them, killing Freya. Fritz then defends his actions to the brothers Otto and Erich as necessities of the New Society.

MGM's attempts to have its cake (not specifying Germany) and eat it too (making clear that Germany was the setting) prompted some bizarre moments in the film. To begin with, there weren't too many other European countries separated from Austria by the Alps where the natives wore lederhosen and congregated in beer gardens to sing German songs. Although Roth is shown wearing a J on his prison uniform, nobody is explicitly identified in the film as a Jew, least of all his daughter Freya or son Rudi.[19] Even after Freya's death at the end, an offscreen narrator imparts the moral as being of some nebulous religious truth rather than of some political order.

The Germans were not so easily charmed, and, as Robert Stack recalls, they reached at least one member of the cast. Stack:

> One morning a representative from the Swiss Consulate showed up on the set in a vested suit and announced that he'd been told by the Germans to tell us that *Confessions of a Nazi Spy* and our picture would be remembered by Berlin after they won the war. I didn't give a goddam about what they were going to remember, and that was the attitude of Jimmy, Maggie, the director Borzage, and most everybody else. But Bob Young was very affected by this little announcement, and he kept asking me, "What about my children? What about my kids?" I'm not saying he was wrong, because Warners ended up having to assign guards to the family of Edward G. Robinson after *Confessions of a Nazi Spy*. Maybe I was just too young and dumb to worry about it. The Germans had just gone around the Maginot Line and France was going to fall any day. But except for Bob Young, nobody had the brains to take what the Swiss guy said seriously.

The MGM publicity department did, though. Still concerned more about offending European distributors that accounted for a substantial part of the grosses on every release than about acknowledging the political and military realities on the continent, the office headed by Howard Strickling opted for a publicity campaign that removed

---

[19] Call sheets during the production of the picture specifically mention "the Jewish Professor," but make no reference to other family members.

practically every trace of politics from the picture's content. Instead, the focus was on the fourth teaming of Stewart and Sullavan, a typical poster showing the co-stars kissing over the reminder that they were "the popular sweethearts from *The Shop Around the Corner*." With little help coming from MGM, it fell to individual theater owners to suggest some of the dark political moments that awaited audiences, and some of them only made matters worse. A theater operator in Stanton, Nebraska, for example, decided that the best way of underlining the picture's connection to current events was to promise "free admission to all fifth columnists who confess at the box office." The promotional subterfuge proved academic: Seven weeks after the general release of *The Mortal Storm* in the United States, Germany banned all American films in territories under its control, and Italy followed suit shortly afterward.

What added up to a mediocre box-office return wasn't helped, either, by the reviews, even by some of the well-meaning ones. For *The New York Times*, Stewart and Sullavan, especially, "brought to vibrant and anguished life the two young people who resist the sweeping system." New York's *Herald Tribune*, a traditional Stewart backer since his theater days on Broadway, thought he "act[ed] with such intense sincerity that the personal tragedy which is the core of the piece is the most sustaining note in the proceedings." But the same newspaper also found *The Mortal Storm* as a whole "dated and romantically distorted"—a note that was sounded by other critics as well because of the nasty volume of military events in Europe between the filming and release of the picture. Even *Variety*, which had earlier predicted that *The Mortal Storm* would "dispel public equanimity" about Naziism "with the devastating directness of a Stuka diver," decided that it was only effective in its "mood of tragic impotence," implying that this was no longer the proper response to the ongoing wave of German and Italian invasions.

Time hasn't been kind to *The Mortal Storm* since then, either.[20] More than fifty years later, it stands mainly as an example of the kind of glossy artifacts that MGM did better—and worse—than other studios. The same elements—cultural approximation, round-robin confrontation, and narrative melancholy—that had worked for Lubitsch as charm with

---

[20] Contemporary distractions might also include the fact that the film's Nazis are played by Marcus Welby (Young), Elliot Ness (Stack), *Wagon Train*'s Major MacAdams (Ward Bond), and Dizzy Dean (Dan Dailey).

The Shop Around the Corner lacked an internal integrity as tragedy (a situation made more evident by the use of the same lead actors—Stewart, Sullavan, and Morgan). To a certain extent, in fact, *The Mortal Storm*, for all its individually agile performances, underscored the creative limitations of the studio system as a whole—a system that operated by channeling its contractually obligated talents toward properties primarily valued for their ductility. If Hollywood has been at the mercy of The Deal since the fall of The Big Eight, with all the restrictions that mentality has imposed on imaginative work, The Deal is still only the younger brother of The Wheel, whereby production teams were assembled on the basis of work rotations dictated by contracts and options, and stories were viewed more for their potential for accommodating disparate house talents than for giving expression to coherent, genuine passions. From that perspective, *all* MGM films were *Grand Hotel* and *Dinner at Eight*. In singling out the scenes between Morgan and Rich or between Stewart and Sullavan as the most powerful in *The Mortal Storm*, what critics were effectively saying was that those were the moments that these actors were so able to establish a dramatic unity between themselves that it was possible to forget about the indiscriminate and glib production expanse around them.

No Time for Comedy (Warner Brothers – 1940)

Although they never appeared on the screen together,[21] Stewart and Olivia de Havilland were the key parties in a 1939 trade between MGM and Warner Brothers. The exchange permitted de Havilland to do *Gone With the Wind*, while Stewart got to do *No Time for Comedy*.

Based on a S. N. Behrman play that ran on Broadway for about six months with Katharine Cornell and Laurence Olivier, *No Time for Comedy* was, according to the movie billboards of the day, about A SHY FELLOW NAMED JAMES WHO KNEW NOTHING AT ALL ABOUT DAMES TILL HE MET A MISS RUSSELL. AND AFTER A TUSSLE HE LEARNED ABOUT WOMEN (HE CLAIMS!).

Well, something like that. The plot actually deals with novice playwright Gaylord Esterbrook (Stewart) who writes a hit comedy for actress Linda Paige (Rosalind Russell), falls in love with her, marries her, then writes several more successful comedies for her. But just when the couple

---

[21] They did, however, have separate screen time as fellow cast members of *Airport '77*.

are the toast of Broadway, Gaylord gets it into his head that he is wasting time writing only fluff and, abetted by a flirtatious, feather-headed socialite (Genevieve Tobin), sets out to write a drama of "social significance." When Linda voices skepticism, Gaylord escalates an argument into a divorce demand. Philo (Charles Ruggles), the wealthy, habitually bemused husband of the socialite, moves in on Linda in compensation for his wife's dalliance with the playwright. The globe is returned to its axis, however, when Gaylord's serious play flops, the socialite decides that she can't help losers and takes up with somebody else, and Gaylord and Linda resume married life recommitted to the successful ideals of the Broadway comedy.

No Time for Comedy spat out numerous ideas but declined to explore any of them significantly, least of all the *Sullivan's Travels* theme of the role of light entertainment. The picture was generally shrugged off by critics, and more than one of them found it hard to resist throwing the title right back at Warner Brothers and director William Keighley. (This became such a problem that the picture was retitled during a rerelease; the unhappy change was to *Guy With a Grin.*) If it holds any interest today, it is for the unusual sight of a Stewart costar, Russell, running circles around him—most of the time by standing still. While the actor's Gaylord rants and whines about one thing or another, the actress's Linda remains solidly fixed at the center of an endlessly enfolded universe in which every ring she cedes to him seems only to attest further to how secure she is. Even when the script asserts that Gaylord undercuts her self-sufficiency, Russell's manner says otherwise, making the playing out of the plot all the slower and more predictable. It is a performance that never touches ground, and would have been disastrously banal if it had. A more uncompromising version of Margaret Sullavan's entertainer in *The Shopworn Angel*, Russell's actress is a world unto herself—the world of the wisdom, sanity, and box-office receipts to be found in Shubert Alley.

The Philadelphia Story (MGM – 1940)

Unlike Marlene Dietrich prior to *Destry Rides Again*, Katharine Hepburn didn't leave it up to others to rescue her floundering career in the late 1930s. By acting as the driving force behind Philip Barry's *The Philadelphia Story*, she not only secured for herself a Broadway vehicle that ran for more than 400 performances, but she put herself in a position to auction movie rights to the play to the highest bidder.

Knowing that a successful screen adaptation of the upper-class comedy would regenerate her film career, she made it one of her major conditions in negotiations with several studios that she approve her male costars. Left out of consideration were her fellow performers on Broadway, Joseph Cotten and Van Heflin. Hepburn:

> There were 20 million people I wanted to cast for it. With MGM I wanted Gable and Tracy. Even they came up after I'd already talked about Gary Cooper with Paramount and Errol Flynn at Warner's. As far as I was concerned, the main thing was to get two marvelous actors who were also stars. That was why Cotten and Heflin did not figure into it. They both had exceptional careers subsequently, but at the time they didn't have the popularity I was looking for. I heard that Heflin, especially, was annoyed about being passed over. I'm sorry about that, but you can't always please everybody.

In the end, the actress agreed to an MGM package of $175,000 for rights to the property, an additional $75,000 for her services, George Cukor as the director, and Stewart and Cary Grant as her costars. There were varying degrees of enthusiasm about the deal. Aware that he didn't have the best male role in the film, Grant took as consolations top billing, the highest single salary ($137,500), and a great deal of publicity over the fact that he was donating the entire fee to his war-afflicted homeland through the British War Relief Fund. Stewart, on the other hand, reacted with surprise that he was being given the meaty role of the reporter. "When I first read the script, I thought I was being considered for that fellow engaged to [Hepburn]," he has said, referring to the role played by John Howard. "As I read it, I thought to myself, 'Oooh, that reporter part is a good one, but I'll be happy to play the other one.'"

It has remained curious to many, including Hepburn, that he could have ever been under such a misapprehension—or why playing the drab, stuffy fiancé would have appealed to him even minimally. According to the actress, Stewart "was the reporter from the word go, especially after *Mr. Smith Goes to Washington*. He wasn't a debonair Dexter and he certainly wasn't the other stick-in-the-mud. How he could have considered anything else is totally beyond me. He was very funny about that picture, in a lot of ways I've never completely understood."

The Philadelphia Story revolves around the high-society wedding of Tracy Lord (Hepburn) and George Kittredge (Howard). In return for suppressing a scandalistic article about Tracy's estranged father, her ex-husband, C. K. Dexter Haven (Grant), makes a deal with the editor of a magazine to introduce a reporter (Stewart) and a photographer (Ruth Hussey) into the posh Lord household for an exclusive story on the wedding. Dexter's attempts to pass the journalists off as friends of Tracy's brother in South America don't get very far, but by that time Tracy has become interested in the reporter, Mike Connor, for the cynical veneer he wears over a deeper talent for fiction writing; for his part, the reporter finds his antagonism toward the rich ("The prettiest sight in this fine, pretty world is the privileged class enjoying its privileges.") dissolving before a growing love for Tracy. What makes this a problem is not only Kittredge, but Dexter, who is still in love with Tracy, and the magazine photographer, Liz, who is in love with Mike.

The night before the wedding, Tracy and Mike get drunk together, declare their passion for one another, and take a nude swim in the pool together. This outrages Kittredge and makes Liz even more melancholy, but mainly entertains Dexter, who views the removal of Kittredge from the scene more important than Tracy's flirting with Mike. He is also indebted to the reporter for information that the blackmailing magazine editor has some skeletons in his own closet, intelligence that neutralizes the threats about Tracy's father. With the guests all assembled in the house for the wedding, Kittredge takes off in high dudgeon at Tracy's refusal to apologize for her cavorting with Mike. But when Mike offers to take Kittredge's place at the altar, Tracy turns him down, declaring that Liz and his writing are what he really wants. To the relief and approval of family members who had always liked Dexter, she ends up walking down the aisle a second time with her ex-husband.

As an advertisement for being more understanding of the superrich, *The Philadelphia Story* achieves most of its aims humorously and deftly. It remains far more successful, however, in its outlook that successful businessmen (Howard's tycoon and the magazine editor played by Harry Daniell, especially) can be more pretentious than blue bloods than in trying to cover over the fact that the innumerable criticisms made of "snobs" by Tracy and her family emanate from characters who are . . . snobs. The finale is also less than convincing unless it is to be interpreted as an argument that, when all is said and done, reporters belong with photographers and wealthy ex-wives belong with wealthy ex-husbands. Certainly, in comparison with the Stewart reporter's ardent romancing of her during the story, the detached, if sincere, admiration of Grant's former-spouse for Hepburn's Tracy doesn't quite add up to another marriage.

There was little question in the minds of most critics that if any performance dominated the proceedings, it was Stewart's, most markedly in back-to-back drunk scenes with Hepburn and Grant. "Stewart . . . contributes most of the comedy to the show," declared the New York *Herald Tribune* reviewer. "His reaction to a snobbish society built on wealth is a delight to watch. In addition, he contributes some of the most irresistible romantic moments. . . . " As related by Hepburn, however, neither the romantic nor the comic scenes came all that easily to the actor. Without an unexpected visit to the set one day by Noel Coward, the actress has recounted, Stewart might still be wrestling with one of his most famous screen monologues:

> Jimmy was doing the scene. . . . "You've got hearth fires banked in you, Tracy, hearth fires and holocausts." And George [Cukor] said to him, "Now, Jimmy, just do that scene in a romantic way. But *don't* do it as if you were just about to run away to the circus. Don't paw the ground with your feet, just say it." . . . So Jimmy was struggling with this thing . . . it's a bit fancy to say. And just before he did it, Noël Coward stepped onto the set and Jimmy nearly died. So he did the scene, and Noël in one second could see what was going on, and immediately stepped up to Jimmy and told him how devastating he was. And George said, "Roll 'em," and took advantage of that moment of flattery and Jimmy got a wonderful take.

As he had during the shooting of *The Shop Around the Corner,* Stewart also tightened up before the prospect of showing off his legs, in the sequence after Mike and Tracy have had their night swim. Although he joked that his appearance in a bathing suit would be "the end of the motion picture industry," it was the apprehension that went back to his early lack of enthusiasm for making movies, and beyond that to his childhood days in Indiana when he had disliked going to the beach. Hepburn took his misgivings seriously enough to propose to Cukor that both characters play the scene in bathrobes.

The Philadelphia Story broke box-office records at Radio City Music Hall in New York and went on to clean up around the country. A late December release also ensured that it was fresh in the minds of Oscar voters, and nominations were garnered in six categories: Best Picture,

Best Director, Best Screen Adaptation (Donald Ogden Stewart), Best Actor (Stewart), Best Actress (Hepburn), and Best Supporting Actress (Hussey). Stewart himself went around telling people that the Best Actor prize belonged to old friend Henry Fonda for his career-defining role as Tom Joad in *The Grapes of Wrath*. After losing out with *Mr. Smith Goes to Washington* the year before, he also made it obvious that he had little desire for attending another agonizing evening of watching presenters open envelopes. He changed his mind only when he received an enigmatic telephone call from a representative of the Academy of Motion Picture Arts and Sciences shortly before the ceremonies scheduled to be held at the Biltmore Hotel. According to the actor, the man was all archness with such remarks as "I know that it isn't my place to say so, but I really think you would find it in your best interests to attend." Stewart read every conceivable kind of meaning into the cryptic invitation—from an indication that he had won the supposedly secret Oscar race in his category to a warning that nominated actors who didn't show up at the ceremonies could forget about any further nominations. He went.

Stewart was the only Best Actor candidate on hand at the Biltmore February 27, 1941, when presenter Alfred Lunt announced him as the winner. Even before he got to the stage to accept his award, there was a knowing consensus that he was being honored as compensation for having been turned back with *Mr. Smith* twelve months earlier. The actor himself has never disputed that notion: "I never thought much of my performance in *The Philadelphia Story*. I guess it was entertaining and slick and smooth and all that. But *Mr. Smith* had more guts. Many people have suggested that I won it as a kind of deferred payment for my work on *Mr. Smith*. I think there's some truth in that because the Academy seems to have a way of paying its past debts. But it should have gone to Hank that year. That was one helluva performance he gave in *The Grapes of Wrath*."

The only other major Oscar won by *The Philadelphia Story* went to Donald Ogden Stewart's screenplay. But Stewart had some familiar company on the awards stage when Ginger Rogers took Best Actress honors for *Kitty Foyle*. Hepburn, while having fulfilled her objective of relaunching her film career, displayed some of Tracy Lord's snobbishness more candidly than in the picture when she sought to downplay the importance of losing to Rogers by telling reporters: "I was offered *Kitty*

Foyle, but I didn't want to play a soap opera about a shop girl. . . . Prizes are nothing. My prize is my work."

If Stewart's win reflected (as he claimed) an Academy habit of eventually balancing the books, it also flew directly in the face of voter reluctance to hand out Best Actor Oscars for comedy performances.[22] He didn't spend too much time worrying about it. With Rogers, Hussey, and others in tow, he went from one nightclub to another until dawn, interrupting his merry-making only for periodic announcements that he himself had voted for Fonda. When he returned to his Brentwood home the following day, Fonda's was among the hundreds of congratulatory telegrams awaiting him. Also waiting was housemate Burgess Meredith, who had had all night to come up with an appropriate greeting. What he settled for was throwing a scornful glance at the Oscar in Stewart's hand and snapping, "Where'd you get that thing—Ocean Pier Park?"

Meredith's crack was followed by a phone call from Alex. He, too, feigned ignorance about "some kind of prize" that he had heard the radio talking about. Unlike Meredith, however, he maintained the pretense well past initial irony, finally telling his son: "Well, I guess that's fine. You'd better send it over. I'll put it on show in the store where folks can take a look at it." The following morning, Stewart dutifully shipped the statuette to Indiana, where it remained in The Big Warehouse on display for decades.

Come Live with Me (MGM – 1941)

Come Live with Me was the first of three quickies that Stewart squeezed into the final weeks of 1940 and dawning days of 1941, on occasion jumping from one picture in the morning to another in the evening. All three films were made under the shadow of his announced intention of enlisting in the military. Although he had already been turned down once by Army doctors for failing to meet minimal weight standards in early November, MGM—and especially Bill Grady—knew that it was probably only a question of a few more meals before the actor tried again to pass the Army physical.

In *Come Live with Me*, Stewart plays Bill Smith, a down-at-the-heels, cranky writer who agrees to accept a "weekly loan" from alien Johanna

---

[22] The only others to do it have been Lee Marvin (for *Cat Ballou* in 1965) and Richard Dreyfuss (for *The Goodbye Girl* in 1977).

Janns (Hedy Lamarr) in return for marrying her, thus saving her from being deported back to a Nazi-controlled country. What Smith doesn't know is that Johanna is the mistress of publisher Barton Kendrick (Ian Hunter), who agrees to the marriage of convenience while he works up the courage to divorce his wife (Verree Teasdale). While abiding by his arrangement with Johanna not to pry into her affairs, Smith is inspired by their bizarre relationship to write a novel about it. The manuscript ends up with Kendrick, who recognizes the dimly fictionalized characters. Suspecting the truth, the publisher's wife maneuvers him into accepting the novel, then throws in the divorce so that he can marry his mistress. Smith, meanwhile, takes his proceeds from the sale and pays back every penny he has accepted from Johanna. When she in turn hears about Kendrick's pending freedom, she asks Smith for a divorce. The writer, by now in love with his wife-in-name-only, agrees only if Johanna will spend a day in the country with him at his grandmother's house. She has little choice but to go along. Under the tutelage of the wise grandmother (Adeline de Walt Reynolds), Johanna realizes that she is as much in love with Smith as he is with her.

Mainly thanks to director Clarence Brown, *Come Live with Me* is less painful than it might have been, achieving an almost surreal hilarity in a scene where Stewart, Hunter, and Teasdale all try to discuss the novelist Smith's characters without referring to themselves. MGM's most romantic director also elicited a performance from Lamarr that (at least temporarily) stymied critics who were convinced that she was inept as an actress. Some of the worst moments in the picture, in fact, come from Stewart, who is unusually hammy in his opening scenes. The same could be said for him in *Ziegfeld Girl*, one of the films he was doing almost simultaneously, suggesting that his frantic runs between sets left him too little time to settle into character.

Pot o' Gold (United Artists – 1941)

Stewart's last loan-out from MGM was for the only picture he has been quoted as calling his "worst." The experience was evidently not lightened by working with Paulette Goddard, whom he saw more often than he wanted to away from the set.

Pot o' Gold was little more than a movie-screen advertisement for a popular radio giveaway show of the same name that featured the Horace Heidt band. The pretext of a plot has Stewart playing the manager of a music store who would prefer to blow on his harmonica than sell sheet music or instruments to others. He and the daughter of a nearby boarding house operator (Goddard) help Heidt and his orchestra through money struggles to success on a radio show that turns into "Pot o' Gold." The nearest thing to a villain in the proceedings is the store manager's wealthy uncle (Charles Winninger), a food manufacturer who initially hates music (or at least Horace Heidt's music) but ends up being the radio show's sponsor.

Stewart's contempt for *Pot o' Gold* was such that he refused even to see it for many years. Then, in 1950, while staying at a New York hotel, he turned on the television set to see, as he put it, "why the movies are so frightened about this new medium." He decided from the inanity on the small screen that the motion-picture industry had nothing to fear from television—until realizing that what he was watching was *Pot o' Gold*.

If any actress in prewar Hollywood had a personality inimical to Stewart's, it was Goddard, who rejoiced not only in the extravagant and extroverted, but even in her own shallowness. Among other things, the actress never shied away from telling people that her former husband Charles Chaplin had "trained me so I was able to speak for three minutes on any subject, but not four." Among those who found this trait endearing was Meredith, who would eventually become Goddard's third husband. During the production of *Pot o' Gold*, she was also a regular overnight guest at the Brentwood home the actor shared with Stewart. Meredith: "Jimmy and Goddard were as different as people could be. She didn't have any of that canny, reserved quality that de Havilland or Sullavan or the other women he saw more than once, had, and that he seemed attracted to as some kind of basic virtue. The last thing she ever cared about was public reaction to what her folly of the moment was. I think it's fair to say that Jimmy never especially liked her."

What made it even worse, according to Meredith, was that the actress was rarely able to show her spontaneity at work, that once the cameras were turned on, she invariably tensed up. This merely worsened the atmosphere on the set of *Pot o' Gold*, where director George Marshall first tried numerous takes to draw a better performance from her, then just gradually gave up, leaving Stewart, Winninger, and the rest of the cast to hold the bag. Goddard herself was hardly unaware of the effect she was having on her leading man, either in Brentwood or on the United Artists soundstage. Asked once what she thought of Stewart, she said only, "Anyone can gulp."

Ziegfeld Girl (MGM – 1941)

Although impresario Flo Ziegfeld was the nominal inspiration for the last Stewart picture to be released before World War II, the shadow of L. B. Mayer again hung over a tale of the rewards to be had by applying oneself while working for a benevolent, successful producer. The most conspicuous differences from The Ice Follies of 1939 were in never showing Ziegfeld on the screen (thereby fortifying all the more his godlike importance) and in demonstrating what could happen when a would-be star didn't apply herself.

The plot of Ziegfeld Girl is laid out fairly didactically in an early scene of the picture when a Ziegfeld manager (Paul Kelly) warns a group of aspiring showgirls that one-third of them will become stars, one-third will quit the business and become housewives and mothers, and the last third will turn into tramps. The picture then proceeds to vindicate this poll. The star is Susan Gallagher (Judy Garland), who breaks up an act with her vaudeville performing father (Charles Winninger), gets to sing ballads like "I'm Always Chasing Rainbows," falls in puppy love with Jerry Regan (Jackie Cooper), and finally even finds a niche with Ziegfeld for her father. The housewife is Sandra Kolter (Hedy Lamarr), who briefly turns her back on her penniless violinist husband (Philip Dorn) for the attentions of the show's leading singer (Tony Martin), but then sees the light and returns to hearth and Beethoven. The tramp is Jerry Regan's sister, Sheila (Lana Turner), who ditches her truck-driver boyfriend (Stewart) for a socialite (Ian Hunter) who coaches her in expensive tastes. In order to hold on to Sheila, the truck driver tries to make some quick money by getting involved in bootlegging. This leads to his arrest and imprisonment. By the time he gets out of jail, he finds Sheila dying of cirrhosis of the liver from too much bathtub gin. She manages to hold on long enough, however, to see the big Ziegfeld show that she would have been part of if she hadn't taken the wrong path.

Ziegfeld Girl was mainly an excuse for recently signed producer Pandro Berman to show that he knew how to handle a big-budget musical. Choreographer Busby Berkeley added his kind of opulence to that provided by art director Cedric Gibbons and clothes designer Adrian, so that the production numbers moved as lavishly as they photographed.

Despite the fact that the story revolved around the characters played by Garland, Lamarr, and Turner, Stewart, who had an appreciably smaller role, received top billing in order to capitalize on his other successes of the period. His only noteworthy moment comes at the end of the picture, when he delivers a monologue on ducks at the bedside of the dying Turner. He so dominates the scene that Turner, the object of a major launching promotion with *Ziegfeld Girl*, was given a second dying scene with the less formidable Lamarr shortly afterward. Otherwise, the actor's presence on the set was an occasional thing, as he himself admitted some years later. "I was going back and forth between *Ziegfeld* and *Pot o' Gold* all the time. One day I got to MGM and heard that Lana's character was dead, and really couldn't remember whether my character had been responsible for that."

According to Jackie Cooper, Stewart didn't miss too much by not being on the set all the time:

> It all worked out great for me personally because I ended up getting fifteen or sixteen weeks of work out of it, and made more money than anybody else. And this was after they told me they were casting me because they didn't want to "waste" a star like Mickey Rooney on what should have been a small part. But between all the preparations for the big production numbers and all the bitching on the set, there was a helluva lot of downtime. Lana, for instance, was a real expert at announcing that she was having her period so needed three or four days at home. A lot of actresses worked that one, but none of them better than Turner. Then Judy got into the act, and it really disappointed me that she was buying into the same star-attitude thing. Something always seemed to be bothering her and slowing things down. Most of it was Turner, and how Tony Martin seemed to pay more attention to Turner than to her. At least when Jimmy was around, there was a sense of professionalism.

Newsweek spoke for most critical reaction in terming Stewart's role "thankless"; which was more or less what the actor had decided about continuing to make pictures at all. He wouldn't go before the Hollywood cameras again until 1946, and by then he would no longer be an MGM contract player.

IV
THE WAR

THE SLACKER

I N THE SECOND HALF OF THE 1930s, HOLLYWOOD PROVED far more adept than European countries at keeping World War II outside the door. At risk with any screen acknowledgment, let alone denunciation, of what was going on across the Atlantic was the disapproval of Germany and Italy—and tens of millions of dollars in annual film rentals. Practically through the end of the decade, therefore, the studios remained far more focused on the estimated 35,000 European theaters that exhibited American movies than on the extent of the armed forces buildup in Germany, the number of political dissidents imprisoned in Italy, or the volume of casualties suffered by nations trying to resist invasion and occupation. When Germany demanded the removal of Jewish employees from distribution offices within its territory, the Hollywood studios complied with barely a mutter. The German and Italian consuls in Los Angeles were approached for "consultations" whenever a screenplay was deemed potentially hazardous to overseas earnings. Even after Japan's bombing of Pearl Harbor in December 1941, priorities were not forgotten: Louis B. Mayer, for instance, could blithely predict that the United States merely had to wait for the Nazis and Communists of Europe to annihilate each other before the resumption of normal business operations on the continent.

If there was a turning point in Hollywood's attitude about confronting European realities, it wasn't brought on by the fall of any of the numerous countries invaded by Germany or by horror reports leaking out of occupied lands; rather, it came about as a result of back-to-back developments in the middle of 1940 that went directly to the heart of the industry's interests. In August of that year, Germany, followed immediately by Italy, announced a ban on all American pictures within territories under its control—making further kowtowing to Berlin and Rome superfluous. A month later, on September 16, 1940, Congress passed the first peacetime military Selective Service bill, calling for the annual drafting of 900,000 men between the ages of twenty and thirty-six. No sooner had Franklin Delano Roosevelt signed the bill into law than a couple of MGM's most prominent players—Robert Montgomery and Stewart—announced their intention of getting a jump on the draft by enlisting immediately. That, in turn, initiated six years of ambivalent maneuvering by the studio bosses to protect their investments while being careful not to become so protective that the investments shriveled into valuelessness.

Montgomery linked his announcement of intentions to warnings that the United States was going to be dragged into the war whether or not it wanted to be, so the country was better off preparing for the inevitable. This brought him the scorn of isolationist politicians and media for presuming to have a foreign policy independent of that of Washington. At one point, the actor skipped Hollywood for an anticipated six months of ambulance duty with the American Field Service in France, only to have to come home again far sooner once Germany invaded. The weekly *Time*, the chief mouthpiece for anti-interventionist Henry Luce, jeered the precipitous return of "Hollywood's foremost authority on World War II." While awaiting a commission in the Navy, Montgomery took every opportunity to furnish particulars about the horrors that he had seen in France and to assail Mayer and the other studio bosses for burying their heads in the sand. Mayer's response was to soak the actor for all he was worth before he received his commission, putting him in one picture after another during his final months as a civilian. The last of the pictures was *Rage in Heaven*, in which Montgomery did a shallow variation on the psychotic killer he had played so successfully in *Night Must Fall* in 1937. A studio executive at the time insisted that the casting was deliberate, that Mayer had wanted Montgomery's last image with the public to be that of a not particularly convincing lunatic.

While lacking Montgomery's firsthand experience with European events, Stewart hadn't depended only on newspapers or radio broadcasts for knowledge of what was going on, either. Although hardly part of Hollywood's British colony, where European war developments had been the chief topic of conversation for years, he frequented homes where English actors were always in attendance. One was the Italianate Beverly Hills mansion of Barbara Hutton and her soon-to-be husband Cary Grant, where such regular guests as Cedric Hardwicke, Laurence Olivier, Leslie Howard, and the South African Basil Rathbone would invariably withdraw to some corner to debate their own course of action in support of the British war effort. Another common meeting place was the Pacific Palisades home of Mr. and Mrs. Douglas Fairbanks, Jr. "He showed up practically every Saturday night," Fairbanks recalls of Stewart, "and before he got around to the piano playing that everyone usually insisted on, he would sit quietly listening to somebody like David Niven talking about the latest news from overseas. I saw that he was very affected by what he was hearing—as anybody who had a conscience would have been."[1]

Stewart's most conspicuous public foray on behalf of the British war effort came in August 1940, when he went with Fonda, de Havilland, Tyrone Power, Nancy Kelly, Mischa Auer, and Richard Green to a fundraiser in Houston. The show at the Houston Coliseum featured Stewart and Fonda first doing a magic act, then returning for a musical encore; Stewart played the accordion, Fonda the cornet. The actors helped to raise more than $100,000.

Even more important for shaping Stewart's attitude—and actions—for the coming storm were his visits to his neighbors Hayward and Sullavan. There he got himself involved in Hayward's Southwest Airlines project and, later on, could avail himself of his agent's vital mediation role in persuading the War Department of his greater use as a pilot overseas than as a celebrity at home. In terms of the efforts that MGM would make to keep Stewart in the United States, if not a civilian, Hayward turned out to be Mayer's worst nightmare.

Not that Mayer simply accepted the inevitable. Prior to Stewart's initial appointment for an Army physical in November 1940, the MGM boss summoned the actor to his office to try to change his mind. He ran through a laundry list of persuasions: the major pictures in the offing for Stewart, something close to a *mea culpa* for not finding better properties for him in the past, contract revision possibilities, sufficient time for him

---

[1] Fairbanks himself was another important source of anti-isolationist sentiment. Widely known as a confidant of the Roosevelt Administration, he would eventually undertake an intelligence-gathering mission in Latin America for the White House, then, after that, serve as an officer in the Navy.

to participate in events such as the Houston fundraiser if that was what he wanted. All accounts of the conversation depict a Mayer who was very aware of having to proceed carefully. Beyond his general apprehension that *any* prominent contract player might start a stampede to the door by announcing a desire to enlist, there was the further problem that it was the nationally lauded idealist Jefferson Smith who wanted to put on khaki. Moreover, those Jeffersonian principles remained as elusive as ever to would-be trappers. Stewart was not associated with any of Hollywood's left-wing—not to mention Communist—organizations that had supported the Loyalist cause in Spain and had called for a mobilization against the Nazis and Fascists for years. He had never taken a pronounced stand against the studios for trying to keep European realities off the screen. Unlike Montgomery, he showed little inclination to defend his intentions in a political way at all. In fact, what Mayer came to realize he was confronting was the casual ideology of the moral (it was right to go), the hormonal (it was time to go), and the technical (it was time to fly more seriously) that, as then, sometimes seemed to trace out impervious patriotism. Mayer knew he couldn't win.

But he got a postponement of the decision. Stewart was turned down by the Army doctors for being ten pounds under the War Department's height-weight ratio standard. He was mortified, and let Brentwood neighbors, housemates, and housekeepers know it. Being too thin hadn't prevented him from playing football at Mercersburg, becoming a leading man in the movies, or attracting women, he lamented to Meredith, Swope, Fonda, Hayward, and Sullavan; why was the Army suddenly so much more particular? Nor was he easily calmed by arguments that, if it was a question of a mere ten pounds, all he had to do was start a high-fat diet, then take the physical again: He already had been through quite a few fattening programs without any lasting success.

In both his alacrity to join the Army and in his despondency at having failed the physical, two other factors also seemed to have been at work. The first was the Stewart family history, in which military service had been a given for generations. It would have taken a virulent amnesia that Stewart never showed on other occasions for him not to have thought of Alex's stints in the Spanish-American War and World War I when he was told that the Army didn't regard him as fit. In any event, Alex didn't even give him the chance to contract it. As the actor once recalled apropos his troubles with the military doctors:

> When I was rejected because of being underweight, coast-to-coast head-
> lines blared—Movie Hero Heavy Enough to Knock Out Villain But Too
> Light for Uncle Sam. That night, the phone rang, and I picked up the
> receiver to hear, "Jim, this is your father. . . . I'm coming right out to
> Hollywood. . . . I can punch a few noses among those reporters. Then we'll
> start suits." "That wouldn't help things a bit. Only make it worse. You can't
> treat the press that way." "Okay, I'll hire a public relations man for you. I'll
> get the best there is in the business." "No, Dad." "Well, by God, we've got
> to do *something!*"

By Stewart's account, the phone conversation was mainly a reassurance that his father was again in his corner, not at all a reminder that
maybe there was something to be ashamed of. If true, it was just as well,
since he was already feeling enough pressures from the kind of newspaper
headline he described.

When Sterling Hayden told Paramount that he was leaving Hollywood
for the armed forces, he was widely quoted as declaring: "I don't want to go
on imitating men, and that's all there is to it." Few contract players in the
early 1940s were ready to state it so baldly, but Hayden was far from being
the only one who couldn't cope with the notion of continuing to play
fictional heroes on the screen while the authentic kind were being
splattered all over battlefields. "Nobody who had a brain was enthusiastic
about going into the military," Robert Stack observes.

> I never detected any great sentiment of "Let's go!" But at the same time
> there was definitely a feeling of shame for a lot of guys in not being part of
> a group that was working to a common end. For people who had been told
> by their bosses and the newspapers and the public that they were stars,
> leaders of men, firsts among equals, that feeling was only magnified.
> Personally, I felt it even from another direction in that I was ranked
> around that period as the fifth-best shot in the world. I didn't have the
> standing of a Stewart or a Gable on the screen, but there was definitely a
> similar pressure around the idea that, "Hey, if he's so good firing a gun,
> why the hell isn't he firing it where it'll do the most good?"

According to Jackie Cooper, it was a problem that confronted the
studios as much as individual actors, if on an economic instead of
psychological basis:

Mayer tried to talk Jimmy out of enlisting, and he exerted even more pressure on a Culver City draft board to keep Mickey Rooney out of uniform. But even he realized that he was walking a very thin line from his own business point of view. On the one hand, all the studios wanted to keep their stars because they were money-makers. But on the other hand, especially as the war went on, they knew that the regular presence of an actor on the screen was going to get audiences asking themselves, "Hey, why is that one still living it up in Hollywood while my son or father or husband is getting the hell shot out of him in Europe?" Too much of that kind of wondering, of course, and somebody who had been a star could turn into box office poison. That's why studios like MGM handed out more 4F reports than hospitals during the war—to justify before the public the presence of their own employees!

Stewart's evolving sense of what belonged inside and what belonged outside the box marked JAMES STEWART—ACTOR had little room for his rejection by the Army doctors and none at all for the public-relations excuses of the MGM publicity department. Equally important, he showed absolute disdain for the idea of waiting for his Selective Service number to come up so he could perhaps take advantage of relatively more relaxed standards at another physical; the concept of volunteering had been another constant in Indiana. With little practical alternative, therefore, he embarked on a program of two pasta dishes a day, regular milkshakes, and whatever other fattener could be swallowed between dawn and midnight. By the fourth month of such a regime, Meredith, for one, thought he had the weight problem licked. ("He certainly *looked* heavier.") Stewart, though, wasn't so certain, and his bathroom scale seemed to have a change of heart nightly. Finally, in March 1941, only days after taking home his Academy Award for *The Philadelphia Story*, Stewart reported for his second physical. Depending on the source of the story, he either made it by a single ounce or didn't get weighed at all.

As Bill Grady recalled the morning, "I was ready to take him in a studio car. But he refused to let me take him in a limousine. He went by bus instead, leaving me with egg on my face. . . . I tailed after him. . . . I waited, and when a medical officer came out, I asked him if Jimmy had made it. The officer told me he'd made it by one ounce. What the officer didn't know was that Jim was so determined to make the weight that he hadn't been to the bathroom for thirty-six hours! It had been torture, but it had put him over."

Stewart's version has been that he walked up to the officer in charge of the physical and said, "Why don't you rerun a whole test on me and this time forget to weigh me?" When the officer reportedly answered that this would have been irregular, the actor said that his response was that "wars are irregular, too, but sure as hell there's one coming"—a comeback that saved him a second weigh-in. In light of Stewart's concern over the years for sparing his public what he deemed unnecessary personal information, and of Grady's insistence that the bathroom detail was accurate, the casting director's version would appear the more credible. What both men agreed on in their accounts is that, as soon as Stewart was informed that he had passed, he charged out to the waiting Grady with an ecstatic shout of "I'm in! I'm in!"

But there were still a few more bumps—some of them of a literal kind—before the actor was sworn in as a soldier. To begin with, Mayer made another pass at trying to talk him out of his decision, at one point resorting to the contention that since the United States was unlikely to get into the war in any case, what Stewart had actually done was to trade in his screen career for a clerical post on some military base. When that argument went the way of his earlier tries, the studio boss finally threw in the towel, referring to Stewart as being "bullheaded" in his determination. To be sure that he was shown to be on the side of the angels, he instructed the publicity department to play up the actor's induction as one of MGM's proudest moments and also threw a big going-away party at which every studio name was expected to be present. "Mayer wanted to fly the MGM flag at half-mast," Grady recalled later. "Actors gave sentimental, patriotic, impassioned toasts. Actresses couldn't stop kissing Jimmy. Some wept. Rosalind Russell took out her handkerchief to wipe lipstick off his face. Underneath each red stain, she printed the name of the star who did the kissing. Jimmy kept it for a good luck omen."

Only a few days before induction, and a week after receiving his license as a commercial pilot, Stewart survived a scrape scarier than Mayer. While he was enjoying what he thought would be one of his last solo flights in the morning, the engine of his Stinson 105 began sputtering, necessitating a jarring forced landing at Van Nuys Airport. He was hospitalized briefly, but emerged with little more than head and face contusions.

Stewart reported for military service to the Westwood station of the Pacific Electric Company on March 22, 1941. The pickup point reminded

Meredith more of a college football stadium before the big Saturday game than a first step toward what might be war. The entrance was jammed with UCLA students singing and playing instruments, some of them wearing World War I German helmets, all of them mocking Hitler's Third Reich in song, sign, or speech. Adding to the carnival air were scores of children, the sons and daughters of those about to be inducted. After a roll call, the volunteers filed on to a bus for the trip to the induction center in downtown Los Angeles, then were transported to Fort McArthur. By nightfall, James Stewart had become Private James Stewart, and everybody in the country knew about it. Even without the general news interest aroused by the induction of a movie celebrity, MGM made sure to obey Mayer's orders by assigning cameramen and photographers to Stewart's every capturable step during the enrollment process. It was the beginning of another obstacle course he was determined to outwit.

Army life wasn't quite what Stewart had planned. For certain, his intention of gaining anonymity overnight as just another soldier wasn't so easily realized. At one of his very first mail calls at Fort McArthur, he came up against a sergeant who insisted on lining up his troops, then doling out letters one by one to recipients. By the time Stewart had marched back and forth from his position in the ranks ten times, he admitted, his whole body was red with embarrassment. On the other hand, the incident also helped him break the ice with other recruits who had previously shied away from him, expecting him either to be stand-offish or to be accorded very special treatment because of his civilian status.

Five days after being barracked at Fort McArthur, the actor was assigned to the Army Air Corps installation at Moffett Field. News of the transfer brought dozens of calls a day to the military base from female fans—not unlike what was to happen in the 1950s after Elvis Presley was drafted. There was also a regular patrol of women with the photographers who lingered at the front gate of Moffett Field, prompting Stewart to decline overnight passes on several occasions. MGM continued to make things difficult, as well. In addition to trying to make Stewart the running star of its newsreels, it waited merely a few months before bombarding newspapers and magazines with supposedly "inside" stories of what it was like for one of the studio's stars to live on less than $2,000 a month. The articles, some of them written under the actor's byline, were so cloying in their trumpeting of simple American virtues and so heavy-handed about relating those virtues to MGM values, that a number of previously sympathetic columnists ripped into the public relations ploy. On August 24, 1941, for example, Ed Sullivan of the New York *Daily News* moaned that "if the Metro press department doesn't stop these floods of imbecilic, ghost-written letters from Jimmy Stewart, the War Department will court-martial him . . . on the grounds of sabotage." What specifically triggered the Sullivan outburst was an "article" signed by Stewart that claimed that the hottest topic of debate in his barracks was whether the new husband of Deanna Durbin, another MGM player, was worthy of her; which the actor assured his buddies the man was.

For all the distractions, however, Stewart advanced steadily up the ranks, going from a drill-instructing corporal to an aviation officer candidate within a few months. At his request, his commanding officers also helped ease some pressures by running interference for interview and photograph requests, all but declaring a blanket no to the media. Through the summer of 1941, he impressed friends as having found a genuine satisfaction in learning the intricacies of airplane mechanics, in particular.

Too much satisfaction, in the eyes of his father.

In September 1941, Stewart was granted leave to go to Indiana to appear at a weekend benefit for the Allied Relief Fund. The scheduled program called for him to repeat with Bill Neff the magic act he had done with Fonda in Houston the year before, then to pair up with another childhood friend, Dutch Campbell, a pianist for the Fred Waring Orchestra, in a musical number. Although the benefit itself went well, Alex found reasons for grumbling before and after it. For one thing, he didn't like the idea that his son wore a suit rather than his uniform. He wasn't too enchanted, either, when, in asking about the progress being made toward acquiring a commission, he received as a response only something about the vagaries of "Army time."

Shortly afterward, Alex and Bessie made one of their periodic visits to California. Alex's worries hadn't been alleviated in the meantime by some wire service photographs showing Stewart hitting a Hollywood night spot with MGM actress Frances Robinson. What he found upon his arrival confirmed his fears: Not only was Stewart going around in civilian clothes whenever he was off his base, but he was acting decidedly more concerned about pursuing an Earl Carroll dancer than qualifying as a military pilot. According to the actor it was his father's resultant blowup that refocused him on why he had joined the Army in the first place; the main thrust of Alex's criticism was that the onetime writer-producer-director-actor of World War I dramas in his Indiana basement had himself become something of a slacker. Within a few weeks, Stewart completed both the academic requirements and a test flight in a BT-14 basic trainer outside San Francisco to gain his wings and a second lieutenancy.

As embarrassing as it was for Stewart to be accused of being too desultory about obtaining his commission, it would have been appreciably more painful if the dressing down from his father had come only a few weeks later—after Japan's attack on Pearl Harbor. As it was, he blamed himself for having to catch up almost as frantically as the U.S. Navy in Hawaii. America's official entrance into the war also revived pressures on him as an actor—and this time with the encouragement of the War Department and the White House. On December 15, eight days after the Japanese bombing, he joined Edward Arnold, Lionel Barrymore, Walter Brennan, Walter Huston, Edward G. Robinson, and Orson Welles in an hour-long program simulcast on all the radio networks and dedicated to the 150th anniversary of the Bill of Rights. Produced by Norman Corwin, We Hold These Truths had actually been planned before the raid on Pearl Harbor. For reasons never made explicable, some network executives had initially considered shelving the project because of the war, causing Roosevelt himself to point out that under the circumstances they weren't likely to come across a more appropriate subject and to urge that the program go on. Stewart's inclusion on the roster of what were some of Hollywood's most dramatic radio voices of the day was considered desirable not only because of his own skills in the medium, but also because of his standing as an early volunteer for military service.

We Hold These Truths turned out to be the start of something mixed and something bad for the actor. Over the months that followed, in fact, he could have been forgiven for thinking that the War Department had come to share Mayer's vision of how best to use him. Between his normal duties as a flight instructor for relatively light aircraft, first at Moffett Field and then at Mather Field, he drew an increasing number of media and public relations assignments. On January 18, 1942, only days after receiving his commission, for instance, his superiors endorsed the idea of doing a radio guest spot with ventriloquist Edgar Bergen, since the comedy program dealt with the dummy Charlie McCarthy's overzealous patriotism in signing up with all the branches of the armed forces. It was not the only time that Stewart appeared with Bergen, and he has never spoken of the experience with any affection. "My instructions were to make soldiers laugh," he told one interviewer. "For three months I traded so many jokes with Edgar Bergen and Charlie McCarthy that I was beginning to feel that I had been carved out of wood, too."

At the end of January, he was a combination Hollywood-military representative at the White House for a birthday party in honor of Roosevelt. Less than a month later, he received enthusiastic permission to show up in his uniform as a presenter at the Academy Awards. Secret balloting or not, there weren't too many that year who would have bet against the Best Actor trophy going to Gary Cooper for his portrayal of *Sergeant York*; Stewart, spokesman for the modern armed forces, ended up handing the Oscar to Cooper, the screen image of a previous generation's breed of heroic soldiers. (Due to some fumbling on the stage, however, both actors walked off leaving the statuette on the presentation rostrum.) In March, Stewart was asked to lend his dramatic talents to a half-hour NBC story entitled *Letter at Midnight*, in which he played a soldier writing home to explain why it had been so important for him to go to war. In April, he narrated the fifteen-minute-long *Winning Your Wings*, the first of numerous recruitment pictures and documentaries that he would make on behalf of the Air Force over some forty years.[2] (As voiced by Stewart, one of the script's pitches to young males in the audience was to "consider the effect these shining wings have on the gals.") Finally, in July, he contributed to a bond drive by reteaming with Cary Grant and Katharine Hepburn in a *Lux Radio Theatre* presentation of *The Philadelphia Story*.

Through it all, Stewart grew increasingly antsy, especially after one of his superiors at Mather Field suggested that he might be best suited as a morale officer who could be detached for special radio and public appearances assignments. This struck him as Mayer's prediction in spades— except that the United States *was* in the war.

The only person complaining more than Stewart about his situation

---

[2] The War Department reorganized its air services between June 1941 and March 1942, eliminating the Air Corps designation for an independent Army Air Force.

was Hayward. Every time the actor lamented his lack of actual fighting opportunities, the agent passed it on to Washington. The one who ended up listening was General Kenneth McNaughton, one of the War Department officials involved in overseeing the Thunderbird Field project in Arizona. McNaughton had the newly promoted Lieutenant James Stewart assigned to heavy bomber instruction at Kirkland Field in New Mexico. Stewart told Meredith that he finally felt as though he had gotten off Edgar Bergen's lap.

BEAT THE FÜHRER

FROM AN OUTSIDER'S PERSPECTIVE, STEWART'S ASCENT UP the military ladder might not have seemed too much slower than his rise from a bit player on Broadway to a leading man in Hollywood. When he arrived at Kirkland Field, near Albuquerque, he had been in uniform for less than eighteen months, and had already acquitted various assignments on base and off base while winning a steady series of promotions and gaining the confidence of both his superiors and his charges. But that wasn't his outlook. As he knew only too well, serving with distinction meant one thing for the War Department in Washington, a second thing for The Big Warehouse in Indiana, and a third thing for MGM in Hollywood. Moreover, it meant a fourth thing for the calendar. Already thirty-four when he reported for his New Mexico posting, Stewart found nothing comforting in the fact that most of those with his lieutenant's rank, and even some of his superiors, were markedly younger than he was. If no one went around calling him Pappy, his years—on top of the celebrity that everybody made an effort to say didn't matter—were hardly an asset for the combat duty he was seeking; he was, in fact, wary of being *too* successful at some administrative or teaching task.

Kirkland Field didn't ease his anxieties all that much. While training bombardier pilots represented some progress from defending Charlie McCarthy against court-martial charges of making false statements to the United States Armed Forces, Stewart watched each group of pilots that passed through like a teacher in June for whom graduation mainly underlined how he had become superfluous. Finally, in December 1942, he officially requested a transfer to nearby Hobbs Field, where 100 hours of classroom work and piloting a B-17 would entitle him to assignment to a war-bound Flying Fortress outfit. It was a struggle for the actor—in the classroom, if not in the cockpit. "I had to work pretty hard at subjects I'd forgotten, and was never any good at anyway," he has said. "Mathematics, for example. Most of the fellows with me were as much as ten years younger than I was and they'd work out in a few minutes navigational problems I'd have to mull over for an hour or more."

But he got through. Qualified as a B-17 commander in February 1943, he was dispatched with thirty other Hobbs Field graduates to Salt Lake City, where he was supposed to receive assignment to an air group scheduled to be sent to a war front within three months. But while each and every one of his thirty companions did get such orders, Stewart again found himself up against a hierarchical reluctance to commit him to combat. After being left to cool his heels for a couple of weeks, he was assigned to the 29th Group at Gowen Field in Boise. It turned out to be still another dirt road going nowhere in particular. "There must be some hitch about your going into combat," Stewart has remembered his commanding officer declaring to him after a week in Idaho. "I've got instructions to classify you as 'static personnel.' From now on, you are an instructor in first-phase training."

Stewart kept his own counsel. He didn't have much choice. Even Hayward was of the view that there was no particular officer holding him back from being sent overseas, but rather an amorphous Air Force discomfit about taking responsibility for such a decision. So, instead, he got down to the job of squadron operations officer at Gowen at a time when the War Department was demanding twenty-four-hour-a-day activity to turn out new crews to replace the severe losses suffered in Europe and the Pacific. It turned out to be an assignment not at all like the administrative task that he had feared; in another way altogether, it was much worse. After only a couple of weeks on the job, his roommate was killed during a takeoff with a student at the controls. Stewart himself lost three of his charges within a single week, partly because of the incessant Idaho snows. When he wasn't instructing on the ground, he was in the air, conducting dangerous drills on how to avoid crashing if one, two, or three of a crew's four engines were knocked out. On another occasion, as related by Beirne Lay, he himself almost came down with an entire crew of learners: "One night Jimmy was checking a new airplane commander. He had given his co-pilot's seat temporarily to the navigator, who wanted to see how things functioned in the cockpit. The navigator got an eyeful a moment later, when a blinding flash of light came from the No. 1 engine on the pilot's side, accompanied by a loud explosion. Somehow, Jimmy got the navigator out of the co-pilot's seat, so that he could reach the No. 1 fire extinguisher selector valve. He regained control, and he set the bomber down safely."

Actions of the kind, plus his high turnout rate of qualified crews, earned Stewart a promotion to captain by the summer of 1943. He also developed a reputation as an officer who had a special feel for his men. Walter Strawinski, posted at Gowen at the time, thinks that this was noticeable even when he didn't accompany his crews on their test flights:

> Stewart was known for being one of the few officers who never left the airfield tower until every single plane returned. There were a lot of other officers who would just stand up there until they were satisfied that the group coming in seemed to know what landing was all about. They'd watch the lead plane or two come down, then they'd disappear from the tower. On the other hand, Jimmy would never move until every single plane in the air was back on the ground and accounted for. It was the kind of small detail that was very important among the men, and they all tucked it away.

Along with his highest possible performance rating of Superior, Stewart's rapport with his students eventually won over the commanding officer of Gowen to his well-known desire to be assigned overseas. The commander, Colonel "Pop" Arnold, appeared to have been convinced just in time, too, since there were reports during July and August that the War Department had decided that the actor should have been satisfied with his well-earned captaincy and that no face would be lost if he spent the rest of the war on various domestic recruitment assignments. But before those orders arrived in Idaho, Arnold had persuaded Colonel Robert Terrill of the 445th Bombardment Group (Heavy) in Sioux City to take Stewart as a squadron operations officer. A mere nineteen days after reporting to the Iowa base, the actor was appointed commander of the 703rd squadron of twenty B-24 Liberators. There was no further talk of keeping him in the United States.

Before his departure for Europe in November, however, there was considerable talk of another kind. While still attached to Moffett and

Mather fields, Stewart had continued to frequent the Hayward-Sullavan household whenever his passes and leaves permitted. One evening there he met singer Dinah Shore, and the two of them continued seeing each other even as he was negotiating the military course marked by his postings to New Mexico, Utah, Idaho, and Iowa. According to Walter Strawinski and others, Shore visited him "more than once" while he was based at Gowen Field, putting up at a Boise hotel. Although the two generally avoided the gossip columnists and magazine writers who, a few years earlier, had reported assiduously on every development—real or imagined—in Stewart's relationship with Olivia de Havilland, he arguably came closer to marrying the singer than he had the actress. Hal Kanter, who wrote, directed, and produced *The Jimmy Stewart Show* on television in the 1970s, among other projects with the actor, says that Stewart told him that he had come to the very edge of marrying before leaving the U.S. with the 445th Bombardment Group.

> The way he told it to me once, he and Dinah decided to get married in Las Vegas, so they drove there one night from Los Angeles. But along the way, he said, Dinah started talking about how at nine o'clock they were going to do this, at eleven they were going to do that, and how the following morning at another fixed hour, they were going to do something else. According to Jimmy, she had absolutely everything worked out on a detailed schedule that stretched far into the future. That was enough for him, he said, to turn the car around and go back to Los Angeles.

Other Stewart associates have expressed skepticism that a marriage was ever so close, especially in light of his aversion to settling down with show-business personalities. The actor himself has also acknowledged that he was occasionally prone to exaggerating particulars of a story if it suited his storytelling.[3] Nevertheless, he was known to have corresponded with Shore regularly once he was based in Europe; it was, in fact, from one of her letters that he got the "Dear John" news that she intended to marry actor George Montgomery. And, as Burgess Meredith observes, "the imminent prospect of being sent to a war from which you

---

[3] Apropos the skiing sequences in *The Mortal Storm*, for instance, he once admitted initially conceding that they had been done by a double, then subsequently asserting that he had done "some" of them, and then finally claiming that he had done them all because "it's like swimming—something you never forget how to do."

might not return could shake up a lot of convictions" about who might and who might not be acceptable as a wife.

Still single, Stewart had a final meeting with his father in Sioux City on the eve of taking his squadron to Europe. By his description, they were "very self-conscious with one another." The actor once told *McCall's* magazine: "We talked generalities, trying to conceal our awareness that, starting tomorrow, he could no longer walk with me. At the time of the greatest crisis in my entire life, he would have to stand aside. We were both afraid. At the moment of parting, he studied his shoes for a moment, then looked at the sky. I knew he was searching for a final word of advice, of love, of something to sustain me, but he couldn't find it. He opened his mouth, then shut it hard, almost in anger. We embraced; then he turned and marched quickly away."

Only after Alex had gone did Stewart realize that he had an envelope sticking out of his pocket. When he saw his father's handwriting, he decided to wait until he was back in his bunk before he opened the envelope. What the message inside said was:

> My dear Jim boy, Soon after you read this letter, you will be on your way to the worst sort of danger. I have had this in mind for a long time and I am very much concerned. . . . But Jim, I am banking on the enclosed copy of the 91st Psalm. The thing that takes the place of fear and worry is the promise in these words. I am staking my faith in these words. I feel sure that God will lead you through this mad experience. . . . I can say no more. I continue only to pray. Goodbye, my dear. God bless you and keep you. I love you more than I can tell you. Dad.

By Stewart's testimony, it was the very first time that Alex had said explicitly that he loved him, and he began to cry, wondering in the middle of his tears whether the letter had "brought me to weakness instead of strength." The Psalm enclosed said:

> I will say of the Lord, He is my refuge and my fortress. . . .
> His truth shall be thy shield and buckler.
> Thou shalt not be afraid for the terror by night; nor for the arrow that flieth by day; . . .
> For He shall give his angels charge over thee, to keep thee in all thy ways.
> They shall bear thee up in their hands, lest thou dash thy foot against a stone.

On November 11, 1943, Stewart received orders to depart for England with his squadron of twenty B-24 Liberators. They were assigned to the Allied air base at Tibenham, a small village in Norfolk, about 100 miles northeast of London. The necessarily circuitous flight plan entailed a series of refueling stops in Florida, Puerto Rico, British Guyana, Brazil, Senegal, and Morocco. Stewart flew as a copilot with Lieutenant Lloyd Sharrard. According to Sharrard, "Jimmy wasn't much for small talk. When he wasn't talking about some technical particular having to do with the flight or going over something with somebody in the crew, he seemed perfectly at ease with silence." What did get a rise out of him, on the other hand, was something he spotted during a layover of several days in Marrakech while the planes were being fitted with armor plating for the final hop over to England. "One day, we visited the Jewish section of the city, and while we were walking down this very narrow street, there in front of us, there is this old billboard, no bigger than 5' x 8', advertising one of his old movies with his picture on it. He looked totally bewildered for a second to find something like that in such a remote place. Naturally, we didn't let him forget it for the rest of the day."

Once at Tibenham, Stewart had little time to wonder about the pervasiveness of Hollywood's distribution network. In fact, initially, he was more impressed by the thoroughness of Nazi propaganda since one of the first to greet him was radio propagandist Lord Haw-Haw, who sarcastically welcomed the 445th Bomber Group to England a mere couple of hours after its arrival. Even Lord Haw-Haw was quickly forgotten, however. After some tutoring from the R.A.F. in Northern Ireland on how to get 1,000 bombers into the air at the same time without causing an intramural disaster, Stewart took his crews through a couple of shakedown flights, then led them in early December on their first bombing mission, against the Third Reich's naval base at Kiel. It was the first of twenty missions that Stewart would fly as a squadron commander or in some other capacity. Mostly, the targets were plants in Germany and occupied France that produced war materials. While with the 445th, the actor flew in a Liberator that had drawn the nickname of Nine Yanks and a Jerk; the label had stuck from a previous crew.

It didn't take long for Stewart to gain a reputation as a "lucky" squadron leader. In fact, according to then-Lieutenant Howard Kreidler, the two of them were the only ones in the group who didn't lose men either to fire from the Germans or internal psychological pressures.

"Sometimes you'd get crew members who would simply crack up or just wake up one morning totally used up emotionally," says Kreidler, who retired from the Air Force in 1970 with the rank of brigadier general. "But that never happened to my men and it never happened to Jimmy's." Navigator Steve Kirkpatrick also calls Stewart "a damn good commanding officer. . . . I always had a feeling that he would never ask you to do something he wouldn't do himself. Everything that man did seemed to go like clockwork."

Stewart's standing among his men was no lower on the ground. John Robinson, a gunnery sergeant, recalled the day that he and another member of the 445th ran across their commanding officer after being told that the crew would have to continue to wait indefinitely for pay already due for two weeks. As Robinson detailed the episode in his book *A Reason to Live*:

> We all walked into the finance office together. With a clearing of his throat, Captain Stewart said to the lieutenant sitting behind the desk, "Why hasn't [the] crew been paid?" The lieutenant said, "They will be paid, sir, but it will take a few days to get around to it." Captain Stewart put his hand to his chin and started rubbing it. Then he said, "Lieutenant, we just don't have a few days. I believe we ought to pay them right now. Not in a few days. I mean kinda like now—in the next thirty minutes. . . . I will be back here in a little while and, you know, if the crew isn't paid by then, I believe that we will just have to find a new finance lieutenant because this one will be on his way out of here to the Infantry."

The crew got paid immediately. On another occasion, Robinson relates, he and his fellow crew members stole a keg of beer from the officers club and hid it under some blankets in their Nissen hut. A couple of evenings later, Stewart came by to talk about how the beer had been stolen, how the base commander was taking the theft seriously, how Robinson's hut had been fingered as one possible hiding place for the beer, how he himself thought that unlikely—the entire monologue delivered while he uncovered the keg from beneath the blankets, poured himself a beer, finished the beer, and bade everybody a goodnight.

Sometimes the personnel problems were more serious. "We had a point early on there," recalls Howard Kreidler, "when Tibenham must have had the highest percentage of clap in the Air Force. One time there was a picnic, and you'd see these guys disappearing one after another into the bushes where the hookers were. It wasn't as bad in our crews as elsewhere, but Jimmy put an end even to that by making a little speech and then marching everybody over for shots."

To hear Stewart himself, his major problem between air missions was dealing with England's winter cold. According to Kreidler, his roommate for many months, that was true, as far as it went: "It was one of those wet colds—not exactly what you would call polar, but the mist used to make it doubly miserable. The batmen stoked up the fire at 6:30 with four small cups of charcoal a night, meaning that by two in the morning you were freezing. Jimmy always had a running nose and was always complaining about his feet."

But then Alex came to the rescue:

All Jimmy had to do was to write to his father about some practical problem, and the mail never stopped. For instance, he must have had more Vitamin B pills than the infirmary—all sent from Indiana. When he wrote his father about the cold, he suddenly started getting all these contraptions the old man sold at the hardware store. The one I particularly remember were these six or eight gunny sacks that had plastic linings. One day I walked into our quarters and there's Jimmy with all the covers rolled back and he's pouring hot water into the sacks. Then he would place the sacks around the mattress—kind of like a network of super-hot water bottles. Those things from his father were the way that he managed to keep warm.

In Kreidler's view, however, Stewart's most encompassing reality at Tibenham was not the temperature, but his rank. While other members of the squadron have talked about evenings when the actor would play the piano in the officers club or take it upon himself to help make chocolate for a group, stirring a pot for hours, his roommate viewed those moments as exceptions rather than the rule. "I'm not going to call it a problem, because for him I don't think it really was. But a commander lives alone. He has no friends. He gets no drop-in visits because people are wary of being seen as trying to butter up to you. I commanded five units in thirty years, so I know it from experience. Jimmy was always basically a loner, and he lived with it. He was a commander, so he couldn't show emotion about that or anything else. In fact, he was about as unemotional as you can get."

Kreidler arrived at his view not only in the course of official duties with Stewart or as his roommate, but also when they went off together on passes.

> Days off, we'd almost always get no farther than the village of Tibenham. We had a 36' wooden boat with a radio that we rented and went off on alone. It was a kind of hideout for both of us. Jimmy preferred spending his free time that way than going up to London. One time I flew him up to London on a pass, and the mist got so bad that I was hedgehopping. After a little too much of that, he said, "Doc, there is absolutely nothing in London that I have to see so bad that I'm going to let you kill both of us for seeing, so let's get back to the boat." No emotion, of course.

Kreidler's perception dovetails not only with much of what Stewart has said about his wartime experiences, but also with the tone in which he has said it—a tone of measured control, of emotions recognized only for being discounted. Asked, for instance, if he had ever said a prayer before taking off on a mission, he told *The Movies* magazine in 1983: "I always prayed, but I really didn't pray for my life or for the lives of other men. I prayed that I wouldn't make a mistake. When you go up, you're responsible. . . . A few bad mistakes can mean disaster."

Similarly, he told another interviewer that one of his worst nights in England was prior to a mission when he *did* feel fear, and worried more about that fact than about the situation that had triggered it. "I was really afraid of what the dawn might bring. Our group had suffered several casualties during the day, and the next morning at dawn I was going to have to lead my squadron out again, deep into Germany. I got to imagining what might happen, and I feared the worst. Fear is an insidious and deadly thing. It can warp judgment, freeze reflexes, breed mistakes. And worse, it's contagious. I felt my own fear and knew that if it wasn't checked, it could infect my crew members."

But fear was far from being the only thing he had to fear. On one mission, John Robinson recalls, Stewart's plane sustained a direct flak hit in the flight deck, just behind the nose wheel. With another crew at the time, the gunner remembers arriving back at Tibenham and seeing the actor's craft practically split in two on the runway. "The tail of the ship was sticking up in the air and the nose was sticking up in front. Just in front of the wing at the flight deck the airplane had cracked open like an egg. The runway had aluminum scars where the airplane had been dragged. Jimmy Stewart stood by the end of the airplane's left wing tip.

As I walked up to him, he looked up at me and said, 'Sergeant, somebody sure could get hurt in one of those damned things.'"

The crash landing wasn't the only time that Stewart and his crew came close to getting killed. Following a raid on aircraft installations and factories in Brunswick, the actor was leading his squadron back to Tibenham as the commander of the second formation when he noticed that the lead formation had veered thirty degrees off course into dangerous territory above France. When he tried to warn the commander ahead of the navigational error, he was told to observe radio silence and just follow along as he had been. Twenty-eight miles south of Paris, the commander of the first formation paid for his obtuseness when some sixty German fighter planes attacked. But while the lead group was demolished in the air battle that ensued, Stewart's squadron fought off the Luftwaffe and managed to get back to England without the loss of a single life. What followed, according to some of those on the scene at the time, was "a division inquiry that was a court martial in everything but name." The investigators not only gave Stewart a clean bill of health, but established the grounds for awarding him a Distinguished Flying Cross.[4] As Ramsey Potts, who became his commanding officer a short time after the Brunswick raid, puts it, "there were a lot of lives saved that day because he knew what he was doing when he had to do it."

But if his superiors were noticing that Stewart, by now promoted to major, knew what to do when he was in the air, some were also beginning to wonder if maybe, notwithstanding his reputation for luck, he wasn't in the air too much, too often in the wrong locations, and even too reluctant sometimes to leave once he had reached his destination. The doubts stemmed from the fact that, as a commander of a squadron, Stewart was expected to fly only about every fifth mission with his crews and that some of these should have been as close to milk runs as a war would permit. Stewart, however, was having little of those guidelines and, as attested to by Kreidler, Robinson, and others, seemed to have an unerring instinct for picking the most precarious missions, often with minimal rest between them. In the view of Lloyd Sharrard, "you had your chicken-hearted commanders who tried to get out of flying altogether,

---

[4] For the missions that he carried out over occupied France, he would also earn the Croix de Guerre avec Palme twice—once for individual valor and once as a member of the 445th Group, cited as a whole.

then you had the average ones who followed the regulations, then you had somebody like Jimmy, who never tried to hide behind anything. He went to England to do a job and he figured the more he put into doing it, the quicker it got done."

Gunner Robinson saw that trait in one of his very first missions with Stewart, in December 1943: "We had to hit a lot of munitions plants in Bremen. During the raid, Jimmy made an initial pass, then went back for another one. That was pretty unheard of both because of the dangers of a double exposure to antiaircraft fire and because the usual thinking was, 'Well, there're plenty of planes behind me, so they'll get whatever I missed.' Back at Tibenham, I asked him why he had made another pass. He just shrugged and said that he hadn't seen the target the first time and was going to get it 'no matter how long it took.' "

It was in this light, says Robinson, that when the rumor began circulating in March 1944 that Stewart was going to be kicked upstairs to the Second Wing Division headquarters at Old Buckingham, three miles away from Tibenham, "everybody just figured it was due to the brass being afraid that he was going to get himself killed. We were easily sustaining the heaviest losses of any group there.[5] On top of that, Jimmy Doolittle had taken over the Eighth Air Force at the end of 1943 and had immediately raised the minimum number of missions from thirty to thirty-five. That just increased the odds against somebody who flew as often as Jimmy." When the word finally came down that Stewart *was* being transferred to Old Buckingham, as operations officer for the 453rd Bombardment Group and within the joint command for the Second Wing Division, it was "a real blow to morale," according to Robinson.

Ramsey Potts, a career officer and subsequently an attorney, who himself had only recently taken over the command of the 453rd, doesn't reject the speculation that hierarchical fears were a factor in the transfer. "When I was put in command, I needed a new operations officer because I didn't want the man who was there then. I didn't ask for Jimmy by name, but I certainly wanted someone with his kind of credentials. It was General Timberlake at the wing who gave him to me. It's possible he was assigned to me because he had been on too many missions at the 445. I

---

[5] Some estimates have put the group's overall casualties at 87 percent. In September 1944, after Stewart's departure, the 445th lost 237 men and 25 B-24s in a single action during a raid on Kassel.

was never told that directly, as I recall, but I think it's very possible."

When he reported to Potts, then a colonel, at Old Buckingham, Stewart found a unit with a morale problem that was among the worst in the Eighth Air Force. Potts had zeroed in on this as an immediate priority.

> When I first got to the 453, I had a broom with me. Seven combat crewmen, I saw from the records, didn't want to fly, had not flown, and had gotten away with it because nobody there appeared to want to do anything about it. There simply hadn't been much leadership. I called in the seven men separately, had a little talk with them, and got six of them back on active duty. The seventh one didn't want to hear, so I sent him over to medical and got him off the base. Then I went to work on some of the people who had allowed the situation to fester for so long. We didn't have a morale problem after a little while.

Indeed, within a couple of months of the arrivals of Potts and Stewart, the 453rd's proficiency rate on raids rose from near the bottom to near the top among Eighth Air Force units. Close to the change was Andrew Low, then the assistant operations officer with a rank of captain. "I'd gotten there only shortly before Potts and Jimmy," says Low, who stayed in the Air Force after the war and eventually retired as a major-general. "But I'd seen enough to know that it was day and night after a few weeks. There was no more of a I'm-not-going-to-fly-anymore-and-that's-all-there-is-to-it attitude. Obviously, that wasn't just because of Jimmy. But the difference in attitude was as noticeable through him and in the reputation he had brought over as a 'lucky' pilot as in anything else. One day, for instance, he found his jeep scrawled with the words DEATH TAKES A HOLIDAY. That said a lot about the new spirit of the place."

Although it did not suffer the punishments of the 445th, the 453rd wasn't a Coney Island ride, either. Within the two months preceding D-Day, it lost fifty-nine planes. Low himself was later shot down in German territory and held as a prisoner of war. "The most important things about those missions in the spring of 1944," he observes, "is how vital they were to the Normandy landing in June. We knocked out about 1,000 German pilots in that period. Would there have even *been* the D-Day we know if those pilots had still been up there?"

Between his arrival there and his return home in August 1945,

Stewart's responsibilities at Old Buckingham fell into four areas. The first, as the operations officer who earned another upgrading to lieutenant-colonel in May 1944, called for planning and charting duties on daily bombing runs. The second was to supervise the orientation and training of newly arrived crews. The third was to hold briefings, for both military personnel and the media. (Walter Matthau, a staff sergeant and still only an aspiring actor, remembered attending some of the briefings "just to hear him do Jimmy Stewart.") The fourth was to rotate with squadron and group commanders on actual bombing missions. His self-confidence in his piloting role was such that, given command of a thousand bombers for a mission over Germany on one occasion, he took off for the continent but, despite inevitable macho pressures, didn't hesitate to call off the entire operation because he wasn't comfortable with meteorological conditions. Ground command later ratified his decision. All told, he flew some 1,800 hours in uniform.

Because of general military censorship and Stewart's personal desire to maintain a low profile, few details of his activities emerged during the war. But, according to Barney Oldfield, just the fact that the American public knew that Stewart was on serious active duty ultimately had as much of a propagandistic effect for the Air Force as it won popular sympathy for the actor himself. "The Air Force has always owed a lot to movies and movie people. Between the wars you couldn't find better recruitment posters than pictures like *Wings*, *Hell's Angels*, and *Dawn Patrol*. Then both during World War II and after it, you had Jimmy. First as a fighting officer, then in the 1950s with something like *Strategic Air Command*. The only person ranking with Stewart as an important publicist for the Air Force in the middle of the century was Milt Caniff, the artist for comic strips like *Terry and the Pirates* and *Steve Canyon*."

As for Stewart's abilities as an officer, Ramsey Potts argues that they were manifest most of all in his dedication to the cardinal principle that dead heroes were mainly dead.

Obviously, the man was 100 percent as a pilot. And he also had a tremendous rapport with the men—that languid, humorous way he had of settling them down in some pretty stressful situations. But, just as important to me, he grasped immediately what I said to him once about agreeing with Marshal Montgomery's view of war. Monty used to go up to a soldier and ask him what was the most important thing he had. And when the soldier would invariably answer something like his rifle, Monty would jump all over him and say, no, it wasn't, it was your life, so you better hold on to it. I told the 453rd the same thing until it was coming out of their ears. From a military point of view, that meant they better fly in close formation if they expected to return to base. Jimmy understood that, too. He impressed them with living as well as winning, and more than that an officer can't do.

COMING HOME

ON AUGUST 30, 1945, STEWART RETURNED TO THE UNITED States. He didn't exactly rush the transition from the certainty in his high-command duties at Old Buckingham to the uncertainty in resuming civilian life. On the very day of his return, while his family and several friends waited at Manhattan's St. Regis Hotel to welcome him back, the now-full colonel made Leland Hayward linger with him at Pier 90 on West 50th Street while, against the background of music provided by the Sammy Kaye and Cab Calloway bands, he personally saw off just about every one of the 14,860 soldiers, sailors, and nurses who had completed the five-day Atlantic crossing with him on the *Queen Elizabeth*. At a press conference the following day at the Brooklyn office of Major General Clarence Kells, he largely parried questions about his immediate Hollywood plans, repeating an old crack about how his thirty-seven years probably entitled him only to roles as "a grandfather to Mickey Rooney" and noting that he had been in uniform nearly longer than he had worked for MGM. It was an amiable performance whose skittish tones were remarked upon only by Hayward and others close to him. He also made it clear to Alex that he was opposed to plans by the Indiana Chamber of Commerce to stage a parade in his honor.

Professionally, Stewart had plenty of company among actors unsure of what awaited them after the war. As Douglas Fairbanks, Jr., put it: "What on earth was I going to do? I had no plans whatever. It is an old theatrical saw . . . that one should not be away from the public eye for more than two or three years. . . . I had been away from my profession for over four years." Similar insecurities were also about to play havoc with Clark Gable, Robert Taylor, and other MGM stars. While some prewar

Hollywood screen luminaries mediated the difference between the grim realities they experienced in battle and the fictional heroics they were called upon to resume in front of a camera with increasing recourse to the bottle, others took up hobbies that derived much of their allure from the potential danger they posed for life and limb. It was in this context, for instance, that MGM put an end to Gable's sudden passion for motorcycle racing by forcing him to sell his bike. For Stewart, the syndrome passed through two additional filters—the one called Leland Hayward and the one recognized by his friends as his powers of self-containment.

In late 1944, Hayward sold his entire client list to the MCA talent agency in order to concentrate on a new career as a Broadway producer.[6] Before getting out of the representation business, however, he had scored a final coup in signing Gregory Peck as a client and then securing the lead role for the young actor in the MGM production of *Valley of Decision*. Pleased by the outcome of that film, Mayer approached Peck with the studio's customary seven-year exclusive contract offer. Hayward not only dissuaded the actor from the deal, but immediately went from studio to studio, committing Peck to almost a score of pictures on a nonexclusive basis and for extremely high sums.[7] The infuriated Mayer then ordered Hayward kept off the studio lot. Around the same time, Olivia de Havilland won a court case against Warner Brothers in which she contended that a seven-year contract was literally that and could not be unilaterally extended by the studio for covering suspensions or other kinds of absences. With the return of Stewart, therefore, Hayward had legal as well as personal grounds for recommending, as a savvy friend if no longer as an agent, that the actor not troop back to Mayer; on the contrary, he counseled, Stewart should point out that his time in the service had more than wiped out the eighteen months remaining on his studio contract, entitling him to independence right away.

Stewart accepted the advice, and informed Mayer of his position at a mid-September meeting. The MGM chief was as hamstrung with his departing employee as he had been with his enlisting employee before

---

[6] Hayward's wife Margaret Sullavan had never disguised her opinion of agenting as "flesh peddling" and helped trigger his career change by returning to Broadway. The family resettled in Connecticut.

[7] Peck: "After Hayward moved to New York, I found myself with seventeen or eighteen commitments, but with no strings to any studio. *That's* an agent."

the war. While alternately railing against Hayward and de Havilland, and cautioning Stewart that he was embarking on uncharted waters, he also knew that he had no legal footing for his indignation and that, moreover, the customary retaliations of the studio press office against a rebellious player might prove counterproductive against an acclaimed war hero. Not that Mayer didn't try. For some time after the announcement of Stewart's decision to go it alone, writers and columnists dependent on MGM handouts periodically reminded their readers of such particulars as Stewart's age and even of the insipid films (*Come Live with Me* and *Pot o' Gold*, especially) that he had made immediately before joining the Army. Hedda Hopper, who regarded herself as an intimate of both Stewart and several MGM executives, tried having it both ways in an early October syndicated column. On the one hand, she sought to titillate her readers with the news that Stewart and Henry Fonda had been spotted at a Beverly Hills restaurant discussing a screen project; on the other, she reported that a group of teenage girls had gathered outside the restaurant—not to see Stewart or Fonda, but rather a third diner on the premises, the younger MGM contract player Van Johnson. To complete the balancing act, Hopper then issued another of her occasional reminders that Hollywood distributors had missed Stewart more than any other single actor during the war.[8]

Stewart processed it all slowly, living up to his characterization by Margaret Sullavan as somebody who "likes to chew his cud" before announcing a decision of some kind. In his session with Mayer, as both principals attested subsequently, he even floated the notion of giving up acting altogether. If nobody close to him was ready to take that possibility seriously, linking the remark to a passing attempt to lessen Mayer's recriminations over the contract issue, some of the other statements he made shortly after his return did have longer life. One, delivered at his Brooklyn press conference in the office of Major General Kells, was that he was convinced that the movie public had been worn out by World War II pictures and that he could not foresee himself appearing in any film with a modern war background. In the event, with the odd exception of *The Mountain Road* in 1960, he did not appear in any for the rest of his career, rejecting even highly paid cameos in epics

---

[8] To make up for some of the slack, MGM and other studios rereleased practically all his pictures during the war.

mounted around famous battles of World War II. Another remark, which Mayer rashly ignored, was that he was opposed to playing in any picture that sought to exploit his role during the war. Consequently, he didn't feel any greater urge to go back to MGM when, during his meeting at Culver City, he was informed that the studio's first project for him was *High Barbaree*, a tale in which he would portray a flying ace. From that point on for several years he had a clause written into his contract prohibiting publicity departments from mentioning his years with the Air Force as a part of their promotions. Violation of that agreement gave him the right to walk off a picture and/or collect an appreciable indemnity.

What is suggested by both these scruples is that, aside from the basic, sometimes wracking acknowledgment by Hollywood performers that there was a vast divide between what went on in the European and Pacific theaters of war and what they were asked to recreate as reality in neighborhood movie theaters, Stewart was equally on guard against abetting the crossover of even the *memories* from one experience to the other. As far as the public was concerned, that meant the memories fueling legends (the Hollywood Star, the War Hero) that in any confusion would imbue one with too much significance at the price of depriving the other of any at all. He had been through that already in striving to separate the actor James Stewart from the corporal, lieutenant, captain, major, lieutenant-colonel, and colonel Stewarts, and he wanted it to be just as true in retrospect. (He was so attentive to that assumption that, in turning down the proposal for a Welcome Home parade in Indiana, he had found his objection not in some apprehension that other repatriated veterans would resent his reestablishment of special celebrity, but in the much more rank-and-file queasiness that the soldier who had returned with an arm missing or the sailor back home without his legs might not find all that much to celebrate with the ending of the war.)

But there was also the question of *his* memories, and he was equally vigilant against any crossover perceptions in that area. Thus his striking statement to several interviewers over the years that, as much as it was vital to him as an actor, "imagination can become a soldier's worst enemy." Taken at face value, the remark would seem to come down to the assertion that people caught up in the life-and-death situations of battle cannot afford to follow an abrupt inspiration in lieu of obeying orders and proceeding according to established directives. As such, it is hardly remarkable, as it primarily attests to Stewart's comfort with the military chain of command and with the prerogatives of the officer system and having nothing to do with acting. Anyway, that is the conclusion of, among others, Gregory Peck. "I would think that what he is getting at there has to do with his personal perspective about being a military man, his personal sense of dignity, if you will, and isn't meant at all as some artificial constraint that he has imposed on himself as an actor," says Peck. "At least, I would hope so. For an actor, putting on a uniform to play a soldier is exactly the same thing, involves the same kind of imagination, of imaginary process, as putting on chaps and a holster to play a cowboy."

Which, of course, is precisely the point: Where he has been concerned, Stewart has indicated that it *wasn't* the same. While even for accountants "imagination can become a worst enemy," it has been only military characters that he has generally eschewed playing for being "unrealistic" and "not at all the truth of what it's like." (If he had applied the same standard to most of the biographical pictures he made in the late 1940s and 1950s, he wouldn't have appeared in them.) They have, by and large, remained impervious to his very desire to bring his imaginative powers to bear on them.

One thought is this: that as successfully as Stewart separated the actor Stewart from the military man Stewart, he also separated both of them from everything else. Just as the emotional charges he brought to the screen struck friends and associates as a contrast to the way he conducted his private life, not least in the fervor of his commitments to the women he dated, the pitch of his application as an Air Force officer provided a similar study in intense mastery and versatility. If roommates like Howard Kreidler found his on-ground demeanor "about as unemotional as you can get," there was nothing, either, of the military automaton in the pilot who returned for a second pass over Bremen because he was going to hit his target "no matter how long it took," in the squadron commander who took on one dangerous mission after another, or in the operations chief who received his assignment at least in part because of the fears of others that he was about to get himself shot out of the sky. In the most encompassing sense, his emotions *belonged* to his work—as both sheltered specific feelings within the military structure and as a general reflection of the structure's perimeters. In the best of times, which were always the worst of times, that made for a lot of liberty for him.

None of this had to do with some consecutive role-playing—Stewart the actor going on to his longest sustained performance as Stewart the pilot, as some glib analyses of his career have proposed. The roles were, if anything, parallel to one another—mutually independent in their establishment of a desired personal terrain. The turf flying the actor's banner announced itself as a land of imagination; that flying the Air Force officer's banner was the land of responsibility. One was as important as the other, one offered as much self-vindication as the other. They marked separate responses to separate obligations—alike only in the opportunity to play things out *beyond* what others might have assumed was some natural conclusion. They could no more be mixed up in his own mind than a hammer could have been used to play a piano: The effort might have been appreciated and the noise might have been noticed, but it still would have been an inappropriate use of the instruments at hand.

In the meantime, while some Hollywood performers of his stature back home from the war hit the bottle and others raced their motorcycles, Stewart flew kites with Henry Fonda.

V
ACTOR AT
LARGE

AT LIBERTY

STEWART'S RETURN TO AMERICA DIDN'T MEAN A return to his eight-room house in Brentwood, at least not immediately. Both Swope (to Dorothy McGuire) and Meredith (to Paulette Goddard) had married during the war and found their own homes, making it necessary to sublet the place on Evanston Street. Since the sublet lease still had some time to run, Stewart accepted an offer from Henry and Frances Fonda to be their guest at Tigertail, the name they had given to their two-story Pennsylvania Dutch colonial residence in the hills above Sunset Boulevard. He ended up staying almost three months in the small outbuilding that Fonda had put up for his children Jane and Peter and called the Playhouse. The accommodations largely consisted of a daybed, kitchenette, and bathroom. As at Fonda's first place in Brentwood, Stewart didn't have to guess what his host's favorite animal was. Jane Fonda, then eight, remembers: "There was an infinite number of cats around the place, and they made it smell horrible. It was a weird time when I think about it. Here was this Hollywood star living in this place that was the size of some bathrooms and that stank to high heaven. Only practice made me stop holding my nose whenever I went in there. I always liked telling people in high school that I knew Jimmy Stewart when he was living in a cat house."

Oblivious to the cat odors, Stewart and the senior Fonda invariably closed out their social evenings by closeting themselves into the Playhouse; while Frances slept in the main house, they listened to the old jazz records they had scoured the stores for during the day. A particularly precious find might prompt invitations to Hoagy Carmichael, fellow composer Johnny Mercer, and singer-pianist Nat King Cole to join them over the Victrola. On other nights, Stewart spent the wee hours trading war stories with his host, who had been in the Navy. Fifty years later, Jane Fonda recalls those days mainly for how Stewart "cheered up my father. It wasn't that he cracked jokes and things, although he had a great sense of humor. What was more important was how by just being there, he could make my father brighten up, even be goofy at times." Christmas, in particular, she says, seemed to bring out the cartoonish in both of them:

> I had gotten old enough not to believe in Santa Claus, and of course that was a mixed blessing where Dad and Jimmy were concerned. They had this mighty production with Jimmy dressed up as Santa and galumphing over the roof with his bag of toys. They were going to get Peter to believe in Santa if it killed them, and the way Jimmy was going across the roof, it might have. Another Christmas, we had this enormously tall tree and had to put the star up on the top. Because Jimmy was the tallest, he was delegated to do the job. Naturally, the reason I remember that today is that as soon as he leaned over with the star, he lost his balance on the ladder, went right into the tree, and rode it down to the floor.

When they weren't listening to music, talking about their war experiences, or attending the parties that Hollywood hosts and hostesses had once again been throwing regularly since V-J Day, Stewart and Fonda were indulging their new passion for kite flying. A faint snickering from some Hollywood writers that not even the war had matured the "overgrown boys" hardly deterred them. On the contrary, as Stewart was the first to admit as their creations got more and more elaborate, "we were like kids." On at least one occasion, Fonda took on more than he could handle. As Stewart told Howard Teichmann:

> One night I got home later than usual. . . . It was pitch black out and Frances came up to me and said, "You'd better go back there. Hank is in trouble with the kite." Well, I looked out. We'd used swordfish tackle for the kite and the tackle was going straight up in the air, and it was almost off the reel, and Hank was holding this enormous kite. The wind was strong and it was pulling him off the ground. Boy! I grabbed him and the two of us got it down inch by inch. I take full credit for saving Fonda. You see, that kite was ten feet by ten feet, and if I hadn't arrived in the nick of time, well, Fonda would have made Nebraska by morning.

Through it all, Stewart continued to fence with proposals for returning to work. About the only film project that he showed any interest in at all was *My Darling Clementine*, John Ford's rendering of the events lending up to the duel between Wyatt Earp and Doc Holliday and the Clanton gang at the O. K. Corral. But despite Fonda's casting as Earp and 20th Century-Fox chief Darryl Zanuck's promotion of Stewart for Holliday, Ford went with Victor Mature in the role of the alcoholic, gunslinging dentist. The director never spelled out reasons for ignoring Zanuck's championing of Stewart, though he did like to boast that he had known Earp personally and so had some very precise ideas on the personalities involved in the notorious gunfight. Stewart himself never displayed any particular chagrin at not receiving a solid offer for the picture, which became one of Hollywood's most sophisticated westerns and represented Fonda's first screen job after the war.

The lack of concrete offers over his first few months at home made it even easier for Stewart to wonder aloud whether he wanted to return to the screen at all; or, as he was prone to putting it, whether he was an "unemployed actor or unemployed pilot." He was never completely without recourse, however, and one of them—radio— indicated that he himself knew that he was primarily an actor waiting for the right fit. Between November 5 and December 17, he did five broadcasts. Four of them were recreations of prewar film roles (*Destry Rides Again*, *No Time for Comedy*, *Vivacious Lady*, and *Made for Each Other*), reflecting the strategy of his new MCA agent that the best way for him and the public to get reacquainted was on familiar territory. The fifth undertaking, a light drama with the title of *The Sailor Who Had to Have a Horse*, cast Stewart as a sailor who shares his shipboard bunk with a saddle. None of the shows drew any particular critical reaction other than to underscore the actor's retention of his dramatic gifts.

Then Frank Capra came back into Stewart's life.

It's a Wonderful Life (RKO – 1946)

Now, Jimmy, it starts in Heaven. It's all about this small town family man who's in serious financial difficulty and thinks he's a failure. As he's getting ready to jump in the river on Christmas Eve, an angel named Clarence

who wants to earn his wings jumps in first. Since Clarence can't swim, our
hero has to save him. Then Clarence shows the man what a wonderful life
he's had. . . . Gee, Jimmy, it doesn't sound so good when I tell it, does it?

As Stewart has recounted it on numerous occasions, that attempt by
Capra to outline the plot of *It's a Wonderful Life* was his first encounter
with the character of George Bailey; it wasn't an especially productive
one, either. No sooner had the director mulled over what he had been
saying during a meeting at his home in the late fall of 1945 than he threw
up his arms in exasperation, deciding that, instead of a legitimate story
for a picture, he had "the lousiest piece of shit I've ever heard." Capra
then thanked the actor for coming over to listen to him and sent him on
his way with the advice to "forget the whole thing."

But Stewart didn't forget about it. He telephoned the director a
couple of weeks later and, breaking his procrastination about resuming
his film career, announced that he definitely wanted to do the picture. It
was the kind of push that Capra needed; within only a few weeks, he was
ready to begin production.

As both a story and a production, *It's a Wonderful Life* had a tortuous
history. It started life in February 1938 as a two-page outline for a short
story by Philip Van Doren Stern. But the writer couldn't make the
material work to his satisfaction, so he put it on the shelf for five years. In
1943, he made another try under the title "The Greatest Gift," but
collected nothing but rejection letters from magazines for his efforts. As a
last resort, he printed it himself and enclosed it with Christmas cards to
relatives and friends. One of those receiving it was his agent, who
promptly sold it to RKO for $10,000. There followed several months when
the studio sought to tailor it as a vehicle for Cary Grant, first hiring
Dalton Trumbo as the screenwriter, then bringing in both Marc
Connelly and Clifford Odets to rework Trumbo's labors. In September
1945, RKO finally gave up and sold the property to Capra.

At the time, Capra would have been the last one in Hollywood to
claim that there was anything wonderful about life. In even more of a
funk about his career than Stewart was about his, the maker of *Mr. Deeds
Goes to Town* and *Mr. Smith Goes to Washington* was shocked to discover
in the waning months of the war that his absence from Hollywood to
make Army documentaries had not been particularly lamented by
Columbia's Harry Cohn or any other studio boss. Although there were

cumulative reasons for this attitude, two of the largest were the increasingly extravagant shooting schedules of his prewar films and an equally swelling ego.[1] The hostility of the traditional studios prompted him to form a partnership with producer Samuel Briskin and, later, directors William Wyler and George Stevens in an independent venture they called Liberty Films. After discarding a number of other projects viewed as sure legitimizing moneymakers, including a western with Gary Cooper, Liberty announced *It's a Wonderful Life* as its first feature.

As Capra told Stewart at their first meeting about the film, *It's a Wonderful Life* is narrated from the point of view of an angel (Henry Travers) as he is given the background on his assignment to go to Bedford Falls and save the desperate George Bailey, who is on the verge of suicide. Lengthy flashbacks inform both Clarence and the audience that Bailey has always been a generous, industrious man who has put his sense of responsibility ahead of what were once ardent dreams of leaving his town to make his way as a world-famous architect. Every time he has been about to leave, some disaster—the death of his father, a threatened takeover of his savings and loan operation by the evil banker Mr. Potter (Lionel Barrymore), and a bank run, most prominently—has instead committed him more deeply to preserving his savings and loan, which is looked upon by the poor of Bedford Falls as their only hope of rising above misery. He has been further rooted to his home by a marriage to Mary Hatch (Donna Reed) and the birth of their four children. For his part, Bailey tries to act philosophical about his fate, rejecting the idea that he is envious of the business success of a schoolmate (Frank Albertson) or the war heroics of his younger brother (Todd Karnes)— accomplishments that might have been his.

But Bailey loses his tranquil demeanor when his absentminded uncle (Thomas Mitchell) misplaces $8,000, exposing his loan company to ruin and himself to fraud charges. What he doesn't know is that Potter has found the money and, rather than return it, sees it as his opportunity for destroying his competitor. The berserk Bailey snaps at his family, goes into a meaningless tirade against the teacher of one of his children, gets drunk, and gets slugged by the husband of the offended teacher. As snow flutters down on Bedford Falls on Christmas Eve, he stands on the town

---

[1] Edward Bernds: "Capra really started getting caught up in himself as the great artist dedicated only to making the Ultimate Masterpiece."

bridge, chewing over Potter's cutting remark that his $15,000 insurance policy makes him "worth more dead than alive" to his family.

Before Bailey can go through with his intention of jumping into the river under the bridge and killing himself, Clarence arrives on the scene as a drowning man. Bailey saves him, but dismisses the man's claim that he is an angel who has to perform a good deed to earn his wings. Bailey sees the light only when Clarence takes up his muttered wish that he never had been born. Bailey is then forced to see Bedford Falls (or, Potterville) as it would have been if indeed he had not been born. Nightmare leads into nightmare. Not only do the local people (including his wife) not know him, but Potterville is something of an extended juke joint catering mostly to hookers and boozers; even the thousands of lives his war hero brother saved have been lost because he himself had not been around to save his brother's life after a childhood accident on a frozen pond. Persuaded that life is worth living, Bailey returns to his real surroundings in joyful gratitude. His final surprise comes with the overwhelming generosity of all the townspeople he has helped and made sacrifices for along the way: Alerted by Mary of the crisis at the savings and loan company, they pool thousands of dollars to make up for the lost $8,000 and then some, underlining the film's explicitly stated theme that a man with friends can never be considered poor. Bailey's redemption earns Clarence his wings.

Although Stewart has made it sound as if he were being totally whimsical in accepting *It's a Wonderful Life* on the basis of Capra's meandering talk about the angel, the plot was actually not all that radical for the 1940s, when the military uncertainties of the war and the social uncertainties of its aftermath honed Hollywood's taste for kindergarten religiosity. Among the pictures made during the decade in which supernatural creatures (evil as well as good), ghosts, or the dead figured prominently were *Here Comes Mr. Jordan, I Married a Witch, I Married an Angel, The Remarkable Andrew, Happy Land, That's the Spirit, The Horn Blows at Midnight, The Human Comedy, Heaven Can Wait, The Cockeyed Miracle, Angel on My Shoulder, The Ghost and Mrs. Muir, The Bishop's Wife, Down to Earth*, and *Portrait of Jennie*.

Stewart's decades-long consistency in naming *It's a Wonderful Life* as his favorite film has also tended to create the impression that the production resembled the final scene under the Bailey Christmas tree, when in fact the atmosphere was much closer to that of George Bailey discovering that Bedford Falls had been replaced by Potterville. Already something of an outcast because of his problems with the major studios, Capra froze his relations for good with Hedda Hopper when he opted for Reed in the role of the wife, instead of Ginger Rogers, as proposed by the columnist; Hopper thereafter called Stewart's performance in *It's a Wonderful Life* the worst of his career.[2] Counting Trumbo, Connelly, and Odets from the earlier RKO attempts to fashion a screenplay, eight writers took a swipe at the script at one stage or another, precipitating a Screen Writers Guild arbitration hearing to determine who had done what. The writers who emerged with the major credit—Frances Goodrich and her husband Albert Hackett—refused to see the completed picture because of what they described as a "horrid" experience with Capra, who also received screenwriting acknowledgment. During production, the director and cinematographer Victor Milner crossed swords continually, until the cameraman was replaced and many of his scenes had to be reshot by Joseph Walker. Even at the post-production stage, Capra got into hair pulling with Dimitri Tiomkin, charging that the composer was so absorbed with another musical score, for the western *Duel in the Sun*, that he had been giving *It's a Wonderful Life* only the leavings of his energies.

And then there was Stewart.

The actor discovered soon enough that his initial enthusiasm for the project was not the same thing as being able to pull off a convincing portrayal of George Bailey. As he admitted to Elliot Norton of the *Boston Post* shortly after the film's release: "I felt when I got back to pictures that I had lost all sense of judgment. I couldn't tell if I was good or bad. I mean in a given scene. Usually, you can tell what is the right thing to do when you're acting. But I couldn't. I was uncertain."

According to one version of a frequently repeated story, Stewart behaved in such a discombobulated fashion at the start of shooting that he found in his insecurity another reason for quitting acting, and Capra sought out Lionel Barrymore for help before the entire production was compromised. The veteran actor then reportedly took Stewart aside for a lecture about how "acting is the greatest profession ever invented" and about how no other vocation had a similar power to "move millions of

---

[2] Rogers herself disclaimed any keen interest in the part, describing the character of the wife as "too bland" for her taste.

people, shape their lives, give them a sense of exaltation." In case that didn't sink in, at least as Capra remembered the conversation, Barrymore also went after Stewart's expressed doubt about acting being a "decent" profession, asking the war ace if he "thought it more 'decent' to drop bombs on people than to bring rays of sunshine into their lives with [his] acting talent." By the director's telling, the Barrymore allusion to the war "knocked [Stewart] flat on his ass."

Stewart has always denied that version of the talk, especially the assumption that he was so depressed that he was ready to quit acting or Barrymore's alleged references to his war record. "I swear I don't know where that got started," he told *The Movies* in 1983. "I never considered giving it up. What Lionel did was encourage me. I was feeling around and every once in a while he'd come up and say something. It was his encouragement that was a tremendous help to me."

For sure, there were few roles, even if cobbled together by a platoon of writers, that could have offered an uncertain Stewart more personal doors of entry than that of George Bailey. The small-town setting in an eastern area, the shopkeeper ambiance, a young man whose first dreams of escape and success center around making it as an architect, the self-intoxicated spieler, the deft dancer, the immaculate politeness to elders (even while being slapped by one, as with the drunken pharmacist played by H. B. Warner, and being slugged by another, as with the offended husband portrayed by Stanley Andrews)—none of this was exactly foreign territory to him. The same was true of the production, beginning with Capra, running through a slew of actors with whom he had performed before (Barrymore, Warner, Samuel Hinds, Charles Halton, Ward Bond, Frank Faylen), and ending with Beulah Bondi again playing his mother. In the end, as he was to admit, he needed every one of those familiar signposts for what turned into some seventy consecutive days of shooting.

If there is one major note to Stewart's performance in *It's a Wonderful Life*, it's intensity—physical as much as emotional. Throughout the film, his George Bailey is constantly running, yelling, pacing, screaming, and throwing off other kinds of kinetic energy. The most ostensibly relaxed conversational scenes—at the supper table with his father, with the cop and the cab driver on a street corner, with the good-time Violet (Gloria Grahame) in his office, with his wife on their improvised honeymoon in a decrepit abandoned house—all take place within a swirl of rival claims for his attention. All of this makes his raucous surrender to despair, just before the entrance of Clarence, not so much a departure from his previous behavior as a paring down of it—George Bailey finally *alone* in his peripateticism. In fact, about the only moment in the entire picture when the character reflects quietly, even barring the usual noises of his own ambitions and exasperations, is when he stands on the bridge with his insurance policy, tasting the truth of Potter's jibe. Given those contours, the part represented a far more exhausting challenge to Stewart than any previous role, not merely because of the need to be on camera practically every minute from start to finish, but to be there as a man who always had his ears keened to what was going on around him even as he denied the exposure of his own nerve ends.

The never-admiring Jean Arthur once asserted that the role of George Bailey was so rich that anyone could have played him as convincingly as Stewart. That is doubtful. Whoever the anyone was, he would have been unlikely to bring to the role Stewart's innate hostility to the incessant emotional physicality of George Bailey, *and* the intelligence to rationalize that hostility as an additional charge from a sometimes humorous, sometimes rancorous expression of small-town respectability, *and* the technical mastery for bringing about the fusion. Having had more difficulty than Stewart with such a process, another actor—while capable of going off in some other creative direction—would have been next to helpless in suggesting, from just below the surface, the resultant petulance that runs through the character of the filmed George Bailey. This is particularly important since Bailey's petulance is hard to distinguish from Capra's.

In his later years,[3] Capra turned what originally had been intended as a critical needle into a protective halberd by referring to the main body of his work as "Capracorn"—in his eyes, at least, a brew of the comic, the sentimental, the rhetorical, the idealistic, and the melodramatic in which the values of the man on the street were raised above those of official authority and in which, even at the cost of gliding over specific plot points, there was inevitably a happy ending. More than once, he cited *It's a Wonderful Life* as a perfect example of Capracorn, arguing in particular how its theme of Friends Represent the Greatest Wealth (spelled out in the final seconds in a message to Bailey from Clarence) was a basic

---

[3] The director died in 1991.

strength of the common man and a quintessential democratic message.

But comparable to the images offered by Stewart's two previous movies with Capra, the director's "common man" in *It's a Wonderful Life* is, at best, an annoying rash. Just as he figured most conspicuously in *You Can't Take It With You* in a jail sequence when his threatening moves against munitions-maker Edward Arnold seemed to emanate from a lynch mob of hoboes, and just as the generic citizenry depicted by *Mr. Smith Goes to Washington* was either stupid or powerless, *Wonderful Life's* man on the street is most in action (before the finale) when he is making a panicky run on George Bailey's savings and loan. The citizens of Bedford Falls aren't bad people, we are left to understand, but they are easily frightened, they are ungrateful for all that George has done for them, and they are even crass for accepting the offer of his honeymoon trip savings for calming their fears.

Thanks to such sequences, not to mention the flashback device guiding the film from the start, Capra has to labor less than usual to establish his trademark inevitability about what occurs. It is in fact owing only to Stewart's elasticity as an actor that the disappointments and frustrations suffered by his George Bailey day after day and year after year don't make his explosion and breakdown seem even *more* unavoidable. The performer's humor was never more necessary, nor more in concert with his equally long line in the lightly cranky, to disguise for so long a character who is just waiting to give in to his resentments about the hand dealt him by fate. (How wrong is Barrymore's Potter when he observes that Bailey hates everything about his life and the people populating it?) If Bailey is an American Everyman, a notion that both Capra and Stewart came around to endorsing, then America is a glib but profoundly petulant benefactor waiting for its generosity to be repaid—and the sooner the better.

Stewart's ability to convey these interior cancerous rages while maintaining the exterior of the town healer provides *It's a Wonderful Life* with a conflict far more suspenseful than his confrontations with the archly Satanic Potter or the awakenings generated by the archly celestial Clarence. Ultimately, the performance hangs out of the collection basket in the last sequence like the news that George Bailey's successful businessman schoolmate is sending $25,000 to cover his financial problems—reducing the urgency, if not the relevance, of all the other gesturing.

After lengthy postproduction work that inflated the film's budget beyond Liberty's expectations, *It's a Wonderful Life* was dropped into New York and Los Angeles theaters at the end of December 1946 to qualify for Oscar consideration that year, then released nationally in January. RKO made the distribution decision mainly because *Sinbad the Sailor*, its originally planned holiday release, ran into Technicolor processing problems in the lab. Initial critical reception was all over the lot. *Time* called it "a pretty wonderful movie," while *Newsweek* backed up a cover story with the verdict that the picture was "sentimental, but so expertly written, directed, and acted that you want to believe it." James Agee was even more backhanded in his compliments in *The Nation* than *Newsweek*, saying that it was "one of the most efficient sentimental pieces since *A Christmas Carol*." Some of the other critics were more direct. For Bosley Crowther of *The New York Times*, "the weakness of the picture . . . is its illusory concept of life. Mr. Capra's nice people are charming, his small town is a quite beguiling place, and his pattern for solving problems is most optimistic and facile. But somehow they all resemble theatrical attitudes, rather than average realities." *New Yorker* critic John McCarten found the treatment of the story "so mincing as to border on baby talk" and voiced particular solidarity with Henry Travers for "God help him, [having] the job of portraying Mr. Stewart's guardian angel."

When it slipped *It's a Wonderful Life* into theaters for Oscar consideration, RKO appeared to be supporting the film, which garnered five nominations—including one each for the picture, for Capra, and for Stewart. Once down to budgetary decisions, however, the studio threw all its promotional weight behind another heavily nominated production, *The Best Years of Our Lives*, leaving the inhabitants of Bedford Falls in snows over their heads. The failure of the Capra picture to win in any of its five categories at the Academy Award ceremonies in March 1947 was the last straw for Liberty: Stunned by the mediocre box-office reception accorded *Wonderful Life*, Capra decided that being an independent producer-director wasn't so marvelous at that, and company assets were sold off to Paramount before Wyler and Stevens got around to making their scheduled pictures.

Capra's bitter explanation for the tepid responses to the picture was that "perhaps [I] had too much faith in the human race. . . . People called me a kind of movie Pollyanna and I guess maybe I was." Stewart has usually blamed it on the times. "The only thing I've been able to come up with is that people had just been through a war and that this was not quite what they were looking for. The picture, even though there was a comedy side to it and everything, was really a very serious picture. There was a dark side to it. I think movie audiences wanted Red Skelton, slapstick comedy, westerns, escapism. We were finished with the war. Maybe it was just the wrong time to make the picture."

One consequence of the dissolution of Liberty Films was the lapsing of copyright control over *It's a Wonderful Life*, allowing it to resurface on television in the 1970s in the public domain. The Christmas ritualization of its programming since then[4] has forced it to play to even greater sentimental expectations than those designed originally by Capra. What Capra saw as "serious" and "dark" on the big screen has, even without the addition of colorization, gained the wine sheen of a seasonal bauble on the small one.

IMPERFECT CRIMES

AS THOUGH TO DEMONSTRATE THAT HIS CLIENT WAS about as free a free agent as it was possible to be, MCA's Lew Wasserman worked out deals for Stewart to star in five films for an equal member of companies immediately after *It's a Wonderful Life*. The only trouble was, the general mediocrity of his successive screen assignments for RKO, 20th Century-Fox, United Artists, Warner Brothers, and Universal ultimately left the actor looking more vagrant than independent, lending no small comfort to the Hollywood Cassandras who had warned performers off turning their backs on exclusive studio contracts. Stewart didn't help his position, either, by returning to Broadway for the first time since the disastrous *A Journey by Night* in 1935: At the start of what developed into a decades-long infatuation with an invisible rabbit named Harvey, he won scant critical favor as a summer replacement for Frank Fay, the star of the stage comedy. At one point, his fortunes had ebbed

---

[4] NBC acquired the copyright in the early 1990s, announcing a policy of one showing a year around the Christmas season.

enough for a *New York Times* reporter to approach him with the news that the paper was preparing a major article announcing his professional demise.

Magic Town (RKO – 1947)

If there was anything more equivocal than Capracorn, it was Capracorn without Capra. Not that *Magic Town* was without some relevant credentials: Producer-writer Robert Riskin had furnished the screenplays for some of the director's most noted films—*It Happened One Night, Mr. Deeds Goes to Town, You Can't Take It With You,* and *Meet John Doe.* But that proved to be nowhere near enough.

Magic Town casts Stewart as a fast-talking public relations cynic named Rip Smith who discovers that the modest little community of Grandview is so close to the heart of America that its surveyed opinions and forecasts have accurately reflected national events for fifty years. Seeing a way to make quick money as an expert pollster, Smith and his crony Ned Sparks move to Grandview where, behind the front of being insurance agents, they record town opinion on various questions and feed it back to a big-city clearing house. Their accuracy in anticipating national trends brings them big money, but also the suspicions of the local newspaper editors, Ma Peterson (Ann Shoemaker) and her daughter Mary (Jane Wyman). Smith, for his part, is fearful that the strident campaign of the Petersons to bring "progress" to Grandview will deprive the town of its sleepy, intuitive character, so he romances Mary to distract her. In spite of her own amatory feelings, Mary finds out about Smith's deception and exposes him in her paper. The resulting hullabaloo attracts a plague of businesses eager to be associated with Grandview, this in turn undermining the town's supposed innocence and causing general calamity. When Smith realizes what he has set in motion, he joins forces with a forgiving Mary and the children of Grandview to start the community back on the road to sanity.

Magic Town was born as an idea, and just about died in that state. Stewart and Wyman, especially, come off as high school debaters around an abstract premise: They are right, wrong, clever, witty, and manipulative at various junctures, but seldom full-bodied characters with lives off the stage. When Stewart's Smith falls in love with Wyman's Mary, moreover, even the wisp of Riskin's debate floats off, leaving little for the audience to do but to get up and walk out of the auditorium. Even the fan magazine *Photoplay*, in a typical critical comment, said that the picture "is unusual enough to rate a cheer . . . and unrealistic enough to rate a brush-off."

Most of the blame for the failure of *Magic Town* has been laid at the door of director William Wellman; among those who have pointed the finger in that direction have been the actress Fay Wray, Riskin's widow, and Wellman himself. "I don't think anybody can disagree that the main problem was Wellman," says Wray. "He was a derring-do director, perfect for things like *Beau Geste*, but absolutely wrong for something like *Magic Town*." Wellman put it even more succinctly: "It stunk! If you think *Magic Town* has anything good about it at all, there's something wrong with you."

But if nobody is about to suggest that the director deserves belated recognition for creating a masterpiece, it has also always been a little too easy to finger him alone for what Wray says was "a tremendous bitterness" on Riskin's part for what turned into an artistic and commercial fiasco. Among other things, Wellman was not at all a stranger to the *Magic Town* genre, having directed, among other features, *Nothing Sacred*, a story that also plows the terrain of media manipulators moving in on small-town values. The picture also suffered mightily—at least in terms of the box office—from a garish ad campaign that made the Stewart and Wyman characters sound as though they had imported a new strain of Ebola fever with such tag lines as "Their love jeopardized the happiness of thousands." At bottom, however, the central problem remained the Riskin conceit—a Gallup Poll version of *Lost Horizon* that sought to be iconoclastic about a postwar mania but that finally legitimized it by suggesting that it could only be opposed by living in the Himalayas of American Innocence.

As for Stewart, he moved through the proceedings in an *It's a Wonderful World* rather than an *It's a Wonderful Life* mode; similar to the hard-boiled detective in the prewar comedy, he regularly threw off such lines as "It may be a rat race, but I'm out front and I'm gonna grab mine." He later conceded that his performance, like the film in general, "consisted of parts that didn't add up to a convincing whole."

It wasn't too long after *Magic Town* had opened to a general indifference that the actor was approached by a writer for *The New York Times* who informed him that the daily was doing an article on "The Rise and Fall of James Stewart." The main ingredients for the piece, it seemed, were *Magic Town*, a hiccough production entitled *On Our Merry Way* involving friends Fonda and Meredith, his fill-in performance for Frank Fay in *Harvey*, and The Old Gray Lady's overall editorial sense that *It's a Wonderful Life* had been the actor's last hurrah and that its failure at the box office proved that he was out of step with postwar society or postwar entertainment needs, whichever was more important. Stewart has never denied being dismayed by the news that some considered him dead professionally. "I knew, right then and there, that I was going to have to do something. I just couldn't go on hemming and hawing, which I realized I'd overdone at times. I looked at some of my old pictures and couldn't believe what I was watching. One of them, *Born to Dance*, made me want to vomit. I simply wasn't getting across anymore. I knew I had to toughen up."

His first step in that direction was *Call Northside 777*.

Call Northside 777 (20th Century-Fox – 1948)

In addition to portraying such figures as Monty Stratton and Glenn Miller in the late 1940s and 1950s, Stewart also appeared in a handful of films in the period that were inspired by biographical incidents. The most noted of these was *Broken Arrow*; the first of them was *Call Northside 777*, Henry Hathaway's tale of Chicago newspaperman James P. McGuire's crusade to free Thomas Majczek, in prison for an eventual twelve years for a murder he didn't commit. McGuire, who ended up with a Pulitzer Prize, had stirred attention to the case in a December 1946 article, "Tillie Scrubbed On," which appeared in the *Reader's Digest*.

As the story emerges on the screen, Mickey McNeal (Stewart) is a skeptical reporter who is assigned by his editor, Kelly (Lee J. Cobb), to look into a personal notice that promises $5,000 to anybody who can provide information on an eleven-year-old killing. O'Neal reluctantly calls the number in the ad (Northside 777) and goes to see Tillie Wiecek (Kasia Orzazeski), a scrubwoman who has been setting aside nickels and dimes for years in her obsession with getting her wrongly convicted son Frank (Richard Conte) out of prison. Although O'Neal's first instinct is to write only a piece underlining the pathos of a woman who refuses to accept reality, he is pushed by Kelly into journeying to the prison to talk to Wiecek personally. There he discovers a man resigned to his fate, so much so that he has forced his wife (Helen Walker) to divorce him so she can remarry and raise their son in a normal family setting. Sensing big circulation numbers, O'Neal goes to see the wife and son, then writes a story about the visit. This infuriates Wiecek, who wanted them left alone, and he accuses O'Neal of making matters worse instead of better with his mercenary aims. From that point on, the chastened O'Neal looks into the murder case more seriously. Because the victim was a cop on the premises of a speakeasy, he discovers, there was a police cover-up around the circumstances of Wiecek's arrest. Step by step, he unravels a story of official deceit and bitterness on the part of key witnesses. In the end, with the aid of a lie detector and improved photocopiers, he succeeds in winning a pardon for the grateful Wiecek. The real murderer is never apprehended.

One of Stewart's attractions to *Call Northside 777* was its semi-documentary approach—a Hollywood fad after the war, and nowhere more so than at 20th Century-Fox where black-and-white investigation dramas "ripped from the headlines" and frequently starring Conte, Dana Andrews, Victor Mature, and/or Richard Widmark identified the studio almost as much as the James Cagney, Edward G. Robinson, and Humphrey Bogart gangster movies had helped form the image of Warner Brothers in the 1930s. By lending himself to the genre, Stewart sought association with the kind of trendiness he thought he needed to keep obituary notices for his career from surfacing. As was usually the case with such pictures, however, there was as much semi as documentary involved, and not a little silence on potentially awkward details as well. This is particularly striking near the end of the picture where, after 109 minutes of meticulous detailing of the reporter's investigation into the cover-up, the Stewart character bids a hasty goodbye to Conte's freed Wiecek and watches him meet his son, his former wife, and the latter's new husband in front of the prison. In fact, director Hathaway *was* in a hurry to wind up his Chicago location work because the actual Thomas Majczek was then ruffling official feathers by charging that he had been forced to kick back $5,000 of the $24,000 indemnity he had received for his wrongful imprisonment to an Illinois politician who had helped cut some red tape in securing the payment.

Not everybody appreciated the picture's chief cachet of using the real sites where James McGuire had conducted his investigation, either. As Stewart revealed some time later concerning the scenes shot at Joliet State Prison: "I remember waiting to do a scene, and an inmate sidled up to me and said, 'Why don't you bastards get out of here? We want to get our privileges back. We have to stay in our cells the whole time you're shooting the damn picture. Why don't you get the hell out of here and leave us alone?' "

Stewart's performance as the McGuire figure is an anomaly for more than one reason. Although the reporter himself was on hand as a technical consultant, the actor displayed little reservation in playing him as a sarcastic skeptic who had been around every block that Chicago and every other metropolis had to offer. This was noteworthy not only because McGuire was nothing like that, but also because Stewart's other screen impersonations of actual people have gone off in the other direction of total blandness. On the first count, McGuire's daughter, Vivian DeVine, suspects that her father might have been obliquely flattered by the misrepresentation, especially in light of her own knowledge of how the events described in *Northside* truly developed.

> They stood a lot of things in that movie on their heads, starting with my father's personality. Some other things he himself was responsible for. For instance, the movie has the editor spotting the ad and telling the reporter to look into it. What happened in real life was that my father saw the ad and brought it to the attention of his editor, a man named Karin Walsh. Walsh said that there was no story in it, but that if my father wanted to nose around, just be sure he did it on his own time and not neglect the work he was getting paid for. And that's the way my father did it—on his lunch hour, after work, on weekends. But when he had enough to start writing, he was afraid that Walsh was going to criticize him for spending so much more time on his afterhours project than on his regular work, so he made Walsh look smart by writing that *he* had been the one who had kept after the story of the old scrubwoman. All that cynical and sarcastic stuff is movie nonsense. My father was mainly a worrier.

The Stewart approach to the role appeared to have been dictated by several factors. Most obviously, the cutting edge to the journalist O'Neal fell within the actor's new determination to "toughen up" on the screen (although, in fact, the character is as frangibly cynical as Rip Smith in *Magic Town* and several of his prewar predecessors). Producer Darryl Zanuck was also known to have demanded additional doses of "character" in the script before it went before the cameras; he had been apprehensive about the picture coming off "like a recital or a lecture more than a drama." Perhaps most influentially, the sarcasm tack allowed

Stewart the closest thing to his usual emotional character in a picture that was otherwise all gray objectivity. As such, it was a sometimes uncomfortable compromise, with the actor sometimes standing around in scenes as though he had been warned to be on his best behavior.

Call Northside 777 was Stewart's only clear commercial success after the war before *The Stratton Story* in 1949. Artistically, his curt, buttoned-down O'Neal drew mixed notices. For Crowther in the *Times*, the picture was "a slick piece of melodrama that combines a suspenseful mystery story with a vivid realistic pictorial style and which is winningly acted by James Stewart. . . . " The weekly *Variety*, on the other hand, found that the actor had returned to the newspaper well once too often. "Among the film's principal drawbacks," it said, "was Jimmy Stewart's jarring and unpersuasive performance. . . . [He] shuttles between phony cynicism and sob-sister sentimentalism without ever jelling the portrait into a recognizable newspaperman."

On Our Merry Way (United Artists – 1948)

For Stewart personally, *On Our Merry Way* was a goof: He got to play a jazz pianist, he got to work on the screen for the first time with Fonda, and his producer was Meredith. As a production, it was mainly goofy.

Initially entitled *A Miracle Can Happen*, the picture stemmed from Meredith's desire to film a tale about a minister in religious crisis who receives a visit one night from a boy who urges him to visit his dying father. When the minister, after sufficient grumbling, arrives at the house, he is informed that the boy actually died years before; the incident restores the clergyman's faith.

Shot with Charles Laughton in the role of the minister, *none of that* appeared in the released version of *On Our Merry Way*.

As planned by Meredith and coproducer Benedict Bogeaus, the Laughton tale was to have been flanked by three other stories in an anthology format around the question of how a child can affect some-body's life. Among those asked the question by a newsman played by Meredith are jazz sidemen portrayed by Stewart and Fonda, who then recount how they once sought to fix a band contest for a local mayor's son, but got outwitted by a trumpet-playing beauty. As slight as the anecdote is, it holds together more winningly than two other comic segments with Victor Moore and Dorothy Lamour and Fred MacMurray and William Demarest. It also should have, considering the names attached to it.

When Meredith first went to Stewart and Fonda with his general anthology scheme, it was they who suggested the ambiance of jazz sidemen and who also proposed that John O'Hara be hired to write the story. O'Hara delivered, and then John Huston was hired as the director. After shooting the setup scene between Meredith's reporter and the musicians, however, both Huston and Fonda had to go off on other film jobs. By the time the actor was available again, Huston had changed his mind about the picture, and George Stevens came in to shoot the flashback sequences of the band contest. Both Huston and Stevens insisted that their names not be associated with the venture. "It was really an amazingly brilliant team," says Meredith. "Stewart, Fonda, O'Hara, Huston, Stevens—where would you find so many talents on one project today? But it did nothing to save the picture."

In the end Bogeaus, who had the bigger producer say in the venture, discarded the Laughton tale altogether as inconsistent with the comic tenor of the other stories. He also turned down an offer from David Selznick to buy the entire picture as a prelude to enlarging the Laughton segment as a separate film. With no more miracles happening, the title was changed to *On Our Merry Way*. Released at the same time as *Call Northside 777*, the picture reinforced a perception that Stewart was careening from assignment to assignment with little in the way of a career plan.

Rope (Warner Brothers – 1948)

In retrospect, the most surprising thing about *Rope* is that Stewart and Alfred Hitchcock were ever eager to work with one another again after its completion. When the director wasn't giving short shrift to the actor and the rest of the cast in his enthrallment with what he viewed as a technical innovation, the leading man was making it evident that he didn't think all that much of the picture, thought himself miscast, and detested the preoccupation with technical trickery. If they agreed on anything, it was in the opinion often voiced in subsequent years that the filmization of the Patrick Hamilton play was not particularly good.

The Hamilton play was inspired by the Leopold-Loeb case, in which a pair of educated young men in Chicago in the 1920s committed a random murder for the thrill of it and to demonstrate their superiority to society. Confining itself to eighty minutes of "real action" time, the mostly faithful Hitchcock adaptation shows the two killers Brandon

(John Dall) and Philip (Farley Granger) as they host a cocktail party while the body of their victim reposes in a chest being used as a serving table in their living room. The party guests in the single-set drama include the father (Cedric Hardwicke) and the aunt (Constance Collier) of the dead man, his fiancée (Joan Chandler), and, most important, the onetime school housemaster and now publisher (Stewart) whose Nietzschean spoutings in the past lighted the fuse for the killing in the minds of Brandon and Philip. In a cat-and-mouse game with the killers, the publisher bores small, large, and larger holes in their sangfroid until he reveals the truth and, denying that his ideas were ever meant to justify homicide, summons the police.

Rope's numerous problems started with the casting. As originally planned by Hitchcock, the film would have starred Cary Grant in the role of the publisher and Montgomery Clift as Brandon. But the established homosexual relationship between Leopold and Loeb, and the tacit recognition of a similar tie between Hamilton's killers, persuaded the bisexual Grant and the gay Clift to steer clear of the project to avoid long-term commercial repercussions. As he would go to the actor in the 1950s to soften various neuroses of his protagonists, Hitchcock then opted for Stewart, overcoming the actor's doubts about being right for the part with the help of an offer of $300,000 for a production whose entire budget was merely $1.5 million. Farley Granger was just one of the people connected to the picture who saw the casting as a mistake:

> I suppose they got what they wanted in muting the homosexual undercurrents by bringing Jimmy in, but I can't help but think that's all they got. Jimmy never really got comfortable with the idea of playing this real heavy, a true villain. After all, no matter what he says at the end, his is the character that has triggered the killing in the story. He was extremely conscious of being this dark figure, and that made him edgy all the way through. He was a pro, of course, and he worked at it. But off camera he wasn't especially friendly, and on camera I really never got the feeling that we were building a scene together. Of course, a lot of that also had to do with the fact that we were all a little distracted by Hitchcock's technical considerations.

Of far more consequence than the film's adherence to an eighty-minute real-time framework was Hitchcock's decision to shoot the entire picture in eight 10-minute takes, obviating the need for any cutting within scenes. At least during *Rope*'s preproduction and shooting phases, the director proclaimed that this challenge added up to his "most exciting" filmmaking experience:

> Every movement of the camera and the actors was worked out first in sessions with a big blackboard, like football skull practice. Even the floor was marked and plotted with numbered circles for the 25 to 30 camera moves in each 10 minute reel. Whole walls of the apartment had to slide away to allow the camera to follow the actors through narrow doors, then swing back noiselessly to show a solid room. Even the furniture was "wild." Tables and chairs had to be pulled away by prop men, then set in place again by the time the camera returned to its original position, since the camera was on a special crane, not on tracks, and designed to roll through everything like a juggernaut.

Largely to divert attention from what was essentially a static theatrical piece and from the homoerotic assumptions of the film, Warner Brothers also made a show of being enthusiastic about Hitchcock's ten-minute takes, sending out daily press releases on the ingenuity of the director and the prop men and finally even publishing an elaborate brochure describing every move of the camera during production. What none of the literature pointed out was that filming in such a manner made most of the actors miserable. "With the exception of Hardwicke and Collier, who were pretty along in years and who thought the whole thing was a lark that they hadn't been exposed to before, it got very tense at times," says Granger.

> We were constantly redoing scenes because the cameraman had moved an instant too late so that some prop man came into a view with this table in his hand or something like that. It was also Hitchcock's first color film, so he was going to make the most of that by doing every room of the apartment in a different color, and that made for more matching problems. It sounds silly today, but one of my biggest problems was having to trust that when I sat down, there would be a chair under my rear end, that the stagehand had gotten there in time. All of that created a helluva lot of insecurities.

Stewart didn't hide his, especially when Warners pressured Hitchcock into opening the set more than once for the media. Lingering at the edges of one press conference, he suggested aloud to a member of the crew that the studio start charging five dollars a head for tourists who might be interested in all the technical secrets of extended takes. On another occasion, he interrupted a query to the director about the film's lengthy rehearsal schedule by declaring that "the only thing being rehearsed around here is the camera." Screenwriter Arthur Laurents and others involved in the movie have also reported the actor as doing some considerable drinking during the shooting ("certainly more than I ever expected," in the words of Laurents). Stewart himself has said that he was so tense at times that he found it impossible to sleep at night. "It was hard to see how the picture was going to work even while we were doing it," he has said. "The noises made by the moving of the walls was a continual problem, and we would have to do scenes over again just for sound reasons, using only microphones like in a radio play. It was pretty wearing. Nobody but Hitchcock would have tried it, but in the end it really didn't work."

More than didn't work, it didn't matter. Few critics spent words on the technique of the extended takes when *Rope* opened in September 1948, and fewer still thought it rescued the stagy, indifferently acted piece. Seen today, it preserves little sap. The performance of Dall seems especially monotonous, the camera trick of concluding every reel by focusing on some dark jacket or other transition surface becomes predictable, and even the plot suffers from Columbo Syndrome at critical junctures (i.e., just as in the case of the television detective played by Peter Falk, the murderers sometimes get tripped up on details that, though challengeable by logic, were known only to the audience and should never have bothered the investigator within the story). As Granger describes it, Stewart looks mainly "uncomfortable," except for a few minutes near the end when he gets to deliver a trademark monologue, this time on the perfidy of the killers. Before then, even the inevitable question to a character played by the actor—"Are you crazy?"—as he is about to open the chest with the body draws merely a glib "I hope so" from a figure who barely registers any sense of responsibility, let alone vulnerability, for the crime that has been committed. If there is one moment that encapsulates the problems of *Rope*, however, it comes about fifteen minutes before the end of the picture, when Dall's Brandon suddenly silences the whimpering Philip with a slap. It is about the only time in the film's eighty minutes that action takes precedence over motion.

The picture fared little better with the public than it did with the critics. It made its biggest ripples in Sioux City, Memphis, Seattle, and Spokane, where local censors discerned enough of the homoerotic subtext to ban it as immoral; Chicago used the same grounds for barring it, though memories of the real Leopold–Loeb case also appeared to be a contributing factor there. Abroad, West Germany refused to show it without major cuts until 1963, while in other European countries it was a commercial failure. For all his enthusiasm about his extended, single-reel takes, Hitchcock had to wait until 1962 until another filmmaker declared interest in the technique. In that year, India's A. S. A. Swami announced plans for a 15,000-foot Tamil feature based on *Rope*. Swami's picture, never shown in the West, was supposed to run for fifteen hours.

You Gotta Stay Happy (Universal – 1948)

In both 1947 and 1948, Stewart spent part of his summer on Broadway filling in for Frank Fay as Elwood P. Dowd in the highly successful comedy *Harvey*. After his first stint, he went to Chicago to make *Call Northside 777*; before his second one, he spent a little time in New Jersey and more in Hollywood to make *You Gotta Stay Happy*. Considering the rut he admitted his career was in at the time, he might have been muttering the words of that title to himself. But the actor was so bent on following up the dark character that he had created in *Rope* with something light that he even went along with accepting second billing to Joan Fontaine.

You Gotta Stay Happy revolves around millionairess Dee Dee Dilworth, who jilts her husband on their wedding night and flees to another room in their New York hotel. Her haven is occupied by struggling air-freight pilot Marv Payne (Stewart), who will lose his business if he doesn't complete a haul to California the next day. Mainly because Dee Dee overdoses on sleeping pills, Marv and his copilot, Bullets Baker (Eddie Albert), are forced into agreeing to give her a ride to California on their cargo plane. Also aboard are an embezzler on the lam, a young married couple, a cigar-smoking chimpanzee, a casket with a dead body, and tons of frozen fish. Marv starts falling in love with Dee Dee, but is also under the mistaken impression that she is the embezzler being sought by the police. He finds out differently after a crash landing in an Oklahoma field, but then becomes even more annoyed to discover that she is wealthy. Despite losing his business because of the crash in

Oklahoma, he rejects Dee Dee's attempts to bail him out. But he changes his mind rather quickly when she persuades him of her genuine love and throws in a spanking new four-engine cargo plane.

You Gotta Stay Happy was put together by Fontaine's husband of the period, producer William Dozier; according to the actress, the only reason she did the film was for the sake of their independent production company. "I didn't want to do it," Fontaine says. "It was so trivial—one of the dozens of pale imitations of *It Happened One Night* that some genius always hit upon in those days when things were slow. But Mr. Dozier, who was running our production company, said that I had to do it, so I did. It might have killed me."

Shortly after signing to do the film, Fontaine discovered she was pregnant. She not only went ahead with the film, but with a few inadvisable stunts dreamed up by director H. C. Potter. "Everything went along all right until a scene where I had to jump off a hay wagon. I ended up in the hospital. Typical of that picture, the only person who came to visit me was Jimmy. Certainly not Potter."[5]

To nobody's great surprise, *You Gotta Stay Happy* was generally written off as a would-be zany comedy past its time. Again, the character played by Stewart was, for a good part of the story, gruff and even occasionally venal—and again, reviewers seemed to see him only as Jefferson Smith flying a cargo plane and crashing a few miles outside of Tulsa. In the words of *Time* magazine, it was "the kind of role that [he] could play blindfolded, hogtied, and in the bottom of a well."

In the summer of 1948, Stewart would have settled for that being true only of his character Marv Payne.

HOUSE ACTIVITIES

NEAR THE END OF *CALL NORTHSIDE 777*, AS STEWART'S O'Neal accompanies Richard Conte's finally freed Wiecek to the front gate of Joliet State Prison, the reporter makes the observation that "there

---

[5] Director Potter's son ended up marrying the daughter with whom Fontaine was pregnant. The actress ignored the wedding.

aren't many governments in the world that would do it"—that is, admit that they have wrongly imprisoned a man and then release him. As smug and incongruous as such a line of dialogue was in being delivered to a man just at the end of spending twelve years in a cell for no reason, it reflected a postwar Hollywood in which the fear of being called a Communist or a Communist sympathizer triggered innumerable denunciations and betrayals on a personal plane, blacklists and graylists on an industry level, and avowals of patriotism in the most dramatically ridiculous circumstances on the screen.

Although his name has generally remained absent from the operations of such self-proclaimed hunters of Communists as the Motion Picture Alliance for the Presentation of American Ideals (MPAPAI) and has never been explicitly linked to the congressional investigations conducted by the House Un-American Activities Committee (HUAC), Stewart was not merely a disinterested spectator to the political events that almost smothered Hollywood in the late 1940s. Among other items, he starred in one of the first pictures affected by the unofficial blacklist, had one friend turn informer to rebut charges of being a Communist, had another humiliate himself on a witness stand after similar allegations, and came near losing his closest friend of all in an argument over the threat posed by the House Un-American Activities Committee. If he did not meet with congressional representatives behind closed doors to express his solidarity as a friendly witness, evidence suggests, it wasn't because he lacked the opportunity to do so or because he didn't share some of their political assumptions.

In one form or another, Hollywood had been waving a red flag about Communism since the fall of the Winter Palace in 1917. In the 1930s, studio bosses sought to portray the rise of the talent unions as a Moscow-directed conspiracy. Although that tactic didn't work where the writers, actors, and directors guilds were concerned, it was much more successful in the propaganda newsreels turned out by the studios for curbing the California gubernatorial aspirations in 1934 of novelist and social commentator Upton Sinclair.[6] Buffoonery was never too far

---

[6] One typical clip showed a wild-eyed, shaggy-haired man with a thick Russian accent being asked about his voting choice. "Vy, I am foting for Sinclair," he replies. Asked why, he responds: "Vell, his system worked well in Russia, vy can't it work here?"

from the picture, either. In 1932, while still a British citizen, for instance, actor Victor McLaglen captained a band called the Hollywood Light Horse, described as "a military organization formed to promote Americanism and combat Communism and radicalism subversive to Constitutional government." For the most part, McLaglen and his troopers marched around in their specially tailored military uniforms to favorite restaurants and bars. When that bid for social attention began to wane, Hollywood Light Horse members began drifting over to a parallel organization known as the Hollywood Hussars. The more serious purpose of the Hussars, at least as proclaimed by founder and World War I hero Arthur Guy Empey, was to invade the Soviet Republic of Georgia to secure drilling rights for an American oil millionaire who was bankrolling their enterprise. At one point, Empey claimed as members of the Hussars actors McLaglen and George Brent, the sheriff of Los Angeles County, and the city police chief. He also distributed literature naming Gary Cooper as one of his sponsors, but withdrew that assertion after protests by Cooper's representatives. In any event, the Hussars never got to invade Georgia; their most conspicuous public outing was a march one afternoon down to the Los Angeles newspaper offices of William Randolph Hearst, where, in gratitude for his anti-Communist editorials, they serenaded the publisher from the sidewalk in a group sing.

In the first half of the 1940s, the point man for Hollywood anti-Communism was Sam Wood, the director of such noted features as *Goodbye, Mr. Chips*; *Kitty Foyle*; *Kings Row*; *The Pride of the Yankees*; and *For Whom the Bell Tolls*; he had also directed Stewart in the 1937 Annapolis drama *Navy Blue and Gold* and would again in 1949's *The Stratton Story*. One of the founders of the Motion Picture Alliance formed in February 1944, Wood possessed such a phobia of Communism that it almost literally killed him, since he dropped dead from a heart attack shortly after a raging argument with Margaret Sullavan over the actress's refusal to fire a writer on a proposed film because of his left-wing politics. Even from the grave, however, the director remained constant—specifying in his will that no prospective heir could claim any part of his inheritance without first signing a loyalty oath.

It was Wood's rabid Motion Picture Alliance that invited the House Un-American Activities Committee to Hollywood after the war to clean out what it regarded as anti-American influences in the industry.[7] The invitation, taken up in 1947, was crucial to subsequent events in that it assured the congressional panel of finding allies within the Hollywood community, thereby lessening its image as an intruder and enabling it to organize its hearings with the broadest possible political strokes. But even before HUAC set up quarters in the film capital, the Alliance itself was spelling out for studios what it regarded as acceptable and unacceptable screen fare. One organization initiative was a so-called *Screen Guide for Americans* that contained such chapter headings as: Don't Smear the Free Enterprise System, Don't Deify the Common Man, Don't Smear Success, Don't Glorify Failure, and Don't Smear Industrialists. "All too often, industrialists, bankers, and businessmen are presented on the screen as villains, crooks, chiselers, and exploiters," the manual complained. "It is the moral (no, not just political, but moral) duty of every decent man in the motion picture industry to throw into the ashcan, where it belongs, every story that smears industrialists as such."

Other admonitions from the Alliance guide were:

> "Don't give your characters—as a sign of villainy, as a damning characteristic—a desire to make money."
>
> "Don't let yourself be fooled when the Reds tell you what they want to destroy are men like Hitler and Mussolini. What they want to destroy are men like Shakespeare, Chopin, and Edison."
>
> "It is not the American ideal to be either 'common' or 'small.' "

As farcical as these dictates might have sounded to outsiders, they were reinforced almost daily by the japes and commendations of Hopper, Louella Parsons, and other columnists, so that it wasn't too long before the studios were taking extra looks at scripts for possibly offending themes or dialogue. Moreover, there was little secret about the fact that one Alliance member, John Wayne, had arrogated to himself the role of super-personnel chief—ostensibly acting on behalf of political virtue, and certainly on behalf of the Alliance, in reviewing the hiring of writers, actors, and technicians with suspect left-wing sympathies. Among the

---

[7] Other founding Alliance members were directors Clarence Brown and King Vidor; studio head Walt Disney; columnist Hedda Hopper; and performers John Wayne, Robert Taylor, Ginger Rogers, Barbara Stanwyck, Clark Gable, Gary Cooper, Adolphe Menjou, Ward Bond, and Richard Arlen.

films the actor vetted before the HUAC arrived in Hollywood was Frank Capra's *It's a Wonderful Life*.

As recounted by the director, he was approached during the casting of the picture by a member of the cast already signed and advised to check with Wayne about the suitability of an actress he was thinking of hiring.[8] Capra said that he blew up at such a notion, especially since Wayne's 4F status had allowed him to stay in Hollywood "getting rich" during World War II. The director then reputedly called Wayne to tell him to go to hell. ("I didn't care. I didn't give a shit who was a Communist or who wasn't.") That Capra was chronically self-aggrandizing always advised caution in trusting the accuracy of his memory, but his normally skeptical biographer Joseph McBride gave credence to the story, if only because of Wayne's vituperative remarks about the director some years later. As the actor reportedly declared in one instance: "I'd like to take that little dago son of a bitch and tear him into a million pieces and throw him into the ocean and watch him float back to Sicily where he belongs."

But the casting issue on *It's a Wonderful Life* was hardly Capra's only run-in with the Alliance and its kind. As might be deduced from the criteria for acceptable entertainment traced by the *Screen Guide for Americans*, his at least surface championing of the little man in several pictures, not to mention his presentation of such capitalist types as Edward Arnold's greedy munitions manufacturer in *You Can't Take It With You* and Lionel Barrymore's demonic banker in *It's a Wonderful Life* did not correspond to the America that Wayne, Wood, Hopper, and other Alliance members wanted to live in. This led to some retrospective attacks on films such as *Mr. Deeds Goes to Town* as proletarian propaganda and helped swell the Capra file in the offices of the FBI, HUAC, and Army Intelligence. For the director, it all ended fairly miserably, at least to judge from considerable evidence that, not having the stomach for the aspersions being cast his way, he became an informer for the FBI, a reviewer of the political credentials of writers sent abroad by the State Department for various projects, and a proponent of mandatory loyalty oaths for members of the Directors Guild.

---

[8] It would appear that the cast member was Ward Bond, an Alliance member who played the cop in *Wonderful Life*, and the actress Anne Revere, then being considered for the part of George Bailey's mother.

Through it all, Stewart was not to be heard from. It wasn't a question of a lot of scuttering behind closed doors that he might not have been attentive to, either. Even in the unlikely case that Capra had not bemoaned his troubles (a stoicisim uncharacteristic of the director), the actor socialized with Cooper, Rogers, Hopper, and other Alliance members. He was also more than aware of some of the testimony before the House Committee that called *It's a Wonderful Life* directly into cause.[9] For all that, however, his only officially recorded involvement in Capra's political problems was in the writing of a letter in 1951 attesting to the director's patriotism; the character reference, sent to the Defense Department at Capra's request, followed the Pentagon's refusal to grant security clearance to the filmmaker as a civilian member of a think tank looking into questions concerned with the defense of Eastern Europe.

There were, of course, some pretty practical reasons why Stewart was never explicitly associated with the Hollywood Right in the late 1940s. For one thing, he was still fighting in Europe when Wood and the others formed the Motion Picture Alliance. Even after World War II, he remained a member of the Air Force Reserve, where there was at least some official nervousness about mixing military and political ardor. Like Capra, he also had subdued enthusiasm for superpatriots who had sat out World War II at home.[10] But no less important was the cynical attitude of the studios, which might have kowtowed to demands from government agencies and right-wing lobbies to keep leftists unemployed through most of the 1950s, but were equally on guard against the economic consequences of employing performers who were publicly wrapping

---

[9] For instance, one witness, writer Jack Moffitt, went out of his way to exonerate (by his lights, anyway) Capra of subersive intentions in his depiction of George Bailey's travails. While granting that the banker played by Barrymore was what he termed "dog heavy," Moffit noted that the characters portrayed by Stewart and Samuel Hinds (George Bailey's father) were also bankers, concluding: "Mr. Capra's picture, though it had a banker as villain, could not properly be called a Communist picture. It showed the power of money can be used oppressively and it can be used benevolently."

[10] Douglas Fairbanks, Jr: "After the war, Jimmy and I talked a lot about why others didn't go [into military service], but we never really wanted to make a public issue about it. People do what they can do, what they have the courage to do, and that's all there is to it. We were both severely disappointed, however, that a few other actors couldn't find it in themselves to do more than USO tours, especially when some of them claimed to own patriotism after the war."

themselves in the flag. As actor Robert Vaughn, author of a book on the Hollywood blacklist entitled *Only Victims*, puts it:

> The attitude of the Cohns, Warners, and the rest was very pragmatic. They didn't really give a damn if some actor wanted to testify to say that he had been a Red or to say the Committee was doing a wonderful job. Uppermost to them was that an actor not be associated with the Committee *in any way* since that would make their image in the mind of the public hazier down the road a few years. After awhile, would the public remember *how* an actor had testified, or would it simply remember that he had, that he had been mixed up in some kind of political thing that undermined whatever generic image a studio was banking on at the box office? The apprehensions of the studio bosses were first and last apprehensions about dollars and cents.

Certainly, there were few actors who testified before HUAC as advocates of the Committee's investigations who enjoyed better or even equal careers afterward. In fact, about the only one who did was Cooper. On the other hand, there were Rogers and Robert Taylor, who went into professional decline; Richard Arlen, who already had been finding work scarce; Ronald Reagan, George Murphy, and Robert Montgomery, who were on their way to television as a transition to political careers; and Adolphe Menjou, whose anti-Communist ferocities got him blacklisted for some time as surely as many of those accused of having been Communist sympathizers. Conversely, there were several key Alliance members who somehow never made it to the HUAC hearing room. The most striking absences were those of Wayne and Bond, who spent all their time between pictures telling the studios who could be and couldn't be hired. Howard Koch, the screenwriter who was blacklisted in the 1950s for his politics and who died in 1995, didn't find that surprising.

> In some cases, the heads of the studios made deals with the Committee not to put a certain individual on the stand publicly. That was true not only of so-called suspects or what they liked to call the unfriendly witnesses, but also of friendly witnesses that the studios didn't want to have "tainted" by political publicity of any kind. Those deals were worked out mostly when a big name was involved. Somebody like a Wayne is a good example. How are you going to get people rushing in to see him

shooting down the Apaches when they start thinking of him as a guy wearing a suit and tie and saying what a great job all these seventy-year-old politicians with their glasses and bow ties are doing in defending America? Mixed message. In other cases, individuals ignored the studios and made their own private arrangements to meet with Committee members or their agents without telling anybody. You heard Cary Grant's name a lot in that connection.

However plausible, Koch's surmises about who might have said what to what body will have to remain just that for a little longer: Congressional access regulations seal away records of executive session investigations of individuals for fifty years. According to the National Archives in Washington, it is also not unheard of for witnesses at closed-door sessions to testify under aliases as a further protection.

Might Stewart have been one of HUAC's closed-door witnesses? At a minimum, it would have been atypical of the panel not to have approached him. Aside from whatever ideological paranoias were circulating with regard to *It's a Wonderful Life* and Capra, subjects on which Stewart could have been presumed to have firsthand knowledge, there was the fact that the congressmen lived for headlines—one of the reasons they were eager to set up shop in Los Angeles in the first place. And certainly, with the possible exception of Audie Murphy, who had yet to make his first picture, there was no more acclaimed World War II hero within the movie industry than Stewart.

But whether or not he was talking for the record, the actor was definitely talking to other people about HUAC's arrival in California. At one end of the scale there was Fairbanks, who insists that Stewart would never have cooperated in any way with the Washington investigators. "I challenged them to subpoena me as one of their witnesses, and so did Jimmy," Fairbanks recalls. "We dared them to call us up there and question our records. We really didn't expect any takers, and we didn't get any."[11] But while not even HUAC would have been demented enough to question the personal contributions of Stewart and Fairbanks to the defense of the nation, there was still the Committee's larger fishing ground—getting witnesses, including Stewart and Fairbanks, to talk

---

[11] The "challenge" was apparently issued, in Fairbanks's case, through some cutting remarks about HUAC to the press; there is no record of even that where Stewart is concerned.

about the actions, beliefs, and loyalties of third parties. It was substantially through this process that the investigators built their daisy chain of suspects and undesirables.

An elementary part of Stewart lore is that he and Fonda remained friends for fifty years because of their mutual decision never to discuss politics. Willy-nilly, there has arisen the impression (based more on remarks by Stewart than by Fonda, who seemed less amused by the topic) that the stalwart Republican from Indiana and the liberal Democrat from Omaha reached that accord after years of skirmishes over one issue or another. Closer examination, however, suggests that there was one specific discussion that sparked the pact of reticence, and that it took place in the spring of 1947. That happened to be shortly after Fonda had joined with Humphrey Bogart, Lauren Bacall, John Huston, and other prominent industry people in signing an open letter to HUAC, suggesting that it rifle its papers somewhere else. According to Stewart, the discussion was "long" and "pretty heated" at times and came to a finish only when the two of them realized that they were jeopardizing so many years of friendship. It wasn't too long after the argument that Fonda moved out of California back to New York; he really wouldn't return until the mid-1950s. Although part of the reason for his extended stay in the East was his starring role in *Mister Roberts* on the stage, he also confided to friends that he couldn't tolerate the political climate in southern California during those years.

Jane Fonda admits that she never got her father to spell out exactly what was said during the argument with Stewart. "I know that it was definitely about the House Un-American Activities Committee and what became known as McCarthyism later on," she says. "And it's true that their friendship really almost ended over that. That's why, after they had cooled down, they decided they would never again talk politics when they were together. But since they were agreeing to being so close-mouthed with one another, they were hardly going to start opening up to other people."

Through the 1950s and 1960s, Stewart seldom talked about the film industry in political terms; most of his political polemics in the period were reserved for defending J. Edgar Hoover, the Pentagon, or some other institution from what he regarded as unfair criticism. But in 1970, a couple of years after he had retired from the Air Force Reserve and almost a year after his stepson had been killed in Vietnam, he made an unexpected foray in to what many might think of as the past (i.e., 1947). Asked by the New York *Daily News Magazine*, for its June 21 edition, whether he agreed with an assertion by John Wayne that Communists posed a threat to the nation, the actor responded: "I don't think there's any question that the Communists are behind a great deal of unrest in the United States. In addition, I feel they are still a potential danger in show business."

He didn't name names.

AN UNMARRIED MAN

THE MILITARY VETERAN WHO RETURNED TO THE UNITED States in August of 1945 was not quite the prewar "gay blade" of gossip columnists and fan magazines. While Hollywood publicists initially took the predictable tack that the motion-picture industry's most eligible bachelor was back and that nobody had him, it was a news slant that palled as the years crept forward. In a community where youth was celebrated almost as much as the studios that kept local rumormongers furnished with dots-and-dashes items, a Stewart in his late thirties who had walked away from MGM was not exactly hot copy. His pictures in the late 1940s didn't help, either. Aside from the fact that, taken as a whole, they fed the feeling of a career in crisis, the most discussed of them showed him as a tormented married man with four children (*It's a Wonderful Life*), a married man with a scant flesh-and-blood private life (*Call Northside 777*), and a graying, maybe-asexual-maybe-homosexual publisher with an unhealthy influence on thrill killers (*Rope*). In a similar counterproductive vein, at least from the angle of the daily and monthly titillators, was the actor's decision to go back to Broadway for a few weeks in both 1947 and 1948 to do *Harvey*; or, as a fan magazine might have put it: ONETIME STAR AGREES TO BE A REPLACEMENT FOR A NO-NAME AND PLAYS CRAZY OLDER MAN WHO TALKS TO INVISIBLE RABBIT AND HAS NO SEX LIFE.

In the late 1940s, Stewart also demonstrated a greater hesitation about playing the Eligible Bachelor game with interviewers. Together with his other strictures against discussing his actions during the war, it made for stories either exclusively concentrated on the film he was promoting at the moment or buttressed with his most practiced tales about Alex and growing up in Indiana. Inevitably, the picture that emerged was of a man who, while as polite and as disarming as ever, was also on automatic pilot.

"I don't think there's any doubt that he was more contemplative when he came back," says Burgess Meredith. "How could he help it after all that flying and bombing? But he also had a few nuts over here that needed cracking. One was his career. Another was what he'd do with his private life."

Shortly before leaving for Europe, Stewart had served as the best man at Johnny Swope's wedding with Dorothy McGuire, which was held at the Hayward house in Brentwood. When he came home, he might have been forgiven for thinking that he was the only person in America who hadn't walked down the aisle. Not only had Meredith, Dinah Shore, and Josh Logan married in the interim, but both his younger sisters had exchanged vows. His two closest friends, Fonda and Cooper, were both married with families. With Ginger Rogers only briefly between marriages and Hayward and Sullavan spending most of their time back in New England, the eligible bachelor felt more like a stranded bachelor.

Not that he became a total recluse. Especially in the first few months after his return, he made the most of Hollywood's big parties. Sometimes he went with the latest young actress or starlet who had crossed his path (for example, Dorothy Ford from his segment of *On Our Merry Way*); other times, he revived his prowling tendencies from Princeton, showing up as a third with the Fondas and leaving in the company of a fourth. In his autobiography *The Ragman's Son*, Kirk Douglas recalled with notice-able bitterness a party he attended in the company of an aspiring German actress shortly after his arrival in Hollywood. As the actor told it, Frances Fonda took the actress aside at one point, relayed a message that Stewart was intrigued by her, and persuaded her to ditch Douglas. The girl reportedly worked her departure by telling Douglas that she had to go to the bathroom before leaving and, while he waited uselessly for her, sneaked out the back door with Stewart and the Fondas.

But as 1945 rolled into 1946, *It's a Wonderful Life* into *Magic Town*, and *You Gotta Stay Happy* into *Harvey*, Stewart was spotted less often in public. As he explained to friends, he was weary of being photographed at night spots, especially with dates who were sometimes more than ten years younger than he was and whose company was more likely to inspire a story about a cradle robber than about the eligible bachelor. He had also found something of a social compromise while living with Fonda in his host's taste for informal barbecues rather than dress-up parties. Back in his own place in Brentwood and later in another house on Coldwater Canyon, he too began entertaining at home rather than touring the city's restaurants and clubs. "Jimmy hated being photographed when he was out with a girl and he seldom took his dates to nightclubs," June Allyson remembered of the period. "Instead, he fed them steak that he had grilled in his own backyard. If they didn't like that and wanted the limelight, they were not for him."

For his part, Fonda found more "gravity" in the postwar Stewart, but not enough to correct his years-old impression that his basic appeal to women was in "bringing out their mothering qualities." But while that might have been markedly true of some relationships, especially with Dietrich before the war and in his lifelong tie to Sullavan, other women he knew saw a much more mixed attraction in him. One of these was Fay Wray, who got to know him socially during the shooting of her husband Robert Riskin's *Magic Town*. As Wray remembers:

> He was a very curious blend, I thought. On the one hand, he had a very sharp paternal attitude toward everyone, even though he was much younger than some of the people he was acting paternal toward. He never let a formal occasion—a funeral, something more pleasant—go by without showing up, and with the air of some kind of generational duty that he wasn't going to be the first one to neglect. At the same time, there was this big, sweet kid, who could be sweetly ridiculous in some little detail. For example, the night we were about to attend the premiere for *Magic Town*, he came over to our house so we could go to the picture together. He had obviously just gotten his suit out of the cleaner's because I'd never smelled so much cleaning fluid in my life. I had to open the windows to let some air in because Robert and I were both gagging. But Jimmy, he hadn't noticed a thing until we started joking about it.

Actress Myrna Dell, as close to a constant companion as Stewart had in 1948, remembers a similarly gawky scene:

> I got a call one day from Sylvia Sidney saying that she was giving a party at her home for John McClain, the theater critic of the New York *Journal-American*, and she asked me to choose between Jimmy and someone else

as a date for the evening. I didn't think too long on that one because he had always been my favorite actor. Well, Jimmy picked me up and took me to Sylvia's. As the front door opened, he seemed to recognize the man who was holding it and started all this enthusiastic handshaking and how great it was to see the man and all that. The man tried to be polite, but looked mainly embarrassed. Finally, when Jimmy stopped pumping his hand, the man asked for our coats. He was the butler!

Dell says that she was also the exception to his new preference for staying home in the evening:

I never met somebody who danced better than he, and he never seemed reluctant about going to places where we could dance, although I did hear that from some other people. But the business about him being a great womanizer always seemed exaggerated to me. Maybe it had been true earlier, before the war, but I never saw much sign of it. One weekend evening, in fact, I left a dinner early because I was suddenly feeling a little stifled. But I didn't want to go straight home, so I dropped by Jimmy's house, which was nearby. There wasn't a light to be seen in the house, and it couldn't have been more than nine o'clock. Maybe he's out for the night, I thought, but I went around to the window of his bedroom anyway and knocked on it. There he was, already on his way to sleep. He looked very happy to see me.

One story that made the rounds in Hollywood in the summer of 1948 said that Stewart and Dell intended marrying as soon as he finished his second replacement stint for Frank Fay in *Harvey* on Broadway. An even more colorful variation was that Dell was so certain of the nuptials that, in the actor's absence, she had his house completely redecorated, charging it all to him. The actress laughs off the tale as a gossip columnist's invention. "Jimmy and I thought it was hilarious when we read it. And as for him coming back to California to discover what I was supposed to have done and then using that as the reason for calling off our engagement, that was absolutely ridiculous because he *never*, repeat *never*, asked me to marry him."

For all the laughs they might have gotten over the redecorating story, however, Dell didn't have to look hard to discern the various pressures Stewart was under in the period. "There was new baggage and there was old baggage," the actress says. "The new had to do with his career. He was very worried about it until *Call Northside 777* came along and persuaded him that he hadn't become poison at the box office. One night he even asked me whether he shouldn't try to speak differently, maybe flatten out his delivery in some way with the help of a voice teacher. I told him to forget it. It's not you, I told him, it's the lousy scripts you're getting involved with. Just exercise a little more judgment before agreeing to what you're handed. You don't always have to say yes, you know."

But at least where two people (i.e., the old baggage) came in, according to Dell, the actor seemed to find it impossible to say anything *but* yes. "Everybody in Hollywood knew the stories about Jimmy and Margaret Sullavan. I'm about as certain as a third party can be that they didn't go to bed together, but he was still clearly in love with her in the late 1940s. Sometimes when I was at his house, she would call from New York or Connecticut, and suddenly he had this tiny puppy dog voice talking to her. I might as well have not been there. She really manipulated him, even long-distance. Anything she said was right, anything said against her was absolutely wrong. I got the feeling that she'd call him whenever she was in need of a little adoration."

The second dominating presence cast a shadow over the private dinner that Stewart and Dell had on May 20, 1948, to celebrate the actor's fortieth birthday. "He'd just come back from Indiana and he told me that he'd had a talk with his father. That his father had told him that he couldn't keep putting off thinking about the future and had to make a choice. Was he going to go down the lonely road worrying only about his career or was he going to get serious and have children and a family? Then he looked at me in perfect sincerity and said, 'Well, I'm too old to be a father, so I guess it's the lonely road as far as I'm concerned.' This, mind you, on his fortieth birthday! But his father had him thinking that he was eighty!"

Alex also had more opportunity for conveying such ideas: Between his acting work in the East and a new fondness for getting into the cockpit of his Piper Super Cub, Stewart found it easier to visit Indiana in the years immediately after the war. Cryptic remarks that he has made about the visits indicate that his doubts about his acting career met with revived hopes on the part of his father that he would think again about the hardware store, but not to the point of any gleeful I-told-you-sos. Already in his midseventies, Alex saved most of his explicit censure for his son's on-and-off church attendance and lukewarm support of his

Presbyterian congregation in California. It was an admonition that Stewart would carry back to Hollywood with him and discuss with friends and acquaintances as though they too might have had something to learn from his father's dissatisfaction. Or, in the words of Fay Wray, "Jimmy had a way of getting you caught up in his concerns, and a lot of them were associated with his parents and Indiana. One time, for instance, we were talking about how his father back in Pennsylvania had raised horses and still liked to go to the track every once in awhile. My husband had a lithograph of some sulkies, a very beautiful piece, and it seemed like the most natural thing in the world to give it to Jimmy so that he could send it to his father. We had never met the man, but thanks to Jimmy we had become drawn into the father's world in some strange way. We wanted to please him, too."

Alex's concerns about Stewart's bachelor status had been shared for some time by his male friends on the West Coast. Even more after the war than before it, Meredith, Fonda, Hayward, and Bill Grady detected an emotional drift that backyard barbecues instead of nightclub hopping had done little to correct. Whether or not for personal reasons having to do with his own wife's strange relationship with the actor, Hayward was especially active in a marriage-broker role, to the point that Stewart mused aloud about whether his former agent was counting on a 10 percent return from a marriage. On one occasion, while doing *Harvey* in New York, he relented before incessant badgering by Hayward to go on a blind date. "I called her, then went and picked her up. I asked a doorman to get a taxi, and she said, 'Don't you have a car?' That was my first mistake. Then we had dinner and just didn't seem to have much to talk about. Then, to make it worse, she ordered something she didn't like. Then we went to the theater, and it wasn't a very good play. After the theater, we had a terrible time getting a cab and in the end she said, 'I think I'd like to go home now.' She said goodbye and left me in the lobby and that was it."

Even then, Hayward wouldn't let it go, telling Stewart that he remained convinced that the woman was right for him; the problem, the producer said, was that the actor hadn't started off the evening by sending flowers. To repair that oversight, Hayward took it upon himself to send them. According to Stewart, "that didn't get me another date with the woman, but it sure as hell got me a bill for what must have been a thousand roses."

Grady told a story about another woman he had thought Stewart was serious about until he confronted the actor one day with a question about the progress of the romance. "I'm not sure," Stewart was said to have replied. "I just don't seem to understand her." Grady then continued, "Later, I found out that they had been parked outside of her house on a moonlit night. She felt romantic and said, 'It's so lovely, the trolls must be out tonight!' Now if she had said elves or pixies or leprechauns, Jimmy might have gotten it. But trolls didn't register with him at all, so he asked, 'Who're the Trolls—your neighbors?' The woman stared at him in amazement, ran inside, and slammed the door."

Beyond amiable naiveté, however, there was still the Stewart who kept his own counsel and imparted his conclusions in a decidedly miserly fashion. "He's the cagiest man I've ever known," fellow Princetonian Jose Ferrer once told a reporter. "He's cagey with everything—with cars, with scripts, with money, with women. When he does marry, she'll have to have talked a very good script." An accentuated self-absorption when he was fearful about his career hardly lessened this trait. As Myrna Dell remembers, "Jimmy was never really open, and most of the time that set the tone between us. Rifts with him were scenes without words, and sometimes dramas without scenes. One night I got really mad at him, blew up in his living room because he never seemed to ask me about my life or my career. For all you know, I yelled at him, I could be a hooker. He just kind of looked at me and said, 'Myrna, would you like a Coke?' "

Even their last scene as lovers, according to the actress, wasn't played together.

I loved him dearly, and I suppose what really broke us up was my idea of humor. A Hollywood columnist had gone to interview him and spotted a photograph of Ann Blyth in his dressing room. When he asked Jimmy about me, Jimmy's answer was that we were both seeing other people. That was true, though not to any serious degree—mainly, I suppose, so that neither of us would start feeling like some weight on the other. Then the same columnist asked me for an interview. The morning that he was due to drop by, I asked the stills man on the picture I was making to find as many pictures of Ronald Reagan as he could and to put them all around my dressing room. He came up with about nine of them. So here's this columnist, he walks in and sees all these pictures of Reagan and decides that Jimmy's crush on Ann Blyth is nothing compared to mine on Ronnie.

The item appeared in the paper, and two things happened. One, Reagan called me up and invited me out. Two, Jimmy never called me again.

Instead, Stewart was calling his future wife.

THE CHARACTER STAR

COMMENTING ON STEWART'S ACTING DEBUT WITH THE University Players in 1932, Norris Houghton observed that company founders Bretaigne Windust and Charles Leatherbee became the first in a long line of producers and directors who wanted to include the actor in their projects, even though they weren't always sure about *how* to include him. That was still largely the case on the threshold of the 1950s, and one of the major reasons was Stewart's refusal to fit neatly into the division between "stars" and "character actors" so fundamental to the Hollywood studio system.

He wasn't the first one to present such a problem, of course; Edward G. Robinson, Paul Muni, and Wallace Beery, to name but three, had thrived for years while being viewed as both. But Stewart posed the problem from the reverse direction of most of his predecessors: By the traditional standards for the Hollywood distinction, he was a star who insisted upon being a character actor, not a character actor whose successful roles had catapulted him to stardom. Physically, he would always be leading man tall, unlike a Robinson. Vocally, he would always be obtrusively recognizable, unlike a Muni. In the eyes of the public, his loquacious Jefferson Smith would always cut more of a romantic figure than Beery's garrulous Long John Silver. Left alone, his forty years had done nothing to gray or belly him into middle-age submission. But with all those qualifications for James Stewart the star established, he had, especially in the late 1940s, seemingly gone out of his way to devalue his box-office standing as a sex symbol, the ultimate star test. And by so doing, he also issued the first of two challenges that would prove significant in the demise of the big studio system.

By practiced definition, stars were the handsome, the beautiful, the charismatic, the instantly familiar, the stylishly shallow, the astronomically paid, and the never changing. A star's appearance in a film, as Richard Schickel once observed, was "properly seen—if not by him, then by his fans—as but a single event in a much larger drama—the star's career. He came to each new enterprise trailing behind him—and often tripping over—the wisps of former parts, and we were pleased or displeased in the degree that, in his new role, he fulfilled our unspoken expectations." By contrast, character actors, as they were classified by the old studio system, were the old, the fat, the homely, the ethnic, the greatly gifted, the modestly paid, and the continuously working. While stars supposedly excited audiences with their feline, ursine, or equine qualities, character actors impressed as chameleons. Stars were *themselves*, character actors were always *somebody else*. Stars *indulged* their characters. Character actors *became* theirs.

One problem with these distinctions is that they were never true, except to the extent that the studios promoted them as such. As a species, the character actor was a financial child of finite studio budgets (not everybody connected to a production could be promoted equally) and demographic calculations (the trumpeting of young leading players for young audiences); from an aesthetic and artistically technical point of view, he never existed. The only actors who became the roles they played, as Italy's Marcello Mastroianni once noted, were performers who "don't know what acting is all about and who belong in a loony bin." By the same token, the only stars who were *themselves* in their work were performers who didn't know what acting was all about and who belonged in a studio publicist's pipe dream.

Even by the studio system's own lights, most of the qualities it referred to for distinguishing stars from character actors seldom stood up to much examination. While the Gables, Grants, Coopers, and Flynns responded to some notion of classic handsomeness, that could not be said of the Cagneys, Bogarts, Tracys, and Rafts. Audience familiarity was also always a tenuous demarcation line between stars and character actors; it hasn't merely been in recent years that a buzz of recognition has gone through the orchestra seats at the belated arrival on the theater screen of a Charles Durning, an Eileen Brennan, or a Jack Warden, no matter the density of their makeup. John Barrymore once suggested how a supporting actor could be as predictable as a leading man in a characterization with the crack: "As my brother Lionel says in every single picture to some ingenue, 'You have spirit—I like that.'" Something similar could have been said of such other stalwarts as Lee J. Cobb (the snarling gangster or the benevolent man of reason), Agnes Moorehead (the vengeful schemer or the arid widow), Arthur Kennedy (the sneering cynic or the hopeful hypocrite), and Ethel Barrymore (the elderly lady as good sport or the elderly lady as iron will or the elderly lady as both). Unlike the case of a Gable or a Flynn, however, they were never accused of being themselves in such roles, no matter how many times they did them.

One of the consequences of the star system where actors were concerned, in fact, was a kind of reverse snobbery. With their top money and top billing, many leading men and women came to be viewed as talentless beyond the confines of the image that their studio devised for them. For all the serious training they might have had before becoming a gleam in a producer's eye, they were reduced to profiles and mannerisms of some exploitable kind, and basically informed that that was all to be expected of them. This is not to say that some weren't content with their position, or even incapable of much beyond it, but the division between star and character player left all of them somewhat in the situation of a baseball catcher who was able to hit: a genuine ability to act was an extra. Joan Fontaine, for one, thinks it was an extra that wasn't even regarded as desirable by many studio people:

For all the stories about how actresses were mistreated by this or that studio boss, I always thought male stars were in a worse situation in one way. The fact of the matter is, the studio executives—especially those up-from-the-gutter immigrants who had their ideas about what was a man and what wasn't a man—they were never all that comfortable with the fact that their main business asset—the stars—had to be actors. It's absurd to think about it, but if they could've managed the whole thing with automobile mechanics, say, they would have been much happier. For the Mayers and the Warner brothers, actors were always vaguely effeminate—people who wore tights to recite To Be or Not To Be. That was why they were so eager to play up a Don Juan streak in their men—it made them seem less "actorish," more like regular guys. That was also why they preferred talking about their assets as stars rather than actors. Stars were larger than the stage, the acting profession. Stars didn't have the homosexual implications that these people attributed to actors, and probably always had since they'd first seen them in some little village square in Europe.

As an actor given to crying as much as to slugging, to yelping for joy as much as to conceding a grin, Stewart had already exhausted one studio's abilities for molding him according to star fashion. His longest suit, as he himself has always described it, has been in *vulnerability*—the quality that attracted him to parts and the quality that, when all his physical and psychological strengths and debilities were computed, attracted audiences to him. But vulnerability, as exposed as his characterizations often made it, was not the most common commodity of male stars; when it was to be found in men at all on the screen, it was almost always in the supporting players who ran on to explode, bubble, winge, swear, sob, urge, and beg in a couple of scenes, then ran off again. By traditional standards, this particular forte made Stewart an unreliable star—not so much because he might score at the box office with one picture and fail with the next, which could happen with anybody, but because it was impossible to pin to vulnerability the same pretense of a marketing plan as could be pinned to suavity (Grant), integrity (Cooper), or toughness (Bogart). There was no telling in what form—in what volatile shaping— the vulnerability would emerge from character to character, from film to film. That did not make for the continuity that the studios depended on (and that, in the case of Stewart, MGM had failed to develop) for a long-range investment.

Stewart was as aware of the problem as the studios. It worried him, too, because he had never disdained the idea of being a star in the Hollywood sense; he had even toyed with the notion of recrafting his vocal delivery to maintain that status. However much he was open to the challenges of unorthodox roles and whatever he had told interviewers years earlier, he wasn't ready to get along as Donald Meek. The only trouble was, running from genre to genre, from tired role to wrong role, as he did for the most part in the latter 1940s, deepened the problem rather than resolved it.

That he came out of his slump owed to two principal factors. The first was the ascent of Jimmy Stewart—that affable, middle-aged youth who never took himself too seriously, always had a grain of salt ready for dealing with the world's complexities, and assumed a universal respect for elders and the flag. It was, in fact, in the late 1940s that the actor began mocking his own image with some regularity, especially on the Bing Crosby and Jack Benny radio programs. He became a comforting personality over and above the individual roles he played on the screen and even beyond the wartime heroics that his public silence suggested had had their dark aspects. What the major studios did not accomplish, consolidating his stardom, NBC did achieve.

What turned out to be even more important was The Deal.

A 1948 Supreme Court ruling that found the studios in violation of anti-trust statutes in their maintenance of production-distribution-exhibition networks had left Hollywood in business turmoil. Required to divest themselves of their theaters, and of all the financial guarantees secured through them, the studios began decrying the end of an era. Without their exhibition assurances, they lamented, they would be forced to cut back in other areas, specifically in the number of films they turned out every year and, as a result of that, in the number of actors, directors, and producers they could afford to keep under contract. Some studios, however, felt the pressures more than others. For companies like MGM, Warners, and Paramount, with their vast chains of theaters, the court decision was a hammer blow. United Artists, on the other hand, would end up a few years later benefiting enormously from the encroaching trend to independent production. Somewhere between the middle and bottom of the ladder was Universal, a studio that made its overhead and a tad more mainly by churning out modest black-and-white comedies (most prominently with Abbott and Costello) and bleary-colored Arabian Nights adventures with Jon Hall and Maria Montez. There were not many unlikelier settings from within which Stewart would rise to the top of the box-office heap and also drive another nail into the coffin of the studio system.

As the tale has usually been told, the actor's MCA agent Lew Wasserman encountered Universal chief William Goetz at a party during the summer of 1949 and mentioned Stewart's enthusiasm for starring in the film version of *Harvey*, the play he had already done twice on Broadway. Goetz, in turn, was more interested in talking about a western that had been gathering dust at the studio for quite a number of years. The last point on which the principals agreed in later accounts was that Wasserman mentioned that Stewart's asking price was $200,000 and Goetz replied that Universal couldn't manage such a steep salary. Depending on the source, it was then either the studio head or the agent who proposed the idea of Stewart doing both *Harvey* and the western, *Winchester '73*, for a percentage of the profits instead of a straight salary. Where Wasserman definitely proved his abilities, on the other hand, was in a subsequent, bigger deal between his client and Universal that operated from the same premise of percentage participation on a nonexclusive basis. With this loophole, the triumvirate that Stewart formed with director Anthony Mann and producer Aaron Rosenberg was free to do another feature for MGM and, with other producers replacing Rosenberg, a second at Paramount and a third at Columbia.

Stewart was not the first actor to accept a percentage of eventual grosses instead of a salary for a picture. In the 1940s alone, Gregory Peck had forged deals of the kind, as had, at Universal, Abbott and Costello. But the agreement was significant both for the appreciable chunk the actor stood to take out of revenues[12] and for its timing. Goetz's father-in-law Louis B. Mayer was known to be especially furious over the deal, not only for the ideas that it would put into the heads of the MGM stars he was trying to hold on to, but also because it meant that the studios, already under fire for shifty accounting practices in their operation of distribution and exhibition branches, would have to open their books to actors and their representatives. One of Mayer's milder remonstrances to his son-in-law was that he had allowed "the lunatics to take over the asylum." That consideration, at least in the eyes of the MGM chief, far outweighed Goetz's pride at having snagged a top name for a medium-budgeted picture without having to pay a big salary.

Stewart himself didn't need a pencil and paper to tote up the risks and opportunities inherent in the deal. On the minus side, Universal was still a small company with little production distinction since the heydays of Boris Karloff and Bela Lugosi; *Winchester '73* would be going into production even as the smaller, serial-type companies were discontinuing their assorted Red Ryder and Lash LaRue western programmers for lack of audience interest; both the western and *Harvey* would be shot in black and white amid the growing popular demand for Technicolor features; and Stewart might not make a penny from the deal if the Universal promotion department turned out to be as penny-wise as its production department. On the plus side, he would be playing a "toughened-up" hero in *Winchester '73*; he had an opportunity to make

---

[12] Some estimates said that Stewart ended up with 50 percent of the income from *Winchester '73*. A more conservative account said 30 percent.

Harvey his after the two Broadway stints that had not completely satisfied him; and there was the possibility that a percentage deal would not only make him a lot of money, but make it for him over an arc of several years, thereby lessening the bite from the Internal Revenue Service. But what not even his optimism about the contract had yet to make completely clear to him was that, with his partnership with Mann and Rosenberg, he was gaining for himself the basis for the kind of continuity that stars had traditionally availed themselves of under the studio system, while simultaneously being free to choose the roles he would undertake. Using the terminology of Hollywood, what the Universal agreement gave him was the chance to be a "character star."

But for all his negotiating smarts, Wasserman might not have found Goetz so receptive to the deal were it not for two other pictures that Stewart had made at the end of the decade. One was *The Stratton Story*, which made a killing at the box office and enabled the agent to price his client as highly as he did with Goetz. The other was *Broken Arrow*, which, while still not in circulation, eased some Universal doubts about the actor's ability to look at home in a western.

The Stratton Story (MGM – 1949)

The Stratton Story was Stewart's first screen biography and set the tone for the others in being more concerned with packaging family magazine-type perspectives than shedding any special light on the characters being treated. It also marked Stewart's return to MGM after his walkout in 1945.

Monty Stratton is a Texas farmboy who is spotted pitching in a semipro game by Barney Wile (Frank Morgan), a Chicago White Sox scout who is looking for the kind of prospect that will get him in favor again with his employers. Wile is so convinced that Stratton will be his ticket back to the big time that he agrees to work on the farm shared by the pitcher and his widowed mother (Agnes Moorehead) while honing some of his find's rough edges. After overcoming the mother's resistance to the idea, the scout accompanies the pitcher to Chicago's spring training camp, where Stratton duly impresses. After some initial failures that earn him a temporary demotion to the minor leagues, Stratton rejoins the White Sox and becomes a member of the starting rotation. He also finds time to marry Ethel (June Allyson), a blind date he has met through another member of the team.

The film's major crisis occurs after Stratton's second consecutive fifteen-win season, when, on a hunting trip, he falls over a log and accidentally shoots himself in the leg. The leg has to be amputated to save his life. Bitter and morose over the abrupt end of his baseball career, Stratton turns a cold shoulder to the world, including his year-old son. But it is also the child's efforts to walk that finally inspire him to rise above his self-pity and attempt his own fledgling steps on an artificial leg. With the encouragement of Ethel, he also begins pitching again around the farm on the prosthetic device. Even his wife and Wile are startled, however, when he insists on pitching in a minor league all-star game. Despite attempts by opposing batters to exploit his handicap by bunting, he wins the game and proves to himself that he is not a cripple.

The Stewart-Stratton combination took some doing. Mayer, for one, didn't want to do the picture at all, telling an aide, "How do you think people will feel when this man with one leg goes to bat, gets a single, but can't run to first base? How will the pregnant women in the audience feel watching such a disgusting sight?" What the MGM boss could also have said was that, with the exception of Gary Cooper's portrayal of Lou Gehrig in *The Pride of the Yankees* in 1942, baseball movies were notoriously poor box-office performers.

Even when Mayer was persuaded to give the green light to the project, technical advisor Stratton posed another problem with deep doubts about the choice of Van Johnson to portray him. Ethel Stratton recalled from her Greenville, Texas, farm in 1995: "Van was a star and a sweet man, but after he had worked out a little with my husband, Monty said he was gun-shy athletically and would never be convincing as a pitcher. We'd wanted Jimmy from the beginning. He even looked like Monty a little. So Monty finally went to MGM and told them that Johnson would never really work out and that Stewart would be ideal."

If Mayer nursed a grudge about Stewart's departure some years before, he got over it enough to have a script sent to the actor in New York where he was doing *Harvey*. Stewart responded that he was interested, but asked for a postponement of a few months until he had fulfilled other commitments. He also asked that June Allyson be cast as his wife instead of the previously hired Donna Reed.[13] In the view of Ethel Stratton, the

---

[13] Stewart's preference for Allyson was partly the result of never-scintillating relations with Reed during the making of *It's a Wonderful Life* and partly of Allyson's bigger box-office appeal.

wait was worth it. "Monty did a lot of training on the field with Jimmy, and Jimmy kept asking for more. Maybe he wasn't a major league pitcher, but he was an athlete and didn't have to be told fundamental things."

Directed by Sam Wood, who had also done *The Pride of the Yankees*, *The Stratton Story* proved to be even more of a success commercially than its predecessor, taking in $4 million on its first national release and becoming MGM's biggest earner in 1949. The stunned Mayer could only conclude that audiences had responded to the sentimental family elements of the story rather than to its baseball background. If so, it was just as well, since many of the diamond sequences tested credibility to the maximum; among other things, batters were shown calling out to congratulate Stratton the pitcher for having struck them out.

Even more than sentimental, *The Stratton Story* was elliptical. The development of personal relations, the critical hunting accident, and Stratton's immediate reaction to discovering that his leg had been amputated (and his baseball career ended) were just some of the items that happened *off-camera*. The same effort to avert, cushion, or historicize shock was apparent in the dialogue, which was mostly of the caption variety, not all that removed from Stewart's Stratton winding up and shouting, "Here comes a fast ball."

Stewart the actor seldom had his fast ball in *The Stratton Story*. As would happen again with his portrayals of actual people, he moves through the proceedings somewhat breezily, almost glibly, as though his passion for the task ended with his mastery of some technical details (pitching) and that all that was required otherwise was to be as personable as possible. Real historical figures did not challenge his imagination, least of all when they hung around a movie set ready to offer pointers in the interests of accuracy; what *The Stratton Story* and its successors seemed to do more than anything was intimidate him in every way except as *Jimmy* Stewart. At that he was as professional as ever, and Mayer and Wood (the Motion Picture Alliance's drafter of *The Screen Guide for Americans*) ended up with the box-office receipts to prove that it was enough.

Asked five decades after the fact what she thought of the film, Ethel Stratton replied: "It was almost as good as the truth."

Malaya (MGM – 1949)

Between *The Stratton Story* and *Broken Arrow*, Stewart squeezed in another stint at MGM on *Malaya*, mainly in the interests of acting again with Spencer Tracy, whom he had found so encouraging on his debut feature, *The Murder Man*. The venture backfired on more than one level.

Based vaguely on a real incident, *Malaya* cast Stewart as John Royer, a newspaper correspondent who teams with soldier of fortune Carnahan (Tracy) to smuggle rubber out of the Malay peninsula during World War II. With the help of The Dutchman (Sydney Greenstreet), a mercenary cafe owner who might have been imported from *Casablanca*, they round up a crew under the nose of the Japanese occupation forces and manage to get 150,000 tons of rubber to the awaiting United States Navy in two shipments. By the time they get around to hauling a third and last shipment, however, the Japanese are waiting in ambush for them. The rash Royer disparages the signs of the ambush, and gets himself killed. Carnahan, who had refused to go on what he regarded as a suicide mission, changes his mind after Royer's death and engineers the delivery of the third shipment. But he too gets killed for his efforts.

Despite the colorful cast of Stewart, Tracy, Greenstreet, Valentina Cortese, and Lionel Barrymore, *Malaya* was all mechanical plot. Much of the blame was laid on Richard Thorpe, another in MGM's long line of directors out to impress front-office executives through his single-take shootings. His haste was evident in everything from badly played scenes between Tracy and less gifted cast members to such illogical details as having the two heroes sneaking through the jungle at night in glaring white linen suits. If Thorpe had any excuse at all, it was Tracy—a heavy drinker notorious for going AWOL on a project when he felt it wasn't up to his talents. And although *Malaya* had originally been aimed at satisfying the actor's demand for doing an action picture, he made it very clear very quickly that he was in a walking mood. As Arthur Beckhard had once counted on him on Broadway, Stewart was asked to exert a calming influence. He recalled years later: "It was a constantly edgy situation. Spencer was more cantankerous than usual because the film was a real potboiler.... He could walk out and pull one of his famous disappearances any time. So I decided on a strategy to keep him interested in something other than the picture."

The strategy involved showing up on the set every day with a batch of travel brochures for a trip abroad the two actors talked about making together as soon as *Malaya* was completed. According to Stewart, Tracy showed "great excitement" about going to Greece, Italy, and India. Or, at least seemed to. Stewart: "When [the picture] was over, I said to him, 'Well, have you got your passport yet?' He said, 'What passport?' 'For our trip to Europe and Asia,' I said. 'Europe and Asia?' he says to me. 'Why, I wouldn't go across the street with you, you son of a bitch.' "

Broken Arrow (20th Century-Fox – 1950)

Although it was released after *Winchester '73*, *Broken Arrow* began production almost eight months earlier. The delay in distribution was due, first, to protracted editing demanded by Darryl Zanuck, head of 20th Century-Fox, and, then, to a studio decision to wait for the public reaction to *Winchester '73* to see how Stewart would be accepted wearing a six-gun and riding a horse.

Based on the novel *Blood Brother* by Elliot Arnold, *Broken Arrow* was another of Stewart's Biographical Incident pictures, recounting the mediation role played by mail rider and former army scout Tom Jeffords in working out an 1870 peace agreement between the U.S. Government and the Apache tribe led by Cochise (Jeff Chandler). Within this framework of the usual suspicions, betrayals, and rebellions on the part of both whites and Indians over the accord, the film dwells on Jeffords's love for Sonseeahray (Debra Paget), a member of Cochise's tribe. It is her death in an ambush organized by the heavy Slade (Will Geer) that, according to the picture, finally wakes up the two sides to the urgency of completing the peace agreement.

Few Hollywood westerns have been analyzed more exhaustively over the years than *Broken Arrow*. The first to do so was Zanuck, who oversaw a major recutting of Delmer Daves's finished product when he decided that the director had allowed Chandler, Paget, and other members of the cast to fall into Stewart's slow, earnest speech rhythms in their discomfort with the "Apache English" used by the whites portraying the Indians.[14] The studio head also had his editing department laboring long hours to cover up some badly staged action sequences, a couple of which survived into the released film. Among outsiders, most of the discussion around *Broken Arrow* has centered on whether it deserved its reputation as a

---

[14] Stewart's opening narration makes note of the fact that the Apache characters will be speaking English, making it all the more curious that they often lapsed into fanciful movie Indian talk.

sincere attempt to depict Native Americans or whether it was just another Hollywood example of bending over backwards so far to apologize for the mistreatment of a minority that representatives of the group come off more divine than human; that is, *Guess Who's Coming to the Teepee*. Those who have discerned boldness in the film, at least for its time, have associated it with some of the other screen treatises of the late 1940s denouncing racial and ethnic prejudice, such as in *Gentleman's Agreement*'s focus on anti-Semitism in 1947 and *Home of the Brave*'s attention to racism in 1949.

What *Broken Arrow* most conspicuously had in common with other so-called liberal pictures of the period was its fear of rage, at least from what would have been the appropriate characters. The Cochise of Chandler often sounds like a *Newsweek* editorial with his on-the-one-hand-on-the-other-hand dialogue; at other times, he resembles a preacher who comes up with the right sermon topics ("What's a fair peace?" and "A treaty to be changed later?" are two), but then dozes off at the pulpit before suggesting any answers. By contrast, Stewart's Jeffords plays the only scenes of fury—first in almost being lynched by Indian haters and then in screaming that he be permitted to finish off one of the bushwhackers who has killed Sonseeahray. Although dramatic in themselves, and rendered in Stewart's most effective visceral manner, the scenes rely for much of their power on the picture's biggest historical falsehood—that Jeffords undertook his peacemaking mission from solely altruistic motives. (In fact, the real Jeffords went to Cochise originally to negotiate the end of the Apache attacks because they were destroying his mail-carrier business.) The emotional displacement ends up tainting the coherence of the entire film when, to resolve the Stewart character's anguish instead of the Indian-white issue, an abruptly staged last scene has a soldier glibly tell Jeffords that the death of Sonseeahray has sealed the treaty he had labored to conclude. Stewart is left looking as though he isn't sure the movie is over.

Zanuck's anxieties over *Broken Arrow* didn't end even after a July 1950 release of *Winchester '73* had assured him that movie audiences were ready to accept Stewart as a cowboy.[15] Even as Fox's publicity department was whipping up anticipation for an August distribution with an

---

[15] Zanuck also had frayed nerves over the project because the blacklisted Albert Maltz had written it, though he did not receive the screen credit.

emphasis on the picture's open-mindedness about Native Americans, the studio was also hiring four Indians in New York to go around to RKO theaters and whoop it up in rain and hoop dances between projections. One of those hired was Lou Mofsie, a half-Winnebago, half-Hopi who was only fourteen at the time: "Fox called them Indian Pow-wows. Besides myself, there was another Winnebago, a Navaho, and a Cherokee. We'd do the dances and some of us would sing 'Indian Love Call' types of things. The audiences really liked it. We did two shows a day, earned $400 each a week, and even ended up on television with Steve Allen." And the reaction of other Native Americans? "Some of our people didn't like it, said we were lowering ourselves. But as a teenager then, it seemed to me that the overriding point was helping to attract an audience to something that wasn't the usual Hollywood junk. Obviously, you'd hope to see a much better depiction of Indians on the screen today, but considering the time and powers involved in Broken Arrow, it came out okay."

Better than that, according to Stewart. As the actor related the story some time later, after several days of shooting in Arizona's Coconino Mountains, the production was approached by an elderly Apache who warned that there would be a disaster if the camp wasn't struck immediately. The cast and crew voted to accept the advice; some hours later, a wall of water flooded the campsite. Members of the crew said that it was an omen; the elderly Apache said no, it was just the annual melting of the snows.

VI
GLORIA

THE RIGHT WOMAN

WHEN HE WAS ROOMING WITH STEWART AT OLD Buckingham during the war, Andy Low drifted off to sleep many evenings after expounding on what it was like being married. The then-assistant operations officer didn't have much choice: "I was married, but I had never seen my child. Jimmy was fascinated by that—not just about the odd thing that I'd never seen my baby, but how I could have committed myself to marriage and a family. We'd be lying in our quarters waiting to fall off, and he'd keep asking me about the commitment that I had made to my wife—what was it like? How did I ever get around to doing it? He'd known so many people, he said, but he couldn't get serious in the way that I apparently had. What did it take?"

For starters, an invitation to Gary Cooper's house for dinner in the summer of 1948. Like Hayward, Meredith, and his other friends, Cooper and his wife Rocky had also concluded that Stewart was a husband in search of a wife and that the problem was bothering him more than he wanted to admit. Their solution was Gloria Hatrick, the only other single invited for the evening.

Actually, Hatrick hadn't been single for long. A thirty-one-year-old mother of two young sons (Ronald, aged three, and Michael, two), she had gotten a divorce only the year before from Edward (Neddy) McLean, Jr., a millionaire whose mother owned the Hope Diamond. The marriage had ended with McLean's announcement that he intended going off with a Vanderbilt. As Hatrick confided to some friends, the news hadn't exactly come as a shock to her, and once assured that the divorce settlement would provide amply for her sons, she had offered no resistance to dissolving the marriage. One story that circulated after news of the breakup said that McLean had to compete with a crossword puzzle to declare his intentions, that Hatrick had continued to fill in her letters

Down and Across until there was silence; only then, her eyes still on her newspaper, did she reportedly reply, "As long as you're the one who goes to Reno." Mignon Winants, a California socialite acquainted with the McLeans and a guest that evening at the Cooper home, doesn't dismiss the tale. "The way Gloria was, that sounds absolutely right," Winants says. "She wouldn't let hard decisions overwhelm her. The harder they were, the more she seemed to disdain them—or at least wanted you to think she did. Nothing was going to be stronger than she was, least of all Neddy McLean."

Gloria Hatrick had never been intimidated by the rich or the celebrated. Born in Larchmont, New York, as one of three children to Edgar and Jessie Hatrick, she attended the best schools in New York City and Westchester, including Manhattan's posh (and now defunct) Finch College for Women on the Upper East Side. The money was there because of her father, who went from being a New York hype salesman to a pioneer in the newsreel and movie-serial fields.[1] After signing on with William Randolph Hearst in 1908, Edgar Hatrick took over the Hearst Metrotone News (later known as *News of the Day*); as a member of the U.S. Government Information Service in World War I, he assembled the first documentary footage of the hostilities to be shown in public. It was at a social function for Hearst's theatrical features subsidiary, Cosmopolitan Pictures, that his daughter met Ned McLean.

Before marrying, Gloria Hatrick had worked briefly as a model, an Arthur Murray dance instructor, and a fashion design assistant on the East Coast. A tall, slim brunette with flashing green eyes, she had never shown serious interest in the acting opportunities her father's position with Hearst might have provided. On the other hand, she had always exhibited a passion for the outdoors—especially for fishing, hunting, and golf. But if there was one quality that struck everybody about her immediately, it was her sense of humor—not only the kind of sardonic glibness that was always at home at glitzy parties, but also a sense of silliness that often bordered on the burlesque. "She was out-and-out

---

[1] Among his more successful promotions was having a Japanese wrestler publicly challenge President Theodore Roosevelt to a match. Although Roosevelt ignored the challenge, it generated enough publicity for the Japanese to have a run of well-attended bouts.

funny," says writer Leonard Gershe, a friend for thirty years. "There was the wit and there was the clown. A lot of people can say funny things and tell funny stories, and Gloria certainly could. But it was her willingness to be silly at times that was the real mark of her self-confidence." Mignon Winants agrees: "She lived her own way, and didn't give a damn what others might think. If she wanted to clown around, she was going to clown around. Anybody who thought she was foolish . . . well, that was their problem. Nobody had a greater sense of self, and probably nobody appreciated it more or depended on it more than Jimmy."

Although he has always claimed not remembering the episode, it was Stewart who did the clowning at his first meeting with his future wife, during the 1947 Christmas season. Accompanied by Bill Grady and Johnny Swope, he had dropped in on actor Keenan Wynn in search of any liquor that the threesome had missed during earlier stops one evening; their arrival had coincided with Gloria's departure. "They were hardly the most sober trio I'd ever laid eyes on," she would recall years later. "And Mr. Stewart certainly wasn't the Mr. Stewart I had come to know on a movie screen." A second encounter some weeks later was even less memorable, and this time for both parties, when Stewart and some friends entered Romanoff's restaurant for lunch and, without a sign of acknowledgment, walked right by a front table where Gloria was sitting with her two sons. Still, she wasn't ready to turn down the invitation from the Coopers. ("Believe it or not, he was still my favorite actor. And besides, Ann Sothern and some other people I liked were going to be there.")

She was surprised by the Stewart she ended up seated next to at the Coopers' table. "All sorts of rumors and gossip had been printed about his girl friends, but I hadn't really paid too much attention. Nothing, though, had ever been said that I could remember about his being so shy. He hardly said a thing all evening. But between the pauses I could sense that the Coopers were right, that we did have a lot in common. We liked golf, sailing, animal conservation. And, of course, movies."

One of the guests who sensed the chemistry was Leland Hayward, who insisted that Stewart and Gloria accompany him to Ciro's for some dancing before calling it a night. As Gloria remembered it, she realized that her blind date was interested in her when she glimpsed Stewart trying to be subtle about waving Hayward off from breaking in on the dance floor. The couple had their first unarranged date the next day—on the golf course.

Because she lacked the cachet of having her name on a marquee, Hatrick was largely ignored by the gossip columnists for some weeks; instead, they continued to speculate about Stewart's relationships with such actresses as Rita Hayworth, Ann Blyth, his *Call Northside 777* costar Helen Walker, and Myrna Dell. According to Dell, she detected his seriousness about Gloria even before the backfiring joke of plastering her dressing room with photographs of Ronald Reagan. "He talked a lot about her and this huge dog of hers that mauled him whenever he went to visit her," says the actress. "You just had to open your ears to hear that it wasn't the way he talked about other women. I would have had to be pretty thick to miss it."

What Hatrick was missing after some time of golfing dates was a followup around dinner hour. Her recollections on this point turned into the first of decades-long sallies against Stewart's caution with a dollar. "It was amazing. I had quite a time just getting him to buy me a meal. Finally, I had to come right out and ask him. He had invited me to the premiere of *You Gotta Stay Happy*, so I said to him, 'If we go to this movie, does it also mean that you're actually going to feed me as well?' "

Stewart has never denied the essence of that story. But while the antithesis of a spendthrift, his reluctance about going to restaurants also appeared dictated by a desire to escape the attention of gossip columnists, to keep Gloria's name out of the bubbling rumor pot already filled with the Hayworths, Blyths, and Dells. During this phase of their relationship, their steadiest social venue after dark was the Cooper house. Subsequently, they began spending greater time at Chasen's, the Beverly Hills restaurant that Stewart and Grady considered a second home and that the married Stewarts would continue to patronize a couple of times a week until it closed down in the 1990s. It wasn't too long after their regular sightings at Chasen's that Hollywood began to get the idea that Stewart had discovered "the right woman" he had been talking about since before the war. There were even attempts at self-fulfilling prophecy in February 1949, when some reports predicted that the couple would elope to Mexico imminently in order to end the increasing conjecture of newspaper and magazine writers. But Stewart was not about to slink off to Mexico or anywhere else. As he emphasized in various ways during the spring of 1949 (after he had stopped being evasive about his hopes for marrying soon), the relationship in question was between Gloria and him, not between the Hollywood press and him. He grew particularly weary of questions about whether he didn't regard forty-one as a little old to be thinking about raising a family. "Some of these people seem to flat-out resent me getting married!" he once exclaimed to Grady.

But at least some of the blame for the fixation on his age lay with Stewart himself. More than once, he came off in newspaper interviews sounding as though his love for his wife-to-be was just another consideration within obligations imposed by the calendar: "When you're 41, life means more than just a bookful of phone numbers. I needed the security of a permanent relationship with a woman I loved. I needed a family and I needed to put down roots. I could say all the usual things about meeting the right girl and falling in love. But it was also the right time."

Nobody shared that belief—or the manner of expressing it, for that matter—more than Alex Stewart. And clearly, Gloria was the alternative to the "lonely road" of mere careerism that Stewart had been warned against by his father. But the meeting of the Philadelphia Street storekeeper and the divorced mother of two was hardly a bonding of similars. Nobody had ever been divorced in the Stewart family, and Alex didn't view that only as a piece of genealogical trivia. Gloria was not a churchgoer. She was rarely to be encountered without a cigarette in her hand. Larchmont and Beverly Hills were about as close as she wanted to get to small towns. Her idea of cooking was to sit down and eat it. But most of all, she had a personality as strong and as shrewd as Alex's that not even her noted sense of humor always disguised. As her niece Melinda Draddy puts it: "With Gloria an eight o'clock dinner meant precisely that—eight o'clock. If you rang the bell at ten minutes after eight, you received the same cordial welcome as everyone else had, but you could also expect to find the others already eating. She ran everything extremely tightly. She was absolute control in the areas she considered hers."

John Stewart recalls unwittingly crossing swords with Gloria within minutes of their first meeting in California.

I went out to California in the early 1950s looking for a school for my daughter. Along the way, we stopped at Hearst's monstrosity at San Simeon. When we arrived later on in Beverly Hills, I happened to make a crack about the castle practically as I was getting out of my car. Gloria thought that it was v-e-r-y unfunny and made me understand right away that Hearst jokes weren't appreciated. Jimmy stood there kind of awkwardly for a moment, then hemmed and hawed with a reminder that her father had worked with Hearst most of his life. Gloria and I got along fine after that, but I had been given one of the ground rules.

Stewart himself once let the word *domineering* escape his lips, but in what he considered a positive context. "She's a little like my mother, who was somewhat domineering but always got what she wanted in a very kindly way," he told *Modern Maturity* magazine in the mid-1970s.

Gloria's first run-in with Alex took place shortly before she officially became Mrs. James Stewart. Arriving in Los Angeles for the wedding that was scheduled for August 9, 1949, Alex experienced the same kind of disappointment that he had been dismayed by before the war when he discovered that his son had not been doing as much as he might have been for his ostensible church, Brentwood Presbyterian. Taking matters again into his own hands, he profited from his contacts with slated wedding guests in the weeks prior to the ceremony by suggesting that, instead of the usual gifts, they buy pews in the church. Connie Wald, probably Gloria's closest friend for forty-five years, says the bride-to-be was "furious." "We laughed about it a lot in later years, but Gloria really didn't think it was that funny when it first happened. She was fit to be tied when she heard about it. God knows it wasn't about missing out on another crystal tray or whatever these people had planned on getting. Just the man's incredible presumption. I still don't know how Jimmy patched that one over."

Little of what Gloria told the press over the years indicated any personality conflict with Alex; even when she sometimes presented herself as having disagreed with her father-in-law on something, it was within the familiar framework of Alex as the witty small-town character. On one occasion, for instance, she reported having voiced relief that a baby born with two heads had died a short time after delivery. Alex was portrayed as having "snapped" at her: "Why? The death of anything is a loss." When she pointed out that survival would have meant a pitiable life, "Dad remained somber a moment, and then his unfailing good humor took possession of him. 'Well,' he said, 'that baby might have grown up to be both president *and* vice-president.'"

But such gloss, according to some people, never truly made Gloria someone receptive to either the rhythms of small-town life or especially enthusiastic about those who sought to conduct them. "I must confess that I'm in the minority about how Gloria was basically so simple, just plain folks," says Eleanor Blair, widow of Stewart's oldest friend from Indiana. "She wasn't that way at all. I always thought of her as having a real salon air to her. There were social expectations to her. She preferred just about anything to eating, for instance, but that didn't stop her when she and Jim were visiting with us from sneering at my food as a little bit too plebeian for her tastes. There was nothing at all plain folks about her."

One gap that was never bridged between Gloria and Alex, according to Blair, was the religious question. "Alex was already dead by the time her son was killed in Vietnam and that story came out about how she swore never to go to church again because of the mix-up at the memorial service. But Gloria had never gone to church much before then, either, and Alex was only too aware of it. He had never really understood her where that was concerned. For that matter, Jimmy didn't, either. He once told my husband and me that one of his greatest regrets in life was never being able to convince his own family—Gloria and the kids—to go to church regularly."

In November 1955, columnist Hedda Hopper caught another fleeting glimpse of Gloria's discomfort with the values of her husband's Indiana background. Suggesting that, if he ever decided to leave Hollywood or the public decided to leave him, Stewart would always have architecture to fall back on, the actor replied with a similar airiness: "Oh, no, the hardware store comes first." Gloria, described by Hopper as sitting nearby and doing needlepoint, immediately piped up: "Over my dead body."

But all of that was still years away on August 9, 1949, when the Stewarts were married at Brentwood Presbyterian. News accounts described the bride as wearing a gray satin, ankle-length gown and the church altar as being decked in delphiniums, one of her favorite flowers. She herself later admitted that she had shaken every step of the way down the aisle past 600 guests, who included Spencer Tracy, Gary Cooper, Ray Milland, Jack Benny, David Niven, Frank Morgan, and the rest of the Hollywood male elite that had thrown an elaborate bachelor party at Chasen's the night before for Stewart. Grady served as best man,

Gloria's sister, Ruth Draddy, as maid of honor. If there was a blight on the ten-minute ceremony for the new Mrs. Stewart, it was caused less by the reminder that some of the pews around her bore her name than by the absence of both her parents. While her mother was recovering from an operation in a New York hospital, her father was near death in a Colorado Springs clinic.

Even by design the couple had prepared themselves for a honeymoon in pieces; it got much more fragmented than that. After several days in a California retreat at Ojai Valley, they flew to Akron, Ohio, where Stewart had been committed to serve as an official at the Soap Box Derby. From there they went to Honolulu for what was supposed to be a month of touring the Hawaiian Islands. But on September 15, Edgar Hatrick died in Colorado Springs, necessitating an immediate return to the mainland. Sixty-four when he succumbed to a lung ailment, Hatrick left some jagged edges behind him, not least an estrangement from his wife caused by a lengthy affair with an actress more than thirty years younger. It fell largely to Gloria and her sister, Ruth, to conduct mourners around those social pitfalls during the funeral and its immediate aftermath.

When the Stewarts got back to Honolulu to resume their honeymoon, they ran into more unexpected grief. Helen Hayes, a Stewart acquaintance from evenings at the Thursday Night Beer Club in midtown Manhattan in the early 1930s, and her writer-husband Charles MacArthur were in Hawaii trying to piece their lives together again after the death of their daughter Mary to polio. Hearing that the MacArthurs were in the city, Stewart called them and insisted on taking them to dinner. The dinner led to a breakfast, a lunch, several sightseeing tours, more meals, a deep-sea fishing expedition, and yet more meals. As Hayes described it some years later, "there was no talking to them. They took us in tow . . . and helped us back to life."

According to Hayes's son, actor James MacArthur, his mother never forgot those days in Hawaii.

Mary's death had really devastated my parents. They were at the end of their rope when Jimmy and Gloria came along. And when you consider that the Stewarts were on their honeymoon and that Gloria had just lost her father . . . well, there was no way that my mother *couldn't* have been grateful to them. Years later, when Jimmy was doing *Harvey* with my mother, they talked a lot about that time. With Gloria's father and everything, I suppose there was a lot of mutual grief to get through. Not your average honeymoon.

But, at the start of a forty-five-year marriage, it was the only formal one that Stewart would have.

HITTING THE JACKPOT

IF STEWART HAS HAD A GOLDEN AGE PROFESSIONALLY, IT was in the 1950s. In the course of the decade, he starred in no fewer than twenty-two released features for six different studios, received two Oscar nominations and prizes from both the New York Film Critics and the Venice Film Festival, and not only debuted as a dramatic actor on television, but also took a turn at directing for the medium. On a commercial plane, only John Wayne and Jerry Lewis[2] matched his drawing power at the box office. The irony behind his success, of course, was that it corresponded with the collapse of the traditional big studio system that he has always defended as the ideal way of making motion pictures. But it was only his independence from MGM in particular and from the studios in general that, together with the smart negotiating of his agent, Lew Wasserman, opened the doors for him to play roles as varied as hard-bitten cowboys, clowns, absentminded scientists, lawyers, photographers, doctors, convicts, Federal agents, and private detectives.

Most of the actor's success in the 1950s was due to two directors— Anthony Mann, with whom he made eight pictures, and Alfred Hitchcock, with whom he made three. But the other half of his twenty-two big-screen appearances not only filled in the picture of a performer available for a wide range of parts, but also won him, at least in the short term, even better critical notices than he garnered through his work with Mann and Hitchcock. It was, in fact, for films made by Henry Koster and

---

[2] Stewart, Wayne, and Lewis were the only ones to finish in the Top Ten at least nine times. Lewis did it six times as Dean Martin's partner.

Otto Preminger that he won the Academy Award nods and the awards from New York and Venice.

The Jackpot (20th Century-Fox – 1950)

Still on the eve of the television explosion, 1950 Hollywood was more preoccupied with throwing darts at the popularity of radio quiz shows. Two of the more successful comedies of the year took on the national phenomenon as a topic: Ronald Colman's *Champagne for Caesar* and Stewart's *The Jackpot*.

Inspired by the actual misadventures of a Rhode Island family named Caffrey, *The Jackpot* cast Stewart as Bill Lawrence, whose life turns into chaos after he wins $24,000 by giving the correct answer on the telephone to a quiz-show question. Over their first flush of celebrity, Lawrence, his wife, Amy (Barbara Hale), and their children (Natalie Wood and Tommy Rettig) find themselves inundated with junk they don't want and services that threaten their quiet middle-class existence. And even that is only the beginning. In quick order, Lawrence finds himself liable for extraordinary income taxes, loses the affection of Amy when she suspects that the portrait he has won has more to do with the beautiful painter (Patricia Medina) than with a framed oil, gets jailed for trying to sell off some of his winnings to a fence, and loses his job as a department-store manager for having been arrested. Things return to something like normal only after Lawrence's newspaper friend Summers (James Gleason) reveals the truth behind all the misunderstandings and the painter persuades Amy that she has no amorous designs on her subject.

Thanks to Koster's direction, the script by Henry and Phoebe Ephron, and Stewart's playing, *The Jackpot* moves swiftly, generally ignoring the temptation to become sententious about the social significance of its mild material. Except for such details as the character of the painter, the picture retained the amiable tone of the original John McNulty *New Yorker* article dealing with the Caffreys.[3] For Stewart, *The Jackpot* has earned recollection mainly for his experience in attending the London premiere for the film in 1950. "I never believed [during the war] that I'd ever hear such gay laughter in England," he told one interviewer.

---

[3] Not mentioned in the 20th Century-Fox movie is the fact that Caffrey won his money by identifying the voice of MGM chief Louis B. Mayer.

Harvey (Universal – 1950)

Stewart's relationship with Elwood P. Dowd, the most recurrent of his career, might not have started at all except for Bing Crosby's cold feet. When the Broadway producers of *Harvey* were looking around for a summer replacement for lead Frank Fay in 1947, they went originally to Crosby. But after voicing enthusiasm for the project, the actor-crooner backed out behind the claim that his fans would protest at the sight of the priest from *Going My Way* and *The Bells of St. Mary's* playing a drunk who carries on conversations with an imaginary rabbit. It was only then that Stewart was approached to take on the role. Ultimately, he did two summer stints for Fay, starred in the film version, did it again on the stage and on television with Helen Hayes in the 1970s, and bade farewell to it only after another stage production in London.

In Mary Chase's Pulitzer Prize-winning play, Dowd is a fortyish bachelor of independent means living with his sister Veta (Josephine Hull) and niece Myrtle Mae (Victoria Horne). He spends most days at a corner saloon gaining a pleasant glow and chatting with his invisible rabbit friend Harvey. Because his erratic behavior keeps driving off suitors of the marriage-obsessed Myrtle Mae, Veta decides to have her brother committed to a mental asylum. But during the admittance interview, Elwood so discombobulates the staff with his ingenuousness and sincerity that Veta ends up being locked away, the asylum director, Chumley (Cecil Kellaway), also begins to believe in the existence of Harvey, and two young staff members (Charles Drake and Peggy Dow) see that they like each other much more than their constant skirmishing might indicate. Although there are some further attempts to "cure" Elwood of his delusions, he ultimately persuades everyone—even Myrtle Mae, who falls for the asylum attendant, Wilson (Jesse White)—that a mildly inebriated dreamer and his invisible rabbit are hardly the worst company in the world.

When Stewart took over as Elwood P. Dowd from Frank Fay in the summer of 1947, he knew he was walking into a hornet's nest: The play had been going since November 1944, and had won most people connected with it one prize or another. If the actor wasn't exactly roasted by the New York critics, he came out of the experience with more than one searing. For instance, Brooks Atkinson of the *Times*, among the more *favorable* reviewers, acknowledged that Stewart was a better overall performer than Fay and that his tentativeness on the stage (in comparison to the rest of the cast) had to be expected, but equally insisted that the "hokum comedy" required by *Harvey* was more the forte of the actor going on vacation than the one replacing him. A year later, for the second replacement stint, the reviews were merely marginally better.

For the most part, Stewart agreed with the Broadway reviewers. But what he wasn't ready to concede was that the character of Elwood P. Dowd would remain forever beyond his grasp; to this end, he doted on the fact that his 1948 notices did mark an improvement, slight or not, on the reception that he had received the year before. He could also console himself that his two limited runs had been sellouts and that his celebrity had probably brought new commercial energy to the comedy. This made for enough self-confidence to campaign openly for the Dowd part in the film version and to agree immediately to the Universal deal that made *Harvey* the quid for the quo of *Winchester '73*.

More than one theory has been advanced for the actor's fascination over the years with the Dowd role. For some analysts, the charm has been the same as that for audiences that have seen him in the part: the character's striking asexuality, despite the fact that he is presented as being in his mid-forties. Typical of this viewpoint is Dennis Bingham's assertion that "the key to the durable appeal of *Harvey* is the protagonist's complete absence of desire, a fantastic contentment that makes him convincingly insane but still an irresistible figure of fantasy."[4] In other words, the actor and audiences both have been drawn to Dowd as the kind of harmless, reassuring stuffed animal that marketing people have always regarded only Harvey as being. But such a perspective falls short of illuminating the practical dynamics involved in a star actor's readiness to appear "minor" by undertaking a summer replacement role, his (untypical) aggressiveness in pursuing the motion-picture adaptation, and his frequently stated conviction that what the war-torn America of the 1970s needed was another dose of Elwood P. Dowd. What Dowd seemed to bring out in Stewart, both in and out of performance, in fact, was a whole houseful of creative mirrors where he was free to be the opposite of what he was looking at—and without any help from what

---

[4] At least indirectly, Stewart has recognized Dowd's asexuality in some remarks about feeling that he had grown into the character only when he was in his sixties; i.e., when the protagonist's lack of a sexual appetite would be somewhat less noticeable.

was being poured down at the corner saloon. He might have felt that a sixty-two-year-old was a more credible asexual character, but that didn't stop the forty-year-old most eligible bachelor of Hollywood from tackling it. Entertaining the first grave doubts about his career since moving to California, he was able to boast to a New York audience every night that "I wrestled with reality for over thirty-five years and I'm happy to say that I finally won out over it." When he wasn't concluding with his advisors that he had to toughen up his screen image, he was telling matinees that "in this world you must be oh so smart or oh so pleasant. For years I was smart, now I recommend pleasant." He didn't know what he wanted— marriage or a career? Being a star or being an actor? Oh yes, he did. He wanted *Harvey*, where the star could guarantee what the mere actor (Fay) could not—profits.

According to Jesse White, who ended up playing the asylum attendant, Wilson, 2,200 times in the film and in numerous stage versions, Stewart was determined to make Dowd his from the very first rehearsal in 1947. "He knew there was something there that he had to have, but he really didn't know what *Harvey* was about at first. There were a lot of jokes that flew over his head, and he would always be saying to the writer Mary Chase, 'Why don't we cut this out?' or 'Do we really need that?' Mary would just smile and say, 'Trust me, Jimmy.' And that's what he did. They never had a real fight about anything. He trusted her. He trusted the lady who had given him Elwood P. Dowd like it was some kind of a very expensive gift."

And then there was the role from a general professional standpoint. For any actor, Harvey's best friend would have been a succulent prospect; for Stewart, the part not only played into one of his most obvious acting strengths (the monologue), but afforded a new and amiable showcase for the "craziness" of his numerous screen characters. Ever since *After the Thin Man*, it had been a rare Stewart character that hadn't had his sanity questioned at some point, whether jocularly, seriously, or in self-doubt. With *Harvey*, that became the central issue, but without the triggering emotional upheavals of other parts. T. Edward Hambleton, who produced a revival of the play in 1970 with Stewart and Helen Hayes, warns against underestimating that factor in analyzing the play's appeal to the actor.

Jimmy was born to deliver monologues, and the smart producers and directors realized it very early in his career. I think that was always an incentive to his ego for doing the part. Together with how he was always being told that he was crazy for being so eruptive, he was able to integrate those familiar traits into a comedy rather than a drama or western or the other things that he normally did. He could exercise his craft, he could exorcise his demons, and he could still have people laughing at the end instead of having to grind their teeth. Why would *any* actor worth his salt want more than that?

For all his preparation going in and despite the Oscar nomination that he received for his performance, Stewart has declared little satisfaction with the screen version of *Harvey*. Sometimes he has described it as having been "too cutesy"; on other occasions he has wondered aloud whether the Chase play was ever meant to be adapted for the more literal film and television media. He was helped to the latter doubt by Henry Koster's bland and intimidated screen direction; at one point, the director even had the imagined Harvey opening up doors, as though he had become one of the ghosts from the *Topper* series. On the other hand, Stewart has voiced admiration for Josephine Hull (who won a Best Supporting Actress Oscar) and, especially, cameraman William Daniels. According to the actor, it was Daniels, without any suggestion from him, Koster, or producer John Beck, who came up with the notion of always framing Elwood P. Dowd with space enough for accommodating the invisible rabbit.

No Highway in the Sky (20th Century-Fox – 1951)

With *No Highway in the Sky*, Stewart was back to several things. He was back to England, where it was shot. He was back to working under Henry Koster. He was back to costarring with Marlene Dietrich. He was back to sounding authoritative on the screen about aviation matters. And he was back to playing another character who behaves erratically enough to have others question his sanity.

Adapted from a Nevil Shute novel, *No Highway in the Sky* tells of the desperate efforts by Theodore Honey, an aviation scientist in the employ of a British airline company, to persuade his bosses that undetectable stress factors threaten the firm's fleet after about 1,400 hours in the air. To prove his theory, Honey is sent to Labrador to investigate the wreckage of a plane he is sure was victimized by the stress problem. But on the way he is dismayed to discover that even his own plane has entered the risk zone.

His attempts to warn the pilot of the danger are met with skepticism, but an actress traveling with him (Marlene Dietrich) and a stewardess (Glynis Johns) show more sympathy. During a stopover in Gander, Honey wrecks the undercarriage of the plane to prevent it from going on. This wins him the total support of the two women for the strength of his conviction, but also gets him taken into custody.

Back in England, Honey has to face an inquiry board to justify his actions and to save his job. He also has to face the arid intellectual environment in which he has been bringing up his daughter Elspeth (Janette Scott) since his wife's death. The movie star and stewardess both try to take the Honey domestic situation in hand; the former withdraws gracefully when she understands how much better the stewardess would be for the scientist and his daughter. Honey is eventually vindicated by continuing stress tests and a deeper examination of the Labrador wreckage.

Visually, *No Highway in the Sky* is only a back projection or two away from being as drab as *Speed*, when Stewart had been more concerned with cars than planes. The modest Fox production bears all the signs of Britain's struggle to dig itself out from under the war. A couple of hundred technicians and extras were hired right off the dole, while such noted local players as Jack Hawkins and Elizabeth Allan looked as much like volunteers as performers. But as long as he was left to develop the central character of the scientist who firmly believed in his own dire warnings, Stewart turned in one of his most overlooked sturdy performances. His character's naiveté about the practical world assumes especially compelling form in a protracted conversational scene with Dietrich's actress when, without sounding at all apologetic for the Hollywood Dream Factory, he explains to the star how important she was to his late wife. Not surprisingly, he shows equal authority in a couple of monologues (one loaded with technical jargon) dealing with aviation.

But not content to present Honey's eccentric self-assurance for what it is, Koster works hard at undermining the performance by introducing pieces of Absentminded Professor business. Just as the director had to have Harvey pushing open doors in his previous venture with Stewart, in *No Highway in the Sky* he has him habitually forgetting hats or umbrella or even walking into the wrong home in apparent apprehension that the audience won't Get It. Distractions of the kind become especially oppressive in a drama that finally becomes so rushed that the scientist's stirring sensitivity to daughter Elspeth's early teen problems, the somewhat abrupt marriage aims of the stewardess, and the demonstrated fragility of the planes all get resolved in a couple of throwaway scenes.

No Highway in the Sky was not Stewart's happiest filming experience. On the set, there was considerable jostling among the women in the cast for camera prominence; off it, he spent ten days in the hospital after an emergency appendectomy.

The Greatest Show on Earth (Paramount – 1952)

A stunt within a stunt, Stewart's performance as Buttons the clown in Cecil B. DeMille's *The Greatest Show on Earth* nevertheless challenged the actor to get along with minimal dialogue and, within that constraint, play against the excesses of his own makeup, which was on his face for every frame of the picture. That he pulled it off owed in part to the self-confidence of his screen presence and in part to the lack of any competing performance of his caliber in the epic.

A big-screen version of the John Ringling North production of the Barnum and Bailey Circus, with documentary footage thrown in every once in awhile to attest to its authenticity, *The Greatest Show on Earth* depicts the love and career travails of a circus troupe as it moves around the United States. The central relationships are between the circus boss, Brad (Charlton Heston), and the aerialist, Holly (Betty Hutton), fellow aerialist Sebastian's (Cornel Wilde) romantic designs on Holly, elephant girl Angel's (Gloria Grahame) designs on Sebastian, and elephant trainer Klaus's (Lyle Bettger) designs on Angel. Moving in and out of all these aerial chairs is Buttons, a fugitive doctor being sought for the murder of his wife. When the jealous Klaus causes a train wreck to get even with Angel for despising him and with Brad for firing him, Buttons has to reveal his real identity in the interests of saving the life of the circus boss. He is hauled off by a detective who has been on his trail, while Brad, fully recovered thanks to Buttons, leads the circus into another town.

The plotting of *The Greatest Show on Earth* amounted to little more than dialogue bridges between the presentations of actual Barnum and Bailey acts. Paramount also got tremendous publicity mileage from the fact that all the major actors except Wilde did some of their own stunts. As Charlton Heston recalls, "Hutton did significant aerial work, especially in Big Top shows in Washington and Philadelphia. It was in the Philadelphia show too that Grahame let an elephant put a foot on her face. And Dorothy Lamour also did the Iron Jaw act. Wilde had a close physical double. DeMille certainly didn't insist that the actors do their own things, but he didn't mind a bit or two. He was also the producer, and that kind of publicity helped sell the picture."

The Greatest Show on Earth became Hollywood's biggest box-office draw of 1952. Mainly thanks to the political hostility of an appreciable industry segment to *High Noon* and producer Carl Foreman, it also beat out the Gary Cooper western in the Oscar race for Best Picture of the Year. For Stewart, the role of Buttons was mainly an opportunity to realize an old Indiana fantasy. "I had always loved the circus," he would say years later, "and when I heard that DeMille had this project, I wired him and asked if I could be in it in the part of a clown. We all had our dreams about running away and joining a circus, and that was mine."

The picture was a product of its time in more ways than one. Aside from being politically safe entertainment (whereas *High Noon* was considered compromised by Foreman's suspected leftist leanings), it drew no distinction between murder and euthanasia, the crime for which Buttons was being sought. When the clown is hauled off at the end by the detective, there is little sense that he will be treated any differently by the law than a serial killer would be. Such impervious moralism brought the film some critical trouble abroad. As well, Sweden, for one, banned it as being unsuitable for children because of the train wreck and another scene (regarded as too violent) when the Wilde character falls off his trapeze. It was Italy that had the most satiric reaction, however, when the noted comic Totò starred in *The Funniest Show on Earth*. In a parody of the Stewart character, he played a murderer of chickens who gets tracked down by a detective who trails after a circus across Italy measuring footprints in order to match them with those found in a coop.

Carbine Williams (MGM – 1952)

Of all the biographical and biographical incident films that Stewart has done, *Carbine Williams* probably required the most shuffling between fact and fiction, between what was presented and what was hushed over. If the portrayal of Williams sometimes seemed to be less elliptical than those of Monty Stratton and Glenn Miller, it was in part because the developer of a crucial World War II Army rifle did not have the celebrity of the other subjects and in part because his life imposed more extreme standards of what to be cryptic about. The least of David Marshall Williams's problems was that he be seen as a nice guy.

As played by Stewart, Williams is a metalworker in the North Carolina of the 1920s who supplements his scant income by running a still. When federal agents raid the illegal works, one of them gets killed in a shoot-out. A first trial accusing Williams of murder results in a hung jury. Unwilling to put his wife (Jean Hagen) through any more publicity, he agrees to waive a second trial in favor of a plea-bargained admission to second-degree murder charges. But despite assurances that he would get only a couple of years in prison, he finds himself up before a different judge, who sends him away for thirty years. Embittered by this turn of events, Williams cuts off all ties to his wife, father (Carl Benton Reid), and family, and cuts a rebellious figure in prison. This leads to conflict with warden H. T. Peeples (Wendell Corey)—and a long punishment in solitary confinement.

Gradually, Peeples penetrates Williams's emotional wall. It is he who persuades the prisoner to maintain ties with his wife and who allows him to use his metalworking abilities to work on designing an automatic rifle with a floating chamber. When state prison officials get wind of this unorthodox way of serving a sentence for murder and demand an end to Williams's labors in the workshop, Peeples offers to serve the rest of the designer's prison sentence if he turns out to abuse the trust shown in him. The warden's act of bravado removes the last obstacle in the way of Williams's testing what turns into the M1 carbine. The rifle is adopted by the Army, and the prisoner is granted a pardon to return to his wife.

At least in retrospect, *Carbine Williams* is almost more interesting for what it is not about than for what it is. It is not about whether the protagonist ever fired the bullet that killed the federal agent. It is not about whether he ever used his shiv in the murder of a fellow prisoner. It is not about the various troubles he had with the Winchester company after his release, to the point that one fellow designer termed the film "fallacious" in its look at the development of the carbine. The MGM publicity department also clearly had a few problems with what was left out. On the one hand, it circulated posters with an angry Stewart pointing a rifle next to the legend of WHY DO CONVICTS MUTINY? In case that didn't catch the eye, within the same poster, it had Stewart and Hagen kissing above one piece of copy that announced A LOVE STORY AS WONDERFUL AS . . . THE STRATTON STORY and above another copy line that trumpeted that SHE KEPT THE PLEDGE OF HER WEDDING DAY FOR EIGHT LONG YEARS.

As far as what was in *Carbine Williams*, it was mainly more of the Bad Attitude Stewart having to learn that families and wardens care. The actor got little opportunity to show more than stubbornness, with exception made for a droll monologue on how he came to envision the design for his firearm while sitting in solitary confinement. Director Richard Thorpe did not help matters by allowing his star to get away with familiar mannerisms (lowering his chin into his chest whenever he wants to convey helplessness) and by asking him to do things illogical to his character (such as staring at fellow prisoners with keen curiosity as they troop by, and this after he has been behind bars for many years). But more than anything, the Art Cohn script was merely a parade of melodramatic incidents that claimed to worry more about historical accuracy than moral reaction; or, as Corey's Warden Peeples phrases it at one point: "I can only tell you about him, I can't tell you how to feel."

Well, no. In fact, *Carbine Williams* tried to do precisely the opposite.

THE FAMILY WAY

AFTER RETURNING FROM THEIR HONEYMOON IN HAWAII, the Stewarts moved into the Beverly Hills house on North Roxbury Drive that they would live in for their entire marriage. A somewhat plain, Tudor-inspired structure (and once described by the actor as "belonging to a style of Mediterranean Ugly"), its biggest defect in the eyes of its new owners was that it didn't have enough room for the vegetable garden that Gloria was intent on keeping. For comedian Jack Benny's daughter Joan, their solution turned into a boon for the whole neighborhood. "It was a very plush block except for one corner place next to where the Stewarts were," Benny recalls. "There you had this awfully dreary house with an overgrown garden filled with weeds. As kids, we always played ghost stories there. Well, the Stewarts bought it and had it torn down. Then they enclosed it all for Gloria's garden and she went to work with her corn and tomatoes and flowers." For Stewart the garden solution enabled him to crack for years that he was "the only farmer in the United States growing corn at sixteen dollars a cob"; it also started his practice of toting bags of tomatoes and other North Roxbury Drive produce to the casts and crews of pictures that he was working on in the Hollywood area.

Despite the fact that the high garden fence was the only conspicuous palisade on the 900 block, Roxbury Drive residents followed the Beverly Hills manner of not stepping on neighbors' grass. "There were lots of people only yards away, really," Joan Benny remembers. "At one time or another, you had Eddie Cantor, Oscar Levant, Lucille Ball, Hedy Lamarr, and Agnes Moorehead. But it wasn't that you just casually dropped in on one or another. There was a tremendous sense of personal privacy and respecting the privacy of the person across the street and next door. The Stewarts were really the only friends my father had on the street. Certainly, they were the only ones he felt free about looking in on during the walks he took every afternoon. He was in their kitchen drinking coffee in the afternoon when they were in town, and some people in the neighborhood found that a bit odd."

Within his home, of course, Stewart not only had a wife, but also two stepsons. Friends of the family say that there was never a lot of "step-" about Ronald and Michael McLean in the mind of the actor. "It was my impression that Jimmy came along at the right moment to fill a void for the boys," says Mignon Winants. "Neddy liked his sons all right, but from some distance, it always seemed to me. He spent most of his waking hours being the playboy that he was and making sure that he held on to his family's money. With Jimmy, the boys had a real father, and one who really took to the role as well as anyone could."

In the weeks leading up to his marriage, Stewart was regularly assailed with questions about becoming an instant father as soon as he became a first-time husband. For the most part, he fenced away the queries with such replies as, "A big family right away will be fine. When I go in for anything, I like to get it over with." To friends, however, he voiced dismay that some Hollywood writers seemed to be looking for an angle about how fatherhood would consolidate his popularity with middle-class audiences. As late as November 1951, the *Hollywood*

Reporter found nothing questionable about recirculating the old conjecture about Stewart and Fonda, suggesting that it was the former's homosexuality that had caused him to wait so long for marriage and that the McLean boys provided an ideal family "cover." The scurrilous speculation was picked up by the *Reporter* from the readership-hungry monthly *Motion Picture*, which otherwise sought to provoke scandal[5] by naming various Hollywood celebrities as drunks or undeclared blacks and Jews. Stewart never bothered replying to the smears; what he did do for the next several decades was to refer to his sons and daughters as equally his own.

In the fall of 1950, the actor and Gloria sailed for England, where he was scheduled to shoot *No Highway in the Sky*. What was supposed to be a stay of around three months turned into twice that because of an emergency appendectomy in November and a protracted recovery. Stewart also had to throw up his arms again before his eternal weight problem: The twelve pounds that he had put on since his marriage evaporated in a London hospital and didn't return. But what made his sojourn in England seem even longer was Gloria's return to the United States after a couple of months. It was in fact in London that she learned that she was pregnant. Accepting a recommendation that she not try to travel back across the Atlantic when she was too far along, she was already back in Beverly Hills in late November when she was told she was carrying twins. Stewart has made the ensuing weeks in London sound even worse than those he spent some years earlier at Tibenham and Old Buckingham. As he told columnist Louella Parsons shortly after his own return to California in February: "I'm never going to miss another Christmas with my family. We couldn't get our picture made in time because of the old appendicitis. And even though all my friends in London tried to make it a great Christmas, I was never so lonely in my life. It's all right when you're a bachelor to spend your holidays alone, but now that I'm married, I want to be with my family."

There had been no history of twins on either the Stewart or Hatrick side of the family. That didn't stop Alex from assuming that the additions

---

[5] Unlike some East Coast periodicals that ended up having to answer libel suits, the scandal-inventing publications closer to Hollywood were generally left to die of financial exhaustion. In the political witch-hunt days of the late 1940s and early 1950s, the magazines were looked upon as useful in more than one quarter.

were both going to be boys and that one of them would carry his name. "When the boys are born" became a common phrase in his daily conversation at the store. For her part, Gloria pointedly told reporters that she wanted a boy and a girl. Stewart disagreed with the both of them, saying that he wanted either two boys or two girls who were, however, identical.

He got half his wish: On May 7, 1951, Gloria gave birth to the non-identical Kelly and Judy. Then the problems started. While hospital statements admitted to nothing but "minor intestinal complications," Gloria sank into a serious condition following the Caesarean delivery. For more than two weeks, it was very much touch and go as she had to undergo three separate surgical procedures to stop hemorrhaging; five blood transfusions were administered during the crisis. At one point, Stewart became so anxious that he invited Samuel Allison, the pastor of his Beverly Hills church, to his home so they could pray together for Gloria's recovery. Although he doesn't remember Allison being in the house, Michael McLean, then five years old, does recall what "we might call an air of crisis. I knew something wasn't right when the girls came home but Mom wasn't with them. It wasn't anything Dad or anybody else said to me, though." Even when Gloria was released from the hospital after a few weeks, it turned out to be only a pause prior to a fourth operation in July. Only then did attending physicians acknowledge that the crisis had been caused by ovarian and intestinal "complications resulting from birth."

Neither Stewart nor Gloria ever dwelled on the seriousness of her condition with interviewers. In fact, at least partly to get off that subject whenever it was raised, she preferred talking about the day the actor came to pick her up from Cedars of Lebanon Hospital to take her home, pointing to it as a perfect example of her husband's absentmindedness.

> He came to the hospital to help move me and my luggage and all the flower pots I'd accumulated. I was in a wheelchair. Jim said: "I'll go down and get the car out of the garage and bring it around to the ambulance entrance. You go down in the elevator and I'll meet you there."
>
> I went down all right, but Jim forgot to pick me up. He just got into his car and went home. Twenty minutes passed and the nurse asked, "Where could he be?" Knowing the man, I said calmly: "He's forgotten." She protested, "He *couldn't* have forgotten." I said, "Take me back upstairs; he'll phone." We went back and sure enough, the phone rang. Jim had started

home and stopped at a photographer's studio to pick up some pictures. The photographer asked: "How is Mrs. Stewart?" Then he ran to the phone.

From the very beginning, the children growing up on North Roxbury Drive were disabused of any notion that their father's celebrity and their posh address entitled them to special consideration. In the words of Michael McLean, "we were raised with that small-town Christian Presbyterian ethic that nobody owes you a living. If you have bad breaks, get up and move on. That was the attitude of both my parents, and it never changed." As part of that ethic, Michael and his brother Ronald spent their grammar school years at the Black Fox Military Academy in Los Angeles. "It really wasn't like West Point or anything like that," he says, "but you got the idea pretty fast that constant nonsense wasn't part of their curriculum."

The sense of small-town family found regular reinforcement in the almost annual stays of Gloria's mother and visits by Bessie and Alex. Gloria and her sister, Ruth, also found ways to stay together about three weeks a year, whether in California or New York. Other relatives on both sides of the family—if some more than others—were welcomed periodically to Beverly Hills and put up. Michael McLean remembers one outing to Disneyland that gave him an inkling of Alex Stewart's aura. "Alex says he wants to sit down on a bench near the gate and rest there awhile. He tells us to go on, he'll either catch up to us or we know where to find him. After awhile, Dad and Mom decide he isn't coming after us, so we go back to the main gate. He was still there all right. There must have been twenty people standing around and listening to this big discourse he's giving about something. Alex never had a complex feeling like a stranger. He'd made friends awfully fast."

For all that, living in Beverly Hills was never quite the same as living in Indiana. Among other things, the house on North Roxbury Drive was a daily stop-off for the tourist bus that offered passengers glimpses of Hollywood stars. "Fifty of those buses stop by the house each day," Stewart told *Modern Maturity* in the mid-1970s, "and either you adjust to them or you become miserable. Of course it gets on my nerves sometimes, but usually when I see one, I just wave and walk quickly inside the house."

According to the actor, there was a special problem with the buses when Kelly and Judy were small and being looked after during the day by a nurse named Wilson. "Such a big woman you wouldn't believe. And it was the strangest thing: Every day at a certain time she'd take the twins for a walk in their double stroller. One day I happened to come home early, and there was Wilson and a sightseeing bus, and everyone on it was peering out the window at the twins. Apparently, she had made a deal with the driver that if she'd tell the people how many times a day she had to change their diapers and what they ate and how much they slept, he'd give her some money."

Particularly important to the children in their early years was Irene DesLierres, a full-time French-Canadian governess known as Mamselle. Described as a stern woman with a sense of humor, DesLierres took care of first the boys and then the girls for a significant portion of their childhood. Michael McLean credits her solidity with helping him and his brother Ronald negotiate some rough patches during their early adolescence, especially in the inevitable conflicts with his parents.

Friends of the family have offered differing views of the Stewarts as parents. One point of agreement is that they were unusually active in organizing outings with the children, whether to Disneyland or sporting events or family picnics. In terms of emotional expression, however, there appeared to be carryovers from Stewart's upbringing in Indiana, where it took a departure into the unknown of World War II for his father to say that he loved him, and from Gloria's upheavals with her philandering father and first husband. According to Mignon Winants, "Jimmy put a wall around himself as a parent. I actually believe he was a very paternal father when it was necessary and that he loved nothing more than his children. But with a personality like his, so laissez-faire emotionally, you always had to be the one to tell him when it was necessary." John Strauss, the actor's publicist since 1958, doesn't disagree. "You have to remember where Jimmy came from," says Strauss. "In his generation, which is also mine, it was hardly commonplace for parents to be telling their children that they loved them in words all the time. So from that point of view, no, he probably wasn't especially paternal. But I'm not sure it has only been this generation and its attitudes that can define what paternal feeling is all about. And the same with Gloria. She was never a clinging vine as a mother, and she certainly never thought of that as being some kind of a flaw."

In fact, Gloria was given to some unpredictable statements about her children in interviews that undermined the efforts of publicists to present the Stewarts as a gingerbread household where the emotions were all gumdrop sweet. Regarding the differences in the twins, for instance, she declared to one interviewer in February 1954: "Kelly follows Judy except in devilment. Kelly makes my blood run cold sometimes. They adore each other. But when you take Judy on your lap, she completely relaxes. Kelly stiffens."

Writer Leonard Gershe is one who doesn't find such remarks inconsistent with Gloria's "cool—sometimes analytic, but inevitably cool—manner toward the kids. She was certainly never maternal in any Mother Earth sense. Gloria always liked to have room for Gloria, and if that meant an occasional draft, then there would be the draft. I've always had the impression that Judy, who's a lot more emotional than Kelly, felt that lack in a big way when she was growing up."

Even Kelly Stewart Harcourt agrees that her mother could never have been called "sentimental." On the other hand, she disputes assertions by some family friends that both Stewart and Gloria were so distracted when it came to sentimental family matters that they even forgot birthdays and anniversaries. "She did not ignore them," says Harcourt, a member of the Department of Anthropology at the University of California in Davis. "She took them as opportunities to have fun. I remember some great birthday parties that Mom and Dad gave for us when we were growing up. In turn, Judy and I used to give them birthday parties. We'd make them funny birthday cards, decorate the dining room, make lots of noise. Mom threw some wonderfully festive, elegant parties for various birthdays of Dad's. . . . [And] Dad always gave Mom a present on her birthday and on their anniversary."

One constant of the Stewart household was animals. The actor's experiences with cats while living with Fonda notwithstanding, that influence was largely Gloria's. According to Gershe, in fact, Gloria "had considerably more feeling for animals than for human beings." While not going quite that far, Connie Wald concedes that "she certainly cared for animals a great deal more than some people she ran into." "Africa, African animals, and dogs," Mignon Winants confirms, "those were the subjects you could always light her up about. Sometimes she hid behind them as topics because she wanted to brush off another subject that she found intrusive or annoying, but she never faked her enthusiasm for

(Left) Stewart, shown here with Donna Reed, never hid his disappointment over the tepid response that It's a Wonderful Life (1946) aroused critically and commercially upon its initial release. He blamed it on the desire of audiences for more straightforward comedies after the war years.

Stewart cementing his signature and handprint on the sidewalk outside Graumann's Chinese Theater.

The actor, shown here with (left to right) Farley Granger, John Dall, and Alfred Hitchcock, had little to smile about during the production of the technically complicated Rope *(1948).*

(Left) Stewart's 1949 marriage to Gloria Hatrick came when the actor was forty-one, and after years of telling intimates that he was resigned to the "lonely road" of bachelorhood because he couldn't meet the right woman.

(Bottom Left) The newly married Stewarts kiss for a cameraman. Maid of honor Ruth Draddy appears to approve, while best man Bill Grady looks elsewhere.

(Bottom Right) Among those luminaries attending Stewart's bachelor party were Spencer Tracy and Jack Benny.

It took some time for Gloria Stewart to recover from the delivery of her twin daughters, Kelly and Judy. Here she is shown with the girls, her boys Michael and Ronald from a previous marriage, and her husband.

(Above) The Glenn Miller Story (1954), costarring June Allyson, was only one of several film biographies that Stewart made between the late 1940s and late 1950s.

(Right) Gloria Stewart was anything but ecstatic when her husband went to work with Grace Kelly in Rear Window (1954).

(Right) The actor never gave a richer or more tormented performance than he did as Kim Novak's obsessive pursuer in Alfred Hitchcock's Vertigo *(1958).*

(Below) Stewart laughs it up with Danny Kaye and Senator Margaret Chase Smith during an Overseas Press Club dinner in New York in 1955. Shortly afterward, the Maine legislator blocked the actor's promotion in the Air Force Reserve.

(Right) Between the late 1940s and early 1970s, the actor portrayed Elwood P. Dowd on stage in Harvey on three separate occasions in New York, and once in London, and recreated the role both for television and the Hollywood cameras.

(Below) Stewart with costars Joseph Welch, Lee Remick, and George C. Scott in Anatomy of a Murder (1959). The courtroom drama excited furor with censorship boards, but provided one of Stewart's finest screen roles.

Stewart's tour de force performance in Shenandoah *returned him, if briefly, to the top of Hollywood's box office in the mid-1960s.*

Fonda and Stewart relax in Hyde Park during a break from the 1975 London production of Harvey.

Stewart had counted on the 1983 cable-TV film Right of Way *to be the final grace note of his career, but costar Bette Davis cooperated in that objective far less than the alley cat that played a prominent role in the tragedy about a suicide-bent married couple.*

(Above) Stewart had to wait more than forty years to get a second Oscar after the trophy awarded to him for The Philadelphia Story—the honorary Academy Award given to him in 1985. (Right) Indiana honors its favorite son with a statue in his likeness for his seventy-fifth birthday. (Below) Stewart never failed to show his visitors the painting done by Fonda of Pie, the beloved horse that Stewart preferred to ride onscreen for nearly twenty years.

Chasen's on Beverly Boulevard that the staff knew better than to push any specials or improvise any extras. "He really had two separate periods," remembers Ronald Clint, who worked at the restaurant for forty years right up to its closing in 1995. "For a long time, he ate what we called a Bubbly Squeak—sautéed, leftover vegetables. He had another period afterward when it was always vichyssoise, the Hitchcock sole, and one scoop of vanilla ice cream." Leonard Gershe thinks of it as "a minor miracle" that one evening at Chasen's he succeeded in getting Stewart to taste his crab. "He liked it, liked it a lot," the writer remembers, "but of course he never ordered it in place of the usual vichyssoise and sole." Publicist Strauss says he can "count on the fingers of one hand the times I've seen him genuinely relish what was on his plate, and most of those times it was something very simple. He was always a small-town boy with the taste buds of a small-town boy—meat and potatoes, period. Eating is a part of the routine, just that, and the more control you have over the routine, the less bother. If some well-meaning member of Chasen's staff sent him a second scoop of his favorite vanilla ice cream, he'd send it right back. That second scoop hadn't been provided for."

Even before her diverticulitis led her to be more of a picker than an eater, Gloria never attacked meals without a pack of cigarettes handy. When California introduced smoking bans in restaurants, she was still able to count on Chasen's, where, according to Ronald Clint, she spent entire meals holding her cigarettes under the table while passing waiters and other regular diners pretended not to notice. The smoking ban on domestic air flights was not so easily dealt with. John Strauss:

> That ban infuriated her. If it meant that she had to go from Point A to Point B through Alaska but that she could still smoke, that was fine with her. Sometimes she'd joke about having to charter her own plane to get somewhere because that would allow her to light up, and you sometimes had the feeling that it wasn't a joke altogether, that she was feeling out the reaction from Jimmy. He had never really gotten after her about the dangers of smoking that I heard. That wasn't the kind of a thing they would've talked about in front of others anyway. And sometimes he'd go out of his way to accommodate her habit. But if there was going to be some breaking point with him on the subject, chartering planes was going to be it. She sensed that, too, so she never really let the jokes go too far.

John Springer, longtime friend and publicist for Henry Fonda who operated out of New York, remembers one example of Stewart publicly defending Gloria's addiction. "It was one of those big bashes at the Kennedy Center in Washington," Springer recalls, "and there was this very big hall decked out with the Presidential Seal and all the rest of it. But there didn't seem to be an ashtray in the entire place until Lauren Bacall and I spotted one way down at one end in a dark corner. Well, before you knew it, you had more than a dozen of these togged-out guests hovering around this one little ashtray. Along comes Jimmy, he sees what's going on, and he says he's going to go find Gloria. In the couple of minutes he's gone, Tony Randall, a real scourge when it comes to smoking, comes over and tells us how we're all killing ourselves. Jimmy comes back with Gloria and picks up the tail end of what Tony's saying. He puts his arm around Tony's shoulder and starts walking him away. The only words I heard Jimmy say were, 'Tony, you're a great actor, but you got to learn that in this world people are going to do what they want or can't help themselves from doing.'"

For many years, Stewart's stay in the hospital in London was his only significant encounter with doctors. He always attributed that in part to the regular physicals he took (and insisted Gloria take) and in part to the general robustness of the Stewart clan. According to Strauss, however, the appendectomy experience also planted a seed of hypochondria. "It got much more noticeable after a few bad things in the 1980s," says the publicist, "but there was always a trace of it, even before then. His back, his stomach—he was always complaining about something being wrong with him even after doctors had just given him a clean bill of health." Gershe remembers another episode when Stewart's unfounded worries about his physical condition cost him in ways that he couldn't have foreseen.

> He always took his general physicals at the big places like Johns Hopkins in Baltimore or the Mayo Clinic in Minnesota. As though maybe their very size would convince him that nothing had been overlooked. Well, one time when he was at Johns Hopkins he came across this clown of a doctor who turns out to have done Elwood P. Dowd in several community theater productions of *Harvey*. For the entire examination this guy tells Jimmy what he did wrong as Dowd and how he the doctor had done it so much better, the way that Mary Chase had intended it to be done. I asked him why he didn't strangle the guy. Jimmy gives me one of his best reaction shots and says, "Oh, sure! I would've tried to choke him, my

blood pressure would've soared to the ceiling, and they never would've let me out of the damn place!"

The medical news was much graver on July 26, 1953, however, when Alex telephoned Beverly Hills to say that Bessie had suffered a severe heart attack. After making sure that his father had called in specialists from Pittsburgh and New Castle, the actor returned east to find his mother in an oxygen tent at Indiana Hospital. A brief sign of a rally faded as fast as it had appeared, and she died a week later at the age of seventy-eight. During his vigil at the hospital and around the funeral, Stewart kept as low a profile as possible, even though reporters from Pittsburgh and Cleveland, especially, didn't have to ask too many questions to locate him at the old Vinegar Hill house. Aside from references to Bessie's love of music and her influence on him in that area, his public comments were generally as terse and as formal as a communiqué. It was a stance that he would adopt on other black occasions in the years to come.

Bessie's death devastated Alex. After almost a half-century of abiding by her strictures about when to cork a bottle, he resumed his heavy drinking. The last place he wanted to return to after closing up the store in the evening was the big house on North Seventh Street that was now completely empty except for him. Frequently, he compromised by visiting his immediate neighbors, the Dingmans. Matthew Dingman, a dealer in sports equipment in Phoenix, was then in his early teens. He remembers Alex's visits extremely well. "He spent an awful lot of nights in our place. It really seemed to be getting to the point where he was spending more time with us than in his own house. My mother also drafted me a couple of times to go over and stay with him, so he could have a little company. I really didn't like doing that. It was a dark, gloomy house, really very depressing when nobody was living there. Had a smell of old things to it. And dark, very dark. Alex could sit there for hours just playing solitaire under this very dim light. He was really a very lonely man after Bessie died."

Stewart tried to shake his father out of his doldrums by inviting him to California. Alex went a couple of times, but the visits were just that; nobody ever suggested that he leave Indiana for good and move in with his son. Stewart also made sure that, whenever he was on a movie location, he spent at least an hour on the telephone with his father on Sundays. As often as not, the calls carried on some argument that Alex had instigated earlier in the week with his own telephoning. As Indiana *Gazette* editor Frank Hood remembers: "They fought on the phone a lot. Part of it was because Alex had no sense of time but his own, and would get used to calling up Jimmy in California as soon as he opened the store in the morning. Jimmy and Gloria weren't exactly charmed to be getting these calls at four and five in the morning their time. The other thing was that the old man would come up with the oddest requests or try to act like a fixer for some neighbor of his with his famous son. For the most part, Jimmy ignored the requests, but every so often, when Alex touched on something affecting Jimmy's profession, things got a lot stickier."

One thing Stewart agreed to under pressure from Indiana was to do a regional television ad for the leather goods store run by Alex's neighbors, the Dingmans. On the other hand, Bill Moorhead recalls another episode when he was caught between Stewart, Alex, and the choral director Robert Shaw, and that ended badly for everyone.

> I had known Shaw, and one day he calls me from San Diego and asks if I know of any way to get Jimmy to narrate *The Lincoln Portrait* at one of his concerts. I bring up the subject as casually as I can with Alex down at the store, and he grabs the phone right away. In less than a minute, he's not asking Jimmy to do it, he's telling him to do it. Jimmy says no, he can't because he'll be shooting the Glenn Miller movie around the time of the concert. Alex's answer to that is, "Who the hell is Glenn Miller? I know who Lincoln is, everybody knows who Abe Lincoln is. You think they know who this Glenn Miller is?" If Shaw had a shot in hell that he would get Jimmy for the concert, that just about killed it.

Sometimes, the outcome was equally fractious when it was Alex who decided to do a favor for his son. James Reid, who served as the pastor of Indiana's Calvary Presbyterian from the mid-1950s to the late 1960s, was once flagged down by Alex on Philadelphia Street and had a letter from Stewart to his father shoved into his hands. Reid recalls: "The phrases I remember were Jimmy saying 'life has really been good to me, and I really don't want anything I don't have. But if there's one thing more I could have, it would be to be made an elder of the church.' Well, Alex waits until I've finished reading, then he says, 'I expect you to fix that up for him. Go tell that guy in Beverly Hills that Jimmy wants to be an elder in his church.'"

According to Reid, he told Alex that elders weren't chosen in such a way, upon which he had the letter pulled out of his hands. A couple of weeks later, however, the minister was in Pittsburgh for a meeting with Presbyterian church officials in the course of which he mentioned the letter from Stewart. One of those present relayed the information to Samuel Allison, the pastor of Beverly Hills Presbyterian, who voiced surprise that the actor had ever harbored ambitions of being elected an elder. "Well, one thing leads to another," says Reid, "and one day I get a call from Alex. He's received another letter from Jimmy, and this one says, 'Dear Dad, you're aware of the various honors that I've gotten over the years, but the most important one of all came to me the other day when Sam Allison told me that I was being nominated for an eldership.' Alex lets that sink in a second, then he says, 'See? We didn't need your goddam help!'"

Alex had one more big surprise left in him, and it rocked his son, his daughters, and most of Indiana. Even before Bessie's death, he had come to know Anita Stothart, a native of Saint John, New Brunswick, and the aunt of his neighbor Ruth Dingman. Stothart, who visited her niece in Pennsylvania at fairly regular intervals, was painted by those on the scene as somebody who never refused a martini and who never shied away from a four-letter word if it helped her make a point. When she came visiting in 1954, she was also a Stothart only in name, since her most recent of several husbands had died and she was brushing off her maiden name of Golding. By the fall of the year, the seventy-eight-year-old widow had become the principal reason for the visits to the Dingmans by the eighty-one-year-old widower, and by December 12, 1954, they were exchanging marriage vows at the Dingman residence.

The local rumor mill went into overdrive. One inevitable topic was how the apparently coarse-mannered Golding represented the direct opposite of Bessie Stewart. Another was that Golding was a gold digger trying to find her way into the Stewart money. A third was that it was the Dingmans who had arranged everything for similar mercenary objectives. Matthew Dingman laughs today at all such speculation. "To begin with, my mother was never especially enthralled by her Aunt Nita. She used to say that Nita was somebody who had to have everything on a doily with a piece of parsley. My mother usually couldn't wait for her visits to end and she'd get back to Canada. The idea of her playing matchmaker between Alex and Nita is ludicrous because it would have meant having my grandaunt right next door on Vinegar Hill all year. There was no way that my mother was going to encourage that."

As it was revealed subsequently, Alex and Nita worked out their own wedding plans while on the excursions to the drive-in movies, out-of-town restaurants, and horse races that the suddenly reanimated Alex kept busy charting. "They were really acting like kids who had gotten an unexpected shot at the cookie jar," according to Dingman. "Teenage kids didn't 'date' any more traditionally than they did. There was no hiding that Alex was desperately lonely for the kind of fresh audience that would appreciate the stories he always had to tell. Nita was really perfect for that. She'd have a drink or two and pay close attention to whatever he said. How could that not have brightened him up?"

For the record, Stewart's reaction to news of the marriage was that "Dad sure picked a good one. It sure is wonderful." But off the record, a cool politeness was about as positive as it got in the actor's reaction to his new stepmother. According to Bill Moorhead and others, "Stewart didn't like her at all and thought Alex had gone a little crazy." Lucille Gipson, who worked as a cook and housekeeper in the Stewart home during the period, says that Stewart's attitude was shared by his sisters Virginia and Mary. "You couldn't say that any of them liked her," says Gipson, "but they were usually silent about saying it. Just the atmosphere in the house when she was sitting around the living room with the rest of them. Everybody watched his words so they didn't give something away. And she herself, she didn't do much to help her situation by the drinking she did. Maybe nobody likes to handle disapproval, but the way she always acted wasn't the way of an intelligent woman."

Intelligence wasn't in great supply the day of the wedding at the Dingman house, either. Once the radio networks had gotten wind of the ceremony and of Stewart's role as his father's best man, they dispatched reporters to the Vinegar Hill living room. A couple of television and newsreel crews followed suit, and with them came cameras, lights, and cables. The forty invited guests barely had room to edge into the house. What ensued, according to Dingman, was a scene from an old Marx Brothers movie.

The first disaster came when the ceremony was about to start. The movie and television people turned on their lights and blew every fuse in the house. Everything was put on hold while that was being fixed, and during the wait somebody made the mistake of pressing some champagne on the organist to toast the bride and groom. What they didn't know was that he was an alcoholic on the wagon. He fell off it pretty fast, and they ended up having to take him out of the fireplace. But the reason I'll always remember that day is because some radio reporter sneaked in uninvited, took a drink or two, and said something to Gloria that really ticked Jimmy off. The guy had Jimmy by thirty or forty pounds and some years, but Jimmy grabbed him by the elbow and walked him right out the front door. I got there just in time to see Jimmy finishing up on a right hook that sent this character flying off the porch and flat on his back in the snow. Alex and everybody else thought it was great. The only thing that annoyed the movie and television people was that they couldn't move fast enough to get one of Jimmy's greatest chivalry scenes on film.

Stewart paid for a honeymoon trip for Alex and Nita that began in Washington, continued to New Orleans, and wound up on North Roxbury Drive for the Christmas holidays. When the subject of his father's remarriage came up after that, friends say, the actor could be counted on for one of three reactions—making a passing crack, rolling his eyes, or getting up to make himself a drink. Even sometime after that ceremony, he was stuck on referring to Golding as "the bride."

MANN OF THE WEST

IN TALKING ABOUT THE GREAT DIRECTORS HE HAS worked for, Stewart has invariably listed Frank Capra, Alfred Hitchcock, John Ford, and George Stevens. Rarely has he mentioned Anthony Mann, with whom he was partnered for eight films over the first half of the 1950s, who provided the tougher image that the actor had been seeking and then some, and whose pictures more than anybody else's were responsible for making Stewart Hollywood's biggest midcentury male star. When he has referred to such endeavors as *Winchester '73*, *Bend of the River*, *The Glenn Miller Story*, or *The Man from Laramie*, it usually has been in terms of the titles, the production studio, or the deal that agent Lew Wasserman negotiated for him that made them enormously profitable ventures. At times, he has even spoken with greater enthusiasm about the relatively bland westerns he did with Andrew McLaglen in the 1960s than about the gritty rides he took for Mann a decade earlier.

The most obvious reason for Stewart's attitude was a rift in the mid-1950s with Mann that hadn't been completely healed when the director died in 1967. The trouble was sparked by Mann's refusal to call the shots on *Night Passage*—a 1957 western the director regarded as incoherent but that the actor had looked forward to for, among other reasons, the opportunity to do a lot of accordion playing. If there was any chance of patching over that dispute, it ended the following year when Mann went into production with *Man of the West*, which many regard as his finest western of all and totally suited to Stewart, but with Gary Cooper in the lead. Shortly after that, the filmmaker moved to Europe, where he showed more of a taste for such epics as *El Cid* and *The Fall of the Roman Empire*.

But if *Night Passage* was the match to the fuse and *Man of the West* the culminating explosion, the gunpowder in Stewart's relations with Mann had been supplied by earlier factors. One was the actor's promotion of two productions—*Thunder Bay* in 1953 and *Strategic Air Command* in 1955—that Mann had not regarded highly and that had reflected very personal agendas of the star. Also not to be undervalued, according to some close to the pair, was Stewart's building reaction to the steadily sparer and more emotionally uncompromising characters he was portraying in Mann's westerns—specifically, a growing discomfort that his screen figures might have remained vulnerable in their toughness, but that the vulnerability was getting less and less screen time. In fact, as a Jimmy Stewart hedge against this development, James Stewart the actor not only sought the diversity of such movie roles as Glenn Miller in the period, but also starred in a radio series, *The Six Shooter*, in which, in sharp contrast to his movie cowboys, he played an amiable drifter who resolved generally folksy dilemmas. It was as much for such nimble professional balancing acts as for the deal with Universal that the actor owed a great part of his commercial success in the 1950s to Wasserman. As had been the case with Hayward before him, his MCA agent liked to boast that he represented careers, not contracting parties.

Winchester '73 (Universal – 1950)

The Stewart-Mann partnership came together after Austrian director Fritz Lang pulled out of a commitment to make *Winchester '73*. Stewart approved the new director after viewing a rough cut of *Devil's Doorway*, an MGM western with Robert Taylor in which he soon afterward had an additional interest aside from who made it. Although it had a much sharper edge than Stewart's *Broken Arrow* in its picture of Indian–white relations on the frontier, Mann's *Devil's Doorway* died commercially because of the greater publicity lavished on the similarly themed Darryl Zanuck production and the Stewart name.

Narratively, *Winchester '73* has two overlapping dramatic lines. The first consists of the hunt by Lin McAdam (Stewart) and his partner High Spade (Millard Mitchell) for gunman Dutch Henry Brown (Stephen McNally); for a considerable length of time, the viewer knows only that McAdam is bent on avenging an old shooting in the back by Brown. The hunt is given episodic form when McAdam and Brown compete in a shooting contest for a new Winchester '73 rifle; McAdam wins the gun, but then Brown and his men rob him of it. From that point on, McAdam is equally bent on retrieving his prize— which falls into the hands of, consecutively, an arms trader (John McIntire), an Indian on the warpath (Rock Hudson), a coward and his fiancée (Charles Drake and Shelley Winters), and a swaggering bandit (Dan Duryea). By the time McAdam catches up to the rifle again, the bandit and Brown have joined forces, precipitating a series of shoot-outs. Only in the last scenes does it emerge that McAdam and Brown are brothers and that it was their father who had been slain by the outlaw son. McAdam shoots Brown dead after a long rifle duel and faces the possibility of some happiness with the fiancée left behind by the coward.

As he had on *The Stratton Story*, Stewart approached *Winchester '73* with a decided technical concern—that he would look persuasive in his handling of the 1873 firearm. Well over the fear that had seized him in Indiana after discharging the bullet that almost hit friend Hall Blair, he practiced target shooting for long hours with Herb Parsons, an expert from the Winchester company. Although Parsons actually did the trick shooting in the film, Mann, for one, considered Stewart's hours with the marksman well spent. "He didn't seem to realize what a great quality he had in westerns, not at first anyway," the director told one interviewer.

"But it was obvious from my side of the camera. He was magnificent walking down a street with a Winchester rifle cradled in his arm. And he was great too actually firing the gun. He studied hard at it. His knuckles were raw with practicing. . . . It was those sorts of things that helped make the film look so authentic, gave it its sense of reality."

From the title to the very last shot of the film (a close-up of the firearm), there is little doubt about the name of the plot convenience in *Winchester '73*. Costar Shelley Winters still laughs about it. "Here you've got all these men—Stewart, Duryea, Hudson, McNally, Drake, the rest of them—all running around to get their hands on this goddam rifle instead of going after a beautiful blonde like me. What does that tell you about the values of that picture? If I hadn't been in it, would anybody have noticed?"

But for all its prominence, the rifle ended up taking second place to Stewart's edgy, and finally explosive, McAdam. While no novice to the cynicism and suspicion he conveyed for most of the first part of the film, the actor brought gasps from audiences for a scene three-quarters of the way through when he abruptly turns on Duryea's bandit and ferociously bangs his head down on a bar, exuding hate as he demands to know where McNally's Brown is. More than any other single moment, according to screenwriter Borden Chase, that scene marked the emergence of the toughened-up Stewart. "When the picture was given a sneak preview," Chase once recalled, "there had even been some titters in the audience at seeing Stewart's name in the opening titles of a western. This was before *Broken Arrow* was released. But once he smashed Duryea in the bar, there would be no more snickering."

The scene with Duryea was also the first of several in which a Mann western hero impersonated by Stewart seemed on the verge of the psychotic. Another follows shortly afterward in the same movie when Stewart and McNally fire at one another endlessly in a mountain rifle duel that not only makes short work of the realism the film had tried to maintain up to that juncture, but that offers an unexpected neutrality in the camera eye after ninety minutes of showing Brown as the absolute worst of all the heavies that dot the picture. At that point, the only difference between the Stewart and McNally characters appears to be that the former's vengeance-seeking McAdam hasn't yet had the latter's opportunity to shoot somebody in the back. It has been partly because of Mann's predilection for abruptly "objective" perspectives of that kind that, coupled with the usual gnarled family relations of his characters, his westerns inevitably began to be seen by some people almost exclusively in terms of Freudian mythology.

If Stewart's performance in *Winchester '73* signaled the kind of breakthrough suggested by Chase, not everybody caught it. Judging by what one *New York Times* reviewer wrote, some people might not have caught the film at all. In defiance of anything that appears on the screen, the New York daily found that "Mr. Stewart drawls and fumbles comically, recalling his previous appearance as a diffident cowpoke in *Destry Rides Again*." More typical of the critical reaction was *Variety's* finding that, contrary to some of his drawling characters of the past, the actor's portrayal was "lean and concentrated," and the verdict of the New York *Herald Tribune* that he took to the chaps and saddles of a cowboy "as if he had been doing nothing else throughout his illustrious career."

Nobody praised the performance more than Mann, especially in comparison to those he had elicited on previous films from the likes of Robert Taylor, George Murphy, and Robert Cummings. "He was always anxious, always skillful, always cooperative," the director consented afterward. "You could see he *wanted* to be great, and that was not exactly true of some of the other gentlemen I'd worked with."

Bend of the River (Universal – 1952)

With the addition of Technicolor, Mann found in *Bend of the River* Stewart's chief costar for their outdoors projects together: the natural environment. Shot on and around Oregon's Mount Hood, the western provided a striking example of the director's penchant for setting his characters against distant, epic backdrops that, as the story unfolded, would come closer and closer until they served as an immediate setting for a climactic duel.

In *Bend of the River*, Stewart's Lin McAdam from *Winchester '73* becomes Glyn McLyntock, a former border raider during the Civil War who is trying to live down his sordid past. That aim is sidetracked when he saves another ex-mercenary, Cole (Arthur Kennedy), who is about to be hanged by a lynch mob. The pair arrive in Portland, a stopping-off place for a group of settlers led by Baile (Jay C. Flippen) and his daughter Laura (Julie Adams) who want to go farther up the river to establish their own community. McLyntock agrees to take the settlers north, but both Cole and Laura stay behind. After some weeks, McLyntock and Baile realize that the supplies they had purchased from Hendricks (Howard Petrie) are not coming, so they return to Portland to find out why. What they discover is an overnight boomtown where inflation is queen and Hendricks king and where Cole and Laura are both working in the main saloon. When Hendricks announces that he won't release the supplies for the money originally handed over to him, McLyntock, backed by Cole and a fast-draw gambler Trey Wilson (Rock Hudson), steal them and head back north.

The second part of the film revolves around McLyntock's growing awareness that Cole hasn't changed all that much and that, rather than bring the supplies to the settlement, he intends selling them at exorbitant prices to a group of miners. When McLyntock tries to prevent Cole from going through with his plan, he is overpowered and left behind in the wilderness. Day by day, however, he stays on the trail of his betrayer and his seedy gunmen (Harry Morgan, Royal Dano, Jack Lambert), knocking them off one by one. Between McLyntock's pursuit and the constant needling of his hostages Baile, Laura, and Wilson, Cole cracks. He finally gets his comeuppance in a brutal fight with McLyntock in a river. McLyntock, Laura, Baile, and Wilson are finally able to deliver the supplies to the settlement.

Bend of the River, which turned into a cash machine for Universal and Stewart, was completed in six weeks, with most of the work done outdoors. Cast members say that Stewart's zest for the physical requirements of his role and his overall calming influence were major reasons why the shooting wasn't as grueling as it might have been. Concerning a key brawl in the picture, for example, Jack Lambert remembers:

> A lot of actors *say* they like to do their own stunts, or even lie about having done them as soon as they get clear of a production. Jimmy wasn't at all like that. He never said a word, he was simply there for all the action things until Tony or somebody in production thought he was going too far. We had a big fight scene in the mud, and one of the reasons it cut so well was because Jimmy was in it as much as they would let him be. He was damn good doing his own fighting, too—a helluva lot better than all these guys who claim to have rolled around on the floor with me, but hadn't even been on the set. Never once did he give off any "star" airs.

Julie Adams recalls similar help from the star on a scene in which she was supposed to whip a covered wagon team across a river. "Obviously, they had a stunt person to do the hardest part," Adams says, "but I still had to get the team down to the edge. The entire movie he had been coming over to me and, seeing my insecurity, telling me that I was doing just fine. That day, he stayed on horseback with me, talking about nonsense that I wasn't really hearing, laughing at the way I was handling the whip. I think what was he mainly up to was diverting my attention from all these huge rocks that lay at the bottom of the river. Maybe you just don't tip over a covered wagon if you know you'll crush Jimmy Stewart underneath it."

After *Winchester '73*, *Bend of the River* was also the second effort putting Stewart and Mann together with producer Aaron Rosenberg. Harry Morgan remembers them as an odd trio.

> First, you had Jimmy, who was Jimmy. Except when he blew up over the worms in the lunch candy bars, you'd think he was just another actor earning his daily bread. Then you had Mann, who sure knew what he was doing behind a camera, but who also had a little John Ford in him in saving his nastiest moments for the supporting players. When Jimmy was around, he was a lamb. But if Jimmy wasn't there, he usually picked out one of the smaller guys and lashed into him for some imagined grievance. Rosenberg I always found a very unpleasant man. Even on the rare occasions that he tried to be funny, it never came out the right way. In Rosenberg's mouth, what was supposed to be funny sounded mainly surly.

Without a Winchester creating subsidiary story after subsidiary story, Stewart's character in *Bend of the River* was a much more concentrated study in violent determination and unspoken brutality (he wears a bandanna around his neck for most of the film to hide scars from a lynching he, too, had almost suffered). His most striking dramatic moment comes when the Kennedy villain is about to abandon him, and he warns: "You'll be seein' me. Every time you bed down for the night, you'll look back in the darkness and wonder if I'm there. And some night I will be. You'll be seein' me." It was the Duryea scene from *Winchester '73* in words, and made clear that Stewart's persona in the first western had not been a passing novelty.

Many critics found the character of McLyntock less manic and more sympathetic than Lyn McAdam, if only because he ultimately "redeems" his outlaw past by getting the supplies to the settlers. Mann and Chase seemed less romantic about that conclusion. With Kennedy's heavy presented as a combination of the darkness of McNally and the swagger of Duryea from *Winchester '73*, their hero might even be accused of being a little slow about realizing that the man he rescued from a lynching will sooner or later turn on him. But this also allowed the character of Cole to loom over the screen action as fatalistically as the lofty mountains where McLyntock will be stranded and as relentlessly as the swirling waters where McLyntock has his climactic struggle to the death. The temporary human face of such a formidable nemesis might have been disposed of in the showdown river fight, but how far has McLyntock truly redeemed himself with the natural order underpinning the Coles of this world?

Not very far, according to Mann. In fact, immediately after winding up production on *Bend of the River*, McLyntock had to change his name to Howard Kemp.

The Naked Spur (MGM – 1953)

For *The Naked Spur*, Stewart and Mann, availing themselves of the non-exclusive nature of the agreement worked out between Wasserman and Universal, moved to MGM. Of the five westerns done together by the actor and the director, it was the simplest—and also the rawest.

Howard Kemp (Stewart) is a bitter bounty hunter determined to get back land lost during the Civil War by collecting a $5,000 reward on escaped killer Ben Vandergroat (Robert Ryan). Before he can reach his quarry, however, he is forced to cut in a gold prospector, Tate (Millard Mitchell), and an Army deserter, Anderson (Ralph Meeker). With the help of his unwanted partners, he captures Vandergroat and the latter's girlfriend Lina (Janet Leigh).

The brunt of *The Naked Spur* deals with Vandergroat's efforts to sow distrust and jealousy among his three captors as they escort him back to a date with the hangman; even Lina is useful to him for getting Kemp off guard for a (thwarted) escape. The only interruption of the tension among the five comes from an attack by an Indian war party. When Kemp gets wounded in the clash, Vandergroat steps up his pressures on Tate and Anderson to let him loose. The prospector falls for a lie about gold that Vandergroat has hidden away and gets himself killed after releasing the prisoner. Vandergroat waits in ambush for the pursuing Kemp and Anderson, but doesn't count on Lina's belated awareness that he is as bad as Kemp has been saying all along. Thanks to her warning,

Kemp is able to kill Vandergroat in a cliff duel. When the outlaw's body falls into the river, Anderson's fixation on retrieving it as proof for the reward gets him drowned. Kemp reveals the same mania, but even as he is dragging Vandergroat's lifeless form to his horse, he breaks down and realizes that he has become something less than human in his bitterness. Kemp and Lina go off to California.

Shot in the Colorado Rockies, *The Naked Spur* made few compromises either with the sheer physicality of the struggles of its quintet of principals or with the snarling psyches being dissected. On the first count, Stewart's Kemp in particular is constantly shown climbing up cliff faces, dodging rocks and boulders, or being kicked off ledges. Even the hunger for survival that his expressions convey in these sequences is ultimately overshadowed by the ravenous paranoia of his Kemp character: Whether hacking an Indian to death or dragging Vandergroat's corpse toward his horse, Stewart's bounty hunter borders on the demonic in his obsession with the $5,000. Given this premise, the sudden turn in the final moments of the film, when Kemp breaks down in tears in awareness that he has neared madness, probably would have been ludicrous with any other actor but Stewart. In something like ninety seconds, he had to deliver (and did) enough emotional sincerity to counterbalance the impressions left by the previous ninety minutes.

According to Janet Leigh, much of *The Naked Spur*'s effectiveness on the screen, especially with regard to the interplay among the five leading actors, was due to the different personal and professional backgrounds of the performers themselves.

> It was a very macho shoot, with me practically the only woman there off-camera as much as on-camera. Fortunately, I was always something of a tomboy, as was my character. But then there was also the very noticeable differences among the men—and these things fed into the story of the differences among the characters. Meeker was from The Actors Studio, for instance. Ryan was as much of a nice guy off screen as Jimmy was, but he was more stage and not nearly so shy. Mitchell was old-school theater. Isolated like we were, I think the tensions that developed among the personalities and even in just acting techniques fit the tensions among the characters perfectly.

Ryan's sibilant Vandergroat, as much a key to the film as Stewart's hysterical passions and Mann's raw rock-and-river settings, also epitomized the dramatic "out" that the star and the director habitually had for sending their western protagonists off in the end relatively wiser. As with the gallery of heavies in *Winchester '73*, Kennedy in *Bend of the River*, and others in *The Man from Laramie* and *The Far Country*, his captive outlaw was presented as even worse than the hero. In the end, in fact, the Mann villains always *know* that they are up to no good, making even the most violent thrashings around by Stewart's characters seem innocent by comparison. It is in this context more than in the frequently mentioned measures of charm and amiability that Stewart's western roles for Mann marked a complete change from the canny control of Tom Destry in *Destry Rides Again*.

Thunder Bay (Universal – 1953)

Thunder Bay was the first of three films that Stewart did in the 1950s that reflected personal interests that went beyond moviemaking. Unlike the ideological advocacies behind *Strategic Air Command* and *The FBI Story*, however, its spring for portraying the oil industry in a positive light was his heavy personal investment in the sector. Before the end of the decade, he would be the partner of a Texas oilman in major explorations in South America and Ireland. As entertainment propaganda, *Thunder Bay* proved as successful commercially as it was laughable dramatically.

Steve Martin (Stewart) and Johnny Gambi (Dan Duryea) arrive in a small Louisiana shrimping village in 1946 to meet with an oilman (Jay C. Flippen) they hope will finance their new storm-proof drilling platform for getting to the rich bed of minerals they believe lies immediately offshore. The oilman finances the venture, but with a warning that his own board of directors is against the plan. The local shrimpers, led by Bossier (Gilbert Roland), naturally object to the idea of having drillers violate their shrimping grounds. They aren't too much happier about Martin's attraction to Stella (Joanne Dru) and Gambi's to Francesca (Marcia Henderson). A round-robin of conflicts among the oilmen, the shrimpers, the oil company, and the women and their lovers costs the life of a fisherman who tries to blow up the drilling platform. In the end, however, Martin and Gambi hit their gusher, vindicate the faith of the oilman, get their women, and even persuade Bossier that the platform was the best thing that ever happened to the shrimpers because it attracts crustaceans to its pilings (!).

Mann gave himself the best of it when he told *Screen* magazine shortly before his death that "the story of *Thunder Bay* was weak and we never were able to lick it. . . . I don't think it was a very good script." When the picture wasn't lathering on the oil lobby line about peaceful coexistence to the fishermen destined to be displaced, it was making awkward, in-joke references to Stewart himself—to his role on the radio as *The Six Shooter* and to the habit of his motion-picture characters to launch into long monologues. And in case anyone got the idea that the shrimpers might have a case in wanting the oil men out of their town, there was Roland doing his usual *patron* number with such lines as, "These people . . . they are like little children." About the closest *Thunder Bay* came to a dramatic question was, Would you want *your* daughter to marry Dan Duryea?

The Glenn Miller Story (Universal – 1954)

There were as many real original members of the Glenn Miller band in *The Glenn Miller Story* as there had been fellow team members of Monty Stratton's White Sox in *The Stratton Story*—one. And that was the least of the points of similarity between the two biographical pictures.

The Glenn Miller Story traces the trombonist's progress from scuffling for jobs in California, though his two-steps-forward-one-step-backward attempts to form his own orchestra, to his worldwide fame as the crafter of such popular tunes as "Little Brown Jug" and "Moonlight Serenade." The central personal relationship is with his practical-minded wife, Helen (June Allyson), and the only tragic note is delayed until the end for his never-explained disappearance in an Army plane over the English Channel in December 1944.

The Glenn Miller Story was filmed with the bandleader's widow on hand for most of the shooting.[6] Helen Miller had in fact rejected earlier offers by other studios to do the picture because of her contention that the scripts had not given sufficient acknowledgment to her husband's serious musicianship, supposedly viewing him merely as a successful record seller. Although the Universal production satisfied her demands on that score, it laid even more emphasis on Miller the Responsible: From an early scene in which Stewart tells Allyson that "I know exactly where I'm going, what I'm going to do," there is little danger that the middle-brow audiences targeted by the picture will be exposed to the musician as nomadic artist. As with *The Stratton Story*, potentially agonizing scenes are also left outside camera

---

[6] Chummy McGregor, Miller's pianist and friend (played in the movie by Harry Morgan), also served as a technical consultant.

range, most notably in having a military officer pick up the telephone to inform Helen of her husband's disappearance, then having the picture skip forward a couple of days.

Stewart's work was of a piece with the gingerly handled material—in the description of the New York *Herald Tribune*, a "discrete" performance. But behind the scenes he was as fixated as ever about mastering the technical details of a role. As Paul Tanner, the only actual Miller band alumnus to get screen time, recalls: "He learned the slide positions of every single note he was supposed to play, even though Dick Nash, Joe Yukl, or I did the actual playing in the movie. He'd also stuff up the mouthpiece to get the inflated cheek effect. He was incredibly conscientious. Friendly on a need-to-know basis, but kept watching me like a hawk. He was an awfully quick learner."

Mann left little doubt that he considered the project "fraught with sentimentality and banality." With Helen Miller hovering around, he showed little taste for a battle over the agreed-upon script; rather, he took refuge in technical solutions. One was minimizing the number of reaction shots, so that the characters weren't always looking thankful for having been treated to a bromide. Another was in unusually flashy (for him) dissolve effects for introducing songs. Stewart was particularly impressed with the presentation of "Moonlight Serenade." "I was at a piano. I'd hit a note, write it down, hit another. In the background, so faint at first you could hardly hear it, were the chords. Then I'd write, then you'd hear the beat, and then we slowly fade into an enormous dance hall, where the whole orchestra is playing 'Moonlight Serenade,' the first song that really had the Glenn Miller sound."

Despite such moments, however, *The Glenn Miller Story* remained the kind of Eisenhower Era movie where elderly characters always seemed to be covering their mouths to conceal smiles. It also turned out to be Hollywood's third-biggest money earner of the year, trailing only *White Christmas* and *The Caine Mutiny*.

The Far Country (Universal – 1955)

The Stewart-Mann-Chase ingredients for a western were back on display in *The Far Country*. Once again, Stewart is a hard case; once again, Mann dwells on mountainous terrain as a character as much as a background (this time in Alberta's Jasper National Park in the Canadian Rockies); and once again, Chase's plot, as with *Winchester '73* and *Bend of the River*, is a railroad train of interconnecting cars generally heading in the same direction.

Jeff Webster (Stewart) and Ben Tatum (Walter Brennan) drive a herd of cattle by land and riverboat to the Yukon, where they figure on making enough money to buy a ranch in Wyoming. During a stopover in Skagway, however, they get conned out of the herd by Gannon (John McIntire), the town boss who has appointed himself sheriff and judge. Jeff promptly steals the cattle back with the help of the saloon girl, Ronda (Ruth Roman), and gets across to Canada before Gannon can catch him. Once in Dawson, he and Ben postpone their plans for a return to Wyoming to buy a claim to look for gold. At the same time, he resists overtures to get involved in the hopes of other settlers to build a lasting community.

Gannon and his henchmen show up. Although he doesn't have even the facade of authority outside of Skagway, he becomes menacing anyway when he begins driving prospectors off their claims at the point of a gun. The ineffectual Rube (Jay C. Flippen), a drunk serving as a constable, can do nothing to stop Gannon, and Jeff refuses to help. Before Gannon can turn to their claim, Jeff and Ben pack up their gold and take a secret trail out of town back to the U.S. But because Ben has inadvertently tipped off the heavies about their departure, they are ambushed. Ben is killed, Jeff seriously wounded. Only after he has been restored to health by Ronda and Renée (Corinne Calvet), the daughter of a prospector, does Jeff realize how selfish he has been. Gannon and Ronda are killed in a final shoot-out. Jeff settles down with Renée.

Because he is the most schematic of the Mann heroes who opt for community life after thinking they can go it alone, Jeff Webster is also the least interesting. Stewart's playing for most of the film is pure ice. He declares to one character: "I don't need any help. I take care of me." Told by a second that he has to help if people need help, he simply asks, "Why?" Asked by a third one why he hasn't said thank-you for having had his life saved, he replies: "That's a term I never use. Nobody does a favor for nothing." Yet, for all that, McIntire's Gannon doesn't sound wrong when, informed that Stewart is coming after him, he cracks: "I always knew he'd turn into a public-minded citizen." Why he doesn't sound wrong is the almost paper- tiger presentation of the cynicism of Stewart's Webster— every sarcastic utterance neutralized by a knowing look from another character that comes close to a wink at the audience. What this added up to was a posturing at the heart of *The Far Country* that not even the playing of Stewart, McIntire, and Roman, especially, ever quite concealed. The producers were aware of the problem, too, since the picture wasn't released for almost eighteen months after the completion of shooting.

Strategic Air Command (Paramount – 1955)

It said something for the paranoia of the times that *Strategic Air Command*, an all-but-dramaless propaganda piece for the United States Air Force, ended up as the sixth-highest-grossing picture of 1955. It said almost as much for the shrewdness of Paramount in adding enough casting, script, and production elements to make the picture sometimes seem like *The Glenn Miller Story* minus the music.

Dutch Holland (Stewart) is a third baseman for the St. Louis Cardinals who is called up by his Air Force Reserve unit because of a critical shortage of Strategic Air Command pilots with know-how. For all of ten minutes, he complains about having his baseball career ruined. For the next forty minutes, he lies to his wife (June Allyson) that he intends returning to the diamond the second his tour of duty is over. Come another forty minutes, both Hollands accept that they are fulfilling a far more important task at an Air Force base than they would have at third base. Finally, when Holland's shoulder makes him as unqualified to fly a plane as to throw a runner out at first, he goes off in search of a minor league managing job. The general who has manipulated this career change, Ennis Hawkes (Frank Lovejoy), detains the Hollands for one final look at a plane taking off for the wild blue yonder.

The first two people who wanted *Strategic Air Command* made were SAC commander General Curtis LeMay and Stewart. For the general, who had previously persuaded MGM to do another Air Force-themed picture with Robert Taylor entitled *Above and Beyond*, Hollywood presented the perfect medium for gaining public esteem for SAC but without having to dip into the Pentagon budget to do it. For Stewart the picture was an extension of his own Air Force Reserve status and of his own beliefs in the vital security role of SAC.[7] Once the full cooperation of the Air Force had been assured, Paramount not only agreed to having Allyson play Stewart's wife but, to consolidate further the associations with the commercially successful *The Glenn Miller Story*, also brought

---

[7] Since the film was exclusively concerned with SAC training procedures, it didn't, strictly speaking, fall into the category of war films he was averse to making.

back James Bell to play her father again and even constructed a house set for the Hollands that might have been copied from Universal's for the Millers. Last but not least, the studio introduced its sweeping Vistavision screen process with *Strategic Air Command*.

Mann, who initially resisted doing the film and who caved in only under Stewart's persistence, took to Vistavision much too well. The undoubted high spots of the film—at least for those not wearing military uniforms— were his inventive tracking shots of jets taking off and his scene-after-scene compositions of fuel streams in the sky—suggesting that SAC activities amounted to billion-dollar skywriting. Some people in the Defense Department might also have also wondered about the fact that the director seemed so desperate for drama that he accompanied every takeoff and landing of a military plane with tease music more appropriate for Stewart's Howard Kemp hanging off a cliff in *The Naked Spur*. The resulting impression was that it was a small miracle that SAC pilots were able to get into the air or onto a tarmac, let alone defend the country. Mann's own verdict was that *Strategic Air Command* had "no beauty, no emotion."

The Man from Laramie (Columbia – 1955)

The last and most ambitious of Stewart's films with Mann, *The Man from Laramie* also amounted to something of a synthesis of their previous work. Stewart was never more physical, his character fluctuated between Jeff Webster's cold watchfulness and Howard Kemp's hot vengefulness, villains ran the gamut from the vicious to the pitiable, and the New Mexico wilderness layered the desperation and desolation of one and all. Somewhat fittingly, the picture was produced by William Goetz, the Universal initiator of the deal with Wasserman who subsequently left the studio to form his own company.

The Man from Laramie casts Stewart as the appropriately named Will Lockhart, an Army officer who has set aside his uniform to find the gun-runners whose arming of Indian raiders led to the death of his brother. Posing as a freighter, he quickly comes up against the local powers in the town of Coronado. The first is the violence-happy Dave Waggoman (Alex Nicol), who destroys all of Lockhart's mules and wagons for inadvertently stopping on Waggoman land. The second is land baron Alec Waggoman (Donald Crisp), who detests his son's wildness and considers himself a fair man, but whose own brutal elimination of smaller landowners has obviously been Dave's biggest inspiration through life.

The third is Vic Hansboro (Arthur Kennedy), the Waggoman foreman who has become accustomed to cleaning up after Dave while practically running the old man's holdings.

After having his possessions destroyed, Lockhart beats up Dave Waggoman. This prompts Alec to make restitution, but also to issue an ultimatum for Lockhart to leave town. When Lockhart ignores the ultimatum, Dave gets a chance to avenge his humiliation, and shoots Lockhart deliberately in the hand to cripple him. Lockhart is nursed back to health by Kate (Aline McMahon), an old flame of Alec's, and Barbara (Cathy O'Donnell), Hansboro's fiancée. By now, he knows that the Waggoman son is involved in the gunrunning to the Indians.

What neither Lockhart nor Alec Waggoman know, however, is that Dave has been partnered with Hansboro in the arms deals—both men rebelling against Alec's tightfisted ways with money. After hearing from Alec that he will never realize his dream of succeeding the old man as owner of their ranch simply because he isn't blood, the enraged Hansboro gets into a fight with Dave about an arms shipment and kills him. He blames the killing on Lockhart. Alec Waggoman, who has been trying to conceal the fact that he is all but blind, goes after Lockhart, but is easily disarmed. He then begins to suspect Hansboro's role in everything, but before he can act on his suspicions, the foreman tries to kill him, too. The old man survives and passes on what he knows to Lockhart. Lockhart tracks Hansboro to a final rifle cache for the Indians with every intention of killing him. But once down to it, he can't pull the trigger. Hansboro tries to escape, but runs into the Indians to whom he has failed to deliver the arms. They kill him. Lockhart settles down with Barbara, while Kate and Alec renew their old affection, as well.

The Man from Laramie contained what was probably the most effective scene of violence in a Hollywood picture for a good ten or fifteen years after World War II; much of its power was directly attributable to Stewart. The scene, in which Alex Nicol's Dave Waggoman orders his men to hold out Stewart's palm so he can fire a bullet into it, achieved its end without any garish view of the actual firing, relying on Stewart's panicked expression and then, after the off-camera firing of the bullet, a swooning roll of his eyeballs in tight close-up. According to Nicol, the sequence wasn't delivered easily:

> My first idea was to play that scene as cool as I could, to increase the sense

of menace that I represented. But Jimmy and Mann fell apart when I did it that way. We want you roaring mad, the two of them said. So I went off and ran around in a circle by myself, whipping up as much anger as I could. I really went at it like a lunatic, with more fury than I put into any other scene in my entire career. We shoot the scene. I'm exhausted. Jimmy nods that it went great. The other actors are standing around waiting for Mann to say something. What does he say? "Well, I'm sorry, boys, but I got a little distracted there, so let's do it again." Forget Stewart! I was ready to shoot Mann in the hand. And I don't mean with blanks. But then the cameraman came to their rescue. "Tony, I really think we should go with what we've got," he says to Mann. "No way it's going to get any better." Jimmy immediately agreed, and Mann saved himself some fingers.

But while the most noted, the hand-shooting scene was only one of several violent moments in *The Man from Laramie*. As Nicol, Mann, and other members of the production were to attest, Stewart insisted on doing his own riding down treacherous slopes, brawling under the hooves of spooked horses, and even being dragged through a campfire during another tussle. It was no accident, according to Mann, that much of the physical action—from having Kennedy push Crisp off his horse on a ledge (as Ryan had done to Stewart in *The Naked Spur*) to having Kennedy and Stewart shoot it out on a mountaintop at the end (as Stewart had done with McNally in *Winchester '73* and with Ryan in *The Naked Spur*)— echoed scenes from earlier pictures. "I wanted to recapitulate, somehow, my five years with Jimmy Stewart," the director told one interviewer. "I reprised themes and situations by pushing them to their paroxysm."

In retrospect, the physicality of Stewart's performance proved necessary to the degree that it gave him a screen presence that the character of Lockhart could not establish otherwise in comparison to the far more suggestive roles of Crisp's land baron and Kennedy's desperate foreman. Crisp's Waggoman, in fact, wanders through the proceedings somewhat like a displaced King Lear, muttering about the dreams he has had of an avenging angel coming to make him pay for his sins, and his blinded attempts to kill Lockhart confirm him as a figure of more pathos than evil. For all his gunrunning, double-dealing, and even killing, on the other hand, Kennedy's Vic Hansboro maintains a quota of sympathy almost to the end because he has been misled in his hopes by his employer and because neither of the Waggomans will ever understand how much he has sacrificed for them. The more desperate his situation becomes, the more tragic he seems. In the destruction he brings about, it is Hansboro, not Lockhart, who is the avenger Alec Waggoman has been dreaming about—a fatalistic bow to heavies even deeper than the ones Mann had taken in his earlier westerns.

Stewart has always rated *The Man from Laramie* as his favorite western. He had little reason to dislike it: The Cinemascope production helped make him Hollywood's biggest box-office draw of the year. It was a commercial height that Stewart the actor professed to be astonished by, but also sought to define by contrasting himself to the previous year's premier drawing card. "Maybe what it is," he declared to one interviewer, "is that people *identify* with me, but *dream* of being John Wayne."

Shortly afterward, he undertook a couple of characters that few would ever admit identifying with.

THE PROFESSIONAL

AS IN OTHER FIELDS, BEING WHAT COLLEAGUES CALL A "professional" or a "pro" in the acting media is frequently easier to recognize than to define. Two ingredients generally accepted as essential are experience and self-discipline—the former for acquiring confidence in the practice of the craft, the latter for ensuring that its personal practice doesn't come at the expense of the project where it is required. In the best of cases, the two factors can fuse into a working generosity; at worst, they assure a mutual respect among like-minded performers.

Stewart's professionalism has been a source of comment among those who have worked with him practically since he arrived in Hollywood. If he has ever been accused of mailing in an effort, of going into a tantrum solely to get attention, or of trying to make a fellow actor look bad, the charge sheet has not survived. His reputation on a set has always been of, in Ben Johnson's description, "a straight shooter," or in Eddie Albert's, "a no-crap guy." What is particularly noteworthy about Stewart's sense of professionalism, however, is not only for how long and by how many people it has been recognized, but also its breadth. In one way or another, he has been a "professional" with fellow actors in front of a camera, with motion-picture companies about to release one of his films, in social relations, and even in the discretion of his own memories. At times, in fact, the professional in Stewart has seemed like his principal raison d'être.

Alex Nicol, who attended the Actors Studio with Marlon Brando in New York in the 1940s and who subsequently appeared with Stewart in *Strategic Air Command* and *The Man from Laramie*, draws a distinction between the two performers. "To my mind, Jimmy was just as talented as Marlon, with the critical difference that he was also a lot more self-disciplined. He was a pro from the bottom up. Brando was selfish, he never thought of anything except Numero Uno. It wasn't that way with Jimmy at all. When you'd do a scene with him, he knew he needed you in that scene with him or else he was going to look a little crazy talking to himself. Marlon, on the other hand, always *wanted* to talk to himself. When you think about it, he's the one who really should have done *Harvey*."

Although it might seem anything but extraordinary for an actor to acknowledge that he needs another player in the vicinity to acquit lines sensibly, Stewart's openness in this regard has extended regularly to the kind of costars that have been routinely avoided by other performers of his caliber. He has never exhibited any apprehension, for example, about sharing a camera with children and animals, the motion-picture medium's most fabled scene-stealers; on the contrary, he has often gone out of his way to underline their contributions to one of his screen ventures. Billy Mumy, who appeared with him as a youngster in the 1965 comedy *Dear Brigitte*, even admits to having been embarrassed by the actor's unconditioned praise not only during production, but for a considerable time afterward. To hear Stewart discuss the westerns he did for Anthony Mann in the 1950s and for John Ford and Andrew McLaglen in the 1960s, he was often just along for a ride on Pie, the horse he used for work for a couple of decades.

His attitude was usually the same when it came to scene-stealers of a more bewhiskered kind. Asked once, for instance, whether he wasn't a bit wary of the likes of Walter Brennan and Jay C. Flippen in *The Far Country*, the actor admitted that they could sometimes go to outrageous extremes to dominate the proceedings, but lauded what he called their "cleverness" in doing it. "As long as they're not picking their noses or something," he told an interviewer, "it can be pretty entertaining, and that ends up helping the picture as a whole." He applied the same reasoning to Will Geer, Dan Duryea, and John McIntire—none of whom could ever be termed "quiet" in their performing—and, as in the case of Flippen, worked with them many times in films and on television. Probably the most incorrigible upstager he ever worked with was Strother Martin—and he *did* give Stewart pause. In 1970, McLaglen proposed to Stewart that Martin be hired for the big role of his would-be partner in *Fool's Parade*. As the director recalls:

> Strother had done one scene with Jimmy a few years earlier in *Shenandoah*. He'd played this railroad engineer and, as always, turned what should have been a bit into the center of attention. Jimmy said he didn't remember him so well. That may or may not have been true, but he certainly didn't act enthusiastic about going through a whole movie with Strother. He'd have to think about it, he said. It took him four days— Jimmy always thinks things out very, very slowly—but then he called to say Martin was fine. Believe me, you had to have a lot of confidence to take on Strother.

There were no problems until, one morning during production of *Fool's Parade*, Stewart noticed that the call sheet had Martin entering a scene with a pencil, a pad, and a piece of string. According to McLaglen and others present, Stewart went up to the director and, his voice rising into a squeak as he went along, declared: "You got Strother here with a pencil, and that's all right. He's got a pad too, and I suppose I can live with that. But there's no way in hell that you're going to get me in front of a camera with that guy and a piece of string!"

There was no string in the scene. But as with Flippen and others, Stewart ultimately concluded that Martin's antics were more asset than liability and had him as his weekly costar on the television series *Hawkins* later on in the 1970s.

If Stewart has shown himself to be at ease working with extravagant performers, he hasn't attempted, either, to make up for screen-time lost to them by overwhelming those younger to the game. In fact, more inexperienced actors have always been among those most vocal about his behavior on a set. The veteran Dana Elcar, for instance, remembers how "surprisingly easy" he found it in his early Hollywood career to work with Stewart. "Here's a guy who's practically the history of American movies personified," says Elcar, "but it was a completely relaxing experience. Very businesslike, very professional, still strangely smooth and uncomplicated.

He knew where he was going from the beginning and I went along with him for the ride." Shelley Winters remembers how she moaned when she realized that, like her, Stewart was shot as often as possible on his stronger left side. "A couple of Left Profiles don't make for a convincing love scene when the two of them are staring off in the same direction. Since he was the star of *Winchester '73*, I knew who'd be told to turn right. I couldn't have been more wrong. One morning, Tony Mann came to me and said that Jimmy wanted me to be shot from the left because he knew that the whole thing was making me anxious. Naturally, Jimmy never said a word to me directly."

For many of those with whom he has worked, Stewart's professionalism emerged literally off-camera, when he declined the prerogative of most stars to have a stand-in read his lines for shots taken from views over his shoulder. George C. Scott, for one, has spoken about that habit during the shooting of *Anatomy of a Murder* ("not just feeding the dialogue, but rolling down his sleeves and tightening his tie to the collar") as his introduction to what "professional stature" was all about. According to Janet Leigh, that was also standard practice during the shooting of *The Naked Spur*.

> There was one particularly exasperating day in Colorado when the sun was playing tag with the schedule. All morning we had to wait to get some close-ups of Jimmy. Finally, the sun was right and Mann got what he wanted. Jimmy was then free to leave, but he refused to because Bob Ryan and I had to do the same kind of shots. "They waited for me to do mine, so I'll wait for them to do theirs," he said. And the rest of the afternoon that's what he did—fed Bob and me while we all waited, got the sun, waited some more, then got the sun again. Many people in the business say they do that, too, but it's not as common as they would have you believe.

One of the strongest pillars beneath Stewart's sense of professionalism on a set was the meticulous study he gave to his dialogue; conversely, when he blew lines, he became especially anxious and apologetic. When a hearing impairment caused him to keep missing cues during the filming of *The Shootist* in 1976, cast members reported, he needed every covering crack by John Wayne not to appear absolutely ashamed. Two years later, during the shooting of *The Big Sleep* in England, his nemesis was a single line. "He just couldn't get this thing about a girl from Keough or some damn reference like that right," remembers Robert Mitchum.

"He'd be moving along fine with this monologue, then boom, here she comes again, and he'd flub it. And every time he'd flub it, he'd look at me and apologize to me like he'd just committed some kind of atrocious crime. Damned embarrassing, I'll tell you. What the hell is Jimmy Stewart apologizing to *me* about?"

Stewart's commitment to a film project rarely ended with the completion of shooting; he has, in fact, scolded in public other actors for not getting out and promoting their finished work. "He's easily the best about that I've ever known," publicist John Strauss says. "I've represented a lot of people at one time or another—Gable, Bogart, Julie Andrews—but none of them came close to Jimmy in that department. He really thought of it as a *duty* to publicize things. Some of that comes from his MGM background, but I think it goes deeper. You do a job, you do it from start to finish, and you don't cut out midway through. It wasn't MGM that taught him that outlook. That kind of thing is almost inbred."

Not that the actor hasn't had his reservations about some of Hollywood's traditional tub-thumping approaches. After what he deemed unproductive experiences in the late 1940s, for example, he vetoed personal appearances at theaters on the grounds that they promoted the theater more than the picture. In its black-and-white age in the 1950s, he also questioned the value of television as a promotion tool, explaining to one interviewer in December 1957:

> The producer spends money to get the best talent, the studio shoots the picture in color for a wide screen, and then somebody decides to give a black-and-white print of a clip to Ed Sullivan. The viewers sitting at home see a fuzzy production of the clip on their TV screens, then the star of the picture comes out on stage. Nothing has been rehearsed at all. "Oh, just say anything, act natural," Arthur Godfrey told me on one such occasion, and you can imagine how that turned out. I'm sure that when the people sitting at home see one of these $3-million extravaganzas being plugged this way on TV, they say to themselves, "Let's really remember to miss this one."

For the most part, however, he has saved his greatest indignation for those he has considered as having tainted, neglected, or abused the fruit of the professional labors involved in a motion picture. He never voiced anything but exasperation for television's practice of interrupting films for commercials, then just gave up talking about it altogether. In 1959, he blasted the State Department for not having a representative from the United States Embassy in Mexico City present for the screening of *Anatomy of a Murder* at the Acapulco Film Festival. In the 1980s, he was one of the most prominent critics of the colorization process, even testifying before a congressional committee about what he called the "denaturing" of *It's a Wonderful Life*. "If these color-happy folks are so concerned about the audience," he has said, "let them put their millions of dollars into new films, or let them remake old stories if they see fit, but let our great film artists and films live in peace. I urge everyone in the creative community to join in our efforts to discourage this terrible process."

The professional has also been on view socially. Prior to Gloria's death in 1994, Stewart had been an unflagging presence at dinners and other functions organized to honor colleagues. He deemed his participation not only a necessary sign of respect for people whose work he admired, but also an obligation toward the film community in a larger civic sense. "He's really been one of the last who's had that kind of an attitude," remarks Robert Stack. "The truth is, there *is* no more sense of the town and the community that took care of its own, as there once was—the difference between the industry people and what Carole Lombard once called the civilians. Except for individuals like Jimmy, you won't find that kind of feeling about Hollywood, an allegiance to it, anymore. I'm not saying that loyalty was pleasant all the time, but it was certainly simpler. If you were a professional in the business, you were a citizen. Salute the Hollywood flag. Enjoy your rights. Fulfill your duties."

In a dinner jacket or not, Stewart brought the same standards of correct behavior to hotel ballrooms in the evening that he carried to movie sets in the morning; slights, unintentional or not, were not just glossed over. During an awards dinner in the mid-1950s, for example, Carroll Baker created a miniscandal by showing up in a Balmain sequined evening slacks suit. Although then the rage in France, it represented the first time that a woman had worn pants to a formal Hollywood occasion, and the local sentinels of fashion were hardly amused. Baker found out how much disapproval she had incurred after she accepted an award and went backstage for the obligatory photographs with other recipients: They had all disappeared before they had to be snapped with her. It was at this point, the actress has related, that Stewart, taking in the embarrassing situation, walked the length of the ballroom, climbed up on the press platform with her, put an arm around her, and said: "Carroll, I think you're beautiful. Now let's you and I pose for these press boys." It was the longest conversation that she had had with Stewart up to that point.

The actor has been no less alert to social gaffes of his own; as with flubbing lines in *The Big Sleep*, the aftermath was a torrent of apologies. Farley Granger remembers an incident in this connection during the 1982 staging of the Radio City Music Hall's "Night of the 100 Stars" spectacular:

> The afternoon of the show, I see Jimmy and Gloria sitting in the orchestra during rehearsals. They're completely surrounded by people, but I go over and say hello. Jimmy just nods and looks at me vaguely, and I go off. Later that night I'm in a dressing room upstairs, and Van Johnson comes running in and says that Jimmy is hunting all over the endless cavern that is Radio City for me. I find him as he's going from one dressing room to another. "I'm really sorry about this afternoon, Farley," he says to me as though he's done something terrible, "but there were so many people and my head was a little mixed up. I hope you can forgive me." Sure, it was social manners, but it was also more than that. It was like he was truly afraid that he had hurt me, even if by accident. Or maybe that is social manners where he's concerned.

If there has been an Old Hollywood aspect to Stewart's notion of professionalism, as Robert Stack observes, there has also been an Old World side to it on occasion, as well. In this context, Norris Houghton points to the actor's old-fashioned manner of referring to former costars as "Miss Hepburn," "Miss Davis," or "Miss Crawford." "When big people worked together, they always used that form of address, usually over the head of a third party who was present," the designer says. "It was a code of courtliness, an acknowledgment of the professional's status. I would have never imagined calling somebody like Ethel Barrymore anything but Miss Barrymore. I'm a cousin of Katharine Hepburn's, but I still thought of her as Miss Hepburn when I ran into her. And for her, when she's talking about him to another person, he'll be Mister Stewart—the formality reserved by the top talking about the top. Because of his delivery, it comes out of Jimmy sounding ironic sometimes, but I don't think it is at all. He puts stock in things like that."

For Stewart more than most, knowing how to do a job has never exhausted the definition of professionalism—unless the job be perceived as no more than what occurs between the daily arrivals and departures recorded by a time clock. For reasons going beyond geographical convenience and financial self-interest, he has viewed his work as being inseparable from the community providing it (and not wrongly: until he made the barely seen *The Green Horizon* for a Japanese company in 1981, the closest he had come to making a non-Hollywood film had been *No Highway in the Sky*). In another life in another town, he might have been a storekeeper who always made sure that his shelves were filled, that his fellow clerks were acquainted with the stock, that he extended cordial greetings to customers, that he gave value for a dollar—and who, in his "friendly aloofness," in his "businesslike way," in his "straight shooting," and in his "no crap," regarded the entire surrounding community as an extension of that exchange.

HITCHCOCK WINDOWS

WHATEVER HE WAS TO SAY ABOUT IT AFTERWARD, STEWART was not in the most receptive mood when Alfred Hitchcock called him in the summer of 1953 and suggested a second film together. Most obviously, the actor had not forgotten his bad experience on *Rope*. When the director mentioned that the project he had in mind was another single-set tale and was based on a relatively obscure short story, the doubts increased. Then, too, there was the impression of many in the movie industry at the time that, following such stale or even disastrous productions as *Under Capricorn*, *Stage Fright*, *I Confess*, and *Dial M for Murder*, Hitchcock had lost much of his creative energy. But if Stewart needed an excuse to put down the phone altogether, it was when the filmmaker indicated that he was on the verge of signing Grace Kelly for the female lead.

Stewart had nothing against Kelly professionally; on the contrary, friends Gary Cooper, who had worked with her in *High Noon*, and Ray Milland, who had worked with her in *Dial M for Murder*, had sung her praises. Milland, however, had not left it at that. After an affair with the actress, who was half his age, during *Dial M for Murder*, he had pressed his wife into initiating divorce proceedings so he could marry Kelly. The future princess of Monaco put an end to the affair before the divorce talk got too far, but that didn't improve her reputation with Gloria Stewart, who counted Mrs. Milland as one of her closest friends and who had picked her as Kelly Stewart's godmother. There was little doubt that Gloria could have gotten along nicely without Stewart working with Kelly. Even years afterward, the blonde actress from Philadelphia was her primary point of reference when she touched on the subject of her husband's beautiful costars:

> Jimmy was working with some of the most glamorous women in the world [during the 1950s]. My constant fear I suppose was that he would find them more attractive than me and have an affair with one of them. A lot of men in Hollywood became involved with their leading ladies. Jimmy was a red-blooded American male so naturally I thought it could happen to him, too. I was convinced it was only a matter of time before the telephone would ring and it would be James telling me that he had to work late at the studio or that he would be out playing poker with the boys. Well, no such phone call ever came. And I can honestly say that in all the years of our marriage Jimmy never once gave me cause for anxiety or jealousy. The more glamorous the leading lady he was starring opposite, the more attentive he'd be to me.

By that criterion, Stewart must have been particularly attentive at the end of 1953, when he began shooting *Rear Window* with Kelly. His initial resistance to another teaming with Hitchcock gave way before several factors. One was the story itself. Even before admitting that he was intrigued by a John Michael Hayes treatment of the original Cornell Woolrich tale, he had heard from old friends Leland Hayward and Josh Logan that they too thought highly enough of the property to look into filming possibilities. Another reassurance came with Hitchcock's promise that *Rear Window* would not degenerate into *Rope II*—a technical exercise that left the actors feeling like supernumeraries on the set. And, as important as anything, there was the fact that Lew Wasserman was also Hitchcock's agent. The MCA representative worked out an elaborate agreement with Paramount that not only guaranteed the director a core team of his favorite production people over several films and a top-of-the-line budget for his undertakings, but that, with specific regard to *Rear Window*, cut Stewart in for a percentage of the profits.

Rear Window (Paramount – 1954)

L. B. Jeffries (Stewart) is a world-traveling photojournalist who has been confined to his Manhattan apartment by a broken leg. To pass the time, he observes the daily doings of the tenants living in an apartment house on the other side of his courtyard. Among these are a pair of newlyweds, a songwriter, a spinster on the rim of madness, and a salesman named Thorwald (Raymond Burr), who has been all but broken by an ailing, nagging wife. The activities of his neighbors account for much of the conversation that Jeffries has with his physical therapist Stella (Thelma Ritter) and his fashion-model lover Lisa (Kelly). Most of the rest of the talk revolves around Lisa's unsuccessful attempts to persuade Jeffries to give up his globetrotting ways and take a high-paying magazine job in Manhattan so they can get married.

When Thorwald's wife suddenly disappears from his gallery in the middle of the night, Jeffries begins to suspect the worst. Suspicions turn to certainty when he observes the salesman leaving his apartment at odd hours with his briefcase, wrapping some knives and a saw into a newspaper, and driving a dog away from a patch of newly turned dirt in a courtyard garden. But none of that is enough to persuade the photographer's policeman friend Doyle (Wendell Corey) that a crime has been committed. Every time Jeffries comes up with some new indication of foul play, the skeptical Doyle produces some alternative explanation that sounds equally logical. In the end, it is Lisa who causes the truth to come out by sneaking into Thorwald's apartment, getting caught there by the salesman, and giving away Jeffries's observation of the place before escaping. The climax has Thorwald breaking into the photographer's apartment and almost killing him for knowing too much before the police arrive and overpower the salesman. Jeffries, who breaks his good leg in the tussle with Thorwald, ends up sitting at his window with two casts covering him up to his hips.

Few Hollywood films have lent themselves to reductionist analyses more than *Rear Window*. The voyeurism suggested by the central character has been the least of it. Sadomasochism, masturbation, and homosexuality have all been divined in one line of dialogue or another. Cineastes have found it to be a parody on the moviemaking process, the politically minded have discerned in it a commentary on the spying mentality fostered by McCarthyism, and the sociologically inclined have squeezed their chins over the exact meaning of the social mix represented as living in the apartment house watched by the photographer. Lending comfort to almost all such readings at one point or another was Hitchcock, who could be as voluble about his work as any director who ever lived. Some interviewers have taken him at his word. Others have taken the word as only a distraction from a waddling neurosis too good to be true. All have found it hard to abstract the conflicts of his pictures from the rotund and gelatinous little man whom James Mason once called "a squishy eunuch" and whom Hitchcock biographer Donald Spoto saw as casting Stewart for protagonists he considered himself to be and Cary Grant for the ones he would have liked to have been.

If Stewart had reservations about being a surrogate for a cinematic psychodiary, he had cause to be concerned the very first day of production when Hitchcock spent a half-hour shooting the shoes of the Kelly character (an insert never used in the film) and didn't hesitate to shrug off a query about it with a "Haven't you ever heard of a shoe fetish?" It didn't take long, either, for it to become evident that the director was back to the Svengali posture with his female star that he had adopted during *Dial M for Murder* and that would lead him to try to "recreate" Kelly in later years with Vera Miles, Kim Novak, and Tippi Hedren. At another early point, he ordered twenty-seven takes of a shot of Kelly kissing Stewart on the forehead. But initially at least, the actor had more worries about the set that occupied an entire Paramount soundstage and that was the grandest ever built by the studio outside those required for the spectaculars of Cecil B. DeMille. With *Rope*-like familiarity, Hitchcock doted on showing visitors how the set consisted of thirty-one apartments—twelve of which had been completely furnished even though they were never to be seen except through windows and from a distant line of vision of the characters in the photographer's apartment.

But even in the midst of his enthusiasm for the new toy that his technical staff had given him, Hitchcock had enough differences from *Rope* going for him to allay Stewart's apprehensions of another mechanical slog coming. Most obviously, the enormous courtyard set had already been built and so, elaborate to the point of excess or not, it was a stationary object that could not preoccupy the director to the exclusion of the story or the actors. Moreover, it was a stationary object viewed almost totally from the point of view of the Stewart character, in effect giving him not only the role of a photographer named Jeffries, but also that of the *Rear Window* camera. The only exceptions to this double function came when the actor himself was shown on the screen—making him about as omnipresent as any film performer could hope to be. With his technical set problems already worked out in preproduction, it was also a much more amiable, even buoyant, Hitchcock who guided the *Rear Window* shooting; in contrast to the frayed filmmaker who had drunk even more than Stewart during *Rope* or the nasty one who had once cracked after Milland had flubbed a line in *Dial M for Murder*, "I wind it up and put it on the floor—and it doesn't work!" the director of the Woolrich suspense tale struck everybody as being happy and eager at work. However much that had to do with being at the crest of his professional (equaling personal) relationship with Kelly, nobody contradicted Stewart for saying afterward that "the whole production went smoothly. The set and every part of the film were so well designed, and [Hitchcock] felt so comfortable with everyone associated with it, that we all felt confident about its success."

For Stewart, the success was in the phlegmatic rendering of a skittish, self-absorbed man who has not only been laid up by a broken leg, but also laid low by having to rely for intimate company on two women that his career—as revealed by the magazine covers of wars and disasters on the walls of his apartment—would have normally allowed him to ignore (Stella) or fly off from after a couple of rolls in the hay (Lisa). Beneath his sardonic commentaries on the routines of his neighbors and on the East Side ambiance of his lover, he conveys a hardness that seems to have been earned as much from bedrooms as battlefields. The actor's ability to make himself sound boyishly uncertain about career and marital decisions that he has already clearly arrived at works as an inner supporting layer to the structure of the story as a whole—sustaining the kind of a suspense that glamorous fashion models from the real world no less than homicide cops from the real world would have dissipated far more quickly. It is a performance by an actor very comfortable with his powers at the center of what is essentially a lavish seediness.

The seediness has little to do with the voyeurism that countless critics have attached to the character of the protagonist over the years. The voyeurism reading, in fact, is redundant and evasive when it isn't irrelevant altogether. It is redundant because, as a photographer, Jeffries is conceded as a professional voyeur from the beginning. It is evasive because it pretends that photographers disabled for a long period would have "more normally" spent their hours reading Ralph Waldo Emerson or watching the cooking programs and old westerns that a 1950s television set would have entertained them with. It is irrelevant because Stewart's Jeffries carries a much more loaded supply of straightforward misogyny—at least toward wives—than of Peeping Tom self-indulgence; or, as he attempts to be ironic in telling Lisa at one juncture, the disadvantages of being married include, immediately before the threat of having to deal with a nagging spouse, the problems of having to cope with garbage disposals.

Not surprisingly, Hitchcock always preferred the critical interpretations revolving around the voyeurism key. For one thing, it enabled him to take after the hypermoralists who decided that Jeffries's snooping made the whole picture immoral. To these guardians of virtue he liked saying: "That's nonsense. Nine out of ten people, if they see a woman across a courtyard undressing for bed or even a man pottering around in his room, will stay and look; no one turns away and says it's none of my business. They could pull down their blinds but never do; they stand there and look out." Especially in his later years, he also liked tantalizing interviewers who saw the voyeurism motif as fundamental to interpreting *Rear Window* as being primarily a self-critical commentary on his own career as a movie maker; that is, the director as autobiographer, à la Ingmar Bergman. In this he was helped no little by public perceptions of him (fostered especially by his popular television series in the 1950s and 1960s) as somebody drolly detached from the absurdities of Hollywood filmmaking and as somebody more inclined to the surfaces of sexual naughtiness than to the depths of sensual obsession. The Master of Suspense, as he was known, *played*, and had decades of masterful but still basically light entertainments to prove it. Thus when Raymond Burr's wife-killer, arguably the most sympathetic character in *Rear Window*, bursts in on Jeffries at the end to ask pitifully, "What do you want of me? Tell me what it is," he is more diplomatically understood as a neighbor who has been espied in his underwear or as an assistant director looking for a job than as a role model for the marriage-abhorring Jeffries (or for all the other wife-killers who figure prominently in Hitchcock pictures).

Along with *The Glenn Miller Story*, *Rear Window* gave Stewart two of the five highest-grossing Hollywood films of 1954. It proved as successful abroad as at home. In January 1955, Japanese riot police had to be called out to clear the Hibuya Theatre after unanticipated thousands turned out for the opening of the picture attended by the actor and his wife. In good part thanks to the celebrity of the princess of Monaco, the picture did even better during a European rerelease in 1962.

As Gloria Stewart had feared, Kelly had not left her husband indifferent; in fact, aside from Margaret Sullavan, he has probably never praised an actress more openly or more consistently. Asked about her supposed coldness by one interviewer, for instance, he replied, "She was anything but cold. Everything about Grace was appealing. I was married, but I wasn't dead. She had those big warm eyes and, well, if you had ever played a love scene with her, you'd know she wasn't cold. She had an inner confidence. People who have that are not cold. Grace had that twinkle and a touch of larceny in her eye."

Enough twinkle and larceny for the actor to agree at once to costar with Kelly again, under the direction of Josh Logan, in *Designing Woman*, a comedy about the volatile marriage between a fashion designer and a sportswriter. But with the sets already going up, Kelly announced her retirement from acting in order to marry Prince Rainier III of Monaco. Stewart was offered Lauren Bacall as a substitute, but indicated the depth of his expectations in reteaming with Kelly by also pulling out of the project. Some years later, he noted to an interviewer that *Designing Woman*, as directed by Vincente Minnelli with Bacall and Gregory Peck, had been a commercial hit, voicing regret that he had withdrawn from the film. It was one of the few times, he said, that he had "let my heart rule my head."

The Man Who Knew Too Much (Paramount – 1956)

Rear Window's success led Paramount to propose numerous properties to Stewart and Hitchcock for a follow-up. They settled on another version of *The Man Who Knew Too Much*, a spy tale that the director had already done in England in 1934 before moving to the United States. Hitchcock had considered doing a remake as early as 1942, with the plot then centered around frustrating an assassination attempt against the president of Brazil. Concerns about South American political alliances during the war had put a damper on that venture.

In the 1956 version, Dr. Ben McKenna (Stewart), his wife, Jo (Doris Day), and their son, Hank (Christopher Olsen), are vacationing in Morocco, where they run into the mysterious Frenchman Louis Bernard (Daniel Gelin). After inviting the McKennas out to dinner one evening, Bernard calls it off at the last minute, leaving the Americans to dine with the Draytons (Bernard Miles and Brenda de Banzie), an English couple. In a Marrakech market the following day, an Arab with a knife in his back falls dying in front of McKenna. The doctor is dismayed to see that it is Bernard in disguise; before expiring, the Frenchman whispers the name "Ambrose Chapel." While reporting their misadventure to the police, the McKennas leave Hank with the Draytons, who promptly kidnap the boy as a hedge against the doctor saying anything about Ambrose Chapel.

The McKennas go to London, determined to recover Hank. They are greeted at the airport by Buchanan (Ralph Truman), a policeman who knows about the kidnapping and informs them that Bernard had been an espionage agent seeking to identify the target of a rumored political assassination. The McKennas refuse to cooperate with Buchanan, however, fearing that it would compromise Hank's life. McKenna leaves Jo with some London friends while he visits an Ambrose Chapel listed in the telephone directory. It turns out to be a wild goose chase, but in the meantime Jo has realized that Ambrose Chapel is a place rather than a person and goes to a small church where she finds the Draytons serving as a minister and his wife. But before she and McKenna can bring the police down on the place, the villains get away with Hank again.

Jo figures out that the intended murder victim is the prime minister of an Eastern European country and that he is due to be shot in the Albert Hall during a particularly loud crescendo from Arthur Benjamin's "Storm Clouds Cantata." Even though she knows that it will probably doom her son, she lets out a warning scream just as the gunman (Reggie Nalder) has lined his target up in his sights. The prime minister is wounded only slightly, and the gunman is killed trying to escape. Certain that Hank is being held in the embassy of the prime minister's country, the McKennas use the official's gratitude for their intervention to attend a reception on the premises. While Jo keeps the guests distracted by singing, the doctor sneaks up into the private quarters and finds Hank. With a major assist from the repentant Mrs. Drayton, he overcomes Drayton. All three McKennas return to their hotel room, where their (neglected) London friends have sat waiting all day.

Hitchcock made no bones about the fact that he wanted *The Man Who Knew Too Much* to be much more of an American family entertainment than *Rear Window*. To this end he made sure that any highbrow connotations in international intrigues and Albert Hall settings were neutralized by establishing McKenna as the Ugliest of Americans, at sea with just about anything foreign, and by having Jay Livingstone and Ray Evans write the popular (and Oscar-winning) ditty "Que Sera Sera (Whatever Will Be Will Be)" for Day.[8] In more than one instance, he also didn't hesitate to choose melodramatic action before dramatic plausibility or to drop in awkward comedy bits. The result was an often lumpy two hours (the 1934 film had run eighty-four minutes) that the director, without any apparent irony, contrasted to the initial picture by saying that "the first was the work of a talented amateur and the second was made by a professional."

In truth, the picture would have been among Hitchcock's most forgettable exercises if not for two sequences. The more celebrated one is the climactic shooting at the Albert Hall, where the director employed 134 cuts on the music track in little more than four minutes while showing the assassin getting ready for his shot, Stewart's McKenna trying to convince the theater's security guards of the danger, and Day's Jo coming to the decision of her life between thinking only of her son or doing something to prevent the assassination. But most strikingly for a sequence traditionally identified with the progress of the Benjamin sonata to the fatal beat of the kettledrums, much of its power actually derives from the total silence of the actions of the main characters, including a long series of shots that make the Stewart character's urgings to the police inaudible. The same technique is used in the final scenes at the embassy, with Day's singing off-camera playing off what are little more than photographs of the building's upper recesses.

In terms of character, however, the most effective scene in *The Man Who Knew Too Much* comes much earlier in Morocco, when Stewart's doctor tries to get his wife to take a sedative in preparation for telling her that their son has been kidnapped. As emotionally ravaging as the cause of his actions should have been, it develops into a study of cold manipulativeness that centers the tone for a married relationship hollow at the core. The conspicuous difference from other Hitchcock treatments of married life is in the fact that it is the woman in *The Man Who Knew Too Much* who draws all the sympathy—a note maintained for the rest of the

---

[8] He had tried the same thing with the song "Lisa" in *Rear Window*, but with significantly less success.

film in underlining how the doctor has made his wife leave her show-business career, how he is less open to foreign experiences than she is, and how he is continually a step or two behind her in working out the ways to retrieve their son. Interestingly, Day is not only one of the very few Hitchcock heroines in a major picture to portray a wife, but absolutely the only one to play a mother.

There was considerable confusion around *The Man Who Knew Too Much*, much of it occasioned by the fact that screenwriter John Michael Hayes remained in Hollywood for most of the shooting, completing ten pages of script a day and then sending them off to Morocco or London by courier for instant filming. To make matters worse, Hitchcock insisted on running even the belatedly delivered pages past one Angus McPhail, a former British Intelligence officer to whom he was personally indebted but who was so far advanced in succumbing to alcoholism that he couldn't stop shaking long enough to offer his comments on some of the film's espionage details. Bernard Miles was one who confessed to being dismayed by Hitchcock's overall distractedness during production, telling one interviewer that the director "certainly did not annoy the cast with excessive attention." Equally put off was Day, who had seen some of the raised eyebrows when she had been chosen for the part of Jo McKenna and who had interpreted Hitchcock's lack of comments about her performance as a sign of disapproval. After a couple of weeks of the silent treatment, she went to see him. "I told him I knew I wasn't pleasing him, and that if he wanted to replace me with someone else, he could. He was astonished. He said it was quite the reverse, that he thought I was doing everything just right—and that if I hadn't been, he would have told me. Then he said he was more frightened—of life, of rejection, of relation-ships—than anyone. He told me he was afraid to walk across the Paramount lot to the commissary because he was so afraid of people. I remember feeling so sorry for him when he told me this, and from that point I felt more relaxed about working for him."

Having been through far worse with the director, Stewart went around reassuring his fellow players that Hitchcock knew what he was doing. Still, he didn't wait for the filmmaker to suggest that he and Day rehearse the sedative scene. And when Hitchcock arrived on the set for filming, he said little more than ACTION and CUT as the two actors completed in a single take the most revealing sequence in the picture. To this day, Day has no explanation why everything seemed to click on the first try. "It was amazing," she says. "Maybe it was just that God was with me that day." On the other hand, she has had little problem explaining what she brought to the scene: "I actually experienced the feeling that I was losing my little son to a kidnapper. I was living that ordeal."

The Man Who Knew Too Much proved to be another money tree for Paramount. Not all the fruit was wormless, however. The picture was opened in Los Angeles in May 1956 as a benefit for a vaguely defined religious group that declared among its intentions "combating the inroads of Communism" in India. Writer Hayes got into a protracted battle with Hitchcock over credit for the screenplay and, after four films, did not work with him again. And in the mid-1960s, the director and Stewart got into a legal tangle with Paramount over what they regarded as the studio's improper distribution of the picture to television.

Vertigo (Paramount – 1958)

In several ways, *Vertigo* summed up all the previous collaborations between Stewart and Hitchcock, then went on to add some more steps into darkness. Off-camera, the director's manic involvements with his lead actresses took some decidedly nasty turns, first with his badgering of a pregnant Vera Miles to play his heroine and then with his often crude handling of the eventually cast Kim Novak. As well, there was another conflict over writing credits. In front of the camera, Stewart went beyond Nietzschean theorists of acceptable murder, spying photographers, and manipulative physicians to play not so much a man obsessed as an obsession personified. The outcome was easily Hitchcock's most suggestive picture and Stewart's riskiest and most disciplined performance.

Vertigo was based on the French novel *D'Entre les Morts* by Pierre Boileau and Thomas Narcejac. Transplanted to San Francisco, it centers around Scottie Ferguson, a policeman who has gone into retirement after his acrophobia caused a fellow officer to plunge from a rooftop trying to help him. With little else to occupy him except to sit around the studio of his designer girlfriend, Midge (Barbara Bel Geddes), Scottie is open to a request from his former college friend, Elster (Tom Helmore), to keep his eye on the latter's wife, Madeleine (Novak). According to Elster, Madeleine has been acting almost suicidal since becoming obsessed with Carlotta, her great-grandmother who long ago went mad and killed herself. Though he takes on the assignment as a private detective, Scottie laughs off Elster's suggestion that someone dead from the remote past can take possession of a living being.

For some days Scottie follows Madeleine all over San Francisco, becoming increasingly fascinated with her trancelike actions that indeed confirm her obsession with Carlotta. He is forced to confront her directly when she makes a suicide attempt by jumping into San Francisco Bay. He pulls her out of the water and takes her to his place, pretending to have just come across her by accident. Little by little, Scottie falls in love with her, while at the same time trying to clear her head of her obsession with Carlotta. He thinks he has broken through when a mission church that she describes from one of her nightmares is actually only a few miles outside the city, not in the Spain of Carlotta. But once they arrive at the church, Madeleine goes running up the steps to the bell tower. Gripped by his acrophobia, Scottie cannot follow her. He is still stranded on the steps when her body comes hurtling down from the tower.

The combination of having his phobia cause a second death and the loss of his lover deranges Scottie. For months, he sits in a near-catatonic state in an asylum, not even registering the attempts by Midge to get through to him. When he is finally deemed recovered enough to be released, he finds it impossible not to hope that every passing woman will be Madeleine. With Judy Barton (also Novak) he goes further than hope, insinuating himself into her life as a lover and then gradually getting her to change her clothes and looks until she becomes a twin for Madeleine. What he doesn't realize—which is revealed in a flashback thought by Judy—is that she disguised herself as Madeleine in a plot with Elster to set Scottie up as a witness for the dumping of the real wife's body from the church tower; they had counted on Scottie's acrophobia preventing him from following Judy all the way up the stairs, where the switch was made. But then a piece of jewelry gives the game away, and in a fury Scottie drags Judy back to the church, ignoring her protestations of love. He is so bent on avenging himself that he climbs all the way to the tower. Once there, Judy stumbles and falls to the kind of death she faked the first time. Scottie is left standing in terror on the tower ledge.

Despite the success of *Rear Window* and *The Man Who Knew Too Much*, Stewart took his time agreeing to *Vertigo* because of reservations about the screenplay. Only after Samuel Taylor had been called in to replace efforts by Maxwell Anderson and Alec Coppel did he say yes. For his part, Hitchcock approached the production in frustration that he hadn't gotten Vera Miles for it. During his immediately previous film, *The Wrong Man*, he had met strong resistance from the actress in his attempts to reshape her as another Grace Kelly; she had put him off further by using a break from the picture to marry Gordon Scott, then known for playing Tarzan. The disbelieving Hitchcock still didn't give up his pursuit of Miles until she told him she couldn't do *Vertigo* because she was pregnant. The director's widely quoted disdainful reply was that Miles "should have taken a jungle pill."

The director's psychodrama with Miles was hardly alien to the making of *Vertigo*, especially when the unwanted replacement Novak arrived for work announcing that she didn't want the clothes and make-up already prepared for Hitchcock's first choice. The closest Hitchcock came to complimenting the actress from that point on was in his assertion to a reporter that "the perfect woman of mystery is one who is blonde, subtle, and Nordic"—which gave Novak one out of the three. Even after the film had been released, and Novak had received significant praise from critics, the director refused to be gracious. "The thing that fascinated me," he told one interviewer, "was the idea of Jimmy Stewart trying to turn the girl into someone she once had to play as part of a murder plot and is later trying not to be—and I'm not sure Kim Novak had the ability to put that across." On that, Hitchcock was very much in the minority, and for reasons most clearly and concisely explained by writer Taylor: "If we'd had a brilliant actress who really created two distinctively different people, it would not have been as good. She [Novak] seemed so naive in the part, and that was good. She was always believable. There was no 'art' about it, and that's why it worked so very well."

In addition to Novak's direct and almost iconic performance, *Vertigo* owed its success principally to a storytelling gamble by Hitchcock, Stewart's delineation of the haunted detective, and the musical score by Bernard Herrmann. The gamble was in the flashback, which effectively destroyed the plot mystery—sustained for almost two-thirds of the film—about what exactly was going on. But in exchange for that abrupt and somewhat perfunctory disclosure, Hitchcock succeeded in concentrating attention exclusively on the obsessive relationship between the Stewart and Novak characters, magnifying the depths of the detective's torment and, in the bargain, creating the same kind of sympathy for Judy's suddenly "helpless" villain that he had shown for Raymond Burr's wife-killer in *Rear Window* and Brenda de Banzie's child-kidnapper in *The Man Who Knew Too Much*. The choice also underlined how truly nonessential to the proceedings the director regarded all his secondary characters, including the murderer Elster, who presumably gets away with his homicide, and the girlfriend Midge, whose guarded but sincere quest for a more solid relationship with Scottie is depicted as ultimately trivial.

That Stewart was more than up to the challenge appeared to astonish him more than anybody. Even years later, he would assert that "trying to make sense out of that confused plot was hard." On another occasion, he admitted that his avenue to the character of Scottie was plain, unadulterated fear. "I myself had known a fear like that," he said of his detective's complexes, "and I'd known people paralyzed by fear. It's a very powerful thing to be engulfed almost by that kind of fear."

For the most part, Stewart exudes the fear almost politely, from fifty-year-old pores that he prefers not to notice are excreting. His long conversational scene with Novak in his apartment after he has ostensibly thwarted her suicide ebbs and flows with a simplicity that his character doesn't really possess, building fateful tensions. For the next hour of screen action, his Scottie accommodates what is bigger than he is—love, sorrow, mental breakdown, fixation—as though he is being perfectly correct (and, by the by, demonstrating to the photographer from *Rear Window* how disabling voyeurism can truly become). His only moment of real anger comes when Midge tries to be funny about painting herself as the mysterious Carlotta, and he finds that so unacceptable that he walks out of her loft unable even to start explaining how her humor is misplaced. The inevitable explosion comes in the final sequence, with Stewart the actor landing on one of the most powerfully delivered monologues of his career and Scottie the character disintegrating beneath its fury. Not even his director knew what to do with him afterward, so he just leaves both the actor and the character standing on the church ledge.

In a film that practically sanctifies disorientation, Hitchcock achieved his ends visually by regularly tracking back his camera at the same time that he was zooming in. Biographer Spoto called the trick "the visual equivalent for the admixture of desire and distance" that permeates the Stewart character. But even that photographic effect might have done little but draw attention to itself without the support of Herrmann's music. From start to finish, the lush, sinuous score is music lost in itself, with rising panic trying to find some reasonable outlet, some culminating expression. It never quite makes it, its interwound themes leaving only the smallest suggestion of progress as the story proceeds but finally ending up as stranded as Scottie on the bell tower.

Despite good critical notices, *Vertigo* was nowhere near the commercial success that *Rear Window* and *The Man Who Knew Too Much* had been. That didn't prevent Stewart from looking forward to yet another picture with Hitchcock, and specifically *North by Northwest*. What he didn't know was that the director had only discussed the project with him when it had looked unlikely that his first casting choice, Cary Grant, would be available to do it. For months thereafter, as he admitted later, Hitchcock dangled Stewart with a variety of excuses about the script not being ready, financing being a question mark, and other casting being up in the air. "Then one day, he called and said he couldn't put Columbia off any longer, that he had to report with Novak for *Bell, Book and Candle*," the filmmaker recalled to one interviewer. "I was, of course, very relieved, and I simply said, 'Well, Jimmy, that's our loss. We'll have to look for somebody else.'"

At that point, Hitchcock went back to the newly available Grant and made a film centered around a protagonist that he would have liked to have been.

ON THE DEFENSIVE

IN THE MID-1950s, STEWART RECEIVED MORE PUBLICITY AS a pilot than he wanted. Offscreen, he found himself a center of controversy when Maine Senator Margaret Chase Smith blocked his promotion to brigadier general in the Air Force Reserve on the grounds that he didn't qualify for the rank. The Washington fracas, which was not resolved until 1959, followed shortly after considerable snickering in Hollywood over the actor's zealous pursuit of the role of Charles Lindbergh in the film *The Spirit of St. Louis*; he went after the part when he was almost twice the age Lindbergh had been in crossing the Atlantic, the historical focus of the picture. While Stewart ended up getting the promotion and the role, the two campaigns required leaning on old friends for help and left him with some public relations welts.

The promotion controversy blew up in February 1957, when the Air Force forwarded to the Senate nominations for three Reserve major generals and eight Reserve brigadier generals. No sooner had the Senate Armed Services Committee received the nominations than Smith, herself a member of the Air Force Reserve, began receiving protests that Stewart was being favored over worthier candidates because of his celebrity and that his promotion would worsen morale in the Air Force's higher echelons; among those protesting were past and present administrators of the Reserve Officers Association. The senator, who had met Stewart socially on several occasions, including a couple of functions sponsored by the Air Force, looked into the matter and concluded that very few of the eleven officers submitted for promotion were entitled to a higher rank. But she saved her sharpest criticisms for the nominations of Stewart and John Montgomery, a colonel who had resigned from the Regular Air Force after twenty-two years to take an executive post, first, with American Airlines, and, subsequently, with General Electric.

The thrust of Smith's opposition to Stewart was that he hadn't done more than one fifteen-day tour as a Reservist since the end of World War II, with even that one occurring only in 1956; otherwise, her records indicated, the actor had worn his uniform for a mere eight days in eleven years. She also challenged his proficiency with the Air Force's jet aircraft, suggesting that he was incapable of flying anything newer than a B-29. Despite such limited duty and skills, Smith declared in dismay prior to a conclusive committee vote in August 1957, Stewart continued to hold the Reserve post of Deputy Director of Operations for the Strategic Air Command, in effect making him the third most important officer of that critical defense unit.

In an attempt to prevent the nominations of Stewart, Montgomery, and the other candidates from focusing untoward attention on the promotion system, especially as it applied to Reservists, Air Force Secretary James Douglas and other Pentagon officials met with Smith before the vote. As the senator was to recount, they only gave her more reasons for her skepticism:

> In our frank discussion, the opinion was expressed that on the basis of his lead role in the movie *Strategic Air Command*, Jimmy Stewart rated being

made a brigadier general. I observed that, surely, Jimmy Stewart suffered no sacrifice or no loss in making the picture and that undoubtedly was paid several hundred thousand dollars for making the picture and that surely such could not be considered Reserve duty and participation. "You do not really seriously believe Jimmy Stewart rates a brigadier generalship for playing in a movie?" I asked incredulously. "Yes," came the vigorous, decidedly positive response. "Then why don't you make June Allyson a brigadier general for playing the female lead in *Strategic Air Command!*" I was the only one who grinned.

Matters degenerated only further from there. Lieutenant General Emmett O'Donnell, the Air Force's Deputy Chief of Personnel, testified before Smith's committee in support of the promotions, but that was after being widely quoted as declaring that "no skirt" was going to tell his armed forces branch who was and who wasn't worthy of being made a brigadier. The senator ended up calling him a liar for some of his statements, noting with satisfaction that the Air Force subsequently sent in "clarifications" affecting sixty-two of his eighty-three pages of recorded testimony. On the other hand, newspapers and columnists favorable to Stewart began circulating stories that Smith's opposition to the actor was mainly motivated by personal pique—especially by resentment that her staff assistant William Lewis had not been among the candidates nominated for a promotion. She became a target in particular of such right-wing commentators as Robert Ruark and George Sokolsky, who inquired with regularity about what she had been doing while Stewart had been bombing Germany during World War II. Another popular theme was that, as a Republican, she was defying the GOP standard-bearer, President Dwight D. Eisenhower, who had signed the nomination list sent to the Senate.[9]

But Smith held strong. She got one propaganda break when several commentators out to smear her accused the senator of seeking to trade the Stewart and Montgomery promotions for her own elevation to the rank of colonel in the Reserve; as she immediately pointed out, she herself had cosponsored legislation making it possible for only one woman at a time, the head of the WAFs, to hold that grade. The Air Force high command also shot itself in the foot by testifying that the

---

[9] Only a few months before the promotions controversy began, Eisenhower had invited Stewart to be the main speaker at Veterans Day observances at Arlington Cemetery.

main reason that Stewart had not fulfilled even minimal Reserve duties had been, according to the actor, the "press of business" over the years. This caused more committee members than Smith to wonder about the lengthy vacations he had taken abroad during the 1950s. To the astonishment of a vast press sector that had predicted an easy confirmation for Stewart, Smith or no Smith, the Senate committee came out of its August session with a 13–0 verdict for rejecting the nomination. Montgomery was also turned down, by the margin of 11–2.

The Air Force didn't let go, either. In February 1959, it resubmitted both nominations. Over the intervening eighteen months, it had been told that it could expect the same voting outcome unless Stewart were moved out of his operations post with SAC and unless he put in more air time. The Pentagon had gone about halfway. Though the actor had indeed done more qualifying flying, he had been transferred to an almost equally sensitive potential combat assignment as chief of staff of the Fifteenth Air Force Reserve. What was perceived as Air Force truculence on the assignment question prompted the Armed Services Committee to sit on the nomination for five months. Finally, in July 1959, with even Smith declaring herself satisfied with the other conditions for the promotion, the Air Force agreed to repost Stewart as a deputy director for Reserve Information Services, thereby removing him from any hypothetical combat responsibilities. The committee then confirmed his nomination as a brigadier general.

Throughout the controversy, Stewart generally remained quiet, declining in particular to feed the conjecture that he was being used by Smith as a bartering piece for obtaining a promotion for the senator's assistant Lewis. But once he had secured the promotion, he took the somewhat acrobatic position of suggesting annoyance with Smith's opposition, agreeing with her that his age had made him unfit for any potential combat post, and claiming that the Air Force had ticketed him for the Information desk even before being pressed into it by the Senate committee. Typical were remarks made to Pete Martin in the *Saturday Evening Post* in 1961:

> The promotion was approved, leaving me to wonder whether Senator Smith was mad at me personally. I didn't think she was. She was protesting against giving a movie actor an important rank because she didn't think I had done enough recent flying to qualify for a star. I'm not

sure that the senator fully understood that nobody was expecting me to climb into a modern jet bomber and fly it. Anyone who knows that my next birthday will be my 53rd will agree that jets have made the pace too hot for my slowing reflexes. . . . Even before Senator Smith squared her jaw at her me, I was in line for a more suitable assignment—deputy director of the Office of Information.

If there was one man in Hollywood who didn't want to hear about the problems of an aging Stewart flying planes, it was Jack Warner, who called the actor's foray as Lindbergh in the 1957 production of *The Spirit of St. Louis* "the most disastrous failure" ever suffered by Warner Brothers commercially. What always incensed the studio head was that he had known going into the shooting in the summer of 1955 that the then-forty-seven-year-old actor was going to be a hard sell at the box office as the pilot in his mid-twenties who had flown solo across the Atlantic, but had been talked out of his doubts by Stewart, the director Billy Wilder, and the producer Leland Hayward.

Not that Hayward had been easy to convince, either. For months after announcing his intentions of bringing the Lindbergh venture to the screen, in fact, he had been ignoring or rebuffing Stewart's urgings, and very explicitly on the age grounds. What kept the question open was the producer's inability to find somebody instead of Stewart, especially after the original choice, John Kerr, turned down the project on political grounds, objecting to the pro-Hitler stance that Lindbergh had taken in numerous public appearances in the 1930s. What finally broke the ice jam, according to the main parties involved, was Alex Stewart.

As the story has usually gone, Stewart invited Hayward and his wife[10] to dinner at Chasen's one evening during the honeymoon visit by his father and Nita Golding in December 1954. In the course of dinner, Alex suddenly whispered to his son that "I'm going to fix things for you" and promptly began quizzing Hayward about the preparations under way for *The Spirit of St. Louis.* He listened only until the producer mentioned that he was looking for a young unknown actor to play Lindbergh, whereupon he slammed the table, leapt to his feet, and growled so the entire restaurant could hear: "Young unknown! What's the matter with my son? You've been

---

[10] After getting a divorce from Margaret Sullavan in the early 1950s, Hayward had remarried.

one of his best friends for years, and now you're deserting him! There's only one man who can do this part for you—and he's sitting right here!"

Stories about the outburst quickly made the Hollywood rounds, deepening Stewart's embarrassment. But it didn't make him any less intent on getting the role. Shortly afterward, Hayward invited the actor to lunch with Wilder; it turned out to be only the first of several lunches for the trio. "I could hardly eat," Stewart has related. "They watched everything I did and every forkful I lifted. They were studying me, thinking about my age." The good news was that Stewart finally persuaded the producer and the director that, with the help of a diet and some tinting of his hair, he could get Lindbergh down. The bad news was that, in a period when such contemporaries as Gary Cooper and Clark Gable were being mocked for presuming to continue playing lovers with actresses often half their age, Stewart went to the top of the list for trying to be oblivious to the calendar, and, as a popular Hollywood impression had it, simply because of his personal ties to Hayward. For the actor, however, the main point was that he was finally getting to do the role that he had been preparing for since he had mapped Lindbergh's flight across the Atlantic on Philadelphia Street.

The Spirit of St. Louis (Warner Brothers – 1957)

The Spirit of St. Louis was almost as much of a tour de force on the screen for Stewart as the original flight had been for Lindbergh. Most of the fleeting supporting roles went to actors usually seen as sheriffs in television westerns (among them, Bartlett Robinson as Frank Mahoney, the graduate from Mercersburg). The nearest thing to a woman's role was a two-minute bit by Patricia Smith as an airport onlooker who gives Lindbergh her pocket mirror for use during the crossing. In what ultimately amounted to Wilder's most striking invention, in fact, Stewart's most important costar was a fly represented as having gotten into the cockpit shortly before the takeoff from Long Island; it becomes a silent interlocutor for Stewart-Lindbergh musings en route to France.

The few-frills narrative of the picture follows Lindbergh as he persuades a group of businessmen to back him in creating history by flying across the Atlantic, suffers a brief reversal when the owners of the plane he had wanted to fly won't trust him at the controls, and then gets Mahoney and his partner Donald Hall (Arthur Space) to design a craft from scratch. While there is an attempt at some offscreen suspense initially, in having characters report on the progress of other aviators trying to be the first to cross the ocean, this subplot is quickly abandoned in favor of saving most of the screen time of 135 minutes for the actual solo trip and some flashbacks showing Lindbergh's growing passion for his venture. The principal dramatic reversals on the flight are a temporary malfunctioning of a compass and the dangerous forming of ice on the wings. Thirty-three-and-a-half hours after taking off from Long Island's Roosevelt Field, however, Lindbergh completes his trip of 3,610 miles, landing at Paris's Le Bourget Field on May 20, 1927, where he is greeted by a mob of cheering spectators estimated at the time as having numbered more than 100,000.

And so what?

That, unfortunately, seemed to be the question among American moviegoers, and in no small part because of the Warner Brothers publicity campaign that had been geared from the beginning to salvage what even Hayward and Wilder had come around to seeing could be a commercial fiasco.[11] With such defensive promotions as conducting a national poll of high school students, asking them to identify Lindbergh and his plane, the message was either that there was going to be a familiar history lesson on the screen for the price of a ticket or that people had once made a big splash about flying a route that had become commonplace—neither a great incentive for opening wallets. The graphics department was even more insipid with such posters as a Stewart looking more retouched than dyed and differently combed above the type legend—IT WAS AN ERA THAT BELONGED TO YOUNG PEOPLE, BUT MOSTLY IT BELONGED TO A SHY LANKY GUY. Writer Wendell Mayes always insisted, for his part, that, familiar or not as teenagers might have been with the name of Lindbergh's plane, they were never going to be attracted to a movie with a title that sounded like an old Judy Garland musical.

The relative few who did go to theaters saw Stewart again at grips with a biographical subject he was careful not to offend with untoward emotions. As he had done with Monty Stratton and Glenn Miller, he channeled most of his insights into technical emulations—not only in

---

[11] The picture wasn't released until more than a year after the completion of shooting. When it was released, it was dumped into the middle of the Stewart controversy over his Air Force promotion.

details around the flying, but also in the makeup. As initially odd as he may look in Lindbergh's blondish red hair, in fact, the actor succeeds to a surprising extent in covering over the age gap with Lindbergh, to the point that this dies as an issue minutes into the picture. What never quite goes away, on the other hand, is the oddity of Wilder being the director of such a hagiographic exercise. The usually acerbic satirist, it turned out, had been as captivated as Stewart by the Lindbergh feat, from his days as a young Berlin newspaperman, and had aspired to make the picture for years. His main accomplishment, as he himself would acknowledge years later, was to blow an original budget of some $2 million into three times that outlay with his insistence on shooting in as many of the original locations (Long Island, Nova Scotia, Newfoundland, the Irish Coast, Paris) as possible. "I missed creating the character," Wilder once said. "I felt sorry for Jack Warner. I thought of offering him his money back, but then I thought he might take it."

If *The Spirit of St. Louis* has a strong point, it is the music score of Franz Waxman—another ardent admirer of Lindbergh's flight and a flyer himself. Waxman spent more than two years preparing the score, telling friends that the subject matter required special treatment.

Stewart's meetings with his boyhood hero ended up being memorable for the wrong reasons. At a preproduction dinner in which he had counted on picking up a few tips from Lindbergh, the pair found so little to say to one another that they ate largely in silence. "I don't know what he thought when we got up to leave," the actor said afterward, "but I'll be damned if I could think of anything to ask."

Another dinner at Chasen's, arranged when Lindbergh called up unexpectedly from Los Angeles International Airport, ended abruptly. Stewart:

> He was very pleasant. And then we finished the meal, and poor Dave Chasen came up to him and said, "Mr. Lindbergh, I have a terrible thing to tell you. And I apologize, believe me. I made a point to have no one say anything to anyone. . . . But there are forty newspaper people outside. And they have cameras." And Lindbergh said, "Do you have a back door out of the kitchen? Would you get me a taxi?" And Dave went back and he said, "The taxi's there." And Lindbergh said goodbye and walked out the back. And that's the last time Gloria and I saw him.

The only compliment Stewart ever received for his performance from

Lindbergh was for a scene in which the actor tapped on his oil gauge before taking off. Stewart called the gesture, an ad lib, the "natural thing" for any pilot to do.

Night Passage (Universal – 1957)

The picture that caused the breakup between Stewart and Anthony Mann, *Night Passage* still had some familiar elements from their collaborations earlier in the decade. The producer was Aaron Rosenberg, the writer was Borden Chase, the chief villain was portrayed by Dan Duryea, and the cast featured such familiar faces as Jay C. Flippen, Jack Elam, and Robert Wilke, all involved in one or more of the Mann features. As well, there was some physically exhausting location work, this time in the rarefied air outside Durango, Colorado. But none of these ingredients brought the picture any closer to *Bend of the River* or *The Man from Laramie* than James Neilson, a director who would thereafter do most of his work for Disney, approached Mann.

Stewart stars as Grant McLaine, a railroad man fired for suspected involvement in a robbery and for the last five years earning his living as an itinerant musician. During a stop at a railhead, he learns that a gang led by Whitey Harbin (Duryea) and The Utica Kid (Audie Murphy) has been hitting the payroll train so regularly that rail workers in the field are about to quit for lack of money. Ben Kimball (Flippen), owner of the railroad, is coaxed by his much younger wife, Verna (Elaine Stewart), into giving McLaine another chance to show that he was wrongly accused of the five-year-old robbery, by being entrusted with the payroll for the field workers. Despite Verna's heavy-handed flirtations, however, McLaine is clearly more interested in Charlotte Drew (Diane Foster), who works at the railhead canteen; unfortunately for him, she carries a torch only for Utica.

McLaine boards the train in the company of Joey Adams (Brandon de Wilde), an orphan he has befriended. When the train gets attacked by the Harbin gang, he manages to hide the payroll in a box being carried by Joey. One way or another, all the principals, including Charlotte, end up at the Harbin gang's hideout, where there is a steady series of fights and personal showdowns about where the missing money is. What emerges from all the battling is that McLaine is Utica's older brother and that he took the rap for the old robbery to protect his outlaw sibling. In the final showdown, Utica and McLaine shoot it out at an old mill with Harbin's bunch; all the gunmen are killed, but so is Utica. McLaine is finally free to go off with Charlotte.

Mann did some preproduction work on *Night Passage*, and might have even shot a few of the establishing scenes used at the beginning of the picture. Such was the mood of those close to the split with Stewart, however, that declarations of ignorance rather than even denials met queries on that point. In explaining why he pulled out of the film, the director told an interviewer in 1967: "The story was so incoherent that I said the audience wouldn't understand any of it. But Jimmy was very set on that film. He had to play the accordion and do a bunch of stunts that actors adore. He didn't care about the script whatever, and I abandoned the production. The picture was a total failure, and Jimmy has always held it against me."

If nothing else, *Night Passage* gave Stewart his biggest singing opportunity since *Born to Dance*, allowing him to vocalize on the Ned Washington tunes "Follow the River" and "You Can't Get Far Without a Railroad." On the other hand, most of his accordion playing in front of the cameras was subsequently recorded by a professional musician. As an actor, he contributed one of his slow-rage, glaring-eyes portraits, and escaped with some mannered scenes under first-time director Neilson. Even worse were Murphy, who still seemed ill at ease in front of a camera ten years after arriving in Hollywood, and Duryea, who did everything but pick his nose while giving one of his whiniest performances.

According to Jack Elam, most of those involved on *Night Passage* were just glad to get the filming over with. Elam, who played a member of the Duryea gang, recalls:

> It wasn't a particularly pleasant experience. Everybody had heard about the thing between Jimmy and Tony Mann, and that cast a pall on everything even before we started. Then there was the weather. At one point we had a pretty big snow storm in Durango. We'd drive to the location 90 minutes away and discover we couldn't do anything. That made for some pretty bad tempers. Even without the snow, we were 8,000, 9,000 feet up there, so that they even had to have oxygen on hand to give out for the more strenuous scenes, like the dancing and wrestling around. It was a payday, but I could have done without it.

Which was more or less the reaction of critics and audiences, as well.

Bell, Book and Candle (Columbia – 1958)

Even before beginning work on it, Stewart had plenty of reason to resent *Bell, Book and Candle*. He had gotten himself into it as a payment to Columbia for allowing Kim Novak to go to Paramount for *Vertigo*. It had originally been scheduled to star Cary Grant, who was at the same time preparing for the Hitchcock thriller *North by Northwest* that Stewart had wanted to do. And his role as publisher Shepard Henderson was little more than a straight man to Novak and to such aggressive screen performers as Jack Lemmon, Ernie Kovacs, Elsa Lanchester, and Hermione Gingold. Nothing that happened during production lightened his mood.

Based on a John Van Druten play that had starred Rex Harrison and Lili Palmer on Broadway, *Bell, Book and Candle* tells of the attempts by modern witch Gillian Holrody (Novak) to fall in love and lead a normal life. The object of her campaign is her upstairs neighbor Henderson, who is engaged to Merle Kittridge (Janice Rule). Using her sorcery, she gets Henderson to break the engagement and become enamored of her. But then her warlock brother Nicky (Lemmon) decides to make some money by writing a book on modern witchcraft with the seedy writer Sidney Redlitch (Kovacs), threatening exposure of how she has won over the publisher. With the help of the local mistress of charms, Mrs. De Pass (Gingold), Henderson discovers how he has been put under a spell, leading to a break with Gillian. But Gillian's desolation causes the tears that only a human being would be capable of—evidence that she has truly lost her powers of witchery. With the help of her sympathetic Aunt Queenie (Lanchester), she manages to convince Henderson, without the aid of sorcery, that they have always been meant for each other.

If the love scenes on camera between Novak and Stewart lacked something, those between the actress and director Richard Quine proved far too conspicuous for some members of the cast. Janice Rule: "Quine seemed interested only in her. An actor always wants to be treasured, but she was the only one he wanted to treasure. Once a director sends out that signal, there's no collegial atmosphere, everything is killed, and you want to make the best of it and get it over with as fast as possible."

Jack Lemmon, a Quine friend of long standing, doesn't agree that the director paid attention only to Novak, but does concede happier film projects than *Bell, Book and Candle*. "For me, there were two problems. The first was that I was never comfortable with the part. At the first reading I thought there were possibilities, but then it started turning into another animal altogether. At that point you just do the best you can and hope the roof doesn't come down on your head. The other thing was that, aside from me and Ernie, there was never any real contact between the actors. We weren't close at all. Was that Quine's fault? It was probably just a bad mix."

Aside from the glamour radiated by Novak, the picture's strongest point was the use of one color against another to achieve the unworldly effect of a witchy environment. In this, the production had the assistance of *Life* photographer Eliot Elisofon, who had done similar consulting work for John Huston on *Moulin Rouge*. Bosley Crowther of *The New York Times* wasn't the only one who found that *Bell, Book and Candle* "comes close to magic as far as its color values are concerned."

As for Stewart, his role as the publisher was his worst miscasting since *Rope*. While always possessing a long line in the remote, the cranky, and the whimsical, he was called on instead to be stuffy, petty, and first-nighter urbane—qualities far more suited to the Broadway Shepard Henderson, Harrison. His biggest moment comes in the sequence with Gingold, when he vacillates between bafflement and disgust in coping with the anti-spell potion she insists that he drink. Otherwise, he delivers his dialogue like someone who is having worries about his rebellious children at home, about the way he was maneuvered out of *North by Northwest* by Hitchcock, about the shooting of Mann's *Man of the West* with Cooper rather than with him, and about the new box-office slump he hit immediately in the wake of *The Man Who Knew Too Much*. Or, in the words of the weekly *Time*, "James Stewart stumbles around most of the time with a vaguely blissful expression—rather like a comic-strip character who has just been socked by Popeye."

The FBI Story (Warner Brothers – 1959)

If *The KGB Story* had been filmed in the Soviet Union the way *The FBI Story* was shot in the United States, it would have been denounced as a perfect example of a dictatorial state's control over the mass media. The least of it was the distorting of history.

A paean to J. Edgar Hoover based on a bestselling book by Don Whitehead, *The FBI Story* sets out to trace the Bureau's biggest moments through the emblematic figure of Chip Hardesty (Stewart). While his wife, Lucy (Vera Miles), worries about him at home, Hardesty takes on the Ku Klux Klan in Louisiana, such gangsters as John Dillinger and Baby Face Nelson in the Midwest, and Indian killers in Oklahoma. Infrequently as he returns home, he does so often enough to have three children, which only makes Lucy angrier that he continues to risk his life. For a brief period, she even leaves him, but then returns again when she realizes that their love for one another cannot be separated from his devotion to the Bureau.

With the onset of World War II, Hardesty gets busy rounding up enemy agents, both at home and in South America. His major setback is the death of his son in European action. After the war, in what turns out to be the picture's longest sustained sequence, he supervises the capture of a couple of Communist spies in New York. With that as his crowning achievement, he is given the less dangerous job of lecturing recruits—to the enormous relief of Lucy.

If *The FBI Story* was anything, it was the official (read: Hoover) version of the agency's activities from the 1920s to the 1950s. Confirming that stamp of approval was a brief and nonsensical scene showing Hoover himself with his chief assistant Clyde Tolson. Failing to get any mention at all, on the other hand, were people whom the Bureau director viewed as rivals for attention; one particularly glaring absence in this regard was Melvin Purvis, the agent who actually coordinated the raids (shown in the film) against Dillinger and Pretty Boy Floyd. The emphasis on Soviet spies at the end of the picture also fulfilled official policy agendas of the period.

But over and above the elimination of people like Purvis and the picture's propaganda aims (including trying to show the FBI as a traditional defender of blacks and Indians), there was the fact that the agency not only controlled every page of script and every frame of footage, but was also ceded by Warner Brothers and director-producer Mervyn LeRoy the right to have the final hiring say on absolutely everybody connected with the production. Or, as LeRoy once told Hoover biographer Ovid DeMaris: "Everybody on that picture, from the carpenters and electricians right to the top, everyone had to be okayed by the FBI. I did one scene . . . and after I shot the picture, they discovered that one of the extras shouldn't have been in there. I don't know why. So we had to shoot the scene over. I had two FBI men with me all the time . . . [Hoover] and his men controlled the movie."

Asked why he tolerated working under such conditions, LeRoy, earlier in his career the director of everything from *Little Caesar* and *I Am a Fugitive from a Chain Gang* to *Madame Curie* and *Mister Roberts*, stumbled over the answer: "Because I had to. Well, I wanted to anyway. I wanted it to be just as perfect as it could be."

He still wasn't sure how perfect it was, however, the evening he arranged a private screening for Hoover, Tolson, and other FBI officials. "I was never so nervous in my whole life," the film director subsequently recounted. "I perspired. I perspired like you've never seen. I was soaking wet. And for this reason—they didn't laugh in the right places, they didn't seem to show any emotion. . . . So when the lights went up, I was absolutely worn out. And Edgar stood up and he motioned for me to come over to him and he put his arms around me, and he said to me, 'Mervyn, that's one of the greatest jobs I've ever seen,' and they all started to applaud. I guess they were all waiting to see how he had liked it." It was at that point, according to LeRoy, that he broke down in his tears— "partly in relief, partly because it was a beautiful story. It was the story of the FBI."

As grotesque as LeRoy's fawning might have been, Stewart didn't find himself uncomfortable working under such conditions, either; at least to judge from remarks he has made about Hoover. For example, Stewart once told DeMaris: "He wasn't a shy introvert at all. He knew about all sorts of things. He liked to meet people, he liked to be with people, and I thought always that he was very easy to be with, and it always surprised me. Every time I met him . . . it always surprised me that he was always so easy to be with and so easy to talk to and, uh, he put everybody around him at ease."

Stewart also told another interviewer that, in the aftermath of *The FBI Story*, he felt for years as though he had the Bureau's unofficial protection whenever he and his family went abroad. "As we'd land in Spain or Italy or some place, a man would just come up to me, just out of the crowd, and say, 'The Boss asked me just to check with you and see if everything is going to be all right.' And he would hand me a card and say, 'If you need us at any time, here's where we are.' "

As for his performance on the screen, *The FBI Story* was again Stewart in his biographical mode with some borrowing from his MGM past: If there was no actual Chip Hardesty toward whom he felt the need to be deferential, he moved through the film with the equivalent gravity of a Lewis Stone knowing that a stern but yet benevolent Louis B. Mayer was supervising his every gesture for the benefit of everybody.

Anatomy of a Murder (Columbia – 1959)

If *Anatomy of a Murder* was not exactly a case of Stewart saving his best for the end of the 1950s,[12] it was the film that brought him his last across-the-board enthusiasm from critics and that enabled him to close out the decade as strongly as he had entered it in *Winchester '73*. Although he still had at least two major performances on the screen awaiting him in the 1960s and an equally forceful one on television in the 1980s, none of them would receive the attention of his turn as Paul Biegler in the Otto Preminger courtroom drama.

A small-town Michigan lawyer who does more fishing and noodling at the piano than practicing, Biegler gets drawn into defending Frederick Manion (Ben Gazzara), an Army lieutenant accused of killing a bartender after the latter allegedly beat and raped his wife, Laura Manion (Lee Remick). Complicating the task for Biegler is Manion's reputation for violence and possessiveness and Laura's for sleeping around. The key to the defense attorney's strategy is discovered in an old law book by his alcoholic friend McCarthy (Arthur O'Connell), who sees the case as a way of recovering his own legal skills. With both insanity and self-defense out of the question, McCarthy persuades Biegler, the defense was to take the tricky tack of "irresistible impulse."

Most of the film's 160 minutes are devoted to trial interrogations and to Biegler's forensic duels with Claude Dancer (George C. Scott) from the prosecutor's side. The lawyer's most important hours away from the trial are spent trying to convince Mary Pilant (Kathryn Grant), a waitress at the tavern of the slain bartender, to testify about the man's questionable character. Pilant finally shows up in the courtroom carrying a pair of panties that have already been described by Laura Manion; she testifies that she found them in the dead bartender's laundry. When Dancer tries to discredit the discovery as the work of a jilted lover, the waitress reveals that she is the daughter of the bartender and always knew that he was capable of the violence charged by the Manions. The jury acquits Manion. Biegler and McCarthy celebrate only briefly: The Army officer and his wife skip town without paying them.

---

[12] *The FBI Story*, though released four months after *Anatomy*, had been shot before.

Anatomy of a Murder was shot in the Michigan peninsula communities of Ishpening and Marquette, with local citizens drafted for the roles of the jurors and courtroom spectators. Because Preminger wanted to exploit the original novel's continuing popularity,[13] he rushed through the shooting in less than two months, beginning work March 23, 1959, and winding up on May 16. Even before ordering his first take, he had an agreement to hold a sneak preview in San Francisco in mid-June. He made the schedule in the face of some daunting obstacles, especially a major casting problem for the role of Laura Manion, the amateur and near-amateur status of some of the performers, and the mountains of dialogue that had to be learned by the principals, particularly by Stewart and Scott.

The original choice for the part of Laura had been Lana Turner, but she walked off the picture when Preminger refused to let her wear Jean-Louis gowns in the character of an Army wife. Remick, who had earlier turned down an offer to play the waitress, was brought in as the wife a month after having a baby. The film's most notable casting, however, was in the choice of Joseph Welch, the lawyer who had taken on Senator Joseph McCarthy in nationally televised hearings a few years earlier, as the trial judge. Although clearly a novice at his task, Welch delivered his lines (most of them in the form of compact speeches) with appropriate authority; ultimately, in fact, he was far more convincing than such ostensible professionals as Grant and Brooks West in the role of the local prosecutor.

Hollywood columnists of the period liked reporting that Preminger had eschewed his usual Gestapo manner of directing during *Anatomy of a Murder* and that this was one of the big reasons that he was able to complete the shooting in less than two months. Ben Gazzara remembers things slightly differently:

> Compared to what he was on other pictures, I suppose he was more of a pussycat. But I don't think he had much choice, either. He had all these local citizens around he wanted to impress. He had Welch. He had Jimmy. He also had John Voelker, the Michigan state Supreme Court judge who wrote the novel.[14] There was no way Otto could pull his usual shit on the

---

[13] The book had been a bestseller hardcover for forty weeks, and was about to go into paperback when production on the film began.

[14] Voelker wrote the book under the pseudonym of Robert Traver.

set with them around all the time. But when they weren't around, look out. He was still a vile prick. He was really abusive to his assistants and to the day players who came in for a scene or two. He's still the biggest bastard I've ever known, and I've known a lot of them.

Stewart not only had reams of dialogue to master, but generally had to deliver it in markedly long takes. One of the actor's techniques in the past for dealing with such a situation had been a kind of meandering into monologues for, apparently, warming himself up to the task; with his character of Biegler, however, there is little of that—the overall folksy front of a lawyer with a steel trap for a mind inducing him to dart immediately to his objective, with no attempt to gild the gradual with the laborious. His playing off Scott's clipped, suave delivery accounts for most of the picture's best moments. Crowther of the *Times* spoke for many critics in his observation that "slowly and subtly, he presents us a warm, clever, adroit, and complex man and, most particularly, a portrait of a trial lawyer in action which will be difficult for anyone to surpass."

Whatever the critics thought, *Anatomy of a Murder* stirred up guardians of moral and social virtue around the globe. The Legion of Decency found that its detailed references to rape put it beyond the "bounds of moral acceptability and propriety." In Chicago, Preminger went to court after Police Commissioner Timothy O'Connor, who doubled as the head of the censor board, refused to grant the film a license; O'Connor had insisted that the filmmaker edit out mention of contraceptives in the dialogue because he didn't want his own daughter, then eighteen, hearing such a word. A federal judge in Chicago watched the film with his two preteen sons and then ordered O'Connor to issue a license immediately. In England, British critics went to war against censors because twenty minutes of cuts were made in the picture after the reviewers had seen it; the critics protested that the censors had made them look bad for recommending a work that had become almost unintelligible subsequently. In South Africa, the picture was banned altogether for a scene in which the Stewart character shares a piano bench with Duke Ellington.

Stewart himself acknowledged receiving many letters from fans who were dismayed to be hearing one of his characters delving into a subject like rape. As he put it in the February 1961 series in the *Saturday Evening Post* with Pete Martin: "You let us down, they said. I'm not going to your pictures anymore. I take my family to see a Jimmy Stewart picture and you're up there in court talking dirty and holding up women's panties. But I didn't think *Anatomy of a Murder* was in bad taste or offensive. And if anything like it came along again, I'd just have to take it. Parts like that don't come along every day."

Among those who questioned him was Alex, who reported in one telephone call that customers had been complaining at the hardware store about the "dirty" movie his son had made. According to the actor, however, his father eventually went off by himself one night to see the film and agreed that there was nothing to get excited about.

Stewart's performance as Paul Biegler won him Best Actor honors from both the New York Film Critics and the Venice Film Festival. The picture as a whole was also named the best of the year by several publications; among these was *The Film Daily*, which placed it ahead of both *The Diary of Anne Frank* and *The Nun's Story*. With regard to the Oscars, Preminger was shut out, but nominations went to the film for Best Picture, Best Actor, Best Supporting Actor (both Scott and O'Connell), Best Screenplay Adaptation (Wendell Mayes), and Best Black-and-White Cinematography (Sam Leavitt). It was the year of *Ben-Hur*, however, and *Anatomy of a Murder* lost in every category. But at least for Charlton Heston, the eventual winner in the Best Actor category, Stewart deserved the Professional Class Award of the year. Heston:

> We were posing for the obligatory photos at the Oscar show. As a rule, you don't have the nominees coming in together, but that year for some unknown reason we were thrown together. I'd always considered him a role model, so you can imagine how stunned I was when he came over to me, took my arm, and said, "I want you to win, Chuck. I really mean that." He truly meant it. It wasn't the normal courtesy you hear between people who are competing in a situation like that. He was absolutely sincere. There's being a professional and then there's being Jimmy Stewart.

But that didn't mean that Stewart had written off his hopes of winning altogether. As Gloria Stewart told Pete Martin:

> One of the protective devices the nominees use to soften the pangs of suspense is to crouch down in their seats muttering to themselves, "I can't win, I won't win." But Jimmy was quite honest with himself. He surprised

me. He kept saying, "I might just win. I can't help thinking I've got a good chance." I had my hand on his arm and it was like keeping in touch with a tuning fork. Thank heaven it was over quickly. As soon as Hugh Griffith won the supporting actor award for *Ben-Hur*, Jim and I knew that it would be a clean sweep; so when Charlton Heston won for best actor, it wasn't much of a shock. By that time *Ben-Hur* had swept the board. I don't mean Jim wasn't disappointed, but I was more emotionally rocked than he was.

For Stewart, there would be another Oscar, but no more nominations.

VII
MIDDLE AGE

PASSAGES

ON JANUARY 1, 1960, MARGARET SULLAVAN committed suicide in a hotel room by taking an overdose of sleeping pills. For Stewart, it marked the beginning of a decade in which phone calls and doorbells brought one piece of grim news after another. On a professional level, it was also a period in which the then-fifty-plus actor found fewer and fewer alternatives to being "just Jimmy Stewart." Most times he didn't seem to mind and involved himself in film projects that largely challenged him to be professional on his own terms, with little inspiration from directors and nothing but complicity from writers. Other times he did seem to object, and took on roles that, beyond reflecting a general acceptance of his age, galvanized him into assembling a gallery of men as determined, troubled, and/or embittered in their fifties and sixties as those he had created in his younger years. Whether he minded or not, friends detected a new melancholy—and sometimes testiness—in his demeanor; some of them attributed it to a worsening hearing problem.

Impaired hearing was also cited as one of the reasons for the Sullavan suicide. According to colleagues, the actress, forty-nine when she died, had grown despondent over her inability to pick up cues while trying out a Broadway-bound play in New Haven. Her anxiety over the impediment had made it impossible for her to sleep, prompting a doctor to give her the sleeping tablets. For his part, Stewart had little to say in public except to underline Sullavan's acting skill and to reiterate his gratitude for her part in getting him noticed on a movie screen.[1]

---

[1] Before the year was out, one of Sullavan's daughters also took her own life.

In April of the following year, however, he almost broke down on national television in accepting a special Academy Award for Gary Cooper. In fact, it wasn't until Stewart began choking on the words "we're all very proud of you Coop, all of us are very proud" at the Oscar ceremonies that Hollywood realized how ill the absent Cooper was from cancer. The twenty-five-year ties between the two actors had been based on numerous things, not least their mutual love of the outdoors, individualistic notions of what went into American manhood, and senses of humor that pinched without puncturing. They also shared the trait of being perfectly comfortable about deferring to—even seeking out—stronger personalities in social and business situations, beginning with their own wives. If Stewart was "an educated Cooper," as Frank Capra liked to say, Cooper was also something of "a self-taught Stewart"—someone who took a quiet middle-class pride in having attained the kind of position where his hunting companions included Ernest Hemingway and his wine-drinking companions Pablo Picasso.

Quiet was also the keynote of the time the actors spent together. Gloria Stewart liked telling of the time that Cooper drove up to their Roxbury Drive house, waved to Stewart who was standing outside, and over the next thirty seconds proposed a hunting trip—and received a positive reply—without a word being exchanged. On another occasion, she related, Cooper pulled up and asked Stewart to help him kill an afternoon by going for a drive in the California hills. For what turned out to be three hours, she told an interviewer, the two of them drove around averaging a monosyllable per hour. When Stewart returned home and Gloria asked how Cooper was, her husband reportedly responded: "I don't know. I didn't ask him."

The star of *Mr. Deeds Goes to Town, Sergeant York, The Pride of the Yankees,* and *High Noon* died less than a month after getting his honorary Oscar, at the age of sixty. Stewart, who had passed long hours at Cooper's bedside over the final weeks, was a pallbearer at the funeral. For some time afterward, he seldom touched on the subject without saying that the final years of his friend's life had been his best because Cooper had "finally realized" how much he had loved his wife—a reference to the actor's highly publicized affair with actress Patricia Neal around the turn of the 1950s. Like the Millands over Grace Kelly, the Coopers had pulled back from divorce at the last minute over Neal—a decision that accorded with Stewart's views on marital commitment.

The deaths of Sullavan and Cooper were hardly a tonic for a weariness that had begun to creep over Stewart even before the suicide of the actress. The trips abroad constantly promoted by Gloria and F. Kirk Johnson, an oil millionaire friend from Texas, as respites from work had begun to pall, too. At the beginning of 1959, in fact, the actor had been uncharacteristically sarcastic with a New York interviewer about a trip he had just begun to India, prior to having to start work on *Anatomy of a Murder*. He told the reporter: "We took a plane from California to here. We'll be taking a jet from here to London. Then we'll board a third plane there for a two-day flight to Calcutta. Then we'll take a small plane to a jungle site. And a jeep will bring us to the tent from which we'll start hunting a tiger I never saw for food we don't need. I would prefer my home in Beverly Hills."

Stewart and Gloria later concluded that at least part of the problem was trying to squeeze their trips into a schedule that never eased where work was concerned; even during his trip to India, for instance, the actor spent hours every evening committing to memory the long speeches he had to deliver in *Anatomy of a Murder*. Following the completion of *The Mountain Road* in the summer of 1959, therefore, Stewart began his longest voluntary hiatus from the making of motion pictures. Although he made a couple of appearances on television in the interim, he did not go before a big-screen camera again until reporting to John Ford for *Two Rode Together* in October 1960; after that, almost another year passed before he worked under Ford again in *The Man Who Shot Liberty Valance*.

The time off did not produce wondrous results. With *The Mountain Road*, a critical and commercial failure, his last film in circulation, career worries accompanied him on his vacation. They didn't ease even when he returned to work for Ford; on the contrary, they only got worse when it became obvious that the aging director of *The Informer*, *The Grapes of Wrath*, and *The Searchers* was close to running on empty for *Two Rode Together* and *The Man Who Shot Liberty Valance*. That did not come as good news for an actor already concerned about the constraints his age was putting on the roles being made available to him, and melancholy soon started flirting with depression. In his as-told-to book with Howard Teichmann, Henry Fonda spoke of an evening in the early 1960s when he and Stewart slipped into a theater on New York's East Side to see one of the latter's pictures. Coming out afterward, Stewart said: "Know something, Hank? I'm depressed. I don't know if I'll ever get another picture again." Fonda's reply was: "You, too? That's the way I feel."

But at least where Stewart was concerned, his despondency at the beginning of the 1960s had more triggers than the deaths of Sullavan and Cooper or his fretting about his career. There was also his awareness that Alex, who was in his late eighties and who had been going to the Cleveland Clinic for a variety of ailments for some time, was not going to be around forever. Indeed, one of his father's checkups in Cleveland had coincided with the January 1959 trip to India, suggesting one motive for his short temper about the tiger hunt. Those who knew Alex in Indiana say that, if that was the criterion, Stewart might as well have stayed holed up at Roxbury Drive 365 days a year since, in the words of the Reverend James Reid, the old man "went to Cleveland at the drop of a hat." It was during one of those medical trips, according to Reid, that Alex demonstrated that he had come to think of his second wife Anita in much the same way he had once thought of Bessie. "This one time he talked Anita into going with him to the Cleveland Clinic so she could get a checkup, too. They go through everything and then go down to Union Station for the trip back home. Alex says he has to go to the john. Anita says she has to, too. They go to their separate johns. Anita comes out. There's no Alex. She looks around, starts getting desperate. She gets a porter to go into the men's room. Nobody's there. Alex had already taken the train home without her."

It was also the familiar Alex who made his annual holiday visits to California, on either Thanksgiving or Christmas, causes for near-desperation by Gloria when he simply dropped out of sight without explanation. One Thanksgiving, according to Michael McLean, his mother came close to calling the police when the oldest Stewart sent Anita over to the house ahead of him from their quarters at the Beverly Hills Hilton Hotel, saying only that he would be along later. Hours later, Stewart found his father holding court at the hotel bar, his turkey dinner not having been forgotten so much as dropped down on his list of priorities. Matthew Dingman says that on another occasion, after hours of futilely looking for him, the old man showed up at Roxbury Drive in the company of a drinking companion he had met in a bar. When he told Gloria to put up the man for the night, it fell to Stewart to slide his wife into one room, Alex into another, and the bar companion to the front door.

In the late summer of 1961, however, Alex was diagnosed by Cleveland

Clinic physicians as having terminal stomach cancer. He returned to the hospital several times over the rest of the year, before being sent home to die in December. He was eighty-nine when he passed away at his Vinegar Hill home on December 28, 1961. Stewart and his two sisters were there for the end. Shortly before the funeral service at Calvary Presbyterian a few days later, the actor approached Minister Reid and asked him to include a reading of the 91st Psalm in the prayers. According to Reid, the reading, which he put off until the burial at Greenwood Cemetery, "shook Jimmy to tears because that was the psalm that his father had stuck in his pocket in Sioux City before he'd gone off to war in Europe."

In talking about his father some years later with *McCall's*, Stewart went out of his way to dismiss his stepmother as a significant presence— not only by failing to mention her whatsoever in the course of a lengthy reminiscence, but also by claiming that Alex had all but lost his will to live after the death of Bessie. As he told Floyd Miller: "With his wife gone, he lost his old appetite for forays and contention. Without her, he could work up no enthusiasms. She had been the only thing in his life with which he had been completely satisfied, the only perfection he had ever found. Her quiet strength had sustained him, and with her gone, he quickly withered away."

In actuality, of course, the "withering away" had taken seven years of marriage to Golding and more than eight years overall, during which, however much he had genuinely mourned Bessie's loss, Alex had behaved as extravagantly and prepossessingly as he had previously. Nor, except by the standards of the Stewarts, where surviving into the nineties had become commonplace, could death at eighty-nine be viewed as an unnaturally shortened life. But Golding's grandnephew Dingman, for one, says he has never been bothered by such pettiness. "I really don't think Jimmy's reaction was all that extraordinary," he says. "I don't think I would be all that thrilled, either, if my father married somebody else in the circumstances that Alex and Anita were married. Now whether Alex was really miserable in his second marriage, I think that's something else. Jimmy wasn't a part of those years in Indiana, so I'm not sure he would know. For sure, that's not the kind of thing that Alex would ever talk to him about. But the main thing is, Jimmy's going to defend what he lived and what he knew, and Anita Golding wasn't part of that."

For all practical purposes, Stewart stopped his visits to Indiana following his father's death, returning thereafter mostly when he was at the center of some special tribute. Even the matter of Alex's will was left up to his business manager, Guy Gadbois. James Reid remembers the evening that Gadbois came to town to settle the family estate. "I was invited to the Dingmans one evening for dinner at Gadbois's suggestion. It was a pretty edgy evening because everybody knew Guy was there to implement Alex's will. After dinner I thought it was best that Gadbois and Anita go back to her house to discuss the will, but he wouldn't hear of it, said he wanted me there."

What Golding and Reid heard was that Alex had left his assets outside the Vinegar Hill house to his daughters; among these were a small, "country bank" coal mine near the town of Willet and The Big Warehouse. Golding was left the use of the house for the rest of her life, after which it too reverted to Mary and Virginia. As had been arranged beforehand, Stewart received nothing. "Some people liked to say it was because Jimmy didn't want the tax burden," says Reid, "as if that would have made such a big difference for the tax bracket he was already in. The real reason was that he simply wanted his sisters to have everything because they weren't as well off as he was. Alex wasn't too happy about it, either. For him, it wasn't the economic value involved, it was the symbolism of a son inheriting at least something from his father. But Jimmy said no—everything to the sisters. Of course, Alex had to have the last word even in that, so the will included a clause that said it was against his better judgment that Jimmy was receiving nothing."

Golding remained on Vinegar Hill for only a brief time, after which she returned to Canada. She died there a couple of years later in her late eighties. With neither of Stewart's sisters desiring to live in Indiana, the house was sold.

For Stewart, however, the store had been even more symbolic of Alex than the house, and it took him only the evening of his father's burial to make up his mind about its future. As he once described it, he wanted to be alone after all the funeral commotion, so ended up walking down to The Big Warehouse on Philadelphia Street. "I let myself in with a key I hadn't touched for thirty years. The interior smelled of metal, leather, oil, and fertilizer—the odors of my childhood. I sat at his scarred oak desk, and idly pulled open the middle drawer. It held a clutter of pencils, paper clips, bolts, and paint samples. Something glinted dully among them. I picked up the funeral train penny with the flattened Indian face and the burst grain. I had lost mine, so now I took his. Then I left the store, locking the door behind me."

During his moments alone in the store, the actor recounted, he had decided that he "could not endure the thought of another man's standing in the middle of Dad's life." So, ignoring offers he had already received for buying the business, he opted to close it and give the proceeds from the sale of the merchandise to his sisters. A couple of days later, a sign was posted in the window of what had become Indiana's oldest surviving business. It said:

> Due to the death of Mr. Alex M. Stewart on December 28, 1961, the hardware store operated under the name of J. M. Stewart & Co. will not reopen. It is desired that all open business transactions be completed as promptly as possible.

DUSTY ROADS

TAKEN AS A WHOLE, THE PICTURES THAT STEWART MADE in the first half of the 1960s were the dreariest of his career. The most that could be said for some of them, especially a trio of comedies made for 20th Century-Fox, was that they demonstrated that the more the actor sought to cater to the image of the apple-pie American Jimmy Stewart, the more he appealed only to senior fans prone to staying at home to watch television versions of his big-screen sitcoms. In their hearts they admired what he stood for; in their living rooms they waited for him to appear for free on the *Jack Benny Show*.

The Mountain Road (Columbia – 1960)
The Mountain Road marked Stewart's only departure from his stated aversion to appearing in a war movie. Why he chose the film adaptation of a novel by Theodore White for the exception has never been clear. The actor himself has said only that he liked the basic premise of an Army officer who discovers that there is considerably more to commanding than wanting to command. But in fact the central situation is much more layered than that.

The setting of *The Mountain Road* is 1944 China, where Major Baldwin (Stewart) and a seven-man demolition squad under his command have the task of destroying roads, bridges, and anything else that will slow down an advancing Japanese force. Baldwin is so taken with his opportunity to demonstrate that he has field know-how that he ignores the warnings of Sue-Mei Hung (Lisa Lu), an American-educated Chinese, that he has left human compassion out of his ambitions. The result is the destruction of a bridge, which the officer justifies as a military necessity, that leaves thousands of stranded Chinese refugees homeless and without provisions.

Worse follows. Collins (Glenn Corbett), the demolition team member with the most sympathy for the plight of the Chinese, naively offers a ravenous mob what turns out to be far too little food and is brutally killed. Two more of the major's squad are slain by Chinese military renegades. In retaliation, the enraged Baldwin orders the destruction of an entire village, murdering men, women, and children—again rationalizing his actions as a military necessity to block the Japanese. Sue-Mei, who had been falling in love with the American, responds with pity and contempt. Baldwin is left with the realization that he didn't have what it takes to command.

Despite its fertile dramatic material, *The Mountain Road* never quite delivers on it. Stewart's persuasive turn as the arrogant, often manic, Baldwin is continually undermined by the screenplay's fuzziness about whether it is a portrait of an insecure man willing to go to any lengths for personal aggrandizement, a treatise against the horrors of war, or a depiction of white American racism in Asia. The irresolute point of view becomes particularly conspicuous with the denouement, which effectively argues that the destruction of the village had the positive consequence of making the character of Baldwin have doubts about his command proficiency.

According to Harry Morgan, who played one of the members of the demolition team, Stewart never talked about breaking his rule about doing a war film for *The Mountain Road*. "But when you think about it," Morgan says, "the classic war movie thing was just like an elaborate background. The real story wasn't about the Japanese as a war enemy, but about these people Stewart's character was responsible for. All the real destruction was turned against them or provoked by them. You could've had the same kind of situation in a lot of other settings."

Stewart's attempts to promote the picture were no more successful than the film itself. During a May 1960 appearance at a convention of theater owners in Pittsburgh, he infuriated most of his audience with an off-the-cuff remark about how pay-per-view television was inevitable. A spokesman for the theater owners suggested that he "stick to acting and leave business to businessmen." At a subsequent appearance in Philadelphia, all mention of *The Mountain Road* was eclipsed by the recent shooting down of Gary Powers's U-2 spy plane in Soviet territory and the actor's defense of such missions. As some gleeful columnists pointed out, none of this did a great deal for the contentions of director Daniel Mann that the motion picture being promoted was to be interpreted in an antiwar key.

Two Rode Together (Columbia – 1961)

Fifteen years after he had been thought about for the role of Doc Holliday in *My Darling Clementine*, Stewart got to work for John Ford. It was the first of four collaborations between the actor and the director in less than four years, and the one that was the most provocative in its failure. According to those associated with the production, it also provided a behind-the-scenes study of the differing, often conflicting, egos of its three principals—Stewart, Ford, and costar Richard Widmark.

In *Two Rode Together*, Stewart plays Guthrie McCabe, a cynical sheriff who is asked by the local army commandant, Frazer (John McIntire), to go to the Comanche chief, Quannah Parker (Henry Brandon), and swap rifles and other goods for the return of white captives being held by the Indians. McCabe insists that he be free to collect $500 each for every white he recovers from a wagon train of relatives that has come to Frazer for help. The desperate relatives, some of whom have not seen their abducted kin for many years, agree to the $500 price; among them are Marty Purcell (Shirley Jones), who carries a guilt that she let her brother be captured by the Comanches while she saved herself, and Wringle (Willis Bouchey), a crass businessman who will settle for any white teenager if that will shut up his new wife's constant laments about the son she lost during a Comanche raid. He offers to pay McCabe double for the delivery of any plausible candidate.

McCabe goes to Quannah Parker in the company of army lieutenant Jim Gary (Widmark), who detests his mercenary outlook. Once at the Indian camp, however, they discover that most of the whites on their list have either died a long time before or have so adopted Comanche customs that they no longer regard themselves as white. One exception is Running Wolf (David Kent), a wild teenager whom McCabe counts on handing over to Wringle for the extra price. Quannah Parker also gives them Elena (Linda Cristal), a Mexican captive who is the woman of Stone Calf (Woody Strode), his chief tribal rival.

On the way back to the army post, McCabe sets a trap for the pursuing Stone Calf and kills him. He has considerably less luck at the fort, however. When Wringle sees the savagery of Running Wolf, he refuses to accept him as his stepson, leaving the Comanche teenager in the hands of a crazed woman ready to accept any boy as her missing son. When McCabe tries to attend an officers' dance in the company of Elena, they are met with racist scorn from the other guests, prompting the sheriff to lash into them. The crazed woman is killed by Running Wolf who is himself lynched by the other members of the wagon train; just before he is hanged, however, he responds to the sound of a music box Marty has been carrying around as a remembrance of her brother. Marty screams futilely as she realizes it is her brother being lynched. McCabe returns with Elena to the town where he has been sheriff, only to find that he has been replaced during his absence. He and Elena go off together to California.

The main interest of *Two Rode Together* lies with director Ford's rancid view not only of humanity in general, but in particular of the Old West characters he had previously viewed as a romantic (*Stagecoach*), a mythographer (*My Darling Clementine* and *The Searchers*), or a political apologist (*Fort Apache* and a couple of other U.S. Cavalry stories). The Comanches are brutal opportunists, the army officers are crude, hypocritical racists, the civilians are a naive conglomerate waiting only to become a rabid mob. In the center of all the muck stands Stewart's McCabe, who is so much of a cynical mercenary that even his defense of Cristal's Elena and decision to go off with her at the end come across as the actions of somebody more contrarian than principled or infatuated. The one potentially earnest figure, Widmark's Gary, is the most underdeveloped and awkward character in the proceedings—a situation made more prominent by the casting of an actor a good ten years too old for the role.

For all that, however, *Two Rode Together* still lacks a final commitment to its misanthropy. The presence in the cast of Ford regulars Bouchey,

Andy Devine, Harry Carey, Jr., John Qualen, and Ken Curtis assures sentimental *shtick* that undermines a coherent tone. A number of key scenes—the killing of Stone Calf, the lynching of Running Wolf—are acquitted so perfunctorily as to suggest a contempt by the director for his audience as much as for Comanches, army officers, and white civilians. Carey, for one, calls the result on the screen "a hodgepodge of incidents and pieces of business from every western Jack ever made—a good old Irish stew." Shirley Jones goes further: "I thought it was pretty bad. I never figured out what it was all about, and I'm not at all sure Ford knew, either. Of course, Jimmy Stewart went at it like he was doing a masterpiece. Without him and Widmark, it might have been—*would* have been—an all-time turkey."

To hear Carey, Jones, Cristal, and others, the skirmishing that went on behind the scenes was far more dramatic and entertaining than anything caught by the cameras. For openers, there was the fact that Ford had never worked with Stewart or Widmark before, considered them both "real actors" (as opposed to many of the people he had been directing in recent years), and embarked on the production with more care than usual about when to stage one of his customary "humiliation" scenes with his star players. Widmark's attitude going in, according to other cast members, was that Ford was past it, but a Ford in his twilight years remained more of a director than 90 percent of the filmmakers in Hollywood. As for Stewart, he impressed others as being happy to work with Ford and Widmark, intent on proceeding as he usually did, and unconcerned about the stories of Ford's inevitable antics. He was lulled even more into a false sense of security when, shortly after arriving at the main shooting location near Bracketville, Texas, Ford insisted on welcoming him with a version of "Bringing in the Sheaves," as sung by Carey and Curtis.

"Jack worked with Jimmy a lot near the end of his career," Carey observes, "but I don't think he was ever quite as comfortable with him as he was with Wayne and Fonda. They had a flippant kind of relationship, lots of humor between them, but I had a feeling that Jimmy made him edgy, had something that Jack knew he could never quite control the way, say, he ran roughshod over Wayne for so long. Maybe it was just Jimmy's talent and Jack's awareness that he had the real stuff in front of him."

At least on *Two Rode Together*, however, Ford was just biding his time. Not that he didn't have distractions. For one thing, there was an almost daily need to rework scenes radically because of Ford's basic contention that the original screenplay was "lousy." (Jones: "There was a typewriter on the set for the whole movie. It was very unnerving, drove me crazy. And, of course, that alone seemed to appeal to Ford.") Then there was Widmark. As Cristal saw it: "I thought Dick was very defensive from the beginning. He really admired Jack, but that was with his head. He and Ford were like a couple of roosters on the set, always circling each other in the barnyard. Everybody knew what crazy things Jack was capable of, but Dick had a pretty good reputation too for eating up directors. They always seemed to be waiting for the other to move first, and I think that insecurity really clouded their talents."

It was Ford who moved first—against *both* his stars—during a long scene in which Stewart's McCabe and Widmark's Gary converse on a riverbank. As Stewart has usually told the story, the real victims were members of the crew. Thus he was quoted in *Films and Filming* in April 1966: "It was early in the morning and [Ford] was sort of grouchy and he walked out and for some reason put the camera in the river. He didn't have to put the camera in the river, but I think he did it because that meant that all the crew had to walk out there up to their waists in the river. He's like that. And it was terribly cold. Widmark and I did it—it was a long, long scene—we did it in one take and left."

Not quite, according to Carey:

> You could feel something building up with Jack for some time. All the deference he'd been showing Jimmy and Dick, that went completely against the grain. So he latched on to the two things that Jimmy and Dick had in common—they both wore toupees and had hearing problems. So he's out there in the middle of the river, with them sitting on the bank, and he starts talking lower and lower. You could hardly hear him if you were standing right next to him, but Jimmy and Dick, they're not ready to admit that they can't hear a damn word. They just keep nodding and nodding. Finally, Jack has established his point and he yells for everyone in the crew to gather around him in the water. When everybody's sloshed over to him, he throws up his arms in this great dramatic gesture and goes, "Fifty years in this goddam business, and what do I end up doing? Directing two deaf hairpieces!"

With the exception of the performances by Stewart and Cristal, *Two Rode Together* was roundly scored by critics. It was also a commercial failure. Ford, who usually despised talking about his movies, made an exception in this case, probably because the project hadn't been his, but had been offered to him by Columbia. "It was a load of crap," he told one interviewer.

The Man Who Shot Liberty Valance (Paramount – 1962)

Deaf hairpiece or not, Stewart returned to work for Ford with *The Man Who Shot Liberty Valance*. If *Two Rode Together* indicated on the screen a director at some advanced stage of curdling, *Liberty Valance* suggested a similar attitude from the studios toward Ford. Having taken a bath on Marlon Brando's *One-Eyed Jacks* only shortly before, Paramount was not at all enthusiastic about another western, and acceded only after Ford had raised some of the production money himself and John Wayne and Stewart agreed to costar. Even then, the studio insisted that the picture be shot in black-and-white and on its own sound stages to minimize potential losses.

Senator Ranse Stoddard (Stewart) and his wife, Hallie (Vera Miles), return to Shinbone to attend the funeral of their onetime friend, Tom Doniphon (Wayne). When a group of reporters asks Stoddard how he came to know Doniphon, a man who had been little more than an impoverished drunk for years, the senator introduces the flashback that takes up most of the film.

The young Stoddard is on his way to Shinbone to practice law when his stagecoach is attacked by the Liberty Valance (Lee Marvin) gang and he is beaten almost to death. Doniphon, a small local cattleman, comes along and takes him to the town cafe where Hallie works with her parents. With no demand for his legal talents in a town intimidated by Valance, Stoddard takes work as a dishwasher in the cafe. He draws Doniphon's jealousy when he begins to teach Hallie how to read and starts persuading her of his belief that laws are more important than guns for maintaining order. Valance comes in one night and again humiliates Stoddard, but Doniphon steps in and prevents more serious trouble. Embarrassed that Doniphon has defended him, the lawyer talks the cattleman into shooting lessons, but shows little skill with a six-shooter. Then the town newspaper editor Peabody (Edmond O'Brien), an advocate of statehood for the territory, is also beaten up by Valance, which prompts the unready Stoddard to challenge Valance to a duel in the street.

Valance is killed in the duel, and Stoddard gains notoriety as his slayer. He becomes a spokesman for statehood and eventually gets elected to the Senate; he also marries Hallie. The secret that he carries with him, however, is what Doniphon has told him on the eve of the statehood vote: that it was actually he, Doniphon, who killed Valance, from the shadows of the street. Doniphon insists that Stoddard tell nobody the truth because he is more important as a statehood spokesman than as a gunman. The cattleman then goes off on a drunken tear because he knows he has lost Hallie, winding up back at his ranch and burning it to the ground.

When the older Senator Stoddard finishes his tale, the newsmen around him decline to print the truth. In the film's most noted line, one of them justifies himself by saying to Stoddard: "This is the West, sir. When the legend becomes fact, print the legend."

As expansive a theme as that might sound, there is little in *Liberty Valance* beyond the basic premise to support it either visually or dramatically. Visually, the picture was made on the cheap[2] and looks it every frame of the way. Interior sets consist of tables and chairs, and little else; some of the soundstage "exteriors," such as where Stoddard is beaten by Valance early in the story, are about as convincing as similar sets on the old *Bonanza* television series. Aside from a couple of background framings of Wayne, there is little in the film to suggest the director of *My Darling Clementine* or *The Searchers*. Structurally, the narrative has the Stoddard character having to live with the main revelation of the film—who actually killed Valance—for all of about three minutes in the scene with Doniphon before the vote. What it does spend a lot of time on, on the other hand, are tedious, scene-chewing performances, most conspicuously from O'Brien and such resident Ford company players as Andy Devine, John Carradine, and John Qualen. Given the often ludicrous levels reached by some of these actors, *Liberty Valance* occasionally seems headed for some operatic vision of the western, somewhat in the key of Sergio Leone's Italian westerns a couple of years later; if so, Ford got cold feet somewhere in the middle of his objective, leaving many of his actors in the middle of his indecision.

The principal beneficiary of all the histrionic noise on the screen is Wayne, whose stalwart quiet becomes all the more commanding by

---

[2] The film as a whole was budgeted at $3.2 million, but much of that went to the actors and the director.

contrast. As in *The Spirit of St. Louis*, Stewart is asked to play twenty-five years younger than his actual age—and again manages to make it a nonissue for the most part. If he gives away his middle-age at all, it is in medium and long shots where his gait is shown to be not quite limber enough; on what might have been the more betraying close-ups, by contrast, his idealistic intensity as Stoddard swats aside the decades. On the other hand, the actor nears caricature in the framing sequences of the older Stoddard at the opening and closing of the film, fitting in much more with the hamminess of many of the supporting players.

Given Ford's dependence on his two stars for *Liberty Valance*, it did not come as much of a surprise that he was even more abusive to Wayne during the shooting than he normally was. He was more selective about going after Stewart, but when he did, he achieved equal humiliation ends. The director's weapon was black actor Woody Strode. As Stewart was to recall:

> There was a funeral scene with a coffin. Woody Strode . . . had been made to look old—plus overalls and a hat. Ford came over to me and asked what I thought of the costume. I said it was a bit Uncle Remus-like and then immediately wished I'd bitten my tongue. I knew I'd made a mistake. "Well, what's wrong with Uncle Remus?" he asks. And then he's yelling, "Hey, Woody, Duke, everybody come over here. Look at Woody, look at his costume. One of the *players* seems to have some objection. One of the *players* here doesn't seem to like Uncle Remus. As a matter of fact, I'm not at all sure he even likes Negroes."

Students of Ford cruelty have voiced doubts that the director landed so accidentally on Strode to rattle Stewart. "He planned his provocations as much as he planned his films," says Harry Carey, Jr. "Typical Ford," says producer-director Hal Kanter, who had more serious black-and-white problems with Stewart a few years later. "He'd discover the vulnerable spot and then jump up and down on it like it was a new mattress. Stewart might not have even known it at the time, but Ford knew that a Woody Strode was a Jimmy Stewart vulnerability."

Mr. Hobbs Takes a Vacation (20th Century-Fox – 1962)

The first of three *Father Knows Best* comedies that Stewart made for Fox in partnership with director Henry Koster, *Mr. Hobbs Takes a Vacation* was totally reliant on the actor's range of expressions for incredulity for its own credibility.

Roger Hobbs is a banker who is looking forward to a calm vacation on the California coast with his wife Peggy (Maureen O'Hara) and smallest children. Peggy has other ideas, however, and rents an enormous eyesore so she can also invite her married daughters (Natalie Trundy and Lili Gentle), their husbands (Josh Peine and John Saxon), and assorted grandchildren. Before long, Roger is trying to mediate a marital crisis for one daughter, keep another son-in-law away from a bikini-clad flirt, put his bored youngest daughter together with a local boy (Fabian), and persuade his preteen son that there is more to life than television. Thrown into the mix are a stuffy couple (John McGiver and Marie Wilson) who abhor all social activities except drinking. By the end of the film, Roger has mended all the family's problems, only to be informed that Peggy has taken a lease on the same house for the following summer.

Mr. Hobbs Takes a Vacation got no further with critics than *Variety*'s summation that "the picture has its staunchest ally in Stewart, whose acting instincts are so remarkably keen that he can instill amusement into scenes that otherwise threaten to fall flat." Cast member John Saxon says that was no accident:

Jimmy was of the old school, where you do everything right or you don't do it at all. I mean, even back then I remember thinking, does any of this have anything to do with anybody? It was a geriatric project from the start, with these dull jokes about television and other things not even having the immediacy of a TV sitcom. But Jimmy, he didn't want to hear any of that. There was this one line, for example, that kept foxing him. Koster would keep saying, "Okay, Jimmy, that's fine." But Jimmy, he'd keeping saying, "No, it's not there yet. Let's do it again." For this one line, they must have ended up doing thirty takes before he was satisfied. We're not talking about a Hamlet speech here. We're talking about a fairly minor line in a lifeless comedy that wasn't going to shake the world whether it was done right or not. The man simply refused to let down.

How the West Was Won (MGM – 1962)

A $14-million spectacular shot in Cinerama, *How the West Was Won* featured Stewart in an all-star cast that also counted Gregory Peck, Henry Fonda, John Wayne, Carroll Baker, Debbie Reynolds, Richard Widmark, Karl Malden, and George Peppard. With Henry Hathaway, John Ford, and George Marshall directing different segments of the 155-

minute-long saga, it was a lumpy mess that seemed to have little time for male actors younger than fifty. For all that, its promotion as the first full-scale Cinerama feature made it one of the box-office hits of the year.

Directed by Hathaway, Stewart appears in the opening segment as Linus Rawlings, a grizzled trapper who comes across the Prescott family (parents Malden and Agnes Moorehead, daughters Baker and Reynolds) on its way west through the Ohio Valley. He is attracted to the daughter played by Baker, but is more attracted to his solitary life. A river pirate named Hawkins (Walter Brennan), however, alters his plans by trying to kill him and steal his furs; Hawkins also has designs on the Prescotts. Linus succeeds in defeating Hawkins's gang, but is too late to save the older Prescotts from drowning in a treacherous river. He helps the daughters bury their parents and settles down with the one played by Baker. After fathering two sons, he runs off to join the Union Army in the Civil War, never again returning.

Stewart appears uncomfortable for much of his appearance, in particular when describing himself as "deep dark sinful" or in delivering such lines as "You make me feel like a man standing on a narrow ledge face to face with a grizzly bear—there just ain't no ignoring the situation." Typical critical reaction came from *The New York Times*, which asserted in part: "The atmosphere of contrivance is further nourished by the endless parade of familiar stars punching out stereotypes of people. Thus the fur trapper that James Stewart plays is not an authentic character, he's a rubber stamp of Mr. Stewart. . . . It should be called How the West Was Done to Death."

Stewart's segment was shot on a desert island off Paducah, Kentucky, where the Tennessee, Ohio, and Clark rivers meet in a triangular fork. It turned out to be the setting for more misadventures than the tussles with Walter Brennan's river pirates. A plague of rattlesnakes was followed by a set-destroying oil fire sparked after the martinet-like Hathaway got into a fight with his special effects people. Near the end of the shooting, an unexpected gale blew up, practically submerging the island and forcing an emergency evacuation. According to Baker, she, Stewart, and Reynolds took the last boat out because they were "aroused by the adventure."

Take Her, She's Mine (20th Century-Fox – 1963)
Whatever *Mr. Hobbs Takes a Vacation* was, *Take Her, She's Mine* was worse of the same. A Phoebe and Henry Ephron comedy that had run on

Broadway for 404 performances because of the television popularity of star Art Carney, it was gussied up for the screen not merely with the substitution of Stewart for Carney, but with the addition of alleged Paris locations aimed at internationalizing its appeal. There was little disguising, however, the Fox lot sets that stood in for foreign exteriors, giving the picture as much of a chintzy look as a hollow sound.

In *Take Her, She's Mine*, Stewart stars as Frank Michaelson, a lawyer and school board head who is constantly suspicious of his oldest daughter Mollie's (Sandra Dee) activities as a free speech advocate and modernist painter and whose dogging of her inevitably gets him into more trouble than she ever finds. Before the picture has ended, Michaelson is jailed twice, dumped into the Seine, and accused of distributing pornography. Even after marrying off Mollie to a French art teacher, he faces the prospect of even greater trouble from his younger daughter.

Screenwriter Nunnally Johnson was the first to admit that the additional sequences with the Paris setting didn't work. They had been ordered by 20th Century-Fox chief Darryl Zanuck, whose own residence was in the French capital and who, since the studio had been devastated shortly before by *Cleopatra*, was reluctant to okay any project without some kind of international box-office peg. "What it comes down to is I just wrote a lousy third act," Johnson acknowledged to an interviewer some time later. "The French didn't understand it any more than the Americans did. But Zanuck was very international then, and he insisted on it."

Long before *Take Her, She's Mine* got to the purported Paris scenes, it was sagging under its patronizing views of campus protests in the early 1960s and a parade of inside jokes about Stewart and his former (and better) films. One benevolent critic called the result a picture about "happy people with happy problems." More scathing was *The New York Times*, which found Dee "such a hideously vulgar creature that she makes an average sensitive grownup cringe. The best thing that can be said for Mr. Stewart is that he fulfills the requirements for stupidity with the deliberations of a mechanical clown."

Cheyenne Autumn (Warner Brothers – 1964)

There have been conflicting stories about how Stewart ended up portraying Wyatt Earp for John Ford in *Cheyenne Autumn*. Certainly, the extended cameo (one fourteen-minute sequence) has little to do in tone or narrative with the rest of the film, which depicts the forced march of the Cheyenne from a bleak Oklahoma reservation to their homeland in the Dakotas and their pursuit by the Army. Some speculation said that Ford was ordered to insert a comic interlude to break up an otherwise lengthy (156 minutes) and solemn portrayal of Indian suffering. Other reports said that Warner Brothers threatened to abort the entire film without another marquee name to go with Richard Widmark, who played the commanding officer of the pursuing cavalry. But Harry Carey, Jr., for one, thinks there was a third reason. "Jack knew that he was composing his valedictory to the western and he wanted as many familiar faces from his earlier westerns as he could get. Some of the guys were dead and Wayne was shooting something else, but there was me, Ben Johnson, George O'Brien. He cast Mike Mazurki as the sergeant because Mazurki reminded him of Victor McLaglen. Then in the sequence with Jimmy, he was able to squeeze in John Carradine and Ken Curtis. He really just wanted to direct us one more time and say Adios." [3]

In what was called "The Battle of Dodge City" sequence, Stewart as Earp and Arthur Kennedy as Doc Holliday do a lot of broad scowling and laughing around a poker game with the Carradine and Curtis characters. When word comes that the migrating Cheyenne are nearing town, Earp pompously announces his defensive "plan of campaign"—which consists of fleeing. Stewart has described the ensuing sequence:

> John Ford rarely told you what he had in mind and kept you guessing. He does it by all sort of means—terrible means sometimes! . . . There were 200 people in the square and Arthur Kennedy and I were supposed to get in a wagon with two horses and drive out of the square. Well, he told us to go in one direction, but he had all his assistants tell the crowd that we were going in a different direction, so that when we charged into the crowd, they didn't know what was happening. There was tremendous confusion. People got pushed by the horses. They screamed, they yelled, they ran. It was just a wonderful scene!

---

[3] Ford, who died in 1973 at the age of seventy-eight, made two more pictures. He codirected Young Cassidy with Jack Cardiff, then did Seven Women with extra help from his assistants.

Response to the Dodge City sequence generally depended on how affected critics were by the main narrative of the Cheyenne migration. Those who thought *Cheyenne Autumn* was an effective tribute to Native Americans, even something of an apology by Ford for his earlier caricatured treatment of Indians, found the Stewart-Kennedy interlude an oafish interruption—another instance of the director relying on tried-and-true routines instead of seeing his objectives clearly to the end. Those who discerned just more sentimental Hollywood Indiana in the main story applauded Stewart's bit as the best thing in the picture; or, as *Newsweek* put it, as its "only twitch of life." Theater owners around the country were equally divided, with many cutting out the sequence altogether as too high a price to pay for the loss of another screening during the day.

Dear Brigitte (20th Century-Fox – 1965)

Dear Brigitte is marginally the best of the treacly trio of comedies that Stewart made for Fox, if only because it allowed him to play cantankerous more than incredulous, gave him some credible scenes with Billy Mumy as his son, and presented the sitcom wife of Glynis Johns as a stronger figure than usual. Its sire, however, was still the Fred MacMurray family comedies made for Walt Disney in the 1950s.

Robert Leaf (Stewart) is the ultimate absentminded professor who teaches English in the Bay Area, lives on a reconverted riverboat with his family (wife Johns, son Mumy, daughter Cindy Carol) and wants nothing to do with modern technology. His personal humanities program has included naming his children Pandora and Erasmus and insisting on family musical evenings together. He takes it hard when he realizes that the cello-playing Erasmus is tone-deaf, harder still when attempts to turn his son toward painting trip over the fact that the boy is also color-blind, and hardest of all when he realizes the boy is a mathematical wizard. From that point on, Leaf and his son get in and out of hot water with con men, government agents, and university administrators who are interested in Erasmus's talent for picking winning horses. At the same time, the professor also helps Erasmus fulfill his dream by taking him to Paris to meet Brigitte Bardot.

As with *Take Her, She's Mine*, some bizarrely contorted plot elements were added to *Dear Brigitte* for justifying a sequence in Zanuck's Paris. Because Bardot refused to go to Hollywood for backlot approximations, however, Stewart and Koster actually got over to the French capital this time. Billy Mumy went with them:

> Bardot made it clear to Fox that being in Paris wasn't enough authenticity for her. She insisted that her apartment be copied from the original down to the smallest detail. Fox did it. If not for her cleavage, it would have all been for a couple of hours of work because she, Jimmy, and I went through the scene perfectly the first time we did it. But then somebody started worrying that there was too much of her chest showing for a picture that was going to be seen by kids, so we did the whole thing over again the next day with a corsage covering her up. She thought we were kind of quaint about the things that we worried about.

Bardot or not on the premises, Stewart's character of Leaf exhibits little sexual vitality in *Dear Brigitte*, carrying absentmindedness to a new level. More than one critic suggested it was time for Mr. Stewart to stop taking a vacation.

HOLDING ON

IF THERE WAS ONE AREA THAT SHOULD NOT HAVE CAUSED Stewart any significant concern in the 1960s, it was money. Aside from the regular six-figure fees and accruing seven-figure profits on film percentage deals he had been collecting for some years from his acting assignments, he had invested in numerous oil and real estate ventures that, more often than not, had paid off. Whatever capitalist success grandfather James Maitland Stewart had watched go up in flames at The Big Warehouse in 1929 had been raised from the ashes by his grandson three decades later.

Stewart's financial smarts consisted of one part Indiana background and one part bright partners and advisors. Falling within the former sphere was the frugality that, along Philadelphia Street, had been considered next to godliness and cleanliness as a human virtue. Nobody liked deriding this quality more than Gloria Stewart who, if not telling reporters the story of how hard it had been to get the actor to take her to dinner after they had first met, was talking about how Stewart was always digging into her handbag because he hadn't bothered to take any cash along. Following a 1954 trip to Italy, she also delighted in captioning a photograph of the two of them in front of the Fontana di Trevi as: "I am throwing a coin in the fountain and the expression on Mr. Stewart's face says that I am wasting money, like throwing away the last dime of the Stewart fortune." A particularly troubling transaction for him, according to friends, was tipping. "He always asked me how much to leave," laughs publicist John Strauss, "almost like he was hoping to hear a lower bid."

Certainly, long before Gloria or his percentage deal with Universal had come along, Stewart had impressed Hollywood friends and associates with what might be called his narrowly targeted ways with a dollar. "He was always shrewd about money, " says Burgess Meredith. "One time, and this was before the war, when he was still on a salary with MGM, he started complaining about how he had so much in annuities and in insurance that he had decided to convert some of it to cash. I told him to get a business manager. His first question, naturally, was whether he would have to pay somebody like that. Anyway, he started looking around and he came across a lot of characters you find only in Hollywood. One night I came home to the place we were sharing in Brentwood and I hear this one saying, 'Mr. Stewart, I can guarantee there's a 95 percent profit in operating a popcorn concession. All you need is a place twenty feet square. . . . ' Needless to say, that one never darkened the doorway again."

By the time he was resettled in Hollywood after the war, however, Stewart had in place, instead of a believer in popcorn futures, three crackerjack financial advisors. One was Lew Wasserman, who negotiated his movie deals. Another was F. Kirk Johnson, a Fort Worth oilman with whom he was partnered in numerous enterprises, not only in the oil field but in race horses and television stations as well. (It was also Johnson and his wife who spurred the Stewarts into heavy travel abroad in the 1950s, touring Europe with them, and especially, helping Indiana's onetime Great White Hunter realize his childhood dream of going on an African safari. It was another blow to Stewart in the early 1960s, after the deaths of Margaret Sullavan, Gary Cooper, and his father, that Johnson also died, succumbing to a heart attack while on a visit to Los Angeles.)

No less important was Guy Gadbois, who operated as the actor's business manager for some thirty years while simultaneously acting as a partner in numerous undertakings. A stockbroker by trade, Gadbois was also a troubleshooter in thorny situations, such as problems related to Anita Golding after Alex Stewart's death. One of his financial specialties was ranchland, and at one time or another, for either personal use or investment purposes, he and Stewart held title to appreciable spreads in California, Nevada, Texas, and Hawaii. A favorite Stewart tale has been how Gadbois talked him into buying a goat ranch in Texas in the early 1950s. "It turned out that the goats were not to be eaten or milked. I was supposed to clip them for the mohair that was then being used for upholstering sofas. . . . So I bought the goats, paying eight or nine dollars apiece. Each one I clipped was supposed to bring me two, maybe three dollars for its hair, then run off and grow some more real fast. The first clipping season came around, leaving me with a mountain of shredded mohair. Naturally, the bottom fell out of the mohair market just then."

Stewart's solution was to store the mohair in a vast warehouse until the prices started rising again. He found the storage facilities "suspiciously ample," leading him to conclude that the warehouse owners "did better than the ranchers." "Then mohair became popular for men's suits. The price bounded back up, and I hurried to sell my goat hair. Every time I saw a fellow wearing a mohair suit in Hollywood, I felt like shaking his hand. For a while there, everything seemed rosy. But the mohair suits didn't seem to take up the slack; we had too much hair again, and once again I was carting it to the storage bins."

Stewart and Gadbois thought about leasing the ranch as a permanent campsite for the Boy Scouts, but that plan foundered on the organization's demands. "They were just too canny for me," the actor has said, "so we just decided to sell the ranch altogether. I can't say that my goat-hair venture was a success from a tax standpoint, but it was educational. Whenever I meet a mohair baron, I can speak his language."

Stewart's personal fortune in business dealings did not carry over all the time into his attempts to speak on, or even interpret correctly, broader economic trends. Sometimes he was right in principle, but wrong about the setting for enunciating it, as in telling the theater owners in Pittsburgh that they could count on pay-television coming in the near future. Other times he was wrong in several directions at once. In 1958, for example, he put his foot in his mouth within the film industry with another lament about the demise of the old studio system and the rise of independent producers, asserting that this had brought about a decline in both the quality and profitability of

American movies. Producer William Perlberg led the charge of ripostes, shooting back, in words similar to those used by the theater owners in Pittsburgh, that the actor was "in over his head, in a field he hasn't given much thought to." Among other things, Perlberg pointed out, the four most recent Best Picture Oscars had gone to independent productions, fifteen of the twenty films nominated in that category over the four-year span had been done independently, and all of the features had made money.

Somebody else who thought Stewart got in over his head on a financial matter was Sheldon Abend, who went all the way to the Supreme Court in 1990 to press a complex copyright claim on *Rear Window* on behalf of the widow and children of original writer Cornell Woolrich and against Stewart, Wasserman, and the estate of Alfred Hitchcock. The claim targeted the 45 percent each that the actor and director gained on the photoplay in putting together the movie deal in the 1950s, declaring the accord as legally lapsed. For Abend, however, the real culprit was Wasserman, who had 10 percent:

> I always considered Stewart a passive defendant. He didn't understand what it was about, and the people around him had no reason to enlighten him. When the whole thing arrived at the Supreme Court, they tried to be smart about it, phrasing the case as "Jimmy Stewart versus Abend," making it sound like I wanted to spit on Mom, apple pie, and the Stars and Stripes. It was a tacky move. The only thing missing was Stewart walking into court in a military uniform. But it was also an idiotic move because the Supreme Court wasn't made up of blockheads. They voted 6–3 in our favor to reaffirm the Second Chance concept of the copyright privilege.

The two sides subsequently settled for a sum reported as being in the neighborhood of $9 million. "I've always thought—or maybe just wanted to believe—that if Stewart had really grasped the copyright issues involved, he would have come down on the side of the widow and the kids long before we ended up in the Supreme Court," says Abend. "But maybe that's just the power of the image. After all, Wasserman was his agent and partner."

At the very least, none of Stewart's business activities and connections contradicted the outlook of the white Protestant Republican America that he had grown up within, that had thrived as official policy during the Eisenhower years, and that would seldom be better than obstreperous in different social circumstances. Within such a purview, there was little incentive for embracing the disruptive as a necessary advance or the new as a necessary conflict. There was, at best, a tolerance of what was first rendered harmless: Jack Lemmon as the symbol of all bongo-beating beatniks in *Bell, Book and Candle*, Sandra Dee as the symbol of all free speech and abortion concerns in *Take Her, She's Mine*, and the big-sisterish Brigitte Bardot as the symbol of all sensuality in *Dear Brigitte*.

None of this made for anarchist social circles in the actor's private life. As the years went by, it even made for fewer and fewer film-community people, except for the heirs of the old studio bosses and others who had gained a separate socialite status. Actor William Windom, who was once married to the daughter of Edie Goetz, herself a daughter of Louis B. Mayer, recalls seeing the Stewarts at his mother-in-law's house constantly. "I could never figure out what Jimmy and Gloria saw in Edie," Windom says. "Obviously, Bill Goetz had made Jimmy a rich man with that Universal deal, but that had been a long time before and Bill was dead by then. But whenever Edie, who could put you to sleep as soon as she said hello, had a dinner or a party, there were Jimmy and Gloria at the table."

In fact, Stewart's wealth and reputation as an Establishment figure, more than his status as an actor or even a war hero, proved decisive for his presence in some California homes. As Windom notes about his own profession, "an actor has always had more of a social standing in Des Moines than he's had in Hollywood. You don't get very far up the hill in Beverly Hills to the really luxurious estates if you're just some guy who's done *It's a Wonderful Life*. Actors are shit in Hollywood— always have been and always will be. If the movie industry could have gotten along with a lot of cartoon characters, it would have. Except then all the glitzy people would have looked down on the animators."

Mignon Winants, a socialite who has been close to the Stewarts for decades, doesn't contradict Windom. "I've never really thought of Jimmy as an actor, or in the way you think about actors. Or, let's just say that, for an actor, he's been a solid citizen ever since I've known him. A dedicated taxpayer, very Republican. That sort of thing has always mattered to him enormously. He's had a great reliance on all those things you used to learn in civics class in school, and he's succeeded in putting them to smart use. That's what comes to mind about him before being an actor."[4]

But if Stewart's status as a performer wasn't enough for him to enter some social circles, it was essential to the political favors he did for Ronald Reagan, Richard Nixon, and other candidates he has identified over the years as incorporating his Republican standards. Ironically, the most noted of these relationships—with Reagan—had to overcome a period when Stewart regarded himself as being more of the genuine article than the right-wing politician he ended up energetically endorsing for governor of California and president of the United States. "One time when he was back in Indiana," the Reverend James Reid recalls, "there was an announcement that Reagan was going to run as a Republican for the governorship of California. Jimmy was skeptical, to put it mildly. Where he was concerned, you didn't just forget that Reagan, whether merely in name or not, had been a Democrat for so long. 'He's just one more johnny-come-lately, he'll never get anywhere,' he said to me. As far as he was concerned, Reagan was just being opportunistic in declaring himself a Republican—a Republican by vote, not a Republican by conviction, the way the Stewarts had always been."

But if so, Reagan's opportunism was something that Stewart had abetted on more than one occasion, and long before Reagan had entered the gubernatorial campaign in the mid-1960s. In 1955, when the future president had been hosting the Sunday evening CBS anthology series *G. E. Theater* as part of his career makeover into a friend to big business who would one day be a viable political candidate, Reagan was brought up short by NBC's decision to schedule the popular western *Bonanza* directly against him. With the *G. E. Theater*'s ratings (and Reagan's post-Hollywood prospects) threatened, Lew Wasserman, the agent for both actors, asked Stewart to do a guest shot on the CBS show to divert viewers from *Bonanza*. Stewart agreed, in part for the opportunity it gave him to publicize *Strategic Air Command* on network television. The result was a Borden Chase–scripted western, *The Windmill*, which marked the

---

[4] Posh hotels in both Canada and Spain have also made Stewart the singular exception to rules against putting up actors, no matter how celebrated. Both establishments always insisted on registering him as General Stewart.

end of his boycott of television drama. Twice more, in 1957, he went to Reagan's rescue with G. E. Theater appearances.[5]

Still, as his remarks to Reid reflect, the pith of Stewart's Republicanism has never been Reagan or any other politician simply laying claim to votes through adherence to the GOP. Long before them came the heritage of personal industry and self-sufficiency that Christian morality and patriotic allegiance defined as authority for all, that prosperity consolidated for those who were "lucky," and that, in the ideally quiet nature of things, even Horatio Alger had called too much attention to. It was a historistic canvas that justified itself in every new day of an expanding, lengthening existence: things had to have developed as they had because that was in point of fact the way that they had. Such retrospective fatalism did not demand much social perceptiveness or political introspection from Stewart; with the advance of years, however, it did leave increasingly more room for its emotional corollary of nostalgia, facts often be damned. Within his profession, there have been his defenses of the studio system that didn't know how to use him for maximum benefit and that he helped to dismantle. There was also, among other things, his attack on Italy's so-called spaghetti westerns in the 1960s: "If a western is a good western, it gives you a sense of that world and some of the qualities those men had—their comradeship, loyalty, and physical courage. The vogue for the new kind of western seems pretty unimportant to me. They try to destroy something that has been vital to people for so long."

Where "comradeship" and "loyalty" come into play in such pictures as Bend of the River, The Naked Spur, and The Man from Laramie, the actor didn't mention. In the same vein has been his praise of the talents of John Ford, even though his own experiences with the director resulted in three extremely labored films and an hour-long television drama[6] that

---

[5] The second of those shows, a western version of A Christmas Carol, also marked his debut as a director.

[6] Entitled Flashing Spikes and aired in October 1962, the drama featured Stewart as a former major league pitcher who is accused of trying to corrupt a young hurler. The TV tale was pretty much kicked around by critics, many of whom used words like "garbled" and "monotonous" to describe its narrative. Ford's penchant for including his regulars on his projects (both John and Pat Wayne were members of the cast) extended in the case of Flashing Spikes to giving the then-forty-one-year-old Harry Carey, Jr., the role of a rookie big leaguer.

were more notable for what was accomplished despite the ailing and heavy-drinking filmmaker than because of him.

Common to all such pronouncements, of course, is the overriding desire to have an idea triumph over the facts—an idea whose time might not have come in actuality, but that might still be delivered in retrospect. James Stewart as Jefferson Smith would not have settled for that, but James Maitland Stewart as Jimmy Stewart has never had a great problem with it.

THE OLDER WEST

IF STEWART LIMPED THROUGH THE EARLY 1960s professionally, he found his footing again in the middle of the decade with three performances that were among the most textured he ever delivered. But with the exception of *Shenandoah*, which returned him briefly to the list of the country's biggest box-office attractions, he worked to the increasing indifference of industry marketing people, who in a couple of cases dumped his efforts into second-run or suburban movie theaters with little more than nominal publicity. In a period in which the media's favorite casserole consisted of sex, grass, and rock 'n' roll, old, crusty, and cynical was lucky to get out of the oven at all.

Shenandoah (Universal – 1965)
Shenandoah marked the first of four films in which Stewart worked with director Andrew McLaglen, and was easily the best. It was also the only picture in which the actor went beyond his periodic paternalistic figures to the character of a full-fledged patriarch.

Stewart stars as Charlie Anderson, a widower who works his big Virginia farm with six sons and a daughter and with a decided indifference to the Civil War raging all around them. Although a couple of his sons, James (Patrick Wayne) and Jacob (Glenn Corbett), feel uneasy about sitting out the war, they don't dare rebel against the wishes of Charlie, and join eagerly to drive away both Confederate recruiters and Union agents who try to seize the farm's horses. The family's meals together consist of Charlie surrounded at the table by his children and James's wife, Ann (Katherine Ross), reminding God during Grace that the Andersons did all the work that brought them their food, and then digging in.

The inevitable happens when the youngest Anderson, known only as Boy (Philip Alford) and clearly his father's favorite, is mistaken for a Confederate by a Union patrol and hauled away as a prisoner. Leaving James and Ann at home to take care of the farm, Charlie, his daughter, Jennie (Rosemary Forsyth), and the rest of his sons go off in search of Boy. Their first move is to block a prison train filled with Rebel soldiers and free everyone, including Sam (Doug McClure), a Southern officer whose wedding ceremony with Jennie was interrupted by a call to duty. Neither on the train nor elsewhere, however, do the Andersons find Boy. With Sam now part of the group, Charlie finally accepts that it will be impossible to find his youngest son and starts back home. On the way, he loses Jacob to a Rebel ambusher. Even worse awaits him at home, when he discovers that both James and Ann have been murdered by two deserters. His first consolation is that their baby has been spared. His second comes in church the following Sunday when, on crutches, Boy stumbles in, having escaped from his Union prison. The remaining members of the family, including son-in-law Sam, sing a hymn of thanksgiving.

As far as Stewart was concerned, *Shenandoah* was more than a tour de force, it was practically a highlight film of his career. One moment he is a gregarious storyteller, the next a bitter, even cruel man; in one scene he is fastidiously preparing a "bridal suite" in an abandoned house for his daughter and son-in-law, in the next, he is conveying more raw hatred than he did even as one of Anthony Mann's characters. To go along with the sentimental piety of the final sequence, there is an earlier scene in the church in which Stewart's Charlie is positively hearty in the malice that he directs at another parishioner (Dabbs Greer). The dialogue given to the protagonist embraces the same broad territory. When Sam tells Charlie that he loves Jennie, the hardened Anderson replies: "But do you *like* her? When you love a woman without liking her, the night can be long and cold and contempt comes up with the sun." Realizing that he is on the verge of choking a boy to death for killing Jacob, the patriarch retreats from his scalding rage no further than to a cold hatred, declaring: "I won't kill you. I want you to be an old man. And I want you to have many, many children. And I want you to feel about them the way I feel about mine now. And when someday somebody comes along and kills one of them, I want you to remember." And in a gloomy, resigned talk to his late wife's headstone, there is the further color of: "It's like all wars, I guess. The undertakers are winning it. The politicians talk of the glory of it. The old men talk of the need of it. The soldiers? They just wanna go home."

"To the day they put me in my own grave," director McLaglen says, "I will never understand why Jimmy didn't get at least a nomination for what he did in *Shenandoah*. The range of the man was never clearer, his conviction never more moving. They even gave it a Tony when it was done on Broadway a couple of years later, but as far as Hollywood was concerned, it wasn't anything serious."

According to McLaglen, one of the first people who had to be convinced of *Shenandoah*'s merits was Lew Wasserman, whose MCA agency had taken over Universal in 1962. "Universal never bothered us about the picture while we were shooting it in Oregon. They considered it a very minor thing, just one more entry on the books. Then when it got released, the critics jumped on it as an unexpected find and people started going to see it in droves. It turned out to be Universal's biggest moneymaker of the year. Suddenly, Wasserman couldn't tell enough people how it had been his company that had made it and how proud he was of it. But during production he hardly knew that it existed."

Overall, *Shenandoah*'s biggest drawback was its chief strength: Stewart so dominated the proceedings that none of the other characters had much of a reality beyond their function of feeding his Charlie Anderson cues for snappish replies or discourses on the state of human nature. After such debacles as *Take Her, She's Mine*, however, that was enough for most critics. For *The New York Times*, the actor was "perfectly cast" and "played his role to the hilt." In the eyes of *Newsweek*, "what Stewart . . . achieves must be a source of some discouragement as well as instruction for the young, unskilled actors working with him. He is far from young. His role of paterfamilias is more tired than his eyes. Yet Stewart compels belief with his strength and his simplicity."

The Flight of the Phoenix (20th Century-Fox – 1966)

If *Shenandoah* allowed Stewart to run the length of a countryside in acting colors, *The Flight of the Phoenix* forced him to mine one desert tone. The result was his last great combination of a big performance in a big role within a big picture. It also put him in the company of the most prestigious international cast of his filmmaking career; the other players under director Robert Aldrich included Richard Attenborough, Peter Finch, Ian Bannen, Hardy Kruger, Christian Marquand, Ernest Borgnine, George Kennedy, and Dan Duryea.

Frank Towns (Stewart) is a grizzled pilot flying a group of men back from a Saharan oil field to civilization. Because his alcoholic navigator Moran (Attenborough) makes a plotting error, he is more than 100 miles off course when his battered plane gives out and he crashes in the desert. From this point on, the rest of the film's 147 minutes are devoted to the relationships among the crash victims as they try to get out of the desert.

The major conflict of *The Flight of the Phoenix* is between the fractious old-timer Towns and Dorfmann (Kruger), a designer who comes up with an ambitious plan to construct a new plane from the remnants of the crashed craft and fly the survivors to safety. As the reconstruction work progresses, Dorfmann becomes increasingly tyrannical in driving the men on, while Towns shows equal bitterness about having to cede authority to what he describes as one of "the little men with the sliderules and computers [who] are going to inherit the earth." It falls to Moran to mediate the quarrels between the two, but even the navigator is dismayed to learn on the eve of the attempted takeoff of the rebuilt plane that Dorfmann has never designed anything besides model planes. In spite of that, Towns manages to get Dorfmann's Rube Goldberg contraption into the air and rescues Moran and the remaining passengers. The picture ends on a note of uneasy coexistence between Towns's kind of old-fashioned derring-do and Dorfmann's technological priorities.

Little about *The Flight of the Phoenix* was easy, and some of it was tragic. To begin with, there were the mutual adaptation problems between Stewart and such European heavyweights as Attenborough, Finch, and Kruger. According to director Aldrich's son William, who played a passenger killed in the desert crash, matters got particularly sticky at the first cast read-through on location outside Yuma, Arizona:

[Jimmy] sits down and all of these guys close their scripts and know their lines, everything memorized. And Jimmy was looking at the script and flipping the pages, trying to figure out where the hell they were.... I think he was very much embarrassed by that: Everybody knew his lines, and he didn't. It was the English training.... [But] the next day we all came to the table again, and Jimmy sat there, with *his* script open, and when we begin, everybody closes his script again. Jimmy looks around—and then closes *his* script and knew all *his* lines for the rest of the rehearsal. He must have stayed up all night.

In the view of Hardy Kruger, however, the biggest initial problem wasn't so much between Stewart and his fellow players as it was between the actor and the Hollywood rumor mill. "I've heard it said that he showed up to work with us very shy, even a little intimidated. That isn't true at all. I mean, he was Jimmy Stewart, after all. The real obstacle was a lot of things he had been hearing about how all these Europeans were going to be elbowing one another out of camera range and how he'd have to be on his guard every second of every take. He was curious, even suspicious, but I wouldn't say shy."

Stewart's second worry, according to Kruger, was just the opposite of his first one.

He was surprised to find that we weren't all these grave egotists out to do in one another once the camera started turning, that on the contrary we were all a little nuts. We laughed and joked and painted Yuma red. He was astonished at first. You could see him always asking himself, "Was all this juvenile behavior off camera going to affect our ability to do our job?" It took him a long time to come forward with the confidence that we were not fools and that we weren't going to foul up the picture by the way we behaved when we weren't working. But once he did come forward, he was the leader of us all. We'd drive back to Yuma from the set with these dummies used in the picture and play Al Capone, giving the dummies the old rat-a-tat, then throwing them out of the car. We weren't drunk, we were having fun. And Jimmy, who'd apparently never had that kind of an atmosphere on a set before and who seemed surprised that it wasn't affecting his work either, he had more fun than anyone.

At the opposite end of such escapades was the death of stuntman Paul Mantz during the filming of the climactic takeoff sequence. After building the plane shown in the picture from little more than a Boxer engine and a crate, Mantz decided that it was top-heavy, so he added rocks and other weights to the fuselage for trimming. That addition proved fatal when, responding to radio directions to come in lower at his 80-mph speed, the pilot couldn't prevent one wing from grazing the ground, causing an immediate crack-up. A second stuntman had been uneasy enough about the planned action to keep his seat belt off, enabling him to leap clear of the plane at the last second and get away with only a broken hip.

On screen, the clash between the Stewart and Kruger characters over the viability of the latter's craft challenged the leading man with one of his most self-contained explorations of hardened melancholy for the good old days. As coldly as the technocrat Dorfmann is presented for most of the film, he also cuts regularly to the heart of Towns's ambiguity with such crisp questions as, "You behave as though stupidity were a virtue; why is that?" Although the climax of the film comes with the takeoff of the jerry-built plane, the two actors reach the peak of their own clash shortly before when the astounded Towns, letting it sink in that Dorfmann has been bluffing from the start, listens as the latter enumerates all his accomplishments as a model-plane builder. Befuddlement vies with admiration in the awareness of the great gamble that Dorfmann has been taking—and not at all harmlessly—with the lives of the surviving passengers at stake. It is a moment horizons beyond the patronizing characters that Stewart had been playing with increasingly regularity in the years leading up to *Phoenix* and strikingly redeems all the anger, guilt, and self-pity he has been meting out until then. With the character of Dorfmann, Towns has found somebody as obsessed as he is—but also somebody not paralyzed by his condition.

Commercially, *The Flight of the Phoenix* never got off the ground. Even the gratuitous insertion of a "mirage" dance by Barrie Chase did little to disguise the fact that the film was two-and-a-half hours in the company of a group of middle-aged men stranded in a desert. Critics, on the other hand, were almost uniformly enthusiastic, with Stewart and Kruger singled out for particular praise. "Measured against the ordinary run of adventure epics," *Time* declared, "*Phoenix* is a bonanza." *The New Yorker* backed that view, saying that the picture "deserves to be especially recommended for . . . succeeding in seeming so fresh and ingenious."

Kruger, a pilot himself, says that he and Stewart spent several conversations speculating about whether somebody might actually fly the kind of craft depicted in *Phoenix* any distance. "What we both decided," the German actor says, "is that it was theoretically possible as long as there was use of a ramp to take off, that there was no way that wheels would be enough. We also agreed that, even with a ramp, neither one of us wanted to be the one to attempt it."

The Rare Breed (Universal – 1966)

Although he had actually completed filming it before going to work on *The Flight of the Phoenix*, *The Rare Breed* was the first of four consecutive westerns that represented Stewart's only contact with the moviegoing public between 1966 and 1970. All four of them gave him moments, and one of them considerably more than that, but none of them were able ultimately to overcome splayed scripts and/or perfunctory direction.

In *The Rare Breed*, Stewart plays Sam Burnett, a cowboy down on his luck who agrees to transport a Hereford bull named Vindicator to a flamboyant Scots rancher named Bowen (Brian Keith). Like a number of other western traditionalists, Sam scoffs at the notion of the bull's owner, Martha Evans (Maureen O'Hara), that crossing the Hereford with Bowen's longhorns will breed a new and hardy species of cattle. Although initially tempted to doublecross Martha and her daughter Hilary (Juliet Mills) by delivering the animal to another cattleman, Sam is won over by their conviction and does the job he has been paid for. This prompts a fight to the death with the gunman (Jack Elam) who was supposed to take delivery of Vindicator in the planned doublecross.

Sam needn't have bothered. Martha finds out about his scheme to betray her and treats him with scorn. Bowen turns out to have more interest in Martha than in Vindicator and sets the animal loose on his range convinced that it will not survive the winter. But suddenly infected with Martha's old confidence, Sam goes off during a howling blizzard sure that he will find Vindicator alive. But his search is unsuccessful until the following spring, when he finds the animal's carcass under a snow bank. Even then, however, he refuses to despair, and his faith is vindicated when he comes across a calf that is clearly the issue of Vindicator and a longhorn. Martha marries Sam, Bowen's son Jamie (Don Galloway) marries Hilary, and the four of them preside over their new crossbred herd.

Veteran actor-wrangler Ben Johnson anticipated most critical response to *The Rare Breed* during the shooting: "McLaglen did everything like he was doing it for TV—hurry, hurry, and save. You don't get great work doing it like that." Stewart, naturally, never saw it that way, or at least didn't admit that he did, during production. Whatever McLaglen's worries about the budget, he had heard them before while working at MGM for One-Take Van Dyke and others. The result on the screen of acting under such conditions was some familiar sloppiness in early scenes, with Stewart's drawl accented to near braying, and then a gradual clearing of delivery and character. The payoff in *The Rare Breed* was the sequence in which his character of Burnett finds the calf that proves the possibility of crossbreeding. As James Powers of *The Hollywood Reporter* observed: "The scene . . . with the camera entirely on Stewart's face is one of great poignance and tenderness. It is only one shot, that of Stewart's face, but it is the crux of the picture, and Stewart once again, as he has a hundred times, shows what it means to understand acting and to make it meaningful."

Firecreek (Warner Brothers – 1968)

For the most part, Stewart stayed away from so-called psychological westerns that traded off big action scenes against panoramic settings in favor of focusing on the relations among a handful of characters in equally few town or cabin locations. According to the actor, that western subgenre, which was particularly in vogue in the late 1950s with such films as *3:10 to Yuma*, *The Lonely Man*, and *The Tin Star*, came too close to television in its physical restrictions and wasted the big screen's possibilities for lending an epic air to stories of the Old West. With *Firecreek*, however, he overcame his reservations, not least because it teamed him in a full-length motion picture for the first time with Henry Fonda.

Firecreek is the name of a sleepy town that is disrupted forever one day by the arrival of Larkin (Fonda), Earl (Gary Lockwood), Norman (Jack Elam), Drew (James Best), and Willard (Morgan Woodward)— mercenaries on the run after lending out their guns to cattle wars. Still bleeding after extracting a bullet from his side, Larkin announces his intention of leaving Firecreek again after a few hours of rest, but his stay in a boardinghouse bed leaves his henchmen free to stir up various kinds of trouble. Earl, in particular, is quickly revealed as a paranoid thug—first almost raping the teenager Leah (Brooke Bundy), then disrupting a church service being conducted by Preacher Broyles (Ed Begley), then firing his gun to cause the elderly Broyles to fall off his horse.

The town's main defense against the outlaws is Cobb (Stewart), a farmer who lives outside Firecreek with his pregnant wife and two sons and who has been sheriff in name only. As the Larkin band escalates its terror, Cobb tries to use reason and humor to defuse tensions. When the dim-witted stable boy Arthur (J. Robert Potter) guns down Drew to protect a local woman, however, Cobb is forced to lodge him in the rinky-dink jailhouse to protect him from the other gang members.

Cobb returns to his farm when his wife, Henrietta (Jacqueline Scott), goes into labor crisis. It is a false alarm, and leads mainly to a lament by Henrietta that the two of them have let life pass them by in settling in a dead-end place like Firecreek. Going back to town, Cobb discovers that the outlaws have lynched Arthur. Waving aside the cynicism of the storekeeper Whittier (Dean Jagger) that the town isn't worth defending, he kills Willard, Norman, and Earl in a showdown. He himself is about to be shot by Larkin when Evelyn (Inger Stevens), a bitter woman with whom the outlaw leader has been dallying, saves him by shooting the last of the gunmen.

In more than general outline, *Firecreek* bears a strong resemblance to *High Noon*. The final duel alone contains several parallels, including the number of villains (four) against the protagonist, the killing of the second one in a stable, the crucial assistance of a woman in dispatching one of the heavies, and even the arrival of a buckboard to take the wounded hero out of town after he has completed his cleaning up. Director Vincent McEveety, however, was not Fred Zinnemann; he was, in fact, a veteran of television westerns making his debut on the big screen, and it showed more than visually. Fonda's character of Larkin, in particular, was saddled throughout with the kind of theme-captioning dialogue found most frequently after television commercials for reminding viewers where they were before the interruption.

But that said, McEveety also got a performance from Stewart that matched the actor's best. Fonda noted as much when he told an interviewer a couple of years later that the director deserved to be singled out for not letting his costar "get away with" some of his tried-and-true mannerisms. In fact, despite pushing sixty during the production of *Firecreek*, Stewart constructed the role of Cobb out of borrowings that spanned most of his career, most prominently in an impassioned, Jefferson Smith-like rebuttal to the storekeeper Whittier that the town *had* to be worth fighting for. Equal to that moment were his quivering whimper of a reaction to discovering the body of the lynched stable boy, as emotionally forceful as some of his responses to cruelty in *The Man from Laramie,* and his attentiveness to the character of his wife as she tells him they have both been losers, evidence that his ability to listen as an actor was not confined to scenes with Margaret Sullavan in *The Shop Around the Corner*.

For Fonda, *Firecreek* represented his first major foray as a villain. Thanks to the decision by Warner Brothers to dump the picture directly into neighborhood theaters, however, it was not seen by too many people, making his impact all the greater shortly afterward when he played the vicious child-killer in Sergio Leone's *Once Upon a Time in the West*.

Bandolero! (20th Century-Fox – 1968)

Stewart went back for a third helping of Andrew McLaglen with *Bandolero!*, a by-the-numbers western that was cast before being written and showed it. And unlike McEveety, McLaglen did let the actor get away with a number of mannerisms.

Mace Bishop (Stewart) hears that his bandit brother, Dee (Dean Martin), and his gang are about to be hanged. He impersonates the executioner and helps them flee from the scaffolding. As soon as Sheriff Johnson (George Kennedy) leaves the town unguarded by organizing a posse after the outlaws, Mace also helps himself to the money to be found in the local bank. Shortly afterward, he again has to help out Dee and his henchmen, who have abducted the widow Maria (Raquel Welch) but gotten themselves surrounded by Johnson's posse. Once he has helped them out of the trap by creating diversionary fire, Mace joins the gang and Maria in their flight to Mexico.

Johnson does not give up. Not only is he embarrassed by having lost his prisoners and by having been duped by Mace, but he is bent on marrying Maria. Once he crosses into Mexico, however, his posse begins being picked off by *banditos*. Mace, meanwhile, has decided that he despises Dee's henchmen as much as Johnson does and tries talking his younger brother into giving up the outlaw life in favor of a ranch the two of them have always talked about owning. Dee is tempted, especially when he realizes that he and Maria are in love with one another. But the dreams of the Bishop brothers are cut short—first by their capture in an abandoned town by Johnson and his men, then by a wholesale attack by the *banditos*. In the ensuing showdown, everybody is killed except Johnson and Maria.

Bandolero! was a typical "deal" project in which the content of the film was about the least important item; or as McLaglen explains: "It was a Zanuck thing from the beginning. I was doing another picture when he called me. 'I got a six-page outline for a western titled *Mace*,' he said, 'and I figure you ought to direct it, James Lee Barrett ought to write it, and Jimmy Stewart, Dean Martin, and Raquel Welch ought to be in it. Nobody else, that's the combination I want.' Bing, bang, bing. I showed the outline to Barrett, and he said fine, he'd write it for the people Zanuck had said."

According to Raquel Welch, the same mechanical approach was pervasive during shooting in Pace, Arizona, and Del Rio, Texas. As the actress recalls, "I wouldn't say creativity was the primary concern on that picture. Barrett was there mainly because everybody said nobody could write dialogue for Jimmy like he could. As far as other things in the script were concerned, they weren't really supposed to be questioned. And with McLaglen, it was all by the book. He created a very constrained atmosphere. It was an inoffensive, nine-to-five project, with a lot of very senior people, the old John Ford gang. Very cliquish. Except for Jimmy, who'd always kind of throw out little things, I felt pretty lonely the whole shoot."

Among the "little things" Stewart threw out, Welch says, were a couple of lessons in professionalism.

Kennedy had just won the Oscar for *Cool Hand Luke*, so Jimmy was all in favor of giving him equal billing. And then when we were in Pace, the proprietor of the place where we stayed saw that he had a good thing, so he started advertising autographs and pictures with the stars. When all these people started showing up outside my trailer, I started feeling like a Disneyland ride and complained to the producer. Jimmy overheard me and said, "Don't forget, Raquel, they're the ones who buy the tickets," and then he'd go off signing these autographs and getting his picture taken alongside Joe and Betty from Ohio. It was his old studio mentality and it brought me up a little short. Was I supposed to lecture all these people on how demeaning it was for them to be standing there with their pencils and pieces of paper? Was I supposed to go charging through them as if they didn't exist? It was Jimmy who made me think about things like that, and I like to believe that I learned a little something from it.

But where *Bandolero!* was concerned, what was difficult to stop thinking about was the shoehorned casting of Stewart and Martin as brothers—a fact that even McLaglen acknowledges. "That was what

Zanuck had put together," says the director, "and Dean tried awfully hard to make it work. In the end, though, I guess it just demanded a little bit too much suspension of disbelief. Jimmy could be convincing playing the brother of a tree if he had to, but the tree would have to have something innately Stewart in it to persuade others."

The Cheyenne Social Club (National General – 1970)

The Cheyenne Social Club was the worst filming experience of Stewart's career, and not because of the picture. Halfway along into production in Santa Fe, the actor was informed that his stepson Ronald had been killed in Vietnam. Before that, he had been forced to accept that Pie, the horse to which he had developed "an almost human attachment," as Raquel Welch observed during the shooting of Bandolero!, going back over fifteen films in twenty years, no longer had enough stamina to support him. According to those on the set, Stewart might not have gotten through The Cheyenne Social Club at all without the presence of his costar Fonda.

This comedy western stars Stewart as John O'Hanlan, a cowboy who travels from Texas to Wyoming to claim a mysterious inheritance left by his recently deceased brother; he is accompanied by fellow cowpoke Harley Sullivan (Fonda). When the pair arrive in Cheyenne, they find that the inheritance is a bordello run by Jenny (Shirley Jones). The straightlaced John initially wants to convert the bordello into a saloon, but changes his mind when the men of the town start treating him with scorn and Jenny points out that she and her fellow workers will be without work. John gets into a fight and is jailed for disorderly conduct, and while he is behind bars, the outlaw Corey Bannister (Robert Wilke) beats up Jenny. John is let out of jail and goes after Bannister and, thanks to the opportune intervention of Harley, kills the thug. This brings him the admiration of the town, but also the arrival of several more Bannisters bent on avenging their dead relative. John and Harley fend off an attack on the bordello and decimate the Bannisters. But before anybody can do any celebrating, hundreds of more Bannisters are spied descending on the town. John turns the lease of the bordello over to Jenny and, accompanied by Harley, flees Cheyenne to go back to his life as a cowpoke.

Although Stewart was enthusiastic about the James Lee Barrett script for The Cheyenne Social Club from the start, Fonda was much less so, and tried to get Jack Elam to do his part instead. As Elam tells it, "Hank and

I went back a long time, and he did everything to get me that part. After it was obvious to Jimmy that Hank didn't want to do it, Jimmy started pushing for me, too. They even set up a screening of one of my pictures for Barrett and Gene Kelly, who was producing and directing. But Barrett and Kelly didn't want to hear about Stewart and Elam nohow. They wanted Stewart and Fonda."

What finally changed Fonda's mind was Barrett's building up his role with a long monologue over the opening credits. As the characters of John and Harley are shown riding from Texas to Wyoming, the latter drones on endlessly about friends, lovers, family, and dogs while his friend remains silent. Finally, with the last credit off the screen, John pulls up and asks, "You know where we are, Harley?" "Not exactly." "We're in the Wyoming Territory and you've been talkin' all the way from Texas." "Just been keepin' you company, John." "I appreciate it, Harley, but if you say another word the rest of the day, I'm gonna kill you."

As it turned out, that was the comic highlight of *The Cheyenne Social Club*, with the rest of the film depending on the easy rapport between the stars to glide over plot inconsistencies, capricious dramatic tones, and some dubious japing that simultaneously sought to be daring about its brothel setting and Disneylike about the action within it. Stewart took umbrage even at the PG rating assigned to the picture, saying that it should have been given a G for all audiences. For Kelly, the only problem with the film was a scene in which Stewart's John encounters one of the hookers in a see-through negligee. "That should have come out," the director asserted, "and Jimmy thought so, too. But National General insisted it stay, and that was a mistake." Kelly was in the minority about the number of flaws in the film. *The New York Times* summed up most critical opinion by saying that "the picture never misses a blue chance to suggest there's more going on here than meets the eye in the parlor and corridors. . . . Any bright child will be bored to death."

Once he had learned of Ronald's death, Stewart's fabled powers of concentration were almost destroyed. Many mornings, he showed up on the set haggard and bleary-eyed, admitting that he hadn't been able to sleep and had little energy to play scheduled scenes. "I knew what he was suffering," Kelly told one interviewer. "And whenever that happened, I'd either shoot around him or cancel the work for the day, and we'd all go fishing." Fonda's tack was pulling up a chair next to Stewart and immediately launching into old stories about their times together on

New York's Upper West Side or in Brentwood. "He and I had already been avoiding talk of the Vietnam war even before the tragedy," the actor recalled. "Now, I did everything I could to take his mind off it." On his better days, Stewart responded with reminiscences of his own; sometimes, he just sat silently.

Although hardly at the level of loss as his son, the actor had already gone about his work in *The Cheyenne Social Club* in a melancholy mood because of the inability of the aged Pie to handle the Santa Fe altitude. Stewart had first spotted the mount in 1949, when he had been looking for a horse for *Winchester '73*. The owner, Stevie Myers, supplied film companies with horses, but had kept Pie as her own. Although she always refused to sell him to Stewart, Myers kept the animal available for every one of his films over the next couple of decades. "I just fell in love with him," the actor admitted on one occasion. "Whenever there was a chance to mention him by name in a movie, I did so. He was a wonderful horse. Never known another like him."

Although Fonda had heard about Stewart's affection for Pie a long time before the shooting of *The Cheyenne Social Club*, it wasn't until they were working together on that picture that he saw it for himself. Noting that the horse had been corralled in Santa Fe after showing that it wasn't up to doing the film, the actor told his biographer Howard Teichmann: "After lunch each day I noticed that Stewart would slip away with an apple or a piece of watermelon or a carrot in his hand. I learned that he'd walk two or three blocks to the corral where the horses were kept. And he'd give a 'goodie' to Pie. That's when I began to realize what Pie meant to him. His boy was gone, and I couldn't do anything about that, but now seeing the expression on Jim's face when he reached for something to take to his horse—I had an idea."

The idea was to go down to the corral every Sunday morning and have the horse brought out so Fonda could sketch it. "I planned it to be a surprise for Jim. I finished the watercolor after I got home. I had it framed and gave it to Jim. He was surprised all right. He just dissolved when he saw the painting. He's got a light over it [in his library] now, like it's a shrine. Ole Pie died about ten days later."

Stewart, who afterward made sure that all visitors to his home saw the Fonda painting, also had a tombstone carved for the animal's burial spot in the Myers's corral. It says simply—HERE LIES PIE.

Fool's Parade (Columbia – 1971)

For his fourth and final collaboration with director McLaglen, Stewart turned in a saddle for a mustache and a glass eye. If the intended effect had been to make his character of Mattie Appleyard in *Fool's Parade* more aloof, even colder, the makeup additions proved valuable; but at the same time, they increased the burden on the actor's vocal delivery to suggest textures not always in the lines, and McLaglen again indulged his occasionally overripe drawls.

Appleyard is released from a West Virginia penitentiary after serving forty years for murder. He walks out with a fussbudget of a onetime bank robber, Leo Cottrill (Strother Martin), a youth who was falsely convicted of rape, Johnny Jesus (Kurt Russell), and a check for $25,000 that represents the sum of his earnings while in prison. With the check, Appleyard plans on opening a store with his companions and leading a respectable life. His plans are thwarted, however, by the crooked policeman Doc Council (George Kennedy) and Homer Grindstaff (David Huddleston), the president of the bank where the check has to be cashed. Determined to get their hands on the money, Council and Grindstaff send a killer after it. But Appleyard kills the thug and gets away.

Appleyard has little better luck with old flame Cleo (Anne Baxter), who runs a boat-bordello and who also wants his money. He ends up blowing up both Cleo and the brothel with dynamite that he left on the boat decades before. This gives him an idea for getting his money from the bank guarded by Council, and he enters the institution with dynamite wrapped around his body. Grindstaff has little choice but to cash the check under the threat, but Council doesn't give up so easily. He goes after Appleyard for a showdown, and gets himself blown up. Appleyard surrenders to the police, is turned loose by a sympathetic jury, and is free to pursue his retailing ambitions.

Fool's Parade spends most of its ninety-eight minutes in search of a tone, and never finds it. The Stewart and Martin characters are basically more mocked for their rural outlooks and accents than developed comically, while Kennedy's heavy comes across as a sadistic geek who might at any moment either slip on a banana peel or blow somebody's head off with a shotgun. Critical and commercial response to the picture was indifferent, with Stewart's glass eye drawing as much attention as his performance. He himself gave little time, at least by his standards, to promoting it. What he could not know at the time was that *Fool's Parade* would be his last opportunity to plug a big-screen effort with him as its leading man.

HOME FRONTS

ON THE THRESHOLD OF HIS SIXTIETH YEAR IN THE LATE 1960s, Stewart had more holes to deal with in his normal routine than those opened by his trundling career. His stepsons were winding up their college educations, his daughters were beginning theirs—and all four of them were out of the house on North Roxbury Drive more than in it. In 1968, he reached retirement age as a brigadier general in the Air Force Reserve and mothballed his uniform for the final time. Outings with Gloria were as likely to be for the funerals of friends and business associates as for dinner parties. And then there was what he regarded as one of the biggest holes of all: the "non-accomplishers," as he called them, who allegedly had created a void in the country with their protest demonstrations against university curricula and the war in Vietnam.

Despite his professed gratitude for Alex's heavy hand in directing him toward Princeton, Stewart did not attempt similar tactics with Ronald or Michael, and neither ended up on the New Jersey campus. On the other hand, Michael had earlier received some of the same steering toward Mercersburg from both parents as his stepfather had. "Ronnie talked them into going to Orme in Prescott, Arizona," he says. "He convinced them he didn't like schools in the East and argued that, at Orme, he'd be close to the ranch we had back then at Winecup, near Elko, Nevada. But as far as I was concerned, I was simply told I was going to Mercersburg. I never considered it a harsh thing. Mom and Dad were the hierarchy of the family, Mom had obviously liked what Dad had told her about Mercersburg, and the decision was taken."

According to McLean, he rarely encountered the kind of problems at the prep school that Stewart had in following Alex to Princeton. "There was one teacher who seemed to have some kind of a beef with me because of who my father was. 'I suppose because you have a famous father, you think you can . . . ' that kind of thing. But that lasted only about a semester, and I never had problems with him or anybody else, after that."

From Orme, Ronald went to Colorado State University, to major in business. Michael's choice was Claremont in California, where he concentrated on political science. "Princeton really came up only twice," he recalls. "The first time, it was the dean at Mercersburg, who kind of assumed that I was on Dad's trail and seemed surprised when I told him I wasn't interested. Then one night at dinner, while I was in my last year at Mercersburg, Dad asked whether I had ever considered Princeton. I told him I'd had enough of eastern schools, wanted to stay in the West, and that was the end of it. I don't know if he jumped up and down in glee at my decision, but he didn't seem particularly crushed and he never brought it up again."

By his own admission, if he had had anything to do about it, Stewart wouldn't even have had a Princeton choice to discuss with his daughters, Kelly and Judy; in fact, as a university trustee between 1958 and 1962, he had spoken out against attempts to admit women to the school. "He was against it for the same reason that I was," Lewis Van Dusen, another trustee of the period, recalls. "He liked the school the way it was. It had gotten along without coeds for generations; why fix what's not broken?"

Following the school's 1969 decision to admit women, however, Stewart beat a hasty retreat. During a 1972 visit to the campus, for instance, he acknowledged about earlier opposition of alumni to women students that "none of us had a very good argument." What has received greater circulation were remarks made to several reporters in the late 1960s that he changed his mind when informed by Gloria that both Kelly and Judy wanted to study at Princeton. "When I found that out, I had to backtrack," he declared almost ritually for a few years. But, in fact, according to his offspring, neither of the girls had ever expressed any such interest in the New Jersey university. "I chose Stanford because it was the best school I got into," comments Kelly Harcourt. "And Judy chose Lewis and Clark because she was looking for a relatively small school and because she really liked that part of the country."

Michael McLean remembers it that way, too. "We were all brought up in the West. Princeton really didn't mean to us what it meant for the people of Dad's generation back in the East. The girls felt the same way about it as Ronnie and I did. After all his years in California, I think Dad understood that, too. The question about admitting women at Princeton had nothing to do with anything."

Even before enrolling at college, Kelly and Judy had given indications of being interested in a bigger world than even that of the western part of the United States. While attending Westlake in 1964, for example, they delivered elaborate school reports dressed as Africans—Kelly speaking on the continent in the guise of a game warden, Judy made up as Cleopatra for a paper on Egypt. Eventually, Kelly would receive a B.A. from Stanford in anthropology and a Ph.D. from England's University of Cambridge in zoology before moving to East Africa to study gorilla behavior in Rwanda and Kenya for many years. After Lewis and Clark, Judy worked as a jungle guide in Nepal, then on a Tanzanian coffee plantation before a cholera epidemic persuaded her to return to California. Both have credited their parents, and the trips that Stewart and Gloria took abroad with the Kirk Johnsons in the 1950s, with developing their taste for foreign cultures. As Kelly Harcourt puts it, "Judy and I had not yet been on safari to East Africa, but we were filled with dreams about it because our parents had infected us with their enthusiasm for the experience. Even before that report I delivered on Africa while I was at Westlake, I think I was set upon the course I eventually followed. A year prior to that, for instance, I had written a 'What Do You Want To Be When You Grow Up' essay about being what I called a naturalist. We acquired a love of the outdoors and of animals from our parents before the African experience [in 1964]."

If Stewart goaded the imaginations of his children the way his parents had once aroused his, he saw nothing but destructive fantasies in the campus protests of many of their contemporaries. A supporter of Richard Nixon in the 1968 presidential campaign race, he tossed off numerous dismissals of university and street ferment in the period as representing nothing more than the actions of people who had no respect for authority, no solid information upon which to base their antagonism to Washington policy, and no achievement of their own to offer as an alternative source of trust; that is, they were "non-accomplishers." He saved some of his best heat for draft dodgers, telling one interviewer: "I hate them! I absolutely hate them! Whether right or wrong, their country was at war and their country asked them to serve, and they refused and ran away. Cowards, that's what they were."

As in millions of other families, such views were the stuff of political divisions, most conspicuously in the case of Michael McLean: "I was vehemently opposed to the war, and I took part in all the antiwar protests at Claremont. A lot of people now want to make it seem like a generational thing, but of course it was never strictly that. The parents of the woman I later married, for instance, were as opposed to the war as any of the students. It was a political division, not a generational one. Dad and Mom really didn't understand where I was coming from."

Complicating the rift further in the Stewart household was Ronald McLean's decision to answer his draft call, ultimately going into the Marines. William Draddy, a relative on the Gloria Stewart side of the family, remembers attending a going-away party for Ronald in Westchester: "You couldn't have imagined two kids more different. Michael was definitely the image of the antiwar protesters—long hair, all of that. Ron, on the other hand, was there in his very impressive Marine garb, looking spic and span, not a hair out of place, shoes gleaming like the sun. Maybe it was the Marine uniform he was wearing, but I couldn't imagine a sharper difference between brothers. They might've been poster figures for the opposite sides of the debate. And that, obviously, was the kind of lousy distinctions that war caused in families."

Both immediately before and immediately after his retirement from the Air Force Reserve, Stewart visited the war zone in Southeast Asia. On one occasion, he accompanied a bombing mission near the Cambodian border in the role of observer. His last visit, early in 1969, came as a member of a USO tour. The actor estimated later that he shook some 12,000 hands during the swing. "Some of them were so young," he told one reporter, "that they had never seen my movies. But when I introduced myself, they said, 'Oh, yeah, I've heard my mother and father say you were their favorite.' I could have done without the past tense, but that was good enough for me."

Stewart, who was accompanied by Gloria on the USO tour, also got the chance to visit with Ronald, and to take a photo of his son with his mother. He carried the somewhat fuzzy picture around with him for some years because it represented the last time he saw the boy. On June 11, about three months after the reunion, Ronald was killed while leading a five-man reconnaissance patrol in Quang Tri province; he was twenty-four.

Official word of Ronald's death was brought to North Roxbury Drive by a mixed military contingent the evening that Kelly and Judy were preparing for their graduation prom at Westlake. For his part, Michael was on the road to Arkansas where he planned to be married within three weeks. "My best man and I stopped off at a place in Arizona," he recalls, "and somebody there that we knew said to call home, that 'somebody had died.'"

Gloria knew what was coming as soon as she saw the military uniforms at her front door. Some stories at the time asserted that she thanked the death notice delegation, saw it out the door, then told her daughters to carry on with their preparations for the prom. Kelly Harcourt denies that. "Mom and Dad certainly did not insist that we go to the prom. We all stayed home together. Some of our school friends left the prom to come and be with us later on in the evening. Over the next few days we did participate in Westlake graduation events, and Mom and Dad attended our graduation ceremony. But there was no insistence on anyone's part. It just didn't occur to any of us not to carry on."

Michael McLean, who was married on schedule three weeks later, agrees that not even Ronald's death undercut "the basic outlook that we always had around the house—let's get on with life."

As far as the Stewarts were concerned, however, some people got on with it a little too casually. One culprit was the Beverly Hills Presbyterian Church, which changed the hour of the memorial service for Ronald at the last minute without bothering to inform the organist. Because nobody else had a key for the instrument, the service was carried on without the musical selections Gloria had prepared for the rite. That was all she needed to boycott the church for most of the rest of her life, with exceptions made for Judy's wedding and a couple of television specials her husband made on the premises.[7] For his part, Stewart made his displeasure known by giving his congregational allegiance for a number of months to the First Presbyterian Church of Hollywood.

No less galling to the Stewarts was a second visit to Beverly Hills by a Marine officer a few days after the news of Ronald's death. Sitting in the Roxbury Drive living room, the Pentagon representative began outlining

---

[7] Although never the ardent churchgoer Stewart had hoped for, Gloria had been a Sunday School instructor at the church for some years—mainly, according to some, because it gave her an opportunity to discuss the animals of Noah's Ark. "It was never about religion, it was animals," says actor Billy Mumy, who as a child was so taken with her classes that he repeated them rather than advancing to a higher level.

plans for publicizing the slain Marine as a hero, thereby winning propaganda points for the political approach being taken by the Nixon Administration for coping with the Vietnam War. According to Melinda Draddy and Karin Lopp, Gloria's nieces, their aunt "went into a rage" over such presumptuousness, while Stewart suddenly stood up, grabbed the officer by the elbow, and, controlling his own anger, said, "Let me take you to the door now." "Whatever he thought about the war," says Michael McLean, "it was absolute lunacy on anybody's part to think that Dad was going to allow for some kind of exploitation of Ronnie's death. Obviously, the military knew very little about him and Mom. They had a zone where some things were 'inappropriate' in the fullest sense of the word, and a pitch like that ended up directly in the center of it."

Other hustlers, including one national television network, approached Stewart with schemes for a movie about Ronald; most of them didn't even get a reply. The actor's public stance on his stepson's death has been almost ritualistic in combining a sense of personal sorrow with denials that it amounted to a tragedy. As he declared, typically, to one interviewer: "It's a loss, a terrible loss. I think about him every day. But I can't look on it as a tragedy. He was a good boy—not a very good student, but a very good boy. He tried hard, for us, to graduate from college, and when he did, he enlisted in the Marines. And on the field of battle, he conducted himself in a gallant manner. I don't think that's a tragedy."

It wasn't quite that easy, of course. For a couple of years after Ronald's death, several sources have reported, Stewart would sit by himself some distance away from the set for a movie or television show, often coming close enough to tears that a makeup man never strayed too far from him. At home, according to Mignon Winants and others, he was all but helpless to console Gloria, who cried herself to sleep for a long time. In this context, Eleanor Blair recalls one "near-conversation" with Gloria when the Stewarts returned to Indiana in 1983 for the celebrations marking the actor's seventy-fifth birthday.

Jim absolutely refused to mourn Ron or anyone else in the open way that people mourn after a death. One day, Gloria and I were alone in the kitchen and I could tell that she wanted to talk about Ron and felt that I would understand because I had lost a child, too. But she really got no further than saying that Jim hadn't let her mourn when he suddenly walked in. From that point on, we had to get along on eye signals because it was pretty obvious that he didn't like to talk about things like that. Gloria and I hardly saw eye to eye on everything, but I felt very bad for her. She must have had it very hard at home.

Gloria's friend Winants, however, thinks that's only half of the story. "Jimmy did try to console her," she says, "but he wasn't free of grief, either, and he was hardly a slambang emotional person. If she blamed him for not letting her grieve, part of it was a reflection of the fact that she wasn't one to let things hang out, either. Nobody is exactly *fair* at such times, especially to people very close. I'd have to say that on this, like so many other big and little things over the years, they didn't surprise each other at all. They knew who they were after twenty years together."

In September 1969, Ronald was posthumously awarded a Silver Star at ceremonies held on the Marine base at El Toro, California. It wasn't until considerable time after that, according to Michael McLean, that he had the feeling that the family rifts caused by the war were beginning to heal. As he tells it: "After Claremont I went to Oxford to study law, then began to teach high school in Phoenix. There was always a strain. What was ironic about it was that, while he didn't agree with me, Ronnie had empathized with my position, whereas Mom and Dad could not. We finally got around to talking about it almost four years later. They still didn't feel that I was sensitive to their point of view." The turning point? "The birth of my son Benjamin in 1973. It was their first grandchild. That's when it started healing. The idea of family is stronger than a lot of things."

COLOR CHANNELS

BETWEEN THE END OF SHOOTING *THE CHEYENNE SOCIAL Club* in the summer of 1969 and beginning production on *Fool's Parade* in September 1970, Stewart took still another shot at *Harvey*. This time the Mary Chase play was dusted off by producer T. Edward Hambleton, as a quick fix for the financial problems threatening the survival of New York's prestigious Phoenix Theater. "It was not in the least a typical

Phoenix play," acknowledges Hambleton. "But several people had told me that Stewart would always be open to an offer for doing another version of Elwood P. Dowd, and he struck me as exactly the kind of commercial tonic we needed to get back on our feet."

For Stewart, it was the right offer at the right time. Since Ronald's death, his days at home had been a trance as much as a routine, mostly centered around a morning round of golf at the Bel Air Country Club with Fred MacMurray, some weekend flying in his Super Piper Cub, and watching Gloria's beans and tomatoes grow. He himself would say that he took up Hambleton's offer mainly because he and Gloria were getting on one another's nerves at home and needed to get out. The material, of course, was hardly incidental. On several occasions since filming *Harvey* in the early 1950s, Stewart had discussed doing other productions of the comedy, even staging it in England and Australia. Most of those plans had foundered on either his film commitments or his avowed reluctance to pull the girls out of school for any extended tours or residence abroad. Now in retrospect he saw even those failed ambitions as a blessing in disguise because, as he insisted to interviewers throughout the rehearsing and performing of the Hambleton presentation, only in his sixties did he finally feel that he was "the right age" for the character of Dowd.

All that said, the actor wasn't so grateful for the opportunity to redo Dowd that he agreed as soon as Hambleton telephoned him. What unnerved him no little was an agreement that the Phoenix Theater had with the University of Michigan for staging tryouts of plays at Ann Arbor. This not only put Stewart on a collision course with his apprehensions that nobody of college age even knew who he was, but also aroused fears that his hawkish sentiments about the war in Vietnam would make him a natural target for campus protests. It was mainly because of these insecurities, people close to the production said, that he hemmed and hawed for a few weeks about the proposed casting of Alice Ghostley in the role of his sister. But he was deprived of that excuse when Helen Hayes, a Phoenix board member who had her own interest in saving the theater, agreed to step in as a costar. "Mother was essentially telling him that if nobody had ever heard of him, nobody would have heard of her, either, so at least they would be company for one another," says Hayes's son James MacArthur.

Stewart's fears proved ungrounded. Aside from the fact that the University of Michigan was far down on the list of campus protest centers, everybody knew of the actor's own family loss in the Vietnam conflict. Robert Schnitzer, who was then in charge of the theater program at Ann Arbor, recalls:

> There was absolutely no targeting of Jimmy during the student demonstrations while he was doing the play. On the contrary, the only students who came near him were the ones in the university restaurant who came up to ask for his autograph or just to say how much they liked his work. I suggested that maybe we ought to do something to discourage the autograph seekers from constantly interrupting his meals, but he wouldn't hear of it. "When they *don't* come up to me," he said, "that's when I'll start worrying." I think it was precisely because it was the period of student protests, he valued it even more than usual that kids were responding the way they were.

According to Schnitzer, the only practical problem encountered during the weeks leading up to the February 7, 1970, opening of *Harvey* was what led Stewart and Gloria to the university restaurant in the first place. "We put them up at the best hotel in Ann Arbor. But after a day or so, Jimmy came up to me and said that he didn't like the food at the hotel restaurant, that it was too rich and fancy. He asked where he could eat on campus, and from that point on he and Gloria ate at the university restaurant every single meal."

At both Ann Arbor and at the Phoenix in New York, Stewart won the raves for Elwood P. Dowd that neither he nor critics had thought he had merited as Frank Fay's replacement in the late 1940s and that he had been edgy about claiming for his Oscar-nominated performance in the 1951 motion picture. As Clive Barnes put it in *The New York Times*: "His garrulous, genial presence is a delight. You feel that apart from Harvey himself, there is no one that you would rather encounter in your favorite neighborhood bar." For Stewart himself, the key was that he had finally dispersed all notions of Dowd as a crazy man. As he told *Cue* magazine shortly after the play's opening at the Phoenix in March 1970: "You've got to convince the audience that this big rabbit is your friend, and that the whole idea is wonderful. Elwood can't be a screwball or an imbecile. You have to convince the audience that, if they had rabbits of their own, it would be kind of nice!"

Stewart's triumph was repeated again in 1975 in London, when an

Alexander Cohen production of *Harvey* realized in part the actor's years-long ambition of bringing the comedy to "English-speaking countries around the world." The London *Times*, for one, found it "a tribute to Mr. Stewart's timing that even the most predictable lines exert a comic shock." Before that in 1972, there had also been a television production under the aegis of the Hallmark Hall of Fame. Stewart was less satisfied with that outing, returning to his old argument that the play belonged only on the stage, that television, as much as film, tended to pose the kind of literal demands on invisible rabbits that the theater did not have to worry about. But by then, he had also been licking a few other wounds inflicted by the small screen.

Since doing Ronald Reagan a favor by appearing on *The G. E. Theater*'s 1955 production of *The Windmill*, Stewart had dabbled in television on an almost annual basis. There had been a number of indifferent dramas, such as John Ford's *Flashing Spikes* for the Alcoa company in 1962, and, worse than that, a syndicated celebrity quiz show at the end of the 1960s called *The Movie Game*. In fact, his home-screen forays might have been written off as disaster altogether if not for the yearly guest shots he had done for friend and neighbor Jack Benny. Usually accompanied by Gloria, Stewart took over the role that Ronald Colman had played for many years on Benny's radio show—that of the famous actor in Beverly Hills who was always scheming with his wife to get away from the comedian and his miserly ways, but who inevitably ended up in his unwanted company anyway. The sketches were typically of the order of one in which the insincere Benny makes a move for a restaurant check, has Stewart tell him that it would make him "feel better" if he could pay, and then withdraws his hand in relief, with the comeback: "Well, if it's a question of your health. . . . "

Not only Stewart, but Gloria, won regular plaudits for appearing as themselves with Benny. Beyond that, the actor's guest shots helped to persuade television executives of all three major networks that Stewart would make an ideal star for a weekly comedy series; feeding this hunch were the results of a string of celebrity studies in the late 1960s that named him consistently with John Wayne and Bob Hope as the most popular performers among heads of families, then perceived by Madison Avenue as its most important target audience. As it turned out, it was NBC, and producer-director-writer Hal Kanter, who got to him first. Kanter, who had known Stewart since the Bing Crosby radio programs after the war, who had done the screenplay for *Dear Brigitte*, and who had also supplied him with material for special public occasions, such as accepting Gary Cooper's Oscar in 1960, recalls:

> They came to me and asked if I had a regular television idea for Stewart. I said no, but give me five minutes. Then we had a meeting. The pitch was that he was the best comedy actor in the business, so let's stop wasting all this time and get on with it. How do you think he'll photograph, they asked me. He was pretty frail looking at the time, so I said seventy-three. They were shocked. But he's still the only sixty-three-year-old Jimmy Stewart around, I said, so we'll pay Makeup extra. No question they were scared, though. Fortunately, just the idea of the show got it sold over in Japan before it was ever on the air in the United States.

What became known as *The Jimmy Stewart Show* went through a lot more labor pains than the star's physical appearance, however. One big question was the female lead, the middle-aged wife of Stewart's college professor character. The actor's proposal was that Gloria be tested for the part; she had been anything but an embarrassment with Jack Benny, displaying surprising professional poise in long scenes heavy on dialogue. Not to be discounted, either, was Stewart's attitude when it came to television—that it was a medium that would never be quite as serious as motion pictures and could therefore accommodate the kind of lark he was proposing. But what weighed in as much as any other factor, according to friends of the family, was Stewart's desire to help Gloria find a productive outlet for dealing with a devastating series of personal losses that she kept bottled up within her; within roughly fifteen months around the death of her son in Vietnam, in fact, she also lost her mother, her sister, and her brother. "That was a monstrous testing time for her," Leonard Gershe recalls, "and since she was Gloria, she was going to take all the tests by herself."

But as far as Kanter and NBC were concerned, there were other priorities besides work therapy. "It was a very delicate thing," the producer-director says. "On the one hand, we did tons of tests of actresses, were talking to people like Vera Miles and Kim Hunter. Then Jimmy would insist that I look at movies of Gloria, which were really just home movies. Finally, one day I said to him, 'Jim, have you really thought this through? You're going to be getting up every morning with Gloria, you're going to be putting in very long days on a soundstage with Gloria, and then you're going to go home with Gloria. And the two of you are going to be together like that for a whole season.' And he just looked at me as though that had never occurred to him before."

The whole question turned out to be academic when NBC refused to consider Gloria for the show, opting finally for Julie Adams, who had appeared with Stewart two decades earlier in *Bend of the River*. Worse, in Kanter's view, the network wasn't diplomatic about announcing its decision. "There was something a little brusque in the way they did it, and Jimmy didn't forget it. After our first season was over and the network was on the fence about a renewal, he only had to lift his finger to push them over to a yes. But he wouldn't do it. I'm convinced that letting the show die was his way of getting even for the brusque dismissal of Gloria."

For once, the critics were on the side of the network. Certainly, there was no new series pasted harder during the 1971–72 television season. While Stewart talked about "traditional family values in a comic setting," *Variety* referred to the show's premise of an anthropology professor's travails with an extended family as *Life with Grandpa* and *The New York Times* described it as "a show heavy with integrity—and heavier with banality and boredom." What made the twenty-four, thirty-minute episodes an even easier target than usual was their blithe depiction of campus life as a sequence of *My Three Sons* misunderstandings in a period of nationwide political unrest at universities. Ellen Geer, who played Stewart's daughter on the show, says the atmosphere was equally unreal on the studio set. Geer, whose father Will Geer appeared with Stewart in several films, recalls:

> It could be eerie, even mind-boggling. Kanter, for instance, came up to me and John McGiver one day and said we were never to talk about politics or what was going on in the country while we were on the set. McGiver, who'd been around forever, couldn't believe what he was hearing, but the fact is that the two of us always had to run off into a corner and whisper if we wanted to talk about the latest debacle from Vietnam or Cambodia or Washington. I don't think that order came from Jimmy, it was just Kanter and the network trying to keep a calm set. But it could really give you the creeps to read something in the paper, walk onto that set, and then see, as did happen one day, Jimmy standing around with a lot of generals from the Air Force. It was like being on another planet.

Both Geer and Julie Adams also sensed that Stewart was fighting a losing battle throughout production to find enthusiasm for the medium he had agreed to work in. Geer: "We rehearsed three or four days, then shot an episode in two. The whole thing moved far too fast for him. He wasn't used to television's addiction for taking shortcuts. About the only thing that changed in his attitude as we went along was his gradual loss of bafflement. But he never accepted the production process, not in any real way."

"I always thought he should have been perfect for the medium," says Adams, "but that was the wrong vehicle for him. It was absolutely too soft, not at all challenging. It was totally dependent on his charm, and the further we went along, the less he seemed to want to be charming about all the realities of television." Kanter goes further than that, saying that Stewart's behavior on the show cost him a "personal hero." Triggering most of the problems, according to the producer-director, was the actor's right of approval for scripts and casting. "On one show, he played the double role of his professor character and his grandfather. The script referred to the grandfather character as being illiterate, mean, and a coward. Jimmy called a halt to everything. 'He can be illiterate and mean,' he says to me, 'but he can't be a coward. My grandfather just couldn't ever be a coward.' He wasn't joking, either. He took it as though we were talking about Jimmy Stewart's grandfather, not this TV character's grandfather. Everything could get very personal with him, and in very eerie ways."

But the worst episode, the one that Kanter says "undermined [his] respect" for Stewart, revolved around the scheduled casting of black actor Hal Williams for a role in one of the episodes. As Kanter tells it:

One day somebody comes running into my office and says you better get down to see Jimmy, he is absolutely furious. I go down to his dressing room, and he's really hot. The problem was he had just found out that we were casting Hal Williams and he related that to a script for a show in which there was a cop lashing into the professor character. "Blacks are bossing white people all over the country," he says to me angrily, "and now we're going to have the same damn thing on prime time television? A black is going to be lecturing me with millions of people watching? No way. I get casting approval and Williams is out." I couldn't believe it. Aside from everything else, he'd screwed up the shows, because Williams had been hired to play an FBI agent on another episode. But his anger about the thing was frightening. He acted chagrined when I told him about the mixup he'd made, but both of us knew that he'd let one cat out of the bag that he would have preferred not to. He didn't have an easy relationship with blacks even as fictional characters.

Others had seen the cat at least in the bag for some time. One was John Ford, who had picked on race as Stewart's Achilles heel during the making of *The Man Who Shot Liberty Valance*. Readers of interviews over the years might also have been struck by everything from his descriptions of the antics of "dusky" housekeepers before World War II, to his complaints in the 1960s and 1970s that motion pictures had fallen under the influence of special interest audiences, among them "teenagers and colored people." Lucille Gipson, an extra cooking and serving hand in the Stewart household in Indiana on the actor's visits home, finds none of this surprising. "The biggest difference between Jimmy and his father on a lot of things was their style," Gipson says. "Jimmy, you'd call a gentleman, Alex, he wasn't. The old man never thought twice about talking about 'niggers.' One time, he was told his regular woman couldn't come to work for a while because her husband had bone cancer and was dying. 'We can't have that nigger back here,' I hear him telling his wife, being all insulted because this man's dying had interfered with his pot roast or something. Jimmy, on the other hand, he would never use words like that. But he would never come near us, either. One time he even donated some money to help save our Baptist church in Indiana after he heard me talking about it, and he sent Alex into the kitchen to ask how much was needed. He *hated* the idea of having to say more than a hello directly to us. Alex and Gloria were kind of messengers whenever he had something to say to us. He didn't know how to act with black people, like it was something special he was afraid of not being able to do right, so better stay away from us altogether."

Beverly Hills friend Leonard Gershe admits to having reached a similar conclusion. "I don't think there's any question that Jimmy was uncomfortable with black people," says Gershe. "But I wouldn't lay it all on Indiana, either. This is Beverly Hills, U.S.A. It is possible to go to dinner parties for years and, except for maybe Greg Peck's home, never run into a black person, even the rich ones like Sidney Poitier and Quincy Jones. When you consider that Jimmy has spent almost his entire life in either Indiana or Beverly Hills, and is of a certain generation, you're not talking about someone who figures to be particularly sensitive to race. Like a lot of people with his mentality, any kind of militancy, like the civil rights demonstrations in the 1960s, made him very uneasy, were just another threat to the way he was used to living, like admitting women to Princeton."

As for Stewart himself, he has generally deflected the reasons for the failure of *The Jimmy Stewart Show*. At his most sardonic, he has blamed the fiasco on golfing partner MacMurray, whose own series *My Three Sons* had made him a rich man while leaving him most of the year to walk around country club greens. "What I didn't realize," Stewart has said, "was that the networks wised up after giving Fred a contract that allowed him to work only thirteen weeks a year. They saw me coming." On other occasions, he has blamed his own production control, as when he told one interviewer: "The trouble was, I had too much authority. And I made too many errors. I was given approval of all the characters, the scripts, the shooting schedules. It just didn't work. People should stick to what they do well. I'm an actor. Someone else should have been calling the shots."

On the other hand, he has never conceded that the actual tone and content of the show might have been its undoing.[8]

Despite the debacle of *The Jimmy Stewart Show* and his ambivalent feelings about the subsequent Hallmark production of *Harvey*, the actor was tempted back to television early in 1973 for the ninety-minute mystery, *Hawkins on Murder*. Reuniting him with the kind of astute, folksy character he had played in *Anatomy of a Murder*, *Hawkins on Murder* was aired by CBS partly for testing viewer taste for a limited-run series. Reaction proved positive enough for seven more installments to be produced and broadcast on the network through the following spring. Stewart snared the lead role only after producer-writer David Karp had pulled back from an earlier partnership with Andy Griffith. "Griffith wanted to control everything, reduce me to an employee," Karp recalls. "So I went to MGM and asked for a young Jimmy Stewart, and they gave me the original."

According to Karp, and others connected to the series, Stewart's main problems during the *Hawkins* shoots had to do with his age. One such difficulty stemmed from his serious loss of hearing: "He was very vain

---

[8] Stewart's commitment to the show also prevented him from playing Sam the Lion in Peter Bogdanovich's *The Last Picture Show*. Ben Johnson won an Oscar for the role.

about wearing a hearing aid, wouldn't hear of it, though he needed one badly. For a time, everybody pretended not to notice. But then Lew Ayres came on as a guest on one of the shows and was astonished to see him lip reading for his cues. He really gave Jimmy a lecture about how he shouldn't be ashamed of something that would help him not only hear better, but work better with his fellow actors. I think it was that subtle appeal to his professionalism that got to him. A little while after Ayres went after him, Jimmy was walking around telling everybody what a great invention a hearing aid was."

Another constant problem was the volume of dialogue. "I have to do more damn talking in this thing than I ever did in the movies," Karp remembers the actor complaining to him regularly. "It became a ritual, really. And I'd always say to him that he was playing an attorney so he could hardly do the thing in sign language. And I'd also keep offering to have his speeches put on cue cards, to which he usually replied, 'But I can't see the goddam things!' And of course, after all that was said and done, he knew the monologues perfectly."

For series costar Mayf Nutter, however, the problem wasn't the monologues per se. "Jimmy came in to my trailer one day looking very worried," Nutter recalls, "and he asks me how I go about memorizing this ton of dialogue. And like this is Jimmy Stewart who's memorized lines for forty years and he's asking *me*! Well, I tell him the routine I go through, and he's nodding along, listening intently to every word, though he had to have heard it all a million times. Only when I'm finished does he finally admit what's troubling him about the script. 'It's not the lines, Mayf,' he exclaims in that very high-pitched voice of his, 'it's these damn names! Henry, McCoy, Fletcher, Billings, Mason. McCoy did this to Billings, but Billings was with Fletcher thinking about Mason at the time! I can't keep so many damn names straight!' It was the plottiness— if you can use that word—of the script that was getting him down. All the usual third-person reference stuff that gets in the way of being able to focus on a character."

In the end, however, neither the hearing nor memorizing obstacles conditioned the production of *Hawkins* for Stewart as much as being back within what had become a shell of his former studio, MGM. When he wasn't needed for work, he took to wandering around on the sets of old Judy Garland and Clark Gable pictures that had been allowed to deteriorate or been ransacked for prop pieces over the years. The result was a continual wistfulness relieved only by his efforts to provide an informal history of their surroundings to Nutter.

I would've listened anyway, but it was obviously very important to him to point out all these things to me. And sometimes he could maintain a sense of humor about it. One day, for instance, we were shooting a scene on what had once been the set for *The Philadelphia Story*. We're just sitting together in this car waiting for the director to give us a signal for a drive-up. In the meantime, a hundred things go wrong. Lights are spitting, props are falling all over. He'd tell me about *The Philadelphia Story*, we'd get the signal to do the drive-up, we'd do it, another technical foul-up of some kind, and back to the starting gate again. Finally, Jimmy ran out of history just as the director said hit it again. I step on the gas, Jimmy glances around at the set in this kind of mock saintly way, and says: "Then, having seen where Mister Grant and Miss Hepburn once worked, Jimmy and Mayf drive off into the sunset." And that is exactly what we did—drove right on out through the main gate and home. As far as he was concerned, they'd had enough opportunities to shoot a simple scene. And nobody said a word the next day.

On more than one occasion during the production of *Hawkins*, Stewart told his fellow workers that the ideal actress for a woman's role in one of the scripts would have been Margaret Sullavan. "He'd light up at the very thought," says producer-writer Karp. " 'Want to know who could really do this well?' he'd ask. 'Maggie Sullavan. I tell you, it would have been a great part for her.' You didn't have to know the whole story to see this was somebody he had never gotten over."

As for *Hawkins* itself, it was a darker version of the *Matlock* series that Andy Griffith, the original choice for the role of Billy Jim Hawkins, popularized a few years later. With such strong performers as Julie Harris and Bonnie Bedelia guesting on each episode, it featured exceptionally long dialogue scenes with the Stewart character in plots that kept the producers in constant wrangles with the CBS censors. Euthanasia and gay love among the wealthy in southern California were just two of the story triggers. "Jimmy never worried about the themes," says Karp. "As long as the stories made sense to him, he trusted me. But our executive producer Norman Felton was always having to threaten the censors that CBS was going to have a big hole in its schedule if they kept harassing us about the most idiotic things. No question, it also helped to have Jimmy and his image saying what we were doing was okay."

Most critics were enthusiastic about Stewart's appearances in *Hawkins*, even those who constantly compared them to his *Anatomy of a Murder* character and those who found his folksy banter with costar Strother Martin terminally cute. The Hollywood Foreign Press Club was another booster, giving him Best Actor honors for the year among television performers. For all that, he called it quits after a season, saying that he was worn down by the production schedule. There was also a sense, however, that he might have done another season if CBS hadn't repeatedly juggled the program on its schedule to accommodate special events, at one point keeping it off the air for nine weeks. It was the kind of treatment Stewart hadn't received at MGM since immediately after making *The Murder Man* forty years earlier.

VIII
FINAL FLIGHTS

GROUNDINGS

WHILE HE WAS WORKING ON THE *HAWKINS* television series in 1973, Stewart was informed of the death of John Ford. He attended funeral services for the director a couple of days later, then returned to the set for what costar Mayf Nutter describes as "probably the single worst day" in the production of the shows. "If he wasn't being just gloomy," recalls Nutter, "he was being terribly short-tempered with everybody. Nobody— the director, other actors, some crew people—could do anything right. Finally, he got into such a state about some trivial thing that even he heard how badly he was carrying on. And that's when he looked at me and he said, 'Mayf, what am I supposed to do? All my friends are dying, and I haven't really made any new ones in thirty years!' "

In fact, Ford's death came around the midpoint of a ravaging period for people particularly close to the actor. The first to go, in 1971, was Leland Hayward. A year later, it was restaurant owner Dave Chasen, whom Stewart liked to say had been the only inhabitant of Hollywood that his father had liked. A year after that, in 1973, it was Bill Grady. In 1974 it was Jack Benny, and in 1976 it was both Rosalind Russell, the only former Stewart costar who had been a regular visitor to North Roxbury Drive, and Guy Gadbois, his longtime business manager and partner. More often than not, the actor was called on at these funerals to deliver the eulogy or serve as a pallbearer. And even that wasn't all of it, since between 1972 and 1977, he also lost both of his younger sisters.

If Bessie Stewart always took second billing to Alex when Stewart began reminiscing about his family, his sisters Mary (or Dotie, as friends called her) and Virginia rarely gained more than walk-on mention. The initial reason for this was the fall of years between them: With Dotie four years younger and Virginia six, they had impressed the teenage boy living in Indiana simply as pests a good amount of the time, or, when Alex and Bessie took the odd evening out, as baby-sitting charges. Their main time together away from Vinegar Hill was in New York City in the 1930s, when Stewart had been trying to make it as an actor. In a piece she wrote for *Coronet* magazine some years later, Virginia, then a freshman at Vassar, described a "mournful" Thanksgiving meal with her brother in a midtown restaurant once it became obvious that *Carry Nation* was going to be a flop. In the *Coronet* article, Virginia also depicted Stewart as being leery of any effusive praise for his performance, falling back on a family code phrase at one point to mock her with the warning "not to get sensitive."

It was hardly the only time that Virginia received such a warning, seriously or not, and surviving friends and acquaintances in Indiana claim that she would have been better off if she had heeded it more than she did. "Ginnie was always a dreamer," says longtime friend Elizabeth Simpson, "but not the aggressive kind who would show you this hard tenacity. She not only looked a lot like her brother, but was easy-going like he was, and in her case that was a bad combination. She didn't get beyond freshman year at Vassar, and whatever the academic record said, the fundamental reason was her distractedness. First and last, she was a lovely dreamer."

Eleanor Blair agrees. "Ginnie was really quite beautiful in a remote sort of way. She was also Bessie's favorite, and her mother really spoiled her. She was going to be a writer, she always said, and that seemed good enough for Bessie to indulge her. Ginnie really didn't have Jimmy's kind of self-discipline for that kind of a career, though." As it turned out, Virginia's most noted piece of writing was the *Coronet* article, entitled "My Brother Becomes a Star," and published in February 1940. Much of the piece is taken up with her expressions of disappointment that Stewart never lived up to his promise to write her in detail from California about the lives of Hollywood stars; instead, she said, his letters to Indiana seldom contained more than weather reports or updates on his efforts to put on weight. The youngest of the three Stewarts financed her writing aspirations for some years by working as an editorial assistant at the Scribner publishing house in Manhattan. In June 1943, she married designer Alexis Alexander Tiranoff. Although the wedding took place in Indiana, that was one of the few things about it that was to prove agreeable to Alex, Stewart, or many of the people in town.

"A Russian, of course," Elizabeth Simpson says, not disguising her disapproval even a half-century later. "That fit perfectly into Ginnie's image of the great romance."

The recurrent description by Stewart family members and Indiana friends for Tiranoff has been "lightweight." "That's the word that comes to me right away," says John D. Stewart. "Something of a happy-go-lucky lightweight who always seemed to have trouble in finding a job and who was really like oil and water with the Vinegar Hill Stewarts. There were some people in Indiana who even saw him as a fortune hunter, but I don't think that was true at all. They said the same thing about Alex's second wife. Any outsider was obviously going to have to hear that accusation. What it came down to was that Ginnie was always a little flaky and Tiranoff fit the bill."

If Tiranoff's ethnic background and unstable job record weren't enough to make Alex cool about accepting him as his son-in-law, there was always the religious factor. As Bill Moorhead recalls: "When Ginnie and Tiranoff had their first child, they had it baptized in the rites of his religion, not the Presbyterian. That really irritated Alex. It was his first grandchild, and there was no way, from his viewpoint, that it should be anything but Presbyterian. What was Ginnie thinking about that she would let that happen, that kind of thing. In a way, I think that bothered Alex even more than Gloria not being a churchgoer, although it was probably six of one and half a dozen of the other."

Lucille Gipson also draws a comparison between the treatment of Tiranoff and Gloria during visits to Vinegar Hill. According to Gipson, "neither one of them was ever all that popular with Alex, but Gloria was a strong personality who didn't care what he had to say, while the Russian was always walking around like he was afraid of breaking something. When Gloria wanted to get away from Alex, she'd come into the kitchen and talk with us. You always had the feeling that she'd promised Jimmy ahead of time to be on good behavior and she was bursting to keep her word. The Russian, though, he'd go down to the basement and kind of stay there by himself when it wasn't meal time. And none of the others seemed to miss him."

"I think it would be a little extreme to say that the family ostracized Tiranoff," says Elizabeth Simpson, "but he certainly wasn't any kind of favorite son. More like both sides were very uneasy with each other.

There was also a lot of annoyance, it seemed to me sometimes, with the two daughters Ginnie and Tiranoff had. It wasn't anything you could put your finger on, or even deny was warranted in some cases, but it was something you noticed."

In that context, Gipson remembers a day when one of the Tiranoff girls threw up in Stewart's car. "He always seemed to have a shorter temper with that family than with anybody else. When one of the nieces got sick in the car, he really went at it a long time. It was like no child had ever done something like that before. It was his sister's fault, it was the Russian's fault. Why couldn't they have brought her up better? Why hadn't they been watching how much she'd eaten before getting into the car? That sort of thing."

By all odds, however, the most shriveling scene took place before Virginia's funeral in Indiana in April 1972. The atmosphere had already been thickened more than usual by some medical opinion that the strangulated hernia that had killed Virginia would not have been fatal if she had taken care of it as soon as it had been discovered and not postponed treatment because of preparations under way for the wedding of one of her daughters. This led to "a kind of feeling of blame in the air," remembers Gipson, adding, "It wasn't a smart thing for the mother to do, obviously, but mothers aren't always smart if it's about their children. But there was this one point that the Russian just broke down in tears with a whole lot of people around, and Jimmy got livid. 'Who are you to start crying with all these people to see you?' he started saying. 'Remember where you are. You want to do that, do it in private.' Like the man hadn't been married to the woman, hadn't lost a wife. And the Russian, he didn't answer him, just tried to control himself. It was a terrible thing."

In contrast to her younger sister, Dotie Stewart played by Alex's rules for the most part, and received almost as much recognition from her father as her brother did. Attracted to art and illustration at an early age, she, too, moved to New York, where, among other things, she worked in the graphics department of *Mademoiselle* magazine. During World War II, some of her drawings were used as nationwide posters by the American Red Cross—a fact that Alex celebrated by hanging samples in the hardware store. An entire room of The Big Warehouse was eventually festooned with her work, including some nude studies that the old man liked to point out to customers when he was beginning to feel oppressed by questions about the actor in the family. "Dotie wasn't at all as physically attractive as Ginnie," says Eleanor Blair. "In fact, had a bad jaw that required a major operation. But Alex was as proud of her, I think, as he was of Jimmy."

Elizabeth Simpson thinks that was inevitable. "In every way, she was close to Alex's idea of what an imaginative woman ought to be, certainly closer than Ginnie. Dotie was a curious combination, really. She was gifted—very gifted—artistically, and still also down to earth. Very responsible, head on her shoulders, none of Ginnie's dreaminess. There were really a lot of the same qualities in her as there were in Jimmy. It always seemed ironic to me that the painter in the family, with all those bohemian preconceptions we have of painters, should be so much more steadfast than her sister was."

It didn't hurt Dotie's standing with Alex, either, when she married Robert Moorehead Perry, her brother's former classmate and fellow accordionist at Princeton, in March 1944. After teaching at New York University for a few years, Perry became a minister in the Bucks County district of Pennsylvania. The couple eventually had four children. Dotie Stewart Perry succumbed to cancer in June 1977.

Even before Dotie's death, Stewart had been firing off some uncharacteristic admissions that it had become impossible for him to ignore his own advanced age. Interviewed for the December-January 1976–77 issue of *Modern Maturity*, for instance, he clearly saw little reason to sugarcoat the truth for the periodical's largely elderly readership in declaring: "I'm 68 years old and I feel every goddam day of it. I don't feel young. I feel old. And I'm resigned to it. I'm not fighting it. People get old, and that's all there is to it."

Adding to his agitation in the period was his hearing disability; hearing aid or not, the impairment was not merely the source of small daily frustrations, but posed an ever-encroaching deadline for curtailing his recreational flying on weekends.[1] With increasing frequency, he depended on others to run interference for him in potentially embarrassing situations. One who took on this task was his longtime stand-in Ted Mapes, who, prior to the start of a film, made sure to speak

---

[1] Stewart finally grounded himself for good in 1981. "It got so that I couldn't understand communications from the tower," he confessed. "I would have to have them repeat everything. Then I tried putting a loudspeaker in the plane. Only trouble was, they could hear me all over the airport, but I couldn't understand a thing. So I had to give it up." When he called it quits, the actor had been flying for more than forty-five years.

with actors who hadn't worked with Stewart before, his message being that they enunciate very clearly.

Even more important was Gloria, who started accompanying her husband with more regularity on his professional assignments. Even with the 1970 revival of *Harvey* at the University of Michigan, she struck some people as being as much of a sentry as a wife. "He did nothing without her," recalls Marilyn Miller, the general manager of the American Theater Wing and then the company manager of the Phoenix Theater production. "She was the one we had to go to for clearing anything. She was always gracious, but it was understood that she was the keeper of the keys and that she wasn't going to let Jimmy be bothered unless it was absolutely necessary." Stewart's old architecture classmate at Princeton, Peter Schwed, came away with the same impression from university reunion dinners. "She was always very protective of him," says Schwed. "She practically kept him in a cage, away from the idolaters, away from what she regarded as unnecessary conversation. She was always gracious, though. The right combination of pleasantness and firmness."

Still, Stewart was hardly ready to put a blanket on his legs and watch the world go by. In 1976, he campaigned extensively in California for Reagan in the presidential primaries, especially visiting shopping malls and airports. He and Gloria also continued their traveling—visiting Kelly in Africa, attending her 1977 marriage in London to University of Cambridge teacher Alexander Harcourt, going to San Francisco periodically to see the equally married Judy, and staying with Michael and his family in Phoenix. During his numerous trips to Africa, he also honed his decades-old hobby of photography, exchanging rifles for cameras and, under the influence of his wife and daughter, becoming more of a conservationist. The ventures into the Rwanda highland gorilla country allowed him to leaven his nagging worries about his age with some humor. As he told a reporter, "There are only 220 of them left, but I'm getting too old for 11,000 feet and a bunch of gorillas. Kelly communicates with them nicely. But a hairy thing, with long arms that pounds its chest and weighs 800 pounds, well, I simply couldn't quite agree with that. Once I was focusing my camera near a bush when, about six feet away, I noticed this gorilla. He wasn't doing much. Just staring. And I kind of stared back. But it's a good thing I had fast film. It caught the darn thing despite the fact that my hands were shaking."

At home, Gloria kept up an evening social schedule that gave him little time to sit around and fret. Friends say that left to his own devices, Stewart probably would have pulled himself in with the sidewalks in the evening. Greg Paul, the chief operating officer of Castle Rock Entertainment and a Stewart financial counselor since the death of Guy Gadbois, thinks that's somewhat inevitable. "Age differences seem to count the most when you're a kid and when you're really starting to get up there. By the 1970s and 1980s, the eleven or twelve years between Jimmy and Gloria began to kick in. Not so much because of their own relationship, as because of their different friends. Hers were relatively younger and still around for the most part, but his were just about all gone, so, more often than not, they went to the houses of people closer to her than to him."

According to Paul, however, any initial resistance that the actor might have put up against going out regularly was usually gone by the time he reached his destination. "Once he was out there, he enjoyed himself. He was rarely left alone. He'd start to tell some story, and he told it so slowly, in that way of his, that by the time he got to the end, he usually had most of the people in the room standing around him."

Stewart himself, however, has admitted to withdrawing to a corner by himself at even the most crowded affairs, while Gloria danced or kept up her end of the social chitchat. He has also denied that it was because he was feeling melancholy. "At a party sometimes I sit back in a chair, all by myself, and don't quite join in as much as I should. But sometimes being part of a crowd can be the loneliest place of all. . . . Being alone, by yourself, has nothing to do with loneliness. A loner isn't necessarily a lonely person—the feeling you're left out of something and you have no one to turn to. The core of all that is rejection. And that's why I think real loneliness is more like a chronic condition and not at all related to how social a person you are."

For both good reasons and bad, he would refer back to that distinction several times in the 1980s and 1990s.

SPECIAL APPEARANCES

IN HIS TWILIGHT AS A PERFORMER, STEWART OWED HIS two big moments to television rather than to the movies. Compounding the irony, one of the efforts turned out to be the worst disappointment of his career, while the other represented him as a poet instead of as an actor. On theater screens, he wound down his more than forty years in the business largely by contributing cameos to films that sought to make up in recognizable names what they couldn't claim in other areas. By way of compensation, no public figure in the entertainment industry received as many honors as Stewart did in the 1980s, with governments, cultural institutions, film festivals, humanitarian and charity organizations, and universities, both in the United States and abroad, staging one kind of tribute or another. The award-bestowing ceremonies and retrospectives sometimes showed an actor frail to an apparent point of collapse, but that proved to be deceiving—as much to his own family as to those giving him standing ovations for his life's work.

Following *Fool's Parade* in 1971, Stewart next went before the movie cameras in 1974, as one of the on-screen narrators for *That's Entertainment*, MGM's commercially successful rehash of scenes from some of the studio's 100 musicals. The appearance mainly gave him a chance to mock his own singing in *Born to Dance*. Then came:

The Shootist (Warner Brothers – 1976)

John Wayne's swan song, *The Shootist* gave Stewart only a couple of scenes as the doctor who has to inform the gunfighter-protagonist (Wayne) that he is dying of cancer. After turning down several meatier roles in other projects, he agreed to do the cameo only when Wayne specifically requested him. His short time on the set of *The Shootist* proved to be trying. The bad acoustics of the enormous, hollow sound-stages only worsened his hearing difficulties, and he stayed by himself most of the time. He and Wayne muffed their lines so often in the main scene between them that director Don Siegel accused them of not trying hard enough. Wayne's rejoinder was a variation on an old John Ford line, advising the director that "if you'd like the scene done better, you'd better get a couple of better actors." Later on, the star told friends that Stewart had known his lines, but hadn't been able to hear his cues; that was what had triggered his own fumbling, he said.

Airport '77 (Universal – 1977)

The third in the series of similarly titled air-catastrophe films, *Airport '77* saw Stewart as a billionaire who anxiously waits for the United States

Navy to pull his luxury jet up from the bottom of the ocean to save the passengers and crew members still alive inside. His character chiefly has to look admiring as Navy officers explain to him how they will use balloons to float the craft and worried when the balloons take an extra second or two to inflate.

Despite his brief appearance in a picture that was generally written off as a dramatic sausage, the actor did a favor for Universal executive Lew Wasserman by helping to promote it. Asked why he was extending his association with the film, his rote reply was on the order of "nobody starts out to make a bad picture," after which he returned to his familiar stories about Indiana and Hollywood.

The Big Sleep (Winkast/ITC – 1978)

A remake of the popular Humphrey Bogart mystery made immediately after World War II, with the location switched from the United States to England, *The Big Sleep* gave Stewart two scenes as the superwealthy General Guy Sternwood who hires the private detective Philip Marlowe (Robert Mitchum) to unmask a blackmailer. As cursory as the scenes might have been, the actor elevates the first of them with a grimly accurate old man's snicker to a crack by Mitchum's detective that one of the general's wild daughters has just tried to sit on his lap even though "I was standing at the time."

Mitchum admits to having been taken aback by Stewart's physical appearance. "The picture was all about corpses," he says, "but Jimmy looked deader than any of them."

The Magic of Lassie (Lassie Productions – 1981)

The actor appeared relatively more frequently in *The Magic of Lassie*, as a vineyard owner who strives to reunite the collie of the title with his grand-daughter. He also sang a couple of songs. Overall, however, he accurately described his role as "a grouchy old grandfather . . . who stands around in the background."

Stewart insisted that he got involved in *The Magic of Lassie* because he shared its G-rated "moral values," as opposed to "so many violent, depressing pictures around that don't give audiences a choice when they want to go to the movies." Few people took him up on his alternative, and the critical reaction was tepid, when not condescending.

The Green Horizon (Sanrio Communications – 1981)

The most bizarre big-screen project of Stewart's career, *The Green Horizon* was shot by a Japanese company on a Kenyan game reserve during a visit there by the actor and Gloria. He has no more than a handful of lines in the never-defined role of The Old Man, a veteran of the African wilds who hates cities and loves animals. More often than not, The Old Man and the other characters are shown gazing off into *Speed*-like back projections of floods, fires, and stampedes. The surrounding cast appears to have been drafted from a bad community theater.

The Green Horizon was shown once on cable television in the United States in 1981, then dumped into video stores. Asked why he had agreed to be in such an amateurish project, Stewart said that he had been "hoping to get the wildlife conservation idea through the back door."

As it turned out, the Japanese production would have been the actor's last working association with a theatrical feature if not for the voice he gave to the character of Wylie Burp a decade later in the cartoon *An American Tail: Fievel Goes West*. Either way, it wasn't a high-note exit.

Whatever real hopes Stewart might have had for publicizing animal conservation through *The Green Horizon*, they were insignificant compared to his ambitions for *Right of Way*, which went in front of the cameras for HBO in October 1982 with the promise of being the first American film made directly for cable television. For the actor, the Richard Lees play about an elderly couple who decide to commit suicide and the daughter who tries to stop them was to be his equivalent of friend Henry Fonda's *On Golden Pond*. What he did not foresee was that another noted survivor of the old studio system, his costar Bette Davis, was more intent on making it a *Dark Victory*-type vehicle for herself.

It was Lees who first approached Davis after *Right of Way* had already attracted some attention through stage productions in several theaters around the country and in West Germany. Although the actress rejected the notion of bringing the play to Broadway, saying that she no longer had the stamina for such an effort, she passed the script along to director George Schaefer, who saw possibilities for the play as a small film. Stewart was signed, at Lees's urging and over initial objections from Schaefer and coproducer Philip Parslow, only when he passed a physical to show that he was insurable.

The actor's enthusiasm for the project was such that he arrived at the first rehearsal with his lines completely memorized. But Davis instantly set the more prevalent tone of the production by starting a fight with a member of the crew—the kind of tantrum she had been indulging in for decades to keep her juices going. Over the ensuing shoot, the only person she spared off-camera was Stewart, who usually sat off to one side looking bemused with her antics; her favorite target was costar Melinda Dillon, who played the couple's daughter. According to those on the production, Dillon got no further than a greeting to Davis at the first rehearsal when the older actress cut her off, turned to Schaefer, and said, "No daughter of mine is going to look like this." From that point on, Dillon was practically ostracized by the crew in order not to draw Davis's wrath. "The only real exception was Jimmy," says Lees. "He really kept Melinda sane. He was always coming up with some new pretext to discuss the characters with her."

As the filming progressed, Lees wasn't the only one who got the feeling that "the performance of a lifetime" was unfolding before the cameras. "He had so many moments in that role," recalls director Schaefer, "that it got eerie at times. And once it got absolutely embarrassing."

The red faces were prompted by the shooting of the turning-point speech in the drama, when Stewart's character announces to his wife: "It happens that I am tired. I am tired of my feet and my nails and my hair and my shadow. It happens that I am tired of being a man. I'm tired of living." Schaefer:

> Jimmy was bothered by a hum in his hearing aid. When we got to that scene, he asked us to stop a second and pick it up again. We mis-understood what he meant and turned off the camera. Then he launches into the most incredibly heart-tearing version of the speech you could want to hear. I didn't dare interrupt him, but it was all so exasperating because it was for nothing. When he finally finished, you could hear a pin drop. Everybody was drained. He'd never been more magnificent. Then I had to tell him what had happened. Obviously, that got him pretty steamed. What we got on film is almost as good, but nothing will ever be at the height of that unrecorded reading.

And that wasn't the only scene never seen by the public. "You could go on and on," says Lees, still disgruntled fifteen years later. "I never saw a crew shaking its head through an entire production, but that's what they were doing over Jimmy's scenes. There was another moment, for instance, when his character is supposed to be hooking the garden hose into the car's exhaust pipe in the garage, a very grim moment. Suddenly, one of the cats in the story jumps away from the trainer and runs under the car with Jimmy. Instead of asking for a cut, Jimmy's suddenly using this nuzzling by the cat—affection, deliberation, warmth, cold calculation. I would have never dared to write that, but there wasn't a moment that he didn't turn to some comic or dramatic effect. Of course, that too ended up on the editing room floor."

By Lees's account, Davis was "the main reason I had to go along with the critics that the movie shown on HBO was very cold and remote. Number one, because she had this influence over the director and producer that led to Jimmy's performance being mangled to death in the editing room. Number two, because she refused to take the extra step with Jimmy during shooting to create some real warmth and chemistry. There was a scene, for example, with the two of them sitting on the bed together and he ends some speech by kissing her on the cheek. The first time they did it, she immediately turned away so he couldn't kiss her. You could hear a gasp on the set. The second time he just hugged her. He never showed anger or rejection at what she had done. But after that there was really no way of hoping for something special between them."

For Schaefer, on the other hand, many of *Right of Way's* problems lay with a year-long saga about how to end the drama. At one time or another, the elderly couple was allowed to die, they were hauled off to jail, and they were hauled off to jail but with the implication that their daughter would post bond for them so that they would be free to go ahead with their suicidal plans. "One of the great paradoxes of the play," Schaefer notes, "is that what we would call the happy ending is to let them die and the tragic ending would be to have the cops arrest them 'for their own good,' as they say."

Stewart agreed with that distinction, telling Bob Thomas in November 1983: "The morality of the question is something that has been with the country for years and years. It's a matter of how far survivability can go. If it's carried to the extreme, we'll end up with a large part of the population in bed or helpless. I know that I don't want to be on a respirator with intravenous feeding. If I get to that point, you can pull the plug on me."

Instead, the actor had the plug pulled on him at the private screening of the film for cast and crew members. First, he saw that the entire picture had been cut around Davis's performance. Then he saw that the ending being used was the one in which the police intervened in time to save the suicide-bent couple. "There was a loud *shish* from him when we got to that," Schaefer recalls. "He absolutely hated it. He wanted the happy ending." According to Lees, however, that was only the crust of the humble pie: "After the screening I saw Jimmy and Gloria standing in the lobby. He looked stunned, she was crying. They didn't say anything, didn't have to. The picture was not going to be his *On Golden Pond* and they knew it. They were both cut to the quick."

So was HBO program director Michael Fuchs, who got into a protracted battle with Schaefer about how to end *Right of Way*. A good year passed by, with the film gathering dust on a shelf and forfeiting its claim as the first American movie made for cable, before Stewart himself called up with a proposal for an ending that would have Dillon's daughter smelling gas and knowing what was going on, but letting her parents end their lives the way the two of them had decided. It was shown that way in the United States.[2] Fuchs went along mainly to get the picture off the shelf, but refused to approve any significant publicity for it.

As was his custom, Stewart refused to criticize Davis explicitly. But by his own standards he managed to insinuate that there were troubles during the production by telling interviewers that the actress had been ailing during the shooting. "That wasn't at all true," Schaefer comments. "She was in good shape. It wasn't until the following June—more than six months later—that she was hospitalized for a mastectomy and then had a stroke." Both Greg Paul and John Strauss also remember the actor referring to his costar as "challenging." "That's about as close to a criticism as Jimmy would ever let himself make," observes Paul.

For his part, Lees carried away one further resentment from the project. "There was a lot of garbage that came out about how a big problem with *Right of Way* was Jimmy blowing his lines, losing his concentration, that kind of thing," says the writer. "That was utterly absurd, a malicious joke spread around by the people who were really responsible for sabotaging everything. He didn't blow a goddam thing. I hated the ending that he proposed and that they used because I thought

---

[2] The BBC showed it with the intervention ending.

it left the relationship between the daughter and the parents up in the air and because it ignored the social ramifications of the issue being treated. But writing wasn't Jimmy's job, acting was, and they used him just to save their own face. Somebody else in his position might have cracked some heads together, but they knew that wasn't his way, so they exploited it."

But if writing wasn't Stewart's forte, it was precisely in that role that he gained his greatest notoriety in the 1980s—as a periodic guest on Johnny Carson's *Tonight Show* who recited the doggerel rhymes that he had turned out on his experiences in Africa, his devotion to his dogs, and other soft topics. It was the apotheosis of the Jimmy Stewart persona in later age: venerable, humorous, slightly cranky, mildly naughty, and completely reassuring. *Tonight Show* producer Fred DeCordova, who had known Stewart since his association with Jack Benny and who talked him into going on with Carson, remembers how even the NBC censors accepted that image on one occasion. "He wrote one poem that ended with a line like 'such a lake was a pain in the ass.' Naturally, Standards and Practices were on the phone right away because this was back before using *ass* became almost commonplace. I told them if Jimmy Stewart could use that word, it certainly couldn't be offensive. And they bought it. I don't think I could have pulled that argument off with anybody else, including Bob Hope."

Stewart's jingles became so popular that several publishers approached him with the idea of putting them out in book form. But he resisted the offers until he came across a children's book called *Buffalo Girls* and decided that that was the simple format he had been looking for. Leonard Gershe called Crown Books for him, and a short time later *Jimmy Stewart and His Poems* was climbing up the bestseller list. With as much white space as print in it, the volume's popularity was helped no little by the fact that it sold for less than ten dollars and it was issued just in time for the Christmas season in December 1989. As he had always done with his movies, the actor promoted his poems dutifully, going to New York, Washington, Chicago, Denver, and Dallas for book signings.

If it was only Stewart's name that had gotten his verse published and sold, it was the career behind his celebrity that made him the decade's most honored motion-picture figure. After already collecting lifetime achievement awards from, among others, Variety Clubs International, the Friars Club, and the International Red Cross, he was invited to the Berlin Film Festival in 1982 as a co-honoree with Joan Fontaine.

Fontaine remembers it as a particularly emotional evening. "There was a moment when we just looked at one another and tears began swelling in our eyes. We had both been through so much, whole lifetimes really, and here we were in this strange place with these nice people saying all these nice things about us in a foreign language we couldn't understand. It was all very inexplicable—literally as much as figuratively."

The following year, it was the turn of both his hometown in Indiana and the Kennedy Center Awards in Washington. Concerning the seventy-fifth birthday celebrations in Indiana, Eleanor Blair recalls one moment that epitomized for her why it was so natural for the town to be honoring the actor: "Jimmy and Gloria were staying with us, and when they arrived at the house, kids were waiting on the porch to sing 'God Bless America.' But this one little boy holding a balloon that said Happy Birthday got lost in the shuffle and started crying. Jimmy saw him and brought him up to the bedroom where he was staying and showed the boy how he was tying his balloon to the bedpost and promised it would stay there as long as he was in town. When Jimmy was leaving, he deflated the balloon and packed it in his suitcase."

Even without old friend Ronald Reagan sitting in the White House, it was inevitable that Stewart would be a Kennedy Center pick among the five artists chosen annually by the institution for career achievements. But the year that also honored Frank Sinatra, Elia Kazan, Katharine Dunham, and Virgil Thomson provided Reagan with the ideal platform for giving even greater circulation to one of the most noted misquotes ever to come out of Hollywood. As seemingly relished by the President, Jack Warner, upon being informed that Reagan was going to run for governor of California, reputedly cracked, "No, that's wrong. It's Jimmy Stewart as the governor and Reagan as his best friend." Barney Oldfield shakes his head at the familiar anecdote. "It's amazing how these things can take on a life of their own," says the former publicist for Warner Brothers and a onetime speech writer for Reagan. "I was the one who went up and told Warner about the gubernatorial thing, and what he actually replied was, 'No, that's wrong. It's Dennis Morgan for governor and Reagan as his best friend.' Jimmy was never mentioned. But I guess the line ended up getting a bigger laugh when it was said with him than with Dennis Morgan, who was then one of Warner's stars."[3]

In March 1985, the Academy of Motion Picture Arts and Sciences came up with an honorary Oscar to go along with the statuette that the actor had won more than forty years earlier for *The Philadelphia Story*. After being introduced by Cary Grant at the ceremonies held at the Dorothy Chandler Pavilion in Los Angeles, Stewart distributed his gratitude between fans and directors, thanking Frank Capra and other filmmakers in particular for "so generously and brilliantly guiding me through the no-man's land of my own intentions."

Among the decade's other honoring organizations were the American Film Institute, New York's Museum of the Moving Image, the USO, the Cannes Film Festival, the Boy Scouts of America, and Indiana University of Pennsylvania. In 1985, the actor was also awarded a Medal of Freedom. Even the new decade didn't stop the tributes: in 1990, he was the guest of honor at Lincoln Center's annual affair for paying homage to motion-picture personalities.

It was a decidedly elderly looking Stewart who was at the center of attention for most of the tributes; also one who had been ill a couple of times. Still, hesitations during his thank-you remarks stemmed more from his speaking patterns than from any special infirmity. What remained obvious to some people by the end of the decade, however, was that attending the dinners and presentations in his name had become as much of a professional chore for him as going out to promote a picture: He said all the right things, praised all the right people, but also kept his deepest thoughts elsewhere. Among those struck by that reaction was Gregory Peck, who was invited to the University of Virginia in Charlottesville in 1989 for a retrospective of his pictures; at the same time, the university was honoring Stewart on the fiftieth anniversary of the release of *Mr. Smith Goes to Washington*. As Peck recalls:

There must have been two thousand students and people from the town for the screening of *Mr. Smith*. At the great filibuster scene I was suddenly surrounded by sniffling on all sides of me. I looked around to see handkerchiefs all around the theater. Then I looked at Jimmy. He was totally impassive, totally cool. He kept his eyes on the screen, kind of looking at himself in a very critical, analytic way. His face didn't tell me whether he liked or didn't like what he saw. After it was over, they gave

---

[3] Stewart, on the other hand, has never had any rivals for the gibe that Reagan would have never been president if he had married Nancy Davis originally instead of Jane Wyman, because the iron-willed Davis would have seen to it that he won an Oscar or two and remained too much in demand in Hollywood to consider entering politics.

him a standing ovation. He remained cool throughout it all. He really wasn't caught up in it.

Part of it was "the professional being the professional," observes John Strauss. "Plus, important as they were, prestigious as they were, there were a lot of those evenings. And maybe, just maybe, when they're talking about your whole life like that, you start thinking of all the people who aren't there. The people who would have made the special really special. Sometimes, no matter how the room may be crowded, you zero in on the empty chair."

Stewart would have had no trouble zeroing in.

THE BEST FRIEND

FAILURE OR SUCCESS, *RIGHT OF WAY* NEED NOT HAVE BEEN Stewart's *On Golden Pond* since, for a couple of weeks anyway, he had entertained hopes of doing *On Golden Pond* itself. The possibility had been opened by Josh Logan, who had sent him the Ernest Thompson play in 1979 with the news that he was involved in a bid for the property and that he wanted it to mark their first screen effort together as actor and director. Although Stewart voiced enthusiasm, Logan was outbid by his goddaughter Jane Fonda, who acquired the right to the drama for her father and herself. When Logan called to tell him what had happened, the actor responded philosophically, telling the director that "this goes to show you what can happen when you not only have a bright goddaughter, but a bright goddaughter who's also a producer."

On Golden Pond was not the only time that Stewart and his old friend Henry Fonda had circled around the same project or had third parties regard them as rivals for the same role. As far back as the University Players and then Leonard Sillman's 1934 production of *New Faces*, thoughts of one actor led many people to think of the other. In 1948, the same Logan approached Stewart with the idea of touring select cities with a road company version of *Mister Roberts*, Fonda's Broadway hit; the actor begged off only after trying futilely to get out of a couple of film commitments. Also in 1948, David Selznick ordered a rewrite of Graham

Greene's story *The Third Man*, switching the protagonist from an Englishman to an American, to accommodate Stewart or Fonda; the part ultimately went to Joseph Cotten. Then there was the case of *Who's Afraid of Virginia Woolf?* in the early 1960s.

Although playwright Edward Albee had written *Virginia Woolf* as a play for Fonda in the role of the married college professor, the actor was not aware of this until it was too late because his agent had rejected it without showing it to him in favor of sending his client off to do the dreary picture *Spencer's Mountain*. When Fonda got over his fury at his agent, he still had his sights set on doing the film version of the four-character piece. Then Stewart and Gloria saw the play in New York, and she encouraged him to go after the screen role. "You could see that Jimmy was really excited by the prospect," remembers John Springer, Fonda's friend and publicist, "and Gloria talked about nothing else. And about that time Jimmy had a little more box-office cachet than Hank, would have brought less of the 'theatrical' image to it than Hank probably would have. But I don't think there was ever any real question where Jimmy was concerned. As much as he might have wanted to do it, there was no way that he was going to get into any competition with Fonda for something Hank had wanted to do for so long. At one point, when Gloria was talking about it again, he just said 'that's for Hank,' and that was the end of it."[4]

"I don't think there was ever any sense of competition between my father and Jimmy," says Jane Fonda. "It had to be imposed by outsiders even for the appearance—like the year that Jimmy won the Oscar for *The Philadelphia Story* when Dad was up for *The Grapes of Wrath*. Frankly, given the personalities involved, I don't think they'd even have admitted it to themselves if there was any kind of jealousy between them."

Springer agrees. "If they were able to remain so close those years with the Margaret Sullavan business, practically forge their friendship on it, and then through all their very real differences politically, there was no way that they were ever going to destroy their relationship over movie

---

[4] As it turned out, Fonda got to second base with the film version of the play, signing to appear with Bette Davis under director Fred Zinnermann. But then Davis got into a fight with Jack Warner and walked away from the project, followed by Zinnemann. When Mike Nichols took over with Elizabeth Taylor, Fonda decided to withdraw as well because of the age disparity between him and the actress. Richard Burton took over the role.

roles. For the rest, I believe they got a kick out of it when some newspaperman came along and started to pontificate about how, *logically*, they shouldn't be friends, had too many personality differences to have gotten along as long as the two of them had."

In that context, the publicist recalls an afternoon in Fonda's Manhattan apartment in the 1970s after *The New York Times* had published an article dissecting their friendship:

> The piece described Hank as this liberal firebrand who always stood up for what he believed and alienated a lot of people because of that. On the other hand, Jimmy came across as a model of the straight citizen who was always polite to everybody. Hank thought the article was a riot, especially the parts that contrasted him with Jimmy. Jimmy just looked kind of baffled. After he'd finished reading every single word, he put down the paper and said, "Gee, it makes me sound pretty dull, doesn't it?" You could see the words forming on Hank's lips. "Don't say it," Jimmy barked out.

In Springer's view, what mainly bothered Stewart about media profiles of that kind were not the depictions of his present, but oversights about his past. "I think the 'Jimmy Stewart thing,' the solid husband and family man and Republican and apple-pie American was fine with him because it was something he believed in, too. But when he was around Hank sometimes you got impression that he wanted people to remember that he'd once been a pretty good cutup in Hollywood, too, that he hadn't always been this stodgy piece of wood that writers, even those seeking to compliment him, made him out to be. Hank, of course, could never have a word written about him without a mention somewhere of all his wives. I don't think Jimmy would have minded at all if, in the middle of all the praise for Gloria as the center of his life, which she was, there was a little more mention of his old gallivanting days. Just to remind Fonda, if nobody else."

Probably the most marked difference in the professional perspectives of the two actors was Fonda's greater passion for the theater. Although Hollywood's oppressive political atmosphere after the war might have encouraged his move to New York, it was his success in *Mister Roberts, The Caine Mutiny Court Martial, Two for the Seesaw*, and other Broadway productions that ensured that he would never be as tightly associated with motion pictures as Stewart was. And while himself habitually professing his love of the theater and confiding to interviewers in the

1970s and 1980s that he regretted not having done more than *Harvey* on the stage in his later years, Stewart was very much bothered by the number of plays his friend did. During the shooting of *Anatomy of a Murder* in the late 1950s, for instance, Ben Gazzara recalls a private dinner with Stewart where one of the chief topics of conversation was Fonda's career path.

> It was like listening to an older brother saying all the things that he didn't have the nerve to say to his younger brother, but that had been bothering him for some time. He said he was very worried about what Fonda was doing with his career. He said Hank didn't pay enough attention to building up a name for himself as big as his talent, that he seemed more interested in doing little plays or, even when he did movies, doing little pictures shot in New York that didn't give him the boost that he needed.[5] Jimmy really wanted him to give Broadway a rest. He was very sincere, thought Fonda was selling himself short.

For his part, Fonda thought that Stewart's status in the Hollywood film industry, especially with his successes in the 1950s, had sometimes made him less demanding where material, directors, and even his own performances were concerned. It was in this connection that he singled out the firm directorial hand of Vincent McEveety on Stewart during *Firecreek*. On the other hand, Fonda also got the message after some years that his friend did not appreciate always being described as a "natural" actor or as somebody who had slid into everything easily, and began to distinguish between Stewart's beginnings as "a good natural actor" and the matured "great" performer; implicit in the difference was the work Stewart had put into his craft in the interval.

Fellow performers and associates of the two actors have also attested to some fundamental differences in their approaches as professionals and in developing scenes and relationships among characters. Working with both of them in *The Cheyenne Social Club*, Shirley Jones, for example, found that "both of them gave acting classes in just about everything they did, but Hank was far more formalistic. Both of them deviated from the script when they felt the need to do it, but with Hank there was a little more sense of knowing when he was doing it, while with Jimmy it

---

[5] Among the pictures answering this description in the period were *12 Angry Men*, *Stage Struck*, and even *The Wrong Man* for Alfred Hitchcock.

was all conversation. Old lines, improvised lines, there was always this flow that made you listen to every single word as though it were coming from the same exact place. Sometimes with Hank, you knew he had just opened up another well. Just as persuasive as Jimmy, but with that little extra burp in between. He seemed more conscious of the rules."

Olivia de Havilland would deny to Fonda one of the qualities—generosity—that has been traditionally attributed to Stewart by other actors. Concerning *A Gift of Time*, a play she did on Broadway in 1962, she admitted falling afoul of Fonda's legendary impatience with performances he regarded as less than ideal and, in spite of her own status, practically being summoned to a meeting to discuss her effort. As she told an interviewer, she was so incensed with her costar's arrogance that it took her a while to acknowledge that all his criticisms were on the mark, and then so much more infuriated that she almost broke a toe kicking at the wall separating their dressing rooms. "I wouldn't say he was generous, but I would say fair," de Havilland summed up Fonda.

Harry Morgan has not only worked in more films with Stewart than any other actor, but also owed his big break in Hollywood to Fonda's insistence that he be his saddle-tramp partner in *The Ox-Bow Incident*. "I always thought they went about their business in entirely different ways," says Morgan. "Fonda lived to be an actor. He never thought about anything else. Twenty-four hours a day with Hank, it was acting—what he had just done, what he hoped he'd get to do. Jimmy never gave you that feeling until he actually began acting. When you worked with Hank, you knew you had to be set to go before you ran into him. With Jimmy, it was anything else under the sun until the director was ready to shoot. Then the monster of a performer that he is came out."

But on at least one major point, Linda Janklow thinks the difference between the two was only of degree. "Jimmy and Hank are the only two actors of their caliber that I've ever known who were totally insecure," says Janklow, daughter of Mervyn LeRoy and the organizer of The Museum of the Moving Image's tribute to Stewart. "A current job was always going to be their last one, as far as both of them were concerned. The difference was that Hank was absolutely neurotic about it, while Jimmy kind of leveled off at simple anxiety."

But above and beyond individual differences and similarities—from their separate relations with Sullavan, their rival political views, and their contrasting marital experiences, to their mutual zest for teenage pastimes, wariness about spending a dollar, and even hearing problems in later years—the record of friendship between the actors demonstrated the right mixture of each for a compatibility that spanned half a century. Donald Saddler, coproducer of a tribute to Josh Logan at New York's Majestic Theater in March 1975, recalls a glimpse of the pair that has remained with him ever since.

> They came into the Majestic together for a rehearsal. They went up to the mezzanine quietly, didn't say a word to anybody, and folded themselves into a couple of seats and just started staring down at the stage. At a certain point I had to go up and tell them it was time for them to rehearse what they were going to do. As I got near them, I had this overwhelming feeling of two men—veterans of god-knows-how-many-years-of-doing-god-knows-how-many-things—working off a profound bond between them. They were talking very quietly, practically inaudibly—a word or two at a time and everything like it was completely understood between them. They were actors sitting in the mezzanine of the Majestic, but they could have been two farmers watching the cows from a farmhouse porch.

In March 1982, Fonda received the Best Actor Oscar for *On Golden Pond*. By that time, however, heart problems and an accumulation of other ailments had confined him to his Bel Air home, making it necessary for his daughter to pick up his trophy. Over the next few months, Stewart was a regular visitor to the house. Witnesses described him as sitting next to Fonda's bed and, in between long bouts of silence, exchanging laconic shouts with the patient about episodes from their common past. The fact that both of them had to yell to be heard sometimes sent Fonda into a laughing fit, but also tired him. As spring turned into summer, friends said, there were increasingly more silences than reminiscences. On August 11, 1982, Fonda died at the age of seventy-seven.

Soon after the end, Stewart met with reporters outside Fonda's home to say tersely that he had "lost [his] best friend," immediately after which he went back inside to rejoin Fonda's widow, Shirlee, and other family members. Jane Fonda recalls:

> We were all sitting in the library. Just about everybody was talking except Jimmy. He just sat there in this big armchair, absolutely not moving an inch and saying nothing. Nobody wanted to look at him, but it was like

trying to pretend there wasn't this gorilla in the room smoking a big cigar. He must have stayed like that a good half-hour, just staring off somewhere. Then suddenly he lowered his head very slowly over his lap and brought it back up at the same time that he raised his arms out as far as they would go and said: "It was by far the biggest kite we ever flew." Those were exactly his first words after all his quiet and from there, right in the middle of this thing he'd obviously been thinking about, he went into this monologue about how he and my father had flown these kites at Tigertail, going into all the details of what they looked like and how hard some of them had pulled. The tears were running down my face, and I know I wasn't the only one. Then after about five minutes of talking about nothing except these kites, he fell back into the same silence and same position he'd been in before he started talking.

Stewart's last reported remarks to Fonda came a few months later, during the shooting of *Right of Way*. Whenever he had completed an especially strenuous scene, people involved in the production reported, he muttered, "That's for you, Hank."

WITHDRAWAL

STEWART'S FRAIL APPEARANCE AT THE VARIOUS AWARD ceremonies organized in his honor in the 1980s was not just the result of his age; he was also felled in the period by a series of ailments. In 1980, for example, he was hospitalized for five days for an irregular heartbeat—a condition that would resurface three years later and prompt doctors at St. John's Hospital in Santa Monica to install a pacemaker. In 1980, as well, a sciatica flare-up caused him to cancel a visit to New York for a wildlife photographic exhibit that he and Gloria had counted on for helping to promote conservationist causes in Africa. Only a few weeks after receiving his pacemaker in 1983, he was back in the hospital for radiation treatments for what was described as "a minor skin cancer."

But threatening as his illnesses might have been if not treated in time, they did not have the effect on his physical constitution that the mere acknowledgment of them—plus his hearing impairment—had. "He had to face what we all have to face at a certain age," observes John Strauss, "and that's that we're not indestructible after all. That doesn't put you in the best frame of mind, and with a guy as thin as Jimmy, maybe it shows a little more, too."

In glimpsing the actor at the Marshall Field bookstore during the publicity tour for his book, Vivian DeVine, the daughter of the newspaperman the actor had played in *Call Northside 777*, spoke for many in describing him as "not just thin, but frighteningly thin." A year later, at Lincoln Center, he hadn't shown any improvement. Wendy Keyes, one of the organizers of the 1990 New York tribute, recalls:

> We went to the Tavern-on-the-Green after the ceremonies. Jimmy was very fragile looking and incommunicative. If he didn't look sick exactly, he looked like he had just *been* ill. At the Green, he sat very silently while Kim Novak, June Allyson, Jack Lemmon, and some of the other guests engaged in separate conversations on either side of him. Every once in a while, he looked up and blew a kiss to me and gave me the victory sign or some other gesture that meant he was grateful for the evening we had organized for him. But I knew it was useless to do anything but smile because he would not have heard anything I said from such a distance with all the competing voices anyway. He really looked a little forsaken.

By the new decade, in fact, the actor struck friends and business associates as having lost even the resilience he had previously shown at social gatherings that initially he had objected to but had subsequently turned into storytelling sessions; "When we were down at the University of Virginia for the fiftieth anniversary of *Mr. Smith Goes to Washington*," John Strauss recalls, "there was a big party at which Gloria danced the night away with John Kluge, the big media magnate. Jimmy sat off by himself with his thoughts. Everybody kind of took a turn to go up and talk to him, but it was a lot more forced than it had been in the past. He was never a party animal, and he seemed to get more miserable on those occasions the older he got."

Eddie Albert had a similar impression. "To me he looked ill for some time," says the veteran actor. "He was always still there at parties and things, though, and I thought it was a pretty depressing sight. He'd sit in a corner with his head down, not talking with anybody. Gloria hovered a lot, but you got the feeling that everyone was expected to take a turn so she could have a change of pace. I'll be damned if I ever understood why he put himself through those situations when he was so clearly uncomfortable."

The answer, of course, was Gloria. And even friend Leonard Gershe admits to having been confounded on one occasion by the commitments she would make in her husband's name:

I'd just come back to California after being away for a few weeks and I turn on the television and there's Jimmy and Gloria sitting on one of these floats at some minor holiday parade. I said to her, "Look, that's okay for Bob Hope and Miss America, but what the hell do you have Jimmy out there like that for?" And she kind of just looked at me as though I should know better and said, "It got him out of the house for a few hours, didn't it?" Her whole thing was to keep him active because she was afraid that he'd sit down in an armchair one day and never get up again. And once he was through doing a little gardening, Jimmy wasn't the kind of guy who'd find activity in the house, like in reading. Where he was concerned, activity had always meant going, moving, and Gloria didn't want him to lose that sense of mobility.

Michael McLean agrees that, once his father wasn't being sent any more scripts, he was rarely to be found reading. "The house was always full of books, but they were Mom's. Dad seldom read anything but Air Force magazines and scripts. I don't know if he ever really learned how to *relax* reading. The magazines and the scripts were work for him, and he would concentrate on them something fierce. He would read scripts, for example, in the middle of the living room with the television on and the rest of us around him talking. He didn't hear a word that we were saying or that the TV newscaster was saying. Reading was part of the job. When the job wasn't there. . . . "

Other alternatives also dried up. Fred DeCordova recalls an afternoon that he made what he assumed to be an automatic appointment with the actor to play golf at the Bel Air Country Club the following day. "We'd been playing together for almost ten years," the television and film producer says. "Suddenly, Jimmy looks at me and says, 'Fred, I don't *like* golf!' And that was just about it where golf was concerned."

Bill Winants tried to get Stewart out of the house by inviting him to the millionaire's remote-control glider club. "I thought having been a flyer, he would have gotten a kick out of it," Winants says, "but it really turned out to be the opposite. He tried maneuvering one of the models, lost control, and panicked. The thing went down, and he couldn't give me back the controls fast enough. I knew better than to invite him again. I suppose when you've done all the real flying he has, remote-control gliders can seem like a comedown, and remind you only of things that you don't want to dwell on."

In 1991, Stewart traveled to Pittsburgh to pick up a citation for his contributions to broadcasting. It turned out to be the final time that he met in person with such fellow Indianians as Eleanor Blair and Bill Moorhead. Although nothing untoward happened during the visit, the old friends came away with the impression that Gloria had already begun to prepare the children for the day the actor would not be around. "Michael, Kelly, and Judy were certainly of an age not to need diagrams drawn for them," says Blair, "and there was nothing in particular that was bothering Jimmy physically then. But he certainly didn't look like he was in the pink. It would have been a little foolish *not* to think of his mortality. Instead. . . . "

Instead, in the fall of 1993, after a half-century of averaging two packages of cigarettes a day, Gloria was diagnosed as having lung cancer. "We were all stunned," says niece Melinda Draddy. "We were all ready for that phone call that said something had happened to Jimmy. When it turned out to be Gloria, it was like having the rug pulled out."

"I was calling Jimmy every weekend, " Bill Moorhead remembers. "Gloria always answered, and I'd ask her how things were going, and she'd always answer 'Fine.' Except this one Saturday morning, when I asked the usual thing, and she said 'Fair.' That's a typical Stewart announcement of something being very wrong."

Under her husband's urging, Gloria agreed to submit to chemotherapy. But after a single treatment, she began losing her hair and getting sick. At that point, according to Leonard Gershe, she cross-examined her doctors more carefully. "She asked them straight out whether the chemo was going to prolong her life. They did some hemming and hawing about it being their best weapon, but Gloria wasn't buying. Finally, it came out that the chemo would probably only prolong her life minimally. That was it where she was concerned. She cut it out right away. She was back in control. And not once did I ever hear her complain. She had made her decision, Jimmy understood it, and there was only the waiting left."

The waiting ended on February 16, 1994, when Gloria succumbed at the age of seventy-five. The evening before her death, Stewart spent more than two hours by her bedside, delivering what family friends characterized as the most painful monologue of his life—talking about their four-and-a-half decades together and how indispensable she had been to him.

"You're married that long, you're always going to take shots at one another the way long-married couples do," niece Draddy observes. "Gloria, for instance, always had something snappy to say about how long it took Jimmy to answer the simplest question, making some crack like 'It didn't take that long to invent the wheel.' His digs were often about her facelifts. One of his favorite things was telling her that Bette Davis had never needed a facelift, like that was some kind of negative standard. Gloria's usual response was to act as though she was suddenly overwhelmed by the vapors and ask Jimmy to change the subject. Which was, of course, exactly what he had no intention of doing. But aside from that kind of sniping, I always had the impression in their company that Jimmy never forgot for a second that she was the center of his life and she knew that there was no way that she was going to make the same kind of mistake she had made with her first husband by being less than vigilant all the time."

"I always thought there was more between them than love," Mignon Winants says. "There was also a mutual respect and admiration. When you consider how hard it is to find admiration in married couples, that alone was probably what guaranteed them the extraordinary length of their marriage."

But if, as John Strauss describes it, Gloria had been "rudder, anchor, and helm" for Stewart, her death left him lost at sea. And what seemed to bother him as much as anything was that he had outlived her. "'It's just wrong,'" Karin Lopp, Gloria's niece, remembers the actor saying repeatedly at the funeral. "'It's absolutely wrong that it happened this way.'"

The pain and bafflement did not ease. Whatever slender thread of public activity Stewart had maintained up to the discovery of Gloria's illness he cut completely, telling Strauss, Greg Paul, and his family that his public life was over. More than a year later, he was still spending most of his time in his bedroom, coming out mainly at the insistence of his housekeeper for meals or for the visits of Michael, Kelly, and Judy. What he regarded as his public life, it turned out, were not only his contacts with the media and fans, but also those with the overwhelming majority of the people who had appeared with him in films, aided his career in some way, and even lived with him. Lew Wasserman and Janet Leigh were only two of the many who attempted to visit him unannounced at North Roxbury Drive and who got no farther than the housekeeper. Former housemate Burgess Meredith reports a similar experience. "I called him a couple of times when I heard that Gloria was ill," says Meredith, "but he never came to the phone and never called back. After she died, I sent him a couple of cards and notes, but he's never responded." Chasen's Ronald Clint says that he knew better than to expect any other reaction. "After Gloria passed away," says Clint, "I'd send food over to the house. But I know he never touched it. When we were closing the restaurant, some people said that we should at least make the gesture of inviting him in for the farewell dinner. Naturally, he said no. His office, the Prappas Company, sent us an autographed picture. A couple of people were disappointed, but I don't really know why. Shutting down Chasen's was just another closure of so many in his life."

One exception to Stewart's withdrawal was Bill Moorhead, who continued making his weekend calls from Indiana to Beverly Hills to talk about cabbages and kings. "Of course the longer he's shut himself up in the house, the less sharp he's been," the former clothier and university business manager admits. "Sometimes it's happened that he suddenly goes completely quiet. I'd think that he'd hung up, but then I hear his breathing on the other end. It was just some odd thought that came into his mind or something that he thought was important to remember but couldn't. Most times, he doesn't like to say what it is."

Other exceptions have been made for those who share the actor's religious bent. "I don't know why he took my calls and ignored so many others after Gloria's death," says Mayf Nutter, Stewart's fellow player from the *Hawkins* television series. "Maybe it goes back to that day of John Ford's funeral when he admitted that he hadn't made new friends in a very long time. I don't presume to say that by confiding that to me, I was the one he'd been waiting for to come along. But I always thought that by confessing that dread to me, maybe it amounted to pretty much the same thing. Anyway, he came to the phone soon after she'd died, and when I asked him how he was doing, he answered 'Not good.' He wasn't all that communicative until I asked if he wanted to say a prayer together, and he said yes immediately. I couldn't help thinking after we'd prayed that only a short time before I'd called the house and it was Gloria telling me that Jimmy was the one who wasn't feeling so well."

James Morrison, the pastor of the Beverly Hills Presbyterian Church, also reports having prayed with Stewart by phone since the passing of Gloria. But then even that stopped after a few months. By the summer of 1995, the minister found himself in more or less Meredith's position. "The man's obviously very despondent," says Morrison. "For some time he was promising me that he would come back to church, but he really hasn't showed up since Gloria's death and I'm not expecting to look up some Sunday morning and see him in a pew. I must admit some surprise at that, given his religious background. On a couple of occasions I've written him notes about it, but he's never answered them. Should I just walk over to his house and be a little more aggressive about getting him back to church? I don't know. That could be awkward."

Although more a part of the Gloria circle that has gradually faded away from North Roxbury Drive since her death, Leonard Gershe visited the house one day and witnessed a moment not unlike that in the library of Henry Fonda after that actor's death.

Kelly was visiting, and I went over to see her about something. As we were talking in the living room, Jimmy came down from upstairs. Whatever it was Kelly and I were talking about exactly, the Concorde was mentioned, and Jimmy suddenly goes into this long disquisition on what problems have to be solved at airports and in hangars and everything to take full advantage of supersonic jets. He wasn't talking through his hat, either. He'd obviously given the whole thing a lot of thought. It was the most lucid he'd been about anything in months, and Kelly and I were both mesmerized. Of course, once he came down again, he came down again.

Over the 1995 Christmas holiday season, Stewart failed to negotiate a rise leading to a dining area and fell, cracking his head on the bill of a wooden duck that Judy had given him as a gift some years ago. Although initial newspaper reports suggested that the actor had been seriously injured, he actually suffered no trauma, and was released from the hospital after a few days. Back home, he has continued to live as a semirecluse since then.

Some associates distinguish between the depression that Stewart undoubtedly sank into immediately after Gloria's death and the seclusion that he has observed since then. "Don't forget the self-containment of the man," says Burgess Meredith. "Fonda and I were always amazed at how self-contained he was. . . . He was able to live totally within himself in ways that I've never seen anyone else."

"Without minimizing the shock he felt over Gloria," Leonard Gershe comments, "let's not forget that he's always been reclusive. His greatest hobby—flying—was the hobby of a recluse. And then along came his problems with hearing. I really think that Gloria's death just let him be what he always wanted to be. The minute she died, he had no more reason to pretend that he wanted to see people. I don't think he's unhappy. He wants to be by himself, even away from those people at his local church. After all these years, hasn't he earned that?"

Gregory Peck has arrived at the same conclusion. "He's had everything a man can have," notes Peck. "He's had it all and he's done it all. He has no reason to regret anything he's done. And I think it's entirely in keeping with his character, typical of Jimmy, to hunker down and wait for the end by himself. Like some old elephant."

EPILOGUE

WHENEVER HE HAS BEEN ASKED WHAT HE hopes his artistic legacy will be, Stewart has invariably referred back to a day in 1953 when, on a lunch break during the shooting of *The Far Country* in Canada's Jasper National Park, he was approached by an elderly man who wasn't even sure who he was. As the actor has told it:

"You Stewart?" he asked.

"Yeah."

"You did a thing in a picture once," he said. "Can't remember the name of it, but you were in a room and you said a poem or something about fireflies. That was good."

I knew right away what he meant. That's all he said. He was talking about a scene in the picture *Come Live with Me* that had come out before the war in 1941. He couldn't remember the title, wasn't even sure I was the same guy, but that little thing—didn't even last a minute—he'd remembered all those years. And that's what's so great about the movies. If you're good and God helps you and you're lucky enough to have the kind of personality that comes across, you're giving people little, little tiny pieces of time that they never forget.

No American film actor has given more of those pieces of time to memory than Stewart. Over and above the sheer quantity of motion-picture moments that the length and variety of his career has provided, his specific qualities of emotional intensity and searching volubility have forged a very *explicit* bond with audiences that are tied to the core of the history of the American sound film. The pieces of time isolated and framed by a James Stewart performance are not just physical allusions dependent on the resources of spectators for supplying coherent meanings or missing senses; at their most compelling, their measure has been a literally stated, frontal instigation. The starting point for that instigation has been what Jason Robards has called "the responsibility to the character."

While it might seem like an automatic priority for any actor, a responsibility to the character has been practiced far less than it has been preached. Nor have the wayward been exclusive to those caricatures of self-indulgent Method disciples who have been able to render the roles of Zeus and Circe only by first healing their traumas caused by Uncle Bob's mountain climbing and Aunt Mary's incessant humming in the kitchen. Hollywood producers—both those operating under the old studio system and those of more recent vintage—have never found concerns about character more dispensable than when they have had under contract a performer, whether Nelson Eddy or Pauly Shore, who might have the acting ability of a peanut, but who, for a while anyway, has certain audiences always reaching into the box office for more. And while some overripe students of Stanislavsky might adopt as their watchword "Let's see ourselves as Chekhov's characters would have seen us," it was Lucille Ball who actually ran acting workshops at her Desilu studios behind the dictum of "Let's see ourselves as others see us."

At his most saccharine, of course, as in such efforts as *The FBI Story, Strategic Air Command*, and the three Henry Koster comedies that he did for 20th Century-Fox in the 1960s, Stewart could have been mistaken for a graduate of the Desilu workshop—giving back the Jimmy Stewart he assumed others saw in him. With such biographical figures as Monty Stratton and Glenn Miller, he might have been applying his own variation on Ball's celebrity impact approach; to wit, "Let's see them as others see me doing them." For the most part, however, and as attested to by his reiterated assertion over the years of opening up a script and looking first of all for the "vulnerability" in the character he was asked to consider playing, his primary instinct was to acknowledge the autonomy of the fictional creature from himself and to sound out the possibilities for a relationship. Once the vulnerability had been discovered, he would even sign on for films that, by his own testimony, he didn't completely understand (*Vertigo*).

One of the implications of an actor making vulnerability his immediate quest is that other aspects of the character not only are regarded as subordinate, but also, from the point of view of craft, are seen to loom as lesser challenges. This is particularly striking as an emphasis in Stewart's case because of his determination in the late 1940s to "toughen up," to show the public that he possessed a lot more leather and iron than Hollywood's image-vendors had given him credit for. That he was still putting the accent even then on vulnerability, while industry counselors and New York Times reporters were warning him that this should have been his last worry, intimates a confidence in his *skills* that his reputation as a fretter about his *career*—a zone subject to the control of outside parties—did not reflect. In fact, Stewart has voiced dismay on more than one occasion that some people were startled by the *Winchester '73* scene that supposedly announced his toughening up— the slamming of Dan Duryea's villain onto the bar. As he put it with characteristic casualness in an April 1990 interview with *The New York Times*: "The very idea of changing my whole thing from the sort of shy, fumbling fellow to the western was just my work. It's all hard work and dedication, to be able to make a go of it. And those were the things offered to me." Put another way, the cracking heads part of his character, however apparently vital to his popularity at the box office, never excited his energies more than falling into pools or collapsing onto the Senate floor had. Vulnerability remained the principal frame of reference.

If there has been one setting in which the actor has continually demonstrated his confidence in dealing with the vulnerabilities of his characters as much as with their other aspects, it has been in scenes with women. Probably the most conspicuous examples of this have been his four films with Margaret Sullavan, his work with Marlene Dietrich in both *Destry Rides Again* and *No Highway in the Sky*, his playing with Katharine Hepburn in *The Philadelphia Story*, and his pairing with Kim Novak in *Vertigo*. "People don't think of him as the great movie lover," Jack Lemmon observes, "but he's worked with a Who's Who of the great leading ladies and he's never made them or himself look bad. Some people say the chemistry from most of those movies came from the women wanting to mother him and him wanting to be mothered. I don't buy that. I think it goes deeper. His real secret with women on the screen was that he made us look at them through the gentleness and respect he had for them, and he made them think he needed them just as much as they needed him."

It has never been hard to find Stewart coworkers who endorse Lemmon's view. For Linda Cristal, for instance, the actor was "exactly the opposite of the John Fords and John Waynes who were terrified of love scenes and kept putting them off until there was no reason to do them at all. Jimmy wanted constantly to test the waters with me in *Two Rode Together*. He was willing, tender, and vulnerable. He wasn't just 'supportive,' as they like to say in that cold, therapeutic way these days. What he did broke down into so many small, tiny pieces. What we did at work was really a *commingling*."

For Shirley Jones, it was Stewart "who made me an actress in a real sense. For him a scene was a conversation, and sometimes he'd change a question into a statement or vice versa because that seemed more natural to the conversation. There was no way in the world that I was going to get away with memorizing my lines and then unloading them. I had to *listen*. And that gave me the sense of *creating* scenes with him."

"Any take with him," concurs Janet Leigh, "was like starting out from one place, and knowing where you wanted to arrive. It was a very secure trip. He was confident and he made me confident."

One of the most prominent technical skills behind that confidence has been Stewart's singular concentration as a listener—his immersion in the work of his fellow players that makes possible his stated goal of conducting a conversation. If he has never gone quite as far as Alec Guinness and the British actor's claim that "others do the acting for me; I only have to listen," he has made of his extended listening moments in everything from *The Shop Around the Corner* to *Firecreek* silent monologues that suggest as many colors as a speech of his own might have.[1]

Another fundamental technique has been his delivery. Although a source of comment since he first strode onto a stage at Cape Cod, Stewart's painstaking arranging of vocal marbles is often thought of only in terms of his general style. In fact, it has also always been a conspicuous example of how actors can set the pace for the development of a scene. As Lemmon explains it:

> Stewart didn't create his stammering out of whole cloth, saying this would
> be a good way of slowing down the movie-making process and letting me

---

[1] One of the offshoots of Stewart's recurrent, lengthy monologues has been an unusually high number by his fellow players as well.

slip into things more comfortably. If he had done that, for instance, by fluttering his eyelids at the beginning of all his scenes, he wouldn't have lasted a year in the business. But because the stammering was natural to him, what he really had was a control device that didn't seem like a control device. And, boy, could he exploit that. And that's a reason among a thousand why he's always been not just a great actor, but an *astute* one. He has always been a lot more in charge technically than even some of his directors probably were aware of.

But as central as it has been to his performances, Stewart's vocal manipulativeness has been just one aspect of the presence established by his physical movements. The lithe dancer whom Ginger Rogers called the equal of Fred Astaire on a ballroom floor has probably been more conscious of the dangers of exaggeration in that area than he has about his delivery. Prior to beginning work on *Winchester '73* for instance, he told more than one interviewer that he was determined to be "far sparer" in his guise as the vengeance-seeking cowboy than he had been in previous roles—an objective that he maintained for a skein of subsequent films, especially those made by Anthony Mann and Alfred Hitchcock. To some extent, in fact, it was his known potential for uncommon physical energy that furnished the tense counterpoint to the wheelchair-bound protagonist of *Rear Window*, the cockpit-confined Charles Lindbergh in *The Spirit of St. Louis*, and even the legless millionaire in *The Big Sleep*. "What it seems to come down to," says director George Schaefer, "is a tremendous command of the actor's most important instrument—his body."

Others have seen that in smaller ways. "He could cry on cue," recalls Raquel Welch of her work with the actor on *Bandolero!* "No mess, no fuss. Just like that, you could see tears in his eyes." On occasion, the command could save directors and editors a tremendous amount of work. As Andrew McLaglen tells it: "He was incredibly meticulous about the smallest physical thing. If we did a scene eight or nine times, every subsequent take would include absolutely everything he'd done on the previous one. Say, for example, on the third take, he'd scratch his ear on a line. Well, the fourth and fifth takes would have him scratching that ear at exactly the same point. He always *matched* what he had done."

As McLaglen's experience indicates, Stewart's astuteness as an actor has been paralleled by his specific smarts as a *film* actor. Asked once by Michael Caine why there were so many tracking shots that forced the actor to cross tracks without acknowledging them during a scene, director John Huston replied: "If you step over the tracks, Michael, that means they are not there, which in turn means that the camera is not there, either, which is the first principle of directing a movie—*you make the camera disappear*." Stewart would have never asked. As other actors and directors have noted over the years, no motion-picture performer has ever been more knowledgeable about the machinery involved in producing a film—nor so able to forget about it all as soon as he was ready to go. "It was like reconnoitering," says Harry Morgan. "Once he had a lay of the land, he knew where it was safe and where a problem was likely to arise, and he geared himself accordingly. He knew whatever there was to know about lighting, and sometimes he'd make suggestions about angles that turned out to be right more often than not."

Despite his own conflicts with Stewart, Hal Kanter still calls him "the best motion-picture actor I ever worked with. He knows the camera like it was in the incubator with him. He could tell when some light went out anywhere. And he never used his knowledge against other actors. If anything, he used it for them. He was never selfish in front of the camera."

But that didn't mean that the actor was above using his familiarity with filmmaking equipment if it meant a shorter workday. On the set of *Hawkins*, for example, Mayf Nutter remembers: "If things were taking too long and Jimmy knew a floor manager or an assistant director was within earshot, he'd say things like, 'Boy, I sure hope they get it right this time, Mayf, because the bolt in that machine up there has only forty minutes of life under a heat exposure like this and I've already counted at least a half-hour gone. You get that bolt melting down and there'll be hell to pay. Whole production could be held up for days!' And of course the person overhearing this would go scurrying off to make sure that things got done much faster."

As impressed as his fellow professionals have been by Stewart's simultaneous sensitivity and self-confidence on a set, they have been equally disconcerted by the shy figure they have encountered in other situations. "The contrast is startling, really," observes Janet Leigh. "You'll see him at breakfast or something, like I did on *The Naked Spur*, and he'll be this enormously shy guy. But then once the lights and camera go on, he would erupt with this strength that seems to come from nowhere."

Where it came from, every clue points, was the actor's sense of freedom on a movie set and, in the best of cases, with the covering of fictional characters who did not expect James Stewart to act like Jimmy Stewart, Jimsey Stewart, or Jimbo Stewart. And sometimes not even the fictional characters were necessary for that self-contained, artificial world to offer feelings of freedom not available to him elsewhere. It wasn't just his failure to make new friends in thirty years that he had found easiest to acknowledge among lights, microphones, and cameras. Julie Adams, for instance, recalls the actor on *The Jimmy Stewart Show* frequently withdrawing to a chair on the corner of the set and doing what he could even be contemptuous of in private family surroundings—crying. "Tears would just start running down his face," Adams remembers, "and the makeup man Frank Westmore would hover nearby until it was over, then go over to fix him up. I never heard them exchange a word. Frank just accepted it as part of his duties, and Jimmy appeared to think of it that way, too." Although it was Adams's surmise that the crying had been set off by thoughts of Ronald McLean's death in Vietnam, more than two years earlier, it might just as well have been for any of several other things: the loss of close friends, an awareness of advancing physical frailties, the specter of his own career winding down on a television sitcom—which he had felt obligated to deal with stoically in other settings. At bottom, movie sets not only triggered Stewart's creative strengths and technical prowess, they could also incite a recognition of their own artificiality—and of the premeditation required to accept them for it. The set was a warehouse of emotional merchandise that offered an appropriate tool for every fantasy and ambition brought on the premises. Everything was possible along its aisles and within its smells. The compromises with reality started only on the far side of the door. And, whether the set was located in Paris or in 20th Century-Fox's backlot version of the French capital, the door was always to be found fronting on Philadelphia Street.

If Stewart had any education at all in Indiana, it was in what was palpable, what was sensate, what was real. Thanks to Alex in particular, he didn't have to speculate about the heat of a fire, what it might feel like to kill a dog, what even a presidential funeral train might look like screaming through the night. The fantasies of boys his age—about circuses, about riding horses, about going up in a plane, about building saleable gadgets—were his common experience. Ruminations were sponsored and feelings subsidized practically as a matter of course. From his father's point of view at least, there was little danger of his turning out to be a dreamer, as his younger sister would be accused of becoming, for the simple reason that there was no *need* to be a dreamer. As much as was humanly possible, whatever his imagination sought was delivered in the concrete. It was an overwhelming kind of education—one that on initial impression would not have seemed likely to leave much room for a creative nerve. But it did, effectively through its own excess, including that of its teacher. The more expansively the reality was filled in (as it also would be subsequently with the regimens of Mercersburg and MGM), the larger grew the uncharted territory beyond its perimeter that offered the prospect of personal, original achievements.

Throughout his career, Stewart has been accompanied by more shadows than Harvey. One has been the shadow of Jimmy Stewart, the rippling twentieth-century extension of that "agrarian myth" about "fancied innocence" that historian Richard Hofstadter referred to. Another has been that shadow of premeditated ignorance that formally untutored performers have perennially dragged around for self-confidence in their objections to acting schools. What that shadow insinuates is some single secret to talent—some key of individual emotional warping that, exposed through some formal schooling process, might impose the sort of conscientious obligations that would jeopardize an ability to perform freely. Not surprisingly, the dread of such a confrontation has little time for the resulting irony that the antischooling actor ends up on the same plane as the true believer in accepting the premise of any single explicable emotional trove of secrets to talent in the first place. For Stewart and others with his outlook, the priority remains keeping the confidence-building shadow exactly where it is—never having to acknowledge it away from work, never having to pay an extra fare for it in the course of a routine day, but, when it counts, having it there to metamorphose into the elastic, shriveled, or other designs that its owner feels otherwise unable to configure in public.

For all that, the actor's admirers over the years have always included some of the most distinguished alumni of acting schools, especially of the Actors Studio. "Get there, that's the essential factor," says Nehemiah Persoff, "and Stewart always got there. So many of these divisions— acting school or no acting school, the media differences, even culture— they strike me as very secondary, often leading to the tail wagging the dog. Look at what the man's done. End of discussion."

Shelley Winters: "You don't have to agree with him on what he says or thinks as a private person, but if you can't respect what he has been as an actor, in both his performance and in the way he has always approached his work, then I'm afraid for you. You can join all the other people who don't have a clue."

Ben Gazzara: "Stewart is a great actor not just because he's given great performances over a lot of years, but because he's dared to do a lot of things that others wouldn't have. He cries, yelps, screams, explodes—he lets it all go, but always knows *where* it is going. At my age, you look at something like that and you say 'Holy Christ!'"

If Stewart has been denied anything in his career, it has been not going out with a bang—as Henry Fonda did with *On Golden Pond*, John Wayne did with *The Shootist*, and Clark Gable did with *The Misfits*. Because a project to film *The Late Christopher Beane* with Carol Burnett fell through at the last minute when the actress collapsed of nervous exhaustion, his last on-camera work as an actor turned out to be a cameo on the 1986 television miniseries *North and South*. If nothing else, that title suggests the polar range that his acting abilities have spanned over half a century.

THE END

BIBLIOGRAPHY

BOOKS

Allyson, June, with Frances Spatz Leighton. *June Allyson*. New York: Putnam, 1982.

Altman, Diana. *Hollywood East*. New York: Birch Lane, 1992.

Andersen, Christopher. *Citizen Jane*. New York: Dell, 1990.

Bach, Steven. *Marlene Dietrich: Life and Legend*. New York: William Morrow, 1992.

Baker, Carroll. *Baby Doll*. New York: Arbor House, 1983.

Balio, Tino. *United Artists: The Company Built by the Stars*. Madison: University of Wisconsin Press, 1976.

Basinger, Jeanine. *Anthony Mann*. Boston: Twayne Publishers, 1979.

Baxter, John. *Hollywood in the Thirties*. London: Tantivy Press, 1968.

Behlmer, Rudy. *Inside Warner Brothers* (1935–1951). New York: Viking, 1985.

———, ed. *Memo from Darryl F. Zanuck: The Golden Years at Twentieth Century-Fox*. New York: Grove Press, 1993.

Berg, A. Scott. *Goldwyn: A Biography*. New York: Alfred Knopf, 1989.

Bingham, Dennis. *Acting Male*. New Brunswick, NJ: Rutgers University Press, 1994.

Brown, Peter H. *Kim Novak: Reluctant Goddess*. New York: St. Martin's Press, 1986.

Brown, Peter H., and Jim Pinkston. *Oscar Dearest*. New York: Harper & Row, 1987.

Capra, Frank. *The Name Above the Title*. New York: The Macmillan Company, 1971.

Carey, Harry, Jr. *Company of Heroes*. Metuchen, NJ: Scarecrow Press, 1994.

Ceplair, Larry, and Steve Englund. *The Inquisition in Hollywood: Politics in the Film Community*. Berkeley: University of California Press, 1979.

Christensen, Terry. *Reel Politics*. New York: Basil Blackwell Inc., 1987.

Collier, Peter. *The Fondas: A Hollywood Dynasty*. New York: Putnam, 1991.

Collins, George B. *Wildcats and Shamrocks*. North Newton, KS: Mennonite Press, 1976.

Considine, Shaun. *Bette & Joan: The Divine Feud*. New York: Dell, 1989.

———. *Mad As Hell: The Life and Work of Paddy Chayefsky*. New York: Random House, 1994.

Cronyn, Hume. *A Terrible Liar*. New York: William Morrow, 1991.

Davidson, Bill. *Spencer Tracy: Tragic Idol*. New York: E. P. Dutton, 1987.

Davis, Bette, with Michael Hershowitz. *This 'n' That*. New York: Putnam, 1987.

DeCordova, Fred. *Johnny Come Lately*. New York: Simon & Schuster, 1988.

De Havilland, Olivia. *Every Frenchman Has One*. New York: Random House, 1961.

Demaris, Ovid. *The Director*. New York: Harper's Magazine Press, 1975.

Dewey, Donald. *Marcello Mastroianni: His Life and Art*. New York: Birch Lane, 1993.

Dick, Bernard, ed. *Columbia Pictures: Portrait of a Studio*. Lexington: The University Press of Kentucky, 1992.

Dooley, Roger. *From Scarface to Scarlett*. San Diego: Harcourt Brace Jovanovich, 1979.

Douglas, Kirk. *The Ragman's Son*. New York: Simon & Schuster, 1988.

Dunning, John. *Tune in Yesterday: The Ultimate Encyclopedia of Old-Time Radio*. Englewood Cliffs, NJ: Prentice-Hall, 1976.

Eames, John Douglas. *The MGM Story*. New York: Portland House, 1990.

Edwards, Anne. *Early Reagan: The Rise to Power*. New York: William Morrow, 1987.

Englund, Steven. *Grace of Monaco*. Garden City, NY: Doubleday, 1984.

Eyles, Allen. *James Stewart*. New York: Stein and Day, 1984.

Fairbanks, Douglas, Jr. *A Hell of a War*. New York: St. Martin's Press, 1993.

Fonda, Henry, as told to Howard Teichmann. *My Life*. New York: New American Library, 1981.

Fontaine, Joan. *No Bed of Roses*. New York: William Morrow, 1978.

Friedman, Lester D. *The Jewish Image in American Film*. Secaucus, NJ: Citadel, 1987.

Friedrich, Otto. *City of Nets*. New York: Harper & Row, 1986.

Frischauer, Willi. *Behind the Scenes of Otto Preminger*. London: Michael Joseph, 1973.

Gabler, Neal. *An Empire of Their Own*. New York: Crown, 1988.

Gilbert, Julie. *Opposite Attraction: The Lives of Erich Maria Remarque and Paulette Goddard*. New York: Pantheon Books, 1995.

Gingold, Hermione. *How to Grow Old Disgracefully*. New York: St. Martin's Press, 1988.

Goldman, William. *Adventures in the Screen Trade*. New York: Warner Books, 1983.

Grobel, Lawrence. *The Hustons*. New York: Scribner's, 1989.

Hadleigh, Boze. *Hollywood Babble On*. New York: Birch Lane, 1994.

Harris, Warren G. *Lucy and Desi*. New York: Simon & Schuster, 1991.

Harvey, James. *Romantic Comedy (in Hollywood from Lubitsch to Sturges)*. New York: Alfred Knopf, 1987.

Haskell, Molly. *From Reverence to Rape: The Testament of Women in the Movies*. New York: Holt, Rinehart, and Winston, 1973.

Hayes, Helen, with Katharine Hatch. *My Life in Three Acts*. San Diego: Harcourt Brace Jovanovich, 1990.

Hayward, Brooke. *Haywire*. New York: Alfred Knopf, 1977.

Hepburn, Katharine. *Me: Stories of My Life*. New York: Alfred Knopf, 1991.

Heston, Charlton. *In the Arena*. New York: Simon & Schuster, 1995.

Higham, Charles. *Marlene: The Life of Marlene Dietrich*. New York: Norton, 1977.

————. *Sisters: The Story of Olivia de Havilland and Joan Fontaine*. New York: Coward-McCann Inc., 1984.

Hirsch, Foster. *A Method to Their Madness*. New York: Norton, 1984.

Holden, Anthony. *Behind the Oscars*. New York: Simon & Schuster, 1993.

Hoopes, Roy. *When the Stars Went to War: Hollywood and World War II*. New York: Random House, 1994.

Hopper, Hedda. *From Under My Hat*. Garden City, NY: Doubleday, 1952.

Houghton, Norris. *But Not Forgotten*. New York: William Sloane Associates, 1951.

Hudson, Rock, with Sara Davidson. *Rock Hudson: His Story*. New York: William Morrow, 1986.

Jowett, Garth. *Film: The Democratic Art*. Boston: Little, Brown and Company, 1976.

Kaminsky, Stuart. *Coop: The Life and Legend of Gary Cooper*. New York: St. Martin's Press, 1980.

Katz, Ephraim. *The Film Encyclopedia*. New York: Harper Perennial, 1994.

Kitses, Jim. *Horizons West*. Bloomington, IN: Indiana University Press, 1969.

Kobal, John. *People Will Talk*. New York: Alfred Knopf, 1986.

Koppes, Clayton, and Gregory Black. *Hollywood Goes to War*. Berkeley: University of California Press, 1987.

Kotsilibas-Davis, James, with Myrna Loy. *Myrna Loy: Being and Becoming*. New York: Alfred Knopf, 1987.

Kroeger, Brooke. *Nellie Bly: Daredevil, Reporter, Feminist*. New York: Times Books, 1994.

Lambert, Gavin. *Norma Shearer: A Life*. New York: Alfred Knopf, 1990.

Logan, Joshua. *Josh: My Up and Down, In and Out Life*. New York: Delacorte, 1976.

———. *Movie Stars, Real People, and Me*. New York: Delacorte, 1978.

McBride, Joseph. *Frank Capra: The Catastrophe of Success*. New York: Simon & Schuster, 1992.

McClelland, Doug. *Forties Film Talk*. Jefferson, NC: McFarland, 1992.

McClintic, Guthrie. *Me and Kit*. Boston: Atlantic Monthly Press, 1955.

McGilligan, Pat, ed. *Backstory 2: Interviews with Screenwriters of the 1940s and 1950s*. Berkeley: University of California Press, 1991.

MacLaine, Shirley. *My Lucky Stars: A Hollywood Memoir*. New York: Bantam Books, 1995.

McNulty, John. *The World of John McNulty*. Garden City, NY: Dolphin Books, 1961.

Madsen, Axel. *Stanwyck*. New York: HarperCollins, 1994.

Meredith, Burgess. *So Far, So Good*. Boston: Little, Brown and Company, 1994.

Miller, Mark Crispin, ed. *Seeing Through Movies*. New York: Pantheon Books, 1990.

Moldea, Dan. *Dark Victory: Ronald Reagan, MCA, and the Mob*. New York: Viking, 1986.

Molyneaux, Gerard. *James Stewart: A Bio-Bibliography*. Westport, CT: Greenwood Press, 1992.

Moses, George. *Ring Around the Punch Bowl*. Taunton, MA: William S. Sulliwold Publishing Company, 1976.

Navasky, Victor. *Naming Names*. New York: Viking, 1980.

Overy, R. J. *The Air War (1939–1945)*. New York: Stein and Day, 1980.

Parish, James Robert. *Ghosts and Angels in Hollywood Films*. Jefferson, NC: McFarland, 1994.

Perry, Louis B., and Richard S. Perry. *A History of the Los Angeles Labor Movement*. Berkeley: University of California Press, 1963.

Peters, Margot. *The House of Barrymore*. New York: Alfred Knopf, 1990.

Pickard, Roy. *Jimmy Stewart*. New York: St. Martin's Press, 1992.

Preminger, Otto. *Preminger*. Garden City, NY: Doubleday, 1977.

Prindle, David F. *The Politics of Glamour: Ideology and Democracy in the Screen Actors Guild*. Madison: University of Wisconsin Press, 1988.

Quirk, Lawrence. *Margaret Sullavan: Child of Fate*. New York: St. Martin's Press, 1986.

Robbins, Jhan. *Everybody's Man: A Biography of Jimmy Stewart*. New York: Putnam, 1985.

Roberts, Glenys. *Bardot*. New York: St. Martin's Press, 1994.

Robinson, John Harold. *A Reason to Live*. Memphis: Castle Books, 1988.

Rogers, Ginger. *Ginger: My Story*. New York: HarperCollins, 1991.

Rooney, Mickey. *Life Is Too Short*. New York: Villard Books, 1991.

Rosenfield, Paul. *The Club Rules: Power, Money, Sex, and Fear—How It Works in Hollywood*. New York: Warner Books, 1992.

Sarris, Andrew. *The Primal Screen*. New York: Simon & Schuster, 1973.

Schatz, Thomas. *The Genius of the System: Hollywood Filmmaking in the Studio Era*. New York: Pantheon Books, 1988.

Schickel, Richard. *The Men Who Made the Movies*. New York: Atheneum, 1975.

———. *Richard Schickel on Film*. New York: William Morrow, 1989.

Schwartz, Charles. *Cole Porter: A Biography*. New York: Dial Press, 1977.

Selden, William: *Club Life at Princeton*. Princeton, NJ: Princeton University Press, 1994.

Shepherd, Donald, with Robert Slatzer. *Duke: The Life and Times of John Wayne*. Garden City, NY: Doubleday, 1985.

Shipman, David. *Judy Garland: The Sweet Life of an American Legend*. New York: Hyperion, 1993.

Sinyard, Neil. *The Films of Alfred Hitchcock*. New York: Gallery Books, 1986.

Sklar, Robert. *Movie-Made America*. New York: Random House, 1975.

Smith, Margaret Chase. *Declaration of Conscience*. Garden City, NY: Doubleday, 1972.

Spada, James. *More Than a Woman*. New York: Bantam Books, 1993.

Speck, Gregory. *Hollywood Royalty*. New York: Birch Lane, 1992.

Spoto, Donald. *The Dark Side of Genius: The Life of Alfred Hitchcock*. Boston: Little, Brown and Company, 1983.

Stack, Robert. *Straight Shooting*. New York: Berkley Books, 1981.

Stacy, Pat. *Duke: A Love Story*. New York: Atheneum, 1983.

Steinberg, Cobbett. *Reel Facts*. New York: Vintage Books, 1982.

Stenn, David. *Bombshell: The Life and Death of Jean Harlow*. Garden City, NY: Doubleday, 1993.

Sterritt, David. *The Films of Alfred Hitchcock*. New York: Cambridge University Press, 1993.

Swindell, Larry. *Screwball: The Life of Carole Lombard*. New York: William Morrow, 1975.

———. *The Last Hero: A Biography of Gary Cooper*. Garden City, NY: Doubleday, 1980.

Tanner, Paul, and Bill Cox. *Every Night Was New Year's Eve—On the Road With Glenn Miller*. Tokyo: Cosmo Space Co. Ltd., 1992.

Thomson, David. *The Life of David O. Selznick*. New York: Alfred Knopf, 1992.

Tozzi, Romano. *Spencer Tracy*. New York: Galahad Books, 1973.

Vaughn, Robert. *Only Victims*. New York: Putnam, 1972.

Wagenknecht, Edward. *Stars of the Silents*. Metuchen, NJ: Scarecrow Press, 1987.

Wayne, Aissa, with Steve Delsohn. *John Wayne: My Father*. New York: Random House, 1991.

Weis, Elisabeth. *The Movie Star*. New York: Viking, 1981.

Wills, Garry. *Reagan's America*. Garden City, NY: Doubleday, 1987.

Wilson, Ivy Crane, ed. *Hollywood in the 1940s*. New York: Frederick Ungar, 1980.
Winters, Shelley. *Shelley*. New York: William Morrow, 1980.
Wright, Will. *Six Guns and Society*. Berkeley: University of California Press, 1975.

PERIODICALS

Since the early 1930s, Stewart has been the subject of literally thousands of magazine and newspaper articles. Among the most illuminating have been a Chicago *Sun-Times* profile by Roger Ebert on June 2, 1985; a special *Film Comment* issue dedicated to the actor in March–April 1990; the 1970 fall-winter edition of *Film Culture*; Floyd Miller's as-told-to piece in the February 1971 issue of *McCall's*; the profile by Joan Wixen that appeared in the December 1976–January 1977 edition of *Modern Maturity*; and the five-part as-told-to-Pete-Martin series that ran in *The Saturday Evening Post* in February and March of 1961. *The New York Times* and the Pittsburgh *Post-Gazette* are just two of the many dailies that have published scores of profiles of the actor over the years.

The most important sources for periodical matter on Stewart are the Lincoln Center Library for the Performing Arts and the Museum of Modern Art in New York City; the Firestone Library, Mudd Library, and Alumni Records Office at Princeton University in Princeton, New Jersey; The Jimmy Stewart Museum and the Indiana Historical Society in Indiana, Pennsylvania; the Thomas Jefferson and James Madison buildings of the Library of Congress in Washington, D.C.; the film department at Brigham Young University in Provo, Utah; and the Academy of Motion Picture Arts and Sciences in Beverly Hills, California.

INDEX

Spring in Autumn (stage comedy), 118, 119,
122
Springer, John, 341–2, 486–7
Stack, Robert, 141, 170, 212, 213, 214n, 233,
369, 370
Stanislavsky, Konstantin, 7, 97, 100, 500
Stanky, Eddie, 143
Stanwyck, Barbara, 18, 159, 182, 287n
Stars in Your Eyes (Broadway musical), 180
Stevens, George, 3, 6, 157, 265, 271, 279, 347
Stewart, Alexander (Alex) (father), 1, 12,
34, 38–9, 40, 41, 42, 43–51, 52–3, 54–5,
56, 57, 59–62, 65, 68, 73, 74, 77, 79,
80–1, 82–4, 85–6, 88, 91, 96, 109, 110,
118, 122–3, 142, 176–7, 191, 221, 232–3,
237–8, 244, 247, 253, 294, 297–8, 319,
320, 321, 335–6, 337, 343–7, 389–90,
402, 410–13, 428, 429, 462, 469, 470,
471, 472–3, 505–6
Stewart, Anita (Nita) Golding
(stepmother), 345–7, 389, 410, 411, 412,
429
Stewart, Donald Ogden, 220
Stewart, Elizabeth (Bessie) Ruth Jackson
(mother), 1, 12, 34, 43–6, 47, 50–1, 53,
54, 56, 58, 59, 60, 65, 68, 73, 77, 79, 83,
85, 86, 116, 136, 237, 320, 337, 343, 345,
410, 411, 469, 470
Stewart, Emma (cousin), 80
Stewart, Ernest (uncle), 41, 42, 48, 51, 80
Stewart family, 38–49
Stewart, Gloria Hatrick (wife), 1, 16, 18, 24,
65, 133, 177, 178, 189, 191, 300, 315–23,
333–70, 372, 376, 377, 392, 402–3, 408,
409, 410, 427–8, 431, 449, 450, 451, 452,
453, 454–5, 456, 457, 458, 459–60, 462,
471, 474–5, 478, 481, 483, 486, 487, 491,
492, 493, 494–5, 496, 497, 498
Stewart, James Maitland
—as an accordionist, 53, 59, 77, 89–90,
91, 92–3, 96, 97, 102, 103, 115, 119–20,
122, 142, 145, 231, 348, 394
—as an actor, 1–3, 4–12, 13–18, 111–12,
184–5, 303–4, 442–3, 499–507;
boyhood theatricals, 59–60; on

Broadway, 109–27, 141, 283, 293, 296,
488; at Mercersburg, 81–2; as an
MGM beginner, 126–7, 131–43;
monologues, 3, 147, 151, 156, 166, 225,
327–8, 329, 333, 357, 384, 491, 502;
physical traits and movements, 9,
10–11, 125, 144, 171–2, 503; at
Princeton, 5, 88, 89-90, 93-5;
professionalism, 6, 14–16, 162, 225, 280,
364–71, 402, 422, 444, 456, 485;
questionable sanity of characters,
9–10, 151–2, 194, 282, 327, 328, 350,
355; on radio, 169–70, 238–9, 263, 303,
348, 357, 458–9; *see also subentry
television appearances and title entries
for specific films and stage works*; with
University Players, 97–109, 110, 111;
voice, speech patterns and delivery, 2,
3, 77, 112–13, 124, 170, 297, 310, 502–3
—birth, 32, 46
—boyhood, 49–62
—as a director, 172, 433n
—education, 2, 57; interest in
Annapolis, 74, 82, 83, 154;
Mercersburg Academy, 57, 60, 73–9,
81–2, 85, 86, 133, 204, 232; Model
School, 57, 60, 73, 77, 204;
postgraduate plans, 87, 95, 109, 110;
Princeton, 2, 5, 12, 57, 74, 77, 79, 82–97,
204
—family background, 38–44
—as a father, 13–14, 334–5, 334–9, 338,
449–55
—finances: donations and requests,
28, 62–3, 66–7, 462; frugality, 80, 91,
318, 427–8, 490; investments, 356, 427,
429; percentage deals with studios, 16,
141, 304–6, 348, 372, 427, 430, 431
—health problems, 491–2;
appendectomy, 330, 335, 342;
depression, 24, 409–10, 497; hearing
impairment, 367, 407, 418, 463–4,
473–4, 476, 479, 490, 491, 492, 498;
scarlet fever and kidney ailment, 58,
77, 79, 81; thinness, 10, 49, 58, 77, 136–7,

Warner Books now offers an exciting range of quality titles by both established and new authors. All of the books in this series are available from:

Little, Brown and Company (UK),
P.O. Box 11,
Falmouth,
Cornwall TR10 9EN.

Fax No: 01326 317444.
Telephone No: 01326 372400
E-mail: books@barni.avel.co.uk

Payments can be made as follows: cheque, postal order (payable to Little, Brown and Company) or by credit cards, Visa/Access. Do not send cash or currency. UK customers and B.F.P.O. please allow £1.00 for postage and packing for the first book, plus 50p for the second book, plus 30p for each additional book up to a maximum charge of £3.00 (7 books plus).

Overseas customers including Ireland, please allow £2.00 for the first book plus £1.00 for the second book, plus 50p for each additional book.

NAME (Block Letters) ....

....

ADDRESS ....

....

....

☐ I enclose my remittance for ....

☐ I wish to pay by Access/Visa Card

Number ☐☐☐☐☐☐☐☐☐☐☐☐☐☐☐☐

Card Expiry Date ☐☐☐☐